ALLE ZEIT WACH
1842

W. Land J. B. Dossetor (Eds.)

# Organ Replacement Therapy: Ethics, Justice Commerce

First Joint Meeting of ESOT and EDTA/ERA

Munich December 1990

Springer-Verlag
Berlin Heidelberg New York
London Paris Tokyo
Hong Kong Barcelona
Budapest

Professor Dr. Walter Land
Abteilung für Transplantationschirurgie
Ludwig-Maximilians-Universität
Klinikum Großhadern
8000 München 70, FRG

John B. Dossetor, M. D.
Joint-Faculties Bioethics Project
222, 11420 University Avenue
Edmonton, Alberta T6G 2J3, Canada

---

The editors gratefully acknowledge sponsorship for the cover design received from SANDOZ – Nürnberg, Germany

---

Cover figure: Hippokrates. Byzantine miniature from a handwriting of the Biblioteque Nationale, Paris, 14th century
From: Hans Schadewaldt, Kunst und Medizin Köln 1967 (The picture was provided by the Institute of Medical History, University of Munich)

ISBN-13: 978-3-642-76446-2 e-ISBN-13: 978-3-642-76444-8
DOI: 10.1007/978-3-642-76444-8


Softcover reprint of the hardcover 1st edition 1991



2123/3140/543210 – Printed on acid-free paper

# Forewords of the Presidents

The European Society for Organ Transplantation (ESOT) has a tradition of concern for the ethics of transplantation. It was under ESOT's very first president, Sir Roy Calne, that the Society's position on the use of organs from paid donors was officially formulated as follows:

> "Transplantation operations involving payment for donor organs are an unacceptable ethical practice that is not consistent with continuing membership in the Society. It is a responsibility of the clinicians involved to make reasonable inquiries into the proposed arrangements organ donation, in order for avoid participation in operations involving sale of donor organs."

This position has remained unchanged. Questions of ethical conduct have been discussed at the Society's international congresses and membership business meetings, and Society officers and council have reaffirmed their commitment to the original position concerning the sale of organs.

More recently, the question of equitable distribution of organs from cadaver donors has moved into the focus of attention. The Munich conference has dealt extensively with this very complex issue – as can be read in this volume. Because many diverging viewpoints exist, a firm ESOT position has not yet been formulated, it is hoped that these proceedings of the Munich conference will contribute to a better understanding, and that first steps will be taken soon to reconcile the different positions. ESOT will work toward the common goal of all those active in the field of clinical transplantation, to find fair and acceptable means of organ allocation.

ESOT was involved in the planning of this conference from the very beginning. Our past president, Hans Brynger, and I assisted and supported the conference chairman, Walter Land, throughout the planning phase. Moreover, The ESOT council was explicitly supportive. ESOT welcomes in particular the opportunity to hold a joint meeting together with the European Renal Association, a society that shares our viewpoints and concerns in the area of ethics and justice in organ transplantation.

Heidelberg, January 1991

*Gerhard Opelz*
President of ESOT

In September 1989, the Council of the EDTA unanimously accepted Dr. Hans Brynger's proposal to hold a joint meeting with the European Society for Organ Transplantation on the moral and legal problems which the use of artificial organs and the transplantation of organs pose for society.

The EDTA Council has always believed that scientists cannot live outside society and ignore the fact that their scientific activity has a personal and collective dimension far beyond the purely professional level. In 1986, the EDTA Council studied the problem of paid or coerced donors in renal transplantation. The result of the Council's reflections was a document approved by the general assembly and which was published in *The Lancet* and in our own journal *Nephrology Dialysis Transplantation*. This document comprises five points, but I only wish to mention two of these here. The first and the last:

The first one says, "The practice of organ transplantation, involving coercion or payment to a donor to induce him to donate an organ, is unacceptable within ethical medicine".

And the last one says, "The deliberate use of paid or coerced donors is incompatible with membership of the EDTA-European Renal Association".

I believe that these two paragraphs clearly express the EDTA's position, as far as this type of problem is concerned. Nevertheless, the subject of paid or coerced donors is only one of the many ethical and legal problems the scientific community faces today, and I hope that, in the proceedings of this conference, we will be able to find an answer, or at least guidelines, to all of these.

Madrid, January 1991

*J. Botella*
President of the EDTA-ERA

# Preface

This volume presents the Proceedings of the First Joint Meeting of the European Society for Organ Transplantation (ESOT) and the European Renal Association (ERA/EDTA) on Ethics, Justice and Commerce in Organ Replacement Therapy, which took place under the patronage of Dr. Gebhard Glück, the Bavarian State Minister of Labour and Social Affairs in Munich, Germany, on December 11–14, 1990.

In fact, it was not only the pre-Christmas season which called for a meeting with such a title; everyone involved in this area, particularly in transplant medicine, who is sensitive and attentive to public opinion is aware of a slowly growing public antipathy towards allegedly unethical events in this field, particularly at the international level. Interestingly enough, the source of almost all those ethical questions is the desperate search for the medium or agent of treatment: the suitable donor organ. Indeed, its shortage represents the main barrier to treatment.

This desperate search for vital donor organs has undoubtedly stimulated a large number of ethics-orientated discourses concerning living and post mortem organ donation, as well as the use of organs from transgenic animals, products of gene transfer and genetic engineering. Commercialism of organ donation from living persons represents the culmination of the public debate, but is not the only controversy of importance. Just as critical in the question of scarcity of post mortem donor organs is the necessity for equitable organ allocation systems; this has introduced another dimension into the ethical disputes which surround organ donation.

Charged with responsibility for all these considerations, the function of the organizers of our First Joint Meeting was clear: the two European medical societies responsible for issues of organ replacement therapy should come together in order to demonstrate their commitment and competence to address the ethics and justice issues of this new exciting field of modern therapy.

Further, the meeting should not be understood as a conference where ethical issues were just debated in terms of "l'art pour l'art" discussion. Far from it. There was a definite intention not only to intensify, but also to regain the public's trust in the ethical probity of transplant surgeons and physicians, as well as associated nephrologists.

It is gratifying to see that there is ample evidence today to believe that most members of national and international medical societies are willing to contribute to this goal. There is wide recognition amongst professionals of the need to intensify understanding of the principles of medical ethics, and use them analytically in the care of patients undergoing organ replacement therapy.

The final goal is to arrive at conclusions which can be defended on ethical principles, case by case, as well as to isolate those problems which cannot be resolved that way. Some ethical conflicts cannot be resolved in a way that is satisfactory for all.

Ultimately, this competence expressed should also include the ability to use these analyses and assessments for a proper interaction with the public.

Looking back to the meeting we conclude that most of these goals and aims really were addressed. One of the characteristics of the conference was that all the difficult ethical issues were approached on the basis of dialogue – a dialogue between medical ethicists, philosophers, lawyers, theologians, transplant surgeons and physicians, nephrologists, etc. Indeed, so wide was its scope, we can claim that the Munich meeting provided an appropriate European Forum where all the relevant issues were addressed.

The meeting turned out to be very productive and a pioneer occasion in medical ethics. It ended up with an attempt to reach consensus on some congress resolutions on certain topics. They are printed at the end of the book.

January 1991

*John B. Dossetor*
Edmonton, Alberta, Canada

*Walter Land*
Munich, Germany

# Contents

## Medical Risk and Benefit in Non-Renal Donors

## IV. The Dilemma of Post Mortem Organ Donation: Are There Any Donation-Facilitating Factors Which are Potentially Suppressed on the Basis of Ethical or Legal Considerations?

### Post Mortem Organ Donation and Brain Death as Death of a Person



### Legal/Aspects Post Mortem Organ Donation and Psychological

## Allocation and Organ Transplantation

# VI. New Frontiers in Organ Replacement Therapy

## Fetal Cell Transplantation



## Xenografting and Cardiac Surgery

## VII. Congress Resolutions



## VIII. Index

# International Boards

# Contributors

Numbers indicate the title page of the contributions; bold indicates that a contributor is the first author of that contribution.

# I. Introduction

# Theories of Medical Ethics: The Professional Model Compared with the Societal Model

R. M. Veatch

The organizers of this meeting showed great wisdom in choosing the topic of "Ethics, Justice, and Commerce in Organ Replacement Therapy." Justice in the allocation of scarce health resources is destined to become the dominant medical ethical issue of the decade of the 1990s. I am a member of the Board of Governors of the Regional Transplant Consortium for Washington, D.C., and a member of the committee that has the awesome task of allocating organs as they become available for transplantation. The problems we encounter I am sure are similar to yours.

In July 1990, the last month for which data are available, there were 17 506 patients in the United States alone awaiting kidney transplant. Another 1 732 were awaiting hearts transplant, and a total of 1 792 were awaiting lungs, livers, or pancreases (Anonymous 1990). It does not take great insight to realize that human organs are a very scarce, life-saving medical resource. It is a dreadful ethical responsibility to make the ethical choices to determine who lives and who dies. It is important to take time out from the day-to-day chaos of transplanting organs to stop to think about the ethics of the choices we are making.

Not long ago an American transplant center was confronted by a 67-year-old, physically vigorous man who desperately needed and wanted a heart transplant to continue to live. The policy in most American transplant centers is that no one receives an organ over age 65. The question posed by that man was: Is that fair? But if one believes age discrimination is unfair, would it be fairer to take the organ from some younger person who is now scheduled to receive it and give it to the older patient?

We routinely tissue match potential kidney recipients with donors. It at first seems obvious that the kidney should go to the person who is most histocompatible. Yet, in the United States we have come to the conclusion that sometimes ethics requires that the organ is given to someone who is not the best tissue match. We need to develop a theory of the fair use of tissue typing in organ transplant.

What about those in need of transplants because of life-style choices they have made in the past: alcoholics who need livers? We sometimes have people on our waiting list who are human immunodeficiency virus (HIV) positive.

The Kennedy Institute of Ethics, Georgetown University, Washington, D.C., 20057 USA

W. Land, J. B. Dossetor (Eds.)
Organ Replacement Therapy:
Ethics, Justice and Commerce

How should their HIV status affect their position on the list? Should organs from HIV-positive donors be made available to these patients? What about potential donors who are HIV negative, but from high-risk groups? Can their organs be transplanted? We need an understanding of the fair assessment of life-style factors in deciding who gets organs for transplant.

We are discovering that wealthy patients can do things to improve their chance of getting an organ. We are seeing wealthy patients relocate – nationally and internationally – to position themselves to be recipients. We know of patients who have simply bought the organs they desire. Can money be the basis of a just or fair allocation system? We need a theory of the role of commerce in allocating organs.

When hemodialysis machines were new and scarce, it was common practice to decide who should get the machine by determining not merely medical need, but also social usefulness. We found ourselves having to decide which was more valuable: a housewife with two small children, a great poet, or a corporate executive. When we allocate organs or dialysis machines, is this the kind of business we want to get into?

It is clear that organ replacement therapy is the definitive challenge in medical ethics for the coming decade. Organs are inevitably scarce, at least for the foreseeable future. The procedures are dreadfully expensive, but gloriously life-saving. Where can we turn for help? The cover of the program for this meeting at first seems to hint at an answer. The wonderful, medieval, Byzantine representation of Hippocrates seems to suggest that the ancient medical ethical tradition growing out of the Hippocratic Oath might provide a standard for our deliberations in this meeting. Let us see how far it takes us.

## The Hippocratic Tradition of Professional Ethics

For over 2400 years, Western physicians have been able to turn to the Hippocratic writings for guidance in their clinical ethical problems (Edelstein 1967). For problems of devotion to patients during the medieval plagues, it worked well. For most (but not all) problems of confidentiality, its wisdom has been adequate. For "garden variety" sexual temptations in relations with patients, it has been profound. But what does it tell us about organ replacement allocation decisions?

The heart of the Hippocratic Oath – what I shall call the Hippocratic principle – is the maxim that the physician should always do what is for the benefit of the patient according to the physician's ability and judgment. That works well when a single patient has an obvious need that the clinician can fulfill, but it has arguably also been the source of tremendous ethical controversy in the current generation of medical ethics. What are the problems?

First, the core principle of the Hippocratic tradition is dramatically paternalistic. As a clinician you are to benefit the patient according to *your* judgment, not the patient's. Imagine that you had a patient who, in your judgment, could benefit from dialysis or a transplant, but who decided on balance that the organ replacement therapy was not worth it. The Hippocratic Oath tells you to do what will benefit him. Often this has been taken to mean benefit the patient even against his will. We are now recognizing that the classical Hippocratic ethics of professional medicine has to be amended to add a principle of autonomy: a basis for a right of patients to decline treatment when they conclude it is not worth it.

There is an even more important challenge from organ replacement therapy to the classical Hippocratic ethic of professional medicine. Imagine that you are a nephrologist with two patients in need of a kidney. One is younger, healthier, and more histocompatible. The other has been on the waiting list longer and appears to be in greater medical need, but because of poorer antigen match has a somewhat smaller chance of a successful graft. How would the Hippocratic ethic help you decide? It would tell you to do what you think will benefit your patient *(in the singular)*. But how does that help? You already know you want to benefit not one patient, but two. But benefiting the one necessarily comes at the expense of the other.

This is a second great problem with the Hippocratic tradition of professional medical ethics. It is relentlessly, militantly individualistic. It is as if in all the world there were only one physician and one patient. Transplantation and dialysis make clear, as no other contemporary therapies, that the Hippocratic ethic is not good enough. It is silent at just the point where we, at the end of the twentieth century, need help the most. We need to know what to do when, by the very nature of the case, we cannot do what will be most beneficial to all our patients at the same time.

Can we get help by turning to the more modern versions of a professional ethic for medicine? The World Medical Association has accommodated us by providing an updated version of the Hippocratic ethic. It removes the old-fashioned irrelevancies and immoralities of the old Oath: the swearing by the Greek gods and goddesses, the flat-out prohibition on surgery, and the pledge not to tell patients any secrets of the profession. But the core Hippocratic principle remains, and it remains individualistic. It commits the physician to place the health of his patient (in the singular) as his first moral priority. It tells us nothing about what we can do when two patients need the organ.

The problem is not limited to organ replacement therapy: it is the moral dilemma of cost containment in health insurance, of acquired immunodeficiency syndrome (AIDS)-patient contact tracing, of research on human subjects, and of just about every really interesting and difficult ethical problem of the day. And it is just at this point – at the point of helping decide how to allocate the benefits medicine can provide that the Hippocratic Oath is silent.

It is equally silent on the other issues of this meeting. You want to know whether a patient with a dead brain is dead or alive. Science cannot tell you. Just as we thought we had almost world-wide consensus supporting a whole-brain definition, a few of us have been pressing the claim that persons with irreversible higher brain function loss are really dead – even if lower brain centers survive. The Hippocratic Oath is as useless in resolving the controversy as is modern neurology.

Likewise, if we want to know whether is it acceptable to procure kidneys or liver lobes from living donors, it does little good for the Hippocratic Oath to tell us to do what we think will benefit the patient.

The time has come in medical ethics to move beyond individualism. The time has come to develop a social ethic for medicine. Only then will we have guidance in allocating expensive machines and inherently scarce organs. What are the possibilities?

## A New Social Professional Ethic?

One option would be for national and international associations of physicians to develop their own social ethic. It would have to spell out what should be done when patients are seen as competing for a scarce resource such as an organ or a dialysis machine. It would have to deal with competition between patients and nonpatients – between potential living donors and living recipients – as well as between the health sector and other goods in life.

Some national associations have, in fact, long acknowledged that the Hippocratic Oath has to be amended to recognize the physician's social ethical duty to the community. The American Medical Association made the change in the nineteenth century and remains committed to a social responsibility for its members. The World Medical Association likewise abandons a purely Hippocratic individualism in its Declaration of Helsinki when it accepts the legitimacy of physician participation in so-called nontherapeutic research. (In Hippocratic terms it would always be immoral for physicians to participate in such research; it could never be consistent with putting the welfare of the individual patient first.) Only with some kind of social ethic for medicine would a clinician have a basis for allocating organ replacement therapies. As in the case of nontherapeutic research, it is the nature of the problem that the interests of a patient must be traded off. In this case they are traded off against the interests of other patients, but the moral problem is essentially the same.

There are real problems, however, in expecting medical professional organizations to come up with a social ethical replacement for the Hippocratic ethic that would provide a basis for allocating organ replacement therapies. The real issue is not the conflict between the individual and society. Some social conflict is inevitable. The real conflict is what the ethical basis should be for adjudicating disputes among the interested parties – among patients competing for organs or machines.

It might at first seem that, if we must turn to social ethics, the only principle is to expand the patient-benefiting principle to a social benefit principle: choose the arrangement that will do the most good overall, considering the interests of all parties. That is what philosophers call the principle of (social) utilitarianism. Following Bentham and Mill, we would calculate the expected net effects of each alternative and choose the one that produced the greatest net good in aggregate. In allocating organs, this would lead to giving the organ or dialysis machine to the patient for whom the most good could be expected.

That principle is very controversial, however. Do we mean *medical* good or *total* good including the *social* good the patient can be expected to contribute if his life is preserved? A pure utilitarian would consider all possible kinds of good, not just medical good. Many, especially clinicians, are very worried about that approach.

An alternative would be to choose the patient who could get the most good medically, but that too is controversial. Do we mean by medical good, immediate preservation of life, the number of predicted years of life added, the relief of morbidity, or the satisfaction of the patient with the procedure. Especially when we are dealing with patients of different ages, the results using different medical criteria can be radically different. Most fundamentally, it is not clear that the proper moral goal is to maximize any kind of good in aggregate, whether it be medical or social. Many critics of utilitarianism hold that a social ethic should consider how goods are distributed as well as how much good is done in aggregate.

Consider the social ethics of the kidney allocation formula. Striving for the greatest possible medical good (measured, for simplicity, in terms of 1-year graft survival) would, at the present state of our knowledge of immunosuppression, plausibly give great weight to measures of histocompatibility. The present United States allocation formula gives approximately two-thirds of its total weight to tissue matching. Yet a formula that allocates organs on the basis of expected medical benefit, as predicted by histocompatibility, raises a serious ethical question. First, histocompatibility is not the only predictor of graft survival: age and, to a small degree, gender also correlate with success. A pure medical benefit principle should be forced, by logic, to take any predictor of success including these into account.

More importantly, we know that not all racial and ethnic groups are equally easy to tissue type and, among those that can be typed, not all have the same statistical chance of matching those in the donor pool. In particular we know that blacks and Hispanics are harder to type and match than whites. A policy that allocates organs on the basis of predicted medical benefit as estimated by degree of tissue match is, de facto, a whites–first policy. Although it is not intended, criteria based on expected medical benefit raise serious questions of justice. Critics of utility criteria argue that justice requires that all groups contributing to the donor pool should have a fair chance to get an organ. A second social ethical principle – justice – conflicts with the more obvious principle of utility – whether measured by the criteria of social or medical utility. Any social ethic for medicine must decide the relative importance of aggregate benefit and justice in distribution. Before we can know what is an ethical allocation of organ replacement therapies, we must know what the proper relation should be between these two social ethical principles.

## Social Versus Professional Ethics

The choice between the two social ethical principles could, theoretically, be made by various national and international professional medical organizations. But is there any reason to believe that this choice should be theirs to make? We are clearly not dealing with medical matters at this point. In fact, traditional, professionally generated, medical ethics of the Hippocratic variety has eschewed these social ethical principles altogether. Moreover, if medical professionals are asked to make these choices, there is every reason to expect they would make them atypically. This is not because they are biased or self-interested. There is every evidence that medical professionals are truly altruistic and concerned about patient welfare. Rather, there are idiosyncratic ethical orientations existing in all special groups including medical professional groups.

In particular, if medical groups were asked to pick between the criteria of medical benefit and total social benefit, it seems clear that physicians would express an unusual interest in medical benefits (just as lawyers would express an interest in legal welfare, clergy in spiritual welfare, and so forth). It is not that they are prejudiced; it is rather that, presumably, they believe medicine to be unusually important, or they would not have chosen it as a profession in the first place.

Likewise, there is evidence that, if forced to choose between maximizing aggregate good for patients as a whole and distributing benefits justly or fairly, clinicians may not give the same answer that would come from the broader general society. Since the issue is clearly not a medical one and society's views may be expected to differ, many are now convinced that the social ethical principles upon which dialysis machines and human organs for transplant should be allocated must be chosen by the society rather than by the profession.

## Conclusion

If this is true, then the problem before this gathering is a complicated one. We in the medical community now literally have the power of life and death in our hands. With organ replacement therapies it is inevitable – at least for the foreseeable future – that there will not be enough to go around to all patients who would like to receive the benefits we have to offer. The great problems – allocation, using live donors, markets in organs, and defining death – are all ignored by traditional professional ethics.

The classical professional Hippocratic ethic proves worthless to give us guidance. It is relentlessly paternalistic and individualistic in its focus.

Modifications by medical professional groups could add a social perspective, but it is not at all clear whether the social ethical goal should be to maximize total good in aggregate, maximize medical good, or give all persons a fair chance of getting a chance at what, for them, is literally a matter of life and death. The question is not a medical one; it is one of basic social philosophy best decided by societies as a whole. This means that clinicians and others gathered at this meeting need to understand that there are alternative social ethical principles available that will make a real difference in who gets organs and there is, in principle, no way medical science can provide a basis for choosing among them.

Let us move into the days to come with fear and trembling, exploring the issues and the implications of the alternative principles available for allocating organ replacement therapies, and realizing that it is, ultimately, the task of the broader society to make the final choice of ethical principles.

## References

Anonymous (1990) Number of patients on UNOS waiting lists by organ needed and ABO blood group, (September–October 1990). UNOS Update 6 (8): 18

Edelstein L (1967) The Hippocratic oath: text, translation and interpretation. In: Temkin O, Tempkin C. L. (eds) Ancient medicine: selected papers of Ludwig Edelstein. Johns Hopkins, Baltimore, pp. 3–64

# *II. Living Organ Donation in Western Countries*

# Legal Implications of the Principle *Primum Nihil Nocere* As It Applies to Live Donors

H.-L. Schreiber

## Introduction

The removal and transfer of organs or parts or organs from living donors to another person is ethically and legally not without problems and it is controversial.

In the early days of transplantation medicine, the idea of donations from living donors was considered especially inadmissible. Even Catholic moral theology concerning living donors was based upon a totality principle developed since Aristoteles and Thomas Aquinus which forbade injury to the physical completeness of a human being. The removal of a healthy organ cannot, according to this opinion, be justified because every organ fulfils its natural purpose as a part of all organs as a whole and only then can they fulfil their common function. Once removed from the organism, the separate organ has no actual purpose. The natural purpose of this organ is completely absorbed by the organism to which it belonges.

The totality principle, when correctly developed, is not against the idea of organ donations for the purpose of saving lives or healing others. The principle, when correctly understood, excludes the idea of the human body or parts of the body being considered objects which can be used for the purposes of others. It rejects the intrusion of a totalitarian society in the integrity of man and his physical being. Human integrity and identity should be protected. This also sets the boundaries for organ transplants but does not, however, forbid it. The principle is not based upon the damage or the mutilation done to the donor, but rather upon help for the recipient. Only in connection with this view can organ donation be judged.

Another basic ethical objection aimed at the donation of organs is the universally accepted elementary medical ethic which is attributed to the Hippocratic oath, namely, the *primum nihil nocere* principle. This principle states that a surgical operation may in no way harm the patient. The removal of an organ for transplantation does not bring the donor any advantage to his health; it leads rather to the risks and dangers due to the surgical operation which may later come to light.

From the legal perspective, the removal of an organ is not a curative surgical operation, but rather a case of physical injury. This is independent of

Juristisches Seminar, Platz der Göttinger Sieben 6, 3400 Göttingen

W. Land, J. B. Dossetor (Eds.)
Organ Replacement Therapy:
Ethics, Justice and Commerce

the argument which claims that every surgical operation represents a factual and legal case of physical injury justified only by consent. Healing or improvement of the health of the donor is not the medical goal; the removal of an organ is advantageous only to the recipient of the organ. For the donor it represents a medical operation without any indication of illness. This constitutes a violation of the no harm principle, which is in part explicitly conceded. However, it would be narrow minded to just focus on the donor. The physician has two patients to consider, both the donor and the recipient. The no harm principle is not an absolute and unlimited one: limitations in compliance with the consideration of values according to the interest in higher ranking values are possible. It is, however, not possible, to sacrifice the life of the donor as a means of saving the recipient.

For instance, the death of the donor resulting from the removal of a nonpaired organ such as the heart is legally and ethically not acceptable. However, it seems – and this is the essence of the admissibility of donating organs – the acceptance of a certain strain caused by the operation, and a limited amount of danger and risk with regard to the donor is acceptable when it takes place in the interest of the life and health of the recipient. The unique problem in the live donor question is the combination of, on the one hand, the healing of a human being, and on the other hand, the strain and endangering of another. The acceptance of such a jeopardy in the interest of another human being is otherwise ethically and legally permitted. However, it can only be acceptable under limited circumstances and under certain conditions. This characterizes the limitations of the admissibility of a live donor. It is wrong, as Deutsch states, that the donation from live donors would result in relatively few legal problems.

## Preconditions for Live Donors

Four essential preconditions for the admissibility of live donors which represent the maxim of the no harm principle must be insured:

1. The risks to the donor must be compared with the need of the recipient.
2. The donor must be extensively informed before consenting to the operation.
3. The agreement must be made willingly and with no form of pressure.
4. The organ donation may not be made in connection with monetary reimbursement.

In the following, I shall present additional comments to these theses which pertain to both the legal and ethical limitations of live donation.

## Risks for the Donor

The risks for the donor are only acceptable if limited. Operations which change or destroy the personality are not acceptable, and this is apparently not the case in the transplantations of today. The risks connected with organ removal may in no way lead to direct mortal danger or the possibility of serious health damage. These are also the prerequisites of the different European transplantation laws. In Denmark and Norway, for instance, there are such exclusion clauses as "imminent danger" or "any immediate risk to the donor's life".

The surgical risks seem to be an acceptable hazard, as do the general hazards connected with the fact that the donor has to continue life with only one kidney. Since this single organ may then become diseased or otherwise fail, this leads to a profound health hazard.

There has to be a logical proportion between the advantages to the recipient and the detriment or risks on the side of the donor. This will only be the case should the transplantation be urgent and promising for the recipient. The best results are reached when tissue compatibility exists. For this reason donations among relatives are more widely accepted as they are not as susceptible to organ rejection. Because of this, the Transplantation Code of the German Transplantation Centers plans to permit live donations only among relatives. The reason for this is that the dangers of commercialization are minimalized in these cases. The aspect of one's own free will among relatives is, however, questionable, but more about that later: the medical risks are for the present decisive. This also applies to the recent controversy concerning the live donation of a partial liver. Once again, the risks and hazards for the donor have to be made clear.

Because this kind of transplantation has only been practised for a short period of time and there is as a result only a reduced number of cases, many doubt if a judgement of the long-term risks to the donor are at all dependable. Only when dealing with an immense risk, would an organ removal seem unacceptable. As this apparently is not the case, it will be possible to gather experiences within a certain period of time in order to reach a profound opinion in this respect.

## Donor Consent

The donor must be extensively informed before consenting to the operation. The requirement of the consent is to protect the individual from being handled as a mere object which can be used for inappropriate purposes. The individual is thus not obliged to donate his organ, even in case of a grave emergency. He may not be forced to donate his organ even in case of a justified emergency via access according to paragraph 34 of the German Penal Code.

Prerequisite for an effective consent is extensive information about the risks and hazards of an explantation and its possible consequences. As we are dealing with a nonindicated operation, the necessity of an information is much higher than in a curative operation. The patient should not be spared the details out of therapeutic consideration. The patient should, furthermore, be acquainted with the indirect hazards of such an operation in order to be in the position to accept these hazards or to reject the operation.

## Voluntary Agreement

The most difficult legal problem lies in the voluntary agreement. An agreement demands a conscious and voluntary authorization of an operation which injures the physical integrity. "Voluntary" is not to be interpreted as a problem of one's own free will, and thus does not comprise the problem of determinism/indeterminism; consequently the question is whether an individual is actually free to decide on the basis of his own free will. In this context, the donor is autonomous, that is, he may decide on his donation knowing the connected risks, rather than deciding under pressure of force from others. The psychological pressure from the family to save a child or brother can be so large in such a situation of severe illness that one can no longer talk of a voluntary, in the sense of free will, decision.

Furthermore, economic motives might play a role with regard to the decision to donate and may thus hinder or exclude a voluntary decision.

The actual problem is to dependably determine whether the donor expresses his own free will or mere consent. His motivation will often be hard to identify. The donors may easily hide their real motives. The physician will generally not be able to determine the exact motives and background in a donor. In the case of a severely ill relative, it will be difficult to decide whether he is dealing with a so-called obligation case. It is a fine line which separates the "obligation" from the "appeal" deriving from the situation and hindering the free will of the donor. This fine line is not always easy to see. When in doubt, the physician may refuse the operation. Especially among relatives, the aspect of one's own free will may be impaired. To insure the donor's free will, he must be able to revoke his consent at any given time.

## Commercialization and Reimbursement

The live donation may not in any case be subject to reimbursement. This is vital in view of the grave dangers associated with commercialization, which are listed in the Transplantation Code of the Society for Transplantation Centers in Germany: diminution of the medical indication by financial aspects threatens to induce the risk of blackmail between the donor and recipient and, consequently, we face the danger of a considerable detriment to the voluntariness of the agreement to donate. According to the proposed laws which have been produced by the German Society for Transplant Centers, physicians should not go through with a transplantation if they have an idea that the donor has received some kind of reimbursement for the organ donation.

## Donor Age

Another difficult problem is in setting an age limit for the consent. For minors, that is, those under 18 years of age, there is a discrepancy in the laws which I know of. In France, the live donation of organs may only take place between siblings, and then only if approved by a special committee. This committee must be made up of at least three experts, of whom two must be physicians. In the Scandinavian countries, such an organ donation may only take place for special reasons and under extraordinary circumstances. According to the German law proposal which was previously mentioned, organ removal in the case of minors is only acceptable if the organ is going to be transplanted to a close relative and if the transplantation deals with organs or cells which can regenerate, for instance, bone marrow.

## Conclusion

If one takes the no harm principle and the "primum nil nocere" principle seriously, then live donation is only legally and ethically acceptable in accordance with the above-mentioned limited and often not easily clarified requirements.

## References

Deutsch E (1983) Arztrecht und Arzneimittelrecht, Springer, Berlin Heidelberg New York

Häring B (1981) Frei in Christus, vol 3., Herder, Freiburg

Illhardt FJ (1985) Medizinische Ethik. Springer, Berlin Heidelberg New York

Laufs (1988) Arztrecht, 4th edn., C.H. Beck, Munich

Lilie H (1989) Juristische Aspekte der Lebendorganspende. In: Albert FW (ed) Praxis der Nierentransplantation (III). Fischer, Stuttgart, p 89

Löw R (1990) Bioethik und Organtransplantation. In: Löw R (ed) Bioethik. Köln, p 125

Wolfslast G (1989) Transplantationsrecht im europäischen Vergleich. Z Transplantationsmed 43

# Voluntarism of Consent in Both Related and Unrelated Living Organ Donors

R. A. Sells

Voluntarism, which is defined as acting of one's own free will, the condition of unconstrainedness, or acting intentionally in the *Concise Oxford Dictionary* [1], forms the basis of all transplant procedures where rules exist to control such procedures. We insist on voluntariness because transplant donation is an intrinsically charitable act: societies which support the development of transplantation have generally refused to assign a monetary value to transplantable organs or tissues.

That fundamental fact, the non-commercial nature of an organ (our resistance to commodification of tissues), preserves the dignity of donor and recipient, imposes a duty on the involved doctors to do their very best to achieve success, and keeps the costs of transplantation down. I hope to show that voluntariness, and particularly altruistic voluntariness (i.e. voluntary action based on a regard for others) is and must remain the moral cornerstone of clinical transplantation. But first the place of voluntariness in existing legislation is worth examination.

## Legislation

In the Western world, there is no law which makes the removal and transplantation of cadaveric organs compulsory. While alive, people generally have the right to direct the manner in which their body will be disposed of after death. The notion of a collective national (or societal or medical) need which justifies the compulsory dissection of a body (whatever the deceased wishes in life), has allowed post-mortem examinations to be ordered by coroners, but has not yet extended to the compulsory removal of transplants. Laws in China allow the extraction of organs from executed criminals. The suggestion by doctors that surgeons in the West might do likewise has sparked off an intense debate [2] because, amongst other things, voluntariness would be transgressed. Western laws generally permit organ removal from corpses under the following conditions:

1. When the donor has stated his willingness in life (voluntarism).
2. Where the deceased's wishes are undocumented, and bereaved relatives do not object (permission given by surrogates, probably acting in accordance with the deceased's attitudes and character).

Royal Liverpool Hospital, Prescot Street, Liverpool, L7 8XP, UK.

W. Land, J. B. Dossetor (Eds.)
Organ Replacement Therapy:
Ethics, Justice and Commerce

3. Where the deceased had not expressed his objection during life, the authorities may assume that he does not object and may release the body to a surgeon for transplant removal (presumed consent).

In cases (2) and (3) the knowledge or assumption that a person had not refused to donate organs after death is taken as sufficient evidence to proceed. Here the principle of expressed voluntariness is rejected as a necessary criterion for organ extraction. It is interesting that in Middle Eastern countries, where transplant services have recently been developed, the prevailing Muslim religion condones the use of a dead person's organs in the public interest and emphasizes the "collective obligation" (i.e. obligation to society) which should be met by doctors: however, that obligation is subjugated by the permission of the donor or next of kin, which is necessary prior to cadaver donation [3]. In Britain, the two-tier design of the transplant law [4] combines principles (1) and (2), but does not go as far as allowing presumed consent (3). Attempts to introduce opting out in Britain have failed despite efforts by politicians and lawyers [5, 6].

Although political inertia is the accepted reason for the failure of these attempts, critical press comment alleged that opting out legislation would disadvantage those incapable of understanding how to register their objection, and those who mistrust computerized registers. So principles (1) and (2) persist in the UK as the basis for organ removal. Yet the way in which the law is used in one particular scenario illuminates well the beliefs held by British surgeons in the necessity for voluntarism: where the deceased has signed a donor card (allowing legal organ removal), but where the deceased's family at his bedside object, most surgeons acquiesce to the donor family's wish. Here, the organs are wasted, but not at the cost of excessive, perhaps harmful grief suffered by an angry family, that extra grief inflicted by a surgeon who mistook the voluntary declaration of willingness to donate for a statement of obligation that the deceased *had* to donate. In laws which govern donation of tissue from living relatives [7] and in guidelines and regulations issued by professional bodies [8], voluntarism is a necessary condition for all acts of donation.

This necessary condition of voluntariness means that an individual's right to refuse, his autonomy, is respected. When the World Medical Association prescribed the conditions for clinical research or volunteers, the two binding codes of Nuremberg (1947) and Helsinki (1964) stressed the need for the subject [8] to be able to exercise the free power of choice without any force or coercion, and that informed consent must be obtained [9]. It is hardly surprising that transplant surgeons (being in the forefront of medical research) and their medical advisers have retained the same elements in the ethical rules of transplant donation.

## Permission and Refusal

Why should people refuse to give permission for cadaver donation?

1. Surgical incision of a corpse is mutilation, irrespective of the intention beyond that incision. The corpse no longer comprises an individual, although the previous identity is inseparable from its features, but the kinship between appearance and existence is too strong in some people to allow the belief that life has stopped, and the request for organs is refused.
2. Religious conviction may prevent any acquiescence to post-mortem surgery of any kind. Shinto-derived beliefs hold that dying is a process which may take days beyond the point of cardiac arrest; if organs were removed preventatively, families would be very worried [10]. This fact may explain the negligible rate of cadaver renal transplantation in Japan. Survival has been provided instead by a massive programme of dialysis: 88 000 patients dialyse there at present; technological solutions have come more easily than changes in religion.
3. Some people do not trust the brain – death criteria [11].
4. Others may not understand the meaning of brain death, nor the concept that life is absent in this condition although the heart beats, the chest moves, and the skin is warm. A relative's disbelief in death is his biggest problem: asking him to agree to organ donation at such a time would be injurious.

I have purposely used the model of *cadaver* organ donation to explore the role of voluntarism in transplantation because the law is more explicit, and is more illuminating of society's attitudes than it is about living donation. Can we use the criterion of voluntarism to draw the line between permissible and non-permissible living donation? In particular, is this a useful discriminatory tool to help us make up our minds about the rectitude of buying and selling organs?

## Motivation

One may draw up a scale of influences and motivational impulses which motivate people to donate, or not to donate, in life:

| *Attitude* | *Motivation* |
|---|---|
| Compulsion (attitudes ignored) | An obligation (a compulsion, personal fears and wishes are overridden) |
| Willingness | A duty to a relative, spouse or close friend.<br>A duty to any other unidentified person. |
| Uncommitted | Indifference |
| Against | Opposed |

As in the case of cadaver donation there is no legal or other enforceable obligation to donate an organ in life. A duty is however widely accepted as sufficient reason to proceed. In motivational terms, what is the difference between an obligation and a duty? An *obligation* is an externally applied constriction of an individual's right to choose not to donate. In addition to legal compulsion, I would include in this category blackmail (within families as well as between unrelated people), the use of organs from criminals in custody (whose voluntariness is compromised by the imperative to shorten their sentence by agreeing to donate), and all cases where a person sells one of his organs during life (here the financial benefits have such an impact on the life of the donor and his family as to be irresistible: the element of voluntariness of donation must be at least compromised, or in extreme cases, abolished).

*Duty,* however, I define here has an internal motivation arising from love of, friendship with, or respect for another individual. A sense of duty can be sufficiently strong in a person as to make it difficult to distinguish between duty and obligation. For example: a volunteer donor of a kidney to his ailing brother was asked by a surgeon whether he felt compelled to donate a kidney. The donor replied that he could not conceive of any stronger pressure than the obligation of a close brother to donate a kidney whatever the risks; the benefits to the recipient would be such that the demands imposed on the donor by his love for his brother amounted to compulsion. Does such internal pressure amount to an obligation as defined above? I think not: the brother still has the freedom to choose not to give, and, in my experience, other no less well-motivated relatives have decided not to donate when the hazards are pointed out to them, though their decision may only be taken after much agonizing thought and self-examination. So the organ can be withheld (at the cost of harming the recipient) or can be given (at a cost of hurting the donor). In these cases, the recipient's plight has forced the dilemma onto the relative, the degree of compulsion (duty) experienced by the brother being proportional to the strength of their relationship. The donor is compelled to make the decision one way or the other. He is not compelled to donate. Voluntariness survives.

The moral difference here between obligation and duty is that obligation is involuntary and, therefore, cannot be altruistic, whereas duty here I would define as altruistic voluntarism, and I would suggest that all living donors must be shown to exhibit that quality of motivation for them to be considered as organ donors [12].

## The Benefits of Altruism

The utility and benefits of this line of thinking in selecting organ donors has been demonstrated by Roberta Simmons [13]. She tested the state of mind of donors 5–9 years after altruistic voluntary donation using standard psychological testing, and compared them with a group of non-donor controls. Few (8%) regretted their act, and donors scored higher in self-esteem and low depressive affect after donation than before, irrespective of whether the transplant failed or not: there is much evidence in this case material of the act of donation having been psychologically beneficial and having improved family ties. We have no data with which to judge the consequences of donation under compulsion, but can speculate that such cases would be less likely to result in such beneficial outcomes.

The selling of an organ necessarily excludes altruistic voluntarism. To the acquisitive or needy donor the payment may compensate or even abolish any disquiet on the donor's part that his organ was not a gift but a commodity. But the fact that the seller of an organ has not voluntarily and altruistically sacrificed his own comfort and taken the risk of donation without payment must also have an effect on the surgeon's attitude to the graft. If the kidney is bought, then the wishes of the donor after its removal can effectively be ignored: the organ is for disposal as the surgeon alone thinks is best. Whereas an altruistically given kidney brings with it an obligation on the surgeon to use that gift in the best possible way, to exert the highest standards of recipient choice (if no recipient has been specified) and to provide the best possible operative and post-operative care, for that is the least that the altruistic donor can expect after this sacrifice.

## Reimbursement or monetary incentive?

Daar, elsewhere in this volume, subdivides the act of "rewarded gifting" [14] into (a) compensated donation (where identifiable costs to the donor are reimbursed) and (b) donation with incentive (where payment is made in addition to identifiable cost). On the face of it, compensating the donor for lost earnings and travel would seem just and unexceptionable, whereas donation with monetary incentives belongs firmly in the class of paid donation. Problems start however when we introduce the solatium, defined as additional money given to compensate risk, pain, discomfort and convenience – "a little something for your trouble." This is the idea which Thiagarajan et al. have used to recruit paid kidney donors in Madras, India, and which has strong precedents in legal compensation for injury and in the sale of blood. Should similar schemes develop to promote cadaver donation, the solatium would presumably be given to compensate for the extra pain inflicted on the bereaved relatives by the request for donation.

But how may we measure the monetary value of pain and inconvenience? How could such a valuation, even if it were possible, be assigned without consideration of the financial needs of the donor? The purest humanitarian motives might lead an assessor to award higher compensation for pain to a beggar, and a lower sum to a wealthy donor. This decision would of course be made easier if the beggar were ignorant, timid, and with a low pain threshold, and the wealthier individual a tough, stoical ex-marine. My point is that incentives for donation may masquerade as compensation payments: in such a case, a monetary transaction has taken place, and any law which permits such subversive coercion must be flawed.

Another argument against the solatium for transplant donation is as follows: since the long-term survival of living kidney donors is essentially normal, and since the donor is not normally preoccupied with the absence of one kidney after the scar has healed, the extent of his or her sacrifice is the sum of his pain, discomfort, and inconvenience, plus the blemish of a nephrectomy scar. For altruism to survive, he must make that sacrifice. If that sacrifice is paid for, however his compensation be measured, altruism vanishes. He becomes a paid volunteer not an altruistic one.

## Summary

The debate on the role of voluntarism in related and unrelated living organ donation benefits from a study of the laws relating to cadaveric organ donation. These laws reflect societies' attitudes and values concerning what rewards should or should not be allowed for the act of donation. In the West, the legal consensus is that coerced donation is wrong, an organ must not be commodified and, therefore, cannot be paid for; any rewards come in heaven, and result from an act of altruism. Applying this principle of altruistic voluntarism to living donation is helpful: the test of altruism distinguishes between compulsion and voluntarism; altruistic donation has a good prognosis for the donors' well-being and state of psychological health: altruism imposes specific duties on surgeons, and the application of the "gold standard" of altruism to the debate on rewarded giving and compensation may help us in the dilemmas posed by the shortage of organs for transplant. In countries where no cadaver organs are available, non-altruistic voluntary live donation is used. The justification for that practice may be pragmatic. Nevertheless, I believe that no doctor should abandon the principle of altruistic voluntarism in live organ donation without a full awareness, and careful consideration, of the possible adverse consequences of that abandonment.

## References


1. Fowler HW, Fowler HG (eds) Concise Oxford Dictionary Oxford University Press, Oxford
2. Meredith (1990) Transplantation proceedings
3. Ail Qatton M (1984) The juristic regarding transplant donor. In: Abowmelha MS (ed) Organ transplantation: proceedings of the second international Middle East symposium. Medical Education Services, Oxford, pp. 1–4
4. Human Tissue Act (1961) Her Majesty's Stationery Office, London
5. Dalywell T (1974) Hansard (December 11). Her Majesty's Government, London
6. Kennedy I (1979) The Donation and Transplantation of Kidneys: Should the Law be Changed? J Med Ethics 5. 13–21.
7. Organ Transplant Bill (1990) Her Majesty's Stationery Office, London
8. The British Transplantation Society (1986) Recommendations on the use of living kidney donors in the United Kingdom. Br Med J 293–257
9. World Medical Association (1947) Nuremberg Code, (revised 1975)
10. Lock M, Hande C (1990) Reaching consensus about death: heart transplants and cultural identity in Japan. In: Social science perspectives on medical ethics. Academic, Dordrecht, pp. 99–119
11. Conference of Medical Royal Colleges and their facilities in the UK (1979) Diagnosis of death. Lancet i: 261–262
12. Lamb D (1990) Organ transplants and ethics. Routledge, London, pp. 106–108
13. Simmons R (1983) Long-term reactions of renal recipients and donors. In: Levy NB (ed) Psycho-nephrology. Plenum, New York, pp. 275–287
14. Thiagarajan CM, Reddy KC, Shunmugasundaram D, et al. (1990) The practice of unconventional renal transplantation at a single center in India. Transplant Proc 22 (3): 912–914

# Medical Risk and Benefit in Renal Donors: The Use of Living Donors Is Justified

V. Bonomini

In today's world of technomedicine, the key topics of discussion circle round molecular biology and organ replacement therapy. In organ replacement especially, two subjects always spark off the liveliest debates:
1. the definition of death;
2. the ethics of living donation.

Controversy, however, seems to be the rule today, especially when the subject, like the present one, arouses such strong feelings in the public. It has been debated time and again, even in unscientific networks; it involves various interdisciplinary fields inside and outside medicine, and often creates a sort of "cross-fire" discussion which is neither productive nor clear, but simply confirms the trend towards "microphone disease" and "logopollution" of present times. There is a crying need for clarity which, once again, medical science is in a position to provide by taking a stand on the established scientific and clinical criteria.

The dispute over living donor transplantation (in our case kidney donation) might well seem unjustified today in the light of the following facts:
1. Living donor kidney transplantation has been the teacher in organ transplantation;
2. Without it, cadaver transplantation would never have occurred;
3. It has not become obsolete, owing to the shortage of cadaver donors;
4. Religious reservations no longer exist (at least in most countries);
5. The clinical risk-benefit ratio fully justifies it;
6. Ethical reservations concern commercialization of the programme and/or professional incompetence in enacting it.

These are facts which deserve some comment.

## Ethics Behind the Programme

The dawn of living kidney donation took place a few decades ago in Paris (Hamburger's group) and in Boston (Merril's group).

Institute of Nephrology, University of Bologna, Via Massarenti 9, 40138 Bologna, Italy

W. Land, J. B. Dossetor (Eds.)
Organ Replacement Therapy:
Ethics, Justice and Commerce

The excellence of living donor protocols in the 1960s enabled the poor initial results of cadaver kidney transplantation to be progressively improved on, and today out of over 250 000 renal transplantations in the world, about 60 000 are from living donors. The annual rate is considerable in both the USA (1800) and Europe (1200), and the differences between the continents (USA 26 %, Europe 11 %, Australia 5.8 %) seem to reflect the varying availability of cadaver donors, rather than any ethical frameworks. Table 1 reports our experience on the matter.

**Table 1.** Renal transplantations performed from 1967 to 1989 (Institute of Nephrology, University of Bologna)

| Type | *n* |
|---|---|
| Living donor | 131 |
| Cadaver donor | 411 |
| Total | 542 |

The ethics of living donor transplantation must take into account both the ethics of the programme (*moral ethics*) and the professionalism required to enact it (*professional ethics*) [2]. The key question in living donor transplantation is: if a recipient has a suitable living donor, does the physician have a moral right to consent to the surgical mutilation of a healthy individual in order to improve the life of another individual? The operation may benefit the patient, but may jeopardize the quality of life of the donor, and *primum non nocere* is an age-old ethical rule in medicine.

The various problems (religious, organizational, legal, and clinical) encountered in living donor kidney transplantation have progressively been surmounted. Sixty years ago, the Catholic Church was against organ donation, as Pope Pius the Eleventh stressed in the Encyclical *Casti Connubi* [6]. Subsequently, the Catholic Church has brought its religious thinking into line with the reality of clinical results, and today the present Pope John Paul the Second defines spontaneous donation as "an act of supreme charity" [5]. Only a few months ago, this viewpoint was confirmed before an international group of nephrologists [4]. Other religions (Islam, Buddism, etc.) also allow living donation, provided that profit is not involved.

The latter point deserves a comment, since it reflects the most delicate and least ethical side to living donor transplantation.

As we know, there is an established shortage of cadaver donors: in part a real shortage, in part due to the failure to turn potential donors into actual donors; in part due to the emotional rebound among population of mass media "crusades" (on subjects like the definition of death) which, even though devoid of scientific value, have a considerable effect on their audience. Whatever the cause, the shortage of cadaver donors is certain, and this has produced a progressive widening of living donation criteria which now include related and unrelated donors, with and without emotional commitment. Profit is here involved, and donation may occur through the most varied channels, including advertising in the popular press. Such trafficking may lead to a sort of spiral commercialization of medicine, which is generally, but not universally condemned. For there are some who argue that financial incentives to promote kidney donation are morally justifiable and do not diminish the nobility of the gift [3]. Official institutions and scientific societies, on the other hand, have taken issue with this conclusion [12]. We have no official data on the real extent of the problem, but whatever the data may be, in our opinion, it is certainly unacceptable on ethical grounds.

## Clinical Risk and Benefit

In clinical terms, the ethics of living donation need to be seen in a professional light; professionalism in terms of skill, performance, and follow-up, which all influence the clinical results and, hence, the ethics of the programme.

We talk too much of ethics, and too little of non-ethics. Glossing over the differing results from center to center (not casually, but causally related to differing degrees of professionalism) is absolutely non-ethical. In appropriate centers the ethics of living donor transplantation, in terms of risk-benefit, are acceptable [1]. The mortality after surgery is extremely low. Starzl reports at least 20 deaths occurring throughout the world [10]. But although Starzl does not personally transplant from living donors, in his center living donor transplants are carried out and today account for around 10% of his yearly transplantations (TE Starzl, 1990, personal communication). In a literature survey, we have found five cases of death in over 8 000 kidney donors (0.06%) and major and minor complications in a low percentage of cases. Of extreme interest are the possible risks in the long term [8]: the reported incidence of urinary signs is 22%, and of hypertension 19% (which is similar to that occurring in the general population. In our experience (Tables 2, 3) the overall results are even better in the short and long term, probably reflecting stricter criteria of donor selection.

**Table 2.** Short- and long-term complications observed in kidney donors (Institute of Nephrology, University of Bologna)

| | |
|---|---|
| *Short-term* (131 donors) | |
| Major complications | 0.5% |
| Minor complications | 11.8% |
| *Long-term* (64 donors) | |
| Urinary signs | 8.2% |
| Hypertension | 3.7% |
| Renal insufficiency | 0.0% |

**Table 3.** Donor psychology after transplantation: survey of 72 donors (Institute of Nephrology, University of Bologna)

| | |
|---|---|
| *Attitude towards recipients* | |
| Improved | 25.9 % |
| Unchanged | 74.1 % |
| *Efficiency at work* | |
| Unchanged | 100.0 % |
| *Physical health* | |
| Improved | 9.2 % |
| Unchanged | 90.8 % |
| *Depression* | |
| Absent | 88.9 % |
| Increased | 9.2 % |
| New onset | 1.9 % |

**Table 4.** Half-life in renal transplantation according to the source of the donor (Institute of Nephrology, University of Bologna)

| | |
|---|---|
| HLA-identical living related donor | 20 years |
| HLA-nonidentical living related donor | 14 years |
| 1st cadaver donor | 8 years |

Concerning some psychological reactions towards donation, a Gallup poll [9] showed a difference in attitude that varied according to the relationship between donor and recipient. A total of 93 % of parents would be willing to donate to their children; up to 57 % would donate to friends. In our experience (Table 4), negative psychological reactions from the donor are minimal, even in the long term, and even in the case of unsuccessful transplantation.

If the risks to the donors are minimal, the benefits to the recipients are quite tangible. In living donor transplantation the 5-year patient survival rate was 98 %, compared with 84 % in cadaver donor. Graft survival too was significantly better (Fig. 1): 89 % versus 58 %, respectively. The steady improvements year by year reflect the continual growth in experience.

According to Najarian's group, the graft survival at 5 years is 90 % in human leukocyte antigen (HLA)-identical patients, 64 % in non-HLA-identical patients, and 50 % in cadaver donor transplantation [7].

The half-life for kidney tranplantation from identical siblings, parents, and cadaver donors is 20, 13, and 7 years, respectively, according to the latest UCLA Kidney Transplant Registry [11]. Our data are 20, 11, and 8 years, respectively (Table 4). These differences are felt by some authors to be sufficient justification for pushing living donation (in Najarian's center 45 % of the total; JS Najarian, 1990, personal communication).

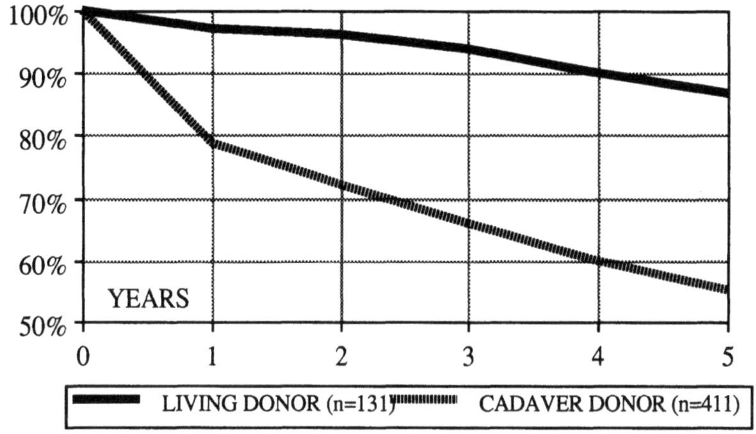


**Fig. 1.** 5-year graft survival in living and cadaver donor transplantation (Institute of Nephrology, University of Bologna)

Three main factors account for the excellent results in living donor transplantation:

1. experience of the staff;
2. more adequate dialysis schedule pretransplant;
3. better donor-recipient compatibility.

This last along with the use of cyclosporine in the last 10 years has afforded a reduction in steroid therapy, which has certainly played its role in reducing clinical complications in transplanted patients.

## Conclusions

Nowadays there is enough experience to define the history, the present extent, and the future prospects of living donor renal transplantation.

*In historical terms:*

1. Living donor kidney transplantation is, and has always been, a unique biological model in man, yielding decisive information on: a) clinical genetics; b) immunological response c) immunomodulation.
2. The modern organ transplant era would never have grown to its present size without the "lessons" of living donor kidney transplantation.

*In present-day terms:*

1. Clinically speaking: a) the living donor transplantation occupies the first place; b) transplantation gives better results than dialysis; c) living donor transplantation gives better results than cadaveric donation.

2. The long-term results show that no reservation – ethical, religious, legal, or clinical – exist against living donor kidney transplantation.
3. Some ethical reservations were perfectly justified 25 years ago, when the programme was still a "shot in the dark." Nowadays, some of the "cons" seem to reflect personal mistrust rather than a condemnation of the program itself.
4. Carried out under strict ethical and medical guidelines, living donor transplantation has grown to be an acceptable and necessary practice, which should not be denied patients or families if they genuinely seek it.

*In future terms:*
1. In medicine all forecasts are tenuous, especially if they also involve extramedical fields, where the borderline between science and ethics, the known and the unknown is constantly shifting.
2. Broadly speaking, one may expect living donor kidney transplantation to become obsolete in future only if cadaveric donation is sufficient to meet the demand.
3. This is devoutly to be wished. Unfortunately, it remains a very distant target.

*In conclusion*, on the basis of the literature results and our personal experience in the field, our credo on living donor kidney transplantation is as follows:
- If there is an "emergency" clinical condition in the recipient;
- If there is a suitable living donor available;
- If no cadaver donor is foreseen in the immediate future;
- If the center responsible provides the guarantee of proven professionalism.

*We feel that the dignity of the donor's spontaneous wish to donate should be fully respected.* These remarks, however, should not be taken as a poem on living donation. Personally, I should be only too happy not to plan for any more renal transplants from living donors, especially in view of the vastly greater emotional strain they place on me and my whole group. If only the number of cadaver donors were high enough!

## References

1. Bay WH, Hebert LA (1987) The living donation in kidney transplantation. Ann Intern Med 106: 719–727
2. Bonomini V, Gozzetti G (1990) Is living donation still justifiable? Nephrol Dial Transplant 5: 407–409
3. Daar AS (1989) Ethical issues – A middle east perspective. Transplant Proc 21: 1402–1404

4. Pope John Paul II (1990) L'Osservatore Romano, May 1st
5. Pope John Paul II (1980) Speech to blood and organ donors. Rome, October 15th
6. Pope Pius XI (1930) Litt. Encycl "Casti Connubi." AAS 22: 565
7. Roberts JP, Fryd DS, Ascher NLN, Migliori, Payne RWD, Dunn DD, Sutherland DER, Simmons RL, Najarian JS (1988) Living related kidneys continue to provide superior results over cadaveric kidneys in the cyclosporine era. Transplant Proc 20 [Suppl 1]: 26–27
8. Spital A (1988) Living kidney donation: still worth the risk. Transplant Proc 20: 1051–1058
9. Spital A, Spital M (1988) Living kidney donation, attitudes outside the transplant center. Arch Intern Med 148: 1077–1080
10. Starzl TE (1987) Living donors: con. Transplant Proc 19: 174–176
11. Terasaki P, Mickey MR, Iwaki Y, Cicciarelli J, Cecka M, Cook D, Yuge J (1989) Long-term survival of kidney grafts. Transplant Proc 21: 615–617
12. The Council of The Transplantation Society (1985) Commercialization in transplantation: the problems and some guidelines for practice Lancet 2: 715–716

# Medical Risk and Benefit in Renal Donors: The Use of Living Donation Reconsidered

P. Michielsen

Opinions are divided on the ethical acceptability of using living kidney donors. Everybody will, however, agree on the absolute necessity of a free decision of the donor after complete and objective information. In this short survey, we will first examine the difficulties in avoiding coercion and the unreliability of the data, on the basis of which objective information of the donor is supposed to be given. We will then critically review the alleged advantages of living donor versus cadaver kidney transplantation.

## Absence of coercion

Most surgeons feel confident that coercion can be avoided by offering a private, dignified route of withdrawal to the potential donor. This point of view has been recently challenged by Tilney (1985). He pointed out that "the selection of a donor from within the family takes place largely beyond the view of the transplant team.... Few donors admit to experiencing coercion by the recipient, other family members, their peers or their physicians, although we have no doubt this occurs, albeit subtly". This puts into question the first fundamental prerequisite: the possibility of being sure of a free decision. In the absence of objective data however, this crucial issue will remain a matter of personal judgment.

## Objective Information of the Donor

In many instances it is the surgeon responsible for the transplantation who informs the donor. As there is a conflict of interests between the donor and the recipient, this is not compatible with the requisite for objective information. This is especially so because the data on which the information must be based are often conflicting. It is, therefore, highly regrettable that no registry of the donors has been established. Most of the studies on the risk of organ donation are retrospective and incomplete, as many donors are lost to follow-up or refuse to participate in the study. According to established clinical epidemiology theory, studies on the course of a disease are suspect if

Department of Nephrology, Universitair Ziekenhuis Gasthuisberg,
3000 Leuven, Belgium

W. Land, J. B. Dossetor (Eds.)
Organ Replacement Therapy:
Ethics, Justice and Commerce

10 % of the original population cohort is lost and studies with a loss of more than 20 % are probably not worth reading (Department of Clinical Epidemiology, McMaster University 1981). Among 13 recent retrospective studies, we found only 2 with a retrieval rate higher than 80 %, and the mean retrieval rate was only 58 %. It is, therefore, not surprising that the opinions on the risk of organ donation differ widely.

– In a recent textbook on transplantation, Haag et al. (1989) conclude "... kidney donation from living donors is a procedure with a proven record of years of extremely low morbidity and mortality....". Another optimistic view is given by Cosimi (1988): "Because of the unusually careful follow-up of thousands of renal donors, in addition to the extensive information available from other unilaterally nephrectomized patients (e.g. trauma victims), the long-term risks can also be assessed quite precisely.... A number of studies, however, including over 900 living donors followed for as long as 20 years, have been unable to identify any convincing evidence of long-term functional abnormalities associated with unilateral nephrectomy...".

– In another recent textbook, a completely different view is given: "Such a donation involves a major operation with the potential for significant morbidity or even mortality. Reported complication rates have varied between 15 and 47 percent, a broad range reflecting differing definitions of complications. Major postoperative complications include important wound infections, pneumonia, acute renal failure, psychosis, upper gastrointestinal hemorrhage, serum hepatitis and halothane-induced hepatitis.... There is no accurate data on mortality for living donors, although in most series it is a fraction of 1 percent" (Tilney et al. 1986). A similar concern is expressed by Engset et al. (1987): "Although the risk to the donor's life is small some recent long-term follow-up studies of donors have found an incidence of hypertension in 35 % of all donors. These results, although not fully confirmed, are worrying....".

These opinions are given by well-known surgeons in standard textbooks on transplantation published between 1986 and 1989. It is likely that the information given to the potential donors will be as different as the conflicting opinions expressed in these textbooks, and it is difficult to imagine how the condition of objective information can be met.

## Early Surgical Risk

The major early surgical complications reported include damage to the spleen or to the adrenal glands major bleeding, retroperitoneal infections, pulmonary embolisms, etc.. The incidence varies between 0 % in a series of 247 patients (Yasumura et al. 1988) and 7 % in 314 patients (Dunn et al. 1986). In a series of 628 patients from Minneapolis there were 2.5 % major complications (Weiland et al. 1984), 4.3 % in 300 donor nephrectomies in Boston (Tilney et al. 1985) and, 6 % in 148 donors in Lyon (Canton et al 1985). The total number of complications, including the minor ones varies between 17 % (Bonomini et al. 1990; Weiland et al. 1984) and 46 % (Dunn et al. 1986). It is unlikely that these different incidences reflect only differences in skill or experience or different selection criteria. It is more likely that they reflect differences about what is perceived as a significant complication by the surgeon.

## Late Surgical Complications

Chronic urinary infection has been reported in from 1.9 % (Weiland et al. 1984) to 16 % (Fehrman et al. 1985) of donors, and incisional hernia in 3.6 % (Weiland et al. 1984; Dunn et al. 1986). Bowel obstruction has been occasionally reported (Dunn et al. 1986). Interesting is the high incidence of local wound pain: 11.4 % of 427 patients followed for between 1 and 19 years as reported by Weiland et al. (1984) and 7.6 % in the series of Dunn et al. (1986). Depression has been reported by some investigators: 25 % in an Australian study (Liounis et al. 1988) and 11 % in an Italian study (Bonomini et al. 1990). Simmons et al. (1985) reported that 8 % of the donors of a successful transplant and 12 % of an unsuccessful transplant regret their decision to donate.

## Proteinuria and Focal Glomerulosclerosis

In the rat model, especially in males, unilateral nephrectomy is a well-known method for inducing and accelerating focal glomerulosclerosis. In man, Kiprov et al. (1982) described focal glomerulosclerosis in five of eight patients with unilateral renal agenesis, but not in ten patients with unilateral nephrectomy. Schmitz et al. (1989) found an increase in albumin excretion in one out of five patients with renal agenesis, but not in uninephrectomized patients. This is in contradiction with the data of Zucchelli et al. (1983), who found proteinuria in 7 of 46 nephrectomized patients. In four of these, renal biopsy showed focal glomerulosclerosis. Taking into account the frequency of renal agenesis, these results suggest that focal glomerulosclerosis is an unfrequent complication, possibly induced by contributing factors other than glomerular hyperfiltration. Several retrospective studies (Hakim et al. 1984; Ferran et al. 1985; Miller et al. 1985; Talseth et al. 1986) indicate that between 30 % and 40 % of living donors present proteinuria. This proteinuria is usually mild, not exceeding 0.5 g/24 h. There is no tendency for this proteinuria to increase with time, at least during a period of observation seldom exceeding 15 years. A careful pre- and postoperative study by Williams et al. (1986) indicated that protein excretion increases in all donors, with a mean value of 100 mg/24 h. more in men, less in women. At the present time there is no proof that this increase in proteinuria will lead to focal glomerulosclerosis, at least not within 10–15 years after nephrectomy. There is however experimental evidence that unilateral nephrectomy accelerates the progression of existing glomerular diseases. For many forms of glomerulonephritis, there is a human leukocyte antigen (HLA)-linked genetic predisposition. It could therefore be inferred that the closer the genetic relationship between donor and recipient, the greater the risk for the donor to develop the same nephropathy as the recipient. The risk of nephrectomy could thus be higher in living related donors than in persons nephrectomized for other reasons. There are also human data indicating that in diabetics, a reduced renal mass could increase the risk of developing nephropathy (Sampson et al. 1990), and recently, Parfrey et al. (1984) reported the development of glomerulosclerosis in a renal isograft recipient and in its identical twin donor.

In this regard it is interesting to note the high incidence of recurrence of glomerulonephritis in patients receiving a kidney from an identical twin: 65 % recurrence in a review by Glassock (1968); 20 % recurrence in an EDTA inquiry (Kramer et al. 1982). It is well known that recurrence of immunoglobulin A (IgA) nephropathy (Berger 1984) (Bachmann 1986) and membranous glomerulonephritis (Obermiller 1985) is more frequent in patients who have received kidneys from related living donors. The closer the relationship, the higher the risk of recurrence. Recently O'Meara et al. (1989) reported an 11.9 % recurrence rate in 134 recipients of a living donor kidney against a recurrence rate of 1.3 % in 603 cadaver kidney recipients.

## The Risk of Hypertension

It is well known that in spontaneously hypertensive rats, unilateral nephrectomy accelerates the hypertension. Retrospective studies in 27 children who underwent nephrectomy for various reasons indicated only a 3 % prevalence of hypertension after a mean follow-up of 23.3 years (Robitaille et al. 1985). In 40 normotensive adults, nephrectomized between the ages of 20 and 72 years, Smith et al. (1985) found that 15 % developed hypertension after a mean follow-up of 11.8 years. This incidence was not considered different from that expected in the general population. These data, obtained in patients nephrectomized for medical or surgical indications, cannot be extrapolated to the living donor situation as the kidney donor population differs from the general population at least in two aspects. First, they are selected on the basis of the absence of significant hypertension; second, they are genetically related to renal patients, in whom the incidence of hypertension is high. Retrospective studies in kidney donors have led to conflicting conclusions. The reported incidence of hypertension varies between 2.4 % (Yasumura et al. 1988) and 48 % (Hakim et al. 1984). Several authors estimate that kidney donors are not more at risk for hypertension than the general population (Yasumura et al. 1988; Weiland et al. 1984; Liounis et al. 1988; Vincenti et al. 1983), others consider that there is an increased incidence or at least an increased risk in some patients (Dunn et al. 1986;

Schwarz et al. 1989; Talseth et al. 1986; Fehrman et al. 1985; Miller et al. 1984; Sakillariou 1985; Hakim et al. 1984).

The reasons for these discrepancies are multiple, the main reason being probably the loss to follow-up of a large number of patients. From the quoted studies, only two (Talseth et al. 1986; Hakim et al. 1984) have a retrieval rate above 80 %. Both studies examine a long-term follow-up of more than 10 years after donor nephrectomy. Talseth found a 15 % incidence of hypertension in 68 patients. From the ten patients found to be hypertensive, only three were completely normotensive preoperatively. After exclusion of these hypertensive patients, the mean systolic pressure in the remaining patients increased from 130 mm Hg before nephrectomy to 140 mm Hg afterwards. The expected increase over a similar follow-up period in the Norwegian general population was only 2–4 mm Hg. In the study by Hakim et al. (1984) concerning 52 patients, 60 % of the men and 30 % of the women were hypertensive postoperatively. At the time of donation only 18 % of the men and 10 % of the women had already been hypertensive. Both these studies conclude that there is a significant increase in blood pressure after kidney donation, more than expected in the general population. In a detailed analysis of 99 patients followed for more than 10 years after kidney donation, Torres et al. (1987) found that, as expected, the frequency of hypertension in their renal allograft donors prior to nephrectomy was lower than in the general population. They concluded that donation of one kidney seems to accelerate the development of definite hypertension in patients with a preexisting disposition to the development of hypertension. The role of donor nephrectomy on the development of hypertension is clearly demonstrated by Dunn et al. (1986) in a retrospective study of 250 donors. In this study, there was a progressive increase in the incidence of borderline and definite hypertension with time after donor nephrectomy, whereas the mean age of the patients was the same in the different time groups, in contrast with the general population where an increase in the incidence of hypertension with age can be expected. From these retrospective studies, it can be concluded that, after donor nephrectomy, blood pressure increases faster than expected in the general population. Patients who are already at risk for hypertension at the moment of nephrectomy are more likely to develop significant hypertension after donation.

These retrospective studies are confirmed by two prospective studies. In 21 white donors, carefully followed for 1 year after donation, Friedlander et al. (1986) observed an increase in diastolic blood pressure to more than 90 mm Hg in 7 of 12 men and 3 of 9 women. All these donors presented an increase in parathyroid hormone level and lower serum phosphorus. Bertolatus et al (1985) followed 22 donors for from 1 week to 36 months after donation. There was a statistically significant increase in both systolic and diastolic blood pressure with time after nephrectomy. The average increase in diastolic blood pressure was 5 mm Hg at 2 years.

## The Benefit for the Recipient

It is generally accepted that the results of living donor transplantation are superior to those of cadaver kidney transplantations. From the point of view of HLA compatibility, transplantation between HLA-identical siblings presents an obvious advantage, as a similar degree of compatibility can seldom be obtained with cadaver donors. For one-haplotype identical transplants, as in the parent-to-child combination, the advantage is less obvious, and similar or better compatibilities can be achieved with cadaver kidneys. It is, therefore, intriguing that better results are still being reported for transplants with parental kidneys. In the interpretation of these results, one must, however, take into account the different patient selection for living and cadaver donors. In centers performing both living donor and cadaveric transplants, there is a negative selection bias for those who are receiving a cadaveric kidney. Recipients of living donor kidneys tend to be younger and belong usually to the good-risk category; their psychosocial environment is also likely to be better, and this could significantly contribute to a better compliance and increased survival rate, as noncompliance has been shown to be a main factor in long-term loss of the graft. Recently Wynn et al. (1988) compared the late results from 258 primary cadaver and 233 primary living-related donor kidney transplants in a single center. With the usual univariate analysis, living related transplants showed greater graft and patient survival than cadaver donor grafts. Multivariate Cox analysis, however, failed to identify a significant association between the type of graft and graft or patient survival. In a retrospective analysis, Cave et al. (1989), in a center known for its excellent results, came to the conclusion that with a 5-year living donor graft survival of 69 %, the results were no better than those of cadaver grafts. In our own center, we never accepted living donors and, since the introduction of cyclosporine, we have obtained in 638 consecutive first cadaver kidney grafts a 5-year patient and graft survival of 85.6 % and 75.6 %, respectively. If we consider only the 250 recipients under 40 years of age, who would have been the most likely candidates for a living donor graft, the corresponding 5-year patient and graft survival is 95.4 % and 81.9 %, respectively. Our data refute the affirmation of Cosimi (1988), that "the 5-year success rates of over 80 % which can be attained using living donor kidneys remain well above any reported cadaver donor results." With appropriate care in comparable patient groups, similar results can be obtained with cadaver kidneys.

## Conclusion

Taking into account the difficulty in avoiding coercion, the early and late surgical risks and the increased incidence in hypertension and in proteinuria after donation, the risks for the donor are out of proportion to the benefit for the recipient. The only remaining argument for using living donors is the shortage of cadaver donors. Experience in Austria and Belgium demonstrates, however, that with appropriate legislation more than 40 kidneys can be retrieved per million population and per year. This covers the need for transplantable kidneys. The statement by the Council of Europe (1987) that: "The use of organs from living donors should be restricted and, where possible, gradually eliminated" seems timely and appropriate.

## References

Bachman U, Biava C, Amend W, Feduska N, Melzer J, Salvatierra O, Vincenti F (1986) The clinical course of IgA nephropathy and Henoch-Schönlein purpura following renal transplantation. Transplantation 42: 511–515

Berger J, Noël LH, Nabarra B (1984) Recurrence of mesangial IgA nephropathy after renal transplantation. Contrib Nephrol 40: 195–197

Bertolatus JA, Friedlander MA, Scheidt C, Hunsicker LG (1985) Urinary albumin excretion after donor nephrectomy. Am J Kidney Dis 5: 165–169

Bonomini V, Gozzetti G (1990) Is living donation still justifiable? Nephrol Dial Transplant 5: 407–409

Canton F, Dubernard JM, Gelet A, Codas H, Martin X, Kamel G, Devonec M, Henriet M, Chabrol B, Mongin-Long D (1985) Surgical complications of living donor nephrectomy. In: Touraine JL et al. (eds) Transplantation and clinical immunology XVI. Excerpta Medica, Amsterdam, pp. 3–5

Cave MH, Doherty CC, Douglas JF, McGeown MG, Donaldson RA, Kennedy JA, Middleton D (1989) Live donor renal transplantation – the experience of the Belfast Renal Unit. Ir J Med Sci 158: 267–268

Cosimi AB (1988) The donor and donor nephrectomy. In: Morris PJ (ed) Kidney transplantation. Saunders, Philadelphia, pp. 93–121

Council of Europe (1987) Third Conference of European Health Ministers, Paris

Department of Clinical Epidemiology and Biostatistics, McMaster University Health Science Center (1981) How to read clinical journals: III. To learn the clinical course and prognosis of disease. Can Med Assoc J 124: 866–872

Dunn JF, Nylander WA, Richie RE, Johnson HK, MacDonnell RC, Sawyers JL (1986) Living related donors. A 14-year experience. Ann Surg 203: 637–643

Engset J, Youngson GG (1987) Surgical aspects of renal transplantation. In: Catto GRD (ed) Clinical transplantation. MTP Press, Lancaster, pp. 31–55

Fehrman I, Widstam U, Lundgren G, Bergström J (1985) Renal donation. Long-term consequences in man. In: Touraine JL et al. (eds) Transplantation and clinical immunology XVI. Excerpta Medica, Amsterdam, pp. 31–38

Ferran NL, Delano BG, Beyer MM, Uribarri J, Friedman EA (1985) Hypertension and proteinuria post renal donation (PDx). Kidney Int 27: 137

Friedlander MA, Lemke JH (1986) Divalent ion handling in human kidney donors with increased blood pressure after uninephrectomy. Am J Med 80: 1079–1085

Glassock RJ, Feldman D, Reynolds FS, Dammin GJ, Merrill JP (1968) Human renal isografts: a clinical and pathological analysis. Medicine 47: 411–454

Haag BW, Stuart FP (1989) The organ donor: brain death, selection criteria, supply and demand In: Flye MW (ed) Principles of organ transplantation. Saunders, Philadelphia, pp. 176–193

Hakim RM, Goldszer RC, Brenner BM (1984) Hypertension and proteinuria: long-term sequelae of uninephrectomy in humans. Kidney Int 25: 930–36

Kiprov DD, Colvin RB, McCluskey (1982) Focal and segmental glomerulosclerosis and proteinuria associated with unilateral renal agenesis. Lab Invest 46: 275–281

Kramer P, Broyer M, Brunner F, Brynger H, Donckerwolcke RA, Jacobs C, Selwood NH, Wing AJ (1982) Combined report on regular dialysis and transplantation in Europe XII 1981. Proceedings of the EDTA 19: 27. Pitman Medical, London

Liounis B, Roy LP, Thompson JF, May J, Sheil AG (1988) The living, related kidney donor: a follow-up study. Med J Aust 148: 436–437, 440–444
Miller IJ, Suthanthiran M, Riggio RR, Williams JJ, Riehle RA, Vaughan ED, Stubenbord WT, Mouradian J, Cheigh JS, Stenzel KH (1985) Impact of renal donation. Long-term clinical and biochemical follow-up of living donors in a single center. Am J Med 79: 201–208
Obermiller LE, Hoy WE, Eversole M, Sterling WA (1985) Recurrent membranous glomerulonephritis in two renal transplants. Transplantation 40: 100–102
O'Meara Y, Green A, Carmody M, Donohoe E, Campbell E, Browne O, Walshe J (1989) Recurrent glomerulonephritis in renal transplants: fourteen years' experience. Nephrol Dial Transplant 4: 730–734
Parfrey PS, Hollomby DJ, Gilmore NJ, Knaack J, Schur PH, Guttmann RD (1984) Glomerular sclerosis in a renal isograft and identical twin donor. Transplantation 38: 343–346
Robitaille P, Mongeau JG, Lortie L, Sinnassamy P (1985) Long-term follow-up of patients who underwent unilateral nephrectomy in childhood. Lancet: 1297–1299
Sakellariou G (1985) Long-term follow-up of living donors. In: Touraine JL et al. (eds) Transplantation and clinical immunology XVI. Excerpta Medica, Amsterdam, pp. 23–30
Sampson MJ, Drury PL (1990) Development of nephropathy in a diabetic patient with a single kidney. Diabetic Med 7: 258–260
Schmitz A, Christensen CK, Christensen T, Solling K (1989) No microalbuminuria or other adverse effects of long-standing hyperfiltration in humans with one kidney. Am J Kidney Dis 13: 1312–1316
Schwarz A, Offermann G (1989) Vorteile und Risiken der Nierentransplantation von verwandten Spendern. Klin Wochenschr 67: 929–935
Simmons RG, Anderson CR (1985) Social-psychological problems in living donor transplantation. In: Touraine JL et al. (eds) Transplantation and clinical immunology XVI. Excerpta Medica, Amsterdam, pp. 47–57
Smith S, Laprad P, Grantham J (1985) Long-term effect of uninephrectomy on serum creatinine concentration and arterial blood pressure. Am J Kidney Dis 6: 143–148
Talseth T, Fauchald P, Skrede S, Djoseland O, Berg KJ, Stenstrom J, Heilo A, Brodwall EK, Flatmark A (1986) Long-term blood pressure and renal function in kidney donors. Kidney Int 29: 1072–1076
Tilney NL, Hollenberg NK (1985) Considerations of kidney donation using living related sources. In: Touraine JL et al. (eds) Transplantation and clinical immunology XVI. Excerpta Medica, Amsterdam, pp. 207–213
Tilney NL, Kirkman RL (1986) Surgical aspects of kidney transplantation. In: Garovoy MR, Guttmann RD (eds) Renal transplantation. Churchill Livingstone, New York, pp. 93–123
Torres VE, Offord KP, Anderson CF, Velosa JA, Frohnert PP, Donadio JV, Wilson DM (1987) Blood pressure determinants in living-related allograft donors and their recipients. Kidney Int 31: 1383–1390
Vincenti F, Amend WJC, Kaysen G, Feduska N, Birnbaum J, Duca R, Salvatierra O (1983) Long-term renal function in kidney donors. Transplantation 36: 626–629
Weiland D, Sutherland DER, Chavers B, Simmons RL, Ascher NL, Najarian JS (1984) Information on 628 living-related kidney donors at a single institution, with long-term follow-up in 472 cases. Transplant Proc 16: 5–7
Williams SL, Oler J, Jorkasky DK (1986) Long-term renal function in kidney donors: a comparison of donors and their siblings. Ann Int Med 105: 1–8
Wynn JJ, Pfaff WW, Patton PR, Peterson JC, Salomon DR, Fennell RS, Scornik JC, Howrd RJ (1988) Late results of renal transplantation. Transplantation 45: 329–333
Yasumura T, Nakai I, Oka T, Ohmori Y, Aikawa I, Nakaji K, Yoshimura N, Nakane Y (1988) Experience with 247 living-related donor nephrectomy cases at a single institution in Japan. Jpn J Surg 18: 252–258
Zucchelli P, Cagnoli L, Casanova S, Donini U, Pasquali S (1983) Focal glomerulosclerosis in patients with unilateral nephrectomy. Kidney Int 24: 649–655

# Attitudes to Using Living Related Kidney Donors in The Netherlands

M. A. Bos and J. M. Wilmink

## Introduction

Since the start of kidney transplantation in the Netherlands in 1966, the use of living related donors (LRD) has been a regular and accepted phenomenon. However, as transplant programs became established and began to expand in the 1970s, the proportion of living donor transplants remained at a stable 4%–5% of the total volume of transplants. In the 1980s, with the introduction of donor-specific transfusions (DST), the number of living donor transplants rose to approximately 10%. Unrelated living donor transplants are now also performed in some centers, but in very limited numbers, and are restricted to spouses and partners.

## The Position of the Netherlands Among European Countries

In 1988, the number of transplants using LRD totalled 9% of all kidney transplants in the Netherlands. Table 1 shows the position of the Netherlands among the other European countries in this respect.

## The Development of Transplant Programs in the Netherlands

Figure 1 shows the development of the kidney transplant program in the Netherlands in the period 1981–1990, indicating the number of transplants with LRD and cadaveric donors (CAD), as well as the total number of transplants. The graph shows that the number of LRDs has remained rather stable over the years, with a minimum of 10 (3% of all transplants) and a maximum of 46 (10% of all transplants). The number of CAD transplants has fluctuated between 289 and 413, with an average of 350. If we look at the individual centers, we see differences in the proportion of living donor transplants in their transplant programs. Table 2 represents the situation in 1989, giving the total number of kidney transplants and the percentage of LRDs.

Dutch Health Council, The Hague, The Netherlands
University Medical Center, Amsterdam, The Netherlands

W. Land, J. B. Dossetor (Eds.)
Organ Replacement Therapy:
Ethics, Justice and Commerce

**Table 1.** CAD and LRD transplants in European countries and the United States in 1988

| Country | All transplants per million population (*n*) | LRD as % of all transplants |
|---|---|---|
| Sweden | 42.7 | 25 |
| Austria | 40.9 | 11 |
| Norway | 40.4 | 38 |
| Belgium | 38.3 | 9 |
| France | 32.5 | 4 |
| Switzerland | 32.1 | 7 |
| Finland | 31.8 | 10 |
| United Kingdom | 31.5 | 8 |
| Denmark | 28.6 | 14 |
| Netherlands | 28.6 | 9 |
| Germany | 28.5 | 2 |
| Spain | 26.2 | 3 |
| Ireland | 21.6 | 3 |
| Portugal | 19.8 | 3 |
| Luxembourg | 15.0 | 17 |
| Italy | 11.5 | 10 |
| Greece | 9.1 | 72 |
| Turkey | 5.3 | 80 |
| USA | 39.7 | 20 |

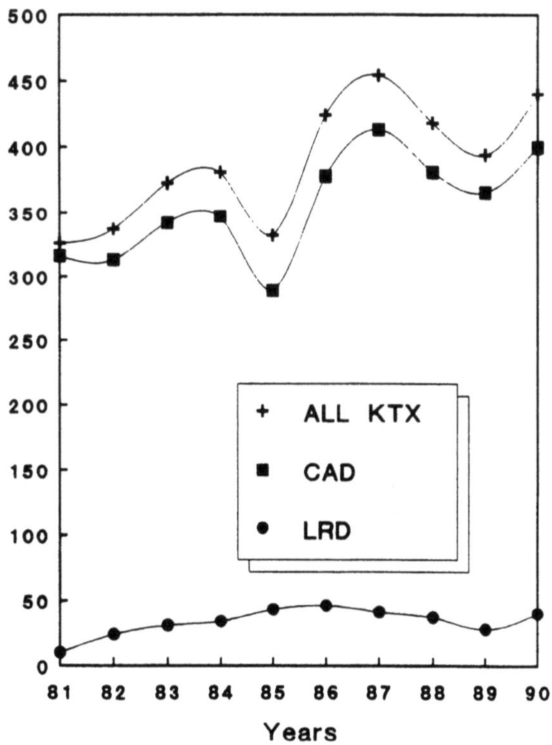


**Fig. 1.** Development of the kidney transplant program in the Netherlands from 1981 to 1990 showing the total number of transplants (*plus sign*) and the number of transplants with cadaveric (*black square*) and living related donors (*black circle*)

**Table 2.** Proportion of LRD grafts performed in Dutch kidney transplant centers in 1989

| Centre | All kidney transplants (*n*) | LRD *n* | | LRD (%) |
|---|---|---|---|---|
| Maastricht | 41 | 1 | | 2.5 |
| Groningen | 63 | 2 | | 2.8 |
| Nijmegen | 85 | 5 | | 6.2 |
| Rotterdam | 48 | 3 | | 6.6 |
| Amsterdam | 63 | 5 | | 8.6 |
| Leiden | 61 | 10 | | 19.6 |
| Utrecht | 28 | 5 | | 21.7 |
| Total | 394 | 28 | average | 7.6 |

## Information on the Results of LRD Transplants

The issue of living donor transplants has not been widely discussed in the Netherlands, neither among kidney patients nor among medical professionals. There has never been a situation of extreme shortage of dialysis facilities, in which people were forced to consider live donation, as was the case in the United States and Scandinavia. The media have also paid little attention to this subject over the years. This may partly be an explanation for the relatively modest use of LRDs in the Netherlands. On the other hand, this does not mean that the public and the doctors have been completely unaware of the possible benefits of transplanting live donor organs. In 1985, an article appeared in the *Dutch Medical Journal* reporting on the long-term follow-up of living donors in two Dutch centers. All living donors in the period 1966–1983 had been regularly examined. In summary, the results were: no deterioration of renal function, very low risk of developing hypertension, and no major postoperative complications. On the basis of this evidence (and similar reports from abroad), the Dutch Health Council, in its 1986 report on dialysis and transplantation, concluded that "the actual risk to living kidney donors is very low indeed and should not be an impediment to continue to perform live donor transplants." In 1988, the results of another study were published, in which the outcome of 1 000 kidney transplants (1968–1988) in the center in Nijmegen was analyzed. Figure 2 shows the graft survival in these transplants. These data show there is significantly better graft survival after 2 and 3 years in the LRD group than with CAD transplants. With the introduction of cyclosporine, this difference has been reduced but it is still present if one looks at long-term survival.

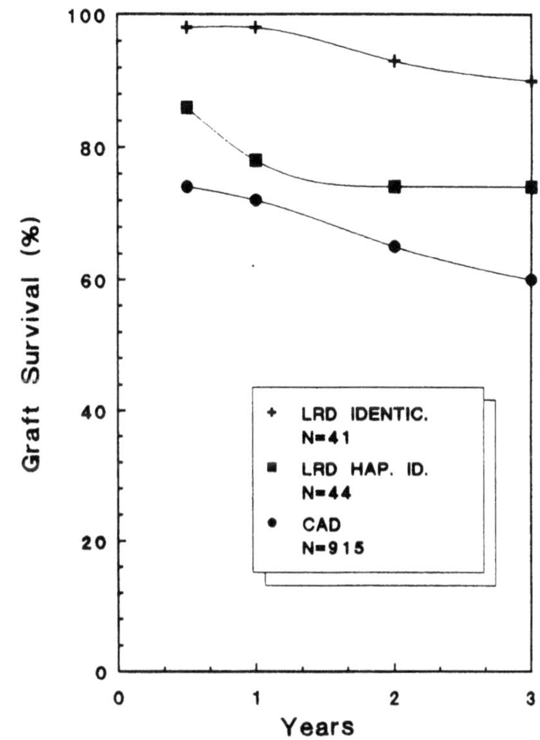


**Fig. 2.** Analysis of graft survival in the Nijmegen transplant center based on 1 000 kidney transplants performed between 1968 and 1988

## Attitudes to LRD: Results From an Inquiry

To get a better view of the attitudes of doctors to living donor transplants, we recently interviewed the heads of the nephrology departments in the seven transplant centers, as well as the heads of ten regional dialysis centers. The results, in summary, are the following:

1. Living donor transplants are almost unanimously accepted in Dutch transplant centers (86 % positive), but less so in the dialysis centers (50 % positive).
2. Unrelated living donors are accepted by most transplant centers (5 out of 7), but restricted to spouses and partners.
3. Transplant doctors agree that with LRD transplants, the initiative should always lie with the donor and his family; they will restrict themselves to giving information. Only few doctors are willing to take further initiative.
4. There is wide feeling among transplant doctors that in the general public, but also in patients and dialysis doctors, information on LRD is lacking.
5. Most transplant doctors would like to see the number of LRD transplants go up in view of the persistent donor shortage.
6. They see an information campaign, especially focusing on kidney patients and dialysis doctors, as the best way to bring this about.

# Living Organ Donation in The Netherlands and in Some Other Countries

J. E. M. Akveld and F. Th. de Charro

## Introduction

In Dutch society, integrity and self-determination are central values which have obtained fundamental protection in the Constitution. In point of fact, the *salus aegroti suprema lex* principle is an elaboration of this. At the same time, this principle creates a key problem in the case of donation ex vivo. In the case of 'regular' medical operations, permission granted by the patient, combined with the fact that the purpose of the medical action is oriented toward improvement of the patient's bodily and/or mental health, is seen as sufficient justification for an operation. The situation, in this respect, is different in the case of donation ex vivo. Here the purpose of the 'treatment' lies outside the treated person. It can be stated that extirpation ex vivo, in the strict sense of the word, is not a medically indicated operation. This fact in itself makes it less obvious that permission granted by the donor should offer sufficient justification for such an operation. Nor does the improvement of a third party's condition offer sufficient supplementary justification for extirpation by a physician. This leads to the conclusion that a legal judgement on the permissibility of this kind of medical operation is necessary. The Danish legislator had already reached this conclusion in 1966, when he stated: 'Nevertheless, it must be desirable to establish the legality of this practice and the conditions under which it can take place, in a law which otherwise contains rules on transplantation'. This was also the opinion of the Netherlands' legislator in 1990, as appears from the Explanatory Memorandum on the Organ Donation Bill. The latter proposes an equilibrium between, on the one hand, protection of the independent donor and his/her self-determination and, on the other hand, the patient's interests (see also [1]).

Another reason for legislation, which is also connected with the character of organ transplantation, is the following: with this type of medical operations, a so-called third party's interest is at stake. Here the legislator cannot remain inactive, also because of the vital interests at stake, and cannot leave the weighing to one of the parties concerned. In those cases the legislator will have to take into consideration the partly opposed interests of both donor and recipient.

Erasmus University, Centre for Health Policy and Law, P.O. Box 1738, 3000 DR Rotterdam, Holland

W. Land, J. B. Dossetor (Eds.)
Organ Replacement Therapy:
Ethics, Justice and Commerce

## A Closer Look at Issuing Rules

It is beyond discussion that organ or tissue extirpation involves a risk for and damage to the donor. The extent of the risk and damages may vary and is, for example, smaller in the case of extirpation of bone marrow than of a kidney. It seems undesirable to lay down *exactly* the boundaries of what is permissible in a law, in the sense that the law stipulates *which* organs and tissues may be extirpated. This, on the one hand, because it might be interpreted as *carte blanche* for extirpation, and on the other hand, because it might result in rigidity and block new possibilities. A certain limitation in more general terms must be considered appropriate, though. There are various possibilities to this effect. The Swedish legislator considers a boundary crossed if serious risks to the donor's health are expected. The Danish legislator takes a step further and puts the boundary there where direct danger to the donor arises. The Netherlands' legislator has chosen as criterion for his bill on this issue that organ extirpation, where permanent effects for the donor are involved, is only permitted in cases where the recipient is in peril of his/her life and these permanent effects for the donor cannot be diverted equally succesfully in another way. The latter opinion requires some critical notes. Firstly, the Netherlands' legislator, in his Bill, makes a direct link between donor and recipient, and he explicitly orders a weighing of interests. Secondly, the requirement that the recipient should be in peril of his life seems less opportune, because if the recipient's life is in peril, the operation will not be of any avail anyway, in most cases. Moreover, the potential donor's freedom of decision will come under heavy pressure in this case.

One might, however, consider formulating a permissibility condition for a donation to take place that states that such an operation may take place exclusively for the purpose of one particular transplantation. In that interpretation, organ extirpation would not be allowed in as far as that might happen with the purpose of building up a certain stock. Another issue is whether or not donorship should remain restricted to genetically related persons. This question becomes the more relevant, the easier it becomes to prevent rejection with the help of new medicines. When, from a medical viewpoint, the necessity to restrict donorship to genetically related persons, no longer exists, the time has come for the legislator to reconsider his stand. In this connection, the Netherlands' legislator has stipulated that adults may grant permission for an organ extirpation for the benefit of a certain individual without strictly limitating this to relatives only. A much stricter regulation holds for minors. It has been laid down in the Bill that donation is only permitted for the benefit of a blood relation as far as twice removed. In this way the Netherlands' legislator categorically cuts off the possibility of building up of a stock.

Another point of interest is the information supply. In this paper we shall confine ourselves to information to the donor, in view of the fact that the recipient's position is more or less comparable to that of other persons undergoing a medical operation. But it is of utmost importance for the donor to be completely informed, in view of the unique character of the operation, not only as to its medical consequences, but also as to the possible material consequences. One might think in this respect, among other things, of the problems of (non)insurability in connection with heightened risks. In our opinion, the donor should also be informed about the chances the recipient receives from the transplantation. It is true that this implies a violation of the recipient's confidentiality position, but it is indefensible to ask someone to take such a far-reaching decision without being able to grasp what he is actually doing it for. All this does mean, though, that the donor has knowledge of the recipient's identity and that he is obliged to keep this confidential. In order to assure that the donor feels as free and independent as possible to take a decision, it is recommended that donor and recipient have separate doctors. In this way an entanglement of interests for a single doctor may be avoided. It naturally follows that the same holds true for pressure – perhaps out of proportion – on a possible donor and, at the same time, on the doctor. Neither the legislation in the Scandanavian countries nor that in Belgium, France, Austria or the Netherlands' Bill comprise a provision in the sense indicated above.

There is consensus on the requirement of permission: it should be voluntary, as a first priority. It is also beyond discussion that permission, once granted, may be revoked at any time. In which case, the recipient's doctor is left with not only the task but even the obligation of translating such a last-minute refusal into a medical reason.

There is a difference of opinion on the matter as to whether or not, in the case of married partners or two people living together, the partner's permission is required as well. Matthijs [2] considered a decision for donation of such weight that even intervention of the judge in summary proceedings should not be excluded. Apart from the fact that we would not be willing to burden a judge with such a divine judgement, we are of the opinion that this kind of solution is not in accordance with the generally accepted opinion in the Netherlands regarding the individual's right of self-determination.

A point to be considered is whether or not certain requirements of form should be laid down for granting permission. A number of legislators, among them the Danish and the French, have stipulated that permission should be granted in writing. The same is found in the Netherlands' Donation Bill. In order to avoid, as Koichi Bai argued in another context many years ago, that permission in writing provides a legitimization for a permission which is lacking in content, a statement in the donor's handwriting, dated and signed, seems most preferable, as laid down in the Netherlands' Bill.

Finally, a separate problem is formed by those persons who are unable to determine their own will, for whatever reasons. We shall first go into the position of minors. In general, provisions for donation ex vivo comprise an age limit which varies between 12 (the Netherlands) and 21 years (Denmark). Usually, though, age does not form an absolute limit. Exceptions are considered acceptable under exceptional circumstances. The Danish legislator has stated on this issue: 'Situations may arise where there are very strong reasons for granting a wish by a person under the suggested age limit to act as a donor'. The Netherlands' Donation Bill runs along the same lines, albeit that organ extirpation with permanent damage for the donor is not permitted. The Donation Bill explicitly excludes, e.g., the extirpation of one kidney in the case of minors, as such an operation is interpreted as permanent damage. Apart from the minor himself, those who exercise authority over the child are required to grant permission as well. Moreover, most legislation on donation by minors comprises additional provisions. Swedish legislation, for example, states that the final permission must be granted by the National Board of Health and Welfare. French legislation also includes a similar provision, stating that permission must be granted before a committee specially created for this purpose. Finally, the Netherlands' Donation Bill states that, apart from the child and its legal representatives, a magistrate in a juvenile court, after having heard the Child Welfare Council, must grant permission as well. Seen in the light of cautious and meticulous action, this type of provision is worth following. On the other hand, it should always be kept in mind that no official, whoever it may be, can take the responsibility for a donation decision away from parents or legal representatives.

Seen by us in a different light is the situation for persons who are incapable of determining their own will as a result of mental disturbance. Based on the viewpoint that self-determination should be a key factor in the donorship decision making, we are of the opinion that this category of persons must not be considered as donors. This holds even in the case that the result of transplantation would benefit the donor. An important consideration for this opinion is the fact that this kind of person will not or hardly understand the reach of such an operation, as a result of which such an operation will only be extremely burdensome without the plus point of any understandable advantages.

Finally, we are not opposed to the use of detainees as donors. It is true, the situation in which a detainee finds himself may make it uncertain whether or not he may come to a free decision, but detaineeship does not mean that someone lacks the possibility to determine his own will freely and independently. Thinking along these lines, we consider it wrong to deprive a detainee from his right to act as a donor, as a matter of course. That would comprise a restriction of self-determination, which does not naturally follow from deprivation of liberty.

## References


1. Land W (1989) The problem of living organ donation: facts, thoughts and reflections. Transplant Int 179
2. Matthijs J (1971) Bedenkingen ten behoeve van een transplantatiewet (Considerations regarding a law on transplantation). Rechtskundig Weekblad, p. 174

# Allowing Relatives to Bridge the Gap: The Norwegian Experience

A. Jakobsen, D. Albrechtsen, P. Fauchald, T. Leivestad, G. Sødal, and A. Flatmark

Traditionally, one has looked upon the duty of physicians and surgeons as directed towards an individual patient. Increasingly, it is becoming clear to many of us that we also have a duty to organize medical services, so that we can offer the best possible therapy to as many members of the community as possible and to provide this service at as low a cost as possible to the payer, whether to the tax payers or to insurance companies. (Jakobsen et al. 1982; Albrechtsen et al. 1990; Jakobsen 1990; Jakobsen et al. 1990). Looking at the treatment for terminal renal failure, such a view has certain implications: there should be a high transplant rate and few contraindications, and the services should be organized in such a way that a large proportion of renal transplants are carried out in a predialytic stage, i.e., just before dialysis treatment becomes necessary.

The population of Norway is only 4.1 million and these people are spread over a distance which is about half the length of Europe. If Norway were piroted around its most southernmost point, the North Cape would nearly reach Rome. It is not unusual for patients on the west coast and in the north of Norway to have to travel up to 3, perhaps 4 h to get to the dialysis center. In the shire of Finnmark, which is larger than Denmark and about two-thirds the size of Scotland, the dialysis center is in Tromsø, 3/4 h flying time from Kirkenes on the eastern border. This means that some patients would have to stay in Tromsø during the week and commute back home at the weekends.

The number of cadaver donors in Norway over the last 10 years has been quite steady at around 50, or in the region of 12–13 donors per million. In spite of considerable effort on our part in trying to increase this figure, we have not been very successful.

What would happen to the waiting list if we had only been performing transplants with kidneys from this actual number of cadaveric donors? With a waiting list in 1985 of 100 patients, that is 24 per million, and with 50 new patients per million per year, the waiting list would have been close to 500, or nearly 120 per million, in 1990. But it is not, it is just short of 100 patients, or 23 per million. The answer lies in the vigorous use of living donors. The relative proportion of living donors has, in fact, increased since 1983, when it was just short of 30 %; at the moment it is nearly 50 % of all renal transplants.

Departments of Surgery, Medicine, and Transplantation Immunology The National Hospital, Rikshospitalet, 0027 Oslo 1, Norway

W. Land, J. B. Dossetor (Eds.)
Organ Replacement Therapy:
Ethics, Justice and Commerce

So far this year (i.e., up to December 7, 1990) we have performed 194 renal transplants, and of these 94 (48 %) were living donor transplants. As the waiting list has not increased over the last 5 years, we have in other words managed to transplant patients at the rate they are presenting as needing treatment for terminal renal failure. We have estimated that about 80 % of all patients in Norway with the diagnosis of uremia eventually receive a renal transplant. The proportion of predialytic transplants is close to 25 %, and the number of patients older than 55 years receiving cadaveric transplants has during the last 4 years been close to 50 %.

We have so far carried out 893 transplants with a kidney from a living donor. Before cyclosporine became available, we only accepted HLA-identical and one haplo type mismatch combinations. Since the introduction of cyclosporine, we have accepted all types of mismatches within the family, including spouses, and have carried out about 50 transplants of this type. The 893 donor nephrectomies have been performed without any mortality. We have observed one case of pulmonary emboli, one case of coronary infarction and three cases of deep abscesses. Some 10 % of the donors have received antibiotica for suspected pneumonia (Fauchald et al 1991). We have also looked into the quality of life of 485 kidney donors, who were asked whether, if they had the chance to reconsider, they would consent to donating their kidney again. Only 14 persons (less than 3 %) would not. Approximately 94 % of the patients did not consider donating a kidney had done them any harm (Westlie et al. 1990).

So, in addition to all the medical benefits to the individual recipient in terms of the chance of long-lasting well-functioning transplant, and in addition to the effect on reducing the number of patients on the waiting list for a cadaveric transplant and time on dialysis for those patients who do not have a living donor and, thus, reducing the total cost for society, we have to do here with the phenomenon of persons who are willing to donate an organ to someone they love. The question really is, do we as doctors have the right to deny them this opportunity?

## References

Albrechtsen D, Sødal G, Jakobsen A, Brekke I, Flatmark A, Fauchald P, Talseth T, Thorsby E (1990) Nyretransplantasjon i Norge. Tidsskr Nor Laegeforen 110: (3) 327–331

Fauchald P, Sødal G, Albrechtsen D, Leivestad T, Berg KJ, Flatmark A (1991) The use of elderly living donors in renal transplantation Transpl Int (in press)

Jakobsen A (1990) A second opinion: in defence of the living donor transplant. Health Policy 16: 123–126

Jakobsen A, Bondevik H, Sødal G, Jervell J, Thorsby E, Flatmark A (1982) Organization for the care of patients with terminal renal failure in Norway. Transplant Proc 14 (1): 216–217

Jakobsen A, Albrechtsen D, Sødal G, Flatmark A, Fauchald P, Vartdal F (1990) Kostnader ved uremikeromsorg. Tidsskr Nor Laegeforen 110 (3): 334–341

Westlie L, Talseth T, Fauchald P, Flatmark A (1990) Quality of life in living donors in Norway. Kidney Int 37: 1984–1989

# The Living Donor in Kidney Transplantation: The Gothenburg Experience (1965–1990) From 490 Consecutive Donor Nephrectomies

H. I. Karlberg[1], G. Norden[2], H. Brynger[1], and I. Blohme[1]

## Introduction

In the Final Communiqué from a Conference of European Health Ministers held in Paris, 16–17 November 1987, it was concluded that donation of organs from living persons should be reduced and if possible completely stopped. Although long-term results of kidney transplantation were considered superior when using an organ from a related donor, it was felt that the short- and the long-term risks to the living donor were unacceptable. In this report, we present data on complications from 490 consecutive living donor nephrectomies in Gothenburg from 1965 to 1990.

## Patients and Methods

Routines and procedures have been reported in detail previously (Blohme et al. 1981). Donor numbers by era and donor-recipient relations are presented in Table 1. Technically or otherwise suboptimal kidneys were used

**Table 1.** Living donor nephrectomies in Gothenburg 1965–1989

| | | Donor status | | | |
|---|---|---|---|---|---|
| Era | Number | Parents | Siblings | Relatives | Non-blood relatives |
| 1965–1975 | 105 | 54 | 46 | 3 | 2 |
| 1975–1980 | 109 | 66 | 42 | 1 | 0 |
| 1980–1989 | 276 | 138 | 127 | 3 | 8 |
| 1965–1989 | 490 | 258 (53 %) | 215 (44 %) | 7 | 10 |

Total number of kidneys transplanted up to November 1990, 2400; number of kidneys donated by relatives up to November 1990, 530 (22 %)

[1] Transplant Unit, Department of Surgery, Sahlgrens Hospital, 413 45 Gothenburg, Sweden
[2] Department of Nephrology, Sahlgrens Hospital, 413 45 Gothenburg, Sweden

W. Land, J. B. Dossetor (Eds.)
Organ Replacement Therapy:
Ethics, Justice and Commerce

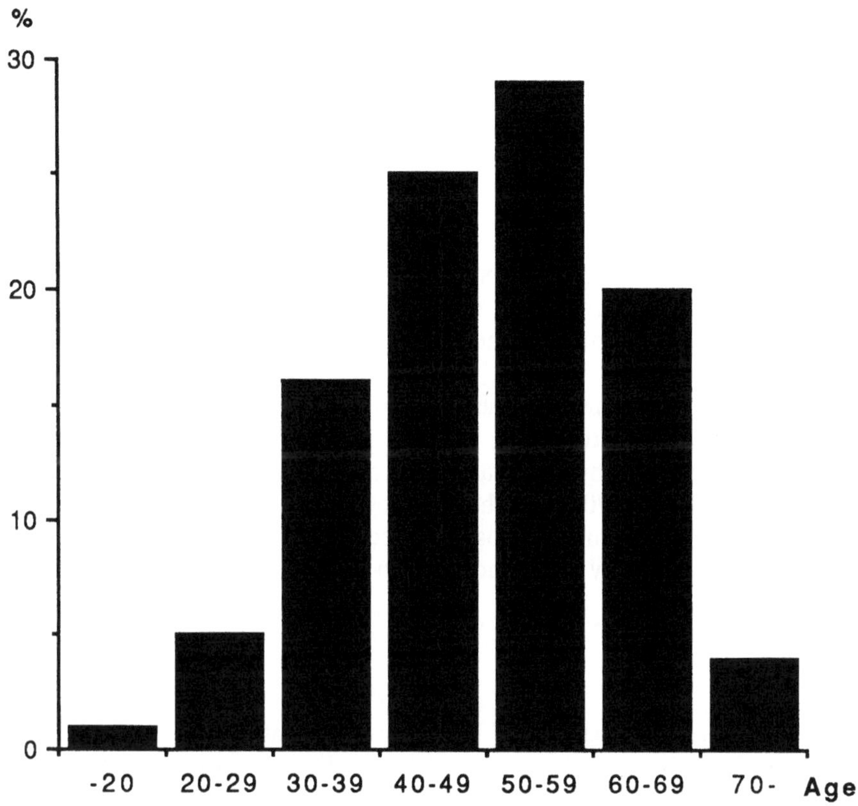


**Fig. 1.** Age distribution of the kidney donors

**Table 2.** Postoperative complications in 490 living donor nephrectomies in Gothenburg 1965–1989

| | 1965 – 1980 | 1981 – 1989 |
|---|---|---|
| Number of nephrectomies | 214 | 276 |
| Mortality | 0 | 0 |
| Postoperative hemorrhage | 4 | 1 |
| Thromboembolism | | 1 |
| Septicemia | 1 | 0 |
| Wound infection | 5 | 5 |
| Bronchopneumonia | 9 | 14 |
| Other minor complications (Bacteriuria, mental, allergic) | 13 | 24 |
| Major complications | 5 ( 2.3%) | 2 ( 0.7%) |
| Minor complications | 27 (13.0%) | 42 (15.0%) |

in 79 cases (multiple arteries or ureters, renal artery stenosis or aneurysms, calyceal cysts, renal adenomas, pelvic stones, and unilaterally reduced size). Age distribution of the kidney donors is given in Fig. 1.

## Results

There was no mortality. Complications are given in Table 2. Major complications occurred in seven donors; in five patients postoperative bleeding required surgical exploration; in one donor septicemia occurred, and one donor required anticoagulation therapy for postoperative pulmonary embolism.

In all cases kidney function was measured pre- and postnephrectomy as glomerular filtration rate (GFR) (ml/min per 1.73 $m^2$ body surface area, BSA) using chrome ethylene diaminetetroacetic acid (EDTA) clearance. Data from 150 donors (70 below the age of 50, and 80 over 50 years) are given in Fig. 2. Six to twelve months post nephrectomy the GFR of the remaining kidney had increased by 38 % and 32 % in the two groups, respectively.

## Discussion

Recent data from large studies of kidney transplantation such as the UCLA and the CTS registries still show superior results with organs from blood-

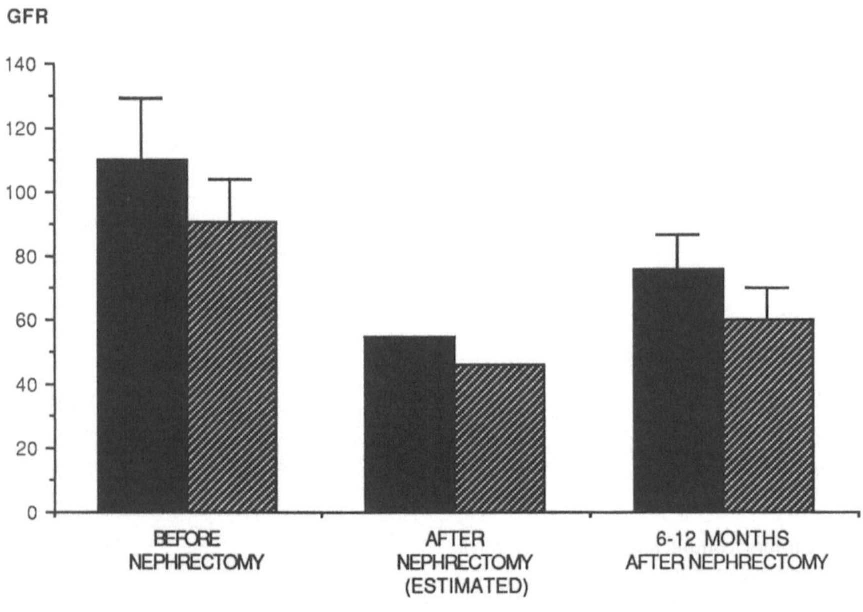


**Fig. 2.** Kidney function measured pre- and postnephrectomy as glomerular filtration rate (GFR)

related donors even when cyclosporine was used. However, the use of healthy individuals as organ donors is not uncontroversial, and the procedure must carry an accepable low morbidity. In two previous reports on long-term follow up, we found no serious disability related to the nephrectomy (Ewald et al. 1976; Mathillas et al. 1988). In those reports, renal function, blood pressure, and proteinuria were studied 10–18 years after nephrectomy. The present report summarizes the early postoperative complications after 490 consecutive donor nephrectomies. Major complications occurred in seven donors (1.4 %). There was no mortality. Minor complications occurred in 14 %. All donors recovered completely. However, one donor, who today is without signs or symptoms, developed a non-A-non B hepatitis, probably from a blood transfusion.

In conclusion, we continue to accept living related donors, since graft survival is superior to that achieved even with well-matched cadaveric kidneys. The basis for this acceptance is the voluntarism and the gratitude expressed by the donors in being able to help, and the facts presented here showing that donor-related complications were few and acceptable, both short and long term.

## References

Blohme I, Gäbel H, Brynger H (1981) The living donor in renal transplantation. Scand J Urol Nephrol [Suppl] 64: 143–151

Ewald J, Aurell M, Brynger H, Hansson L, Nilsson A, Bucht H, Gelin LE (1976) The living donor in renal transplantation: a study of physical and mental morbidity and functional aspects. In: Gelin LE (ed) Renal transplantation. Almqvist and Wiksell, Stockholm, pp 59–69

Mathillas Ö, Attman PO, Aurell M, Brynger H (1988) Glomerular filtration rate, hypertension and proteinuria after renal ablation: A long-term follow-up study in kidney donors. Scand J Urol Nephrol [Suppl] 108: 49–55

# Living Donor Kidney Transplantation in the United Kingdom and Ireland: Does Donor-Recipient Age Difference Matter?

P. K. Donnelly[1], A. R. Simpson[1], and D. G. Clayton[2]

## Background

There is an ever increasing discrepancy between the demand for renal transplantation and the supply of donor organs [1, 2]. Much of the recent increase in transplant waiting lists has been due to a rise in older patients (over 50 years). One possible solution to the shortage of cadaver donor organs would be to increase the use of living donors [3]. Recent studies have suggested that older living donors are an important source of organs [4, 5], however, physiological studies suggest that functional renal tissue decreases with age [6, 7]. Analyses of multicentre data [8] have also confirmed earlier reports [9] indicating that donor recipient age difference is a risk factor for graft survival, particularly when transplanting older donor organs. A survey was undertaken to investigate the extent of living donor transplantation (LDT) in the United Kingdom and Ireland with special reference to graft survival and the relative ages of donors and recipients.

## Patients and Methods

Questionnaires were sent to 32 transplant centres representing 18 health regions in the United Kingdom and Ireland. The following topics were covered: extent of LDT experience, donor source, donor and recipient ages, and transplant outcome. The analysis for graft survival versus time from transplant was complicated by the fact that the date of graft failure was not always accurately recorded. The construction of survival curves based on such data was based on a method described by Peto [10].

[1] Department of Surgery, Leicester General Hospital, Gwendolen Road, Leicester, LE5 4PW, United Kingdom

[2] Department of Community Medicine, Leicester University, Leicester, LE1 7RH, United Kingdom

W. Land, J. B. Dossetor (Eds.)
Organ Replacement Therapy:
Ethics, Justice and Commerce

## Results

Of the transplant centres contacted, 27 (84 %) replied and these represented 17 (94 %) of the health regions. The data that were available varied enormously between centres, but concerned over 1200 LDTs, representing approximately 10 % of all transplants. Seven transplant centres simply documented LDTexperience as a percentage of their total transplants. South Thames gave a cumulative result for graft survival on 334 LDTs. In all, 654 transplants were recorded in sufficient detail to permit individual analyses.

LDTs accounted for 0 %–25 % of total transplant experience in the various health regions, with the lowest figures being found in the Midlands. Analysis of the relationship of transplant donor to recipient showed that the most frequent donor source was sibling (56 %) followed by parent to child (38 %); 16 child to parent (2.5 %) transplants were recorded. The majority of recipients were aged 25–34, as were the donors although the overall trend was for donors to be older than recipients. The age differences and graft survival with siblings and parent donors are also shown in Table 1. Clearly, the parents were mostly 20 years older than the recipient, whilst the vast majority of sibling donors (84 %) were up to and more than 5 years younger than the recipient. LDT overall graft survival was 89 % at 1 year, falling to 76 % at 5 years and 66 % at 10 years. When graft survival was plotted in relation to source of donor there was an inferior graft survival for parent to child transplants as compared with sibling transplants (Table 1).

**Table 1.** Donor-recipient age difference and graft survival for living donors

| Donor-recipient age difference (years) | Sibling donor (%) | Parent donor (%) |
|---|---|---|
| Younger | | |
| >20 | 1 | – |
| 10–20 | 8 | – |
| 6–10 | 15 | – |
| 0–5 | 24 | – |
| Older | | |
| 0–5 | 41 | – |
| 6–10 | 10 | – |
| 10–20 | 4 | 9 |
| >20 | 2 | 91 |
| Graft survival | | |
| At 10 years | 75 | 53 |
| At 20 years | 66 | 42 |

## Discussion

In the United Kingdom and Ireland, living donors accounted for only 10 % of all transplants whilst there were major variations between centres. The explanation for these differences is uncertain. The advantages of LDT are claimed to be the absence of waiting time and the excellent long-term results [2]. This study confirms earlier reports that long-term graft survival is superior to that of cadaver donors [3]. However, the parent to child graft survival was significantly worse than that of the sibling transplants. Whilst this is most likely attributed to the effect of a one haplotype match rather than a two haplotype match, as is more common for siblings, it is possible that the relative ages of donor and recipient are also important. Further study of the relative importance of human leukocyte antigen (HLA) matching and age differences is indicated with a larger data base.

It has long been known that renal tissue decreases in mass and functional capacity with increasing age [6]. Over the age of 30 years glomerular filtration rate decreases linearly by 13 ml/min per decade. Since renal function, particularly in the elderly, is further impaired by rejection episodes and cyclosporin toxicity, it is perhaps not surprising that on the basis of age difference alone, parent to child kidney transplants would not survive as long as those from sibling donors. Older living donors are an important source of transplant kidneys from which reasonable function may be obtained. Whilst it is logical to consider more sibling or spouse transplants among the elderly, the effect of donor-recipient age difference should be considered as a risk factor in the aetiology of inferior results from parent to child transplantation.

## References


1. Feest TG, Mistry CD, Grimes DS et al. (1990) Incidence of advanced chronic renal failure and the need for end-stage renal replacement treatment. Br Med J 301:897–900
2. Broyer M, Brunner FP, Brynger H et al. (1987) EDTA Registry Centre Survey 1985. Nephrol Dial Transplant 2:475–487
3. Bay WJ, Lee AH (1987) The living donor in kidney transplantation. Ann Int Med 106:719–727
4. Compistol JM, Manalich M, Andrea J (1989) Rising age limit for kidney donors. Lancet ii:744–745
5. Fauchald P, Sodal G, Albrechsten H et al. (1991) The use of elderly living donors (LD) in renal transplantation. Transplant Proc (in press)
6. Anderson S, Brenner BM (1986) Effects of ageing on the renal glomerulus. Am J Med 80:435–442
7. O'Conner KJ, Franklin C, Bradley JW (1986) The effect of increasing donor age on kidney transplant outcome. Transplant Proc 18:480–481
8. Thorogood J, Persijn GG, Zantvoort FA (1990) Matching for age in renal transplantation. N Engl J Med 332:852–853
9. Donnelly PK, Simpson AR, Nicholson M et al. (1989) Age-matching improves the results of renal transplantation with older donors. Br J Surg 12:1349–1350
10. Peto R (1973) Experimental survival curves for interval censored data. Appl Stat 23:86–91

# Retrospective Evaluation of Psychosocial Factors in Former Living Related Kidney Donors

H. Bunzendahl, K. Wu, H. W. Künsebeck, G. Offner, U. Frei, H. Freyberger, and R. Pichlmayr

Since living related kidney transplantation has a long tradition in several countries, most of the relevant medical and ethical questions were asked early on, and many answers and conclusions have been published. In addition to surgical and medical factors, some of them are related to psychological and social factors. These may reflect thoughts and feelings of a particular society or nation. The number of living related donor kidney transplants is low in Germany. It has been in the range of 2 % of the total number of transplants for many years. In Hanover, this fraction has been higher. With some fluctuation over the past 16 years, about 7.5 % of all transplant kidneys were procured from living related donors. In pediatric recipients, this has been even higher, approaching 25 % in some years.

The immediate availability of a kidney with the highest possible quality was an important reason for choosing living related donors, especially in urgent recipients. Short-term and long-term function have been consistently higher with these kidneys in comparison with cadaveric kidneys matched for time of transplantation and recipient age. Although our results are not different from published results of Scandinavian, North American, and Australian series, the total number of utilized living donors has remained relatively low. To exclude the possibility of adverse psychological and social effects after transplantation in our country, a retrospective study of these factors related to previous kidney donation was carried out using a questionnaire.

Between October 1973 and January 1989, 121 living related donor kidney transplants were performed by our group. The addresses of 106 donors were still available; 83 (78 %) responded and sent back the completed questionnaire. Statistical analysis was carried out using $\chi^{2*}$ and $t$ test analysis wherever applicable. $P$* Values of less than 0.05 were considered significant. The mean donor age at the time of operation was 42.3 years (range 21–70 years); 27 donors (36.1 %) were men, 56 (63.9 %) were women. The time since the donation was 1.2–14.9 years. A total of 26 symptoms were listed, and four choices of severity were suggested ranging from "never present" to "always present". These symptoms were: fatigue, exhaustion, abnormal blood pressure, headaches, sleeping disorders, water retention, impaired memory, irritability, frightening dreams, restlessness, weight gain, back pain, nervous-

Klinik für Abdominal- und Transplantationschirurgie, Abteilung für Psychosomatische Medizin und Kinderklinik der Medizinischen Hochschule Hannover, Konstanty-Gutschow-Straße 8, 3000 Hannover 61, FRG

W. Land, J. B. Dossetor (Eds.)
Organ Replacement Therapy:
Ethics, Justice and Commerce

ness, feeling of loneliness, fears concerning future, oppressed moods, lack of interest, fears concerning complications, kidney disease, involuntary urination, indigestion, nausea, tremor, cardiovascular complaints, perspiration, and itching. The results were grouped according to common psychological techniques and their presence was determined. The data thus collected are presented in Table 1.

Sex-related differences in response patterns did not achieve statistical significance. "Irritability" was a more frequent complaint in men (26.9 % vs 8.9 %; $p = 0.07$). Symptoms related to "anxiety" were slightly more frequent in women (23.2 % vs 18.5 %). These symptoms or syndromes do not represent illness by themselves and did not require treatment. They are helpful in determining the psychosocial setting and make data more readily comparable with other studies.

The influence of the transplantation result was analyzed in detail. No symptoms or group of symptoms were significantly influenced by the transplant outcome. The question whether the donor would donate again, if possible, includes several aspects of the experience related to donation. The answers were distributed as presented in Table 2.

**Table 1.** Analysis of the effects of transplantation on donor health

| | % |
|---|---|
| Presence of groups of symptoms | |
| Depression-related | 21.7 |
| Anxiety-related | 24.1 |
| Psychovegetative | 7.2 |
| Self-evaluation of the donor's present state of health | |
| Good | 74.7 |
| Fair | 21.7 |
| Not good | 3.6 |
| Bad | 0 |
| Self-evaluation of the donor's quality of life after the donation | |
| Better than before | 12 |
| Unchanged | 79.5 |
| Somewhat worse | 6 |
| No comment | 2.4 |

**Table 2.** Analysis of influence of transplant outcome

| Grafts | Number of donors (*n*) | Donor would donate again *n* (%) | Donor would not donate again *n* (%) |
|---|---|---|---|
| With function | 58 | 52 (89.7) | 6 (10.3) |
| Without function | 25 | 21 (84.0) | 4 (16.0) |
| Total | 83 | 73 (88.0) | 10 (12.0) |

**Table 3.** Correlation of data on whether the donor would donate again with data on initiative for transplant operation

| | Number of donors (*n*) | Donation without donor's initiative *n* (%) | Donation with donor's initiative *n* (%) |
|---|---|---|---|
| Would donate again | 73 | 9 (12.3) | 64 (87.7) |
| Would not donate again | 5 | 0 (0) | 5 (100) |
| Undecided | 3 | 2 (66.7) | 1 (33.3) |
| Total | 81 | 11 (13.6) | 70 (86.4) |

It is reasonable to assume that the initiative to donate the kidney may influence the attitude afterwards. The results were surprising, especially if correlated with the question whether the donor would donate again (Table 3).

Satisfaction with pre- and postoperative care may play an important role in the donor's final evaluation of his overall experience. "Very satisfied" or "satisfied" were 79.3 %, "not satisfied" were 21.7 %. This is an indication of a reasonable performance of the donor program. The results of our questionnaire are in good agreement with a previously published study (Smith et al. 1986). The vast majority of donors experience a donation as a positive event that leads to improved self-esteem with few psychological and social side effects. The final outcome of transplantation apparently has no significant influence on the donor's overall experience. In contrast to other series (Smith et al. 1986), a higher percentage of donors in our series felt that the initial stimulus to donate came from themselves and not from medical personnel. This may indicate a very skillful information strategy that enables the donor to initiate donation himself, but it could also be interpreted as a sign of excessive and unjustified caution in recommending living donation.

Psychosocial factors in our series are not different when compared with the series studied in regions with higher utilization of living donors. Our questionnaire did not lead to a detection of additional obstacles in using living related donors in Germany. These findings may indeed influence patient teaching in our center and elsewhere and could possibly help to increase living donation in our country.

## References

Smith MD, Kappell DF, Province MA, Hong BA, Robson AM, Dutton S, Guzman T, Hoff J, Shelton L, Cameron D, Emerson W, Glass NR, Hopkins J, Peterson C (1986) Living-related kidney donors: a multicenter study of donor education, socioeconomic adjustment, and rehabilitation. Am J Kidney Dis 8(4):223–233

# Results of an Audit of Living Related Renal Allograft Donation From a Single Centre

P. A. Rowe[1], E. A. McGregor[1], M. A. Watson[1], and S. G. Macpherson[2]

## Introduction

The renal transplant unit in Glasgow serves a population of 2.75 million, and performs over 100 renal transplant operations each year. The first transplant from a living related donor was carried out in 1969. Since nephrectomy in a healthy person involves a small but appreciable risk, the procedure of living related transplantation needs careful evaluation. Both patient and graft survival in the recipient, and donor assessment protocol and outcome require audit. This study reviews the experience of 20 years, with particular regard to the assessment of and outcome for the donor.

## Patients and Methods

This initial report considers only the families of those patients who actually received a kidney from a living donor, and excludes families where no volunteer was deemed suitable. Patients were identified from renal unit records, and the hospital, departmental and laboratory records of each potential donor examined.

A potential donor was defined as an ABO-compatible first-degree relative who offered a kidney, with one exception of a living unrelated donation from wife to husband. The tissue type, length of time taken for assessment, reasons for rejection if more than one donor was available, operative complications, and outcome of grafting for all potential donors of each recipient were extracted from the case records.

The stages in prospective donor assessment are shown in Table 1. A haploidentical or identical human leucocyte antigen (HLA) match was sought in each case, and potential donors with less than this degree of HLA matching were rejected. The transplant surgeon and an independent medical team judged the psychosocial suitability of the potential donor and no formal psychiatric evaluation was conducted. The same independent physicians also carried out the medical assessment, which consisted of a short hospital

[1] Renal Unit Western Infirmary Glasgow G11 6NT Scotland
[2] Department of Surgery, Western Infirmary, Glasgow G11 6NT Scotland

W. Land, J. B. Dossetor (Eds.)
Organ Replacement Therapy:
Ethics, Justice and Commerce

**Table 1.** Stages in assessment of potential donors

1. Confirmed offer from first-degree relative
2. ABO blood grouping
3. HLA typing
4. Interview with transplant surgeon
5. Medical assessment by independent physician
6. Multidisciplinary discussion

admission for full examination and investigation. A haematological and biochemical profile, an intravenous urogram, supervised creatinine clearance, and formal bilateral selective renal arteriogram were undertaken in every case.

## Results

Since the first renal transplant in this centre in 1968, 1084 transplant operations have been performed, and 100 patients have received a kidney from a living donor. Seven patients underwent surgery elsewhere, and were excluded from the analysis of donor assessment. The age, sex, and relationship of all the potential donors are shown in Table 2. Sufficient information to permit evaluation of selection was available in 64 of the 93 cases. In 37 cases (58 %), only one donor was assessed; in 17 cases (27 %), two donors were assessed; in four cases (6 %) three donors were assessed; in five cases (8 %) four donors were assessed; and in one case, six donors were assessed, giving a total of 109 offers. Rejected donors were assessed more

**Table 2.** Details of potential donors

| | Accepted ($n$ = 93) | | | Rejected ($n$ = 45) | | |
|---|---|---|---|---|---|---|
| | Mean | SD | $n$ | Mean | SD | $n$ |
| Age (years) | 36.0 | (9.8) | – | 32.7 | (13.3) | – |
| Assessment interval (weeks) | 44.0 | (45.1) | – | 17.7 | (22.6) | – |
| Relation | | | | | | |
| Sibling | | | 64[a] | | | 32[b] |
| Parent | | | 28[c] | | | 13[d] |
| Spouse | | | 1[e] | | | 0 |

SD, Standard deviation: [a]33 women, 31 men; [b]21 women, 11 men; [c]16 women, 12 men; [d]8 women, 5 men; [e]1 woman

**Table 3.** Reasons for rejection of a potential donor

| Cause | Number (%) |
|---|---|
| Immunological | 15 (33) |
| Social | 10 (22) |
| Psychological | 5 (11) |
| Medical | 3 (7) |
| Donor offer withdrawn | 3 (7) |
| Anatomical | 2 (4) |
| Unknown | 7 (16) |

quickly ($t$-test; $p = 0.001$). The reasons for rejection of potential donors are listed in Table 3. In some cases two factors were judged to have contributed and these have been scored as 0.5 for each.

Immunological grounds for rejection comprised less than haploidentity (5.5 cases), or the existence of another donor with identical HLA type (9.5). Social reasons included family commitments such as young children (4.5), or general unease about motivation (5.5). Psychological problems such as drug or alcohol abuse (3), fear of operation (1) and lack of insight (1) also led to rejection. The medical contraindications were mitral valve disease (1), hypertension and hyperlipidaemia (1), anaemia (0.5), and age, obesity and smoking (0.5); two patients had bilateral multiple renal arteries and were considered unsuitable.

Early postoperative complications arose in ten cases (19%), only one of which was classified as serious – a pulmonary embolism. The remainder were wound haemorrhage requiring blood transfusion in one case; wound infection in six cases; and lower respiratory tract infection in two cases. There have been no deaths. Late complications have been observed in four donors: one suffered from depression for 6 months; two have developed hypertension requiring drug therapy; and one has required surgery to remove a calculus from her remaining kidney. The outcome of grafting for all 100 recipients is shown by actuarial life table analysis in Fig. 1. Ten-year graft survival (where death with a functioning graft is treated as loss to follow-up) was 78.8%. The majority of graft losses occurred early, eight within the first month, and the cause or graft failure was rejection in five patients, arterial thrombosis in one, recurrent oxalosis in one and uncertain cause in one.

## Discussion

The demand for renal transplantation continues to exceed the availability of cadaveric kidneys [1] and the long-term survival of grafts from living related donors is better than survival of grafts from cadavers [2]. For these reasons, many centres still practice living related kidney transplantation. However, such elective surgery in healthy individuals requires careful and continuing

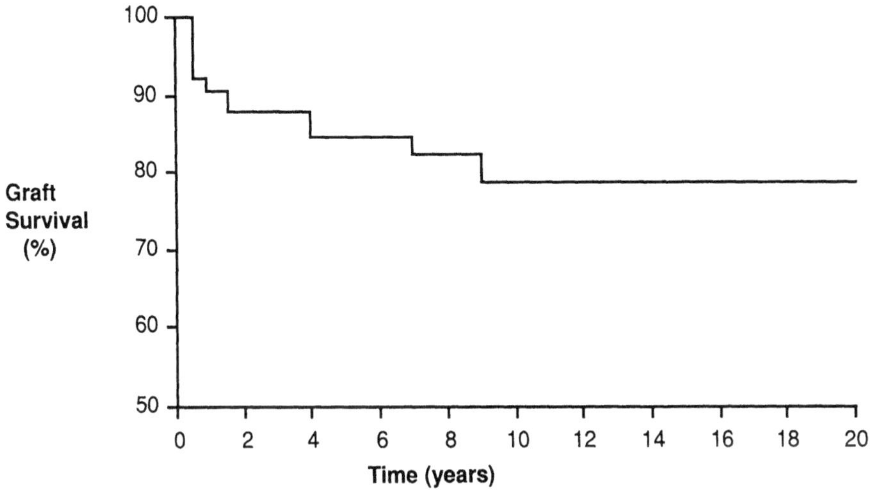


**Fig. 1.** Overall results of living related renal allograft transplantation (1969–1989)

audit and can only be justified by a consistently superior outcome with minimal and acceptable risks to the donor.

Our results demonstrate that the risk to the donor of serious complications is low, and the minor problems encountered were not of an unexpected nature. The possibility of such complications had been discussed with the donors during their preoperative counselling. Unsuitable donors were rejected reasonably quickly, usually for immunological or social reasons, but assessment of accepted donors was lengthy. This permits considered appraisal and is appropriate, since only well-motivated donors are likely to complete the assessment.

The long-term results of the procedure for the recipient were good, and compared favourably with the results of cadaveric transplantation. However, there remains a significant risk of early graft loss from acute rejection, even in these well-matched donors, and further effort should be made to reduce this.

Living related renal transplantation offers the prospect of long-term graft survival to the recipient at small risk to the donor and should continue to play a role in the management of end-stage renal disease.

## References

1. UK Transplant Service (1989) Annual report, p 22
2. Morris PJ (1988) Results of renal transplantation. In: Morris PJ (Ed) Kidney transplantation, 3rd edn. Saunders, Philadelphia, pp 737–741

# Renal Transplantation From a Living Related Donor

E. Alexopoulos[1], G. Sakellariou[1], D. Memmos[1], Z. Polymenidis[2], A. Antoniadis[3], K. Karamitsos[1], D. Lazaridis, and M. Papadimitriou[1]

## Introduction

Living related donors (LRD) still remain the main source of kidney transplants for several countries. The superiority of graft survival from LRD is undoubted. On the other hand, the shortage of cadaver kidneys and the better histocompatibility between relatives argue in favor of LRD [1]. Thus, in some centers in the United States, up to 25 % of transplanted kidneys come from this source. In Europe, the center policy differs considerably regarding the potential donors. In Norway, 56 % of all grafts performed in 1987 came from LRD, and in Sweden and Denmark more than 20 % of all first grafts came from that origin. However, in other countries like the United Kingdom, Spain, France, and Germany, LRD are accepted only in a minority of the centers [2]. In Greece, out of a total of 758 renal transplantations performed over the last 20 years, 584 (77 %) came from LRD.

The aim of this study was to analyze the results of a single center experience, based on 231 LRD renal transplants which have been performed over a 20-year period and which represent more than one-third of the total number of renal transplantations done in this country during that period.

## Patients and Methods

Among 294 kidney transplants performed at our center from July 1968 to July 1989, 231 (78.6 %) grafts came from LRD. The mean age of the recipients was 33 years (range 9–58 years) and of the donors 53 years (range 19–78 years). Mean period of observation after transplantation was 58 months (range 6–234 months). The primary renal diseases of the patients are shown in Table 1. Of the donors, 145 (62.8 %) were mothers, 60 (26.0 %) fathers, 25 (10.8 %) brothers and 1 (0.4 %) aunt.

[1] Department of Nephrology, Aristotelian University of Thessaloniki, Hippokration Hospital, Thessaloniki, Greece
[2] Department of Immunology, Hippokration Hospital, Thessaloniki, Greece
[3] Department of Transplantation Surgery, Aristotelian University of Thessaloniki, Hippokration Hospital, Thessaloniki, Greece

W. Land, J. B. Dossetor (Eds.)
Organ Replacement Therapy:
Ethics, Justice and Commerce

**Table 1.** Primary renal disease in 231 LRD renal transplantations

| Disease | *n* |
|---|---|
| Glomerulonephritis | 143 |
| Interstitial nephritis | 37 |
| End-stage kidney disease | 20 |
| Diabetic nephropathy | 9 |
| Alport's syndrome | 7 |
| Polycystic kidneys | 7 |
| Lupus nephritis | 4 |
| Nephrosclerosis | 3 |
| Hemolytic-uremic syndrome | 1 |

Donors and recipients were ABO compatible. Prior to 1982, histocompatibility testing included typing for HLA-A, -B and -C. Starting in 1982, determination of HLA-DR was introduced in the histocompatibility profile of the donor and the recipient, as well as the mixed lymphocyte reaction (MLR) in selected cases. All patients received at least 1 unit of whole blood before operation.

Until 1984, postoperative immunosuppression consisted of prednisolone (Pred) and azathioprine (Aza). Cyclophosphamide was used only in selected cases. After 1984, cyclosporine A (CyA) was introduced in combination with Pred and Aza (triple drug regimen). Pred was administered in a tapering schedule reaching 10 mg/day at the end of the 3rd month after transplantation. Aza administration started 2–3 days before transplantation in a dose of 1.5–2 mg/kg BW. Its dose was further adjusted according to the presence of side effects. Oral CyA was given in a dose of 5–6 mg/kg BW and then adjusted to keep whole blood levels at 200–400 ng/ml as determined by a radioimmunnoassay method (Sandoz).

Rejection episodes, diagnosed by clinical criteria, were usually confirmed by percutaneous renal biopsy. Antirejection treatment consisted of daily bolus of methylprednisolone i.v. up to a total cumulative dose of 2–3 g. Antilymphocyte globulin (ALG) or antithymocyte (ATG) globulin were used concomitantly with methylprednisolone in a daily dose of 10 mg/kg BW for 7–10 days. Plasma exchange was rarely used, except in cases of acute vascular or accelerated rejection resistant to conventional treatment.

The diagnosis of CyA nephrotoxicity was suggested by elevated serum creatinine in the absence of histological evidence of rejection and by the response to CyA dose reduction. Posttransplant follow-up included hematological, biochemical, and routine urine analysis at frequent intervals. Sonographic and radionuclide functional and anatomical evaluations were routinely performed. Also, the lymphocyte subpopulations and the changes of the OKT4/OKT8 ratio were closely followed.

## Results

Among the 231 graft recipients, 149 received conventional immunosuppression (Pred plus Aza) and 82 CyA in combination with Pred and Aza.

Patients and graft survival of the 231 recipients are shown in Fig. 1. Overall the group displayed a patient survival rate of 96 %, 80 %, and 61 % at the end of 1,5, and 10 years after transplantation, respectively. Graft survival at the same intervals was 89 %, 70 %, and 55 %, respectively.

The patient survival for CyA-treated recipients at 1 and 2 years posttransplant was 97 % and 97 % (Fig. 2). Graft survival for the same group of patients and for corresponding intervals was 88 % and 82 %, respectively

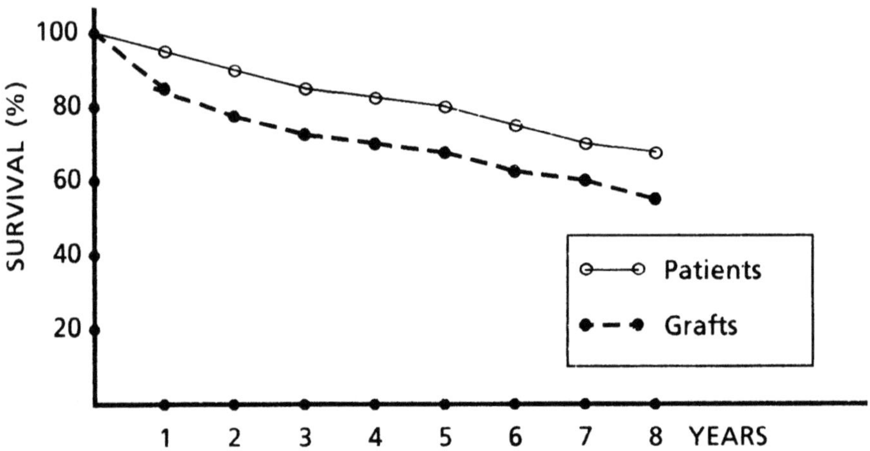


**Fig. 1.** Cumulative patient and graft survival in 231 LRD renal transplantations

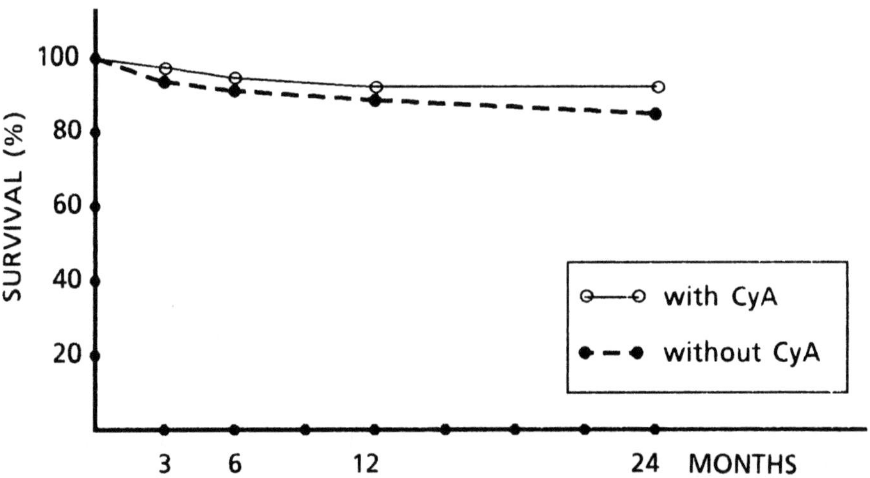


**Fig. 2.** Comparative patient survival in CyA-treated and conventionally treated groups of patients

(Fig. 3). Most importantly, no significant differences were observed in the conventionally treated group, regarding patient (95% and 89%) and graft survival (87% and 77%) for the same periods of observation.

Irreversible graft rejection was the most frequent cause of graft loss. A total of 72 grafts were lost owing to rejection. Interestingly, the rate of graft loss was higher during the first 3 months and in the 2nd year after transplantation (Fig. 4). Almost half of the patients had at least one episode of acute rejection. More specifically, episodes of acute rejection were observed in 91 of 149 patients (61.9%) in the conventionally treated group and in 28 of 82 (34.1%) CyA-treated patients ($p < 0.001$).

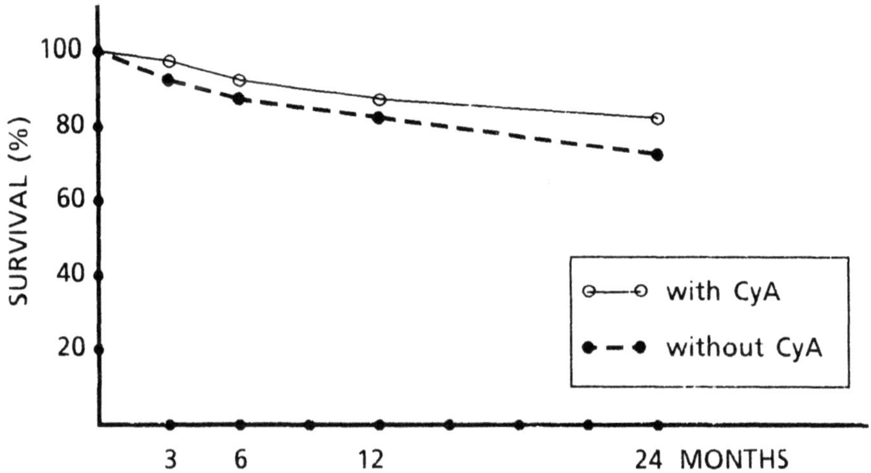


**Fig. 3.** Comparative graft survival in CyA-treated and conventionally treated patients

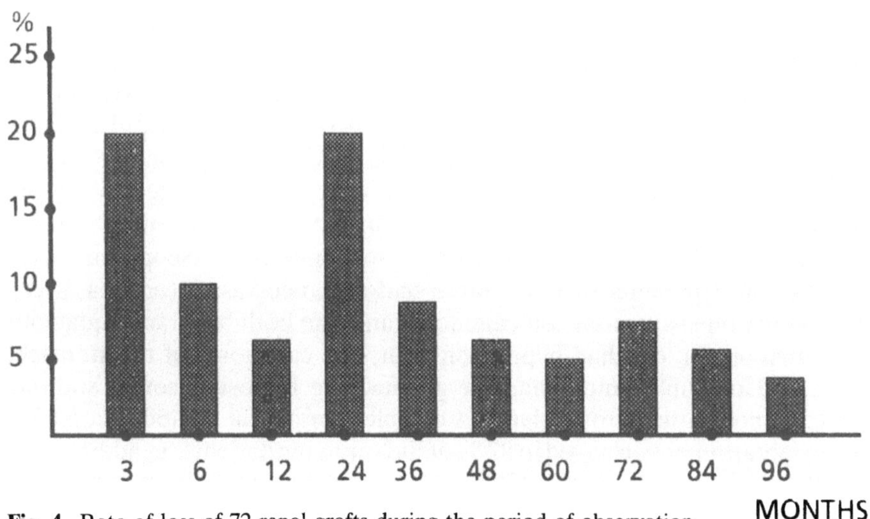


**Fig. 4.** Rate of loss of 72 renal grafts during the period of observation

**Table 2.** Causes of death in 46 patients

| | *n* | % |
|---|---|---|
| Infections | 13 | 28.2 |
| Liver disease | 12 | 26.0 |
| Cardiovascular disease | 11 | 23.9 |
| Neoplasms | 5 | 10.9 |
| Gastrointestinal bleeding | 4 | 8.7 |
| Uremia | 1 | 2.1 |

In all, 46 patients died and 58 returned to dialysis or continuous ambulatory peritoneal dialysis (CAPD) during the period of follow-up. The main causes of death were infections (28.2 %), liver diseases (26 %), and cardiovascular complications (23.9 %) (Table 2). Relatively early deaths (occurring less than 1 year after transplantation) were seen in 12 of 149 (8.05 %) conventionally treated patients, and in 2 of 82 (2.43 %) CyA-treated patients ($p<0.001$). Early deaths in the former group were attributed to hepatitis in four cases, infection in four, gastrointestinal bleeding in three and myocardial infarction in one. The two early deaths in the second group were due to infection and myocardial infarction respectively.

A total of 127 patients are still alive with functioning grafts and a current mean plasma creatinine level of 1.48 mg/dl (range 0.6–6.5 mg/dl). Mean plasma creatinine of the CyA-treated patients is 1.78 mg/dl (range 1–6.5 mg/dl), and of those treated conventionally 1.35 mg/dl (range 0.8–5.4 mg/dl) ($p<0.05$).

Arterial hypertension requiring treatment was the most frequent complication and was recorded in 88 patients (38 %). The incidence of hypertension was higher in the CyA-treated group (48 %) than in the group that received conventional treatment (26 %). Severe infections necessitating hospitalization were observed in 23 patients (10 %), and cataracts with unilateral or bilateral involvement in 23 (10 %). The latter complication required a drastic reduction in the steroid dosage in the majority of the cases, while extraction of the cataract was carried out in seven instances. Steroid-induced diabetes mellitus was diagnosed in 19 patients (9.3 %) and avascular bone necrosis in 14 (6.9 %). All patients with bone disease were initially treated by a rapid reduction of the dose of Pred; however four patients unterwent a total hip replacement and three are candidates for operation. Neoplasms were detected in 9 patients (4.1 %); three had skin neoplasms (one basal cell carcinoma, one squamous cell carcinoma and one both basal and squamous cell carcinomas), one had hypernephroma, one carcinoma of the stomach, one non-Hodgkin's lymphoma, one glioma, one Kaposi sarcoma, and one mixed tumor of the parotid gland. A complete or partial rehabilitation after transplantation was achieved in 87 % of the surviving patients. In addition, 13 healthy children have been born from nine transplanted patients (six female and three male).

The long-term impact, of nephrectomy on the renal function was studied in 86 donors. The mean age at the time of donation (± SD) was 59 (± 7 years) and the mean follow-up 55.2 (± 42.9) months (range 3–140 months). During this time mean plasma creatinine level rose from 1.16 (± 0.11) mg/dl to 1.38 (± 0.23) mg/dl ($p < 0.001$). In 20 donors, plasma creatinine levels exceeded 1.4 mg/dl at the last admission. Urine tests after nephrectomy disclosed traces of protein in 12 donors (13.9 %), but in three cases the daily protein excretion was greater than 500 mg. Seventeen of the donors (19.7 %) had mild hypertension at the time of donation, while at the endpoint of observation, 28 of them (32.5 %) were found to be hypertensive.

## Discussion

The results of the present study confirm previous observations that kidney transplantation from LRDs offer the best chance of excellent long-term outcome. However, there are several salient points in our experience. Patient and graft survival in our transplant population are comparable to the rates obtained in other centers [3, 4] although, over the last 8 years we have not excluded from the transplant program patients with severe renal diseases such as diabetes mellitus or systemic lupus erythematosus (SLE). The excellent survival rate may be due to the improvement in our knowledge regarding the use of the immunosuppressive drugs, increased clinical experience, and the introduction of CyA as a first-line immunosuppressive drug.

Of course other factors such as improvement in tissue typing, MLR, and transfusions cannot be ruled out. We have recently shown that identity in certain superhaplotypes between donors and recipients resulted in a significant prolongation of LRD graft survival [5]. Also, the presence of low mixed leukocyte culture (MLC) stimulation index before transplantation was associated with an increased graft survival rate as well as improved renal function, as indicated by the plasma creatinine levels [6].

Despite the initial difficulties encountered in learning to use a new drug like CyA, the overall short-term clinical results for the first 82 LRD kidney recipients treated with CyA are at least as good, if no better, than those obtained with the conventional immunosuppressive agents as used by us for 16 years [7, 8]. However, in a mixed population of living and cadaveric transplants in our center, CyA increased the graft survival by almost 15 % and this difference could be attributed to the better survival of cadaveric grafts. It seems likely that LRD renal transplants have an excellent prognosis, and any improvement, even with CyA, may be difficult to attain, at least in the short-term [3, 8]. Whether or not the small, although not significant, difference observed by the end of the 2-year follow-up will increase is unknown at the moment.

However, the institution of CyA had two main advantages. First, the incidence of acute rejection episodes was significantly reduced, and this is in agreement with other reports [9]. This has led to the development of safer and more flexible protocols with the use of steroids in concert with Aza and CyA in low doses for long-term immunosuppression.

Second, the death rate during the early posttransplant period was lowered; especially reduced was the number of deaths due to infections and liver disease which almost characterized the pre-CyA era. This could be the result of the less aggressive immunosuppression and more aggressive approach to the infection that permitted early diagnosis of common and rare infections and early institution of antimicrobial therapy [10, 11]. Of course, we cannot exclude improvement in disparate background factors such as medical management and technical experience which may contribute to the superiority of the recent results.

The increased graft loss during the first 3 months after transplantation while patients are receiving high doses of immunosuppressive drugs indicates that most of these rejections are not preventable. On the other hand, the later peak of losses, observed during the 2nd year after operation, relates rather to the suboptimal immunosuppression, regarding control or prevention of side effects [12].

Hypertension has been a significant problem in many patients. Its incidence rose to almost 50 % in CyA-treated patients despite the use of low doses of CyA and the presence of normal plasma creatinine levels. It usually appeared during the 2–3 days after the institution of the drug and required antihypertensive therapy in almost 8.5 % of the patients during the 1st month [4, 13].

Severe infections are still a serious problem. The majority of the infections were bacterial in origin and primarily involved the upper and lower respiratory tracts, the urinary tract, and the skin. It is worth noting that among 22 severe infections in the conventionally treated group which required hospitalization, 12 led finally to death. In contrast, only one patient in the CyA-treated group died because of pneumonia, a fact that confirms the lower incidence of fatal infection in this group of patients [4].

Interestingly, the incidence of aseptic bone necrosis was higher in our patients than in other reports [14], and this may be due to higher doses of steroids which were used in the past. In addition, there was also a relatively low incidence of neoplasms as compared with other reports [15]. Of particular significance is the fact that all but one of the tumors were observed in the conventionally treated group. This may reflect the less aggressive immunosuppression that has been used recently, but also, the relatively short follow-up of the CyA-treated patients.

CyA nephrotoxicity has been recognized in 20 % of the patients who received CyA and, 5 years after its institution in our transplant program, the distinction between CyA nephrotoxicity and acute transplant rejections remains an unresolved problem [16].

Our experience, based on a recent analysis of our cases, indicates that the best basis for diagnosis of CyA nephrotoxicity is to evaluate all the features of CyA overdosage, i.e., whole blood through levels, clinical and histological signs of toxicity, as well as the persistently stable or low ratio of OKT4/OKT8.

Each of the above parameters separately is of limited diagnostic value [17].

Infections, cardiovascular complications, and liver disease were the main causes of death. Interestingly, gastrointestinal hemorrhage has no longer been a cause of death in recent years. In addition, deaths due to infections and liver disease have considerably decreased in CyA-treated patients. Among the total number of deaths, only three occurred in this group of patients. This is a most important point, relating to a great extent to the introduction of CyA that permitted the use of combinations of drugs in lower doses and decreased the incidence of rejections and infections. The long-term effects of CyA on renal graft function still remain a matter of controversy [18].

The rehabilitation of the patients is almost complete in the vast majority of the cases. Most of them are back to work, and they enjoy a full family and social life. Parenthood is not risky if patients have normal renal function and receive the immunosuppressives in relatively low doses [15, 19].

Donation is a safe procedure without major risks for the donors. The slight increase in plasma creatinine levels and blood pressure are relatively early events, which tend to stabilize during follow-up and do not complicate significantly the general well-being of the donors. Of course longer follow-up is needed to evaluate more precisely the long-term implications of the nephrectomy [20, 21].

In conclusion, LRD renal transplantation is an accepted form of therapy for patients with chronic renal failure. Patient and graft survival is excellent in the short- and long-term. CyA does not improve graft survival significantly, at least after a short-term period of observation. However, it has led to a lower incidence of infections, acute rejection episodes, and early deaths. The rehabilitation of the patients is high, while no significant early or late complications related to the donation were noted.

## Summary

Living related donors (LRD) still remain a significant source of kidney grafts in several countries. Over the last 2 decades in this unit, from a total of 294 renal grafts, 231 (78.6 %) came from LRD. The mean age of the recipients was 33 years (9–58 years) and of the donors 53 years (29–82 years). Actuarial patient survival rates at 1 and 5 years were 96 % and 80 %, and graft survival 89 % and 70 %, respectively. In 82 recent cases, CyA was also included in the therapeutic protocol.

Patient survival at 1 and 2 years was 97 % and 97 % in the CyA-treated group, and 95 % and 89 % in the conventionally treated group. Graft survival at the same intervals was 88 % and 82 % in the former group, and 87 % and 77 % in the later. CyA-treated patients had a much lower incidence of acute rejection episodes than those treated conventionally ($p < 0.001$). In addition, the number of early deaths was significantly higher in the second group than in the CyA-treated group ($p < 0.01$). Rehabilitation was achieved in 87 % of the surviving patients. All but one of the donors now have normal plasma creatinine levels, and no lethal complications related to the donation were observed.

In conclusion, LRD renal transplantation seems to give the best chance for long-term patient and graft survival. The use of CyA has led to a lower incidence of acute rejections and early deaths, but up to now it has not improved significantly the short-term patient and graft survival. On the other hand, LRD renal transplantation is a safe procedure for the donor, without affecting the renal function in the long-term follow up.

## References


1. Roberts JR, Fryd DS, Ascher NL, Migliori R, Payne WD, Dunn DD, Sutherland DD, Simmons RL, Najarian JS (1988) Living related kidneys continue to provide superior results over cadaveric kidneys in the cyclosporine era. Transplant Proc 20 [Suppl 1]:26–27
2. Brunner FP, Fassbinder W, Broyer M, Brynger H, Dykes SR, Ehrich JHH, Geerlings W, Rizzoni G, Selwood NH, Tufveson G, Wing AJ (1987) Combined report on regular dialysis and transplantation in Europe XVIII:5–32
3. Stratta RJ, Armbrust MJ, Oh CS, Pirsch JD, Kalayoglu M, Sollinger HW, Belzer FO (1988) Withdrawal of steroid immunosuppression in renal transplant recipients. Transplantation 45:323–328
4. Kahan BD, Flechner SM, Lorber MI, Golden S, Conley S, Van Buren CT (1987) Complications of cyclosporine-prednisolone immunosuppression in 402 renal allograft recipients exclusively followed at a single center for from one to five years. Transplantation 43:197–204
5. Polymenidis Z, Papadimitriou M, Sakellariou G, Memmos D, Vergoulas G, Daniilidis M, Alexopoulos E, Metaxas P (1985) Superhaplotype haploidentity and renal graft survival from live relative donors. Transplant Proc 17:2207–2210
6. Daniilidis M (1988) The significance of certain antigen of the HLA-D/DR region in graft survival from living related donors. MD Thesis, Thessaloniki, Greece
7. Mickey MR (1986) Center effect. In: Terasaki PI (ed) Cinical transplants 1986. UCLA Tissue Typing Laboratory, Los Angeles, pp. 165–173
8. Cicciarelli J (1986) Cyclosporine and trends in kidney transplantation. In: Terasaki PI (ed) Clinical transplants 1986. UCLA Tissue Typing Laboratory, Los Angeles, pp. 223–230
9. Flechner SM, Kerman RH, Van Buren CT, Lorber MI, Barker CJ, Kahan BD (1987) Does cyclosporine improve the results of HLA-identical renal transplantation? Transplant Proc 19:1485–1488
10. Papadimitriou M, Alexopoulos E, Memmos D, Efstatiadis G, Proia E (1985) The management of nosocomial infections in chronic uraemic patients. In: Ishigami J (ed) Recent advances in chemotherapy. University of Tokyo Press, Kyoto, pp. 2065–2066
11. Alexopoulos E, Sakellariou G, Memmos D, Kirou A, Papadimitriou M (1985) Urinary tract infections after renal transplantation. Drug Exp Clin Res 11:101–105
12. Mickey MR, Cho Y, Terasaki PI (1988) Early graft loss. Tranplant Proc 20 [Suppl 1]:31–33
13. Chapman JR, Marcen R, Arias M, Raine AGG, Dunill MS, Morris PJ (1987) Hypertension after renal transplantation. A comparison of cyclosporine and conventional immunosuppression. Transplantation 43:861–864

14. Delpin-Santiago EA, Gonzalez Z, Mora-Rive E, Amadeo JH, Ramirez-Gonzalez R (1986) Results of living-related kidney transplantation in Puerto Rico. Transplantation 41:606–610
15. Rao KV, Andersen RC (1988) Long-term results and complications in renal transplant recipients. Transplantation 45:45–52
16. Thiel G, Harder F, Lörtscher R, Brünisholz M, Landmann J, Brunner F, Follath F, Wenk M, Mihatsch M (1983) Cyclosporin A used alone or in combination with low-dose steroids in cadaveric renal transplantation. Klin Wochensch 61:991–1000
17. Alexopoulos E, Leontsini M, Daniilidis M, Sakellariou G, Visvardis G, Papadimitriou M (1991) Differentiation between renal allograft rejection and cyclosporine nephrotoxicity. A clinicopathological study. Am J Kidney Dis (in press)
18. Kahan BD (1986) Cyclosporine nephrotoxicity: pathogenesis, prophylaxis, therapy and prognosis. Am J Kidney Dis 8:323–331
19. Tabakoudis P, Alexopoulos E, Papadimitriou M, Kalogeropoulos A, Mandalenakis S, Metaxas P (1985) Parenthood after renal transplantation. Mat Med Greca 13:75–79
20. Conrad M, Wahrman J, Williams S, Jorkasky D (1987) Living-related donation: a sibling controlled study. Transplant Proc 19:1492–1493
21. Sakellariou G, Alexopoulos E, Kokolina E, Daniilidis M, Gakis D, Papadimitriou M (1989) Impact of donor age in relation with graft survival and quality of remaining kidney of donor. In: Andreucci VE, Dal Canton A (eds) Current therapy in nephrology. Kluwer, Boston, pp. 449–451

# Organ Donation with Living Related Donors with Cancer

N. Ivanovski, K. Čakalaroski, A. Ončevski, G. Masin, Ž. Popov, and M. Polenaković

## Introduction

Kidney transplantation is currently considered a routine treatment of chronic renal failure. Nevertheless, in spite of its expansion nowadays, it has grown mostly in the highly developed countries where there is good organization and effective organ sharing. Less developed countries such as those in Eastern Europe are significantly behind in the application of cadaveric kidney transplantation, either as a result of the bad organization of the transplantation service or because of a lack of legal rules for organ donation. On the other hand, the number of candidates for chronic hemodialysis treatment is increasing almost equally in all countries, and, thus, the need for kidney transplantation is equal, too (Tufveson et al. 1989).

Some countries have tried to solve the lack of regular organ supply by forcing living donor transplantation, mostly with a matched haplotype or fully identical human leukocyte antigens (HLA). In recent times there has been a growing tendency for transplantation using unrelated donors, which, under the codex of the Council of the Transplantation Society, may be performed only if not associated with the buying or selling of organs, or if it is emotionally justified. The living donor transplantation certainly takes into consideration the complete safety of the donor: his complete fitness and the exclusion of any kind of contraindications. From that point of view, we are reporting two cases of voluntary kidney donation made when the donor is suffering from a malignant disease, and where the primary principle of safety (of the donor) appears to be broken.

## Case 1

In the first case, the kidney donor was the father. He was 70 years old, with advanced laryngeal carcinoma, and he donated a kidney to his son, who was 40 years old and had chronic glomerulonephritis; the son had been treated with hemodialysis for 7 months. The surgical procedure, postoperative

Department of Nephrology, Skopje School of Medicine, University of Cyril and Methodius, Vodnjanska 17, 91.000 Skopje, Yugoslavia

W. Land, J. B. Dossetor (Eds.)
Organ Replacement Therapy:
Ethics, Justice and Commerce

course, and the general condition of the donor as well as of the recipient were good. The recipient underwent therapy with azathioprine, methylprednisolone, and cyclosporine A from the very beginning. The graft function normalized on the 15th postoperative day, without any need of dialysis treatment. Because of the slow normalization of the graft function, a minor degree of initial tubulopathy could not be excluded. Eleven months after transplantation, we had normal morphology and function of the graft. In the meantime because the donor was suffocating, a total laryngectomy was performed. He is now in a relatively good general condition and has normal kidney function.

## Case 2

In the second case, the kidney donor was the mother. She was 53 years old, with lymphoepithelioma and local lymphonodular metastasis. She donated her kidney to her 32-year-old daughter, who had chronic glomerulonephritis and had been under dialysis treatment for 4 years. The surgical procedure and postoperative course of the donor as well as of the recipient were good. From the beginning the recipient was under therapy with azathioprine, methylprednisolone, and cyclosporine A. We did not confirm either a tubulopathy or rejection episodes. Eighteen months after transplantation, the morphology and function of the graft were normal. The donor is in a good condition after undergoing local radiation therapy.

## Discussion

### Current Need of Organ Supply

The area of S. R. Macedonia with a population of 2 million has 13 dialysis centers available and 650 dialysis patients. The annual increase in the number of new dialysis patients is 70; the total number of patients on the waiting list for kidney transplantation is 225. The local kidney transplantation center performs about 20 transplantations per year, 12 from cadaveric and 8 from living donors. Under these circumstances, our team is simply obliged to take into consideration all the organ donations offered.

### Ethics of Donation Under Existence of Malignancy

Starting from the Hippocratic Oath that human life is of primary concern, as well as from the principle *"primum non nocere"* (Bonomini 1990), taking a kidney from a person with a malignant disease should certainly be considered a handicap for the donor, because he/she is left without one organ of vital importance in conditions of malignant disease. The decision for accepting such a donation is to be motivated with a high degree of sense, strong emotional relationship, and high human motives for donation (Morris et al. 1985). On the other hand, the decision is to be influenced also by the nature of the malignant disease and the potential risk of its appearance in the recipient who is under permanent immunosuppresive therapy.

## The Curse of the Physician's Decision

Looking at God giving life to Adam in famous fresco Michelangelo's, it seems that life comes from heaven. But, Adam stands firmly on the earth, and the physician's job is cruel, unsparing and permits no compromises in the struggle to maintain life here on earth. In these cases, we accepted the donations, next time, perhaps we shall not.

## References

Bonomini V, Gozzeti G (1990) Is living donation still justifiable. Nephrol Dial Transplant 5:407–410

The Council of the Transplantation Society (1985) Commercialization in transplantation: the problems and some guidelines for practice. Lancet 2:715–716

Tufveson G, Geerlings W, Brunner FP, Brynger H, Dykes SR, Ehrich JHH, Fassbinder W, Rizzoni G, Selwood NH, Wing AJ (1989) Combined report on regular dialysis and transplantation in Europe, XIX, 1988. Nephrol Dial Transplant 4 [Suppl 4]:S5–S29

# Social Aspects of Kidney Donations in 300 Living Related and Unrelated Renal Transplantations

N. Simforoosh, B. Amir Ansari, A. Bassiri, and S. Gol

## Introduction

Renal transplantation in humans started with a living related donor transplant in 1953 [1]. Later on, cadaver transplantation found a special place in organ transplantation, especially in kidney transplantation. Since, with organized efforts, there were not enough cadaver kidneys to fulfil the ever-increasing demand for kidneys [2], living renal transplantation has strongly maintained its place in transplantation today, especially living related donation with its good results on a long-term basis [3]. We have not only used living *related* donations [4, 5], but also living *unrelated* transplantation which has been the only hope for life for many of our recipients without a proper donor [6]. We present here our results of related and unrelated renal transplantations.

## Methods and Materials

Renal transplantation was started a Shahid Labbafi Nejad Medical Center in June 1984, and, since then, a steady upward trend has emerged with 300 consecutive transplantations performed as of December 1989 (Fig. 1). All kidneys were acquired from living donors. In 185 cases, the kidneys were obtained from family members (brother, 60; sister, 43; mother, 61; father, 18; child over 18 years old, 3). Of these family donations, 47 cases were human leukocyte antigen (HLA)-identical, while 133 cases were HLA-haploidentical. There were 115 cases of unrelated kidney donations, of which 19 were from spouses. There were many cases of donations from devoted persons such as friends, distant family members, and nonrelated persons with humanitarian intentions (emotionally related).

Donor nephrectomy was performed via midline transperitoneal incision in 20 donors, but in the remaining 280 cases, the flank approach with 12th rib resection were used for donor nephrectomy. Kidneys were irrigated with chilled Ringer's solution (500 ml, containing 1000 U heparin, 10 ml of 1%

Shahid Labbafi Nejad Medical Center, Boostan 9th, Pasdaran Ave, Tehran, Islamic Republic of Iran

W. Land, J. B. Dossetor (Eds.)
Organ Replacement Therapy:
Ethics, Justice and Commerce

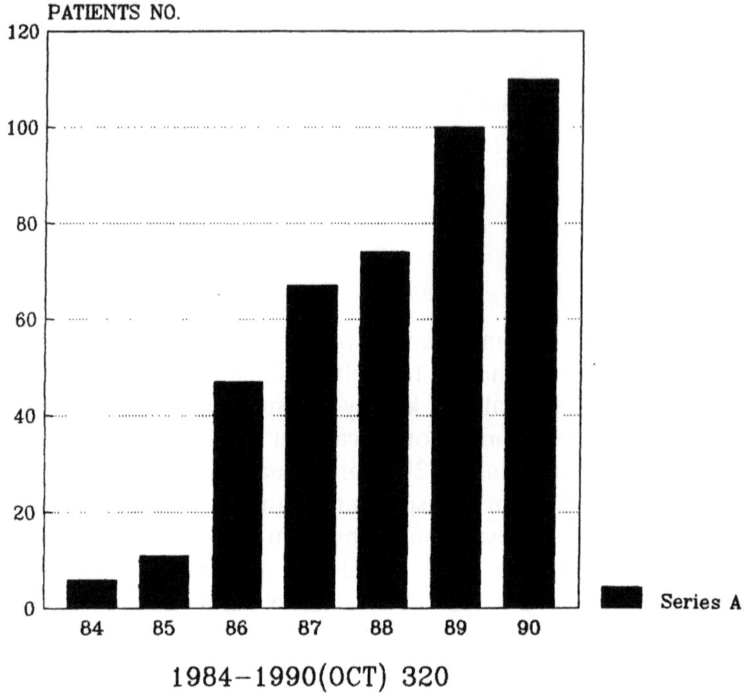


**Fig. 1.** Growth of renal transplantation in Shahid Labbafi Nejad Medical Center

lidocaine, and 1 ml bicarbonate). Immunosuppression was achieved with azathioprine and steroids in all HLA-identical cases, while cyclosporine was used with steroids in all unrelated cases (starting with 10–12 mg/kg and tapered gradually to about 4 mg/kg maintenance dose within about 6 months). Donor specific transfusion (DST) was used in 89 cases, while it was not in 38 unrelated cases. Donors were mobilized the day following surgery and usually were discharged within a week.

## Results

We compared our graft survival rates in cases of related donations with those of unrelated donations. One-year graft survival was 80 % for all patients (Fig. 2), about 81 % for haploidentical relatives, and 74 % for unrelated transplantations (CTS registry, Heidelberg, FRG; Fig. 3). In donors, there were two cases of pneumothorax which recovered with chest tube insertion and one case of acute tubular necrosis (ATN) following inadvertent prolonged use of anticoagulation therapy, in a patient who recovered with medical management achieving normal creatinine levels 3 years postoperatively. Two cases of lower limb thrombophlebitis were also controlled by conservative means. In almost all donations, the donors' self-esteem was

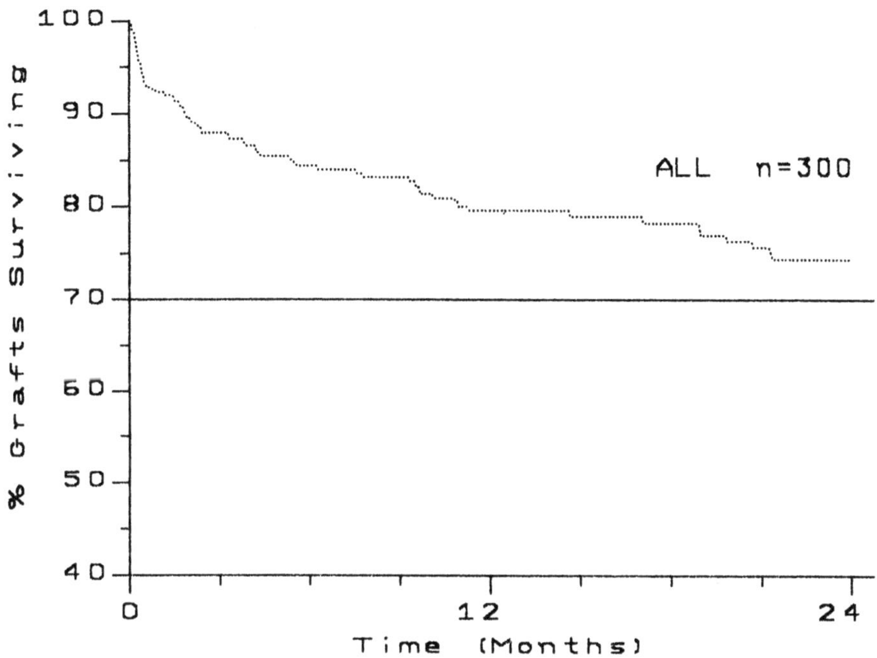


**Fig. 2.** One-year graft survival in 300 kidney transplantations at Shahid Labbafi Nejad Medical Center (CTS Registry, Heidelberg, FRG)

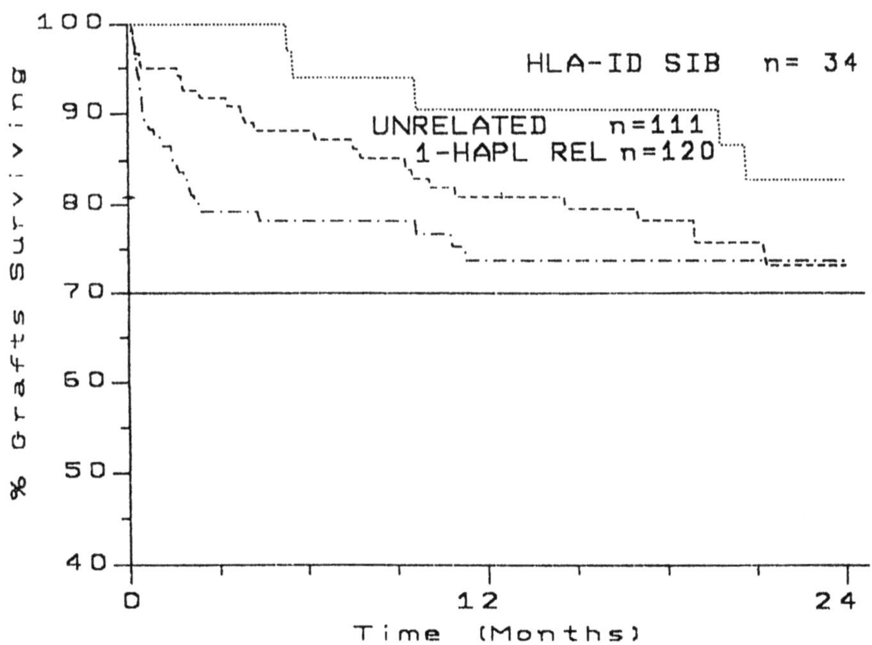


**Fig. 3.** One-year graft survival in 120 haploidentical and 111 unrelated kidney transplantations at Shahid Labbafi Nejad Medical Center (CTS Registry, Heidelberg, FRG)

increased significantly. There were no cases in which the donor regretted what he or she has done.

## Discussion

Renal transplantation was started in Iran 22 years ago [7, 8], but it did not play a significant role in the management of uremic patients until 1984 [4, 5, 8, 9]. In fact, the two first main centers started their function in the problematic circumstances of wartime, with its resultant shortages and difficulties. But in spite of the long-standing war, the number of transplantations grew steadily and at a rapid pace, and it was not interrupted even at times when both centers in Tehran were under heavy air and missile attacks [6, 9]. Five new centers were started by colleagues trained at our center in five different cities, two of them in cities at the war fronts (Urmina and Bakhtaran Provinces). Together with nine other centers, more than 1100 renal transplantations have been performed throughout Iran.

We started with HLA-identical live transplantations, then moved to haploidentical cases. Since we were unable to start cadaver transplantations, many recipients were left without a proper donor. This made us think about and start unrelated renal transplantations. The first of these was from a wife to husband on January 11, 1987, and here the kidney is still functioning after 30 months.

This opened up a new hope for many recipients on the list, and then other centers, having witnessed the successful results of unrelated donations, began to use this as a potential source for their own transplantations. This is now being performed in all 14 centers in Iran.

Our preference has been for live related donors, and that is why we placed them on our priority list. When a family donor was unavailable, we accepted spouses, friends, and other unrelated souces. No member of the medical team was involved in the act of kidney donations. Buying kidneys was discouraged, and written consent was obtained from recipient and donor that no commerce was involved; no money was transferred as a buying act. If any gift was exchanged between donors and recipients, we were not aware of this and the patients were told if they talked about money transfer the surgery would be cancelled. It is true that besides families, there were many donations through humanitarian intentions. Three of our donors were volunteer soldiers. We have refused to accept kidneys from some of our war-wounded people, as, for example, in the case of an injured combatant who had an amputated leg, which distressingly for him, made him unable to donate.

We have to remember that one side of our problem is always a desperate patient who needs a new life, and if we had not started unrelated renal transplantations, many recipients, especially children, who are now in good shape would have been left in the unfortunate state of end-stage renal disease (ESRD) and on dialysis or may have lost their lives. We encourage cadaver transplantation, but many efforts are necessary to overcome problems with this issue in countries like ours, in which dead bodies are treated very specially by their families. Even though cadaver transplantation has increased in Iran (30 per million population per year), a public opinion poll held by a Japanese national newspaper in December 1989 showed that only a fifth of those who answered would agree to donation if a doctor diagnosed a relative to be brain dead. These figures show that Japanese people still have much resistance to accepting brain death. Yet three-quarters agreed to donation from living donors [11]. Besides, in many countries such as Canada the demand for kidneys is increasing while the good supply of cadaver kidneys is not only not increasing, but is actually decreasing due to the use of seatbelts and the enforcement of speeding laws, which is leading to fewer accidental deaths [2]. In Iran, we could not have seen such a rapid growth and success in transplantation if we had not started living related and unrelated transplantations. So, with a proper awareness of the community and good surgical care, both living related and especially the newly developing unrelated transplantations could save many lives, whereby careful consideration of humanitarian intentions is encouraged in this type of donations.

In conclusion, there are several benefits involved in living renal transplantation. The superiority of family donations to cadavers donations has been shown well, especially in the long-term. Therefore, we still have to prefer kidneys from family sources, especially siblings. If the use of a cadaver kidney is not feasible in particular social settings, or if there are not enough living related and cadaver kidneys available, we recommend living unrelated transplantation as a potential source with comparable results. With this type of transplantation, a good approach is taken by society and especially the medical team, and humanitarian standards are held at the highest possible level.

## Summary

From June 1984 to December 1989, a total of 300 renal transplantations were performed using organs from living donors. Recipients from family sources were placed on a priority basis to encourage family donations. There were 185 cases of family donations (brothers, 60; sister, 43; mother, 61; child over 18, 3; father, 18). In 115 cases kidneys were obtained from unrelated donors, preferably from spouses, distant relatives, and friends (emotionally related). All recipients were informed that in case of any money transaction, the transplantation would be cancelled, and consent was taken in this regard. However, if they wanted to transfer any gift, we did not interfere and were not aware of it. It was made sure that no person on the medical team was involved in the donation aspect. The donors' self-esteem was usually increased following donations. They were well aware of what they were doing, and in the majority of cases a humanitarian act was involved. One-year graft survival was 81 % for all patients; it was 80 % for haploidentical relatives, and 74 % for unrelated transplantations (CTS Registry, Heidelberg, FRG). Living related transplantation, especially from siblings, is preferred due to better long-term results. With good humanitarian intentions, we recommend unrelated kidney transplantation as a potential source of donation for many uremic patients in desperate need of a kidney when cadaver transplantation is unavailable.

## References


1. Hume DM, Merril JP, Miller B, F et al. (1953) Experience with renal homotransplantation in the human report of nine cases. J Clin Invest 24:227
2. Cook GT (1983) Transplantation today: a commentary. The Renal Family 5:4
3. Terasaki PL et al. (1985) Patient, graft and functional survival rates: an overview In: Clinical Kidney Transplant. UCLA, Los Angeles, pp 1–26
4. Simforoosh N et al. (1987) Renal transplantation in living related donors. In: Haberal M (ed) Chronic renal failure and transplantation. Semih, Turkey, pp 199–204
5. Simforoosh N et al. (1987) Renal transplantation: a better quality of life for uremic patients. Review of results in 69 kidney transplantations. Med J Islamic Rep Iran 1:1–6
6. Simforoosh N et al. (1990) Low dose cyclosporine with DST. A less nephrotoxic protocol. In: Haberal M (ed) recent advances in nephrology and transplantation. Pelin, Ankara, Turkey, pp 209–213
7. Kadjbafzadeh M et al. (1984) Renal transplantation: report of 25 cases. J Iranian Med Council 9:114–121
8. Ghods. Results of 319 successive renal transplantation from living related and unrelated donors. Iranian J Med
9. Fazel I (1988) Report of 200 renal transplantations from living donors. Med J Islamic Rep Iran 2:165–170
10. Land W (1989) The problems of live organ donation: facts, thoughts and reflections. Transplant Int 2:168–179
11. Yamauchi M (1990) Transplantation in Japan. Br Med J 301–507

# Living Related Liver Transplantation in an Adult and a Child

M. Haberal, H. Telatar, N. Bilgin, N. Büyükpamukçu, B. Kayhan, Y. Bayraktar, G. Arslan, M. Karamehmetoğlu, H. Gülay, Ş. Sert, B. Uzunalimoğlu, M. Turan, M. Koç, and E. Hamaloğlu

## Introduction

Orthotopic liver transplantation is the most effective treatment for end-stage liver diseases in adults and children; however, the lack of convenient donors is the main restrictive factor existing in this particular area. The paucity of infant and child donors remains a worldwide problem, especially in developing countries where the number of adult cadavers is also very limited. The desperate search for organ sources has led surgeons to transplant a portion of the liver from an adult into a child, and this approach has been accepted by some centers [4, 6, 9].

It is well known that as little as a quarter of a whole liver can be sufficient for an adult to survive with normal liver functions. This has been proven through the numerous experiences gained during liver resections from benign and malignant conditions and transplantations of reduced-size livers performed in various centers [1, 2, 3, 4, 8, 10]. This fact makes it possible to transplant the left lobe of a living donor's liver to the recipient.

When the first successful orthotopic liver transplantation was performed by our team at our hospital in Turkey [5], a lot of chronic liver disease patients were referred to us for transplantation. Unfortunately, the second cadaver donor was only available 1 year later. During this time, we realized that approximately 50 % of the patients (both children and adults) on our list had died. It was this unfortunate consequence that led to our decision to perform living related, partial liver transplantations in both children and adults.

Turkish Transplantation and Burn Foundation Hospital Fevzi Çakmak Cd., 10. Sk., No: 45, 06490 Bahçelievler, Ankara, Turkey

W. Land, J. B. Dossetor (Eds.)
Organ Replacement Therapy:
Ethics, Justice and Commerce

## Case Reports

### Case 1

A child with biliary atresia was referred to us at the age of 7.5 months for assessment of a possible liver transplantation. The child was jaundiced at birth, and, at the age of 6 weeks, a Kasai portoenterostomy was performed at another hospital. No improvement occurred in the jaundice, and recurrent cholangitis and anemia continued.

At the time of referral, the child weighed 6.4 kg and had a temperature of 37.5 °C, jaundice, and moderate hepatosplenomegaly. Laboratory examinations revealed the following data: hemoglobin, 9.5 g/dl; white blood cells (WBC), 8000 $mm^3$; alkaline phosphatase (ALP), 450 U; serum glutamic oxaloacetic transaminase (SGOT), 90 U; serum glutamic pyruvic transaminase (SGPT), 40 U; total bilirubin, 8.0 mg; direct bilirubin, 6.0 mg; total protein, 6.0 g; albumin, 3.0 g; and prothrombin time, 18″ [1, 2].

The child was prepared for cadaver liver transplantation and required blood transfusions and antibiotic therapy with good enteral feeding. He was discharged with some clinical improvement and put on the waiting list for a blood group A liver. Approximately 1 month later, the child was admitted with anemia (hemoglobin 7.0 g/dl) and a more advanced hyperbilirubinemia (total bilirubin, 9.2 mg; direct bilirubin, 6.0 mg). It was during this time that the parents were informed about living related partial liver donations. The mother, a 31-year-old woman with blood group A, volunteered to be the donor. Human leukocyte antigen (HLA) typing showed haploidentity, with the cross-match being negative. The hematologic, biochemical, and urological analyses and the scintigraphic, radiologic, and tomographic evaluations of the donor showed no abnormality. Angiographic evaluation showed the recipient and donor hepatic and left hepatic arteries to be suitable (Fig. 1a, b).

After psychological consultation and at the beginning of the 10th month, a mother-to-child segmental liver transplantation was performed. Donor laparotomy was done with a bilateral subcostal incision with xiphoid extension. The liver was mobilized, the left hepatic vein, left hepatic artery, and left portal vein were skeletized, and the left hepatic duct divided. With the use of the dissection and ligation technique, the left lateral lobe was detatched from the main part, leaving the left portal vein, left hepatic artery, and left hepatic vein intact.

The recipient hepatectomy was performed in a separate operating room, leaving intact the retrohepatic inferior vena cava. Just before the recipient hepatectomy, the donor's left lateral lobe was removed and the via portal vein and hepatic artery perfused with cold UW solution. Following the recipient hepatectomy, the left hepatic vein in the allograft was anastomosed end-to-side to the recipient's inferior vena cava with a 4/0 continuous prolene suture. The recipient's portal vein was anastomosed end-to-end to the left portal vein with a 6/0 prolene suture. The recipient's hepatic artery was

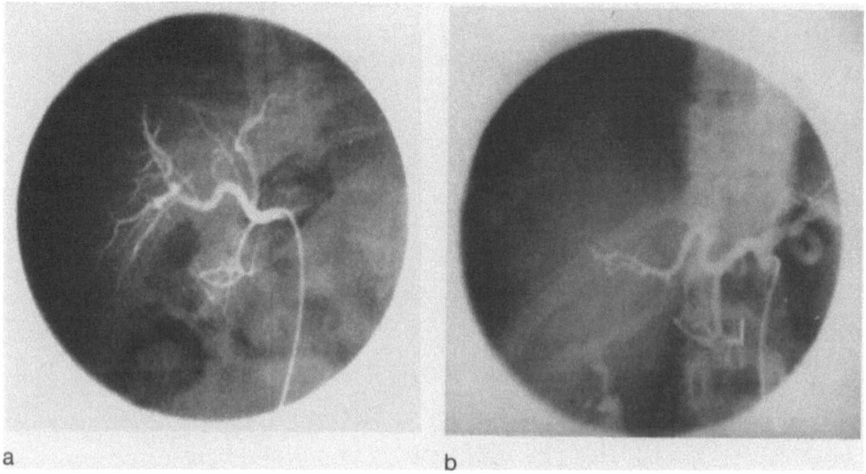

**Fig. 1a, b.** Normal hepatic angiograms for (**a**) recipient and (**b**) donor

anastomosed to the donor's left hepatic artery with an interposition vein graft (inferior mesenteric vein) with a 7/0 prolene suture. The total ischemic time was 4 h and 20 min. Following the arterial anastomosis, the transplanted liver started to function. Proceeding this, the left hepatic duct was anastomosed end-to-side to the jejunal roux-en-Y loop with 6/0 interrupted vicyrl sutures. After securing hemostasis, both the donor and the recipient abdomens were closed in planes by placing one drain for each patient. The donor received 3 U blood, and the recipient received 6 U during the procedures.

Postoperative immunosuppression consisted of triple drug therapy, namely 2 mg/kg per day azathioprine administered intravenously, with 2.5 mg/kg per day prednisolone and 3 mg/kg per day cyclosporin A also administered intravenously. The early postoperative day was uneventful. The child began to recover. Unfortunately, on the 3rd postoperative day, cerebral edema developed, and the liver functions began to show signs of deterioration as well. Therapy with OKT3 2.5 mg/day was started and continued for 5 days. After some improvement of liver functions, progressive deterioration began again and a hepatic angiogram was performed; this revealed the graft artery and portal vein to be patent (Fig. 2a, b). Following severe cerebral edema, the patient became unresponsive to medical treatment. Progressive deterioration of brain and liver functions led to the eventual death of the child on the 14th postoperative day. The postoperative course of the donor was uneventful. A slight elevation of the bilirubin (total, 4.2 mg; direct 3.0 mg) occurred during the first 48 h, but returned to normal within a couple of days (Table 1), and she was ready to be discharged on the 7th postoperative day. Three months after surgery, she became pregnant and is still doing well.

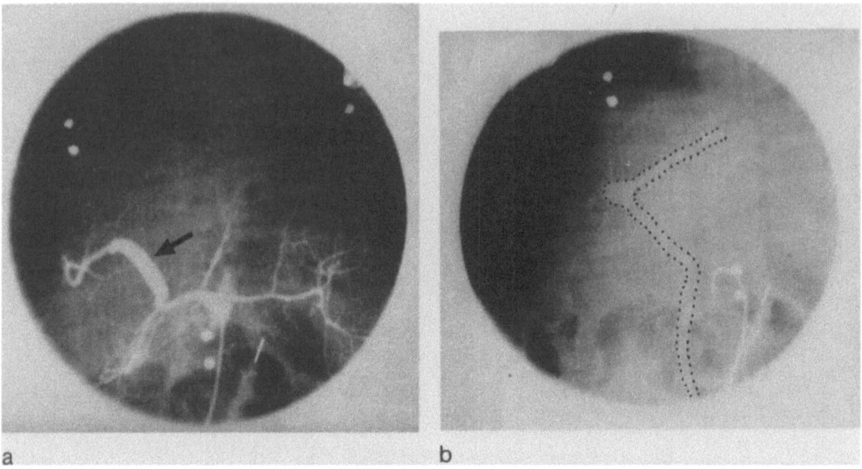


**Fig. 2.** a Postoperative graft arteriogram showing patent graft artery. *Arrow* shows inferior mesenteric vein graft. **b** Superior mesenteric arteriogram demonstrating patent graft portal vein

**Table 1.** Pre- and postoperative results of liver function tests in donor to 10-month-old male child

| Liver Function | SGOT (U) | SGPT (U) | Bilirubin (mg) Total | Direct | Total Protein gr. (%) | Albumin gr (%) |
|---|---|---|---|---|---|---|
| Preoperative | 15 | 14 | 0.8 | 0.4 | 6.9 | 3.8 |
| Postoperative | | | | | | |
| After 1 week | 40 | 35 | 1.2 | 0.6 | 7.0 | 4.0 |
| After 1 month | 38 | 32 | 1.1 | 0.6 | 7.0 | 4.0 |
| After 6 months | 10 | 18 | 0.8 | 0.4 | 6.0 | 3.2 |

SGOT, serum glutamic oxaloacetic transaminase; SGPT, serum glutamic pyruvic transaminase

## Case 2

A 20-year-old male with cirrhosis due to chronic active hepatitis was referred to us on January 10, 1990, for liver transplantation. Three years before this, he was jaundiced and hospitalized at another hospital with a biopsy revealing chronic active hepatitis. When accepted to our hospital, he was jaundiced with marked splenomegaly.

Liver function tests were disturbed (ALP, 160 U; SGOT, 20 U; SGPT, 18 U; total protein, 5.2 g; albumin, 2.2 g; total bilirubin, 5.2 mg; direct bilirubin, 2.2 mg; prothrombin time, 24″) [1, 2]. The esophogogram showed obvious varices (4/6). Numerous albumin infusions were required. The blood group was A Rh(+), and the patient was put on our waiting list. His hepatic functions tended to worsen. Unfortunately, no cadaver donor was available during the patient's hospitalization period of over 3 months. The parents were then informed about living related partial liver donations. The father was found to be a volunteering and suitable donor.

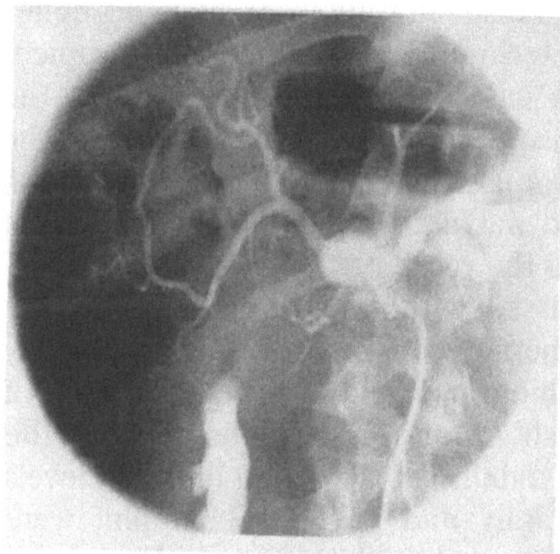

**Fig. 3.** Recipient hepatic angiogram showing normal anatomical structure

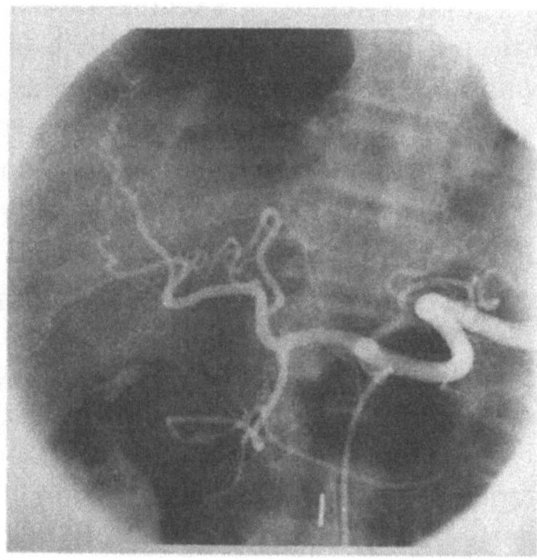

**Fig. 4.** Donor hepatic angiogram showing normal arterial structure

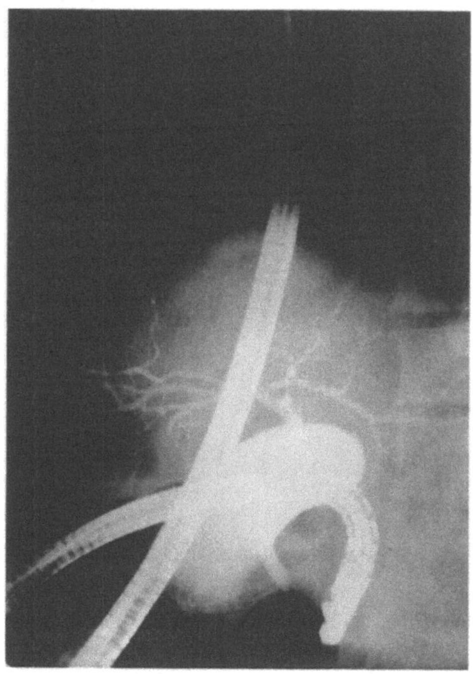

**Fig. 5.** Endoscopic retrograde cholan giogram showing normal bile system in donor

During the preoperative period, complete clinical, biochemical, and radiologic examinations were done for both the donor and the recipient. The radiologic and angiographic evaluations of the recipient showed that the portal system and hepatic arterial system were patent (Fig. 3). Donor hepatic arteriography and endoscopic retrograde cholangiography showed left hepatic branches to be in correct anatomical positions (Figs. 4, 5). HLA-A, -B, and -DR typing showed one haplotype matching. After the cross-match, which resulted as negative, a segmental liver transplantation from the living donor was performed on April 29, 1990. The technique of the donor and recipient operations was about the same as in case 1, with the exception of the stabilization of the transplanted liver, which was provided by putting the tissue expander in the right subdiaphragmatic area. During left lateral segmentectomy of the donor no blood was used for the donor operation; however, 4 U blood were transfused to the recipent.

The early postoperative period passed without any problem for the recipient. Triple immunosuppressive therapy consisted of 1 mg/kg per day prednisolone, 2 mg/kg per day azathioprine, and 3 mg/kg per day of cyclosporin A administered intravenously. On the 3rd postoperative day, the recipient was orally fed. However, the stability of the serum bilirubin levels tended to increase. Hepatic angiography and portal venography were performed postoperatively. Both vessels were found to be open (Figs. 6, 7), and antirejection therapy with OKT3 was started on the 6th postoperative day. Unfortunately, the patient died on the 12th postoperative day, from cerebral hemorrhage.

The early postoperative course of the donor was also uneventful. The bilirubin level showed an early rise of up to a total of 11.0 mg and returned to

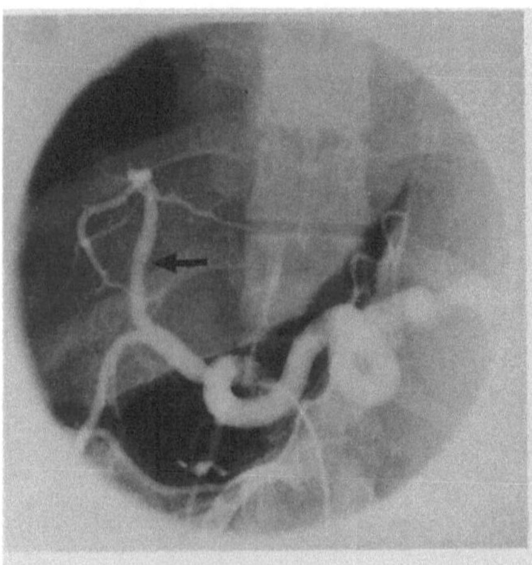
a

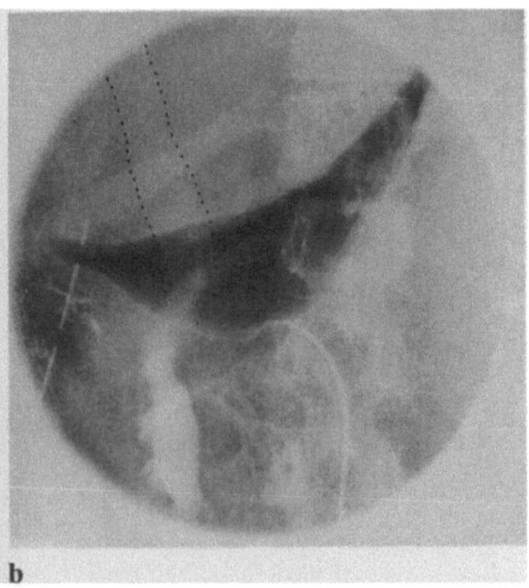
b

**Fig. 6a, b. a** Graft hepatic arteriogram showed patent arterial circulation. *Arrow* shows inferior mesenteric vein graft. **b** Superior mesenteric arteriogram demonstrating patent portal vein. *Dotted line area* shows portal vein

**Table 2.** Pre- and postoperative results of liver function tests in donor to 20-year-old male adult

| Liver Functions | SGOT (U) | SGPT (U) | Bilirubin (mg) Total | Bilirubin (mg) Direct | Total Protein gr. (%) | Albumin gr (%) |
|---|---|---|---|---|---|---|
| Preoperative | 16 | 18 | 1.0 | 0.5 | 7.0 | 4.0 |
| Postoperative | | | | | | |
| After 1 week | 22 | 20 | 10.4 | 5.6 | 7.0 | 4.0 |
| After 1 month | 30 | 50 | 1.8 | 1.0 | 6.8 | 3.8 |
| After 6 months | 50 | 47 | 1.4 | 0.6 | 7.2 | 4.5 |

SGOT, serum glutamic oxaloacetic transaminase; SGPT, serum glutamic pyruvic transaminase

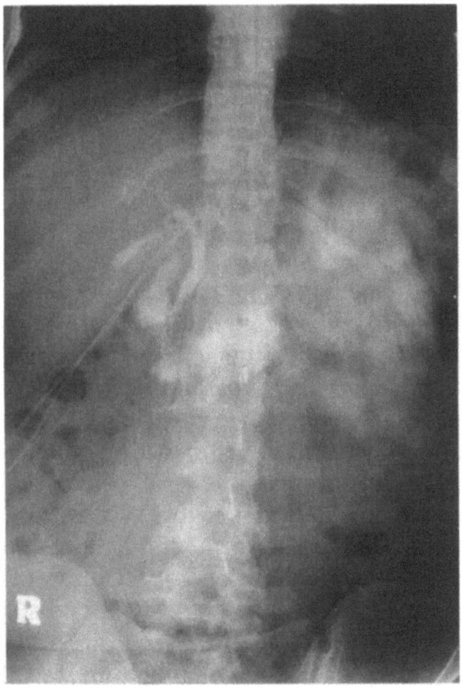


**Fig. 7.** T-tube cholangiogram showing normal drainage, but no bile leakage

normal after 4 weeks (Table 2). A bile leakage from the cut surface of the liver was detected on the 10th postoperative day, and the bile collection at the left lobe pouch was drained with a percutaneously placed pigtail catheter and, at the same time, a T-tube cholangiogram was performed, which showed normal drainage (Fig. 7). The bile leakage healed spontaneously without any other access, and, 3 months later, the donor's condition became completely normal. The liver scan taken during this period (Fig. 8) showed a normal hepatectomized liver. At present the donor is doing very well and working.

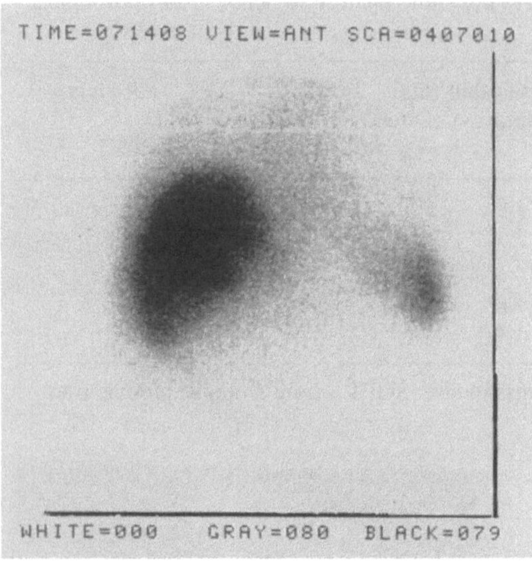


**Fig. 8.** Liver scan image showing normal hepatectomized liver

## Discussion

The first living donor partial liver transplantation in a child was performed by Raia et al. [6] and, immediately after this, Strong et al. [9] and Broelsch et al. [4] accomplished the next living related partial liver transplantations. These three separate groups later individually studied and discussed the controversial points concerning the topic of transplantation and, later, through these discussions and in-depth studies, a technique for this type of transplantation evolved. Through these series of experiences, it has been proven that this type of transplantation is highly successful, since living donor partial transplantations can be performed in children without causing severe complications and risk factors in donors. Therefore, through this procedure, not only are people able to save the lives of end-stage chronic disease patients through donating their kidney, but they are also able to save the lives of chronic liver disease patients by donating a part of their liver.

Extended right hepatic lobectomy and hepatic trisegmentectomy procedures have proven to be capable of prolonging the lives of adults by providing appropriate liver function [10]. Through this procedure, it occurred to us that chronic end-stage liver disease adult patients would have a chance of survival if partial liver transplantation were performed as well.

Obtaining cadaveric organs has long been a problem throughout the world and still continues to be one today, to the extent that, since our hospital began liver transplantations within the last 2 years, only seven cadaveric organs could be obtained and six of these were used for liver transplantations. Unfortunately, approximately 50 % of the other patients on the waiting list for liver transplantation died during their term of waiting for a liver.

Approximately 100 liver transplantations are required per year at our hospital.

At our hospital, each living donor transplantation recipient is admitted for a couple of months, and, even then, finding the organ required is a practically dim hope. Therefore, the living donor partial liver transplantation procedure has been accepted at our hospital, though our results in this field of transplantation have not been able to match the high success rate in living related partial liver transplantation achieved by Broelsch et al. [4]. Our experiences and the experiences of others show that, like living donor kidney transplantations, living donor partial liver transplantations can be another alternative to prolonging the lives of these chronic end-stage liver disease patients both children as well as adults. It would definitely mean giving these patients another chance to live.

## Summary

Due to the severe shortage of liver cadavers, two segmental living related liver transplantations were performed. One of these transplantations was performed in a 10-month-old boy with biliary atresia, and the other was performed in a 20-year-old male adult with cirrhosis due to chronic active hepatitis.

In the case of the 10-month-old boy, the mother was the donor for the segmental living related liver transplantation, and the operations in both the donor and the recipient were uneventful. However, unfortunately, the recipient showed signs of cerebral edema and deteriorating liver functions on the 3rd postoperative day. On the 14th postoperative day, the child died of severe cerebral edema. The child's mother, the donor, underwent an uneventful postoperative term, and was discharged from our hospital on the 7th postoperative day. She became pregnant, three months later, and is still doing well.

In the case of the 20-year-old male adult, the father was the donor. The operations in both the donor and the recipient, including the early postoperative stage, were uneventful. Unfortunately, the 20-year-old recipient died on the 12th postoperative day due to cerebral hemorrhage. The donor (father) underwent an uneventful early postoperative term. At present, the donor is doing very well and leading a normal life.

Our experiences show that left lateral segmentectomy is a safe procedure for living related liver donors; however, meticulous surgical technique is necessary. Through our in-depth studies, it has become apparent that segmental living related liver transplantation may be used for the treatment of chronic liver disease in children as well as in adult patients.

## References


1. Bismuth H, Houssion D (1984) Reduced-sized orthotopic liver graft in hepatic transplantation in children. Surgery 3:367–370
2. Bismuth H, Morino M, Castaing D et al. (1989) Emergency orthotopic liver transplantation in two patients using one donor liver. Pr J Surg 76:722–724
3. Broelsch CE, Emond JC, Thistlethwaite JR et al. (1988) Liver transplantation, including the concept of reduced-size liver transplants in children. Ann Surg 208(4):410–420
4. Broelsch CE, Emond JC, Whitington PF, Thistlethwaite JR, Baker AL, Lichtory JL (1990) Application of reduced size living transplants as split grafts, auxillary orthotopic grafts and living related segmental transplants. Second International Congress of the Middle East Society for Organ Transplantation, March 1990, Kuwait. (Abstract), p 47
5. Haberal M, Erbengi A, Erbengi G, Telatar H, Topçu M, Büyükpamukçu N, Bilgin N, Arslan G, Karamehmetoğlu M, Gülay H, Sert Ş, Öner Z, Turan M, Bayraktar Y, Kayhan B, Sanaç Y (1989) Brain death criteria and heart beating donor. Fourth International Symposium on Organ Procurement and Preservation, September, 1989, Minnesota. (Abstract), p 73
6. Raia S, Nery JR, Mies S (1989) Liver transplantation from live donors. Lancet ii:497
7. Singer PA, Siegler M, Whitington PF, Lantos JD, Emond JC, Thistlethwaite JR, Broelsch CE (1989) Ethics of liver transplantation with living donors. N Eng J Med 321(9):620–622
8. Strong R, Ong TH, Pillay P, Wall D, Balderson G, Lynch S (1988) A new method of segmental orthotopic liver transplantation in children. Surgery 104(1):104–107
9. Strong RW, Lynch SV, Ong TH, Matsunami H, Koido Y, Balderson GA (1990) Successful liver transplantation from a living donor to her son. N Engl J Med 322(21):1505–1507
10. Starzl TE, Bell RH, Beart RW, Putnam CW (1975) Hepatic trisegmentectomy and other liver resections. Surg Gyn Obst p 141

# Medical Risks and Benefit of Pancreas Transplants from Living Related Donors

D.E.R. Sutherland, F.C. Goetz, K. Gillingham, K.C. Moudry-Munns, and J.S. Najarian

The rationale to perform transplants of any organ from living related donors (LRDs) rather than cadaver (Cad) donors is two-fold: there is a shortage of Cad donors for the number in need of a transplant, and the rejection rate will be less with grafts from LRDs. Either reason by itself will justify the use of LRDs, and for kidney transplants both pertain.

In most parts of the world, there is not a shortage of Cad donors for the number of diabetics who are currently considered for pancreas transplantation. Thus, the main benefit of an LRD pancreas transplant is the need for less immunosuppression and less rejection long-term. For kidney transplants, the technical failure rate is equally low for LRD and Cad donor transplants (or lower for LRD kidneys). For pancreas transplants, the technical failure is actually higher for LRD than for Cad donor transplants because only a segment of the organ can be used, and only short lengths of vessels are available [1]. The higher technical failure rate with pancreas grafts from LRDs than from Cad donors partially offsets the immunological gain in the overall results. However, in an individual recipient, if the pancreas transplant is technically successful, the probability of long-term success is better with an LRD.

The University of Minnesota began to use LRDs for islet and pancreas transplants in the 1970s [2,3]. Of 401 pancreas transplants performed at this institution from December, 1966 to December, 1990, 74 were segmental grafts from LRDs; 28 were human leukocyte antigen (HLA)-identical siblings, (17 sisters, 11 brothers) 10 were identical twins (9 female, 1 male), 34 were HLA-mismatched relatives, including 19 siblings (12 sisters, 7 brothers), 16 parents (11 mothers, 5 fathers), and 1 male cousin. In addition, 2 of 24 islet allografts performed during this period were from LRDs of a pancreatic segment, one from an HLA-identical sister and one from a one-haplotype matched sister, both of whom had previously given a kidney to their sibling. Thus, our total experience with hemipancreatectomy in LRDs is 76. All recipients had been diabetic for at least 10 years, and all donors were at least 10 years older than the age of onset of diabetes in the recipient; in the case of sibling donors, no other siblings or family members other than the recipients

University of Minnesota Hospital and Clinic, Box 280, 420 Delaware St. SE, Minneapolis, MN 55455, USA

W. Land, J. B. Dossetor (Eds.)
Organ Replacement Therapy:
Ethics, Justice and Commerce

were diabetic. When these demographic features pertain, the risk of future diabetes developing is no greater than for the general population [4].

Changes in blood glucose and insulin levels have occurred in most donors postoperatively, but oral glucose tolerance tests have remained normal in two-thirds of those tested and only three donors have been identified who were not completely normoglycemic during the follow-up (fasting and post prandial blood sugars within the range of the nondiabetic, nonpancreatectomized reference population). Of the donors who had abnormal glucose tolerance tests postoperatively, all but one was in a group whose sum of plasma insulin levels during preoperative and intravenous glucose stimulatory tests were below a cutoff of 62 μU/ml [5]. Approximately one-half of the donors whose preoperative insulin secretory response to stimulation was in the lowest thirtieth percentile of the entire group on preoperative testing had abnormal glucose tolerance test results postoperatively. The three who developed postoperative elevated fasting and postprandial glucose levels were in this group, and are classified as Type II diabetics. One takes insulin to aid in maintenance of glucose homeostasis. Since this correlation was made, only individuals with a post intravenous glucose stimulatory first phase insulin level above the thirtieth percentile of normal have been accepted as donors [6]. The donors continue to be studied prospectively and retrospectively [7,8]; so far, all donors meeting current criteria have remained euglycemic after hemipancreatectomy.

Surgical complications of segmental pancreatectomy have occurred in 10 (13.8 %) of the 76 related donors: need for splenectomy in three (4 %), one at 2 days because of a total infarct, one at 1 month for rupture occurring during minor trauma, and one at 4 years for bleeding from esophageal varices formed in the splenic venous collaterals; sterile fluid collections treated by percutaneous aspiration without recurrence in four (5.3 %); an abscess drained percutaneously in one (1.3 %); and need for reoperation in two (2.6 %), one to religate the pancreatic duct at the site of transection, and one to retrieve a sponge.

The islet allografts have been divided into several series, and the courses of the two LRD islet allograft recipients have been previously described as case numbers 3 and 6 in the second series of eight transplants performed during 1977 and 1978 [2]. In brief, the LRD islet allografts functioned initially, with elevation of C-peptide in both recipients and temporary insulin independence in one. However, both lost function, one at 3 and one at 4 weeks post transplant from presumed rejection.

The first LRD pancreas transplant was performed in 1979. All the LRD pancreas transplants were solitary (without a concomitant kidney transplant), either a pancreas transplant alone (PTA; $n = 47$), or a pancreas after a kidney transplant (PAK; $n = 27$). Twenty-one donors of a pancreas to a PAK recipient had also been the donor of the kidney (6 parents, 15 siblings). Six others (2 siblings, 4 parents) gave a pancreas segment after another family member had given the kidney (in one case, the other family member had given a kidney and a failed pancreas graft). In two PTA cases, a family member (1 sibling, 1 parent) donated a pancreas segment after one from another family member (sibling) had failed.

The LRD pancreas transplants have all been performed since 1978. During this time there were 210 solitary Cad donor pancreas transplants (PTA, $n = 114$; PAK, $n = 96$). (In addition, we did 102 simultaneous pancreas/kidney (SPK) transplants, and one simultaneous pancreas/liver (SPL) transplant, all the pancreas grafts being from Cad donors; there were no LRD pancreas transplants performed simultaneously with a kidney transplant or any other organ. All SPK and the SPL transplants were done with the bladder drainage, BD, technique.) For the solitary pancreas transplants (Sol Px Tx), a variety of duct management techniques were used, including open duct intraperitoneal drainage (OD) in 15 (5 LRD, 10 Cad), duct occlusion (DO) in 44 (6 LRD, 38 Cad), enteric drainage (ED) in 92 (54 LRD, 38 Cad), and BD in 136 (9 LRD, 127 Cad). The overall results and results in technically successful LRD and Cad donor pancreas transplants performed since July 1, 1978 were analyzed on October 30, 1990. Two solitary (1 PTA, 1 PAK) and 3 SPK transplants performed from November 1 to December 5, 1990, all with less than 1 month follow-up, were not included in the analysis.

In the overall series of Sol Px Tx, the 1- and 4-year functional survival rates for grafts from LRDs ($n = 74$) were 44 % and 36 %, and for grafts from Cad donors ($n = 207$) were 40 % and 17 % (ns). For the SPK cases ($n = 99$) 1- and 4-year pancreas graft functional survival rates were 63 % and 55 %. In the two Sol Px Tx subgroups, there also were no significant differences. For PTA, 1- and 4-year pancreas functional survival rates for LRD grafts ($n = 47$) were 43 % and 32 %, and for Cad grafts ($n = 113$) were 42 % and 17 % (ns). For PAK transplants, 1- and 4-year pancreas functional survival rates for LRD grafts ($n = 27$) were 44 % and 40 %, and for Cad grafts ($n = 94$) were 38 % and 18 % (ns). Even though the differences between the LRD and Cad donor pancreas functional graft actuarial survival curves overall were not statistically significant, long-term ($\geq$ 3 years) pancreas graft functional rates were significantly higher for LRD transplants.

In addition, a Cox proportional hazard regression analysis of our institutions total experience from 1978 to 1990 disclosed four factors that had a significant impact on graft outcome [9], of which one was donor source (Table 1). The other factors of significance were recipient age (those over 45 years are at increased risk for graft loss), methods for management of graft exocrine secretions (relative risk for graft loss with BD was 0.5 versus other techniques), and recipient category (relative risk for graft loss was 0.5 for SPK compared with Sol Px Tx). The use of a living donor was associated with a decreased risk of graft loss (0.6 versus a cadaver donor, $p = 0.0192$). Thus, when one accounts for the myriad of factors that influence pancreas transplant outcome, the expected beneficial effect of a genetically matched graft clearly emerges.

To return to the current univariate analysis, patient survival rates showed the same trends as graft survival, and for all Sol Px Px cases at 1 and 4 years were 94 % and 91 % for recipients of LRD and 91 % and 79 % for recipients of

**Table 1.** Factors found to be significant on multivariate analysis of 355 pancreas transplants over nearly 12 years (July 1978 – May 1990; modified from [9])

| Variable | Levels | Beta | SE (Beta) | Z Score | *p* Value | Relative risk |
|---|---|---|---|---|---|---|
| Recipient age | >45 (≤45) | 0.6 | 0.2 | 2.3 | .0192 | 1.8 |
| BD | Yes (no) | −0.6 | 0.1 | −3.8 | .0000 | 0.5 |
| SPK | Yes (no) | −0.5 | 0.2 | −2.4 | .0136 | 0.5 |
| Pancreas donor | LRD (Cad) | −0.4 | 0.1 | −2.3 | .0192 | 0.6 |

BD, bladder drainage; SPK, simultaneous pancreas and kidney transplant

Cad donor grafts ($p<0.06$). In the two Sol Px Tx subgroups, patient survival was high at 1 and 4 years, being 93 % and 93 % for LRD PTA and 91 % and 86 % for LRD PAK cases (ns).

The immunological advantage of LRD over Cad pancreas transplant was best seen in the univariate analysis of technically successful (TS) cases (Table 2). The reason this difference did not appear in the analysis of all cases was because of the high technical failure rate, leading to early graft losses, but by 3 years this handicap had been overcome. The technical failure rate for all Sol Px Txs was 35 % for LRD and 19 % for Cad donor grafts (compared to 20 % for SPK Cad pancreas transplants). In an analysis of all TS Solitary transplants (8 OD, 39 DO, 59 ED, 108 BD), 1- and 4-year pancreas functional survival rates for grafts from LRDs ($n = 48$) were 65 % and 53 %, and for those from Cad donors ($n = 167$) were 48 % and 21 % ($p<0.01$). For TS SPK transplantations; $n = 79$, the 1- and 4-year pancreas graft functional rates were 80 % and 69 %. In the two subgroups of the Sol Px Tx cases, similar

**Table 2.** Functional survival rates of living related versus cadaver donor solitary pancreas transplants compared with combined pancreas/kidney transplants: analysis of technically successful cases

| | Graft survival rates of all technically successful cases 1978–1990 | | | | | |
|---|---|---|---|---|---|---|
| | Cases (*n*) | | 1-Year function (%) | | 4-Year function (%) | |
| | LRD | Cad | LRD | Cad | LRD | Cad |
| Solitary pancreas transplants[a] | 48 | 167 | 65 | 48 | 53 | 21 |
| Combined pancreas/ kidney transplants (all bladder drainage) | – | 79 | – | 80 | – | 69 |

[a]124 in nonuremic pts. 91 after a kidney transplant; 8 open duct, 39 duct occlusion, 59 enteric drainage and 108 bladder drainage; $p < 0.01$ LRD vs Cad LRD, living related donors; Cad, cadaver donor

differences were seen in one. In the PTA group, the 1- and 4-year pancreas graft functional survival rates for LRD transplantations ($n$ = 32) were 60 % and 45 % and for Cad donor transplantations ($n$ = 92) were 51 % and 20 % ($p$ = 0.16). For TS PAK Txs, 1- and 4-year pancreas graft functional survival rates for grafts from LRDs ($n$ = *16)* were 75 % and 68 % and for grafts from Cad donors ($n$ = 75) were 44 % and 24 % ($p$ = 0.02).

The higher patient survival rate when the pancreas grafts came from LRD donors was also seen in the analysis of TS cases, indicating that it is not a difference in tolerance of technical failures between the two donor groups that account for the survival advantage. For PTA cases patient survival rates at 1 and 4 years were 97 % and 97 % for LRD and 96 % and 94 % for Cad cases, while for PAK cases 1- and 4-year survival rates were 100 % and 93 % for LRD and 94 % and 74 % for Cad cases ($p$ = 0.11).

The advantage of LRD pancreas transplantations is also reflected in the large number of long-term functioning grafts. We have a very large experience with Cad pancreas transplantations, but very few have functioned for more than a few years. In contrast, we have 32 LRD grafts functioning between 1 and 10 years, 20 in the PTA and 12 in the PAK categories (Table 3).

There is one aspect of the LRD experience that deserves special comment: the course of seven TS identical twin transplantations and the serendipitous observation that in the absence of immunosuppression the graft is susceptible to isletitis and recurrence of disease [10,11]. The first three twins were not prophylactically immunosuppressed; all three became hyperglycemic between 6 and 12 weeks, and biopsies showed isletitis (appreciated in retrospect in the first case). The second and third twin recipients received antilymphocyte globulin (ALG) and azathioprine (Aza) after the diagnosis of recurrence of disease was made. In the second case, Aza was stopped because of the lack of a clinical response; this patient was the only one with end-stage nephropathy and had previously received a successful kidney transplant from her twin without the use of immunosuppression. In the third

**Table 3.** Number of long-term (> 1 year) functioning LRD pancreas grafts of 72 at risk

| Time post transplant (years) | Pancreas transplant after kidney ($n$) | Pancreas transplant alone ($n$) | Total ($n$) |
|---|---|---|---|
| 10 | 1 | – | 1 |
| 8 | 1 | 1 | 2 |
| 7 | 1 | 2 | 3 |
| 6 | 1 | – | 1 |
| 5 | 3 | 2 | 5 |
| 4 | 2 | 5 | 7 |
| 3 | – | 3 | 3 |
| 2 | 1 | 3 | 4 |
| 1 | 2 | 4 | 6 |
| All | 12 | 20 | 32 |

twin, the need for a permanent return to exogenous insulin was obviated for 1 year by introduction of Aza; this recipient remains on Aza with a partially functioning graft at 7 years, and a recent biopsy showed beta cells to still be present in approximately 10% of the islets. The fourth TS identical twin transplant recipient received Aza prophylactically and was normoglycemic for 3 years, at which time hyperglycemia occurred and a biopsy showed isletitis; a course of ALG and Cyclosporin A (CsA) was added to her regimen, with an initial clinical response, but at 5 years post transplantation resumed insulin permanently. The fifth recipient of a TS identical twin transplant received Aza and CsA prophylactically; a biopsy of the pancreas graft at 1 year showed normal islets, and the patient remains normoglycemic at 3.5 years. The long-term courses of the first five TS identical twin cases have been described in moderate detail [12,13]. The sixth TS identical twin also received Aza and CsA prophylactically; at 6 months, plasma glucose levels were slightly elevated and a graft biopsy showed mild isletitis; she received ALG, and remains normoglycemic at more than 2 years post transplantation. The seventh TS identical twin had the most advanced nephropathy of all but the second case, with a creatinine clearance of 50 ml/min; thus, she was placed on triple therapy with low dose CsA and Aza as well as prednisone (the only steroid-treated identical twin recipient), and is normoglycemic at 3 months post transplantation.

Type I diabetes mellitus is known to be an autoimmune disease in which the beta cells are selectively destroyed [4]. The natural history of pancreatic pathology in diabetes was recapitulated in the first few twin transplantations, and this observation provided one of the strongest bits of evidence that Type I diabetes has an autoimmune etiology. Isletitis has also been seen in grafts transplanted from non-twin HLA identical siblings to recipients who were only minimally immunosuppressed with low-dose CsA alone, or low-dose Aza and prednisone [11–13,15], but the clinical manifestation of recurrence of disease was at a slower rate, and the process was reversed in some by an increase in immunosuppression [12,13]. It is apparent that recurrence of disease can be prevented by adequate immunosuppression, and this may be why such a process has not yet been recognized in any Cad donor pancreas transplants, where immunosuppressive doses have been higher because of the known greater propensity to rejection [16]. However, the observations are also consistent with recurrence of disease being major histocompatibility complex (MHC)-restricted to grafts sharing the critical HLA alleles. Against this hypothesis is the observation that the functional survival rates are significantly higher for Cad pancreas allografts from donors that share than those who do not share HLA antigens with the recipient [17,18]. The strongest effect of matching is seen at the DR loci [19,20]. On the other hand, the amount of immunosuppression needed to prevent isletitis may be less than that needed to prevent rejection of Cad pancreas allografts. Recurrence of disease also appears to be mitigated by adequate immunosuppression in twins as well as in non-twin cases, and steroids have not been used in any of the twin cases that currently have long term function.

In summary, in 76 LRD islet or pancreas transplants, metabolic changes were seen in one-third of the donors. The insulin secretory response to intravenous glucose can be used as a screening test, and individuals with first phase insulin response above the lowest thirtieth percentile can be chosen as donors with the assurance that they will remain normal after segmental pancreatectomy. In recipients of TS Sol Px Txs, long-term functional survival rates are higher with grafts from LRD than from Cad donors. Scientifically, the detection of recurrence of isletitis in the absence of immunosuppression and the prevention of recurrence of disease by adequate immunosuppression has been the most interesting aspect of the LRD pancreas program. If the technical failure rate can be lowered, LRD pancreas transplants could be applied more liberally, since the long-term graft functional survival rates are superior to Cad transplants for TS cases. If immunosuppression is improved to the point where pancreas transplants could be considered in all diabetic patients, the number of Cad donors would be the limiting factor, and the rationale for LRD pancreas donation would be completely analogous to that of the kidney.

LRD pancreas transplantations are performed only when the donor, recipient, and the entire family understand the trade-offs and accept a higher probability of an immediate technical failure for a higher probability of long-term function, if the graft is technically successful. Only in a diabetic individual who is so highly sensitized that a Cad donor transplantation is extremely unlikely to occur, and in whom a negative crossmatch can be obtained only with a family member, is an LRD pancreas seen as the only practical option if transplantation is deemed the best treatment for the patient.

One subset of our living related pancreas donors were able to give consent with more assurance of being fully informed than the usual renal donor, namely those who had previously been a donor of a kidney. In addition, for LRD re-transplantations, the situation is similar to LRD kidney retransplant, prospective donors are aware of what was involved for other family members who were donors.

At this time, pancreas transplantation is an appropriate treatment for diabetic patients already obligated to immunosuppression in lieu of a kidney transplant, or to a non kidney transplant recipient whose problems with diabetes are more serious than the potential side effects of the antirejection drugs or of immunosuppression in general [21]. Since the need for immunosuppression is less with LRD transplants, this option expands the diabetic subpopulation than can benefit from this procedure.

The University of Minnesota is not the only institution to use LRDs for pancreas transplants, and the Stockholm group has reported on their experience [22,23]. The total number of cases reported to the International Pancreas Transplant Registry as of October 30, 1990, was 83 cases, or nine in addition to those from Minnesota, including three identical twin transplants, all three currently functioning.

The ethical issues of LRD pancreas transplantation are, in some respects, akin to those for LRD kidney donors [4]. Both organs are transplanted to improve the quality of life and not to save a life, since alternative therapies are available for both diseases, dialysis for renal failure and insulin for Type I diabetes. For the kidney, both early and long-term success is clearly better and less immunosuppression is needed for grafts from LRDs than from Cad donors. In addition, there is a shortage of kidneys. With the pancreas, however, the high technical failure rate offsets the lower rejection rate, and the only advantage of the LRD is the lower dose of immunosuppression and lower rate of late rejection; a shortage of Cad grafts does not exist now, except for the highly sensitized group of prospective recipients, but this will change in the future as all Cad pancreas grafts are used. Presently, the annual incidence of Cad donors is less than the annual incidence of new cases of Type I diabetes. Unless the procurement rate can be increased, LRD pancreas transplants will be necessary to treat all who can benefit.

The degree to which LRD pancreas transplants will be used in the future depends in part on lowering the technical failure rate, but at least for the highly sensitized patients or for those who desire to accept a higher technical failure rate as a trade-off for less immunosuppression, and for those who have problems such that the high dose of immunosuppression should be avoided, LRD pancreas transplantation is a rational option.

## References

1. Sutherland DER, Goetz FC, Najarian JS (1984) Pancreas transplants from living related donors. Transplantation 38:6740–679
2. Sutherland DER, Matas AJ, Goetz FC, Najarian JS (1990) Transplantation of dispersed pancreatic islet tissue in humans: autografts and allografts. Diabetes 29 [Suppl 1]:31–44
3. Sutherland DER, Goetz FC, Rynasiewicz JJ, et al (1981) Segmental pancreas transplantation from living related and cadaver donors: a clinical experience. Surgery 90:159–169
4. Barbosa J, King R, Goetz FC, et al (1977) Histocompatibility antigens (HLA) in families with juvenile insulin dependent diabetes mellitus. J Clin Invest 60:989–999
5. Kendall DM, Sutherland DER, Goetz FC, Najarian JS (1989) Metabolic effect on hemipancreatectomy in donors: preoperative prediction of postoperative oral glucose tolerance. Diabetes 38 [Suppl 1]:101–103
6. Kendall DM, Sutherland DER, Najarian JS, Goetz FC, Robertson RP (1990) Effects of hemi-pancreatectomy on insulin secretion and glucose tolerance in healthy human donors. N Engl J Med 322:898–903
7. Seaquist ER, Robertson RP (1990) Metabolic effects of hemipancreatectomy on human donors. Clin Res 38:156A
8. Seaquist ER, Robertson RP (1990) Metabolic effects of hemipancreatectomy on human donors. Diabetes 39 [Suppl 1]:5A
9. Morel P, Gillingham KJ, Moudry-Munns KC, Dunn DL, Najarian JS, Sutherland DER (1991) Factors influencing pancreas transplant outcome: Cox Proportional Hazard Regression Analysis of a single institution's experience with 357 cases. Transplant Proc 23 (1):1630–1633

10. Sutherland DER, Sibley R, Zhu X-Z, Michael A, Srikanta S, Taub F, Najarian JS, Goetz FC (1984) Twin-to twin pancreas transplantation: reversal and reenactment of the pathogenesis of Type I diabetes. Transplant Assoc Amer Phys XCVII:80–87
11. Sibley RK, Sutherland DER, Goetz F, Michael AF (1985) Recurrent diabetes mellitus in the pancreas iso- and allograft. A light and electron microscopic and immunohistochemical analysis of four cases. Lab Invest 53:132–144
12. Sutherland DER, Sibley RK (1988) Recurrence of disease in pancreas transplants. In: van Schilfgaarde R, Hardy MA (eds) Transplantation of the endocrine pancreas in diabetes mellitus. Elsevier, Amsterdam, pp. 60–66
13. Sutherland DER, Goetz FC, Sibley RK (1989) Recurrence of disease in pancreas transplants. Diabetes 38 [Suppl 1]:85–87
14. Eisenbarth GS (1986) Type I diabetes mellitus: a chronic autoimmune disease. N Engl J Med 314:1360–1368
15. Sutherland DER, Goetz FC, Elick BA, Najarian JS (1982) Experience with 49 segmental pancreas transplants in 45 diabetic patients. Transplantation 34:330–338
16. Sibley RK, Sutherland DER (1987) Pancreas transplantation: an immunohistologic and histopathologic examination of 100 grafts. Am J Pathol 128:151–170
17. Squifflet JP, Moudry K, Sutherland DER (1988) Is HLA matching relevant in pancreas transplantation? Transplant Int 1:26–29
18. So SKS, Moudry-Munns KC, Gillingham K, Minford EJ, Sutherland DER (1991) Short-term and long-term effects of HLA matching in cadaveric pancreas transplantation. Transplant Proc 23 (1):1634–1636
19. Sutherland DER, Moudry-Munns KC, Gillingham K (1990) Pancreas transplantation. Report from the International Registry and a preliminary analysis of United States results from the new United Network for Organ Sharing (UNOS) registry. In: Terasaki, P (ed) Clinical transplants 1989. UCLA Tissue Typing Laboratory, Los Angeles, pp. 253–266
20. So SKS, Minford EJ, Moudry-Munns KC, Gillingham K, Sutherland DER (1990) DR matching improves cadaveric pancreas transplant results. Transplant Proc 22 (2):687–688
21. Sutherland DER, Dunn DL, Goetz FC, et al (1989) A ten year experience with 290 pancreas transplants at a single institution. Ann Surg 210:274–288
22. Groth CG, Tyden G, Ostman J (1989) Fifteen years' experience with pancreas transplantation with pancreaticoenterostomy. Diabetes 38 [Suppl 1]:13
23. Bolinder J, Gunnarsson R, Tyden G, Brattstrom C, Ostman J, Groth CG (1988) Metabolic effects of living related pancreatic graft donation. Transplant Proc 20 (3):475–478
24. Sutherland DER (1985) Living related donors should be used whenever possible. Transplant Proc 17:1503–1509

# Medical Risk and Benefit in Living Pancreas Segment Donors

R. Margreiter

Any consideration and discussion of the problem of medical risk and benefit of live pancreas segment donation must be primarily based on the experience of the Minneapolis group, since the vast majority of these procedures were carried out at that center and only three cases at the Huddinge Hospital. The aspect that renders the task even more difficult is the fact that, to our knowledge, the whole Minneapolis series has never been published in its entirety. The program of transplanting pancreas segments of human leukocyte antigen (HLA)-matched, living related donors to patients with type I diabetes mellitus was initiated at the University of Minnesota in 1977 [1]. By August 1989, a total of 69 such transplants had been carried out [2]. Together with the three cases reported from Sweden [3], they form the basis for this risk-benefit analysis.

## Risk and Benefit for the Donor

The main risk to the donor is that of partial pancreatectomy. The Minneapolis group recently reported on 28 donors who were reevaluated approximately 1 year after surgery in order to determine the metabolic consequences of this procedure [4]. Three of these donors had complications, two of whom required reexploration for splenic vascular compromise leading to splenectomy or for accumulation of intraabdominal fluid in the region of the pancreatic resection. There was no death as of August 1989 [2]. However, there were a few patients requiring prolonged treatment at the intensive care unit (DER Sutherland, personal communication). In two of the three donors in Stockholm, the spleen was removed together with the tail of the pancreas. One of these patients developed a peripancreatic pseudocyst, which was percutaneously drained and did not recur. A small infarction of the spleen, as demonstrated by an uptake defect on a $^{99}$Technetium scan was observed in the patient who retained the spleen [3]. Since all these pancreases were procured from healthy donors, the perioperative risk associated with partial pancreatectomy cannot be compared with that of distal pancreatectomy for trauma or tumor.

Department of Transplant Surgery, University Hospital, Anichstraße 35, 6020 Innsbruck, Austria

W. Land, J. B. Dossetor (Eds.)
Organ Replacement Therapy:
Ethics, Justice and Commerce

With regard to pancreatic function 1 year after distal pancreatectomy in the patients of the Minneapolis series as well as in those investigated in Stockholm, mean fasting serum glucose levels were significantly higher 1 year after the procedure than before pancreatectomy. Fasting serum insulin levels again were significantly lower, as was the 24-h urinary C-peptide excretion. Oral glucose tolerance tests were clearly abnormal in 7 donors, but normal in the remaining 21. Insulin secretion, however, in these 7 donors was indistinguishable from that in the 21 donors with normal glucose tolerance. The authors concluded that hemipancreatectomy in healthy donors results in deterioration of insulin secretion and glucose tolerance [4]. It remains to be seen whether hemipancreatectomy leads to the development of clinical diabetes mellitus. It must be said, however, that no further deterioration occurred in the eight donors with abnormal glucose tolerance restudied from 1 to 6 years later. The Stockholm group came to a similar conclusion. In addition, they did triolein absorption studies, showing reduced absorption after 3 and 12 months [3]. Thus, removal of the tail of the pancreas results in significant loss of endocrine and exocrine pancreatic function after 1 year. Whereas grafts in Stockholm were procured from mothers [3], in Minneapolis most pancreses were harvested from HLA-identical siblings [2]. For the case of a parental donation, a high degree of motivation and therefore altruistic gains may be assumed providing the transplant was successful. This psychological benefit for the donor should be minor compared with the donation of a hepatic lobe, which can save the life of a child. There is, however, a certain surgical risk involved in related pancreas donation. Whether this risk is acceptable or not must be calculated from case to case on the basis of the medical benefit for the recipient.

## Benefits and Risk to the Recipient

The benefits to the recipients of transplantation from a living donor are obvious: donor and recipient operation can be scheduled, long waiting times for a suitable transplant avoided, and cold organ ischemia kept to a minimum. Since hemodynamic instability frequently associated with the occurrence of brain death is prevented, optimal initial graft function can be expected, provided the graft is handled with great care in order to not cause vasospasm and thus organ damage. If the pancreatic graft is harvested from parents or siblings, most donors and recipients will be at least haploidentical with respect to HLA. It is known from the International Pancreas Transplant Registry that matching for HLA-DR results in improved graft survival [5]. This may at least theoretically be a strong argument in favor of live pancreas donation. There are, however, some risks to the recipient. The rate of graft loss due to surgical complications is reported to be 37 % and, thus, significantly higher than in transplants from cadaveric sources at the same institution (24.1 %). The main complication was graft thrombosis, which was encountered in 15 out of 69 (21.7 %) patients in contrast to 9 out of 207

(4.3 %) when using cadaver organs [2]. This, in our opinion, might be due to the shortness of graft vessels, which does not facilitate optimal positioning of the transplant, thus predisposing for this kind of complication. Another disadvantage, if not risk factor, of using pancreas segments from live donors is the fact that less than 50 % of the total islet cell mass is transplanted. The risk of the recurrence of diabetes in the recipient seems to be minimal, even when donor and recipients are HLA-DR3 or -DR4, or both. Pharmacological immunosuppression seems to overcome the genetically determined predisposition to develop the disease. The greatest benefit of living donation of a pancreas to the patient should be better graft survival. Even in the most recent Minneapolis series, however, 1-year graft survival is somewhat inferior to that achieved with pancreases from DR-matched cadaver donors [6]. Graft loss in the live donation group was mainly due to technical failures. In Stockholm all three grafts transplanted were ultimately lost to rejection (CG Groth, personal communication).

When discussing the justification for live pancreas donation, organ availability has to be taken into account. Since only a few centers perform single pancreas transplants, pancreas transplantation is so far mainly restricted to type I diabetics with end-stage diabetic nephropathy. Here again, according to the International Registry, combined pancreas kidney transplants from cadavers are carried out in most instances [5]. This would leave only a few patients for a single pancreas transplantation, namely those who had received a kidney from a live or cadaver donor and for whom the pancreas transplant was postponed for one reason or another. Furthermore, some special cases of patients with brittle diabetes or lacking insulin counterregulation would be candidates for a single pancreas transplant. Altogether, there are certainly many more donors than candidates for single pancreas transplantation. From this point of view, there seems to be no need for live pancreas donation.

For the time being, the medical benefits of pancreas transplantation from a living related donor do not seem to outweigh the certain risks associated with this procedure. If the technical failure rate can be reduced to an acceptable level and thus survival rates increased to over 90 %, which is achieved in renal transplantation with kidneys from living related donors, this policy might be reevaluated. The same is true for a more liberal indication for pancreas transplantation, resulting in an increase in the number of such transplants. If it is possible to achieve low rates of immunological and nonimmunological graft loss through improved surgical technique and immunosuppression without severe side effects, pancreas transplantation will be performed before secondary complications of diabetes mellitus occur. In this situation, live pancreas donation will probably be neccessary in order to meet demand.

## Conclusions

1. Hemipancreatectomy for living related donation is associated with: no mortality and a low perioperative complication rate, but loss of endocrine and exocrine function.
2. Pancreas transplants from living related donation have a high technical failure rate and graft survival rates inferior to DR-matched cadaver pancreases.
3. Because of the hitherto rare indication for pancreas transplantation alone, there appears to be no need for living donation.
4. A possible altruistic gain for the donors does not outweigh all the risks and disadvantages of living pancreas donation.
5. Once the indication for pancreas transplantation is broadened due to better results and less toxic immunosuppression, the concept of living related pancreas donation will have to be reevaluated.

## References

1. Chinn PL, Sutherland DER, Goetz FC, Oliphant UJ, Elick BA, Najarian JS (1984) Metabolic effect of hemipancreatectomy in living-related graft donors. Transplant Proc 16:11–17
2. Sutherland DER, Dunn DL, Frederick C et al. (1989) A 10-year experience with 290 pancreas transplants at a single institution. Ann Surg 210:274–288
3. Bolinder J, Gunnarsson R, Tydén G, Brattström C, Östman J, Groth CG (1988) Metabolic effects of living related pancreatic graft donation. Transplant Proc 20:475–478
4. Kendall DM, Sutherland DER, Najarian JS, Goetz FC, Robertson RP (1990) Effects of hemipancreatectomy on insulin secretion and glucose tolerance in healthy humans. N Engl J Med 322:898–903
5. Sutherland DER, Moudry-Munns KC (1990) International pancreas transplantation registry analysis. Transplant Proc 22:571–574

# Medical Risk and Benefit in Living Pancreas Segment Donors

R. Landgraf

## Arguments for Pancreatic Tansplantation

Under conventional insulin therapy, morbidity and mortality in type I diabetic patients is still high [20]. Prerequisite for prevention of diabetic complications is long-term normoglycemia [5]. However, normal glucose homeostasis is up to now still only achievable with pancreatic grafting [10]. In recent years, pancreatic transplantation is quite a safe and successful mode of treatment for carefully selected type I diabetics [13,14,17].

## Arguments for Living Pancreas Segment Donors

1. There is no doubt that parents and siblings of type I diabetic patients have a high motivation for organ donation, not only for kidneys but also for pancreas segments. This has been amply demonstrated by the Minneapolis group [7,8] and has also been reported from other transplantation centres.
2. In addition, a well-planned grafting is possible with an optimal preparation of the recipient physically as well as mentally.
3. The surgical removal of the pancreas segment under optimal conditions increases the quality of harvesting which is extremely important for the outcome of grafting.
4. The pancreases from human leukocyte antigen (HLA)-matched living related donors seem to have better graft survival rates, mainly due to fewer rejection episodes [17].
5. The morbidity of the donor peri- and postoperatively (early) is rather low, and mortality has not been reported [2,3,8].
6. Development of clinical diabetes in the donor is low (4%; [7]).
7. Animal experiments have shown that comparable pancreas resections did not lead to overt diabetes although long-term follow-ups are missing [6,11,12,15,18].

Department of Internal Medicine, Klinikum Innenstadt, University of Munich, Ziemssenstraße 1, D-8000 München 2, FRG

W. Land, J. B. Dossetor (Eds.)
Organ Replacement Therapy:
Ethics, Justice and Commerce

## Arguments Against Living Pancreas Segment Donors

### Donor Related

1. Major surgery has to be performed, with the possibility of peri- and postoperative morbidity and mortality. Reoperations for splenectomy or infections have been reported [2,8].
2. Deterioration of glucose metabolism after hemipancreatectomy can be demonstrated in all living donors, and one-third of the donors showed impaired glucose tolerance – some of them in the manifest clinical range – 1 year after transplantation [8].
3. Since the islet mass is closely related to the insulin secretory capacity [19], diminution of this reserve might become relevant with aging, which is associated with progressive disturbances of glucose tolerance and with states of insulin resistance like obesity, catabolic situations, and certain drug regimens (e.g., glucocorticoids, thiazide diuretics).
4. In addition, there are no markers available for the prediction of the development of type II diabetics. The test battery for judging the endocrine function of a potential donor [8] is probably insufficient, especially when the longevity of the donor can be expected to be high. Also the empirical risk for developing type II diabetes might be increased in first-degree relatives of type I diabetics [9].
5. Markers for the prediction of the development of type I diabetes in potential donors have not been considered (ICA; IAA) before pancreas segment donation [8]. Also it cannot be ruled out that diabetes may develop in a family member of a diabetic patient 10 years after the onset of diabetes in the patient, as reported by Barbosa et al. [1].
6. At the moment there is no shortage of suitable cadaveric pancreas organs, which might however become a problem when more centres start pancreatic grafting or when organs are used for other purposes (e.g.) isolation of adult islets and research projects.
7. Ethical problems might arise, especially when family members apart from parents are considered for pancreas segment donation.

### Recipient Related

1. HLA identity or haplotype matches might lead to a recurrence of the autoimmune process in the grafted organ [16]. Therefore, chronic immunosuppression is also necessary in living related pancreas recipients.
2. Graft survival is still not optimal, and the method of choice for the surgical procedure and the handling of the organ is not available.
3. The islet mass in a pancreas segment is less than in a whole organ which might become critical after rejection episodes or recurrent pancreatitis.

4. Drainage of a pancreas segment into the bowel or the urinary bladder is less advantageous than drainage via pancreaticoduodenal jejunostomy, or cystostomy. In this context, it is interesting to note that the rate of technical failures in living related pancreas grafting is higher than in cadaveric pancreatic transplantation (35% vs 19%; DER Sutherland, personal communication).
5. Recently, graft survival rates from living-related donors and from cadavers have been comparable (DER Sutherland, personal communication).
6. Metabolic control of the recipient of a living related donor's pancreas is not better than that with a cadaveric donor's organ.
7. Effect of pancreatic grafting on the secondary diabetic lesions, especially in the advanced stages, is not predictable [10]. Primary prevention trials are, therefore, necessary at a rather early stage of the diabetes, which might lead to ethical and legal problems, since the recipient is often minor and the potential donor is also very young.

## Conclusion

Since pancreatic grafting is not a life-saving procedure, except for patients with an extremely labile diabetes leading to unavoidable severe hypoglycemic attacks, living pancreas-segment donation should not be performed when the risk/benefit ratio for the donor and the recipient is considered.

## References

1. Barbosa J, King R, Noreen H, Yunis EJ (1977) The histocompatibility system in juvenile insulin-dependent diabetic multiplex kindreds. J Clin Invest 60:989–998
2. Bolinder J, Gunnarsson R, Tydén G, Brattström C, Östman J, Groth CG (1988) Metabolic effects of living related pancreatic graft donation. Transplant Proc 20:475–478
3. Chinn PL, Sutherland DER, Goetz FC, Oliphant UJ, Elick BA, Najarian JS (1984) Metabolic effect of hemipancreatectomy in living related graft donors. Transplatn Proc 16:11–17
4. Dubernard JM, Sutherland DER (eds) (1989) International Handbook of Pancreas Transplantation. Kluwer, Dordrecht
5. Hanssen KF, Dahl-Jørgensen K, Lauritzen T, Feldt-Rasmussen B, Brinchmann-Hansen O, Deckert T (1986) Diabetic control and microvascular complications: The near-normoglycemic experience. Diabetologia 29:677–684
6. Imamura T, Koffler M, Helderman JH, Prince D, Thirlby R, Inman L, Unger RH (1988) Severe diabetes induced in subtotally depancreatized dogs by sustained hyperglycemia. Diabetes 37:600–609
7. Kendall DM, Sutherland DER, Goetz FC, Najarian JS (1989) Metabolic effect of hemipancratectomy in donors. Preoperative prediction of postoperative oral glucose tolerance. Diabetes 38 [Suppl 1]:101–103
8. Kendall DM, Sutherland DER, Najarian JS, Goetz FC, Robertson RP (1990) Effects of hemipancreatectomy on insulin secretion and glucose tolerance in healthy humans. N Engl J Med 322:898–903

9. Köbberling J, Tillil H (1982) Empirical risk figures for first degree relatives of non-insulin dependent diabetics. In: Köbberling J and Tattersall R (eds) The genetics of diabetes mellitus. Academic, London, pp 201–209
10. Landgraf R, Nusser J, Scheuer R, Fiedler A, Scheider A, Meyer-Schwickerath E, Müller-Felber W, Illner WD, Abendroth D, Land W (1989) Metabolic control and effect of secondary complications of diabetes mellitus by pancreatic transplantation. Ballière's Clinical Gastroenterology 3:865–876
11. Leaky JL, Bonner-Weir S, Weir GC (1988) Minimal chronic hyperglycemia is a critical determinant of impaired insulin secretion after an incomplete pancreatectomy. J Clin Invest 81:1407–1414
12. Mizumoto R, Kawarada Y, Goshima H, Tamaki T, Sekoguchi T, Tomikawa J (1982) Carbohydrate metabolism and endocrine function in the pancreas remnant after major pancreatic resection. Am J Surgery 143:237–243
13. Land W, Landgraf R (1987) Clinical pancreas transplantation: The world experience. Transplant Proc 19 [Suppl 4]:1–102
14. Najarian JS, Sutherland DER, Groth CG (Guest Eds) (1990) Second International Congress on Pancreatic and Islet Cell Transplantation. Transplant Proc 22:569–883
15. Sun AM, Coddling JA, Haist RE (1974) A study of glucose tolerance and insulin response in partially depancreatized dogs. Diabetes 23:424–432
16. Sutherland DER, Sibley R, Chinn P, Michael A, Srikanta S, Taub F, Najarian J, Goetz FC (1984) Twin to twin pancreas transplantations: reversal and reenactment of the pathogenesis of type I diabetes. Clin Res 32:56
17. Sutherland DER, Dunn DL, Goetz FC, Kennedy W, Ramsay RC, Steffes MW, Mauer SM, Gruessner R, Moudry-Munns KC, Morel P, Viste A, Robertson RP, Najarian JS (1989) 10-year experience with 290 pancreas transplants at a single institution. Ann Surgery 210:274–288
18. Ward WK, Wallum BJ, Beard JC, Taborsky Jr GJ, Porte Jr D (1988) Reduction of glycemic potentiation. Sensitive indicator of β-cell loss in partially pancreatectomized dogs. Diabetes 37:723–729
19. Weir GC, Bonner-Weir S, Leaky JL (1990) Islet mass and function in diabetes and transplantation. Diabetes 39:401–405
20. WHO Study Group (1985) Diabetes mellitus. WHO Technical Report Series 727

# Medical Risk and Benefit in Living Small-Bowel Segment Donors

E. Deltz

## Introduction

In contrast to transplantation of kidneys, liver, heart, or pancreas, small-bowel transplantation has not yet gained the status of a routine clinical procedure. At present small-bowel transplantation is leaving the state of a mere experimental procedure to enter the field of clinical application. Thus, the general discussion on small-bowel grafting and especially on living small-bowel organ donation resembles to the situation that was to be encountered when kidney transplantations started and during the first clinical attempts at liver transplantation in the 1960s.

The only causal therapy which can be offered to a patient with short bowel syndrome is this new type of organ transplantation. The decision making in this early phase of development of clinical small – bowel transplantation requires careful systematic analysis and the sensitive application of ethical principles. According to Caniano [1], who has dealt extensively with the therapeutic problems in cases of massive intestinal loss, a systematic ethical analysis involves several steps. Caniano states:

> "First of all a clinical description of the diagnosis and prognosis is necessary. In addition, the physician's responsibility must be to communicate completely and clearly the range of therapeutic or experimental options. The anticipated results of these options and their complications should then be identified and assessed according to degrees of probability. Finally, ethical principles should be applied to the options and results so that an ethical base will support the decision."

These considerations have to be taken into account especially when an organ donation, i.e., the removal of a small bowel segment, has to be carried out from a living donor. According to international rules and the codex of German transplantation centers, organ donation from living donors should be performed only from direct relatives. This type of living related organ donation played a major role in the early era of clinical small bowel transplantation.

Department of General Surgery, University Hospital, Arnold-Heller-Str. 7, 2300 Kiel 1

W. Land, J. B. Dossetor (Eds.)
Organ Replacement Therapy:
Ethics, Justice and Commerce

## Case Reports

The first clinical attempt at small bowel transplantation was undertaken by Detterling in 1964 [2], using a segment of ileum from the mother of the recipient. The recipient survived only 12 h. In the second attempt, which was performed by Alican and coworkers [3], a 90-cm ileum graft from the donating mother was used and the child survived 7 days before he died from a generalized sepsis. In 1971, Fortner [4] used an allograft of 170 cm of lower jejunum and upper ileum obtained from the sister of the patient. The patient died of sepsis caused by E. coli and with the signs and symptoms of consumption coagulopathy 76 days after transplantation.

In our first case of small-bowel transplantation [5] in a 4-year-old boy, we grafted a 60-cm segment of jejunoileum, which was donated by the recipient's mother. The graft had to be removed on the 12th day postoperatively, because of an untreatable rejection episode. The recipient recovered quickly and is still alive under total home parenteral nutrition (HTPN). This was the first time a small-bowel recipient survived the operation despite a definite graft rejection.

In our second case [6], a 42-year-old female patient received a 60-cm graft of lower jejunum and upper ileum which was donated by the patient's half-sister. This was the first transplantation with a long-term graft survival. At present, the patient is in a good clinical state without the need for parenteral nutrition.

Besides these two patients, 13 small-bowel transplants using cadaver donors have been performed in 12 cases altogether in Paris, Kiel, Innsbruck, and Uppsala since March 1987 [7]. Two grafts are currently functioning and their recipients are nourished enterally alone. In addition to this a successful small-bowel liver transplantation has been carried out by Grant [8]. This group performed a couple of small-bowel transplantations this year; in both cases cadaver donors were used and, as far as I am aware, they are successful up to now.

## Total Parenteral Nutrition

The issue of small-bowel transplantation and especially that of small-bowel grafting with living related organ donation must always be discussed with regards to the conservative option of treatment in those cases of short bowel syndrome in which the small-bowel remnant had failed to adapt so that the patient is left with an indefinite period of total parenteral nutrition (TPN). Since HTPN began in 1970, its effectiveness in the treatment of small-bowel failure has been proven[9]. In large centers dealing with HTPN, patients with short bowel syndrome are the prevailing group, but, in spite of experienced care, the total mortality rate amounts to 28 % while it is 33 % in patients with short bowel syndrome [9].

Similar figures can be found in pediatric patients, in whom, besides malignancies, diagnoses include a number of short bowel syndromes caused by connatal malformations. The mortality rate in this group is as high as in the group of adult patients. As reported by Caniano et al. [11], the survival rate in neonates with extensive short bowel syndrome and TPN was 86 %, but 8 of 12 survivors presented intestinal adaptation and could therefore discontinue their TPN.

In all three groups of patients, adults, children and neonates, with short bowel syndromes, the same characteristic TPN-associated complications occurred. Catheter sepsis is the most acute and life-threatening complication. Cholestasis with bileduct proliferation and subsequent fibrosis as well as metabolic bone disease characterized by osteomalacia, bone pain, and fractures are long-term complications [10,12,13]. Despite the fact that some patients with TPN can be fully rehabilitated and lead an active occupational and social life, the constant dependency on an artificial life-supporting system, together with the high rate of morbidity, leads to a state of severe depression in a lot of cases, which may eventually cause some patients to become suicidal.

The costs of TPN have to be mentioned in this context too. Talsma [14] gives a sum of 40 000 – 60 000 US dollars per year for TPN-related expenses, and, according to Caniano [11], the average costs of the initial hospitalization in neonates with short bowel syndrome amounted to 31 500 US dollars, with a mean duration of hospitalization of 450 days.

## Living Versus Cadaveric Small-Bowel Organ Donation

In the light of these data, the problems of small-bowel organ donation by relatives have to be discussed. What are the advantages of living organ donation in small-bowel transplantation over the use of cadaveric donors?

During the waiting period for a cadaveric donation, an exact timing of the transplantation cannot be done by the patient and medical staff in contrast to living donation which can be done after optimal preparation of the recipient and before all the aforementioned complications occur. Living donation by relatives enables the surgeon to plan and organize the operation in an optimal fashion. Graft and donor pretreatment, i.e., irradiation of the graft or cyclosporin A (CsA) medication, can be done electively.

Up to now the role of ischemia in small-bowel transplantation is not completely understood, but the small-bowel graft seems to be extremely susceptible to ischemic damage, especially by injury induced by free oxygen radicals [15]. Thus, a short ischemic time period appears to be a prerequisite for a successful small-bowel transplantation, a condition that can be guaranteed in a scheduled transplantation of a living donor graft with simultaneous donor and recipient operations. It is a matter of course that living donor organ donation is only indicated in case of a certain degree of human leukocyte antigen (HLA) compatibility between donor and recipient.

The donor operation with the removal of a jejunal segment in continuity to an ileal segment, which secures an optimal adaptive capacity and the maintenance of the absorptive functions, does not offer major technical problems; the preparation of the mesenteric vessels as well as the reestablishing of the donor's gut continuity by end-to-end anastomosis is a procedure demanding only average surgical skills. All these factors help in putting less strain on the patient in this operation than in a living donation of a liver or pancreas.

## Surgical Techniques

The type of organ harvesting depends on the vascular architecture of the distal small bowel and the ileocecal region [16]. For the removal of a well-vascularized jejunoileal graft, it is necessary to remove a section of the superior mesenteric artery and vein together with the graft. This technique requires end-to-end vascular anastomoses between the proximal and distal stumps of the mesenteric vessels.

If there are sufficient vascular arcades and connections between the right colonic vessels and the terminal ileum, the ileocecal artery and vein, which otherwise provide the major blood supply to the cecum and terminal ileum, can be ligated without jeopardizing ileocecal viability so that a safe anastomosis can be constructed. This was the technique used by Fortner and colleagues in their clinical attempt in 1971 [4].

If the ileocecal artery is retained with the graft and there are no arcades to the colon, the cecum should be removed to avoid a resulting insufficient blood supply, and the intestinal continuity should be reastablished by an ileoascending intestinal anastomosis. This type of operation leaves the donor with the typical risks of a major surgical procedure including a certain rate of anastomotic leakage that cannot be neglected. In a healthy donor, the length of the remaining small bowel is sufficient for an impaired absorptive capacity even after removal of a segment of 60 – 100 cm, provided that a segment of ileum is left to ensure the patient's absorption of bile acids and fat soluble vitamins. For these reasons, we only removed a graft of 60 cm in length in our two attempts of living organ donation [5,6], cutting the mesenteric vessels directly at the point at which they leave the ileocolic artery and vein, thus obtaining a graft with a mesenteric vessel diameter of 2 – 3 mm and ensuring no impairment of the donor's bowel blood supply or absorptive capacity.

Preparatory irradiation in order to decrease the activity of immunocompetent cells, which are localized mainly within the mesenteric lymph nodes of the small-bowel segment, in order to avoid graft versus host disease (GVHD) cannot be carried out in living organ donation for ethical reasons. Inactivation of lymphocytes in the gut-associated lymphatic tissue therefore has to be done by treating the donor with CsA for 24 h before transplantation; this can only be done with the informed consent of the donor. Side effects of this short-term CsA course are not to be expected.

From the technical point of view the recipient operation using living donor's small-bowel grafts holds the problem of microvascular anastomoses. Iliac vessels seem to be suited for vascular anastomoses, as the mesenteric vessels, aorta, inferior vena cava, or the portal vein are not very easily accessible in most recipients due to multiple previous intraabdominal operations.

## Postoperative Treatment and Complications

It is a matter of course that the recipient is subjected to all the problems and complications associated with continuous, effective immunosuppression. In small-bowel transplantation, a very strong immunosuppression seems to be a prerequisite for sufficient long-term graft function. Even in case of a good histocompatibility, multiple rejection episodes may occur requiring an aggressive therapy which, in addition to the side effects of CsA medication, causes the recipient to become susceptible to various infectious diseases.

In the long-term follow-up after small-bowel transplantation, all the complications and side effects of immunosuppression can be observed. Besides recurrent septic episodes caused by the permanent central venous catheter, our patient had a severe cytomegalovirus (CMV) encephalomeningitis 5 months after the transplantation, and 18 months postoperatively, she suffered from a widespread herpes zoster infection. The immunosuppressants CsA and steroids had caused a rise in serum creatinine which necessitated a dose reduction; a subsequent cataract formation in both eyes required operative treatment.

Besides these somatic problems, the patient had severe psychological disorders as she refused to eat and drink and suffered from episodes of recurrent vomiting; at the same time the graft's absorptive capacity was proven to be sufficient along with a normal motility pattern. This may in part have been induced by the long duration of parenteral substitution of electrolyte solution and caloric support; the small-bowel graft had gained full adaptation 20 months after the operation, and the parenteral substitution could be discontinued. The psychological difficulties could be overcome by a great amount of attention devoted to this patient by the nurses and the surgical staff as well as through the help of a psychologist.

## HLA Matching

A main advantage of living donation by relatives is the possibility of good HLA matching between donor and recipient which exceeds that encountered in cadaveric organ donation; this is why this type of procedure was chosen when kidney transplantation began, too. Which criteria with regards to HLA matching should be fulfilled in living small-bowel organ donation?

There are three reports in the literature with detailed data of HLA typing in living relatives. In Fortner's patient of 1971 [4], there was, according to the HLA typing of that time, HLA identitiy between the recipient, who received a segmental graft from her sister, and the donor. In our first attempt [5], the following situation was found with regards to the HLA typing. Using the mother as a donor, the recipient showed identity at the A and DQ locus and a mismatch each at the B and DR locus in both, the host versus graft reaction (HVGR) and graft versus host reaction (GVHR) direction. This situation was regarded to be adequate to allow clinical transplantation. Nevertheless, this graft underwent an untreatable rejection and had to be removed.

In our second case [6] using the recipient's sister as a donor, in the HVGR direction there was no mismatch, whereas in the GVHR direction the B and DR locus both were mismatched. Despite this good matching, at least in the HVGR direction, multiple severe rejection episodes occurred, which could finally be treated effectively, but there were no signs of an acute cellular GVHR, except for a chronic anemia as a result of a chronic antibody-mediated GVHR. In contrast to these findings, Revillon and coworkers (J. Revillon, personal communication) in Paris observed long-term, i.e., more than 1-year, graft function in two cases of small-bowel transplantation using grafts from totally mismatched cadaveric donors with a graft failure in one case caused by chronic rejection.

From these observations, it has to be to concluded that in small-bowel transplantation the role of the histoincompatibility between donor and recipient at present is far from being completely understood. Especially the interference and delicate balance of GVHR and HVGR alters these bidirectional immunological reactions in an unpredictable manner. Thus, at present we cannot conclude from a certain HLA match situation in living organ donation by relatives, that a small-bowel transplantation will be successful or not. Therefore, organ donation by living donors cannot generally be recommended.

## Summary

With regards to the initial question of how to make a decision in the treatment of short bowel syndromes including medical facts of known treatment and options of new treatment as well as ethical principles with regards to living small-bowel segment donation, I should like to summarize and draw the following conclusions:

1. Successful small-bowel transplantation offers a better quality of life, a lesser rate of morbidity, and a better life expectancy to the patient than permanent TPN.
2. Small-bowel organ donation by relatives seems to be permissible in case of HLA identity (or one mismatch).
3. The role of HLA compatibility between donor and recipient in small-bowel transplantation is not yet completely understood, so that living

small-bowel donation cannot be recommended in general. Nonadult donors, should therefore, not be used.

4. Living small-bowel donation should be carried out only after extensive information of donor and recipient about all the therapeutic options and their complications and side effects.
5. Up to now, living small-bowel donation has not been proven to be superior to cadaveric transplantation. Therefore, cadaver grafts should be used for further clinical attempts.

## References


1. Caniano DA, Kanoti GA (1988) Newborns with massive intestinal loss: difficult choices. N Engl J Med 318:703–707
2. Agnholt JS, Freund LG, Rasmussen StN (1989) Tyndtarmstransplantation. Ugeska Laeger 151/21:1298–1302
3. Alican F, Hardy JD, Cayirli M, Varner JE, Moynihan PC, Turner MD, Anas P (1971) Intestinal transplantation: laboratory experience and report of a clinical case. Am J Surg 121:150–159
4. Fortner JG, Sichuk G, Litwin StD, Beattie EJ (1972) Immunological responses to an intestinal allograft with HLA-identical donor-recipient. Transplantation 45:673–676
5. Deltz E, Mengel W, Hamelmann H (1990) Small bowel transplantation: report of a clinical case. Progr Pediatr Surg 25:90–96
6. Deltz E, Schroeder P, Gebhardt H, Gundlach M, Timmermann W, Engemann R, Leimenstoll G, Hansman ML, Westphal E, Hamelmann H (1989) Successful clinical small bowel transplantation: report of a case. Clin Transplant 3:89–91
7. Schroeder P, Goulet O, Lear PA (1990) Small-bowel transplantation: European experience. Lancet 336:110–111
8. Grant D, Wall W, Mimeault R, Zhong R, Ghent C, Garcia B, Stiller C, Duff J (1990) Successful small-bowel/liver transplantation. Lancet 335:181–184
9. Wolman SL, Jeejeebhoy KN, Stewart S, Greig PD (1986) Experience in home parenteral nutrition and indications for small-bowel transplantation. In: Deltz E, Thiede A, Hamelmann H (eds) Small-bowel transplantation. Springer, Berlin Heidelberg New York Tokyo, pp. 214–221
10. Vargas JH, Ament MW, Berquist WE (1987) Long-term home parenteral nutrition in pediatrics: ten years of experience in 102 patients. J Pediatr Gastroenterol Nutrit 6:24–32
11. Caniano DA, Starr J, Ginn-Pease ME (1989) Extensive short-bowel syndrome in neonates: outcome in the 1980s. Surgery 105:119–124
12. Bohles H (1987) Cholestasis in total parenteral nutrition. A review. Infusionsther Klin Ernähr 14 (S1):3–9
13. McCullough ML, Hsu N (1987) Metabolic bone disease in home total parenteral nutrition. J Am Diet Assoc 915–920
14. Talsma SE, Marks WH, Marks C, Brady M (1986) Potential recipients for small-bowel transplantation in the United States and the United Kingdom, In: Deltz E, Thiede A, Hamelmann H (eds) Small-bowel transplantation. Springer, Berlin Heidelberg New York Tokyo, pp. 258–261
15. Belzer FO, Southard JH (1988) Principles of solid-organ preservation by cold storage Transplantation 45:673–676
16. Schraut WH, Lee KKW (1986) Procurement of intestinal allografts from living related and from cadaver donors. In: Deltz E, Thiede A, Hamelmann H (eds) Small-bowel transplantation. Springer, Berlin Heidelberg New York Tokyo, pp. 203–210

# Living Donor Nonrenal Organ Transplantation: A Focus on Living Related Orthotopic Liver Transplantation

P. F. Whitington, M. Siegler, and C.E. Broelsch

## Introduction

Surgical and medical advances of the last decade have made replacement therapy for organ failure a clinical reality. The supply of organs for transplantation has relied heavily upon the availability of brain-dead, heart-beating cadavers. While there will continue to be a reliance upon this source, organ donation by living volunteers offers certain medical and strategic advantages that have recently prompted some prominent transplant centers to consider increasing the use of this source for allografts.

## Kidney Transplantation

Living related donors remain an important source for kidneys for transplantation, now constituting 21 % of kidney transplants performed in the United States (United Network for Organ Sharing, news release, April 18, 1990). In some major centers, living donors provide more than 50 % of the kidneys transplanted, while substantial differences between centers seem to reflect more a philosophical concern about whether it is ever acceptable to risk any degree of harm to a healthy individual (the living donor) rather than the procedure's medical and scientific merit. Although there appears to be a marginal survival advantage for the recipient of a living related kidney, there remains considerable question whether this advantage outweighs the risk to the donor. Recipients of kidneys from living donors appear to have some immunologic advantage with fewer and less severe rejection episodes, but much of this advantage has been attenuated with the advent of cyclosporine and will be further reduced as better immunosuppression is developed. The donors generally regain their former health. However, the risk of death from kidney donation is about 1 in 1600 (0.06 %), even though 74 of 79 transplant centers that use living donors reported zero mortality [1]. In addition, there is

Departments of Pediatrics, Medicine, and Surgery, The University of Chicago Pritzker School of Medicine, Chicago, IL, USA

W. Land, J. B. Dossetor (Eds.)
Organ Replacement Therapy:
Ethics, Justice and Commerce

a well-documented reduction in renal function after donation that could translate into increased risk for hypertension and renal insufficiency with increasing time for follow-up. At this time, long-term actuarial survival for kidney donation appears to be the same as for the general population. Despite the use of living kidney donors for more than 20 years, the debate continues.

## Pancreas Transplantation

More recently, Sutherland's group at the University of Minnesota have accumulated a large experience with living donor pancreas transplantation with 79 procedures reported from that institution [2]. Again, there seems to be a marginal advantage to the recipient, but the donors may have a higher complication rate than kidney donors. In the first year after transplant, the recipients derive no clear advantage from receiving live donor pancreatic allografts because the procedure is associated with increased surgical and postoperative complications that lead to graft loss. Long-term follow-up suggests there may be some advantage, but it is small. Abnormal glucose tolerance in many of the donors results from the relative lack of reserve for insulin secretion after resection of part of the pancreas. Whether this will translate into reduced donor survival is not yet clear. It should be noted that the number of pancreas transplants being performed with living donors is rapidly shrinking, suggesting a lack of conviction as to the benefit of the procedure on the part of those involved.

## Other Organs

Transplants of three other organs – liver, small intestine, and lung – have recently been performed using living donors. The experience with small-bowel – two cases performed by Deltz's group in Kiel [3] – is far too small to form any opinion as to the balance of benefit and risk. One patient is alive with good small-bowel function, which indicates the procedure can be successful. The donors suffered no complications. The investigator involved has concluded from this limited experience that obtaining small bowel from living donors offers no advantage over cadaver allografting. It seems premature to make that conclusion. A single live donor lung transplant has been performed at Stanford University (lay press communication), but there has been no follow-up to assess outcome. Obviously, these numbers are too small to allow analysis of the advantage of living donation.

There has been a rapid accumulation of experience with living liver donation. Other than the experience at the University of Chicago (to be fully described later), there have been 14 live donor liver transplants performed – 9 in Japan (5 at Kyoto University), 2 in Brazil, 2 in Turkey, and 1 in Australia. The program at the University of Chicago, in which 16 procedures have been performed, was the first structured experimental protocol to use liver segments from living donors for transplantation into children. Of a total of 30 recipients worldwide, 23 are alive (76 % actual survival). If the four deaths in institutions that are not equipped to handle the postoperative management of such complex patients are excluded, the actual survival is an impressive 90 %. No donors have died or suffered major complications. Of course, the follow-up is short, but based on initial results, the procedure appears to be safe for donors and beneficial for recipients. This operation clearly deserves further application, although caution is due.

## The Program of Living Related Liver Transplantation at the University of Chicago

At the University of Chicago, the first liver transplant using a living donor was performed on November 23, 1989. By the end of 1990, 16 procedures had been performed.

### Ethical Issues

The first procedure followed 3 months after our publication of the ethical issues involved in living donor liver transplantation [4]. By announcing our plans in advance and introducing the ethical issues involved in living donation of liver segments, we were responding to Dr. Francis Moore's plea some years ago that the ethical conduct of therapeutic innovation should involve: "... open display, public evaluation, and prior discussion." [5] This publication was the result of extensive discussions involving surgeons, medical physicians, and ethicists. The ethical issues were discussed at a meeting of the Committee on Medical Ethics that was open to wide University participation. We considered a variety of ethical issues including:

1. the risks and benefits to recipients;
2. the risks and benefits to donors; and
3. whether true informed consent could be obtained from living donors.

We concluded that the surgical risk to the donor was the only major obstacle to performing living donor liver transplantation in an ethically acceptable way. Data were collected from published reports of the surgical risk of partial hepatectomy and from our own experience with this procedure. The apparent risk for death following partial hepatectomy ranges in various series from 0 %–10 %. In our own experience involving more than 40 cases (CE Broelsch and JC Emond, unpublished data), there have been no deaths when left hemihepatectomy is performed for the treatment of benign lesions or metastatic carcinoma. These appear to be the circumstances that most closely approximate elective left lobectomy in a volunteer liver donor, so the risk of death was estimated to be very low for this operation when performed by an experienced liver surgeon in a first-rate hospital. However, there can be no argument that there is a finite risk of death for the donor. From our own experience, we estimated the risk of major surgical complications to be in the order of 1 %–2 %, while the risk of minor complications we believed to be in the order of 5 %–7 %.

Much of the discussion related to our protocol focused on the question, "Is any risk to the donor justifiable?" Can anyone be asked to risk death or disability to benefit another? The answers to these questions, of course, depend upon the level of risk and the potential benefit to the volunteer. It was concluded that people are permitted to do many things with finite risks and with no greater justification, so it seemed reasonable that an adult family member should be permitted to donate a liver segment to benefit his or her child. The key goal of the experimental protocol submitted to our Institutional Review Board was to determine if the balance of benefit to risk justified the continued clinical use of living donors for liver transplantation.

Our protocol permits 20 infants to be transplanted in nonemergency conditions with liver segments from adult relatives. Infants were selected because they are affected more by donor availability than are older children and adults. Data from the Bureau of Vital Statistics [6] and from the Cildren's Memorial Hospital in Chicago [7] indicate that 60 %–80 % of children who die with end-stage liver disease are less than 2 years old. Therefore, the average child needing a liver transplant is quite small. Accidents, the major source of heart-beating cadavers, affect mainly school-aged children. As a consequence, there is a donor-to-recipient mismatch and a shortage of liver donors for small children. This has resulted in waiting times that often exceed 6–9 months. For the infant with biliary atresia, this may be more than half of the child's life expectancy. End-stage cirrhosis has profound effects on growth, nutritional status, neurologic development, and immune function of infants. As a consequence, the recipient of a liver graft from a cadaver donor is often a poor surgical risk. Moreover, some of the effects of end-stage cirrhosis, particularly the delay in neurologic development, may be irreversible so the overall benefit even of "successful" transplantation will necessarily be flawed. Donor availability for infants has improved because of the use of segmental transplantation from cadaver donors [9–13], but infants still must be on United Network for Organ Sharing (UNOS) status 3–4 to obtain a donor organ. Infants still die on waiting lists throughout the United States because of the lack of suitable donors. From the recipient's perspective, improving the availability of organ donors and the timeliness of transplantation seem to be overwhelming reasons to perform some liver transplantations with organs from living donors.

There also may be some advantages from the donor's perspective. The process of liver transplantation is very traumatic to family life and difficulty obtaining a donor for a critically ill child worsens that trauma. The long waits filled with uncertainty are perceived by family members as races against death. The fact that children must be in very advanced liver failure to obtain a donor seems unreasonable and unfair to the family. The need for another child to die for an organ to become available produces tremendous ambivalent feelings in the recipient's parents. Moreover, parents and family members desire to participate actively in the transplant procedure, even as donors. Parental willingness to participate is largely a result of altruism, but parental attitudes also may be affected by feelings of guilt that can result from bearing a sick child.

## Informed Consent

The informed consent for volunteer related donors was designed to reduce coercion in several ways. First, parents are informed that at the University of Chicago virtually every child who needs a liver transplant can obtain one from either a whole cadaver graft or a reduced-size cadaver graft (and, thus, living donation is not necessary to save the child's life); and second, only nonemergency cases are considered for the first 20 cases in our experimental protocol. The consent process involves two separate detailed written consents that must be signed by the donor and the spouse. The first permits entry of the donor into the evaluation. If the donor is found to be medically suitable, a second consent is obtained. At the time of the second signing, a donor advocate who is a member of the General Medicine Department plays the "devil's advocate" by asking all unasked questions. If the donor wishes to proceed, our protocol stipulates that 2 weeks must pass before the transplant is performed to give adequate time for reflection and possible withdrawal. Despite this elaborate process, we still continue to question whether the process we have developed represents truly informed consent. Many of our donors deny that they themselves could die as a result of their volunteerism. It is our impression that most volunteers have decided to participate before our discussions, and nothing we can do or say will change their minds. Similar observations have been made for kidney transplantation [8]. However, it is not clear whether we, as health care providers, have the right to prohibit healthy volunteers from donating, particularly if we have assessed the balance of benefit to risk to be favorable.

## Medical Evaluation

The medical evaluation of potential donors involves a general physical examination to exclude medical conditions that the volunteer may not be aware of. This is followed by a broad chemical and serologic evaluation to further assure the absence of hidden medical conditions that could imperil either donor or recipient. For example, we have identified one potential donor who was positive for Hepatitis B S-Antigen (HbSAg) although he was unaware of this condition.

Computerized axial tomography is used to assess the size of the left lateral segment. The two-dimensional images stored on digital tape are reconstructed into a three-dimensional image using computer-enhanced integration. From this, a volume of the left lateral segment is estimated. If the volume of the graft is deemed to be within the limits of tolerance of the recipient, the evaluation proceeds. Two potential donors have been excluded because the graft would have been too large.

The next stage of the evaluation involves assessment by a psychiatrist to assure that the stress of the procedure can be tolerated by the volunteer and the family. Two potential donors have been deemed inadmissible for psychiatric reasons. The final stage of the evaluation involves hepatic arteriogram to assure the adequacy of vessels for transplantation. The arterial anatomy has been found to be highly irregular although no potential donors have been excluded by arteriogram.

## Results

The 16 recipients of living donor liver transplants have included 12 women and 4 men. Twelve have had biliary atresia, two α1-antitrypsin deficiency, one neonatal hepatitis and one cytomegalovirus hepatitis. The ages of the recipients have averaged 12 months, and their weights have averaged about 7.5 kg, placing them far below the 5th percentile of weight for age. Eleven of the cases have been truly elective, equivalent to UNOS status 1, three others have required hospitalization, equivalent to UNOS status 2, and two others have required moderate support in the intensive care unit, equivalent to UNOS status 3.

The donors have been on average 28 years of age and have weighed an average of 67 kg. Nine of the donors have been mothers of the recipients, six have been fathers, and one a grandmother. The computed volume of the left lateral segment has been 252 ± 70 cc, yielding an average of 34 ± 8.5 cc/kg of recipient.

The donor operations have been performed without incident, except in the first case where the spleen ruptured during the period of portal vein cross-clamping. Emergency splenectomy was performed and the patient has recovered. The first three donor operations involved total left hepatectomy. Each of these donors suffered minor postoperative complications, two having minor bile leaks from the cut surface of the liver, and the third having a minor fluid collection. All of these patients have recovered without long-term problems. The last 13 donors have undergone left lateral hepatectomy without operative or postoperative surgical complications. Our experience now suggests that, in the majority of cases, left lateral hepatectomy, which can be performed with minimal risk to the donor, provides an adequate graft for the recipient.

There have been a wide variety of complications in the recipients, but these appear to have been no greater than those observed in recipients of reduced-size cadaver grafts. Two grafts have been lost to hepatic artery thrombosis. Both of these had aberrant arterial anatomy with two arteries to the left lateral segment. Attempted reconstruction was unsuccessful and resulted in arterial insufficiency. Subsequently, we have elected not to use donors with this anatomy, although we have not encountered a similar case. One patient had thrombosis of the hepatic artery and the portal vein related to positional kinking. This patient has subsequently done well, although she did require reoperation for thrombectomy of the portal vein. Another recipient developed arterial thrombosis related to infection along the cut edge of the graft. Treatment of the infection and surgical thrombectomy has left this child with a patent artery and a normal graft function. Another factor that may have been involved in arterial thrombosis was the use of the donor's inferior mesenteric vein as an arterial graft. It seemed too flimsy and prone to kink and clot, so we now use saphenous vein harvested from the groin. Since making that change, there have been no further vascular complications. There have been no instances of primary graft failure.

Table 1 presents a comparison of the recipients of live donor allografts and a group of infants receiving left lateral segmental grafts from cadaver donors. Compared are 12 of each who were treated over the same time period and for whom we have at least 6 months follow-up. As can be seen, the recipients of living donor allografts have had no more surgical complications and have had

**Table 1.** Comparison of 12 recipients of live donor hepatic allografts to 12 recipients of left lateral segmental cadaver allografts

| Recipient | Live donor ($n$ = 12) | Cadaver donor ($n$ = 12) |
|---|---|---|
| Age (months) | 12.6 ± 5.4[a] | 12.1 ± 5.8[a] |
| Weight (kg) | 7.6 ± 1.7 | 6.5 ± 0.8 |
| Complication | | |
| Bile leak | 3/12 (25%)[b] | 2/9 (22%)[b] |
| Bleeding | 2/12 (17%) | 3/11 (27%) |
| Vascular thrombosis | 4/12 (33%) | 4/10 (40%) |
| Primary nonfunction | 0/12 ( 0%) | 2/12 (17%) |
| Secondary graft failure | 2/12 (17%) | 3/12 (25%) |
| Retransplantation | 2/12 (17%) | 3/9 (33%) |
| Rejection | 4/12 (33%) | 7/9 (77%) |
| Mild | 2/12 (17%) | 7/9 (77%) |
| Severe | 2/12 (17%) | 2/12 (17%) |
| Blood in operating room (units) | 2.0 ± 1.0 | 2.6 ± 1.9 |
| Hospital stay (days) | 20 (14 – 93)[c] ($n$=12) | 34 (18 – 83)[c] ($n$=10) |
| Deaths | 1/12 ( 8%) | 3/12 (25%) |

[a] Mean ± standard deviation
[b] Denominator is number at risk
[c] Median (range of values)

fewer life-threatening complications, such as primary graft nonfunction, than the comparison group.

Rejection appears to have been reduced relative to our usual rate in infants, which is about 75 % [14,15]. We have observed six rejection episodes in the 16 recipients. Four of these have been quite mild and have required only pulse corticosteriods for resolution. Both severe rejections required therapy with OKT3 [15], and one was resolved. One patient continued to have chronic rejection while receiving FK-506 and represents the only recipient of a living donor allograft with persistent abnormal liver function. In this case, the grandmother was the donor, and there was a positive cross-match.

In follow-up of the recipients, 14 are alive, 13 with the original graft. All of these have normal liver function with bilirubin values of less than 1.5. Two patients were retransplanted because of arterial loss. One of these patients died from an infection 10 days after retransplantation, and the other has chronic rejection with stable liver function while receiving FK-506. The living donor recipient with chronic rejection requiring FK-506 therapy has also died from overwhelming pneumococcal infection 7 months after transplantation.

The donors are all alive and well in follow-up. There is no indication that chronic medical disability has resulted from donation, but there has been some psychopathology. One father reports that he feels “spent” and has separated from the family, and another had a mild paranoid reaction. One mother feels scarred by the operation and indicates that she would not do it again. Eight of the families remain unchanged with regard to their basic structure. Most of these are strong nuclear families, but one contains significant pathology. Three families have separated. All of these were having difficulties before transplant but were not detected in our social and psychological screening. One family with major difficulties before transplant seems to have been strengthened by the ordeal, now being much closer than they were before transplant.

In conclusion, our experience with living donor liver transplantation demonstrates the feasibility of the procedure in the context of infants receiving segments from adult relatives. The benefits of the procedure appear to outweigh the potential risk to consenting donors, but the actual benefits and risks of the procedure will only be proven after further experience.

## The Possible Benefits and Risks of Living Donor Liver Transplantation

### Recipient Benefits

There are many possible benefits to recipients. Certainly there will be reduced preoperative morbidity and mortality if infants can be transplanted under elective conditions. Infants can be spared the effects of end-stage liver disease on general health, including malnutrition and immune deficits, and the risks of life-threatening complications, such as variceal bleeding and peritonitis, if transplantation can proceed electively. This probably constitutes the strongest reason for performing living donor liver transplantation – a timely transplant for infants with progressive liver disease. There is likely to be improved postoperative survival related only to the improved medical condition of the recipient at the time of transplantation. The uniform good quality of the graft that we have observed to date, including the complete absence of primary graft failure, will also improve outcome and make recovery quicker. Finally, there may be improved long-term survival, which could be related to reduced rejection because of the genetic similarity of the graft to the recipient.

The benefits and the risks to the donor are not purely physical. The benefits include a sense of extreme joy from giving of themselves to their child. One mother has expressed it as having experienced a second birthing process. All donors have commented about feeling good about reducing their child's suffering. After successful transplant, there appears to have been a strengthening of bonding and a sense of investment in the child that is stronger than with the usual transplant family. Some of the donors have experienced a tremendously increased sense of self-worth and self-esteem [8]. On the other hand, this procedure produces immense family stress because two members undergo major surgery simultaneously. There has been a loss of earning power related to the donor's hospitalization and convalescence. Some of the potential donors who were excluded for medical reasons have experienced reduced self-esteem because they were not permitted to participate. Some of the actual donors have experienced reduced self-esteem which has been expressed as feeling spent or used. The donors of children who have died or who have lost their grafts have experienced depression because they gave so much for nothing. If this procedure is to achieve maximal benefits for donors and recipients, more time must be devoted to considering the psychological risks and benefits and establishing support programs for donors and families.

## Benefits For Health Care System

Living liver donation may provide benefits to the hospital and to the health care system as a whole. Obviously, living donation results in an increased supply of donor organs. There will be expected to be a reduced need for pretransplant care that could result in improved utilization of intensive care unit facilities in transplant centers and reduced usage of blood products required to support patients with end-stage liver disease. Elective surgery requires improved utilization of operating room resources through scheduling. Blood usage may also be reduced, and autologous blood donation by the donor and donor-directed blood transfusions for the recipient are feasible. There may be reduced donor-related transplant costs. Our analysis demonstrates that the cost has been quite comparable to the expense of obtaining a cadaver graft, and with streamlining of the evaluation procedure, those costs can be further reduced. Finally, there is likely to be a reduction in postransplant needs and costs related to the improved condition of the recipient prior to transplantation and the excellent quality of the graft. This is exemplified by the fact that the recipients of living donor allografts have required a posttransplant hospitalization that is one-third shorter than the recipients of infants receiving cadaver grafts during the same period of time.

## Conclusions Concerning the Appropriate Use of Living Donors for Nonrenal Solid Organ Transplantation

Transplantation using living donors should certainly continue as investigational protocols in some major transplant centers. Caution must be exercised because two lives are being placed at risk, and one is a healthy person!

Dr. Francis Moore has stated that the ethics of therapeutic innovation depend on three things:

1. the scientific background of the procedure;
2. the "field strength" of the team; and
3. the ethical climate of the institution [5].

Scientific background is often developed in the laboratory; it has immense impact on outcome and is usually controlling. Dr. Moore states that:

> "Field strength is something that the public rarely sees or feels, and legislative bodies rarely understand. Physicians and surgeons understand it clearly. An example is to be found in liver surgery. Here, some persons and teams are very experienced in dealing with and handling the liver, both in the laboratory and clinical work, both medically and surgically, and others are not. Or field strength may lie in transplantation itself. Some teams in hospitals are very experienced in the use of immunosuppressive drugs, and others are not. Therapeutic innovation can occur ethically where there is this field strength, even if the team has not done that particular procedure before except in the laboratory."

He further states that:

> "It is on the third score, the ethical climate of the institution, that my own worries are most severely stressed at this time ... When capital gains, investor profit, institutional reputation, fame, surgeon ego, municipal pride, and chauvinism become the objective of the procedure, then the ethical climate of the institution is no longer acceptable for therapeutic innovation ... Physicians who are close to the institution may be able to make judgements. At the very least, they can raise questions in the open forum of public debate."

The program at the University of Chicago has met all three of Dr. Moore's standards, and other programs undertaking innovative live donor transplantation protocols should also seek to do so.

The use of living donors is a compelling temptation for surgeons who wish to institute a program of transplantation, but lack a track record or procurement system to obtain cadaveric organs. The training of transplant surgeons is such that the operations can be performed in many settings other than highly sophisticated institutions such as the University of Chicago. One reason for presenting the details of our program is to demonstrate the importance of the support systems, particularly for the recipient, but also for the donor – anesthesia, intensive care unit, nursing, gastroenterology, hepatology, dialysis, and psychosocial services – if a successful program is to be developed. Even institutions such as ours rely heavily upon the extended medical system for follow-up. It is unacceptable to engage in a practice that endangers a healthy person, particularly if local medical conditions significantly reduce the probability of success in the recipient as well. This is why liver transplantation using living donors should not be performed in developing countries or in secondary hospitals in developed countries, both of which are not capable of providing maximal sophisticated medical care. Live donor transplantation cannot be called upon to overcome the lack of institutional support, problems with cadaveric organ procurement, or a deficient health care system.

For the same reason, these procedures should be performed only in centers with major experience in cadaver-based transplantation. For example, live donor liver transplantation should be performed after experience has been gained with transplanting whole livers and liver segments. This provides the experience necessary to undertake the more complex live donor operation with a reasonable chance for success. The use of live donors to overcome a systemic deficit of cadaver donors cannot be condoned. In Japan, where live donor liver transplantation seems to be proceeding nicely, there is a social constraint to cadaver donation. This has been overcome by applying extremely advanced medical/surgical care and by learning from the experience of the University of Chicago before cautiously starting. The lack of a backup source for organs in the event of graft failure is worrisome. This situation does not seem ideal, but circumstances warrant such an approach.

There is room for continued debate about whether living donors should be used in any circumstance. It is clear that unless some advantage is to be gained by the recipient, the donor should not be allowed to participate. The program at the University of Chicago has constituted an experiment, the results of which are not yet complete. Our primary aim in conducting this experimental series of 20 cases was to demonstrate that liver transplantation is feasible using segmental grafts from living donors and that the risk-benefit ratio for both recipients and donors was a favorable one. The available data support the continued application of live donor allografting of liver. The advantages to the recipient are easily apparent. Survival approximating 90 % when the procedure has been performed in sophisticated medical settings is evidence of its effectiveness. Reducing pretransplant morbidity and mortality further argue for its use. It clearly should continue as a clinical experimental procedure with expansion into a few additional major centers in which there is experience with cadaveric liver transplantation. Until the results of our experiment are written, it should not be considered a clinical procedure, and when they are written it cannot ethically be undertaken in institutions without adequate field strength in liver transplantation.

The experience with small-bowel and lung transplantation using living donors is too small to warrant much analysis or comment. Certainly, there is no compelling reason to discontinue doing them until further, significant experience is amassed. They should be done in a very limited number of centers under established protocols, such as the one described for our live donor liver transplant program, but only as experimental procedures.

Pancreas transplantation using living donors has been performed in significant numbers in a setting where the value of the procedure and the risks can be properly evaluated. It appears to be of little value as compared with cadaveric pancreas transplantation in today's medical environment. Its use should possibly not continue and certainly should not disseminate. It cannot be recommended as a clinical procedure, and unless changes in surgery and medicine produce new questions as to its value, it should not be the focus of experimental protocols.

Surgeons who are interested in embarking on clinical live donor transplantation protocols, now applicable only to kidney and liver, should carefully review their facilities and backup systems at all levels. The responsibility to provide care for each patient should not lead surgeons to exceed the limits imposed by the surrounding health care systems. Universal ethical considerations command that individual surgical innovation should match institutional capacities to translate the sacrifice of a donor into the best treatment for the recipient. To embark on an experimental live donor transplantation protocol, all of these considerations apply, and, in addition, there should be the scientific capability to produce results that can be used to judge the value of the procedure being studied.

## References

1. Bay WH, Hebert LA (1987) The living donor in kidney transplantation. Ann Intern Med 106:719–727
2. Sutherland DER, Dunn DL, Goetz FC, et al (1989) A 10-year experience with 290 pancreas transplants at a single institution. Ann Surg 210:274–288
3. Hansmann M-L, Deltz E, Gundlach M, Schroeder P, Radzun H-J (1989) Small bowel transplantation in a child. Morphological, immunohistochemical, and clinical results. Am J Clin Pathol 92:686–692
4. Singer PA, Siegler M, Whitington PF, Lantos J, Emond JC, Thistlethwaite JR, Broelsch CE (1989) Ethics of liver transplantation using living donors. N Engl J Med 321:620–622

5. Moore FD (1988) Three ethical revelations: Ancient assumptions remodeled under pressure of transplantation. Transplant Proc 20 [Suppl 1]:1061–1067
6. Anonymous (1986) Vital statistics of the U.S. 1982. Mortality. Part A,B. Hyattsville, MD 2:186
7. Lloyd-Still JD (1985) Mortality from liver disease in children. Am J Dis Child 139:381–384
8. Fellner CH, Marshall JR (1968) Twelve kidney donors. JAMA 206:2703–2707
9. Broelsch CE, Emond JC, Thistlethwaite JR, Whitington PF, Zucker A, Baker AL, Aran PP, Rouch DA, Lichtor JL (1988) Liver tansplantation, including the concept of reduced-size liver transplants in children. Ann Surg 208:410–420
10. Emond JC, Whitington PF, Thistlethwaite JR, Alonso EM, Broelsch CE (1989) Reduced-size liver transplantation: use in the management of children with chronic liver disease. Hepatology 10:867–872
11. Otte JB, de Ville de Goyet J, Sokal E, et al. (1990) Size reduction of the donor liver is a safe way to alleviate the shortage of size-matched organs in pediatric liver transplantation. Ann Surg 211:146–157
12. Broelsch CE, Emond JC, Whitington PF, Thistlethwaite JR, Baker AL, Lichtor JL (1990) Application of reduced size liver transplants as split grafts, auxiliary orthotopic grafts and living related segmental transplants. Ann Surg 212:368–377
13. Sokal EM, Veyckemans F, de Ville de Goyet J, et al. (1990) Liver transplantation in children less than 1 year of age. J Pediatr 17:205–210
14. Emond JC, Thistlethwaite JR, Baker AL, Whitington PF, Ferrari M, Carmellini M, Stuart FP, Broelsch CE (1987) Rejection in liver allograft recipients: Clinical characterization and management. Clin Transplant 1:143–150
15. Woodle ES, Thistlethwaite JR, Emond JC, Whitington PF, Black DD, Aran PP, Baker AL, Stuart FP, Broelsch CE (1990) OKT3 therapy for hepatic allograft rejection: Comparison of results in adults and children. Transplant Proc 22:1765–1766

# Living Related Liver Transplantation: A Note of Caution

P. McMaster and A. Czerniak

## Introduction

Reduced size liver transplantation (RLT) for paediatric recipients has been performed in increasing numbers throughout the world. In Europe, 264 such transplants had been performed by the end of 1989, of which 101 (38 %) have been performed during 1989 alone [1]. The original technique of reduced size grafting described by Houssin and Bismuth [2] was extended by Otte [3] and now gives results not significantly different from those of whole organ transplantation [4]. With such experience and the continued shortage of organ donors, combined with the enormous regenerative capacity of the liver, it was inevitable that the feasibility of living related segmental liver donation would be studied. Programmes have now been initiated in several continents and the procedure seems likely to expand.

The advantages of providing a suitable liver for all children with hepatic disease is clearly an attractive one, while increasingly the evidence suggests that the procedure is indeed feasible. Are there really any reasons not to press ahead with the development and expansion of such programmes at this time?

For the wider dissemination of such procedures three fundamental questions need to be addressed, and these are discussed in the following.

## Is The Procedure Beneficial?

Because living related liver transplantation (LRLT) involves a two-step surgical procedure (donor segmental hepatectomy and recipient grafting), the potential benefits must be considered in both phases.

Firstly, the possible benefit to the recipient. When the segmental donor liver involves removal of segments 2, 3 and 4, sufficient length of portal, arterial and biliary elements are obtained. However, with problems developing in donors, more recently, only segment 2 and 3 have been excised and what may be a safer donor segmental hepatectomy is "paid for" by obtaining

---

Liver Unit, Queen Elizabeth Hospital, Edgbaston, Birmingham, B15 2TH, United Kingdom

W. Land, J. B. Dossetor (Eds.)
Organ Replacement Therapy:
Ethics, Justice and Commerce

a much shorter portal pedicle to the left lobe. This results in the need for vascular interposition grafts. Hepatic artery thrombosis is a significant problem in small children, with up to 25 % of all transplant patients weighing under 10 kg experiencing problems, and it is, therefore, perhaps not surprising that there have been early reports of arterial thrombosis (two of four patients reported by Broelsch [4]).

In addition, the length of bile duct obtained by doing a left lobectomy (segments 2 and 3) may create a difficult biliary-digestive anastomosis. Indeed, two of the seven patients (28 %) reported by Broelsch had biliary leakage [4]. There remains, in addition, the possible problem of hepatic vein outflow obstruction. Although experience is limited at this time, it seems unlikely that living related grafting will be associated with lower morbidity or a lower technical complication rate in the recipient than grafting segments 2 and 3 from cadaveric origins where full vascular pedicle and bile ducts *can* be obtained. Indeed, in that situation of segmental graft, hepatic artery thrombosis has been less common, although biliary leakage and infection have been reported [3]. It seems unlikely, therefore, that the living related donation will provide significant technical benefit when compared with cadaveric grafting.

One potentially attractive aspect relates to the degree of histocompatibility achieved in living related grafts with donor and recipient being at least one haplotype match. The benefits of optimal matching have now been demonstrated for the majority of organ grafts including heart, kidney and pancreas, whereas the benefits in liver grafting remain uncertain. Conflicting evidence relates to the incidents of acute rejection in poorly matched grafts or long-term outcome, suggesting that the degree of vanishing bile duct syndrome or chronic rejection may actually be enhanced by optimal matching. Studies underway at this time may well demonstrate the relevance of tissue matching in liver donation, but for the present this must remain a theroretical potential advantage.

From the point of view of risk to the donor it could be argued that partial hepatectomy now is a standard and frequently undertaken procedure with low morbidity and almost zero mortality in experienced hands [5]. The reduction in mortality has been largely brought about by increased understanding of the anatomy of the liver, a development of isolation techniques and vascular control prior to hepatic transection. Such an approach was adopted in the early living donations with segments 2, 3 and 4 being removed with vascular control and hepatic perfusion and subsequent bench removal of segment 4 prior to implantation.

However, currently only segments 2 and 3 are being excised without prior vascular control, very different from the "standard" partial hepatectomy. In the current living donor technique without vascular control, the liver parenchyma is transected, and excision of the corresponding vascular elements is delayed for as long as possible in order to prevent ischaemic injury and shorten the warm ischaemic time of the resected lobe [4]. At the same time, the various vascular and biliary elements are excised with the aim of preserving as long a length as possible in order to facilitate grafting of the resected liver.

Detailed anatomical studies have been performed in order to evaluate the anatomical feasibility of performing LRLT by using the left liver lobe (segments 2 and 3) [7]. It was found that there are some anatomical problems which are peculiar to the procedure using segments 2 and 3, and in some cases satisfactory anatomical configurations may not be present. Czerniak et al. [7] demonstrated that a satisfactory anatomical lobe could not be obtained in all cases, and only 48 % of livers had "normal" anatomy while in 19 % of cases it was found anatomically difficult or impossible to resect the left lobe and utilise it for LRLT. The problems here included an intrahepatic left hepatic vein or intrahepatic biliary system within the umbilical fissure, as well as multiple arteries and/or bile ducts to the left lobe. While some of these difficulties may well be circumvented, persistent biliary drainage already has been seen in donors, and inadvertent ligation of bile ducts to segment 4 suggest there will be a proportion of patients in whom difficulties will be encountered.

The Chicago experience [6] included three left hepatectomies (segments 2 – 4) and four left lobectomies (segments 2 – 3). When the left liver was resected, it was eventually reduced to a graft consisting only of segments 2 and 3 prior to transplantation. The three donor patients who had the left hepatectomy had the following complications:

1. Splenic laceration requiring splenectomy and laceration of the common bile duct requiring T-tube insertion for 6 weeks
2. Subhepatic fluid collection (abscess ?) treated by subcutaneous aspiration and antibiotics
3. Persistent biliary fistula managed by external drainage

No complications were reported in the two patients who had left lobectomy only (segments 2 and 3). As predicted in [7], the length of the portal vein or artery to the left lobe obtained while doing left lobectomy was not sufficient, and the donor operation also involved excision of the inferior mesenteric vein to be used as an interposition portal graft [6].

It appears that donor hepatectomy for living related grafts may not be possible using conventional "standard" techniques of vascular isolation and control, and so the morbidity likely to be encountered may not be as low as has been reported. The liver in only approximately half the potential donors will be ideally suited anatomically for donation of the left liver lobe.

## Is It Really Necessary?

Even if concerns about the technical aspects both of the recipient and of the donor could be overcome with greater experience, it would be crucial to answer the question of whether LRLT is really necessary. A shortage of organs for organ donation has been widely publicised, and waiting lists for grafting increase each year in spite of expanding transplantation activity. The instability of many patients with advanced cirrhosis, with the ever-present risk of massive haemorrhage from varices or overwhelming sepsis, means that deaths of patients awaiting grafting has been reported. As many as 5 %–15 % of children awaiting grafting may die before a suitable liver is found. Thus, on the face of it, there would appear to be a particular shortage of livers for transplantation at this time, perhaps justifying the need for LRLT.

However, a detailed review of the situation suggests that perhaps the situation is not as clear cut as this. If we take the United Kingdom as an example, it becomes clear that retrieval rates vary enormously from the "best" to the "worst" regions in this country. Heart-beating donor retrieval rates in the United Kingdom range from as low as 10.3 per million population to 22 per million against an overall cadaveric retrieval rate (including non-heart-beating cadavers) of 31.6 per million population [8]. This compared with Belgium and Austria of over 40 per million seems inadequate, and, indeed, the harvesting of organs other than the kidney from these donors also varies considerably. Rates vary in the United Kingdom between 0.6 livers harvested per million population in Northern Ireland, 4.5 in Wales, 4.3 in Scotland and 6.3 in England in 1989. In addition, if we look at retrieval rates by region, we see that of heart-beating cadavers, the proportion who yielded livers varies; Northern Ireland 4 %, Eire 14 %, Northwest Thames region 20 %, West Midlands 57 %, Wessex 37 % and East Anglia 68 %! If the "lowest" regions of the United Kingdom in terms of percentage retrieval of livers from heart-beating cadavers could be brought up to the "highest", a near doubling of livers available in the United Kingdom would easily be achieved.

Even so, the United Kingdom is a net exporter of livers to other countries with 4 livers being *imported* during 1989, yet 32 being *exported* to other countries. In addition, tragically in 1989, no less than 30 paediatric livers in Great Britain could not be used because of unavailability of intensive care beds or theatre facilities.

Lest we feel that this is a parochial United Kingdom problem, evidence from other centres suggests that the same pattern is occurring in Europe. Whereas between January 1990 and September 1990, 429 livers were transplanted under the auspices of Eurotransplant, no less than 399 livers offered during that period were not accepted. Reasons given for failure to accept offers range from non-suitability of recipients to medical reasons about the donor, but no less than 142 livers were refused in 1989 because of organisational problems [9].

It clearly seems likely that at this time a substantial increase in liver transplantation would be possible if there were adequate facilities to utilise *all* the livers which are apparently available and if those regions or countries well below the national and international averages could be improved; thus in 1989 in Austria while 83 livers were procured, only 56 transplants were performed (balance −27), in Belgium 103 livers were procured, and 129 transplanted (balance +26), in the Federal Republic of Germany 208 were procured and 268 transplanted (balance +60) and in the Netherlands 68 were procured and 46 transplanted (balance −22).

## Is It Really Ethical?

Clearly, if doubt is cast on the two primary questions, "Is it beneficial for donor/recipient?" and "Is it really necessary?", one can only conclude that it probably is really not appropriate at this time for a wide extension of this procedure. In undertaking new procedures, the potential benefits and hazards of the new method should, of course, be compared carefully with the best current alternative techniques. Where active cadaveric programmes are present and can perhaps be extended and livers utilised more efficiently, it hardly seems justified at this time for a wide extension of living related grafts experience.

Where no cadaveric programme exists, it could well be argued that such constraints apply. Clearly, this is a fine judgement indeed, and it is not for those not faced with these particular dilemmas to sit in judgement. There will be those who conclude that it is the prerogative of those who wish to donate organs for the benefit of a loved one in the family to do so, and of course, one would be loath to deny them such an opportunity. However, I would seriously ask the clinicians actively involved whether it should not be possible to establish cadaveric progammes. What effort has been made to change the laws and cultural or religious concerns which mitigate against successful cadaveric progammes. Are those clinicians really engaged in educating the public and changing cultural and social habits? It would only seem justified at this time, if every conceivable effort was being made to resolve cadaveric difficulties for such programmes to develop.

One other aspect which clearly could be a matter of concern relates to the matter of "informal consent". While recognising the open and public debate that colleagues have undertaken in addressing the ethical issues [10] and in doing all that is possible to ensure that informed consent is truly free and knowledgeable, there must be anxiety that, particularly in underdeveloped countries, it would be difficult for many parents to decline to offer their organ when faced with a child that is dying from liver disease and who might be "saved". While, clearly, there could be many positive and beneficial aspects of such donation, should major difficulties occur, there could well also be much more negative impact. While individual clinicians and patients will adopt their own attitudes to such dilemmas, we believe that considerable caution needs to be advanced in this delicate area.

## Conclusions

In the development of any new technique, there will always be those who express concern and caution. Where such an endeavour has the potential to jeopardize another healthy human being, those concerns will inevitably be significant. At this time, we are uncertain whether the benefits have as yet been proven for LRLT over and above cadaveric segmental grafting and remain concerned that there may yet be a penalty for the recipient and also for the donor, due to technical problems. Even if the technique were demonstrated to be beneficial, we would have to ask the question, "Is it really necessary?". In most developed countries with active cadaveric programmes, if the least productive areas for procurement could reach the average figure of all other centres, there should be enough livers available to help the majority of patients currently being accepted. Furthermore, the provision of adequate resources to current teams, especially in ITU facilities, would ensure that all organs currently available could be used.

Much more difficult is the situation in which there is no experience of cadaveric liver grafting because of cultural, social, ethical or legal constraints. In that very situation and with clinical teams who are perhaps less experienced than their colleagues fortunate enough to have established cadaveric programmes, there must be real concerns that the technical difficulties outlined earlier might prove significant. It would seem, in our view, only justifiable at this time for grafting to be undertaken if extensive clinical efforts were continuing by all clinicians, politicans and health care workers in the field to establish cadaveric grafting, and we would see living donation as an interim phase only while the establishment of cadaveric progammes is undertaken.

## References


1. European Liver Transplant Registry (1989) Newsletter. Hospital Paul Brousse, Villejuif, France
2. Bismuth H, Houssin D (1984) Reduced size orthotopic liver graft in hepatic transplantation in children. Surgery 95:367–372
3. Otte JB, Starzl TE, Ascher N (1987) Liver transplantation in children. Transplant Proc 19:3229–3230
4. Broelsch CE, Whitington PE, Emond JC (1990) Evolution and future perspectives for reduced-size hepatic transplantation. Surg Gynecol Obstet 171:354–360
5. Strong RW, Lynch SV, Ong TN, Matsunami H, Koido Y, Balderson GA (1990) Successful liver transplantation from a living donor to her son. N Engl J Med 322:(21)1505–1507
6. Broelsch CE, Emond JC, Whitington PE, Thistlethwaite JR, Baker AL, Lichtor JL (1990) Application of reduced liver size transplant, split grafts, auxiliary orthotopic grafts, and living-related segmental transplants. Ann Surg 212:368–377
7. Czerniak A, Lotan G, Hiss Y, Shemesh E, Avigad I, Wolfstein I (1989) The feasibility of in vivo resection of the left lobe of the liver and its use for transplantation. Transplantation 48:26–32
8. UKTS Report (1989)
9. Anon (1990) Eurotransplant Newsletter No. 80, pp. 11–12
10. Singer PA, Siegler M, Whitington PF, et al. (1989) Ethics of Liver Transplantation with living donors. N Engl J Med 321:620–622

# General Discussion: Living Organ Donation in Western Countries

*Davison:* I think one of the more interesting questions has come from Prof. Dickens. This is a question which I think raises a lot of particular issues, it says: is it consistent with the principle of voluntarism that family members can veto a deceased person's voluntary act of consenting to cadaveric organ donation and other tissue donations? This is addressed principally to Mr. Sells, perhaps you would like to give your initial thoughts on that?

*Sells:* In abstract, the duty according to my definition of it – well, I might say actually the obligation of the family of the deceased person would be to do everything they can to carry out or to make someone else carry out the wishes of the deceased. Therefore, if I were a lawyer I would say it is the duty and the obligation of the family not to veto, or not to be allowed to veto, the wishes of the deceased as expressed in the donor card. But the wording of the donor card, certainly in the UK, is "I give permission" or "I wish for my organs to be used after death for purposes of transplantation". I am not familiar with the wording in other countries. How do you as a lawyer interpret that statement? Perhaps I could hear what you have to say before I respond to the question behind the question.

*Dickens:* I believe that legislation frequently says that the completion of the donor card is a complete legal authority fo acquisition of organs. The implication being that a family veto could be ignored; whether it actually is or not is what I am addressing.

*Sells:* That is consistent with my own view, and I believe that the majority of my colleagues in Britain feel the same, that the legal view says that the veto can be ignored. Now, we come to the clinical situation where you have a person on his death bed, brain death is being diagnosed, the person in charge

---

The general discussion sessions were transcribed from tape recordings made during the conference. In the interest of a rapid publication, the individual speakers/discussants did not see their own comments and questions before the book went to press. One of the editors (W. Land) tried to make obviously necessary corrections in the manuscripts derived from the tape recordings and then authorized the publication of the sessions in their present form. Therefore, incorrect publication of the comments or questions with regard to style, content, etc. might be possible in the view of the speakers concerned. We apologize for any possible inaccuracies.

W. Land, J. B. Dossetor (Eds.)
Organ Replacement Therapy:
Ethics, Justice and Commerce

of the body has told the relatives that death has occurred, there is nobody there anymore. The ventilator will be switched off, there is no offer to the relatives of any discretion about that, it is a clinical decision which is going to be carried out. And the deceased person has signed such a donor card. If the relatives then say to the doctor, "we object very strongly to the idea of his body being mutilated" (they don't explain this, but it obviously is going to cause an enormous amount of distress), the doctor is then faced with an excrutiating decision. Does he carry out the letter of the law, if you like, assuming that the law in this sense to be complied with must result in that person's organs being removed at the cost of extra anguish for the family, who probably are at the worst time in their lives as a group, and who are obviously going to have a lot of problems with that. Or do we save the family that extra grief and anguish and we just, if you like, break the law, although I don't think I am breaking the law in these circumstances. My answer is I would do that which gives the least hurt to the survivors, and, therefore, I would accept the family veto. But I know that this is a matter of personal opinion. I am very glad to hear what other people think.

*Veatch:* Let me offer a slightly different perspective. It is clear in the United States that the donation is legally effective and sufficient. It is likewise common practice that clinicians will, nevertheless, yield to the objection of relatives. I have tried to argue on moral grounds as opposed to legal grounds that a clinician who is involved in transplantation has a moral duty to fulfill the wishes of the deceased as best he can, and, therefore, is morally obliged to be polite with the family, but to spend his energies explaining to them why he is morally obliged not to follow their wishes, but to follow the wishes of the deceased. I base this particularly on countries that use a true donation system, i.e., an opting-in-system. That to me is a policy decision that affirms that our first moral priority is to respect the wishes of the actual donor. And if we are going to take the wishes of the donor seriously, it seems to me that that generates a moral obligation, not only to refrain from taking organs when the individual refuses to donate, but also to go as far as we can to take organs when they will be of medical use when a donation has been made. I recognize full well that that will create legal and perhaps psychological embarrassment with the relationship with the family, but it seems to me that the first moral priority is a truly voluntary system, and the wishes of the deceased have to be given priority. I urged clinicians for some time to recognize a moral obligation to tackle the difficult legal and psychological problems that would be generated, and to take the organs against the wishes of the family.

*Davison:* It is not the practice in the UK to take the organs if the relatives refused.

*Veatch:* It is not the practice in the US, either. It is clearly legal to do so, I think, and I think morally that is what ought to be done.

*N.N.:* The moral and legal rectitude of that argument, but what Mr. Sells hasn't said, is another factor that the transplant surgeon necessarily takes into account: if there is conflict with family, the media will be involved. There will be negative publicity, and, for the sake of taking an organ on that day, there may be many organs lost over the next few weeks. And this returns us to the point we made this morning about the transplant surgeon being responsible to the community of patients, rather than to the individual patient. And this is where the conflict, I think, arises.

*Veatch:* We have also had criticism though, of patients where the story gets out that a donation was made, and, nevertheless, the organs were not procured, even though they were medically suitable. So I think the implication for the long-term recovery of organs could cut either way.

*Gomes da Costa:* There is a point that may be useful at least in Portugal. Most of the time, even when families don't accept, almost all bodies have to have a medical, legal autopsy. So the argument that the body won't be mutilated is not true, because either we take out the kidney or not; the body will be mutilated because we will subject it to a medical and legal autopsy.

*Sells:* May I ask the gentleman from Teheran a question? You took some organs from people who had recently been injured in the war. This raised one or two questions in my mind. First of all, how many were there, secondly, what was the nature of their injuries, and thirdly, was there anything special about the fact that they were soldiers and perhaps had already discharged their obligation to their society? If you understand what I mean.

*Simforoosh:* This is a nice subject. What I was trying to say that there is too much love and affection to donate. We refuse to get a kidney from a wounded man whose leg was amputated, and he was so upset that he could not donate as he went to the war front and offered his body to defend his country. Here we had some war-wounded who came to give their kidneys. He had a small pellet in the muscle wall, but was otherwise completely healthy and had otherwise no physical injury, but he was considered wounded. We just recently had one prisoner who was released from Iraq, and he donated to another prisoner in Iran. So, in our society we have many examples like this that our people, and those in other societies too, perform acts of love and concern: that is why I brought up those cases. There are people who always want to act out of altruism or sacrifice to help others with their lives.

*Davison:* It is interesting continuing the question of prisoners, as you have mentioned one there. Janet Radcliffe-Richards wanted to make a question.

*Radcliffe-Richards:* I wanted to bring up the idea that you coerce prisoners to give their kidneys in some way if you offer them remission in return for it. And again, the idea that you are somehow coercing a Turkish peasant by offering £ 3 500 pounds for his kidney. I would have said that this is exactly the opposite of coercion. Coercion happens when you make a threat to make someone's situation worse unless they give the kidney, and not if you offer improvement. It seems to me that this is a great difference between an inducement and a coercion. If you had asked the Turkish man if he was worse off or better off before the offer of the £ 3 500 pounds, he would have said he would rather have the offer.

*Sells:* Thank you. Is that question directed at me? Well I think it was I who first used the term; well, maybe you used the term coercion as well and, on reflection, I think I probably used the wrong word. However, the concept which I was trying to verbalize I believe is right, and that is that in both of the examples you have chosen, which I chose as well and which we are referring to, i.e., the prisoner who is offered remission and the very poor person who is offered a sum of money that is going to completely transform his life and the life of his family (I use the word coercion quite wrongly). I would like a word or a phrase which sums up my lack of confidence in that as a permissible situation, i.e., where a donor kidney can be removed, because in both of the situations referred to, it seems to me that altruistic volunteerism disappears.

*Radcliffe-Richards:* Well, that turns the question into a different one surely. You are concerned about altruism rather than volunteerism itself, and that is a different point.

*Sells:* Yes I agree, because I would agree with you that the volunteerism is not abolished by incentives. Altruism however is extinguished by the sorts of incentives that we have been discussing, would you agree with that?

*Radcliffe-Richards:* It depends on what you want the money for: that might be altruistic, too.

*Sells:* Yes. Thank you!

*Davison:* Altruistic money, another phrase.

*Schreiber:* I think that the donation by prisoners is not allowed. It should be principally not allowed, because there is an assumption that they are not voluntary donors. Not only altruistically, but due to the situation of the prisoner, which is such a bad one that they are not in a position to donate voluntarily. And from this situation, I think it should not be legal to take any donation from them. The prisoner said that it is their free position, their *Grundrecht* as we say in German, i.e., their basic right. I think that is wrong, and think it is very dangerous to take donations from prisoners. They are not free, they are supposed not to be free, and I wouldn't accept any donation from a prisoner.

*Davison:* Dr. Akveld, you commented in your presentation that the Dutch legislation was not opposed to this but you did not say it was in favor of it. I think your words were interesting.

*Akveld:* I didn't say that the Dutch legislation is not opposed to it, but I said that people have basic rights and one of the basic rights is not left behind on coming into a jail. If that were the case, if you couldn't realize your basic rights, you could do as Mr. Schreiber is doing and say that would mean that you could make use of that right, because it is doubtful if it will be realized fully. You could, however, also take it the other way around and say basically you have the right. What difference is there between a brother who needs a kidney and for whom the donor is not in jail, and the other case in which the donor or the potential donor is in jail. That would mean that you impose on the one in jail an extra punishment by saying you cannot be a donor because of the situation in which you are. I would say you have to take only those things from a prisoner which it is necessary to take, and that is freedom to go in and out, but that does not implicate that you also have to take his right to make a positive decision to be a donor. It only means that you have to clearly identify the freedom. But if you are saying (quite categorically) that prisoners, although there will be exceptions, are excluded, in that case I would say that the legislator would be doing too much. And that would not be necessary.

*Schreiber:* A short answer. The freedom of the prisoners is reduced and we do not reduce it more. We protect him, but he won't lose any more of his freedom. We have had such bad experiences with experimentations and prisoners in Germany, and I think we should learn from these experiences. That is a different position.

*Sells:* But I would like to come back briefly to Janet Radcliffe-Richards, because she thought her last question was a rhetorical one, and you must never pass up the opportunity of converting a rhetorical question from a philosopher into a real one. So, your question was, or your statement was, it depends what he does with the money. We are now talking about the rectitude or otherwise of reimbursement, according to how the money is spent. Now I would like to ask you this question: to what extent is it incumbent on a transplant surgeon or his advisor to take into account the way in which the money is spent in coming to a decision about whether or not to accept a donor who is paid, assuming that you don't use my rule of altruistic volunteerism as a necessary criterion for donation? Well, obviously it was not a rhetorical question after all.

*N.N.:* Going back to the subject of volunteerism and altruism: if we accept that commerce and money does not necessarily prevent an action from being voluntary, can we go on to think why commerce should act against autonomy? What evidence do we have that allowing commerce into organ donation reduces the incidence of autonomous and altruistic organ donation? Why should that necessarily be the case? I cannot quite understand why it should necessarily be the case that individuals should cease to want to give up their organs when they die if it is possible to sell them when they are alive. I don't see the necessary logical connection there. Similarly, I do not see that it is necessarily the case that family members should cease to willingly give up their organs to other family members if it is possible to sell them to someone else. I don't see a logical connection between the two.

*Sells:* Well, your second question I am not going to comment on, because I don't really understand it, and we don't really have so much time, I suppose. But the first question I would answer in the following way, I think there are two answers. Number one, you look at the case material which is proven and available for scrutiny, and almost all of it with the possible exception of Dr. Reddy's cases (p. 173) concerns the donation, shall I say the selling by the very poor to the relatively very wealthy. In circumstances where it is quite clear that the opportunity of self-improvement and improvement of the family was such, in my view as to destroy effectively the choice of that individual because he cared very much for his family, and therefore, if you like relatively, the rescue was taken to the point that he could not diminish to the point that he could not honorably continue without donating his kidney. I believe that that takes away altruistic volunteerism as I have defined it.

The other way of seeing your question is a much more sort of pragmatic one, and that is that I think you have too much faith in human nature. If a surgeon is not a servant of society in such a way that society cannot tell him what to do, and a single patient cannot tell him what to do, what he does has to be founded on the basis of a contract between him and the patient – that is the first very important thing – from that stems the idea that the surgeon has to make up his own mind about intention and motive, and motivation is something of which there is an enormous spectrum. Some of Dr. Reddy's patients have spent the whole lot on a horse the following day after their discharge, and some of Dr. Reddy's patients have spent their money in a way that might be construed as responsibly, by buying a corner shop, and setting up the family, and educating the children. Dr. Radcliffe-Richards is probably considering the case of a father who offered to give his kidney so his daughter could get the drugs to treat her leukemia. I don't think the surgeon should be put in the position of making that judgement, and, therefore, we have to draw the line somewhere, and it is an arbitrary line, and that is why I told you this is a pragmatic answer.

*Davison:* We are short of time and I would like to get one or two more questions in, we have had more questions clearly than we can hope to deal with. This is specifically directed to Prof. Schreiber, but also to all other members who have spoken this morning. How do you suggest protecting the rights of the person who becomes a non-donor, that is someone who is suitable to give a kidney, but has denied giving that kidney because of the reluctance of the physician to promote living organ donation. In other words, does the person who wishes to give the kidney, but does not promote it, also have rights? Dr. Bunzendahl, you asked the question. Would you like to elaborate on that?

*Bunzendahl:* As I mentioned in my abstract, there are very few living related transplants being done in Germany, and I think the majority are being done in Hannover. We ran into the problem of the donor family who came to our center and said we have been talking about transplantation, but our physician or our surgeon elsewhere refuses to promote or to proceed to living related transplantation. He also refuses to refer the patient even for information or an information session for potential living transplantation. I think you have made a big point out of protecting the donor's rights. You mentioned the four points under which circumstances living related donation is possible in Germany. But I think that for the area, let's say, *below* deciding on transplantation or not that means that the potential right of the donor to donate for his child or brother or sister is not realized, probably because it is outside jurisdiction and just within medicine, it must be realized that there are rights of the non-donating potential donors as well.

*Schreiber:* A brief comment: This is a medical problem whether someone considers a transplantation suitable. If the physician does not feel competent and he refuses to do it, no donor can force him to do it. No one can demand it of him in the same way that no one can demand of a physician that he carry out some sort of senseless treatment. It's not a basic human right. The centers handle this in various ways, and that is the responsibility of the centers. They cannot be coerced by a donor who is trying to force them to do something. That isn't tenable.

*Veatch:* Perhaps there is a problem in expressing this in terms of the right of the individual to be a living donor. Surely it is correct that there is at least no legal right to be a donor if no one is willing to take the organs: but I think the same problem can be expressed in a very different framework, and that is the framework of suggesting that if a surgeon is willing to participate in an organ procurement and transplant system, he has some obligation to take on certain responsibilities. I have already referred to the responsibility of the surgeon to take organs against the wishes of next of kin. I would suggest that there is a similar kind of moral weight in favor of an obligation to take organs in the case of a medically suitable living donor, whether related or not, and that cannot be overcome by mere trivial resistance; there would need to be some strong weight on the other side. I think perhaps we are excessively troubled in our deliberations over the possibility of understanding volunteerism in situations where most of us, perhaps, would not be inclined to act in a manner to donate. I am troubled by the suggestion that the living non-related donors cannot be truly voluntary, the same way I am troubled by the suggestion that large amounts of money would make on otherwise voluntary choice involuntary. I am also troubled by the possibility that a decision made in an emergency, say in the case of living liver donation, is non-voluntary simply because of the dramatic attractiveness of the offer that is being made. I don't think we should assume that dramatically attractive offers are automatically creating situations that are non-voluntary.

*Michielsen:* I disagree with this point of view. I think Dr. Sells is right, for instance in the Belgian situation where cadaver kidneys are retrieved to provide a kidney for everyone in need, I have the right to feel that it is ethically unacceptable to take a kidney from a living donor. And even if the living prospective donor insists, no one has the right to oblige me to do something against my ethical views.

*Schreiber:* I agree.

*Veatch:* I would agree.

*Michielsen:* And the patient has the possibility to change and to find another doctor. In other centers there will be others who are willing to accept that no such ethical objections, of course, exist.

*Veatch:* All I suggested was that there needs to be a weighty reason. I think you are giving the kind of weighty reasons on the other side.

*Akveld:* Couldn't you accept a certain duty in the sense that if you have your own medical opinion on performing living donations and you are not willing to perform them, you would at least, if there are not medical obstructions for that, refer a patient to a center for him to get help there. Wouldn't that be an obligation you could have? You can say no, I don't perform these operations, you stop over there.

*Michielsen:* I think this question is absolutely theoretical, because all patients are very well informed. If patients know much more about what happens in the various transplantation centers, then we know what happens in the centers of our colleagues. So this is purely theoretical. So my answer would be yes, in the theoretical case that the patient doesn't know, you can say there is a colleague who is doing this and this is possible.

*Schreiber:* I think we should inform him about this, to give him the opportunity, but the surgeon is not forced to do it himself.

*Davison:* On a similar theme, we have had two interesting questions that boil down to the one question which is: Does a living donor program prevent the development of a properly organized cadaver program? Would you care to answer that?

*Michielsen:* I think yes. For instance, in Belgium we have two parts to the country. In one part they take living donors and the retrieval rate of cadaver kidneys in lower than in the other part where living donors are not used. But it is very difficult to see that there is a causal relationship between the two. It is a matter of interpretation.

*Sells:* In Liverpool in my center, we do more living related transplants in terms of percentage per year than anywhere else in the UK, and that is a natural thing. It is also a fact that we have a relatively low cadaver donation rate. In fact, we are one of the lowest in the country, and we are desperately trying to do something about that. But I think there is a reason for that other than the living donor program, and that is that we have one particular hospital where our neuroscience is concentrated, and there have been difficulties in the past. We are maximizing the number of organ donors in that particular place. In the UK, we have an overall deficit of about 30 % or 40 %. As long as there is a deficit, I would think that a living related donor program is absolutely essential, so that we can capitalize on those offers when they do come up in conditions of scarce resources.

*Brynger:* I don't think a donor program for kidneys should influence the number of cadaver kidneys, just due to the fact that the donors are used for more organs than kidneys. If this is properly organized regarding heart, liver, pancreases, etc., this would rather be completely without relation to a live donor program in kidney transplantation. This is our experience of this kind of behavior.

*Abouna:* I just would like to say that if you have an established cadaver program, living donor transplantation is unlikely to affect it. But if you do not have one, as I shall show you in a few minutes, it certainly affects it a great deal.

*Davison:* Finally I would like to thank all the speakers who have given us a superb review of the various situations in a various number of countries. I would like to thank my co-chairman here for taking part in this and in particular I would like to thank those who have asked questions, because I don't recall a meeting that has stimulated so much discussion over such a wide range. And I think it is a tribute to Prof. Land and his organizing committee for having put together such a good program. So thank you very much, and we now move on to the next session which I trust is going to be just as interesting and informative. Thank you.

# *III. The Intra- und Inter-Cultural Commerce in Human Organs and Tissues*

# Is There a Universal System of Ethics or are Ethics Culture-Specific?

H. T. Engelhardt, Jr.

To the two central questions regarding morality, "Is there a universal system of ethics? Are ethics culture-specific?", I will answer both yes and no, and in each case I will couch the answer with important qualifications. These two questions reflect the intellectual challenge and difficulties of the so-called postmodern era, in which we find numerous competing moral visions and no universally justifiable moral narrative in terms of which one can choose among them. The attempt to answer these questions leads to the conclusion that there is no general secular warrant to condemn the sale of human organs. This does not mean that one may not have special religious or other important reasons morally to condemn practices such as the sale of organs. It is just that such a condemnation cannot be justified in general secular terms. Moreover, an examination of the general secular justification of the moral authority of the state brings into question the moral authority to prohibit such sales.

In the first section of this chapter, I will examine the historical roots of the postmodern predicament. In the second section, I will show its intellectual inevitability: that there is no universal content-full system of ethics. Then I will show the implications of this circumstance for the proscription of the sale of organs.

## The Postmodern Condition: Its Implications for a Content-Full Universal System of Ethics and the Prohibition of the Sale of Human Organs

Western philosophy, which in its attempt to give universal answers has shaped philosophical reflection throughout the world, has over its history offered quite different answers to these questions. Western philosophy developed out of the Graeco-Roman world, which was multicultural, polytheistic, and diverse in languages, religions, and moral assumptions. Though from the very beginning there were those such as Plato, Aristotle, and the Stoics who held that the first question could be answered in the affirmative, namely, that there is a universal system of ethics, there was robust skepticism. In fact, from the Sophists to the Skeptics, there was an accent on the individual or cultural-

Center for Ethics, Medicine, and Public Issues, Baylor College of Medicine, One Baylor Plaza, Houston, Texas 77030, USA

W. Land, J. B. Dossetor (Eds.)
Organ Replacement Therapy:
Ethics, Justice and Commerce

relative character of morality. One of the most engaging presentations of this cultural-relative view is provided by Sextus Empiricus (ca. A.D. 200) in his *Outlines of Pyrrhonism* [6].

The de facto heterogeneity of moral, religious, and customary views found in the ancient Mediterranean world was not only personally troubling for many of its inhabitants, but also posed a problem in the administration of the Roman Empire. It was quite natural to hope that one could discover some moral constraints that were plausibly binding on all men. If such could be shown, the task of administering the Roman Empire would at least be theoretically facilitated: one could demonstrate the general moral authority of social and political structures. It is here that one discovers the natural and morally most significant tie between ethics and politics. Political life involves the use of coercive force in the regulation of human interactions. The moral question at the foundation of politics concerns the proper range and character of such coercive force. Put very simply, one wants to determine when and under what circumstances the state may coercively require the compliance of its citizens. From the very beginning, the hope was that one would be able to show that the state was indeed a rational structure, that is, that rational men and women should see why they should submit to its coercive force. However, to provide such moral authority or moral warrant for the activities of the state (such as regulating the sale of organs), it is necessary first to establish at least some thin fabric of a universal system of ethics.

Looking to our concerns here, with regard to ethics, justice, and commerce in organ replacement therapy, one finds the same challenge. If there are to be national or international regulations of the ways in which persons may give, barter, or sell their organs, one would hope to show a general moral justification for such constraints. In particular, one would want to be able to see why one should regard oneself as morally bound by them, and why one should understand the state as having the moral authority to forbid the sale of organs, if those involved understand the risks and conditions, so as to have been able to provide informed consent. Or to put the question somewhat differently, one would like to know how one can resolve moral controversies regarding the propriety or impropriety of selling organs (or engaging in other activities in medicine) so that one can determine under which circumstances there are strong moral considerations, if any, in favor of state intervention. Of course, beyond this question and just as fundamentally, one needs to answer the question regarding the origin of the state's moral authority.

In the ancient world, as today, three obvious ways of resolving controversies were apparent. First, one could appeal to force. Force could be that of either a tyrant, an oligarchy, or a democracy. The ancient world, it should be remembered, recognized that without special constraints, the force of a democratic majority was just as questionable (and fearful) as the force employed by a tyrant or an oligarchy. To put the matter in more modern terms, just as one must be skeptical about the divine right of kings, one must, in the absence of a special argument, be skeptical regarding the divine right of majorities. One needs to ask why a democratic majority should have moral authority over a peaceable minority wishing to buy and sell organs with the consent of all directly involved.

Second, the ancient Mediterranean world understood, as we do, that moral controversies could come to a closure if all converted to a particular understanding of the world. But then, as now, the probability of such conversion was generally seen to be unlikely. It is for this reason again that appeal to sound rational arguments, the third way of resolving moral controversies, seems so promising. If the questions one asks about morality or about the rational authority of the state are rational questions, then if one receives a rational answer the controversy should be closed. Dissidents must be recognized as irrational or holding rationally indefensible positions. Moreover, the appeal to rationality is especially promising with regard to justifying the coercive interventions of the state. If the state imposes on irrational individuals the rational way in which they ought to be acting, the state in fact does not alienate those individuals, but returns them to their true nature as rational, moral agents. In fact, in this way one should be able to meet three general desiderata for justifying the use of coercive force, including the proscription of the sale of human organs:

1. one knows that what one is doing is correct,
2. one knows that one is in moral authority to impose correct action on the unwilling, and
3. one can determine that such an imposition will lead to more benefits than harms.

If one could carry out the project of establishing a rationally justifiable universal system of ethics, one could perhaps justify the state in general and the regulation of the sale of organs in particular. If one can give a conclusive rational argument to establish a particular universal system of ethics, one may be able to show why coercively enforced regulations regarding the sale of organs would need out of rational considerations to be accepted.

This aspiration to a universal ethic was, in the ancient world, reflected in theories concerning the existence of a law of nature, a *jus naturale*, and a law common to the nations, a *jus gentium*. This point was developed by Gaius in the second century[1], by Justinian in the sixth century, and by William Blackstone in the eighteenth century, to choose but a few of a host of thinkers in this tradition. Skepticism regarding such claims that was regnant in the ancient Mediterranean world was set aside by the Christian moral and intellectual synthesis that dominated the European Middle Ages. The Middle Ages, it must be underscored, was marked not just by a faith in Faith, but by a faith in reason. In contrast with the multi-cultural polytheistic ancient Mediterranean world, there emerged a monocultural, monotheistic world view in which faith and reason were seen as pillars of a content-full universal

[1] "Quod uero naturalis ratio inter omnes homines constituit, id apud omnes populos peraeque custoditur uocaturque ius gentium, quasi quo jure omnes gentes utuntur" (See [1], p. 2).

system of ethics. The European culture that broke upon the world at the end of the fifteenth and beginning of the sixteenth centuries included a philosophy taking its first important steps away from this medieval synthesis. Against the background of the Reformation and the Renaissance, the image of a unified moral vision was threatened. The religious wars of the seventeenth century ushered in the Enlightenment, during which one still hoped to be able to justify the Judeo-Christian morality without belief in the Judeo-Christian God. There was a general confidence, though marked by a number of important exceptions, in the project of rationally justifying a moral vision that could then rationally justify the state and the moral authority of the state. From Thomas Hobbes and John Locke to Immanuel Kant, there were different but importantly similar attempts to tie the state and its moral authority to rational considerations. Contemporary aspirations rationally to justify the proscription of the sale of human organs fall within this genre of philosophical undertaking. There is the hope that one will be able to show that the proscription of the sale of human organs is ingredient in some way to the notion of moral rationality, so that one may be able to justify that proscription to individuals from different cultures and with different moral intuitions.

The crisis of the postmodern world, revealed in the difficulty of finding a general moral justification for coercively forbidding the sale of organs, lies in the failure to be able to justify a universal content-full system of ethics rationally. In fact, one encounters competing notions of moral rationality and competing views regarding the propriety of allowing the sale of human organs. This general difficulty of not being able to identify a particular canonical, content-full moral view is described by Jean-François Lyotard as the loss of a universal content-full moral narrative [4]. It is reflected in the titles of such books as Alasdair McIntyre's *Whose Justice? Which Rationality?* [5]. Though there is a considerable inclination to want to be able to say with intellectual justification that one can rationally, outside of any particular moral or religious faith, discover that particular activities, such as the sale of human organs, are morally wrong, this is not possible, as we will see shortly. The crisis of the postmodern world is the recognition of the impossibility of discovering a content-full universal system of ethics on the basis of reason alone. In the end, as the Christians of the fourth century understood, one must believe in order to understand. But the difficulty in a multicultural world marked by a plurality of religious visions is that all do not believe the same, nor do they understand or see the world in the same fashion[2]. Because of the failure to be able to justify in general secular terms a content-full universal system of ethics, it is not morally appropriate for secular governments to forbid the sale of human organs.

---

[2] Because the author is robustly critical of the capacities of reason to provide a justification for a universal system of ethics, the reader may be tempted to conclude falsely that the author is a relativist. This would be in error. Though the author has lost faith in reason, he has not lost faith in Faith, and despite the rationalistic excesses of the Roman patriarchate submits himself to the true teaching and worship of the Catholic Church.

As we will see, there is still a general way in which one can justify a universal system of ethics. However, what will be secured lacks moral content. As a result, the governmental authority that it will justify is that of limited democracy, which must of moral necessity recognize large areas of private choice, precisely those areas where individuals may decide freely to buy and sell organs.

## Postmodernity: The Crisis and Its Solution

The crisis for moral rationality can be put somewhat straightforwardly. There are in general two ways in which one can resolve moral controversies by sound rational argument. Either one can show that there is a logical inconsistency involved in all accounts save one, or one can show that all accounts save one are falsified by the facts at hand. But moral considerations are not simply considerations of rational coherence. Indeed, given different initial premises, quite different moral viewpoints can rationally be justified without logical incoherence. The problem is, which initial premises should be endorsed or embraced. Nor are there moral facts to which one can appeal outside of a particular moral viewpoint. One cannot appeal to consequences without knowing how to weigh or rank different consequences. For example, how ought one to rank liberty, equality, security, and prosperity consequences of any particular institution or rule in order to assess its moral probity? One must already have answered the fundamental ethical issues in order to resolve the derivative ones. Nor can one appeal to preferences without knowing how to rank present versus future preferences, impassioned versus rationally considered preferences. Nor can one turn in to moral rationality itself, to a notion of a hypothetical decision-marker, to a notion of hypothetical contractors, in order to discover a concrete moral vision, without already having presupposed a particular canonical moral intuition, moral sense, or thin theory of the good. However, the problem is to discover which moral theory, moral intuition, or moral sense ought to be canonical. Yet this cannot be done without begging the very question at issue.

It is at this point that the project of morality appears to collapse. If more cannot be said, not only do proscriptions of the sale of human organs come into question, but so as well do many more fundamental moral proscriptions. However, there is still a way out of this moral crisis. It requires understanding, even if one cannot discover a canonical moral authority, that one can still derive moral authority when moral strangers meet from their agreement. That is, even if God is not heard in the same way by all, and moral reason does not possess a univocal moral content, insofar as one is interested in resolving issues other than by means of a foundational appeal to force, one can derive moral authority from mutual consent. It is as if one asked how one could resolve moral controversies among individuals in a large lecture hall, presuming that these individuals are of different cultures, religions, and moral traditions. Even if there are radical disagreements regarding the content-full character of the good life, still, insofar as these individuals are interested in resolving issues peaceably, a source of common moral authority is at hand: mutual respect. That is, mutual respect of actual consent becomes the cardinal point of departure toward creating a general moral fabric. One would know already that one could not murder, rape, or use members of the audience without their consent and still have available this general fabric of common moral undertaking. Moreover, if individuals create a social structure and come to have common goods, they can establish ways in which to deploy these goods to create general welfare rights. But in all of this, they would not have to presuppose a particular common moral viewpoint, nor would they have to presuppose that they had given over to the community ownership of themselves or their bodies. They would have found that they had created a limited democracy.

The point is that, in the postmodern world, one can still discover the basis for a universal system of ethics founded on mutual respect and consent. It does not require that the participants share a common content-full moral vision. It does not require that they value mutual respect and consent. It requires only that they recognize mutual respect and consent as conveying moral authority. They will then be able in terms of this fabric of mutual consent to understand the moral propriety and standing of practices such as free and informed consent and the free market, as well as the institution of limited democracy. But they will not be able to discover a content-full moral ethic that will justify the proscription of the sale of human organs. That is, they will not be able to decide, for example, between

1. those who hold that the sale of human organs is exploitative in some way that hiring individuals to risk their lives as high-rise construction workers is not; and
2. those who believe that the proscription of the sale of human organs is a form of moral exploitation in which some, particularly those in the developed world, impose their particular cultural values on those in the developing world, so as not to allow them freely to acquire funds from the developed world by the sale of their organs.

One group will see those who allow the sale of organs as exploiting the poor on behalf of the needs of the rich. The other group will see those who forbid the sale of organs as exploiting the poor on behalf of the sensibilities of the developed world. There will in principle be no general rational argument to choose between the two viewpoints. As a result, it should fall beyond the compass of a general secular universal morality and beyond the proper compass of a secular state. Forbidding the sale of human organs is coercively to impose one out of many particular culturally determined moral viewpoints. One should turn instead to protect individuals from health risks and from fraud.

## The Morality of Moral Strangers and the Morality of Moral Friends

It is important to recognize what a universal system of ethics can and cannot offer. Universality in secular morality is always purchased at the price of moral content. Content in secular morality is always purchased at the price of universality. What secular morality offers is a language for discourse among moral strangers, the kind of discourse that one finds in large-scale states and at international conferences. The language is framed in order to allow individuals with different moral visions to collaborate[3]. This language of moral strangers should not be seen as a substitute for the language of moral friends, the language one finds that one shares with those in one's own moral community. Thus, in speaking the language of moral strangers, one will recurringly find oneself asserting that "X has a right to do A (e.g., sell humans organs), but it is wrong (e.g., I from my particular moral vision and rich cultural viewpoint understand its impropriety)." Given the history of Western thought, it is understandable that one should hunger after a universal content-full morality, as had seemed achievable in the Middle Ages. In our postmodern world, we will need to satisfy ourselves with procedural ethics and limited democracies, when we meet as moral strangers.

## References


1. De Zulueta F (1976) Institutes of Gaius. Oxford University Press, London
2. Engelhardt HT Jr (1986) The foundations of bioethics. Oxford University Press, New York
3. Engelhardt HT Jr (1991) Bioethics and secular humanism. Trinity, Philadelphia
4. Lyotard J-F (1984) The postmodern condition. (Translation). University of Minnesota Press, Minneapolis
5. MacIntyre A (1988) Whose justice? Which rationality? Notre Dame University Press, Notre Dame, Indiana
6. Sextus Empiricus (1976) Outlines of pyrrhonism (Translation). Harvard University Press, Cambridge


[3] Much more would need to be said about this point and the others in this paper. I have explored these issues extensively elsewhere [2, 3].

# Preventing Commercial Transactions in Human Organs and Tissues: An International Overview of Regulatory and Administrative Measures*

S. S. Fluss

## Introduction

The World Health Organization (WHO) has had a long and continuing interest in organ transplantation legislation since 1948 (the year WHO's Constitution came into force), when a brief summary of what may well have been the first item of national legislation on the subject, a French Decree of 20 October 1947, was reported in the first issue of the *International Digest of Health Legislation*[1]. In 1969, WHO published a survey of legislation on the subject [2] which noted, *inter alia*, that the Italian Law of 26 June 1967 appeared to be the first statute to address the issue of commerce (it prohibited any form of reward or compensation for living kidney donors). Since then, WHO's Health Legislation unit, and its counterparts in WHO's six regional offices, have monitored both national and related international developments. Thus, at the 1989 Ottawa Congress (cited elsewhere in this volume) Fuenzalida-Puelma provided a comprehensive overview of key aspects of the legislation in this area in Latin America [3]. Noting that "the key to organ shortage does not lie in commercialization", he pointed to legal difficulties that may not be limited to that subcontinent. A particularly apposite comment by Gerson is cited:

> *Ultimately, the potential for organ transplantation will depend not only on advanced medical technology, but also on progress in the legal technology of organ donation* [4].

While the issues raised by commercialism are by no means the only ones that "legal technology" must address, it is clear that they are crucial and of broad concern. Few would disagree with Abouna and his co-workers:

Health Legislation Unit, World Health Organization, Avenue Appia, 1211 Geneva 27, Switzerland

* Except where clearly indicated, any views expressed are not necessarily those of the World Health Organization. The author alone is responsible for any errors, omissions, or misinterpretations.

1 See [1]. Virtually all the statutes and international instruments cited in this paper have been reported in this quarterly journal. For more comprehensive information on the subject matter of this paper see the report by the Director-General of WHO on human organ transplantation (unpublished document EB87/12, dated 19 November 1990).

W. Land, J. B. Dossetor (Eds.)
Organ Replacement Therapy:
Ethics, Justice and Commerce

> *...trafficking in human organs has become one of the nightmares of medical and technological advances of our time, and ... represents the extreme of human greed* [5].

Documentary evidence of this "nightmare" [6], and its consequences for the health of organ recipients, is, moreover, becoming increasingly authoritative [7].

## The International Response

It is often the case that, in issues related to bioethics and, more generally, in the newly emerging discipline of "health ethics", nongovernmental organizations react more rapidly to given situations. In this section, we shall initially examine the responses of nongovernmental organizations to the issue of commerce in human organs, before dealing with the intergovernmental organizations that have entered this area.

### Nongovernmental Organizations

#### *Transplantation Society*

The first international effort to confront the issue may well have been a 1970 Statement by the Committee on Morals and Ethics of the (international) Transplantation Society which affirmed, *inter alia,* that: "The sale of organs by donors living or dead is indefensible under any circumstances" [8, 9]. In September 1985, the Council of the same Society published a statement on the subject [10]. This contains two sets of guidelines, viz. "guidelines for cadaver organ distribution" and "guidelines for the donation of kidneys by unrelated living donors". The unequivocal deprecation of commerce contained in these guidelines reflects the Council's view that "the donation of an organ is a gift of extraordinary magnitude and ... transplant surgeons hold a donated organ in trust for society". In a Special Resolution, the Council declared:

> *No transplant surgeon/team shall be involved directly or indirectly in the buying or selling of organs/tissues or in any transplant activity aimed at commercial gain to himself/herself or an associated hospital or institute. Violation of these guidelines by any member of The Transplantation Society may be cause for expulsion from the Society.*

#### *World Medical Association (WMA)*

A statement on live organ trade was adopted by the 37th World Medical Assembly at its meeting in Brussels in October 1985. Noting that "in the recent past a trade of considerable financial gain has developed with live kidneys from underdeveloped countries for transplantation in Europe and the United States of America", the WMA condemned the "purchase and sale of human organs for transplantation", and called on the "governments of all countries to take effective steps to prevent the commercial use of human organs". At the 39th World Medical Assembly, held in Madrid in October 1987, the WMA adopted a declaration on human organ transplantation. Paragraph 8 of this declaration condemns the "purchase and sale of human organs for transplantation".

## Intergovernmental Organizations

### *Council of Europe*

In May 1978, the Committee of Ministers of the Strasbourg-based Council of Europe (which now has 24 Member States) adopted a Resolution (R (78) 29) on the "removal, grafting and transplantation of human substances", Article 9 of which reads as follows:

> *No substance may be offered for profit. However, loss of earnings and any expenses caused by the removal or preceding examination may be refunded. The donor, or potential donor, must be compensated, independently of any possible medical responsibility, for any damage sustained as a result of a removal procedure or preceding examination, under a social security or other insurance scheme.*

A Conference of European Health Ministers, devoted to the topic "Organ Transplantation", was convened in Paris in November 1987 under the auspices of the Council of Europe, at the invitation of the then French Minister of Health and Family Affairs. The final text, stated to contain "guidelines on which agreement was reached and which constitute a foundation for future co-operation in Europe", includes the following paragraphs under the heading "The non-commercialisation of human organs":

> ... *A human organ must not be offered for profit by any organ exchange organisation, organ banking centre or by any other organisation or individual whatsoever. However, this does not prevent the compensation of living donors for loss of earnings and any expenses caused by the removal or preceding examination.*
>
> ... *Neither organisations nor individuals should advertise outside their national territory either for donation or transplantation.*

The Conference recommended that the Council of Europe take appropriate steps to (*inter alia*) "revise existing instruments and draw up new ones to implement the principles set out in this text". It is conceivable that the framework convention on bioethics, now under discussion in the Council of Europe, may include a prohibition on commerce in human organs based on the provisions quoted above.

*League of Arab States*

At the twelfth session of the Council of Arab Ministers of Health (a body that functions under the auspices of the League of Arab States), held in Khartoum in March 1987, a Unified Arab Draft Law on Human Organ Transplants was adopted. Its Article 7 reads as follows:

> *The sale, purchase or remunerated donation of organs is prohibited, and no specialist may perform a transplant operation if he knows the organ to have been acquired by such means.*

*World Health Organization*

The supreme governing body of WHO, the World Health Assembly (which meets annually in May), has only rarely turned its attention to the ethical issues raised by advances in biomedicine. It was consequently somewhat of a break from established practice when the Fortieth World Health Assembly, meeting in May 1987, adopted resolution WHA40.13 on "Development of guiding principles for human organ transplants" (see Appendix 1). This resolution expressed the Assembly's concern at the "trade for profit in human organs among living human beings", affirming that "such trade is inconsistent with the most basic human values and contravenes the Universal Declaration of Human Rights and the spirit of the WHO Constitution". The Director-General was requested to study, in collaboration with other organizations concerned, the possibility of developing appropriate guiding principles for human organ transplants. Two years later, in May 1989, the Forty-second World Health Assembly adopted resolution WHA42.5 on "Preventing the purchase and sale of human organs" (see Appendix 2). This expressed the Assembly's concern at the "commercial trafficking in the organs of healthy donors, which exploits human distress and puts at increased risk the health of the donors", and called upon WHO's Member States to take appropriate measures to prevent the purchase and sale of human organs for transplantation. Member States were recommended to "introduce legislation to prohibit trafficking in organs where this cannot effectively be prevented by other measures". The Director-General was requested to report to the Forty-fourth Assembly (May 1991) on the measures taken by the governments of Member States in pursuance of this resolution.

The development of guiding principles involved extensive consultations with experts (from different countries and cultures) in organ transplantation, medical ethics, health policy, and law, as well as representatives of intergovernmental organizations (the Commission of the European Communities and the Council of Europe) and nongovernmental organizations, notably the Council for International Organizations of Medical Sciences, a WHO-based body which has itself promoted an active dialogue on the policy and ethical issues raised by organ transplantation [11], and the International Academy of Legal Medicine and Social Medicine, which has official relations with WHO, and academic institutions (including the WHO Collaborating Centre for Health Legislation, based at the Harvard School of Public Health in Boston). WHO's Principal Investigator for the project was Professor Bernard Dickens, of the Faculties of Law and Medicine at the University of Toronto, selected for his preeminent expertise in and publications on the topic [12], while the two Informal Consultations convened to discuss successive drafts of the Guiding Principles were moderated by a distinguished Australian lawyer, Russell Scott, who had played a major role (as Commissioner in Charge) in the preparation of the pioneering Australian Law Reform Commission report on the subject [13]. A set of Draft Guiding Principles (accompanied by Commentaries) has now been developed, and will be presented to WHO's 31-member Executive Board session in January 1991[a]. They are intended to provide an "orderly, ethical, and acceptable framework for regulating the acquisition and transplantation of human organs for therapeutic purposes". The Guiding Principles "prohibit giving and receiving money, as well as any other commercial dealing in this field, but do not affect payment of expenditures incurred in organ recovery, preservation and supply. Of particular concern to WHO is the protection of minors and other vulnerable persons from coercion and improper inducement to donate organs".

From the standpoint of this paper, perhaps the four key principles are the following:

1. *Guiding Principle 5.* The human body and its parts cannot be the subject of commercial transactions. Accordingly, giving or receiving payment (including any other compensation or reward) for organs should be prohibited.
2. *Guiding Principle 6.* Advertising the need for or availability of organs, with a view to offering or seeking payment, should be prohibited.
3. *Guiding Principle 7.* It should be prohibited for physicians and other health professionals to engage in organ transplantation procedures if they have reason to believe that the organs concerned have been the subject of commercial transactions.
4. *Guiding Principle 8.* It should be prohibited for any person or facility involved in organ transplantation procedures to receive any payment that exceeds a justifiable fee for the services rendered.

[a] The Executive Board endorsed the Guiding Principles, with only minor emendations, at its session (Note added in proof).

*United Nations*

In June 1990, the United Nations Sub-Commission on Prevention of Discrimination and Protection of Minorities had before it a report on, *inter alia*, the adoption of children for commercial purposes [14]. That report noted that the Government of Mexico had indicated that "the unlawful ends for which Mexican minors were adopted included ... sale of children for profit and even sale of organs ...". In the light of this statement, and other allegations of similar practices, the Sub-Commission has appointed a Special Rapporteur, Mr Vitit Mutabhorn of Thailand, to prepare a report on this and related issues for the forty-third session of the Sub-Commission, scheduled to be held in the summer of 1991. WHO is working closely with the United Nations Centre for Human Rights to compile the necessary information and documentation, including information contained in the general media.

## National Responses

Concurrently with the development of the Draft Guiding Principles, WHO has endeavoured to "inventorize" all known national laws, regulations, and

**Table 1.** List of jurisdictions known to WHO/HQ to have legislation on organ transplantation (by WHO region)

| African region | Region of the Americas | Eastern Mediterranean region | European region | South-East Astia region | Western Pacific region |
|---|---|---|---|---|---|
| Algeria<br>Niger<br>South Africa<br>Zimbabwe | Argentina<br>Bolivia<br>Brazil<br>Canada<br>(all Provinces and Territories)<br>Chile<br>Colombia<br>Costa Rica<br>Cuba<br>Dominican Republic<br>Ecuador<br>El Salvador<br>Guatemala<br>Honduras<br>Mexico<br>Panama<br>Paraguay<br>Peru<br>USA<br>(Federal and all States and District of Columbia)<br>Venezuela | Cyprus<br>Iraq<br>Kuwait<br>Lebanon<br>Syrian Arab Republic | Austria<br>Belgium<br>Bulgaria<br>Czech and Slovak Federal Republic<br>Denmark<br>Finland<br>France<br>Germany<br>(ex-GDR states only)<br>Greece<br>Hungary<br>Italy<br>Liechtenstein<br>Luxembourg<br>Norway<br>Portugal<br>Romania<br>Spain<br>Sweden<br>Switzerland<br>(17 Cantons)<br>Turkey<br>United Kingdom<br>Yugoslavia<br>(+ Bosnia and Herzegovina) | India<br>Bombay<br>Karnataka<br>Kerala<br>Maharashtra<br>Union Territory of Delhi<br>Indonesia<br>Sri Lanka | Australia<br>(all States and Territories)<br>Japan<br>Malaysia<br>Philippines<br>Singapore<br>Tonga<br>Viet Nam |

codes and other measures that address the issue of commerce in human organs. In accordance with the policy adopted for previous legislative surveys undertaken by WHO, every effort has been made to rely solely on primary sources (i.e., legal instruments published in official gazettes or the equivalent). Moreover, a computerized database has been compiled of all known legislation on the subject of organ transplantation. The countries and jurisdictions currently (December 1990) included in this database are listed in Table 1. As a decentralized Organization, WHO has established a regional system based on six regions, and countries and jurisdictions are hence listed here according to the region in which they are located.

Table 2 lists those jurisdictions known to WHO to have legislation that addresses, directly or indirectly, the subject of commerce.

Within the scope of this paper, it is not possible to describe, even superficially, the varying forms that legislation has taken in those countries and jurisdictions listed in Table 2[2]. Nor is it possible to discuss the policies in other countries and jurisdictions where nonlegislative measures have been taken. Thus, in the Federal Republic of Germany (other than the five new states created as a result of the unification process), there is currently no legislation on organ transplantation. However, the Cartel of German Transplantation Centres has formulated a Transplantation Code, binding on all physicians performing transplantations. One of the effects of this Code is

**Table 2.** List of jurisdictions known to WHO/HQ to have legislation on commerce in human organs (by WHO region)

| African region | Region of the Americas | Eastern Mediterranean region | European region | South-East Asia region | Western Pacific region |
|---|---|---|---|---|---|
| Algeria | Argentina | Cyprus | Austria | Indonesia | Australia |
| South Africa | Bolivia | Iraq | Belgium | Sri Lanka | (all States and |
| Zimbabwe | Brazil | Kuwait | Denmark | | Territories) |
| | Canada | Lebanon | Finland | | Singapore |
| | (all Provinces | Syrian Arab | France | | |
| | and Territories) | Republic | Germany | | |
| | Chile | | (ex-GDR | | |
| | Colombia | | states | | |
| | Costa Rica | | only) | | |
| | Cuba | | Greece | | |
| | Dominican | | Hungary | | |
| | Republic | | Italy | | |
| | Ecuador | | Luxembourg | | |
| | Guatemala | | Romania | | |
| | Honduras | | Spain | | |
| | Mexico | | Switzerland | | |
| | Panama | | (8 Cantons) | | |
| | USA | | Turkey | | |
| | (Federal + | | United Kingdom | | |
| | all States and | | Yugoslavia | | |
| | District of | | | | |
| | Columbia) | | | | |
| | Venezuela | | | | |

[2] See also document EB87/12 (referred to in footnote 1), pp. 8–19.

that "any trade in organs or any commercialization of the transplantation ... sector is, in principle, excluded" (W. Schoeppe and A. Fürsch, personal communication, May 11, 1990).

It is hoped at a later stage to prepare a comprehensive survey of legislation on this and other key areas of organ transplantation legislation. In that survey, which is currently still in the conceptual stage, it is hoped to review not only legislation and nonlegislative measures as such, but also their implementation in practice, and their effectiveness in achieving the objectives sought.

## Conclusions

It will be up to WHO's Executive Board to review the Guiding Principles that we have described above, and to advise the Director-General as to whether the text should be submitted to the World Health Assembly in May 1991. One possibility is certainly that the Board may recommend that the Assembly adopt these Guiding Principles in the form of a recommendation to WHO's 167 Member States under Article 23 of the Constitution[a]. Under Article 62, all Member States are required to report annually on the action taken with respect to such recommendations, and, consequently, WHO will have a continuing mechanism to monitor the steps taken by Member States if and when a recommendation is adopted.

The holding of this Congress is timely, and in a sense constitutes a follow-up to the Congress on Ethics, Justice and Commerce in Transplantation: A Global Issue, held in Ottawa on 20–24 August 1989. It will be recalled that resolution 2 (commercialism and transplantation) adopted at that Congress affirmed that "the buying and selling of human organs and tissues for transplantation is unacceptable", while resolution 4 (alleged criminal actions to obtain organs) stated that

> *criminal activity to obtain organs for transplantation is abhorrent. No evidence was presented [to the Congress] to substantiate allegations of illegal and criminal acts to obtain organs but such allegations impose a duty to continue investigation by appropriate authorities.*

Vigilance in this area is certainly necessary, not least in the light of continuing arguments that there is nothing inherently illegitimate in what the author of a recent paper describes as "the kidney trade" [15].

---

[a] In its resolution EB87.R22, adopted in January 1991, the Board did in fact make such a recommendation to the World Health Assembly (Note added in proof).

# Appendix 1

## RESOLUTION WHA40.13
## (Development of guiding principles for human organ transplants)

**WHA40.13** The Fortieth World Health Assembly,

Recognizing the scientific progress achieved in human organ transplants in many Member States;

Concerned at the trade for profit in human organs among living human beings;

Affirming that such trade is inconsistent with the most basic human values and contravenes the Universal Declaration of Human Rights and the spirit of the WHO Constitution;

Commending the measures taken by some Member States to regulate human organ transplants and their decision to develop a unified legal instrument to regulate these operations;[1]

REQUESTS the Director-General:

(1) to study, in collaboration with other organizations concerned, the possibility of developing appropriate guiding principles for human organ transplants;

(2) to report to the Health Assembly on the action taken in this regard.

*May 1987* WHA40/1987/REC/1, 11

[1] Document WHA40/1987/REC/1, p. 47

# Appendix 2

## RESOLUTION WHA42.5
## (Preventing the purchase and sale of human organs)

**WHA42.5** The Forty-second World Health Assembly,

Concerned by the commercial trafficking in the organs of healthy donors, which exploits human distress and puts at increased risk the health of the donors;

Aware that commercial arrangements for organ transplants are nevertheless being undertaken and that to date there has been little success in preventing trafficking in human organs;

Anxious to prevent the exploitation of human distress, particularly in children and other vulnerable groups, and to further the recognition of the ethical principles which condemn the buying and selling of organs for purposes of transplantation;

1. CALLS UPON Member States to take appropriate measures to prevent the purchase and sale of human organs for transplantation;

2. RECOMMENDS that Member States introduce legislation to prohibit trafficking in organs where this cannot effectively be prevented by other measures;

3. URGES Member States, in close cooperation with professional health organizations and supervising health authorities, to discourage all practices which facilitate commercial trafficking in organs;

4. REQUESTS Member States to report as soon as possible to WHO on action taken with respect to this resolution;

5. REQUESTS the Director-General to report to the Forty-fourth World Health Assembly the measures taken by the governments of Member States in furtherance of this resolution.

*May 1989* WHA42/1989/REC/1, 7

## References


1. WHO (1948) International Digest of Health Legislation, vol 1. WHO, Geneva, p. 95
2. WHO (1969) Use of human tissues and organs for therapeutic purposes. A survey of existing legislation. WHO, Geneva
3. Fuenzalida-Puelma HL (1990) Organ transplantation: the Latin-American legislative response. Transplant Proc 22: 961–962; Bulletin Pan Amer Hlth Org 24: 425–445
4. Gerson WN (1987) Refining the law of organ donation: lessons from the French law of presumed consent. J. Int Law Politics 19: 1013–1032
5. Abouna GM et al. (1990) Commercialization in human organs: a Middle Eastern perspective. Transplant Proc 22: 918–921
6. Lillich RB (1990) Transplanting organs from living donors: an international regime or more free enterprise? Finnish Yrbk Int Law 1: 510–527
7. Salahudeen AK et al. (1990) High mortality among recipients of bought living-unrelated donor kidneys. Lancet 336: 725–728
8. Committee on Morals and Ethics of the International Transplantation Society (1971) Ann Int Med 75: 631–633
9. Committee on Morals and Ethics of the International Transplantation Society (1972) Bull Wld Hlth Org 47: 131–133
10. Council of The Transplantation Society (1985) Commercialisation in transplantation: the problems and some guidelines for practice. Lancet 2: 715–716
11. Van der Werff A, Vilardell F (1988) In: Health policy, ethics and human values: European and North American perspectives. Proceedings of the XXIst CIOMS Conference, held in Noordwijk aan Zee, the Netherlands, 2–5 June 1987. CIOMS
12. Dickens BM (1977) The control of living body materials. Univ Toronto Law J 27: 142–198
13. Law Reform Commission (1977) Human tissue transplants. Australian Government Publishing Service, Canberra
14. United Nations, Economic and Social Council (1990) Contemporary forms of slavery. Geneva (document E/CN.4/Sub.2/1990/43, dated 26 June 1990)
15. Brecher B (1990) The kidney trade: or, the customer is always wrong. J Med Ethics 16: 120–123; and Harvey J (1990) Paying organ donors. J Med Ethics 16: 117–119

# The Negative Impact of Paid Organ Donation

G. M. Abouna, M. M. Sabawi, M. S. A. Kumar, and M. Samhan

## Introduction

The enormous advances that have taken place in transplantation during the past decade and the increasing demand by patients to reap the benefits of these advances have created a widening disparity between organ demand and organ supply. This situation has led to a flourishing international trade in human organs which is rapidly increasing, particularly in those areas of the world where cadaver organs are not available and where there is marked disparity in wealth among the different segments of the population such as India and the Far and Middle East. As a consequence, a new and deplorable kind of medical practice has emerged where human kidneys are bought from the poor and the destitute for transplantation into a wealthy clientele with soaring profits for brokers, private hospitals and physicians. According to Dr. C.P. Vas of India, the current President of the Geneva based International Commission of Health Professionals (ICHP), more than 1000 kidneys were sold in India in 1988 to wealthy recipients, of whom 56% came from wealthier countries of the Middle East, the Far East, Europe, and America. Also, since 1986, more than 400 patients from the Arabian Gulf countries received paid kidney transplants in India, Egypt, and more recently Iraq. Trading in human organs has also taken place in Europe and the Americas, albeit on a smaller scale, and recently in England, where some of the physicians involved in this practice were duly reprimanded. It is not surprising that such practices have alarmed both the medical profession and the public and have been rightly condemned by international medical societies and organizations including the International, the European, the American, and, more recently, the Middle East Societies for organ transplantation [1, 2]. In order to get around this professional and public outcry and in an attempt to make this abhorrent practice less disagreeable, a new and more attractive label was recently introduced. It is called "rewarded gifting" [3, 4], which is not only a contradiction in terms, but in our view and from our experience is only another more subtle form of trading in human organs and has the same negative impact on many of our moral, medical, and ethical values. In this

Division of Organ Transplantation, Department of Surgery, Hahnemann University, Philadelphia, PA, USA and the Department of Organ Transplantation, Kuwait University, Kuwait

W. Land, J. B. Dossetor (Eds.)
Organ Replacement Therapy:
Ethics, Justice and Commerce

paper, we shall illustrate and explain some of the negative consequences of organ sale in the light of our observations and experiences in the Middle East.

## Observations on Paid Kidney Transplantation in the Middle East

Between 1986 and 1990, 72 patients were seen and treated at the Kuwait Transplant Center, one of the largest referral centers in the Middle East, after returning from abroad where they had received paid renal transplants. Another 50 patients who had also received purchased kidneys abroad were followed by their referring nephrologist in Kuwait. Of these, 55 % received their kidney grafts in India, 30 % in Iraq, 9 % in Egypt, and the remainder in the Far East. Most of the patients who went to India were transplanted in private hospitals in Bombay from poor donors, supplied by the hospital or through brokers. The 21 patients who underwent transplants in Iraq were operated on at the Al-Khayal Hospital, which is now the busiest private hospital in the Middle East for paid kidney transplantation and purportedly uses the system of "reward gifting" as described by Dr. Reddy of Madras [3]. As we have reported earlier, a large number of serious medical, social, moral, and linguistic problems were observed [5].

The medical outcome for these patients leaves much to be desired. Within the first 6 months of transplantation, 11 patients (15 %) died and 28 grafts (30 %) were lost as a result of complications, many of which are avoidable today. Another 15 recipients (21 %) were "rescued" from possible death and/or loss of their grafts by extraordinary and intensive effort at our center for the treatment of a multitude of technical, immunologic, and medical problems, including a variety of communicable diseases such as hepatitis, malaria, tuberculosis, and human immunodeficiency virus (HIV) infections. Four patients from Kuwait and an estimated 24 others from the Arabian Gulf became HIV positive, with 40 % of them dying from acquired immunodeficiency syndrome (AIDS).

## The Problems of Paid Organ Donation

While it is easy to rationalize that paid organ donation may be one way of coping with organ shortage, especially in the current health care and economic environment of countries like India and the Middle East, we believe this to be a flawed, short-sighted, and self-defeating approach to a complex problem. Paid organ donation has a serious negative impact on many of the medical, moral, and ethical values intimately connected with organ transplantation including the donor, the recipient, the local transplant programs, the medical profession, society, and the international community. We will now consider each one of these areas separately.

## The Impact on the Donor

It is generally agreed that in organ transplantation from living donors, there are three fundamental principles which cannot be violated. First, the removal of an organ from the donor must not impair the health, life, or functional integrity of that donor; second, the consent to donate must be voluntary and without pressure or coercion; and third, the donor should be fully informed of all the possible consequences and risks of the procedure.

From our observations and from the type of environment where paid living donors are sought, most or all of these basic principles could not or have not been fulfilled. Most of the donors come from a section of the society where their health and nutrition are already compromised by poverty and economic hardship. A major surgical operation such as nephrectomy and the removal of a healthy organ is likely to further impair the health and functional integrity of these individuals. A truly voluntary and noncoerced consent is also unlikely in the circumstances of these individuals. The mere placement of a thumb imprint on a consent form is no proof of voluntarism. The desperate financial need of the donor is an obvious and clear economic coercion for, as has been admitted by Reddy and his colleagues: "All donors have only one thing in common, great financial need and most of them come from the lower strata of society" [3, 6]. A truly informed consent is equally unlikely because this involves an in-depth discussion of the nature of the procedure and the likely hazards and complications that may follow. Given the educational and literacy levels from which these donors generally come, it is doubtful that this important principle can ever be met.

There are other problems and injustices arising out of this practice. Exploitation of the donor, by the hospitals, by the physicians, and by the recipients has been common [5, 7, 8]. The mere renaming of this practice by the label of "rewarded gifting" does not entirely remove this possibility. There are many reports of donors who have been cheated by the hospital and by the recipient, and of donors not given the full sum of money promised to them before harvest. It has been recently reported that with the number of poor people wanting to sell their kidneys in India increasing rapidly, the market price for a kidney is falling considerably. Also, many of these donors are known not to receive optimum care during operation and after discharge. Surgery is often carried out in badly equipped hospitals and the patients discharged at the earliest possible time to cut costs and increase profits. Postoperative care and follow-up of the donor, if any, is negligible or limited [7, 8].

## The Impact on the Recipient

Many of the recipients who receive paid kidney transplants do so out of desperation because of lack of cadaveric organs in their own countries. Like the situation with the donor, the recipients have neither the free choice nor a properly informed consent for the procedure. They are at the mercy of the hospital and the physicians regarding costs, choice of donor, and the quality of evaluation and investigation. Many of the recipients in Kuwait had to pay exorbitant charges which are continuing to rise, and when these are compared with the local currency and living costs, they are astronomical. The charge at the Al-Khayal Hospital in Baghdad is 4000 Kuwaiti dinars (US $15000) or approximately 40000 Iraqi dinars, which is the equivalent of the earnings of a physician in that country in 8 years. The situation is similar in India and the Far East [7–9].

Exploitation of the recipients goes further. They are required to bring with them expensive medications including cyclosporine and antilymphocyte globulin in excessive quantities. They are kept in the hospital for the shortest possible time, and in many cases they are discharged with the wounds open or in the midst of rejections and other serious complications. The philosophy is obvious: Once payment is made, get rid of the patient as soon as possible to cut costs and increase profits. The pretransplant evaluation of the donor has been minimal and unacceptable (again to cut costs). Many hospitals, including the ones in Iraq, Egypt, and Bombay, do not carry out tissue typing. Screening of the donor for communicable disease is inadequate or nonexistent, and it is no wonder that patient and graft loss are high, that so many patients have become HIV positive, and that many more have developed other communicable diseases like malaria, tuberculosis, and hepatitis.

## The Impact on the Local Transplantation Programs

There is considerable evidence to indicate that marketing in human organs will eventually deprecate and destroy the present willingness of members of the public to donate their organs out of altruism and charitable deed. Indeed, why should anyone donate his or her organs freely when others are selling them at a price? Why should a living related donor, especially if he is rich, go through an operation to give away one of his kidneys when he can go to India, Egypt, Iraq, or elsewhere and buy a kidney for his relative quite cheaply? Again, why should a government or voluntary organization put great effort and expense into developing a cadaver program when kidneys can be bought elsewhere for no more than US $1000?

Our experience in Kuwait has indeed shown that all of these possibilities did take place. About 50 % of the recipients who went abroad to buy a kidney had potential living related donors, and half of these had already been evaluated and were found to be suitable for donation. However, when they heard they could go to India or Iraq and buy a kidney, they disappeared. They were seen again with their relative upon their return to our center, often with a profound feeling of guilt and remorse, especially when the kidney was lost or the patient died from complications. The two sons of a recipient who died from AIDS following a paid transplant in India wept with shame for not giving him one of their kidneys.

Many of the officials in the Ministry of Health of Kuwait were reluctant to invest in a national program of organ procurement, even though the country had enacted an excellent cadaver transplant law (Law No. 55 for 1987), because they did not consider that there was enough pressure or need to go through such an effort when it was much easier to write a cheque for their citizens to go and buy a kidney abroad. Consequently, very few cadaver kidneys could be obtained, in spite of the fact that the annual death rate from trauma in that country was among the highest in the world (200 per million population). Even though the Kuwait transplant law prohibits the buying and selling of human organs, the opportunity to buy kidneys in India and Iraq and elsewhere for dialysis patients in Kuwait was so appealing to the local officials that they did not allow the news of HIV infections in transplanted patients to be made public, for fear that this would discourage other patients from going to buy kidneys abroad. Finally, the negative impact on the development of a cadaveric program does not only affect renal transplantation, but more specifically, the transplantation of other more life-saving organs such as the liver and the heart.

## The Impact on the Medical Profession

Paid organ donation in all its forms has become a lucrative business in which medical decisions are controlled more by the market forces than by acceptable professional codes of conduct and medical ethics. Examples of exploitation of donor and recipient by the hospitals and by the physicians have been reported [5, 9]. According to Dr. Colabawalla and Dr. Vas of India [7, 8], there have been many instances of false documentation of donor's age and health status, of fee-splitting among physicians and of unnecessary consultations and excessive billing. It is in the nature of things that when a medical service is carried out solely for profit and where there are a large number of patients who are in desperate need of that service, there is often the temptation and the opportunity for deception, exploitation, and corruption with least regard to many of the most cherished moral and ethical values of the medical profession and society. The other aftermath is that when the public knows that the medical profession is engaged in the buying and selling of human organs, they become disillusioned and distrustful and many who would be donors, no longer wish to participate in a system in which there is corruption, exploitation, and an unjust distribution of organs which favors the rich and the influential [10].

## The Impact on Society

In his recent testimony to the American Congress, Arthur Caplan rightly pointed out:

*"What is truly distinctive about transplantation is not technology or cost, but ethics. Transplantation is the only area in all of health care which cannot exist without the participation of the public. For it is the individual citizen, who while alive or, in the case of vital organs, after death who makes organs and tissues available for transplantation. If there were no gift of organs or tissues, transplantation would come to a grinding halt" [10].*

Paid organ donation, under whatever label, will drown all voluntary donation by the public and all serious effort of initiating cadaver organ procurement programs in countries like India, the Far East, and the Near East. In other words, by accepting paid organ transplantation, not only will we be compromising our ethics, but we will lose the very battle which we are fighting to win, i.e., making more cadaver organs available.

We often hear from protagonists of organ sales such dramatic statements as "buy or let die" [3] and that there is nothing wrong with this practice since the rich recipient is restored to better health and the donor receives financial benefits and thus there is some sharing of the wealth. This is misleading, for what is happening in practice is not sharing of wealth, but sharing of health by the rich recipient at the expense of poor donor, with justice to none [8]. Indeed, the past President of the Indian Society of Nephrology, Dr. Chugh stated in 1988, "If the current trend of selling human kidneys continues at the present rate, most of the poor people of India will be minus one kidney by the year 2000." Indeed, according to the reputable journal *"The Times of India"*, there are already colonies and villages of poor people in India where most of their inhabitants have sold one of their kidneys.

If the human body can be treated like ordinary goods to be sold for known and predetermined rewards, we are inviting corruption in society and an unjust and unfair system of access and distribution, for the rich will always be on the receiving end and the poor on the giving one. You corrupt justice if the rich and the powerful can buy his judgement in a court of law or buy himself out of a national duty or buy himself into a powerful and prestigious position in society. It is undoubtedly a sacrifice on the part of a father to sell his organ to feed his children because the circumstances of his environment compel him to do so. We should deplore the system that compels such a father to do this and we should correct rather than exploit a system which equates the desperately poor with the desperately ill since these require quite different solutions. It is sometimes argued that an individual should be free to sell his organs just as he sells his labors and why should there be any objection? This argument, if taken to its conclusion, may easily be used to justify a return to allowing individuals to sell themselves into slavery, which is clearly unacceptable. In a civilized world, one has to consider the needs of the individual and the methods of fulfilling those needs versus the value system of the society in which he lives. The freedom of an individual to behave must clearly be circumscribed by the needs of the society and by the greater good of social order and morality. If an individual is forced to have to sell part of his body at a price dictated by the market forces, it is surely against the autonomy and the dignity of the human individual as well as the many fundamental religious and cultural beliefs. If this is allowed or condoned, then surely society has failed. Another possible negative impact on society is potential criminal consequences which the sale of organs for profit is likely to bring, just as drug trafficking has brought with it. There are already reports from different parts of the world where women and young children have been abducted, have disappeared, or have been sold for their organs.

## The Impact on the International Community

In transplantation, it is very important that we should have one code of ethics regardless of the geography or culture where this treatment is being given especially when the countries of the world are getting closer together. A person from Germany, USA, or UK who knows he cannot buy a kidney in his own country because of existing laws prohibiting the sale of organs can do so by going to India or the Far East. In this way he can easily flout the legal and the ethical standards laid down in his country and by his society and indeed this is what happened in Kuwait when many patients left to buy a kidney in India and elsewhere since Kuwait (Law No. 55 for 1987) prohibits the buying and selling of human organs.

Another reason for having one standard of ethics throughout the international transplant community is clearly to do with the fact that the people and the medical profession in India, the Far East, and elsewhere will consider it an insult if they are relegated a second rate standard of ethics by condoning organ sales in their country while the West prides itself of having a different and higher standard of conduct. In a letter to the President of the Transplantation Society, Dr. Colabawalla and two leading Indian transplant physicians had this to say, "Advocating Reward Gifting" for countries like India, opens the transplantation society to a justifiable criticism of having dual standard of ethics. We, as Indians, feel that a 'second rate' standard of ethics is unacceptable" (BN Colabawalla, 1990, personal communication).

## Conclusions and Recommendations

The sale of human organs, in all its forms, which is one of the evils of current technological advances, is damaging to the cause of transplantation as well as to the many cherished moral, religious, and ethical values and beliefs of civilized society. Indeed, both the Judeo-Christian and the Islamic culture condemn the sale of organs [12]. Organ sale has a negative impact on organ donation through altruism and voluntarism by the public and on the establishment of cadaver procurement programs by national governments. It leads to exploitation of both donors and recipients by private hospitals and physicians. It deprecates some of the fundamental professional and moral values of society by demeaning the dignity and the autonomy of the human individual. It promotes an unjust system of organ access and distribution controlled by market forces which favors the rich at the expense of the poor. It invites social and economic corruption, exploitation, and even criminal dealings in the acquisition of organs for profit.

Since all these negative developments are the consequences of nonavailability of cadaver organs and the poor socioeconomic conditions in the countries of the East, where organ sales are most rampant, the solution to this problem must lie in the creation of appropriate conditions and the introduction of necessary reforms by local governments for the establishment of national programs of cadaver organ procurements. In the current environment of India, the Middle East and the Far East, the key to achieving this goal is by a combination of legislation and creative and morally acceptable incentives as previously outlined by us [9] as well as by Monaco [11] (Table 1).

In view of the profound negative feedback affect of organ sales on voluntary and legitimate organ donation, it is imperative that all forms of paid organ donation be made illegal in all countries of the world if the efforts to create local cadaver procurement programs are to succeed. In this regard, both this International Congress as well as the World Health Organization have a vital responsibility and must play an important role.

**Table 1.** Possible legislation and incentives to achieve reforms in organ transplantation

**Legislation**

1. Legalize removal of organs from cadavers upon the diagnosis of brain and/or cardiac death
2. Introducing presumed consent laws as in some european countries and now in Singapore
3. Legal prohibition of all paid donation to remove the negative feedback effect on cadaver donation

**Incentives**

1. Exemptions from "standard" financial obligations
   A. Funeral costs
   B. Taxes on income or inheritance
   C. Loss of income from disability during and after donation in the case of living genetically or emotionally related donors
2. Providing needed support
   A. To the bereaved family of the donor, eg., widow's pension
   B. Family relief grant
   C. Free medical care to donor in living genetically or emotionally related donors
3. Insurance plans for donor's family
   Government sponsored life insurance payable upon death and donation to be made available to all who wish to donate their organs after death

## References


1. Council of the Transplantation Society (1986) Ruling of the Council Transplantation, 41:1
2. Middle East Society for Organ Transplantation (1990) Resolution condemning the sale of organs. Second International Congress of MESOT, Kuwait, March 12, 1990
3. Reddy KC,Thiagarajan CM. Shunmugasundaram, D et al. (1990) Unconventional renal transplantation in India. Transplant Proc 22 (3): 910–911
4. Sells R, Daar A (1990) Unrelated renal transplantation. Transplant Rev 4 (1): 128–140
5. Abouna GM, Kumar MSA, Samhan M, et al. (1990) Commercialization in human organs – a Middle Eastern perspective. Transplant Proc 22 (3): 918–921
6. Thiagarajan CM, Reddy KC, Shunmugasundaram D et al. (1990) The practice of unconventional renal transplantation at a single center in India. Transplant Proc 22 (3): 912–914
7. Colabawalla BN (1991) Commerce and trade in human organs. In: Abouna GM (ed) Recent advances and current practice in organ transplantation. Kluwer, Dordrecht (in press)
8. Vas CJ (1991) Some ethical concerns in organ transplantation. In: Abouna GM (ed) Recent advances and current practice in organ transplantation. Kluwer, Dordrecht (in press)
9. Abouna GM (1990) Organ transplantation in the Middle East-Problems and possible solutions. In: Haberal MH (ed) Recent advances in nephrology and transplantation. Haberal Educational and Research Foundation, Ankara, Turkey, pp. 233–242
10. Caplan AL (1990) Testimony to the subcommittee on health and the environment of the United States Congress, April 20 (in press)
11. Monaco AP (1990) Transplantation – the state of the art. Transplant Proc 22 (3): 896–901
12. Albar A (1991) The Islamic position on organ transplantation. In: Abouna GM (ed) Recent advances and current practice in organ transplantation. Kluwer, Dordrecht (in press)

# Organ Donation for Consideration: An Indian View Point

K. C. Reddy

No universal yardstick can be used to determine the modality of treatment a patient with end-stage renal disease (ESRD) is likely to get. Two major criteria eventually decide the fate of that patient, and both have little to do with actual medical practice:

1. The part of the world the patient happens to be born in
2. The extent of his wealth

It is unfortunate but true, that the treatment modalities of ESRD in various parts of the world depend in no small measure on the economic strength and, to a lesser extent, on the culture of that individual community, and the poorer the society the greater the social acceptability of less optimal forms of treatment. Scrutiny of Table 1 will illustrate my meaning.

**Table 1.** Treatment modalities of ESRD in relation to national economy

| | | |
|---|---|---|
| Ideal | Maintenance hemodialysis<br>Cadaver donor transplantation | Developed countries |
| | Ethical rubicon – Hippocratic tenet – Primum non nocere | |
| Acceptable practices | Maintenance hemodialysis<br>Cadaver donor transplantation<br>Live related transplantation | Developed countries |
| | Lack of maintenance hemodialysis and cadaver transplantation | |
| ? Acceptable | Living donor transplantation<br>Related and regulated paid donor transplantation | Third world countries |
| | Loss of social and medical values | |
| Unacceptable | Unregulated paid donor transplantation<br>Commercialization of transplantation | Third world countries |

Pandalai Cardio Thoracic Foundation, 157, Poonamallee High Road, Kilpauk, Madras 600010, India

W. Land, J. B. Dossetor (Eds.)
Organ Replacement Therapy:
Ethics, Justice and Commerce

If the cultural yardstick is superimposed on this table, two countries stand out. Japan as one of the most developed economies in the world depends mainly on hemodialysis as the principle modality of treatment of ESRD, with very little transplant activity. On the other and of the scale, India for the following reasons occupies the lower half of that table.

1. Patients with ESRD have few options for treatment other than living donor transplantation as (a) cadaver donor programs are nonexistent, and (b) chronic maintenance hemodialysis is unavailable to most, both on the grounds of impracticality and economics.
2. It is sufficiently medically advanced to effect a living donor transplantation.
3. There are no laws which make the "sale" of organs illegal 'per se'.
4. Dialysis and transplantation are confined largely to the private sector, and only those patients who have the wherewithal to meet that expenditure can hope to have any form of treatment.
5. A large population of poor people, who for both financial and social compulsion are willing to sell their organs.
6. Many ingenious and unscrupulous individuals who exploit the situation for personal gain.
7. Cultural and social acceptability of sacrifice as a way of life in hindu India.

So the scene is set for commercialization of renal transplantation, and as neither the government nor the various medical councils have any statutory power at present to regulate such activity, a wide range of commercial practices occur in the country. Viewing this activity with concern, an expert committee was constituted by the government of India to formulate policy with regard to several controversial issues connected with organ transplantations. On the issue of organ donation for consideration, with respect to renal transplantation, the document says:

> "The use of organs, such as kidney from living donors who are not related to the ill patients who require kidney transplantation is viewed with suspicion because of the likelihood of commercial trafficking in organs. Voluntary donation of paired organs such as kidney by a living person could be made permissable. However while enforcing the legislation it would be difficult to ascertain whether the kidney has been donated voluntarily or whether consideration has been paid. Therefore, the related question which requires to be resolved is whether to permit removal of human organs such as a kidney from a living person for consideration. The various alternatives that could be considered are:
>
> 1. prohibit removal of any organ from a living person for consideration.
> 2. permit removal of a human organ such as kidney from a living person for consideration but prescribe regulations and procedures with regard to such activity.
> 3. allow removal of kidney from a living person and leave it as a matter between donor and donee."

So the crux of the matter is whether one of paired organs, such as a kidney, can be removed from a living person for consideration?

It is our opinion, that with regard to India, until such time as alternative modalities of treatment are available to all patients, the second option would meet the requirements of society. What are our reasons for recommending such a course of action?

## The Need to Buy

What more compelling reason can there be than to save one's life! In the absence of cadaver donor programmes and effective state-aided chronic hemodialysis programmes, patients with ESRD have only one option for long-term survival – a living donor transplantation. More than half of these patients have no suitable living donors, and if paid organ donation is not permitted, these patients must be allowed to die. Whenever any living donor transplantation is considered, the ethical tenet of *primum non nocere* is transgressed. However minimal the risk, there is risk involved. It is illogical to suggest that the risk involved is alright if it is taken in a spirit of love, but not when money exchanges hands between the parties involved for mutual benefit. When money is involved to achieve a good end with harm to none, the use of that money does not make the transaction immoral.

Consider further:

1. Over 40 % or so of genetically related donors in India, receive monetary compensation or are subtly coerced.
2. Laws confining transplantation to the genetically related alone will be difficult to enforce.
3. Prohibition of paid organ donation will only give a stimulus to the black market in organs.

### Responsibilities to the Donor

The arguments above are weighted in favor of the recipients. What then are our responsibilities to the donor? Living donor transplantation is regarded as justified on the following premises:

1. No significant harm comes to the donor.
2. Valid, uncoerced informed consent.
3. Significant emotional benefit to the donor.
4. Secure donor follow up

*Valid uncoerced consent versus donor vulnerability.* In all related and emotionally related transplantations, there is one irreplaceable precondition – donor specificity. So the decision to donate is not one based on the ideal of universal altruism. It gives the donor satisfaction and indeed pleasure to see his loved one live, not anyone live. Although this emotional pressure is importantly different from the pressure of financial inducement, it is nevertheless pressure, and this pressure is acutely intensified when alternative sources of treatment are unavailable [1]. Should one doubt the validity of the consent in either case on this score of external pressure?

*Emotional benefit to the donor* is closely linked to the need to sell and social attitudes to paid organ donation. I am a strong believer that ethics, or, as I would prefer to call it, code of social conduct is culture specific. The Hindu ethos of Dharma, or the fulfilling of one's duty or obligations, is a paramount guiding principle in the average Indian's life: "Perform action which lies in the sphere of your duty" (Bhagavad Gita, Chal 2). If personal sacrifice is required in the fulfillment of his duty, the act enobles rather than degrades that human being. If financial need alone was the motivating factor, donor lists would be filled with the ranks of the destitute; but this is not so. The major social compulsions for donating kidneys for consideration are (a) payment of dowry and settlement in marriage of daughters and sisters, (b) the settlement of crippling family debts, and (c) to improve the donor's own standard of living and to secure a better future for his/her children.

The main donors are young adult males who have responsibility for their siblings, widowed and abandoned women who have responsibility for their children, and young well-motivated couples with complete families looking for a better future. Is there anything wrong in this motivation? Does not the achievement of any of the stated objectives result in deep emotional satisfaction? Is this emotional satisfaction in any way inferior to the satisfaction that the genetically related donor gets from seeing a loved one live? Is there not, then, a mutual transfer of health in the totality of its meaning? Today new donors who come to our centre cite the improved social status and standard of living of previous donors as another reason for wanting to donate their kidneys for consideration.

*Secure donor follow-up*. Initial follow-up of donors indicates no mortality and minimal morbidity in our hands. However, even though in our paid organ transplant programme we provide for 3 years of free medical aid, donor compliance to follow-up is poor (about 20%). Clearly more work has to be done in this area.

## The Right to Sell

If an individual has a right to give a tissue or an organ for emotional reasons, why not for consideration? It is illogical to state that the payment of money alone makes the act illegal. The medical implications of donor nephrectomy are the same in both instances. When social laws are framed they should in general be for the benefit and protection of those they seek to serve. If the state believes that living donor nephrectomy is harmful to the individual, then it has a right, nay, the duty to prohibit all living donor nephrectomy.

When the recipient and the donor are mutually benefited by the financial transaction, the act cannot be deemed to be criminal. If it is the intention of the state to prevent trafficking, then it should act against those who would actually take commercial advantage of the need for organs. The moral evil in trafficking stems not from the organ donation for consideration, but from the profit directed commercial arrangements which would certainly lead to the exploitation of the financially vulnerable [1]. Thus, the proper response is to attack the exploitation of the need for paid donation and not the act itself.

Those against paid organ transplantation condemn the practice as being "victimisation of the poor, a form of corporeal prostitution, resonant with the undertones of slavery". It must be remembered that poverty is one of the grim realities of life in India. Nothing dehumanizes an individual more than poverty and his inability to provide for his family. At the same time, the recipient is faced with the problem of survival, When neither the state nor society can provide a solution, what are these individuals expected to do? When a mutual transfer, dictated by absolute need, is done with full informed consent of all parties concerned, no serious ethical or moral objection can be made to the act of organ donation for consideration.

Let us now consider purely medical controversies regarding paid organ transplantation. Do the results of such transplantation warrant continuation of such practice. No national transplant registry exists and therefore this will have to be evaluated on the basis of our own experience. The results of unrelated paid donor transplantation at our center are given in Table 2. All patients were on triple drug therapy (prednisone, azathioprine and cyclosporin A). All transplants were blood group compatible only; no tissue matching was done.

**Table 2.** Calculation of actuarial patient and graft survival following living unrelated (paid) kidney donation: Pandalai Cardiothoracic Foundation, Madras, 1984–1989 (From [4])

| | Study interval (months) | | | | | |
|---|---|---|---|---|---|---|
| | 0 | 3 | 6 | 12 | 24 | 36 |
| A. Number of patient entering interval | 296 | 296 | 246 | 198 | 171 | 74 |
| B. Number of patients insufficient postoperative period to enter interval | 0 | 20 | 39 | 13 | 87 | 49 |
| C. Number of grafts lost per interval | 0 | 30 | 9 | 14 | 10 | 2 |
| D. Number of patients died per interval | 0 | 23 | 8 | 10 | 9 | 1 |
| Graft survival per interval | 1.00 | 0.8893 | 0.8532 | 0.7885 | 0.7241 | 0.6943 |
| Patient survival per interval | 1.00 | 0.8971 | 0.8651 | 0.8194 | 0.7627 | 0.7493 |

What should these figures be compared with? Firstly, with survival on maintenance hemodialysis in India. Except for Mani [2] of Apollo Hospital, Madras, who believes that chronic hemodialysis is a real alternative for patients of ESRD, most other observers, including Sastry [3] of C.M.C.H., Vellore, believe that the 3 year patient survival on hemodialysis would be in the region of 15 %. From our own records, one-third of the patients registered with us for transplantation, but being dialysed elsewhere, have died awaiting surgery – the waiting period being approximately 4–6 months. So certainly long-term survival rates following paid donor transplantations are significantly superior.

Secondly, against live genetically related (one haplotype matched) transplantation. In our hands, there was no statistical difference in long-term graft survival of one haplotype-matched transplantation on conventional two-drug therapy (prednisone and azathioprine) when compared to unmatched transplantation on three-drug therapy. For the last 18 months, we have introduced three-drug therapy to all related donor transplantation, and the initial results show significant improvement in graft survival, a fact that we now try to impress on patients seeking paid organ donation.

Thirdly, against unrelated live donor transplantation done in India, but followed up elsewhere. The recent report by Salahudeen et al. [3] looks at the results of 130 patients from three units in the United Arab Emirates and Oman, who received paid organ transplants arranged through brokers in Bombay between June 1984 and May 1988. The patients' actuarial survival rates at 12 and 45 months were 81.5 % and 80.7 %, respectively, and graft survival rates, 76.9 % and 74.7 %, respectively. Most of the grafts lost were accounted for by patient deaths in the 1st year. In analyzing the factors contributing to the high mortality, the overseas team cited bacterial and viral infections as the major cause and that these may have resulted from:

1. Aggressive immunosuppression in the initial posttransplant period.
2. Poor patient counseling regarding medication and follow-up and the hazards of immunosuppression.
3. Conditions and facilities where the transplants were done being totally inadequate with a high incidence of postoperative wound infections and other complications.
4. Contaminated blood products or kidneys being responsible for human immunodeficiency virus (HIV) infections and hepatitis.

How would these results be interpreted from an Indian perspective?

Most transplantation in India is a one-shot affair. Few patients can afford to go back on dialysis following rejection, so that patient survival rates are only marginally higher than graft survival rates. The major cause of graft failure besides patient deaths due to infections, are attributable to noncompliance of patients to treatment, due to complacency, economic reasons and occasionally nonavailability of drugs. Hence the figure quoted by the Middle East team would be considered excellent in Indian terms. What is even more remarkable is the very small drop in both patient and graft survival rates between the 12- and 45-month period. So the results in themselves are not a contraindication to paid organ transplantation.

Furthermore, without going into the controversy of whether Arab patients should have been treated in India, the report clearly indicates that much of the mortality could have been avoided if correct medical practices were observed. So the results strongly strengthen the argument that if paid organ transplantation is to be considered as a modality of treatment of ESRD, then it must be under strict control, not only for social, but also for medical reasons.

There is a considerable body of opinion that considers paid organ transplantation an obstacle to the development of cadaver donor programs in India [2]. For over a decade, those at the helm of affairs have not been able to get even a semblance of a cadaver program going, let alone having brain death criteria introduced into our statute books. It is this failure that gave a stimulus to paid organ transplantation in the first place, and the responsibility rests squarely on the transplant fraternity in my country. All of us in this field must work together with the state to get an efficient cadaver donor programme going along with state aided dialysis. Till then, regulated paid organ transplantation will be the only alternative available to these hapless patients.

Having advanced arguments for paid organ renal transplantation in India, what strategies should be employed to make it acceptable in the developing world and to secure the recognition of that acceptability from the developed world?

1. State-funded autonomous bodies with statutory powers to regulate and oversee the process.
2. Institutions which are permitted to do such transplantation must be notified, and be subject to periodic inspection and licensing.
3. The donor selection and counseling process must be independent of the transplantation team and must be responsible for all aspects of donor welfare – pre- and postoperative. Particular emphasis must be placed on (a) ensuring valid informed consent, (b) sociological screening and counseling to see that the benefits derived from the transaction are not wasted, and (c) guaranteed free medical follow-up.
4. Those recipients who request paid donor transplantation must also be subject to independent screening and counseling. All efforts must be pursued to ensure that the advantages of genetically related transplantation are explained to the patient.

The introduction of these measures will bring the practice out into the open and into centers of excellence, and the interests of all concerned can be safeguarded.

The government of India finds itself in an unenviable situation. The treatment of ESRD is not listed as one of the national health care programs, and hence, treatment becomes available only to those who can afford it and that too in the uncoordinated private sector. To compound matters, health is a state subject, and any central law will have to be ratified by the various states. No laws defining brain death have been enacted, and the infrastructure and logistics to provide a national cadaver program simply do not exist. Most of these restraints are the result of a poor economy rather than the lack of expertise or desire. One of the more affluent states in India, Maharashtra, is set to introduce a law banning all paid organ transplantation and to provide for cadaver organ transplantation. The outcome of these measures will probably influence policy in other states of India.

Being part of a team that openly conducts and records perhaps the largest number of paid organ renal transplantations in India, what are our inner sentiments? Given a choice, we would like to be amongst those communities that have the economic might to treat all patients of ESRD with either maintenance hemodialysis and/or cadaver donor transplantation. Or, we could have opted out from making a choice – after all, if the patients blood relations are unwilling to help and the state unable to provide, why should we? The addition of a few hundred more to the several thousands dying of more readily treatable causes should cause us little concern. But we chose to take a stand, to buy rather than to let die, to attempt to return to useful lives some of the patients afflicted with ESRD, and at the same time, give an opportunity to the donor and their families to improve their standard of living.

The system we have introduced at our center is not perfect, particularly in the area of donor follow-up. Absolute shortage of cadaver donors have left us with little option but to consider and practice paid organ transplantation. Further, it is obvious that the moral evil in trafficking results primarily from the exploitation of the act of paid donation rather than in the act itself. The transplant fraternity in India faces a challenging and daunting task ahead – to try and establish alternative methods of treatment, so that paid organ transplantation is no longer needed, and in the meantime be ever vigilant that the paid donor is well protected, so that not only is justice done, but seen to be done in the eyes of the world.

## References


1. Evans M (1989) Organ donations should not be restricted to relatives. J Med Ethics 15: 17–20
2. Mani MK (1990) Needed: a campaign for cadaver donations. The Hindu (August 19, 1990, pp. 19)
3. Salahudeen AK et al (1990) High mortality among recipients of bought living-unrelated donor kidneys. Lancet 336: 725–728
4. Daar A, Sells RA (1990) The problem of paid organ donation in India. Report on behalf of the Ethical Committee of the Transplantation Society to the President and Council of the Transplantation Society

# Rewarded Gifting and Rampant Commercialism in Perspective: Is There a Difference?

A. S. Daar

## Introduction

I consider the question of rewarded gifting as one of the most important ethical issues facing the transplant world today: it has enormous practical implications for the worldwide practice of transplantation, especially that of kidneys. I feel at once both privileged and daunted to have been given the task of dissecting the question of whether there is a difference between "rewarded gifting" and rampant commercialism.

## Recent History: Why the Controversy?

Clinical organ transplantation is approximately 3 decades old, but at least as early as 1970, the Committee on Morals and Ethics of the Transplantation Society was already concerned about the buying and selling of organs when it affirmed that "the sale of organs by donors living or dead is indefensible under any circumstances". Fifteen years later, the Society again felt the need to clearly define its guidelines regarding this matter (Council of the Transplantation Society 1985). Furthermore, partly in response to open attempts by entrepreneurs to introduce the buying and selling of organs, the Council of the Society even passed a special resolution threatening expulsion from the Society of any of its members who violated its guidelines (Morris 1985). During the early 1980s, there were also rumours and newspaper and personal reports that active trading in organs, involving large numbers of rich foreign patients, was taking place in Bombay. These reports, which were subsequently confirmed in the scientific literature (Alkhader et al. 1986; Daar 1988; Abouna et al. 1990; Salahudeen et al. 1990) led to the condemnation of such commerce on ethical and moral grounds by people both in the West (eg. Medawar et al. 1984) and in the East (Mani 1986). The practice has not only continued, but is actually spreading in India to cities such as Madras (Daar and Sells 1990a) and, in a more frightening way, to Calcutta [The Telegraph (India) 1990].

---

Department of Surgery College of Medicine, Sultan Qaboos University P.O. Box 32485, Al Khod Muscat Sultanate of Oman

W. Land, J. B. Dossetor (Eds.)
Organ Replacement Therapy:
Ethics, Justice and Commerce

In the beginning, the matter appeared quite clear: any payment for an organ must be condemned. However, a daring presentation was then made by C.T. Patel at the Pittsburgh forum to honor T. Starzl in 1987. Here we had a physician from Bombay who was actually justifying the practice of some form of payment for living nonrelated donor kidneys thus: "kidney donation is a good act. It is the gift of life. The financial incentive to promote such an act is moral and justified." (Patel 1988). As far as I am aware, it was Patel who first used the term "gift with reward" in this context. A few people, both in the East and the West, did share his opinion at the time, but no one was willing to say so in a public forum. Organizers of the 12th Congress of the Transplantation Society arranged in 1988 a highly acclaimed symposium in Sydney at which four people were asked to contribute: P. Little from Baghdad sympathized with Patel's view and pointed out an important point: "Who can advise on the ethics of transplantation? Is it the Council of this Society, which represents 16th of the world population containing the rich developed world, or should the debate be widened to include the over 5/6th of less fortunate mankind?" (Little et al. 1989). Both J. Dossetor (Dossetor 1989) and I (Daar 1989) felt that there was a clear difference between "rewarded gifting" on the one hand and "frank entrepreneurial commerce" (Dossetor) or "rampant commercialisation" (Daar) on the other. Dossetor maintained that "Western ethics would hold that both these have the same fundamental flaw, though the second variety ("frank entrepreneurial commerce") has obvious risks for donor victimisation, *but no absolute answer exists*". At that time, I perhaps vocalized the fears of many by being "worried about opening flood-gates, for the consequences would be bad." At the same meeting R. Sells called attention to the work of a group of transplanters at the Guest Hospital in Madras, who believed that they were practising transplantation using live nonrelated paid donors with enough controls and modifications as to be outside the ambit of "rampant commercialism." (Sells 1989)

## Our Classification: The Ottawa Meeting

The subject was now beginning to come out into the open, and it was felt by many that there was a desperate need to discuss these questions further and to try to answer "even if societal acceptance is the ultimate arbiter of ethics, where do we as a profession draw the line?" (Daar 1989). Having been thoroughly confused ourselves, we then proposed a classification of the issues involved in living donor renal transplantation. This was presented at the "Ethics, Justice & Commerce in Transplantation – A Global View" meeting in Ottawa in August 1989 (Daar et al. 1990). The five categories we described were: I living-related donation, II emotionally related donation, III altruistic donation, IV "rewarded gifting" and V rampant commercialism. The classification was based on the concept of *gifting* from the principle that "the only circumstance where a kidney may be removed ethically from a living donor is when it is a gift to the recipient." (Morris and Sells 1985) My task today is to look with a "retrospectoscope" to see whether in fact there is a difference between categories IV and V.

At the Ottawa meeting, Reddy et al. (1990) and Thiagarajan et al. (1990) pointed out the good results of their living nonrelated "unconventional" program in Madras, implying that it satisfied the (as yet undefined) criteria of rewarded gifting. In my mind, the most telling aspect of their arguments was the subtitle of Reddy's paper: *"To buy or let die"*[1]. There was limited opportunity, though, to really discuss the issues in detail, and despite the inspired chairmanship of C. Stiller, no consensus could be achieved on whether there was an *ethical* difference between categories IV and V (and therefore, perhaps, acceptability of category IV by the transplant community). A resolution, under the heading of "commercialism and transplantation" was adopted and this read "The buying and selling of human organs and tissue for transplantation is unacceptable". What was clear at Ottawa, however, was that there was universal condemnation of category V transplantation, but not of category IV. In that sense, at least, there was a perception of a difference by some. The need for further discussion obviously persisted, hence part of the reason for the Munich meeting (both W. Land and H. Brynger, who bring us to Munich for this conference, were at the meeting in Ottawa).

## Between Ottawa and Munich

Reflecting Little's view of the need to widen the debate, and perhaps V. Yadav's view from floor in Sydney that the Society needed to familiarize itself with the situation in India, the President of the Transplantation Society, R. Batchelor, responded to an invitation from Reddy to send a delegation to India. The Society asked R. Sells and me, both members of its Committee on Ethics, to be its representatives. Our report (Daar and Sells 1990a) documented the situation as we saw it and understood it. The report's main thrust was that the Society should encourage cadaver organ donation in India, and we made several concrete proposals on how members of the Society could help with this. It was not our mandate to make moral or ethical pronouncements, and we did not do so. The recommendations were discussed by the Council of the Society and by its general assembly in San Francisco and were accepted. A secretariat is now being established in Boston to coordinate this effort (amongst other things). Some of the feedback we have had from India was to the effect that Indians do not want "second rate ethics". We could not agree more.

[1] Perhaps a less dramatic and more generalized form of this ethical conundrum was enunciated by A. V. Hill in his Presidential Address to the British Association (for the Advancement of Science) in 1952: "If ethical principles deny our right to do evil in order that good may come, are we justified in doing good when the foreseeable consequences are evil?"

In September 1990, we published in *The Lancet* an analysis of the results of category V transplantation (patients from Oman and the United Arab Emirates buying kidneys and undergoing transplants in Bombay and being followed up in their own countries), pointing out that during the period of analysis (mid-1984 to mid-1988) the results were poor in terms of morbidity and mortality, and that at that time in Bombay our patients were exposed to dangerous infections, including human immunodeficiency virus (HIV) (Salahudeen et al. 1990). Our message was that *in addition* to the ethical arguments the poor results were another reason to condemn category V transplantation. In a letter to the editor in response to our article in *The Lancet*, Al Khader et al. from Riyadh (who had previously made a preliminary oral report at the Helsinki Congress of their own poor experience of patients transplanted in Bombay; Al Khader et al. 1986) pointed out that the results in more recent years have improved: we are now analyzing our own recent results (the practice continues to this day) to clarify the situation. The ethical and moral reasons for condemnation, though, have obviously *not* changed.

Another interesting development also took place between the Ottawa and Munich meetings and this development, in my view, now significantly shifts the focus for discussion of "rewarded gifting" from India to the United States.

## The Need for More Organs: Developments in the United States

In our analysis and reappraisal of living nonrelated donor renal transplantation (Daar and Sells 1990b), we documented some of the facts and figures for end-stage renal failure and its current management in the United States. All recent figures, eg., from Rapaport (1991), Alexander (1990), and the United Network for Organ Sharing (Peters 1990), point to a worsening of the disparity between kidneys needed and kidneys donated from all sources. The number of kidney transplants in 1987 actually *dropped*, and the average waiting time for a cadaver transplant has nearly doubled in 1 year, from 126 days to 233 days! (Anaise et al. 1990). This has stimulated a vigorous discussion among some of the most prominent members of the profession in the United States about the possible role of incentives to donate. I quote three specific examples.

1. Monaco (1989), noting that modern methods of immunosuppression achieve superior success with living unrelated kidney donors, has recommended that the use of such kidney donors should be encouraged and developed. He adds that:

"At the same time, consideration should be given to development of appropriate motivational incentives. These might include financial ones from government sources, particularly to cover the financial burden from loss of work. If these two concepts for living unrelated donation were pursued widely, the shortage of kidneys might not be so dramatic."

In relation to cadaver donors, he has said:

"One could, therefore, argue that a trial programme should be initiated of testing the effect of providing some type of additional incentives to the donor family. These might be in the form of federal fixed-payment grants for deferral of burial expenses, tax deductions for the donor's estate, tax deductions for the immediate next of kin, and so on" (Monaco 1989).

2. Peters (1990) noted that:

   "Over the past 30 months, 4,350 patients died while on the *active* national waiting list maintained by the United Network For Organ Sharing (UNOS). Because the issue in transplantation today is growing more and more towards the issue of patient death *while waiting* for a transplantable organ, there are those who are supporting the idea that *financial incentives to families of patients who give transplantable organs should be studied.* Altruism, professional and public education, as well as legislative interaction have not increased organ donation in the last 3 years. Air pilots carrying organs to a potential recipient get paid, but the next-of-kin do not." (Peters 1990)

3. While not recommending that the process of organ donation be commercialized, or that the present law prohibiting sale of organs from live donors be changed, Newmann (1990) a health policy consultant who received a kidney transplant in 1987 after 14 years on dialysis, went on to say: "I feel there should be a field test to determine if providing a death benefit to the next-of-kin would increase the supply of organs ..... Financing would be done through the government as part of the current payment for procurement." Talking at the Seminar on "The Regulation of Human Tissue and Organs" sponsored by the Food and Drug Law Institute in Washington in July 1990, Newmann said the family could accept, reject, or designate the money to a charity, adding that "there should be no coercion, *altruism would remain intact*, and the incentive would not benefit the rich, since the government would pay for the process" (Newmann 1990).

## Payment to the donor: What Is Allowed in Current Guidelines?

A donor has to undergo investigations and inconvenience. He/she has to leave work to go to the hospital for these investigations and to then undergo the surgical procedure (e.g., nephrectomy), with its attendant discomfort and the small risk of a complication or (very rarely) death. Obviously, the loss of earnings from being off work before and after the donation and the actual expenditure for investigations and hospitalization (which are *not* borne by the government or by insurance schemes in many instances) can amount to an appreciable sum in any country. In general, professional organizations have taken some of these factors into account in their guidelines, and I quote three:

1. The Transplantation Society: "However, *reimbursement* for loss of work earnings and any other expenses related to their donation is acceptable" (Council of the Transplantation Society 1985).
2. World Health Organization (WHO): "'Payment' means the transfer of money or money's worth, or the giving of an advantage or preference, in exchange for a gift or promise of an organ, but *does not include* any *repayment* in whole or in part of costs incurred or to be incurred in removing, preserving, or transporting in organ for transplantation, or expenses or loss of earnings incurred or to be incurred by a person reasonably and directly related to the supply of an organ from his body" (WHO 1990).
3. Council of Europe conference of European Health Ministers in Paris on November 16–17, 1987: "However, this does not prevent the *compensation* of living donors for loss of earnings and any expenses caused by the removal or preceding examination" (WHO 1988).

Apart from items such as investigations, medications, hospital room, and operating theatre time (which are difficult enough to quantitate in most instances), how does one quantitate real loss of earnings for a businessman or for someone who is not employed? How is discomfort to be valued, and what about risk? Should a donor in Bombay be paid more than one in Boston for the risk component? Legal scholars also do differentiate between tissue donation and a *service* (WHO, proposed guidelines). The (ethical) justification for payment for blood donation is that this is for the provision of a service. Advocates of incentives for organ donation would probably fail to understand what the "service" component is in the act of blood donation that is missing in the more onerous act of kidney donation.

## Future Questions: the United States, Variants of Category IV, and Controls

These fine points certainly need further discussion, but an obvious question arises at present: will the profession in the United States now embark on studies to see whether incentives

a) are possible,
b) will increase donation, and
c) are acceptable to the public (or legislators)?

If these studies are initiated, then in effect our American colleagues are saying that there are no ethical arguments against the use of incentives, and in that sense they are saying there are at least variants of category IV transplantation that *are* acceptable.

This immediately then raises the question as to whether there are in fact variants of category IV, and the key question then reverts to "where do we as a profession draw the line?" and how do you define the "limits of compensation"? (Salahudeen et al. 1990). If this is easy in the United States, it will not be when we try the same exercises for other countries, especially when we do not know the value of the dollar and, therefore, its equivalents in other currencies.

We have recently stated (Daar and Sells 1990b) that "rewarded gifting" is probably better named "compensated donation", or "donation with incentive". It has become clear to me now that these are in fact terms that would encompass two distinct variants of "rewarded gifting" (a) *compensated donation* would fall within the definition of what is allowed by current guidelines as compensation for loss of earnings, hospitalisation and other related expenses "incurred or to be incurred", as discussed above; and (b) *donation with incentive* would be what I predict our American colleagues are about to try, and presumably this would involve controls including at least all of those ones in the following list, which would distinguish this subcategory from category V (Table 1).

Thus, one variant, namely compensated donation is different from category V of our classification (rampant commercialism). This is acceptable practice. Donation with incentive, the other variant, is as yet theoretical, and, as such, it is theoretically different from category V. One way or the other, therefore, rewarded gifting is different from rampant commercialism.

**Table 1.** Analysis of the distinction between rewarded gifting and rampant commercialism

| | Category IV<br>Rewarded gifting variant (donation with incentive)[a] | Category V<br>Rampant commercialism |
|---|---|---|
| Status | Theoretical | Already exists |
| Beneficiary | Recipient and donor | Doctors, middlemen, hospitals, laboratories (windfall profits) |
| Brokers | No | Yes |
| Specific Regulations? | Yes | No |
| Govt. or professional supervision | Yes | No |
| Continuing care of donor (eg., catastrophe insurance) | Yes | No |
| Rich at expense of poor | No | Yes |
| Potential for exploitation | No | Yes |
| Results | ? | Poor |
| Possible at present in: | | |
| India | No | |
| USA | Yes | |

[a] Rewarded gifting is seen as having two distinct variants: (a) *compensated donation* which exists, is practised, and is allowed in current guidelines and legislation; and (b) *donation with incentive* which is what is being considered here (see text).

## Will Category IV Necessarily Deteriorate into Category V?

It is interesting and important to note here that even practitioners of transplantation who claim to have some of the features of the controls of category IV would say that in India today, for example, it would be impossible to have rewarded gifting without this being exploited by middlemen and greedy professionals into becoming rampant commercialism. The reasons given are that voluntary and even legislative controls are likely to be ignored in any society where the involved institutions are not yet strong enough, where the relevant laws are in a state of flux, where the numbers of transplants (even with paid donors) is grossly inadequate to cope with the numbers of patients, where the absence of dialysis facilities makes the choice between life and death stark indeed, where the distribution of wealth is grossly skewed and thus massive wealth (including that of rich foreigners) is juxtaposed to dire poverty, and where both petty and major corruption at all levels of society is a much talked about subject. I suppose in this context an Indian commentator on transplant ethics can be forgiven in thinking that rewarded gifting is nothing but a "terminological subterfuge meant to obfuscate the issue" (Colabawalla 1990). I concur that any society which has at least several of these features is not a place to attempt a practical distinction between category IV and category V transplantations. And it is in this context that we will watch our American colleagues with keen interest, because in the United States it may just be possible to answer whether donation with incentive, theoretically one kettle of fish, can be practised without rampant commercialism, a different kettle of fish.

## Conclusions

1. Rampant commercialism (category V) is unacceptable morally, ethically, and in terms of its effects and results.
2. An analysis of what is actually meant by rewarded gifting (category IV) reveals that this has two distinct variants I propose that these are named (a) compensated donation which is acceptable and is allowed in current guidelines, and (b) donation with incentive, a variant that has not been practised widely and systematically. As a theoretical concept, and assuming the adoption of appropriate controls, this variant is different from category V. Thus rewarded gifting is different from rampant commercialism.
3. To maintain the difference between the two variants of category IV on the one hand, and category V on the other, will be almost impossible in many countries, especially where professional and governmental guidelines do not command widespread acceptance.
4. The increasing shortage of organs has stimulated a great deal of interest in the category IV variants, particularly in the United States, where specific proposals for trials involving incentives have been put forward by eminent members of the profession.

## References

Abouna GM, Kumar MSA, Samhan M et al. (1990) Commercialisation in human organs – a Middle East perspective. Transplant Proc 22: 918
Alexander TW (1990) The cutting edge. Transplantation
Al Khader AA, Abomelha MA, Saltissi D et al. (1986) XI International Congress Transplantation Society, Helsinki, Finland, August (Abstract A 11.4)
Colabawalla BN (1990) Letter to editor. Lancet 2: (Nov 10)
Council of the Transplantation Society (1985) Commercialisation in transplantation: the problem and some guidelines for practice. Lancet ii: 715
Daar AS (1988) Renal transplantation in developing countries. In: Morris PJ (ed) Kidney transplantation, principles and practice, 3rd edn. Saunders, Philadelphia p. 709
Daar AS (1989) Ethical issues – A Middle East perspective. Transplant Proc 21: 1402
Daar AS, Salahudeen A, Pingle A, et al. (1990) Ethics and commerce in live donor renal transplantation. A classification of the issues. Transplant Proc 22: 922
Daar AS, Sells RA (1990a) The problem of paid organ donation in India. Report on behalf of the Ethical Committee of the Transplantation Society to the President and Council of the Transplantation Society
Daar AS, Sells RA (1990b) Living non-related donor renal transplantation – a reappraisal. Transplant Rev 4(2): 128–140
Dossetor JB (1989) Ethics in different cultures: "The West". Transplant Proc 21: 1395
Little PJ, McMullin JP, Macdonald A (1989) Live donor renal transplantation in Iraq. Transplant Proc 21: 1400
Mani MK (1986) Letter. N Engl J Med 315: 714
Medawar P, Dausset J, Snell G (1984) Letter to President Reagan (quoted by the editor) Lancet 2: 1344
Monaco AP (1989) Comment: A transplant surgeon's views on social factors in organ transplantation. Transplant Proc 21: 3403
Morris PJ, Sells R (1985) Paying for organs from living donors. Lancet i: 1510
Morris PJ (1985) Presidential address. Transplant Proc 17: 1615
Newmann J (1990) In: The regulation of human tissue and organs. Washington, DC, July 1990
Patel ČT (1988) Live renal donation: a viewpoint. Transplant Proc 20: [Suppl 1] 1068
Peters TG (1990) The regulation of human tissue and organs. Washington, DC, July 1990
Rapaport FT (1991) Problems of Organ Allocation. Transplant Proc (in press)
Reddy KC, Thiagarajan CM, Shunmugasundaram D, et al. (1990) Unconventional renal transplantation in India: to buy or let die. Transplant Proc 22: 910
Sells RA (1989) Ethics and priorities of organ procurement and allocation. Transplant Proc 21: 1391
Salahudeen AK, Woods HF, Pingle A, et al. (1990) High mortality among recipients of bought living-unrelated donor kidneys. Lancet 2: 725
The Telegraph (India) (1990) The kidney bazaar (January 7), p.4
Thiagarajan CM, Reddy KC, Shunmugasundaram D et al. (1990) The practice of unconventional renal transplantation in a single centre in India. Transplant Proc R2 (3): 912–914
WHO (1988) International Digest of Health Legislation. 39 (1): 277
WHO (1990) Draft Guiding Principles for Human Organ Transplants

# From Him that Hath Not

J. Radcliffe Richards

When the trade in transplant organs from live donors first came to public attention in Britain a year or two ago, what was most remarkable about the immediate response was its unanimity. From all points of the political compass, from widely different groups who were normally hard pressed to agree about anything, came indignant denunciations of the whole business: it was a gross exploitation of the poor by the rich, repugnant in every respect, and should be banned forthwith.

This indignation was not, in the first instance, directed at the worst abuses that are now known to go on. Revelations of such horrors as kidney stealing, failure to pay the agreed price, and even abduction and murder, did not appear until later. The trade in organs from live donors was, in Britain at least, universally denounced as unacceptable in itself, and such remarkable concord must seem to suggest that the case for ending it by law is unequivocal.

Nevertheless, I want to argue that things are not clear as they may seem. Of course there is something repugnant about the whole business, but it is nevertheless very far from obvious that it should be stopped. If we start not with our own feelings of repugnance, but with the situation of the exploited people on whose behalf we profess indignation, the matter begins to look very different, and should at least give us pause.

Consider, for instance, the situation of the young Turkish father swept to the glare of British television by the surge of outrage that followed the revelations. He had arranged to sell a kidney in order to pay for urgent hospital treatment for his little daughter. Now presumably the prospect of selling his kidney was, to say the very least, no less repugnant to him than it seems to us; nevertheless he judged this to be the best option available to him. This very fact shows how unspeakably bad the alternatives must have seemed. To forbid the trade, therefore, is to take away what seems the best option open to someone whose position is already so appalling that this *is* his best option. It is to make the worst off worse off still.

This is not enough to show that the trade ought to continue, but it does show that anyone who wants to stop it needs to produce a very good justification. If we want to implement policies that cause harm, and especially harm to the worst off, we need to show either that the harm is only apparent,

---

Department of Philosophy, The Open University, Milton Keynes, MK7 6AA, UK


W. Land, J. B. Dossetor (Eds.)
Organ Replacement Therapy:
Ethics, Justice and Commerce

or that it is outweighed by more important considerations. So what kind of justification might be offered?

The usual justification we give for interfering with other people's actions is that we want to prevent their harming others. That, however, would be most implausible here. Far from harming anyone else, the father was benefiting his daughter, and probably saving the life of the kidney's recipient as well. (Our desire to protect the poor should presumably not lead us to conclude that the lives of the rich – people like us – do not matter at all.) If we intervene and prevent him from selling his kidney, therefore, we not only cut off what seems to him his own best option and forbid him to sell what is, if anything is, his own; in this case, at least, we also prevent the saving of two other lives. I suppose odd cases might arise in which it could be argued that prospective organ sellers were risking unreasonable harm to other people, but since what the sellers most obviously do is save the lives of the buyers a prohibition would far more reliably cause harm to others than prevent it.

Perhaps, then, the idea is to protect not other people, but the would-be vendors themselves. They may be making what seems to them the best choice available, but perhaps we want to claim that they are simply misguided. This idea is certainly more in keeping with the tone of the popular outcry, which does, after all, express indignation on behalf of the exploited victims of the rich. Nevertheless, most people will find this line of argument equally difficult to sustain.

In the first place, it obviously runs against the fundamental liberal principle that although people's freedom of action may legitimately be curtailed to prevent their harming others, it may not be curtailed to prevent their harming themselves. Anyone who takes this principle to be absolute, as many do, must obviously rule out paternalist intervention completely. Even if is argued that some of the potential vendors are being subtly coerced, or are too ill-informed to make rational decisions, the absolute version of the principle can justify intervention only in particular cases. It cannot permit a general prohibition which curtails the freedom of all.

Most people probably are less full-bloodedly liberal (or libertarian) than this, and are likely to regard paternalism as justifiable in some cases (such as the compulsory use of seat belts, or the prohibition of drug use). But even they have to confront the problem of explaining why kidney selling is so obviously misguided, and why a benevolent paternalist would prevent it. Of course it is a risky business (as is altruistic kidney giving), and no doubt in many cases, at present, the vendors are making choices they would not make if they were better informed. But there is not the slightest reason to think this must always be the case. There is nothing obviously irrational and mistaken about taking risks. We do not usually regard risking life and health as absurd even for people who are rich enough to have other options open to them: normally we think it entirely a matter for individual decision if people are willing to risk their lives for the joys of rock climbing or for danger money from North Sea diving. It is surely far *more* difficult to see why the desperately poor, who see in selling a kidney the only hope of making anything of their wretched lives and perhaps even of surviving, should be regarded as so manifestly irrational as to need saving from themselves.

Of course there is a sense in which some of the vendors are not acting in their own interests; many, like the Turkish man, are taking what risks there are for the benefit of others. It is true that the father would have been greatly distressed by the death of his daughter, but most people would nevertheless count his action as one of altruism, and taken in her interests rather than his own. Even in such cases, however, it is still not clear why a paternalist should feel obliged to intervene. Is it irrational for a man to take risks with his own life to save the life of someone he loves? Should we make a general policy of intervening and insisting on unswerving attention to self interest whenever people are tempted to sacrifice themselves for the good of others? Once again, most people would say not. And anyway, it is quite clear that most of the people who oppose the trade in organs have no such view, since they are the very people who say that only pure altruism can justify organ donation. If the daughter had herself needed a transplant, and the father had offered his kidney, they would have applauded. What difference does it make that there is an extra link in the chain, and that he sacrifices his kidney for money to save her by other means?

In one way or another, therefore, most people are going to find it very difficult to justify a general prohibition of organ selling in terms of concern for the well-being of the sellers. Even if they are not opposed to paternalism on principle, as many people are, they still have the problem of explaining why choosing to sell a kidney is necessarily misguided, and why a well-judging paternalist would ban the trade outright rather than intervening only in particular cases.

Perhaps, then, we should try an argument based on the idea of exploitation. Poverty may not make people irrational, it may be argued, but it certainly makes them vulnerable to exploitation. We have, therefore, a duty to protect them.

No doubt we have such a duty, but if protecting the poor from exploitation is our concern, banning the trade in organs is a very strange way to go about it. An exploiter is typically someone who makes use of the fact that people who are desperately poor will clutch at even the slightest opportunity to improve their situation. Someone whose only alternative is starvation will quite rationally agree to work all day for a loaf of bread, so the exploiter takes the opportunity to get the work done without paying more; someone in grinding poverty may well be prepared to sell cheaply what others would not part with at any price, and the exploiter makes the most of the situation. Now there is of course a sense in which if we intervene to prevent the contract between exploiter and exploited from taking place at all we shall indeed put an end to the exploitation; but only in the way that we should eliminate the miseries of slum dwelling by bulldozing slums, or solve the problem of ingrowing toenails by chopping off feet. In other words, we may end the evil in that particular form, but only at the cost of producing an even worse evil for the sufferers. We may perhaps give ourselves the satisfaction of depriving the exploiters of their ill-gotten gains, or take pleasure in seeing the greedy rich unable to use their money to save their lives (though it is not clear how we can be entitled to any such satisfaction as long as we go on paying as little as possible for luxury goods made by grossly exploited labourers in the Third World), but we do no good to the exploited. We actually make things worse for them.

The simple fact is that there is no short cut to ending what is really evil about exploitation. What makes people vulnerable to exploitation is their having too few options, which means the only way to improve their situation is to give them more. We can do them nothing but harm by taking options away. The only radical cure for exploitation is the elimination of poverty. Failing that (since we lack either the will or the knowledge to do it), the best thing is not to forbid the trade but to subject it to stringent controls: to organize a system that completely rules out all dealings with donors or organs of dubious origin and profiteering by middlemen, to get the highest price for the organs that the market will bear, to counsel prospective vendors fully about both medical matters and the use of money, and to provide insurance and after care. Provisionally, then, it seems necessary to conclude that this is what we should be doing. We should be eliminating not the trade, but the abuses.

It is, however, most important to emphasize that this conclusion is provisional, and to make clear the form this argument has taken.

The argument has not taken the form of advocating some controversial moral principle – such as, for instance, the liberal principle that people ought to be allowed to do what they like with their own bodies – and moving from there to the conclusion that there should be a free market in organs. An argument of that kind would be very easy to counter, since anyone who did not like the conclusion could just reject the principle. This argument has been of a different kind. It has worked on the basis of two much less contentious propositions, both of which nearly everyone involved in this debate is likely to accept: that preventing the trade in organs does cause harm, and that whenever some policy has intrinsically bad consequences it must be presumed unjustified until shown otherwise.

This is a perfectly familiar idea. It is intrinsically bad to stick needles into a child, and if you announced an intention to do such a thing you would expect to be stopped. On the other hand, you would also expect most people to let you go ahead once you explained that you were bent on nothing more sinister than vaccination, because most people would accept that the expected good justified the immediate harm. In the case of organ selling, however, things seem to be much more difficult. The policy of banning organ sales has several consequences that nearly everyone would accept as intrinsically bad – it limits the autonomy of adults, takes away the best option open to the wretchedly poor, and allows potential recipients of organs to die – but so far no justification has been found for allowing these evils to happen. And by this I do not mean that no one has produced a justification that would convert opponents of prohibition. So far it has seemed impossible to justify prohibition in terms of *anyone's* principles, including those of its most passionate advocates.

What the argument does, therefore, is put the onus of proof on anyone who is in favour of prohibiting rather than regulating the trade in spare parts from live donors. It takes the form of a challenge: show that what you are advocating is justified in spite of the harm it undoubtedly causes, or withdraw your objections to the trade.

For what it is worth, I rather hope this challenge can be met, since I find the whole business as intuitively repulsive as does everyone else. Nevertheless, once a properly critical attitude is taken to attempted justifications, it is extraordinarily difficult to find any that will fare at all better than the ones already discussed.

For instance it is often claimed, as if it were self evident, that the donation of an organ should be altruistic and that it is inherently wrong for it to be a commercial transaction. That of course still does not explain what is wrong with kidney selling when money is wanted for altruistic purposes, and raises again the question of why direct altruism should be acceptable but indirect not. But, quite apart from that, there is the problem of why it so unacceptable to have anything other than altruism as the motive. It may be *best* if a kidney is offered out of love by a relative, but that does not in the least suggest that what is less than best must be wrong. It is best if elderly people are cared for at home by loving relatives, but we are not usually tempted to infer from this that people who have no relatives, or who are not loved by them, should go without care rather than have it paid for. Some services to other people are performed for love, but many (including virtually all medical services) are paid for, and no one sees any harm in that. If there is a fundamental difference between services and spare parts, what is it?

A rather more promising line may be seem to be the idea that if some practice is allowed at all, people who do not really want to do whatever it is may be coerced or bullied into it. (This is one of the commonest lines of objection to voluntary euthanasia.) That, however, is true of any kind of freedom, and forbidding something altogether because of the danger of coercion is extremely difficult to justify, because it involves placing a *certain* limitation on the freedom of *everyone* in order to prevent the *possibility* of limitation on the freedom of *some*. If our concern is really to protect people who might be pressed into selling their kidneys against their will, our first impulse should be to institute a careful screening system, and refuse organs from anyone about whose motivation there was doubt. We should resort to an outright ban only after much agonizing, and after careful investigation had shown that allowing kidney trading caused more harm to people who were coerced into it than outright prohibition would cause to people who were prevented from doing what they willingly chose. We certainly have no such evidence yet. And, moreover, even if we had, an argument of this kind could still not be used (as it frequently is) by people who are happy to condone kidney donation by relatives, since within families, surely, lies the greatest scope of all for moral bullying and other assorted pressures. If the willing and the subtly coerced can be distinguished in this context, so they can in others.

Obviously it is impossible to anticipate all the arguments that might at some time be attempted, but there is one general matter that needs to be kept in mind whenever proposed justifications are to be assessed, and which should be mentioned in conclusion. It concerns the relationship between the real reasons people have for wanting something and the justifications they think up afterwards.

The fact that people often have their own private motives for approving some policy does not, of course, automatically vitiate the justifications; we may often have selfish motives for wanting something that is perfectly justifiable for other reasons (as when academics and doctors protest against closure of universities and hospitals). On the other hand, it does need to be remembered that people who are firmly convinced of something are often quite extraordinarily uncritical of any argument that appears to support their preconceptions.

Now one thing that is quite clear about this kidney-selling issue is that the impulse to ban the practice outright was immediate and strongly felt, and not at all the result of complicated deliberations. It was from the outset described as repugnant, and when we call things repugnant what we mean is that they produce in us feelings of disgust and revulsion. Strong feelings, however, are not in themselves reliable guides to either rationality or rectitude. Sometimes they stem from good moral impulses, but on the other hand strong feelings rooted in prejudice and superstition, and often superficially rationalized in moral terms, have been responsible for half the evils of history. We have very strong feelings about organ selling, but we must beware of presuming such feelings must have their foundations in morality.

I do not doubt for a moment that many of our feelings of outrage in this particular context are indeed connected with the plight of the poor. On the other hand, the foregoing arguments do suggest reasons for doubting that our feelings of repugnance are quite as deeply rooted in legitimate grounds for moral outrage as we may like to think.

We are inclined to say, for instance, that we find the trade in organs repugnant because of the harm it does to the vendors. But if that were really true we should find the idea of making their situation worse by stopping the trade more repugnant still. We should find it even more repulsive that the Turkish father should be forced to keep his kidney and watch his daughter die than that he should sell it and save her, since the first situation is worse for him. It seems, however, that we do not, which suggests that it is the sale of the kidney in itself, rather than the wretchedness of the man who is proposing to sell it, that arouses our deepest feelings.

We are also inclined to say that what we find most repugnant about the trade is the abuse and exploitation, but in that case if the trade were regulated and the donors properly paid our feelings of revulsion should go. Once again, it seems that they do not. Most people would probably be even more appalled if the trade were officially sanctioned and regulated than they are by what goes on now. Or we claim that our feelings of repugnance are caused by the thought that organs should be given for any other reason than love, but if that were so we should find it no more repugnant that a father should sell his kidney to save his daughter than that he should give it to her directly. Most of us find ourselves responding very differently to the two.

It seems, then, that our feelings of repugnance are only loosely connected with the moral principles we invoke their justification, and therefore that eliminating the causes of the feelings – whatever those may be – is by no means necessarily the same thing as eliminating what is, morally speaking, repugnant.

This is most important, because it suggests one clear advantage to ending the trade that should give us particular reason for suspicion and caution as we consider putative justifications. It seems likely that if we forbid it altogether we shall, for whatever reason, ease our own feelings of disgust. Prohibition may make things worse for the Turkish family and other desperate people around the world, as well as for the relatively rich who will die for lack of kidneys, but at least these people will despair and die quietly, in ways less offensive to the affluent and healthy, and the poor will not force their misery on our attention by engaging in the strikingly repulsive business of selling parts of themselves to repair the deficiencies of the rich.

Perhaps, indeed, that may in itself suggest a sufficient reason for allowing the trade to continue. If we are forced to recognize that something we find as disgusting as organ selling provides the best option for the destitute and the only hope for the dying it may help us to keep in mind the need to pursue more radical remedies: on the one hand to increase the effort to find dead donors, and on the other to take the despair of the poor more seriously.

But quite irrespective of that rather extreme justification for continuing the trade in human spare parts, one thing does seem to be clear. We must make absolutely sure that there is a better reason than the protection of our own squeamish sensibilities before we rush into legislation whose most striking and immediate effect is – strange as it may seem – to take away, from him that hath not, even that which he hath.

# Aspects of Living Organ Donation with Emphasis on the Fight Against Commercialism

M. Broyer

## Introduction

Ethics has become most important by the progresses of modern medicine, and ethical questions are a part of the day-to-day life in big hospitals, particularly in transplant units. Whatever his level of responsibility, each member of a transplant team should feel that the fact of knowing how to perform a successful transplantation does not automatically give him the right to do so. In this area, the use of living donors is potentially dangerous because exposing to all drifts. What is one to think about this practice today in Europe, and what recommendations have to be made? The aim of this paper is to propose some guidelines which could be applied in developed countries for the use of living donors, taking into account the basic rules of ethics.

## Advantages of Living Donor Kidney Transplant and Drawbacks for the Donor

The advantages of living donor kidney transplants are well known, but have been mainly proved for related recipients. Patient and graft survival are usually higher in most of the reported series of transplantation with living related donors (LRD). The benefit for the donor is more questionable, apart from a sense of moral satisfaction reinforcing his self-esteem which is associated with donation.

The drawbacks constitute the most important consideration from an ethical point of view. The risk of death per operation was estimated at 0.06 %, the risk of serious postoperative complications at 1.8 %, less severe complications occurred in 10 %–40 % of the donors, according to the reports [1]. Postoperative suffering and the anxiety surrounding the idea of an operation must not be ignored. The loss of 4–8 weeks or more of activity must also be considered. The real question that remains is the long-term effect of uninephrectomy 20–50 years later, with the possible development of renal symptoms in a small but unknown proportion of cases.

Hôpital Necker-Enfants Malades, 149 rue de Sèvres, 75743 Paris CEDEX 15, France

W. Land, J. B. Dossetor (Eds.)
Organ Replacement Therapy:
Ethics, Justice and Commerce

## "Ethical" LRD Kidney Transplantations

In spite of these drawbacks, it may be considered ethical to perform a nephrectomy in an adult person in order to perform a transplant in a member of his family waiting on dialysis, if several conditions are fulfilled:

1. perfect health, absolutely normal kidneys, and renal function after in-depth investigation of the donor;
2. reasonable expectation of success of the transplantation for the recipient;
3. complete information about the risks of nephrectomy;
4. free consent after enough time for consideration; and
5. absolute certainty that there is no psychological pressure or monetary inducement.

An additional recommendation concerns the search for a human leukocyte antigen (HLA)-identical sibling. In this case the real willingness of the possible candidates must be formally obtained before HLA typing is performed.

## Unrelated Donors and the Risk of Commercialism

It is so difficult to be sure that an unrelated living donor is not paid that it is better to refuse such donors a priori. The principle to refuse living donors who are not first-degree relatives is one of the articles of an ethical chart about to be adopted by the association France Transplant. Some exceptions could be accepted for unrelated donors who have a deep emotional relationship with the recipient (for example, husband and wife) after the agreement of an independent committee. The existence of a *right* to donate was advocated in order to defend living donor transplantation, but this right is not justified since it may be in opposition to the ethical rules that the physician must follow [3].

The case of unrelated donors who are strangers and receive money for their donation is generally condemned, but we know that an organ market is already in place in some of the poorest countries, either openly through various channels including advertising in newspapers or by way of under the table settlements. It is possible to understand the mechanisms of this market, which are mainly the pressure applied by uremic patients who are able to pay on the one hand, and the vital needs of poverty-stricken people on the other hand. The lack of dialysis facilities and their higher costs are also factors favoring this system.

## The Reasons for Refusing Paid Donors

We must refuse paid donors for several reasons some of which are related, some not related to ethics. Among those not related to ethical considerations, there is a first caveat concerning the real health status of donors who live in insalubrious conditions with the additional risk of transmission of viruses, parasites, or other exotic microorganisms which are not always easy to detect. There are also adverse effects which may be expected in the case of extensive nonrelated living kidney donation. First among them is the depreciation of voluntary free donation and its disappearance, since it would be possible to pay someone to donate. Another more important consequence would be a decrease in motivation not only to develop but also to maintain cadaver kidney procurement programs. As a matter of fact, cadaver organ retrieval is a complex and difficult procedure to set up, whereas the removal of a kidney from a living donor is much simpler and does not disturb the usual work pattern of the hospital [2].

Ethical considerations are yet more constraining. Is it ethical for a surgeon to remove a kidney from a paid unrelated donor? Certainly not for several reasons. The transgression of the old medical dictum *primum non nocere* (do not harm) is not acceptable when at the same time the basic principle of autonomy/self-determination is violated. Donor voluntariness is a key ethical concern and is completely cancelled when the real incentive of the donation is monetary gain. In addition, it is far from sure that the donor would be able to understand fully the information about the sequelae of nephrectomy.

In developed countries, the increasing number of patients on the transplant waiting list and the insufficient possiblities of organ procurement programs are not acceptable reasons for using unrelated living donor transplantation, which inevitably would be associated with commercialism. This type of program would start with a "reward" for a supposed altruistic donation – this would of course concern only very poor people in the country – and, step by step, one may foresee an extension of this program with a search for less expensive donors, that is to say for donors coming from the third World.

One of the main worrying consequences of this generalization of organ brokering is that it would soon appear as a visible and intolerable symptom of the exploitation of the poor by the rich. This type of transaction could undermine the whole edifice of modern medicine, of which transplantation is one of the cornerstones. A large part of public opinion, at least in Europe, would then reject the well-founded intentions, of organ transplantation and that would lead to a general refusal of this mode of treatment.

Another major implication of this market would in the long-term be an additional poisoning of the relationship between rich and poor countries due to the highly symbolic character of the commerce of parts of the human body.

## References

1. Bay WH, Hebert LA (1987) The living donor in kidney transplantation. Ann Int Med 106: 719–27
2. Kreis H (1985) Why living related donors should not be used whenever possible. Transpl Proc 17: 1510–14
3. Singer PA, Siegler M (1988) Whose kidney is it anyway. Ethical considerations in living kidney donation. AKF Nephrology Lett 5: 167–170

# The Ugly Head of Commercialism in Organ Transplantation in Greece

K. Koniavitou-Hadjiyannaki, D. Protogerou, S. Drakopoulos, M. Siakotos, E. Sigounas, Th. Syrakos, A. Antoniadis, A. Tourkantonis, E. Hadjiyannakis, and S. A. Raptis

Organ transplantation depends on a display of public confidence. Health authorities have the duty to protect public confidence against any action that would put in doubt the quality of the health services offered and/or the ethical issues connected with the health services. On the other hand, there has been a period of access to the practice of "transplantation on the free market", something which creeping its way in to several countries and which will hopefully come to an end shortly. Our aim is to present another aspect of commercialism, more complicated than usual, and in which conflicting evidence has been presented at different periods; this aspect will also be ending soon.

During the past 12 years, two major factors influenced organ transplantation in our country, viz:

a) The extreme helplessness of renal failure patients, in relation to transplant access; and
b) the stiffness and practical immobility of health authorities to act in elaborating the necessary budgets and arrangements for the organization of a national transplantation service.

Since 1972, in our country, a few medical teams have been actively involved in organizing by themselves kidney transplantation programs. The Hellenic Transplantation Society was founded in 1976 by medical teams. Shortly afterwards, as a result of the pressure exerted by this society on the Health Authorities, a law concerning living related and cadaveric renal transplantation was voted unanimously by the Greek Parliament. Those same legal provisions were revised in 1983, and the articles prohibiting commercialism remained unchanged.

It seemed that a hopeful start in organizing the issue had been made. Unfortunately, nothing was done officially to activate and promote essential features of the transplantation practice. From 1979 onwards, a tendency among the renal failure community to establish initial contact with transplant centers abroad was obvious, although not scientifically justified. This policy became rather aggressive from a social point of view, and the health

The Hellenic Transplantation Society, 4, Papadiamandopoulou Str., 115 28 Athens, Greece

W. Land, J. B. Dossetor (Eds.)
Organ Replacement Therapy:
Ethics, Justice and Commerce

authorities seemed unable or unconcerned to deal with the matter. A so-called reformation of health services in our country carried out by a new government in 1981 provided an opportunity for foreign agents of the free transplantation market, who had failed in the past, to interfere and provide solutions. Nevertheless, at this stage it seemed that under the pressure of the medical society and the continuous demands from the Hellenic Transplantation Society, the policy towards transplantation would be changed for a national scheme.

Unfortunately, the aggressiveness of a group of patients, and the ignorance and immobility displayed by the health authorities in providing a quick solution to the matter for the benefit of partial social demands become clear after an agreement was signed with the Chicago Regional Organ and Tissue Sharing Program (CROSP), a private organization for organ exchange. Surprisingly enough, this agreement, which was signed by the Consulate General of Greece in Chicago (by authorization of the Minister of Health) and responsible parties of the private bank, was announced in a television program as soon as the first two paid kidney grafts had arrived in Athens. The three-page CROSP agreement consisted mainly of financial terms. There was not even a paragraph making reference to the scientific prerequisites for either the source of donor or graft details, or any evidence of scientific protocol to the potential recipient, except for partial exclusion of the highly sensitized patients. The whole set-up was almost a one-way procedure to allow renal failure recipients access to transplantation.

While the above agreement was in force after 1984, four more became valid through the Ministry of Health, with European Private Clinics in Europe. Again the source of grafts was mainly the United States. It is worth noting that all these agreements have recently been (November 1990) cancelled. We must admit that, at this time, there were "improved" terms, but they were still scientifically unacceptable when faced by the demands of our nephrologists, and few details were given from those European Clinics. In general, human leukocyte antigen (HLA) typing was very poor (maximum one HLA antigen in common, irrespective of loci) and cold ischemia time was usually at 60 h (Siakotos et al. 1989). Between 1982 and 1988, 55 or more patients received a kidney graft under these agreements. Only five grafts have been sent to Athens from CROSP, and the rest of the patients have undergone transplants either in Chicago or in European private centers. There was a 40 % – 50 % loss of grafts, due to irreversible rejection, within the first posttransplant year.

In spite of such results, an increasing number of renal failure patients sought transplantation treatment in centers abroad. In 1986, there were 86 patients, in 1987 142, in 1988 186, and in 1989 224 patients. It seems that the patients were provided with no official information whatsoever. It has been rather difficult, sometimes even impossible, to get specific information, but from two of the major National Insurance Companies, it seems that the average cost for a cadaveric transplant in those private centers reached approximately US $ 135 000, while the average cost during 1980 – 1982 in Greece for a kidney transplantation was approx imately US $ 20 000.

In 1983 the official cooperation offered by Professor Cohen from Eurotransplant to the Minister of Health was denied by ignoring the communication, although ten grafts had been sent from Leiden to Greece between 1978 and 1982 (six of those patients still have functioning grafts and are in excellent condition, 8 – 12 years posttransplantation). It is obvious today that there was an effort to influence the access to transplantation by social utility.

## Proposals

As A.P. Monaco stated in August 1989 at the Ottawa Meeting on Ethics, Justice and Commerce in Transplantation: "Ethical transplantation demands ethical access to transplantation" (Monaco 1990).

It has been also said (Dickens 1990) that morality is not necessarily committed to the promotion, or protection, of market practices. However, societies expect a certain level of morality in the market area and that the market practitioners be found to be ethically accountable.

It is very difficult to classify agreements signed between an official authority of a democratic country in a known private transplantation trading program, as either immoral or unethical. Nevertheless, it can be readily understood that it is unfair for both the patients, and the scientists.

Therefore, an urgent need appears in view of a greater Europe, that strict and specific ethical standards of conduct be duly established, care of a European Ethical Committee. Transplantation Societies throughout Europe ought to reach a consensus, in order to establish effective European containments, as the British Transplantation Society has already done (1989). It may be useful for liaison representatives to proceed to examine shortly any category of paid organ donation and enact throughout the scientific members of the European Community standards of conduct relating of transplantation in general. This will enable the transplant communities to be kept in ethical account and the health care communities to be moral towards patients and scientists, thus safeguarding public confidence.

## References

1. Siacotos M, Homatas I, Kostakis A, Vosnides G, Hadjikonstandinou V, Papasteriades Chr, Vlassis Th, Kyriakides A, Poulopoulos A, Bilis A (1989) The long-term function of cadaveric renal transplantation with prolonged cold ischaemia time. Abstracts of the 38th Scientific Meeting of the Hellenic Society of Nephrology. Hellenic Nephrol 1:383–386
2. Monaco AP (1990) Transplantation. The state of the art. Transplant Proc 22 (3):896–901
3. Dickens BM (1990) Human rights and commerce in health care. Transplant Proc 22 (3):904–905
4. British Transplantation Society (1989) Minute of the Annual General Meeting of the BTS. Report of the Supervising Committee on Organ Transplantation

# Fallouts of Commercialism in Organ Donation as Seen in Pakistan

S. Adib Rizvi and S.A. Anwar Naqvi

Renal transplantation is the preferred method of managing end-stage renal failure (ESRF). This is particularly true for the developing world (Daar 1988), where resource constraints have become a central issue in the modality of treatment, particularly chronic renal failure.

## Facilities for Dialysis and Transplantation

There are 36 dialysis centers in the country, one-third being in hospitals in the public sector. Private dialysis is extremely costly ($ 6000 per year which must be seen against the background of per capita income of only $ 350) and beyond the reach of the vast majority of population.

Transplantation of kidneys in Pakistan began in 1979 in Rawalpindi. At present five centers perform about 100 renal transplants every year. The Institute of Urology and Transplantation at Karachi is the largest public sector center and has performed 110 living related donor transplants so far, 40 of them in 1990. Renal transplants in public hospitals is state supported, although the cost of immunosuppression is sponsored by philanthropic organizations and given free to patients. This ensures an excellent follow-up and drug compliance for the patients. Transplantation in the private sector is limited in number and is predominently a living related donor program. The average cost of renal transplantation privately averages US $ 8000.

## Limitations of Living Related Donors

The shortage of intrafamilial donors is genuine. Although families in Pakistan are large and intrafamilial marriages frequent, unmarried females do not come forward for donation easily as it lessens their prospects for marriage. Married females have to seek permission from husbands whose motivation for organ donation is not encouraging. In general, 31 % of people felt that organ donation was injurious to health, the older population being the most

Institute of Urology and Transplantation, Dow Medical College and Civil Hospital, Karachi, Pakistan

W. Land, J. B. Dossetor (Eds.)
Organ Replacement Therapy:
Ethics, Justice and Commerce

resistant to donation, primarily because they could not identify themselves with the new science of transplantation.

The confidence of patients in the results of living related donor programs in Pakistani centers is also an important factor. In our own experience, patients traveling to India to buy donors started leveling off and, in fact, started to show a downward trend when our own transplant results became visible to them. The quality of life of patients who underwent transplants here was the most important factor in convincing dialysis patients of the benefits of living related donor renal transplantation.

## Growth of Unrelated Donor Transplantation in India

From a reported figure of 50 unrelated donor transplants in India in 1983, the figure has swelled to over 2000 in 1990. The annual turnover in the kidney trade in India is reported to be over 20 million US dollars. Attempts at regulation have not been successful and are not likely to be so, unless the issue is dealt with openly and justly.

Dispassionate analysis will reveal that such an astronomical rise in the number of unrelated donor transplants is the result of unethical commercialism. The private sector in developing countries is generally without sufficient regulatory safeguards, and this is especially true in the case of renal transplantation. The profit motive reigns supreme, and when a patient arrives at the doors of these clinics, ethics recede into the background, and the patient becomes a client seeking a package deal for transplantation and hospitalization. Early discharge is the rule, and patients are encouraged to go back to Pakistan within a month of surgery. The transplant team is, therefore, not able to follow up the patients locally during the critical period after they have received the graft. Moreover, the patients are handed a list of drugs suggesting the tapering off of immunosuppression with no advice on who is responsible for their follow-up after they reach Pakistan. This encourages resistance to any suggestions of manipulating the immunosuppressive regimen by the Pakistani physicians in the event of complications.

## Impact of Commercialism as Seen in Pakistan

The ugly head of unethical unrelated transplantation is not yet a problem in Pakistan, especially after the good results of our related donor renal transplantation program. Ethical transplantation has stemmed the tide and has significantly curtailed the reprehensible traffic to Bombay. However, it is only a question of time that the practice may well start here as well. What is stopping the sale of organs is the fact that transplantation is available predominantly in the public sector where commerce plays little role. On the other hand, as soon as a team decides that "rewarded gifting" can mitigate the organ shortage, there will be several other teams who will start taking a lenient view on the moral issue, and large-scale commercial transplantation will quickly follow. These are some of the realities in the Third World which should be borne in mind before a well-meaning thought is put into practice without analyzing the consequences.

## What Are the Solutions to Curb Commercialism?

1. Dialysis and transplantation in poorer developing countries should be encouraged in teaching hospitals in the public sector, and the state should take the responsibility for such programs.
2. Living related donor kidney transplantation should be promoted initially so as to build the foundations for a successful renal rehabilitation program. Good results are likely to encourage intrafamilial donation, so that transplantation becomes the preferred and cost-effective method of treatment for ESRF.
3. Mass campaigns should be directed through the media, especially television, at educating the public on the benefits of cadaver donation. The message ought to be that when there is no religious sanction in Islam, the state religion, why is it being delayed. Cadaver donation will promote not only kidney but also liver, heart, pancreas, and lung transplantations, benefiting thousands of patients every year.
4. Transplant teams must resist the temptation of offering "rewarded gifting" in the developing world. In a poor country where the rich have a tendency to exploit the poorer population, it is extremely difficult to regulate and supervise any commercial transaction and, thus, unrelated donors will be subject to the same market laws. Societal values and pressure will be applied to transplantation, good intention notwithstanding.

## References

Daar, A.S., Renal transplantation in developing countries, in kidney transplantation. Edited by Peter J. Morris. 3rd ed. Philadelphia, Saunders, 1988, p. 709.

# Organ Grafting and Human Society

S. Bošković

*"Since your eyes are open*
*you think that you see"*
GOETHE

First of all, we would like to discuss the medical ethic in a modern society as an initial factor for solving the important problem of organ transplantation. The traditional attitude and medicoethical education of the most medical staff are still not enough to obtain a big group of physicians for solving this important problem. Generally speaking, from the transplantational point of view some developed countries such as Denmark, the Netherlands, Sweden, and Finland have enabled their society to create a proper social climate for an easier understanding of the whole problem. The complex nature of this problem raises a number of philosophical questions and demands a humanistic altruism and educational practice other than the classical educational process of physicians. What is new in the ethical responsibility of a physician and in an educational attitude is the notion that transplantation brings about a new way of treatment, a treatment based on a *living substance*, in other words on living human organs, which has been quite unknown so far. Excluding the cases of experiments performed on animals which have met with disagreement, resistance, and disgust not only among physicians but among society in general. This kind of medical treatment by "living organs" has not yet become traditional enough. We can still remember those physicians who were banished by the religious organizations and animal protection societies which are still a great obstacle for scientific and experimental work in many countries. All of a sudden, revolutionary news is brought, suggesting that everyone should now accept a method of treatment which was proscribed not long ago Bearing all this in mind, it is understandable that transplantation as a form of medical treatment was not accepted before the appearance of effective immunological drugs to control the immunological reactions of recipients, i.e., organ rejection. Medicine itself is a traditional science, and each new concept has always caused resistance, especially if it was a revolutionary one.

Even in 1960, when the attitude that organ transplantation can enable successful treatment had been accepted, it became clear that something must be done to encourage the number of organ donors. In 1968, a new definition of death was established by a special committee for transplantation from

University of Sarajevo, High Medical School, National Institute for Organ Transplantation, Sarajevo, Yišnjik z/a, Yugoslavia

W. Land, J. B. Dossetor (Eds.)
Organ Replacement Therapy:
Ethics, Justice and Commerce

Harvard High Medical School. Death was defined as a total and irretrievable function failure of the whole brain. The new criteria guaranteed the absence of the slightest fear that taking an organ could cause death. This was assumed as the beginning of solving the problem of popularization of transplantations with organs from cadavers.

More than 20 years after that these new criteria for defining death have received strong support in most countries, and they have been legally formulated. Unfortunately, things do not seem to be so simple: transplantational medicine demands more and more organs for transplantation, while the number of donors is still insufficient, in spite of the fact that it has been growing. The legislation of the new criteria for defining cerebral death does not help either. Out of 20000 patients in the United States in whom cerebral death was diagnosed, only 20% become donors, i.e., about 4000 of them.

The answer to this complex question is not simple, and increasing the number of donors seems to remain the biggest problem. Although social consensus was achieved, the problems still remained underneath the surface, and, according to the detailed study made by the four university clinics in Cleveland, physicians are to be blamed for the discrepancy between the needs of patients and the number of donors.

This anonymous questionnaire included most of the physicians from surgical departments (neurosurgeons, traumatologists, and anesthesiologists) as well as those from intensive care departments. The results of the questionnaire were dreadful, and, in short, they showed clinical, legislative, and conceptual confusion regarding the question whether cerebral death can be treated as a real death. The traditional concept that those patients whose heart is still beating could not be treated as dead, although they are dead according to the general criteria of cerebral death, caused discomfort among the mentioned physicians. They were not willing to talk to the members of a patient's family about cerebral death and the need for taking an organ out of the dead body of their kin. Only 35% of these covered by the questionnaire were absolutely familiar with the criteria for cerebral death and were prepared for an active talk to the members of the family which would result in the successful realization of an organ transplantation. In contrast to such a low percentage of physicians, the active participants in this process, 95% of those covered by the questionnaire agreed that a patient dependent on a machine could be treated as dead. This opinion was based on the fact that the patient has lost his consciousness irretrievably, and that his brain is not able to coordinate other subsystems of the body any longer.

Most interesting was the group consisting of 30% of questioned physicians, who can be blamed for the insufficient number of organs available for transplantation. They accepted the fact that patient dependent on a machine is actually dead, but fell that he must be treated as alive since there were still signs of life. The definition of cerebral death in this group of physicians created conceptual confusion about a new class of dead patients, i.e., those who have totally and irretrievably lost integrative and sensitive brain functions, but whose cells, tissues, and organs with the help of a breathing ventilator remain "alive" and function at different periods of time. Their hearts beat spontaneously, the body is still warm, th color of skin is normal, while digestion, metabolism and elimination go on. These patients, defined as cerebrally dead, are scarcely similar in any way to those dying from some traditional disease. Such patients may become an emotional problem for the physicians who deal with their treatment for a long time, a problem which becomes the important one when the decision that the patient is dead has to be made although his heart is still beating.

This emotional tie influences the attitude of a physician towards the further treatment of a dead man and, because of conceptual confusion, significantly reduces the number of organs which could be taken for transplantation. A special emotional obstacle for taking organs occurs in anencephalic newborn infants, who are born with healthy organs but totally undeveloped brain mass; for this reason, they can live no longer than for a few hours. These infants are well represented in the pool of donors, but very often they are not used for transplantation. Such an attitude remains because although the cerebral death is diagnosed, the breathing ventilator is not switched off. On the contrary, the patients starts to receive special care to prolong his "life" functions further, e.g., organ perfusion, hydratation, diuresis, and heart supporting drugs, and finally he undergoes surgery, where by means of technically very precise surgical acts, in which the surgeon makes every effort to avoid any infection, his organs are taken out. This group of physicians ad quite a number of members of the hospital staff have the feeling that such patients die twice, or that he is not dead for the first time after organ removal. The terminology of cerebral death could not leave them indifferent.

The answers to this questionnaire are very disturbing. If they themselves are confused and misinformed, physicians and their staff are not in a position to explain cerebral death to the grieving families, let alone to the public and press. This group of physicians avoids any conversation with the family of the patients, which leads to dangerous resistance towards carrying out the law on organ transplantation. I would tend to call this group of physicians traditionalists, because they have not in themselves accepted the concept that dead donors should be kept in a suitable condition to have their organs removed in order to save someones else's life. It causes a turnover in their method of work and a certain conflict in their traditional attitude towards medical treatment which lasts as long as a heart beats. These physicians, traditionalists, reluctantly and feeling unpleasant, inform the family that there is no more hope for their relative and explain that his organs should be taken for transplantation.

In contrast to the attitude of quite a number of physicians, indeed a large number of those covered, the questionnaire showed that in about 80% of described cases, the families give permission for taking organs. This percentage of agreements is the result of special conversation. Conceptual confusion about cerebral death in not a small number of physicians (about 30%) is only one step towards open resistance to carrying out the transplantation law. The criteria for cerebral death, the transplantation law, and all the clinical and moral implications of this problem should be a part of a regular program at all university schools of medicine and medical schools in one country.

Finally, let us say something about those patients who die at the end, waiting in vain for the practical solution of our arguments. Five thousand patients in Yugoslavia are waiting for the transplantation of different organs, as a result of the modest possibilities caused by insufficient knowledge about transplantational (unconventional) medicine on the part of a great number of our physicians. In order to enlarge the pool of kidneys for transplantation (a paired organ), the American Federal Health Committee suggested that kidneys for transplantation should be taken between married couples under the same technical conditions as in cases of cadaveric transplantations, since couples are not blood relatives. Transplantation from living donors gives much better results for transplant survival than cadaveric transplantation, even in the cases of non-blood relatives, claimed Prof. Jonasson, head of the transplantation centre at the University of Ohio, Pennsylvania. About 1200 kidneys per year can be provided in this way in the United States. I was lucky to perform successfully, in spite of strong criticism, several such transplantations in our country. I wanted to prove that such achievements of American medicine could be applied here, although taking kidneys from living relatives brings extreme moral and medical responsibility, and only the most experienced centers perform this kind of transplantation. That is why most of the physicians try to avoid living organ transplantation, spreading misinformation on cadaveric transplantation, accusing everyone but themselves for its still poor popularization. They belong to the group of 30 % of American physicians covered by the questionnaire, while their number is much bigger in our country.

About 5 years ago the British press reported on the trade with organs, which astonished all transplantologists. A rich foreigner receives a kidney from a poor peasant, "a relative" for a price of 4500 American dollars. The surgery was done in England. We are threatened by the danger that the organs and the living body they are taken from could be treated according to the market laws as merchandise. This business might also involve market agents, physicians, and bring them financial profit. Some developed Western countries, under the influence of transplantologists, easily accepted an attitude and conclusion that the human body was something you could not trade with and that it should not be treated as merchandise. Soon after that, several Western countries passed very strict laws about it. These laws were designed to protect poor people or foreign workers from themselves, qualifying trading with organs as something that a civilized society must not allow. At the symposium in Ottawa last year, very important conclusions were drawn regarding trade with human body. A paid donor gives a paid agreement for his kidney to be taken, while paying for it should be seen as a kind of forced act and, therefore, treated as a criminal act. The trading with organs automatically makes a division in society into donors, who are always poor, and recipients, who are always rich. Countries which allow this work directly against greater promulgation of cadaveric transplantation, causing great damage to thousands of patients threatened by death. If they continue in this direction, we will be threatened by the presence of a great ethical abyss, into which many cases of organ sacrificing may sink and which may even endanger the lives of those wishing to make financial profit for themselves or their families. This kind of organ sacrificing could become very popular.

Nevertheless, some countries refuse to accept those conclusions. Out of 22 Indian federal states, only one confirmed that it will prepare a transplantation law. The cases of organ transplantation in Bombay clearly testify to why they were not willing to obey this law. The commercialization of organs for transplantation is becoming more and more organized: the list of poor peasants has already been made, out of which the rich recipients, mostly foreigners, can get a needed organ for themselves. The taxes have also been made for donors, surgeons, and agents. Dr. A. Daar reported at the symposium in Ottawa on the tragic destiny of 130 recipients of bought organs. After the transplantation in Bombay, the death rate during the first 6 months was 20 %, while among those who survived longer than that, a large percentage of hypertension appeared, caused by renal artery stenosis, which in most cases was defined as a technical error in the act of transplantation. A large number of recipients were rich Arabs, and three out of ten of them died of acquired immunodeficiency syndrome (AIDS) 6 months after the transplantation.

Another case was described by Dr. Thiagarajan from Madras where 303 kidney transplantations from paid donors were made for the fee of £ 1000 sterling and 3 years' postoperative life insurance free of charge. The survival rate of the received kidneys 2 years after transplantation was 82 %, which can be taken as a good percentage, even in the view of the experiences of some Western countries. In this group, no death was reported, while the selection of donors was made by the group of physicians without an announcement and interference of agents. This was the difference in comparison with the Bombay group, where the donors falsely claimed to be the relatives of the potential recipients. These two different examples show that if the legal medical service of one country interferes in the organ trade, significantly better results are made concerning transplantations, in other words, if all relevant medical standards are taken into consideration. Bearing in mind all the specifities of the medical service in those Indian states such as an insufficient number of dialysis centers, poor technical devices and a permanent shortage of organs from cadavers, it is necessary that the state should interfere in its medical service. That can be done by introducing certain rules of anonymity with moderate financial compensation and strict adherence to modern medical standards. With such a method, the number of wanted organs could be increased, while the uncontrolled sale of organs could be placed under control. Poorer countries tend to accept such "interference" of the state, while the official prohibition of organ market, which has already been done in Europe, has little chances of success in India.

Such a situation brings about various liberal and political organizations in Western pluralistic societies, which in their political programs insist that the state should be prevented from making paternal interventions in the sale of organs for transplantation. Their argument is that no one has the right to protect people from themselves and that previously decided sacrifice of oneself is the free will of each individual. Individuals are not guilty of their poverty and that should be respected, as should the status of the living human body from which organs are taken in cases of so-called family or matrimonial transplantation. In other words, there is no greater difference in that.

The fact that people are ready to do anything today for commercial or financial reasons, or to risk their health and their lives, and the fact that 35000 people per day die of hunger in the world make it understandable that in the regulative Indian medical law, on none of the 400 pages has transplantation been mentioned – as Dr. Yader claimed at the symposium in Ottawa. The ethical attitude of Western civilization, according to these words, cannot be applied to poor regions, which are much more numerous than rich ones. So, unfortunately, the law which prohibits the human body market finds its application only in the other, smaller part of the world. In the poor countries, poor surgeons must operate, obviously in totally different ethical and medical conditions. Nevertheless it must be admitted that these interpolations and objections of liberal movements, as well as the mentioned statements of eminent Indian physicians have met with understanding in Ottawa and in Western countries, but there is no hope that the attitude towards the human body market as a dirty business will be changed.

Meanwhile, the discussion on these matters has only just started in the world, and it is obvious that the time has come to solve this subtle and important problem through an universally applicable theory. The interests of legislators, politicians, philosophers, religious theorisers, and finally the strongest interest of the patients who are condemned to death must be generally represented in a new international law of transplantation. This law should remove all the previous theories and different experiences of different regions and should be applied everywhere, irrespective of nation, medical budget, or religion.

In this way, the new social and legislative problems in treating a group of the most seriously sick patients are brought about. Under new conditions of treatment, the ethical support of human altruism has changed its quality. It asks from a member of urban society an active participation in the new organization of medical treatment with living substance, totally unknown in medicine in previous periods. The confusion in solving these problems appeared when the rights and obligations of each member of the human community had to be defined in view of a new way of treatment, something which had not been done before. Some new aspects already settled in most countries at the moment are the subject of discussion here, the imperative of which is making certain definitions. At the beginning of such debates, in the countries where the definitions have already been made, we are faced with the first dilemma: what can be used as an individual interest from the biological, not from the sociological point of view considering the organization of a society.

The term "biological community" in a modern society has been clearly defined, and means that for its members it brings certain logical rights and obligations. The standpoint of individual interests applicable in medical treatment and human health preserving came into consideration, and soon it became clear that those interests are contradictory to the social welfare of the most healthy members of one society. To speak simply, this problem is seen through a claim: how it is possible for most of the healthy members of one society to watch with no emotions the dying of a large group of the people who are members of the same society. The lives of the sick ones could be prolonged only if the healthy part of the society together with the physicians leave aside the traditional attitude towards efficient medical treatment and decide to become organ donors after their death, in this way prolonging the lives of the sick people who are – also members of the same society. We must ask ourselves where this lack of emotion on the part of healthy people towards the sufferings of sick ones comes from? It is based on an attitude adopted before the transplantational era and consists of many historic, developing, and ethical theories which accepted the ethical axioma of the hippocratic oath on so-called individual benefit as a general benefit in traditional medical treatment ("To whom the bell tolls? To you" – Hemingway).

Bringing logic into clinical practice and new opinions about organ transplantation raised the question of another type of welfare, which is in opposition to or interferes with individual welfare, i.e., *social welfare*. All this demanded a new approach and the regulation of this matter, in order to aim the interests of society towards the interference between individual and social welfare. Accepting these axiomas in legislation enabled a great deal of the population to be educated towards an attitude that efficient medical treatment can be performed using living substance. This new concept has brought new biological consideration of human wishes, aspirations, and reasons for living. Providing food and maintenance for mankind have become old-fashioned preoccupations of the human race, and the new mutual and individual interests of civilized society found in organ transplantation are the fresh confirmation of these old-fashioned ideas.

So we come from the two above-mentioned opposing opinions to a compromise called utilitarism, i.e., that the only type of welfare is that aimed at a great number of people. The principle of utilitarism, which can be applied to medical ethics, brings us to the relevant solutions of moral problems in the treatment of patients using organ transplantation. That demands the establishment of some international decisions, similar to those applied to the control of nuclear energy or of strategic armaments. The possibility of an individual life and survival after many dangerous and almost uncurable diseases is not an individual or family problem but is conditioned by the high degree of reciprocity of individual interest and solidarity of the environment.

It all should come out of our modern urban life as the only one possible and the only one acceptable in the future.

Perhaps these few thoughts will bring more light and contribute to more equilibrium between some extreme and discouraging attitudes in connection with our subject “the commerce of health”.

## References


1. Bošković S (1987) Organ grafting and human society: kidney transplantation. Svjetlost, Yugoslavia, p 34
2. Levy NB (1981) Psychological reactions to machine dependency: hemodialysis. Psychiat Clin N Amer 4:351–363
3. Law Reform Commission of Canada (1983) Euthanasia, aiding suicide, and cessation of treatment. Minister of Supply and Services, Ottawa, Canada, p. 32
4. Vatican Congregation for the Doctrine of the Faith (1980) Declaration on euthanasia. Rome, pp. 9–10
5. Irwin BC (1986) Ethical problems in organ procurement and transplantation. ANNA 13(6):308
6. McKinley R (1984) Right or wrong: how do we decide? A model for making ethical decisions. J Nephrol Nurs (Sept/Oct):80

# European Community Law and its Effects on Import and Export of Human Cells and Tissue

P.F. W. Strengers

## Introduction

After the Treaty of Rome, it is the European act of 1986 which has given new impulses in reaching the goals of a European Community (EC). EC Commissioner Lord Cockfield presented in 1985 his "White Paper", which included a list of almost 300 directive proposals, which once accepted would be the first steps towards a free circulation of persons, goods, services, and capital in the member states of the EC.

January 1, 1993 will be a historic date, and in the EC countries efforts are being made to realize the unification of the European market after 1992.

The EC was originally founded to create an economic community and, therefore, a uniform system of health care was not integrated into the common goals. After 1992, the health care system of the EC countries will still be organized nationally to a great extent, but it is expected that the realization of one internal market, and the harmonization and integration processes necessary to establish this will affect, directly or indirectly, the health care system in the member countries. To give an example, the objective of the EC concerning free movement of persons and services will be also applicable to health care workers. Not only do medical degrees of the medical faculties of all EC universities have to be accepted in all EC countries, but a system of national protectionism, for example on housing possibilities, control, and prescription facilities will not be allowed.

EC directives and protocols on medicines and medical aids will be of main importance in the free movement of medicinal goods. Because of the disappearance of borders between the member countries, a uniform policy on the prevention of infection diseases will be essential, because those diseases pay no attention to invisible lines which divide member states. And, of no less importance, EC directives and legal regulations will be applicable to liability and risk liability to protect the consumer or the patient in case of damage.

Central Laboratory of the Netherlands Red Cross Blood Transfusion Service, Plesmanlaan 125, 1066 CX Amsterdam. The Netherlands

W. Land, J. B. Dossetor (Eds.)
Organ Replacement Therapy:
Ethics, Justice and Commerce

## Health Care Protection

Other aspects of EC directives will directly or indirectly influence the national health care systems and the position of the patient. For major issues in protection in health care, the course of action will be transferred from national to EC level. This area includes not only activities in the protection against infectious diseases, cancer, drug addiction, and radiation, but also medicines, blood and blood products, sera and vaccines, tissues, organs, and other body material. In this course of action, the proposed regulations to create an internal market are of a high standard. Not only activities like acquired immunodeficiency syndrome (AIDS) prevention or AIDS therapy, prevention of cardiovascular disease, education, and research programs but also new technologies, a European medical passport, and technology assessment will be discussed and organized at EC level.

## Role of the Council of Europe

In the proposals for better health care in Europe, the Health Division of the Council of Europe plays a very active role. The Council of Europe, the oldest international organization founded in 1949, has 24 member states, twice as many as the EC. The Council of Europe prepares only recommendations. Directives which become European legislation are issued by the EC. The Council of Europe defends human rights, social rights, and cultural rights. When there was a flood in the mid-1950s and blood products were sent to that country for therapeutic purposes, there were big problems because labeling was not clear, different languages were used, etc. So it was the Dutch authorities which asked that the only international European organization at that time should take up the subject and see what could be done to make things clear for blood products when they travel throughout Europe.

On December 15, 1958, the Council of Europe came to an agreement on the Exchange of Therapeutic Substances of Human Origin. This Agreement 26 was adopted at the meeting of the Minister Deputies and deals especially with human blood, red cells, leukocytes, platelets, and blood products like fresh frozen plasma, dried human plasma, albumin, immunoglobulins, fibrinogen, and clotting factor preparations. Agreement 26 gives recommendations on the character, identification, tests, assays, storage, quality control, and labeling of the products. It fulfills a specific and unique role as concerns the exchange of whole blood and cellular products among all Council of Europe member states, whether or not they are members of the EC. It also concerns the exchange of human plasma and plasma products among the Council of Europe countries and non-members of the EC (e.g., between Switzerland and Sweden) as well as between these countries and EC countries (e.g., between Switzerland and France).

But Agreement 26 dates from December 1958. To update this agreement, a special committee, the Expert Committee on Blood Transfusion and

Immunohaematology of the Council of Europe, has been formed to revise the parts dealing with cellular products. The European Pharmacopeia Commission has been asked to revise the parts dealing with plasma products. It is expected that final publication will not take place before 1992. This recommendation illustrates how important it is that international agreement exists on products of human origin.

On legal affairs, the Council of Europe has adopted two resolutions which are important in organ transplantation. First, Resolution 29 on the Harmonization of Legislations of Member States Relating to Removal, Grafting and Transplantation of Human Substances. The second is Recommendation R5 on the International Exchange and Transplantation of Human Substances. The main purpose of these resolutions is to achieve a greater unity between the members of the Council of Europe, in particular through harmonizing legislations of member states on removal, grafting, transplantation, and transport of human substances. This is important to ensure the protection of donors, prospective donors, and recipients of human substances to enhance the progress of medical science and therapeutics, and to facilitate transportation. In Resolution 29, adopted on May 11, 1978, the issue is focused on removal, grafting, and transplantation of human substances, and the governments of member states have been recommended to adopt provisions conforming to the resolution or introducing new legislation to identify, by appropriate means, the efforts to inform the public and arouse the interest of doctors on the need and importance of the donation of substances, while keeping the confidential character of individual operations.

In Recommendation R5, adopted on March 14, 1979, the governments of member states have been recommended to take all appropriate measures to facilitate the international exchange and transplantation of human organs, tissues, and other substances and to ensure the safe, speedy, and priority transport of these substances. Furthermore, it was recommended to exempt the substances and their containers from all duties and taxes at importation and exportation. The reason for this recommendation was clear. The need in the member states of the Council of Europe for an adequate supply of suitable organs and tissue had caused an increase in the exchange and transmission of such organs and given rise to wider international cooperation.

The exchange and transmission was a relatively new phenomenon in international cooperation, and it was clear that the legislation and administrative regulations of most member states of the Council of Europe did not contain rules and measures which facilitate the success of such treatments by speeding deliveries of required material. Recommendation R5 was intended to fill the gap and to result in the setting up of a legal framework within which the exchanges can take place.

As with the transport of blood across borders, emphasis was being laid on the gratuitous nature of human substances donation. This principle finds its roots in the practice of almost all member states which treat human substances as *res extra commercium*. Therefore, no price, however large or small, should be put upon the substances. And, therefore, the Recommendation recommends member states to exempt human substances, having regard also to their humanitarian purpose, from all import and export duties and taxes. This will facilitate and encourage their transmission and exchange. It is very important to realize that the Recommendation R5 excludes the international exchange and transplantation of human blood and derivatives which are already covered by the European Agreement on the Exchange of Therapeutic Substances of Human Origin. By this, it has been made clear that organs and tissue are not put on an equivalent basis as blood and blood derivatives. Separate legislation is, therefore, needed.

## EC directives

Separate legislation is very important because on June 14, 1989 the Council of the EC adopted the EC directive 89/381, which deals specifically with medicinal products derived from human blood or human plasma. The main objective of this directive is to create a common market for blood products, like albumin, clotting factors, and immunoglobulin, mainly by harmonizing quality standards. The EC member states, therefore, have to take all necessary measures in order to encourage the self-provision of human blood at EC level. Furthermore, the voluntary and nonremunerated donation of blood and plasma in member countries should, therefore, be stimulated. By adopting this directive, member states have to take the necessary measures to prevent the transmission of infectious diseases and to ensure that human blood and human plasma donors and donation centers are always clearly identifiable. Furthermore, it was stated that these safety guarantees must also be given by importers of human blood or human plasma from non-EC countries.

EC directive 89/381 was preceded by a European Agreement. On January 26, 1987, the Council of the EC adopted Agreement 87/67 on the Exchange of Medicines of Human Origin. This directive is also related to human blood and blood derivatives. Considerations of this agreement were that medicines of human origin can only be provided by the gift of a human donor and, therefore, are applicable only in small quantities. Furthermore, it was highly desirable that the member states should help each other by providing these medicines when there should be a necessity to do so. It was also agreed that this mutual help is only possible when the quality insurance and the use of the products are subject to regulations which are the same in all the member states, and emphasis has been laid that the import of these medicines should be free for the necessary facilities and exempt of all import and export taxes and duties. The considerations for this agreement seem the same as the proposed agreements on organ transplantation.

## Quality Assurance

In the free market, the health care of patients has to be set on an optimal level. Therefore, the EC is planning to develop a system to create optimal quality assurance and quality control in health care. This includes activities to create or support data bases, early warning systems, for example, for reporting the side effects of medicines, and a system analogous to the system functioning in the Netherlands of reporting faults, accidents, and near accidents, the so-called Fona system. By new developments in medicine, questions on medical, ethical, and legal issues are rising. In some issues, like genetics, these questions have caused discussion concerned social borders in these developments, in which the legal position of the individual has been put at the center.

In transplantation too, such discussions have taken place at EC level. As a consequence, it has to be clear that common problems within the EC will require a common solution. It is important that the international organ exchange organizations start to be active in Brussels and take part in the discussion.

## Conclusion

Directives of the EC concerning importation or exportation of human cells and tissues are up to now only available for blood and blood products. There are no directives on import and export of human tissues and human organs. It is important that, given the special nature of substances suitable for transplantation, the starting material, human organs and tissue, is subject to particular safety requirements to prevent the transmission of infectious diseases. Furthermore, it is essential that nondesirable side effects can be prevented. The current negative effect caused by the shortage of organs is the commercial trade in organs, and, therefore, emphasis has to be laid on the use of voluntary donors. Especially in this field, directives are very much needed, and, because this has been discussed thoroughly in the field of blood transfusion, it seems a relatively small step to what is necessary in the field of organ transplantation. It is very important that the European Community should not diminish the quality of care, not only for the patient himself for whose care proposals for procedures of good clinical practice are being discussed at EC level. Also, in legal protection of the health care system, it is essential that this medical treatment which goes across borders whould be of the highest quality.

The Council of Europe and the International Organ Exchange Organizations, therefore, have to be constantly active in Brussels to transfer the ongoing Council of Europe recommendations to EC directives. Lots of common effort is very important and especially needed because health care is not the main interest of the EC. But while a successful program of organ transplantation is only possible because of international cooperation, this international cooperation will also be successful on the European scale of directives.

# Legal and Practical Consequences of the Commercial Use of Human Cells and Tissues

S.B. Rodgers[1], L. Reinbacher[2], P. F. W. Strengers[3], and B. Cohen[4]

With increasing frequency, human organs and tissues are being placed in the stream of commercial transactions to be treated as commodities. The transplant community, the media, and legislative bodies are following this commercial development with intense interest. The following three topics – the commercialization of biotechnology products, the media's response to transplant activities, and the European Community's (EC) development of policies and regulations concerning organ and tissue replacement therapy – highlight many of the ethical and legal concerns facing transplant medicine today. Preparation for the challenges of the future begins with honest appraisal and analysis of the evolution of ethical dilemmas confronting organ and tissue replacement therapy.

## Valuing Donated Organs and Tissues – Balancing Donors' Rights Against Commercial Interests

The issue for discussion is whether a patient has the right to be informed about, to consent to and to share in the profits of the commercial development of his/her tissues. This issue was brought to the fore by the California case, Moore vs. The Regents of the University of California [1].

In 1976, John Moore entered the UCLA Medical Center for confirmation of diagnosis and treatment of hairy cell leukémia. As part of his treatment, Mr. Moore underwent a splenectomy. Mr. Moore's physicians, who were also biotechnology researchers employed by the University, discovered that Mr. Moore's cells contained unique morphologic features.

Through the application of genetic engineering, Mr. Moore's physicians developed a permanent cell line from Mr. Moore's spleen, blood, and other tissue samples. The physicians applied for and were granted a patent for the

[1] Atlanta Legal Aid Society, 151 Spring Street, N.W., Atlanta, Georgia 30335, USA
[2] Lessingstraße 68, 8960 Kempten, FRG
[3] Central Laboratory of the Netherlands Red Cross Blood Transfusion Service, Plesmanlaan 125, 1066 CX Amsterdam, The Netherlands
[4] Eurotransplant Foundation, University Hospital, P.O. Box 9600, 2300 RC Leiden, The Netherlands

W. Land, J. B. Dossetor (Eds.)
Organ Replacement Therapy:
Ethics, Justice and Commerce

cell line which they named MO-CELL after Mr. Moore [2]. Subsequently, the physicians entered into commercial agreements with two pharmaceutical firms, Genetics Institute, Inc. and Sandoz Pharmaceuticals Corporation [3].

The physicians were compensated with cash, shares of common stock, and consulting positions. Throughout the 7 years of development of the cell line, Mr. Moore traveled from his home in Seattle, Washington to Los Angeles to provide blood, bone marrow, and skin samples. At no time was Mr. Moore informed that his cells were being commercialized, nor did he give consent for this commercialization. Mr. Moore became suspicious that all of his appointments to obtain specimens were not solely for his benefit.

Mr. Moore filed a law suit claiming that the blood and spleen taken from him were his property and that they were taken without his consent. He sued his doctors, the University, and the pharmaceutical companies.

## Questions Presented by the Moore Case

1. Do physicians have an obligation and a responsibility to inform patients that removed body parts may be used for research which may lead to commercial opportunities?
2. If yes to the above, will the economic incentive to conduct important medical research be destroyed?
3. Is the value in the cell line or in the spleen itself?
4. Does a physician violate a patient's right to control the disposition of his/her cells by using that patient's cells without specific consent to develop a marketable product?

## Basic Assumptions

Medical research depends upon the free exchange of experimental tissue and ideas. At the same time, public policy opposes placing a monetary value on human tissue, and we have a moral aversion to treating the body as a commodity. Moral attitudes and professional medical standards require that patients be fully and adequately informed of the nature of the scientific research in which they participate because moral and philosophical arguments oppose nonconsensual use of the body. Professional ethics support extension of informed consent to include disclosure of the physician-researcher's aims and expectations. Consent to surgery does not equal consent to medical research unrelated to the patient's treatment. Physicians engaged in biotechnological research who use their patients' tissue as raw material from which biotechnological products are developed create tension between their traditional fiduciary responsibility as health care providers and their new roles as biotechnological researchers.

## Possible Solutions

1. Legislation
   a) Informed consent waiver. A patient waives all right of future claims to any profit.
   b) Right of commerciality. This recognizes the newly developed commercial value of human tissue.
2. Free Market Approach
   At the time of consent to surgery, physician and patient negotiate a fair free market price for the tissue to be removed.
3. Profit Sharing
   Upon the potential of development of a commercial product, physician-researcher and patient negotiate a profit-sharing agreement.

## Recommendations

Organs and tissues donated, recovered, but not transplanted must be considered in light of *Moore*. The donor and/or his next of kin voluntarily give for the betterment of society and mankind. If unused tissue subsequently generates huge profits for third parties, donors and their families will become disenchanted – either donations will drop or potential donors and next of kin will demand to negotiate deals. Both scenarios are disturbing. It is general practice to tell the next of kin that donated organs not transplanted will be used for important, perhaps valuable research. Many donor programs are sensitive to wishes that donated organs and tissues should not be used for research. To date, most probably, donor families are not told that "valuable" could mean huge profits for a researcher. Donor families are not told that donated tissue might be used to develop commercial products.

Organ and tissue donor programs need to establish policies for protecting voluntary donorship. Know to whom your research tissue is distributed and for what purposes it will be used. Negotiate firm contractual arrangements with researchers that organ donor tissue will not be used for development of commercial products. Mr. Moore may have been the first, but most assuredly, he is not the last.

# Commercial Use of the Human Tissue and Cells: From the Media Point of View

## Evolution of Media Coverage of Medicine

The media's involvement in the coverage of medical and health care issues has been an evolutionary process. One hundred fifty years ago, publications appeared offering helpful tips on hygiene and medical matters. Following World War II, most physicians began to report medical innovations and developments; however, physicians were hesitant to provide interviews. Professor Christiaan Barnard not only threw open the gates of a new era in medical science, he also motivated medical journalism.

## Media Coverage of Donation and Transplantation

Media coverage of transplantation was slow to develop because the procedures were considered exotic and difficult for the public to understand. Development of cyclosporine changed the face of transplantation and, accordingly, the media's attention to transplant activity, particularly in the area of heart transplantation. Increasing public interest in health issues motivated the media to hire specialty medical journalists to provide improved coverage. Smaller media organizations may still be less inclined to hire specialists because of the cost. Many of the medical journalists strive to fairly and accurately present the facts and, as a result, transplant surgery enjoys almost unreserved approval.

## Sensational Journalism

Mavericks' efforts to commercialize organ donation and distribution have provided fuel for articles detailing the kidnapping of individuals who are then forced to become donors. Much attention has been given to the exploitation of the poor in order to provide organs for the rich. Recent coverage of the London story involving a Turkish farmer who underwent surgery highlighted how the patient was told he had an appendectomy when in fact his doctors had performed a donor nephrectomy. Another topic of much debate in the press is the utility of multiorgan transplants which appear to enjoy limited success while using considerable organ resources. Sensational coverage generates concern in the public about transplant activities.

## Continuing Challenges to Media Interest

Many editors believe that transplant stories require a "local feel." The German press declined to carry a story on the first segmental liver transplant because the donor and the patient were American and only the surgeon was German. In addition, editors refuse to carry potentially unsuccessful stories.

## Media Coverage of the Use of Human Cells and Tissues

The use of human cells and tissues in replacement therapy does not enjoy the same treatment afforded organ donation and transplantation. The public lacks the personal, emotional involvement in the implantation of tissues. Both the public and the media are unconcerned about the sources of tissues, such as inner ear ossicles and blood.

While the coverage of use of human tissue is limited, for the most part, it is positive as evidenced by the high esteem placed on blood donation. Medical coverage of the risk of transmission of the human immunodeficiency virus (HIV) has contributed to the intensifying of efforts to develop appropriate pharmaceutical alternatives to human products. Industry responds to public pressure as represented by the media.

### Recommendations

Form open and honest relationships with the media in your area. Take the time to educate the media concerning the ethical dilemmas facing organ and tissue replacement therapy. The media is a channel for the delivery of information and can be used to great advantage. However, the user must know how to play by the rules.

## EC Law and Its Effect on Import and Export of Human Cells and Tissues

The EC was founded to create an economic community. No uniform system of health care was integrated into the development plan. After 1992, health care will remain, in large part, a national concern; however, the EC will legislate health care protection measures. The objective of the free movement of persons and services within the EC will include health care workers. EC directives and protocols will be developed to facilitate the free movements of pharmaceuticals and medical aids. Review of the following will be transferred from a national arena to the EC level: prevention of and control of the transmission of infectious diseases, treatment and prevention of cancer, treatment and prevention of drug addiction, regulation of blood, blood products, organs, and other bodily materials, acquired immunodeficiency syndrome (AIDS) prevention and treatment, diagnosis, treatment, and prevention of cardiovascular disease, and assessment and development of new technologies.

On June 14, 1989, the EC adopted EC directive 89/381 which deals with products derived from human blood and plasma. The main objective of this directive is to create a common market for blood products, to harmonize quality standards, to encourage self-provision of human blood, and to ensure that donation is voluntary and nonremunerated. Directive 89/381 will form the basis for regulation of organ and tissue donation and distribution.

It is expected that the EC will look to the Council of Europe for recommendations before developing directives in the health area. Although the Council of Europe only makes recommendations, it has been very active in the development of health policy. In 1958, the Council issued Agreement 26 concerning the Exchange of Therapeutic Substances of Human origin. This agreement provided recommendations regarding the identification, testing, storage, labeling, assaying, and quality control of blood and blood products. The Council's goal was to facilitate the exchange of these substances among member states.

Significant development have occurred since 1958, and in response, the Council of Europe has formed the Expert Committee on Blood Transfusion and Immunohaemotology to revise sections of Agreement 26 dealing with cellular products. Recommendations made by the Council of Europe are geared toward enhancing and promoting unity. The Council of Europe has facilitated the process of donation by developing brain death criteria. Resolution 29, pertaining to the removal and transplantation of human substances, and Recommendation 5, regarding the international exchange and transplantation of human substances, ensure protection of donors and recipients of human substances, enhance the progress of medical science, and aid in the transplantation and distribution of human substances.

Human substances should be treated as *res extra commercium*. Rather than placing a monetary value on organs and tissues, international exchange occurs based on the humanitarian value of these substances.

### Recommendations

European transplantation organizations should lobby at the supranational level for legislation and regulations designed to enhance and facilitate organ and tissue donation and distribution. EC directives concerning blood donation and the distribution of blood and blood products offer guidelines from which to develop policies.

## Conclusion

The foregoing presentations delivered three important messages. First, organ and tissue donor programs should establish tissue sharing policies geared to protecting voluntary donorship. Those involved in organ replacement therapy activities should develop open and honest relationships with the media. And lastly, European transplant programs should lobby for legislation designed to support and further develop transplantation.

## References


1. Moore versus Regents of the University of California, 51 Cal. 3d 120, 793 P. 2d 479 (1990)
2. Moore versus Regents of the University of California, 51 Cal. 3d 120, 793 P. 2d 480 (1990)
3. Moore versus Regents of the University of California, 51 Cal. 3d 120, 793 P. 2d 481 (1990)

# General Discussion: The Intra- and Intracultural Commerce in Human Organs and Tissues

*Brynger:* As the moderator of the session, I think it's about time to try to start the discussion. The first question comes from Prof. Thiel; he has a very specific question that we might possibly have an answer to.

*Thiel:* In order to avoid the kidney trafficking to Bombay and Madras from Switzerland, I plan for my own university in Basle to do two things. First of all, pass out the warning of HIV, hepatitis, and early death, this will certainly function, and the second rule, and this is now referring to the question, I want to state officially, also perhaps in the newspaper, that we won't follow up any uremic patient who has got a bought kidney wherever. My first question now, a legal question: Is it legal to say, we won't treat you if you come back with a bought kidney? And the second, a medical ethical question: Am I allowed as a doctor to say: I won't treat you, even if you come with a rejection and all of that, I won't treat you. So, legally, medically and ethically, can I do that?

*Akveld:* I'll try to give you an answer. If I understood you correctly you said, a person who came back to your country from abroad and who was ill in a sense, and he offered himself to you for treatment, you would think about refusing treatment. I can't speak for Switzerland, but I could speak for Holland and I would say that, in that situation, you as a doctor have the obligation to treat the patient, even though you didn't like what he did when he was abroad. But coming back and being in your country, the rules of your country are priorities in that case and I would say that you should help him and ought to see him.

*Thiel:* I spoke about treating the kidney, the rejection, acute renal failure, and giving him prescriptions for Imuran, for cyclosporine. If I refuse to do that, and that's what I'm talking about, am I legally allowed to say I won't accept him in my practice?

---

The general discussion sessions were transcribed from tape recordings made during the conference. In the interest of a rapid publication, the individual speakers/discussants did not see their own comments and questions before the book went to press. One of the editors (W. Land) tried to make obviously necessary corrections in the manuscripts derived from the tape recordings and then authorized the publication of the sessions in their present form. Therefore, incorrect publication of the comments or questions with regard to style, content, etc. might be possible in the view of the speakers concerned. We apologize for any possible inaccuracies.

W. Land, J. B. Dossetor (Eds.)
Organ Replacement Therapy:
Ethics, Justice and Commerce

*Akveld:* What you would be saying is, what the patient did was a fault. He shouldn't have done it. You are playing a judge in that case. People do a lot of wrong things in your eyes, maybe, but you could not draw your own conclusions every time as if you were a judge, or would not do, what a doctor should do and that is help the people. And that's my answer.

*Engelhardt:* I would think that you would treat people who acquire sexually transmitted diseases because they failed to use prophylactics as they should have. I presume you would treat patients who acquire hepatitis or HIV infections from the illegal use of drugs elsewhere. Generally, physicians have treated people, even if the ways in which they have conducted themselves are illegal. I presume you would treat someone who was shot by the police while trying to rob or rape or murder. Usually physicians treat patients who get severely injured, even if they are doing things we all think are terrible.

*Siegler:* I agree with the first two respondents. I think the exceptions to that general rule are limitation of resources and real allocational questions. So if, for example, in the case you gave, the person jumped a queue that existed by going out of the country and getting a transplant, and then returning the country to re-enter the queue at the head of the line, essentially in the face of the rejection, I think you might legitimately invoke the original allocational decision that was delaying whatever, dialysis or transplantation. You can say that bypassing the system does not give you an entitlement to gain a higher level on the queue than you were otherwise entitled to. But it would be that allocational matter, rather than the cause of the patient's problem. I tend to agree that we physicians usually treat people regardless of whether we like the way they got sick or not. We cannot blame them for their illness, but we treat the problem before us.

*Engelhardt:* Dr. Siegler what would you say, though, if the person is not receiving governmental care, but is paying for it himself, and it's not tax-deductable. What is the difference between that and buying a BMW?

*Siegler:* I'm saying that there can still be allocational questions that all of us could face, regardless of the source of the financing of the care.

*Engelhardt:* Then one gets into a view of how powerful a state ought to be, something one should reflect on when having a meeting in Germany.

*Siegler:* I think we should move on to the next question. I think Dr. Abouna has a comment.

*Abouna:* Yes, actually we met that problem in Kuwait in an earlier situation. We asked our ethicist, the legal people, and the religious people, and were told you *have* to treat the patient, regardless of where he received his treatment, whether or not you agree or disagree on how it was done. A exception, we were informed, is if you had informed that individual that when he came back from receiving the treatment in a way that you think isn't correct, your conscience will not be able to treat him, but there is another doctor who can take care of him. Otherwise, you really have to treat him. And we treated all the patients in the same way as if they were our own patients. You have to treat.

*Thiel:* That's the whole point of the thing, it's a preventive measurement. It's a threat.

*Abouna:* May I help, you mean that if you had a system of warning, would it help to eliminate the buying and selling of organs?

*Thiel:* I think in another country, if you put in the newspaper that the medical association states that if somebody goes and buys a kidney in Madras, he won't be reimbursed for the medication, and he will not be followed up at home; he can stay in Madras to be followed up there. I am sure that this would be very brutal and I'm not sure whether it is right to do so. This is what I'm asking all those experts. I don't know whether one should do it, but it would be a very effective and preventive method.

*Siegler:* Thank you. Dr. Henne-Bruns, I think you addressed a question to Dr. Daar; do you want to ask a question?

*Henne-Bruns:* Yes. Dr. Daar clearly draws a line for living kidney donations between the different categories, and you see the line between category IV and V depending on the country where this transplantation is performed. My question is, where do you see this potential line for other organs like lungs, pancreas, bowel, and liver segments? Because we will have to face this problem in the near future. At the moment, there is the argument that these organs or the segments can only be transplanted in highly specialized institutions, but looking forward to the development of transplantation, I think that will change in the very near future. So the question is: Where do you see the limit according to the five categories for other organs except the kidney? Which category could be accepted for living organ donation or living segment donation?

*Daar:* I was trying to describe the historical development with this line of thought, and that really applies only to kidneys. However, that does not mean that it cannot be generalized to other organs, provided that the other organs go to the same state of development and reach the same stage of success and the risk involved is the same. I would think that then the same arguments would apply. But if, and the mere reason why you are asking the question is that it does not apply, other organs have special characteristics, my line of argument wouldn't apply.

*Siegler:* Dr. Sells had one aspect of a question which was addressed to Prof. Radcliffe-Richards. It noted that the adverse consequences of paid donation might include the encouragement of a slippery slope, which might result in a poor man donating everything, including vital organs, for the sake of his family. In a way, the question about unpaired organs, I think, leads us towards that aspect of Dr. Sells' question.

*Radcliffe Richards:* Yes. One of the things I left out in my paper in my rush, was a discussion of the general problem that if you allow some practice at all, there is always the danger that people are going to be pushed into it against their will.

Now, I think that's a line of argument which might possibly work in this case. But it's a line which you have to be very cautious about taking, because it's true of any kind of freedom whatever. If you are allowed to do anything, then there is a chance you may be pushed into it. And it isn't – if you believe in individual freedom – and that's why you don't want people to be cursed, it's no good starting with the idea that you must prevent everyone doing it in order to stop the risk of a few people being pushed into it.

You would have to produce a very good argument that it was worth it in that particular case. There was more harm that resulted from allowing the risk for this to happen to a few people than a blank prohibition on everybody.

*Siegler:* Now, let me just try the question directly: under the auspices of economy someone wants for very good reasons, reasons such as the education of a child, the health of a child or something else, to donate a whole liver or to donate a heart, and has perfectly good reasons, I mean persuasive reasons. Now, is that the kind of gift one would be prepared to accept or to reimburse one for?

*Radcliffe Richards:* A greater love has no man than this that he should lay down his life to his friends.

*Sells:* I must respond to that. One of the legal, I'm sorry, one of the political forms was discussed, namely, the House of Commons committee before the UK passed the Organ Transplant Bill. Now, "greater love has no man" applies specifically to a concept of a soldier laying down his life involuntarily for his friends. Now, are we going to try and draw any parallels between that sort of mental condition and a phenomenon, the bottom end of that slippery slope, which I just mentioned to Prof. Siegler and which could ultimately lead to the, if you like, legalized homicide by a surgeon.

*Radcliffe Richards:* You say legalized homicide, but this is supposed to be with people who are saying they want to do it. This is not the matter of the surgeon going and pinching people's organs.

*Sells:* Well, it's killing by a surgeon and it's legal, that is legalized homicide.

*Radcliffe Richards:* Why do you call it killing rather than, if you like, assisted suicide.

*Sells:* As a matter of fact, I don't care about the semantics. It's the image I have in my mind which I think is very important. No, the serious point about this is that of a surgeon who sees this as a possible consequence of his action of taking an organ from a paid donor, no matter how remote this possibility actually is. And it's not really remote in some countries, particularly in Latin America. A possible consequence of that is a slippery slope which leads to commodification, a relaxation of the standards of society which could ultimately cause the political condoning of the ultimate sacrifice. The best way to prevent that ever happening is to stop now, and I believe that's a very popular response to that objection.

*Engelhardt:* I take it there are only three ways that one can transfer money and organs or interdict the transfer: 1. by state power, 2. by market choices, 3. by altruism. Those are the only ways in which organs and money get transferred. You have to look at the history of the world to decide where the greatest abuses have come from. That is, state attempts to do the good or freedom in chaotic choices. Now, if you want to place things into very global circumstances, that's where the discussion begins.

Good answers are made in terms of partial solutions to difficult problems. What so impressed me when Dr. Abouna spoke about the problems of prohibiting or allowing the sale of organs in all of the examples which involved areas where good oversight was not possible, was that there were no intrinsic difficulties. If I understood correctly the interesting thing that you did was to make reference to the similarity with the prohibition of drugs. And I would just ask you how successful has the prohibition of drugs been in allowing the interdiction of world-wide commerce, etc. I don't think you have a picture, if you try to look at global understandings, you have to look at the way in which you have little institution alization, and probably a good example is prostitution. Probably no one here wants to support prostitution. In the United States, it is generally forbidden, and one has a great number of prostitutes who are HIV infected. In Germany, prostitution is regularized. I take the point that Dr. Reddy was making, that if you look at a problem that's unlikely to be solved in terms of general prohibition, (and where you don't have a good argument to show what's wrong with commercialization in another setting) then you look for partial solutions and partial regulations. I've yet to hear any good argument about what's wrong with commercialization in another setting.

*Abouna:* If I could answer that: the fact is that we have failed, or the system has failed, in the control of drugs. What you are saying is that we will fail also in what we are trying to do in the case of the sale of organs. This is an argument against trying. The worst thing that a man can do is not fail, but not try. I mentioned the example of drugs, only in the context of a crime being committed as cause of the buying and selling of drugs. It's the same as the sale of drugs; there are a lot of criminal things happening in the sale of organs, if you follow the same methods, and I only emphasize that aspect. The reason I mention that is I did not equate the trafficking of drugs with the sale of organs, except that both of them are exposed to crime.

*Engelhardt:* I can't understand what you are doing, because you are appealing to an example that undercuts your position. If you appeal to the example of drugs, you appeal to where an absolute prohibition has failed.

*Abouna:* There is no other way in which you could do it. Can I just comment on what Dr. Daar said? Dr. Daar said that he is against the rampant commercialization of organs because it is organ sale. But he does not think that so-called rewarded gifting is wrong. Now, as I said earlier, rewarded gifting is a contradiction in itself, because you cannot have a gift and also have a reward. The issue here is, the so-called rewarded gifting is the same as organ sale, except it is a controlled sale of organs. That's the only difference. The actors in both of these acts are as follows: the donor and the recipient, a broker, a doctor and a hospital in the rampant sale of organs. With rewarded gifting you have the same actors, you just remove the brokers only. So the right term for it is really a controlled sale of organs.

The other comment I have is, it is not true of what is happening in the United States, and I think this may have been misunderstood, that there is now the tendency to pay for organ donation. I think this is unfair, because that's not what's happening.

What is happening in the United States is to encourage the donation of organs by instituting a number of incentives, and these are of three categories. I think all of these are ethically and morally acceptable. One is to exempt the donor's family from financial obligations, such as income tax, for example, or inheritance tax, or funeral costs. This exemption of that is an incentive. The second group of incentives is to pay for the loss of work, if this is incurred, and also to give pension to a widow who has lost her husband and who has allowed his organ to be donated. This is done by the state and not by any individual or hospital. The third incentive is to provide some kind of insurance for the family of the donor after his death and after his donation. This is again done by the state.

I think all these categories of incentives are ethically acceptable. And none of them involves the direct sale of organs in which approaches or contracts are made between a donor and a group of doctors or a hospital. And I think this could also be done in the Middle East or in India, when a cadaver organ program is established. It will help, and I think this is the way that you should be encouraging our Indian colleagues, rather than to accept or condone a so-called controlled sale of organs.

*Siegler:* Thank you. I want the audience to recognize that the three incentives that Dr. Abouna has just referred to are not yet policy. We should understand that these, as Dr. Daar pointed out in his paper, are really proposals that have been brought in by one or several people in the transplant community. None of these is currently legislation. I wonder, if I could ask Bernard Dickens to raise the question that he addressed to Dr. Radcliffe-Richards. And I just wonder if that same question might not be addressed to Dr. Fluss at the WHO.

*Dickens:* Yes, in part. The last observations that Dr. Abouna made are related to this. The question is, whether the repugnance that was felt in the United Kingdom to the experience of a Turkish donor is not so much the repugnance to the exploitative sale, but to the unfair approach, that is, the wealthy people obtaining services not available to others. One approach might be to unlink sale and purchase. An agency such as the National Health Service, which of course in enduring costs to maintain patients on dialysis, might pay for an organ and then allocate according to medical need, not according to personal wealth.

*Radcliffe Richards:* I'm only guessing about the causes of repugnance, but it's the idea that it's repugnant that people should get care, because they are rich. It should apply equally to any sort of care, and I felt it would apply equally to things like having a better diet and all the other things that keep you in better health, because you are rich. It seems to me that people don't go into that degree of repugnance towards these things. Now, if they do, they are morally justified, as far as I am concerned, but then the issue is not the transplant and not the living donor.

*Engelhardt:* I think we have all kinds of disparities which we live with, and if we don't want to correct that, we are hypocritical. The poor have to engage in risky labor, much more risky than being kidney transplant donors, and all this is sustained in many parts of the world. If you think that that risk invalidates their consent, then you must think that everyone in the developed world is engaged in pressed labor.

But beyond that, when I drive around Houston, I drive around in a small compact car, because I don't have enough money to have a crash-resistent expensive one. I don't think that's unfair, it's a real difference.

*White:* A couple of quick points I wanted to make: One relates to the prohibition of drugs. It seems to me that the point about prohibiting drugs is not so much that it has failed, as that the attempt to prohibit them has been counter-productive in that it stimulates criminal activities, which are arguably orders of magnitude worse than the drug problem in the first place. I think we have to bear this in mind, if we are talking or prohibiting the sale of kidneys.

The second point relates to slippery slopes. And that is, that it seems to be just as logical to put the slope between altruistic organ donation, live related organ donation, and going all the way down to the donation of a non-paired organ on a commercial basis. We must then say that you draw the line at the level where people give up their non-paired organs, rather than drawing the line between altruistic donation and commercial donation. It seems to me that this is not at all logical, that the altrustic is not on the same slope.

*Engelhardt:* Anti-drug laws are price-support systems for drug dealers.

*Fluss:* All that I can say is, I think it is extremely important that we've had here a very free and very frank discussion. I think that it's very important that individuals from different backgrounds express points of view which are not in line with the general global consensus from this issue.

But I don't think we should forget for one moment that as a single professional society, a professional grouping around the world – I stand to be corrected, perhaps in South East Asia – there has been virtual unanimity in every government which has addressed this issue, whether it's a national government a sub-national government, a group of transplantation surgeons, or groups such as the World Medical Association or Ministers of Health. And I don't think the unanimity indicates that all of those individuals and all of the institutions have been guilty of faulty reasoning. I think one can rationally come to a decision using philosophical arguments, that there is basically nothing wrong with slavery, and, of course, the case was made by respectable philosophers. These are religious arguments. Whether it be slavery, whether it be prostitution, whether it be altruistic suicide, in order to save someone else's life, these are all true. But the fact remains that we are dealing with a situation which has been examined in different cultures, in different religions, and in virtually every case. There has been a strong unanimous agreement that the practice of mutilation of the human body, for whatever reason, is, in general, (with the exceptions we have all discussed here such as limitations) not something the global community can live with where commerce is involved.

*Radcliffe Richards:* There are several points there. John Stewart Mill pointed out that one of the commonest arguments for keeping women in their inferior position to men was that this had always been done, and all society has agreed about it. I don't think the fact that all societies have agreed about slavery in the past argues for its continuation; we've got beyond that. It doesn't seem to me that it's so clear.

Many societies have also practised mutilation as parts of their culture. It's quite a different point.

*Fluss:* For commerce!

*Radcliffe Richards:* No! Could I just make a general remark about slippery slope arguments? There are very well-known forms of fallacy. Normally, if you have something at one end of the slope that's good and at the other end something that's bad, and there is a slope between them, what we try to do is alter our behavior at the two ends of the slope. If people can give will-informed consent to something, we let them decide, and, at the other extreme, they are manifestly incapable of giving consent to either side. In between this there is a grey area where we really don't know what to do. The only people who say we must treat everybody as if they were at one end of the scale are the people who have other reasons for everyone to be treated at the end of the scale.

The impulse, if you really care about getting it right is to say, let's try to make a distinction. This is an argument used about euthanasia. It's often said that we cannot allow voluntary euthanasia, because it's a danger to the people who will be pushed into it against their will.

If we really care about letting people do what they want, we will see whether we can devise safeguards and regulations. We'll do all we can. If we rule out at the outset the possibility of creating these safeguards, it shows that what we really want is to prevent euthanasia.

Now, I'm not denying that there are dangers in implementing this paid donation. I'm just saying that, if what we are against is the exploitation and the pressure, we will aim at that first and only outflow the whole thing as a last resort. We won't jump immediately to that.

*Siegler:* Thank you. Dr. Freund, would you like to ask your question please?

*Freund:* The question is especially to Mr. Fluss, Mr. Akveld, and Dr. Abouna. What we heard about today was some asking for some legislative consequences, and this sanctions, again, the organ transplantation tourism from certain second world countries to the Third World.

Mr. Fluss, what do you think you would vote for in the case of legislative consequences. And if you would vote for them, what kind of law would you prefer with what kinds of punishment and for whom? For the donor, for the recipient, for the broker or, maybe, for the surgeon?

*Fluss:* Let me answer that question very briefly: I don't think that there is any universal recipe to that question. I think it depends tremendously on national context. For example, in a country such as the United Kingdom, it was deemed appropriate for the offending members of the medical profession to be put into prison or even fined, but to be subjected to penalties, professional penalties, imposed by their peers and by their fellow colleagues in the medical profession. This, of course, was done in the United Kingdom by the General Medical Council.

Now, that might be appropriate in one country. Elsewhere there might be a need for penal sanctions, but I don't think anyone can really answer that question in a universal, global way. This will depend entirely on traditions and contexts.

*L. Cohen:* I wanted to agree and to make a few statements and comments about the panel and whether to agree with Dr. Abouna that the term "rewarded gifting" is misleading. I would simply view it as an awful euphemism.

It's a desire to create a market, and one person may believe the market has virtues in this area and another person may not. This euphemism adds nothing to it. I was rather confused because the suggestion that Prof. Abouna found attractive would have been made with regard to the US cadaver donor market and precisely that, a *market!* These are creations of some sort of market incentive "in other forms" such as paying for funerals and rewards to widows. But it's nothing more than a market. And to quote something else, perhaps an ineffective market adds no great virtue to it.

Let me also say, a number of the panelists have suggested that instead of paying for organs from live donors, one should encourage post cadaver donation. Well, in the United States, we have been trying to encourage post cadaver donation for about 35 years without a great deal of success. So, this touches again on Prof. Engelhardt's point of the three ways in which goods can be transferred. By government affairs, by altruism, or by a market. And, although, I am an altruistic person and would gladly give you one of my organs, I don't think that's a universal characteristic. To waste resources in that attempt, rather than to rely on the institution that provides us with beautiful buildings and nice meals, also provide us with organs. I think this is a mistake.

Finally, with respect to Dr. Reddy, the universality of the repugnance to organ donation by many nations that have assed on this and by learned societies, I think, is morally persuasive in the sense that, when many people agree on something it is worth looking at more closely.

But when you look at it more closely, first of all you can find that there is a special interest at work, second, you can also find that what we have here is something that may be an anachronism. Prior to 35 years ago, there was no good use for the parts of other people's bodies and perhaps we are simply carrying on this moral anachronism at a time when it's no longer relevant, no longer appropriate.

*Abouna:* I'd like to answer this. The reason why I accepted the group of incentives which you mentioned is not because the paid sale of organs from one individual to another or to a hospital is open to the exploitation of the donor or recipient. Secondly, they do not force a donor to sell his organs. There is no coercion here. And three, they give equity of access. Anybody who donates, rich or poor, gets the same. And four, I think, they are not open to abuse in the market place, where the price would go up and down, depending who is doing it, who is selling it. It's the state that is controlling it for everybody. And I think for these reasons that they are acceptable.

*Daar:* Being an optimist, I knew a day would come when Dr. Abouna would agree with me! He has exactly described what rewarded gifting is. He is telling us that it's alright to tell the wife of a deceased that she's going to get 10 000 US dollars worth of tax rebate or funeral expenses, or whatever, and this is not a contract. But it's wrong to say, 10 000 US dollars will be paid to you, madam, if you allow me to take the kidney from your husband.

This is donation with incentive, which is the second type of rewarded gifting. Now, you may think that the term "gifting" cannot go with the term of "rewarded": I would like to comment on that, but let me just remind you, and this is purely from the linguistic point of view, that this is not a judgement on whether it's right.

In society, gifts would have absolutely no meaning if they were not returned. And, therefore, a gift by definition needs to be returned, otherwise it has absolutely no meaning. It increases solidarity, it only exists because it is returned. If you didn't get Christmas cards back from the people you sent them to, then you'd stop sending them.

So, to say that gifts are meant to be a one-way traffic, is just self-deception.

But that does not mean I condone it. And the reason you were not able to discern my position was that I did not state it. I have never stated my position, and in order to remain a commentator on this subject, I will never tell you what my position is.

*Abouna:* Could I just say one thing very quickly: the incentives which I mentioned and which are now being discussed in the United States, are to do with cadaveric transplantation.

*Daar:* I talked about living nonrelated donation!

*Abouna:* Well, maybe he did. However, if we have no organ shortage from cadavers, the problem which we are now discussing will not even arise. So there are two solutions to the problems that we are facing today: First of all more organs should be made available, and secondly, the economic system of the third world should be improved.

And these are the two reasons, why people are selling their organs. The various organs which are now being obtained, represent one-tenth, both in Canada and in the United States, of what could be obtained.

And, therefore, before we go into this problem of buying and selling, let us see if we can improve that. These incentives are simply one way to improve the supply of cadaveric organs and this would be a solution, one solution, to the problems of buying and selling human organs from living individuals and the coercions and other forms of exploitation.

*Daar:* The wife agrees to give a gift of her dead husband's kidneys. And the state rewards her by excusing her from some taxes. This is exactly rewarded gifting.

*Abouna:* This is *after* death!

*Siegler:* I do want to call to the attention of the audience to a problem there has been all through the afternoon, I don't know if you share it with me, and that's the problem of incentives to increase the use of living donors and incentives to increase the use of cadaveric organs. This seems to me to be an ongoing impressing question, as to which of these mechanisms we are dealing with at a particular moment in terms of increasing incentives.

*Hanggardner:* Two things really, a comment about what just Mr. Fluss said a few moments ago about the situtation in the UK. He said that the matter that was discussed by the GMC was handled in a professional ethical form. I mean, that is correct, because at that time there was no legislation in the UK.

Since the passage of the Human Organs Transplant Act 1989, there is scope to proceed against virtually anybody who has had anything to do with commercial trafficking as defined in the Act in Human Organs. And that would include the surgeon, the donor, the recipient, and the authorities controlling the institution in which it took place.

There is an important caveat in the Act, which is that any prosecution is brought by the director of public prosecution. And he would actually determine if it was appropriate to prosecute without prejudicing his view. The other thing, I have a question which is related to what you just said a moment ago, Mr. Chairman, namely, does the state have the right to offer incentives to people to donate, in order to avoid having to meet the costs of a properly organized hemodialysis program or to meet the costs of a properly founded cadaveric donation program?

Because it seems to me that you could argue under these circumstances that the state is in fact doing exactly what one is objecting to which is exploiting people.

*Daar:* A very difficult issue. It would seem that that is what my American colleagues are now proposing, that you pay – because it does ultimately constitute payment to the potential donor – in order to reduce the waiting lists and in order to relieve the pressure on dialysis facilities and save money ultimately.

It's an investment on part of the government. So, if this is going to be done by the Americans, it would be exactly what you were saying, and the answer would be: yes.

However, my position in this is – as I keep saying – I'm a commentator on this, and if you are going to say that this is alright, I will quote you next time.

*Siegler:* I just want a point of clarification. I don't want the audience to leave this meeting with the sense that the only proposals going around in America at the moment are for the commercialization of organ donations. That is, I would still suggest, at best a minority prospective. I have been to three meetings in the last 3 months and here they are still figuring out ways to increase traditional organ donation through educational means and a variety of other incentives.

The second approach which is reemerging, and I suspect will have greater power in the wake of the decisions in the United States Supreme Court 6 months ago, is a return to the right of individuals to make advance statements as to what they want to have done with themselves, when they die. That was the old uniform Anatomical Gift Act in America, which failed, and which was involved with the signing of a driver's license.

I think there is a big movement to try to revive advanced directives on the part of individuals to increase organ donation. So I just don't want to appear, that that is the only proposal currently on the table. I would agree with the speakers that it is one of the proposals that is circulating.

*Simforoosh:* I think it's unfair to say that all of the recipients are on the rich side. In our country in the last 4 years, most of the recipients were poor people who had their dialysis programs sponsored by the government. And, in fact, either the government or other people had helped the recipients to be able to find a kidney.

Secondly, we should not merely close our eyes to the recipients' ethical rights. As I see from the morning's papers, all the discussion has been focused on the ethical aspects, on the donor's aspects, and the little child with no hopes for life, but there have been many cases in which unrelated donation has been their only hope. We have 4 years of experience in unrelated donor transplantation in a controlled way. We have had about 400 unrelated donor transplantations in our country, with excellent results of between 80 % and 90 % for 1-year graft survival.

*Siegler:* I'm sorry, that's for liver, kidney?

*Simforoosh:* Kidney, unrelated. To be realistic about this governmental and legislative aspect and realistic to the community, so that nobody would be harmed, what we recommend, as we have done, is that exploitation should be stopped, and illegal practices and middlemen avoided. Only the recipient, donor, and a medical team should be involved. We choose the schedule, and the families were on priority lists. Altogether I can say, if the governments support the poor recipients in despair and if we encouraged altruism, if we take all this into account, there are common advantages, and all have benefited from this, and it has been done in a right and fair way. I think this could be a model and could be studied in detail. We have no time to discuss that now.

*Brynger:* Thank you everybody. I would really like to thank all the speakers of today for making this afternoon very full, and I would like to thank the audience for their patience. Thank you very much everybody now.

# IV. *The Dilemma of Post Mortem Organ Donation: Are There Any Donation-Facilitating Factors Which are Potentially Suppressed on the Basis of Ethical or Legal Considerations?*

# *Post Mortem Organ Donation and Brain Death as Death of a Person*

## Brain Death as Death of a Human Being: A Matter of Image of Man

H. Angstwurm

Brain dcath signifies the complete and irreversible loss of all brain function as a consequence of the brain having died in its entirety, while intensive care and mechanical respiration initially keep the remaining parts of the body alive. This form of death can only assume importance in the intensive care unit. In terms of outward appearance, it is characterized by the fact that the person who has suffered brain death looks as if he were still alive.

A subsequent autopsy, however, shows that the phenomena of decay resulting from death have advanced further in the brain than in the other organs, proving that the brain has been dead longer than the other organs. The brain dies as soon as pressure in the cranial cavity, increasing to a level above the blood pressure, prevents blood from flowing through the brain. The definition of brain death is based solely on the pathological process, on the death of the whole organ in its entirety, and cannot be applied to the death of just one part of the brain. For this reason medical science makes a definite distinction between brain death and any defective development of the brain, however severe it may be, any injury leading to only partial absence of brain activity, and any temporary absence of brain activity such as is evident in a specific state of embryonic development.

The diagnosis brain death means a specific, recognizable condition which has developed previously at an unknowable moment in time. This means that it is a purely technical question, not an ethical one, and certainly not a question that can be determined on the basis of the patient's earlier wishes. It is not a question of the physician's judgment or a question of prognosis, nor is it a declaration of death that is only binding in legal terms and which could be revoked.

Although brain death is self-evident and its diagnosis beyond doubt, the physician can be thankful for the fact that it is also accepted outside the field of medicine as a certain sign of death in human beings, as seen in the joint publication of the German Conference of Bishops and the Council of the Protestant Church of Germany *Organtransplantationen,* as well as in the

Neurologischer Konsiliard der Innenstadtkliniken, Neurologische Klinik der Universität München, Ziemssenstr. 1, 8000 München 2, FRG

W. Land, J. B. Dossetor (Eds.)
Organ Replacement Therapy:
Ethics, Justice and Commerce

answers from Islamic and Jewish theologians and from lawyers to our written inquiries.

Medical science needs the support and counsel of the humanities to counter some philosophers who question this interpretation of brain death, these very humanities to which, in the words of Buchborn, medicine owes its humaneness, and to which medicine has proposed and will continue to propose the statement that in brain death man loses two characteristics of his earthly existence as an intellectually and spiritually gifted organism.

Intellectually and spiritually gifted denotes the basic, immutable difference between man and other living beings. Intellect and spirit mean awareness, discernment, reason, freedom and responsibility, joy and sorrow, the ability to transcend the material world and sensual perception, and to relate to a superior world independent of man. It also implies the capacity for cultural achievement. This spirituality also pertains to the human soul as the embodiment of inner unity, the essence of each individual human being. For Christians, man is the image of God (*imago Dei*) and each individual intellect and soul has been created by God as the intrinsic characteristic of the body. When it comes to the connecting link between the human intellect and the human body, scientific medicine can only state – but *can* state with certainty – that the brain is necessary and irreplaceable for this link. This outstanding attribute of the brain makes it neither the "seat" of the soul, nor the "origin" of the intellect, regardless of whether one interprets man dualistically, as consisting of a body and a soul, as in two separate parts, or monistically, as existing as a unity of intellect and soul and a body transfigured by the latter (*anima rationalis forma corporis humani* according to Thomas Aquinas). But the importance of the brain for the human spirit suffices to maintain that with the death of his brain, man will lose that essential bodily prerequisite for his intellect to partake in, or to have any effect on this world.

The organism is the form of existence taken by man and any other living creature on this earth. The human body as the organism is so essential for man that Christian doctrine teaches it will be awakened on the Day of Judgement.

The organism of plants, animals, and human beings is a superior entity, and, as such, essentially different from the mere sum of the individual parts of the body and their functions. The individual parts exist only for the sake of the whole, and only through the purposeful orderliness of their interactions do they become the whole, the organism, the living being itself. In human beings, as in a large number of animals, it is the brain that controls the individual parts of the body and the way in which they work together. It controls the purposeful coordination of their interactions to give an expediently arranged whole and also the many and varied interrelations between the living being and its environment. The complete and irreversible loss of brain function destroys this independent, self-determined and self-acting status, which means governed by internal laws, unity, and order.

The organism, the living being, then ceases to exist and becomes a collection of organs which can only continue to function with continued external support, and which no longer fulfil any meaningful purpose. The condition of what remains of the body following brain death – and hence the difference between the dead organism and those parts of the body that are being kept alive with external help – can be most clearly shown by the fact that, after brain death, the individual organs can survive only if transplanted into another organism. Every person living with a transplanted heart is living proof of the fact that the loss of one's own heart function by no means implies death, whereas the total loss of brain function would.

Medicine thus regards brain death as a certain sign of death in humans, since it regards man as an organism gifted with spirit and intellect.

But there are further aspects to this meaning of brain death. A person who has suffered brain death can only be distinguished from an unconscious living patient by means of special examinations. This demands of physicians and medical staff particular carefulness both in behavior and in the choice of words. A person who has suffered brain death is not a "living corpse", not an "anthropoid", not a "humanoid" being, not a "subhuman", and for these reasons alone (not to mention any others), may only be referred to as what he actually is, namely a dead person. Therefore the same respect is due to him as to any other dead person. The fear voiced by a philosopher that a person who has suffered brain death, and who consequently appears to be completely at the mercy of others could be abused, for example as a "surrogate mother", or a "convenient source of blood and hormones" or as an "object of study" or an "aid to education" is yet unfounded, although certainly to be taken seriously. History shows that it was never the physicians alone who had to decide who was entitled to do what – and when – to the body of a deceased person. These problems were, and still are, dealt with differently in different parts of the world. And in Western Europe too, the solutions agreed on in the twentieth century differ from those of the eighteenth century. If the current attitude of respect for persons who have suffered brain death were to undergo a change, the humanities as well as our inherent sense of responsibility would help us all, not just the physicians, to act in a responsible way. Brain death and its significance for the post mortem donation of organs are typical for the "medicalisation of death" (Ph. Aries). At the same time, however, it becomes evident to what extent the medical aspect of death remains only a partial aspect. In addition, the fact that organ transplantations can be undertaken only after brain death has occurred reveals the foolishness of the question as to whether present-day medicine is striving for unlimited prolongation of human life. It is precisely in the case of organ transplantations that the life and well-being of one person are dependent on the misfortune and death of another.

The distinction made on the basis of the diagnosis brain death between the death of human being and the death of his separate organs, together with the chance of survival of organs transplanted into another organism, will probably influence our sense of body awareness. For it is obvious that the life of a human being indeed depends upon the functioning of organs, but not exclusively upon the functioning of his own, original organs. It is equally evident that the survival of the organs is dependent upon an organism, but not upon a specific organism, as one version of the legend of the leg transplantation by the saints Cosmas and Damian may signify. According to this version, the saints instructed the recipient to give the transplanted leg back to the donor upon the resurrection of the dead on the Day of Judgement. The unity of spirit and soul and the organism make it possible for human beings to incorporate what is originally part of a foreign body into their own.

## Summary

Critical care medicine confronts us with the situation that the whole brain is dead, while the rest of the body is kept alive by mechanical manipulations. This leads us to the question: is this person dead or still alive? We pointed out, that the human being can only be understood as a unity consisting of intellect, soul, and body. We also pointed out, that intellect, soul, and body need the brain in order to fulfil human life on this earth. We conclude, therefore, that with the death of the whole brain the unity of spirit, soul, and body – necessary for human life on this earth – is destroyed and ends finite existence.

# Theological Aspects of Brain Death with Regard to the Death of a Person

J. Gründel

Transplant medicine has been extremely successful in the last 20 years. It need not be specially justified. In Christian understanding the voluntary readiness to make one's own vital organs available as a means to save the life of a sick person is a magnanimous act of charity.

From the Christian point of view, every human being is a person independent of his social standing, his achievements, or his health – God's creature in the Creator's image, and called to life beyond death; consequently, his dignity is inalienable. As our respect for human life forbids killing a human being, vital organs may be explanted only after the death of the donor. This precondition is a reliable definition of death. The confidence in transplant is a reliable definition of death. The confidence in transplant medicine can only thus be maintained. We also must understand the difference between heart death (or clinical death) and brain death. The death of a human being is, therefore, the basic fact and prerequisite for the explantation of vital organs for transplant purposes. When, however, is a human being dead as a person?

## The Different Competences of Medical Doctors and Theologians for the Definition of the Moment of Death

In the past, various criteria were assumed to determine the moment of death. At one time it was the death of the heart, then the death of the brain, then again total death with the breakdown of the complete organism. But, as Prof. Angstwurm has just pointed out, brain death alone is, from the medical point of view, the sufficient criterion to ascertain death.

The question is whether the theologian can endorse the view. The answer seems to require some clarification of the respective competence and of the limits of what can be said about the termination of human life as a person. The scientist's statements relate to human life as biological events that can be approached empirically, but his science does not qualify him to pass judgment on a human being's personhood. This is the domain of the humanities, above all of philosophy and theology.

Institut für Moraltheologie und Christliche Sozialethik, Ortsstr. 1, 8050 Freising-Hohenbachern

W. Land, J. B. Dossetor (Eds.)
Organ Replacement Therapy:
Ethics, Justice and Commerce

But because of the close union of body, mind, and soul in man, philosophers and theologians cannot talk about the beginning and end of human life without regard to the findings of science. They must take them into consideration, just as the scientist must not pass by the ethically meaningful statements of philosophy and theology, if his interference in human life is to be ethically responsible.

## The Definition of the Human Being as a Person

First of all the philosopher and the theologian must say what they mean by 'a person'. Boethius (480–524), the Roman philosopher, formulated it thus: *Persona est naturae rationalis individua substantia* [1], defining a person as an indivisible or inexchangeable rational being, even if the mental faculty has not fully developed yet. The theologian understands by 'a person' God's ultimate acceptance of a particular human being. Man is in the image of God and his life will continue beyond death or is called to the resurrection from the dead. The easily misunderstood term 'immortal soul' means exactly this. For classical philosophy and theology the mind-soul is the form-giving life principle. Experimentally, the scientist cannot grasp the unifying principle, yet it is physically conditioned by the brain. The mind-soul of man cannot be simply localized in the brain, but it is to the brain we must attribute the most important part in the process of human consciousness, in the regulation of life and the functioning of all organs.

## Brain Death As a Reliable Criterion for the End of Human Life [2,3]

In 1968 an ad hoc committee of the Harvard Medical School proposed that the death of man as a person be equated with the end of the functions of the brain. The irreversible cessation of these functions cannot be determined selectively as occurring at a certain moment. Irreversibility can only be stated retrospectively after some time has passed. The transition from brain death to total death is flowing. The death of the individual, however, occurs at the very moment the form-giving and regulating life principle gives out. This is what the scientists call brain death. Even if the event occurs at a certain moment, the irreversible breakdown of the cerebral functions can be ascertained only retrospectively. As such, the exact moment of an individual's death cannot be determined.

But it is the position of defining death as brain death that permits the explantation of vital organs whose ability to function is artificially maintained from a person just deceased. "With brain death man lacks the irreplaceable and never again attainable physical foundation for his mental existence in this world" [3]. Human consciousness, thought, and feeling are exclusively linked to the brain. Brain death, therefore, implies individual death, even if the heart and the blood circulation still function artificially. It is a matter of medical competence to diagnose the occurrence of brain death and to define the respective criteria. The fact of brain death having occurred should be established by, at least, two medical doctors of whom one must expect that they will not participate in the ensuing organ transplantation.

In Japan and some other Asian cultures the definition of death as brain death has not been accepted even today. As the human body is considered inviolable, it is dead only when all organs have died. As the explantation of a vital organ terminates human life, it is permissible only when the human being is no longer alive. The crux of the matter is that the organ intended for donation must be biologically alive or it will not serve the purpose. Whoever postulates – as Joachim Gerlach once did – that man is dead only when all bodily organs have ceased to function vitally cannot allow any organ transplantation whatsoever. In such an opinion it would be the very explantation of the organ that causes the respective individual's death.

Recently also in Europe – especially from German philosophers – opinions have been voiced that refuse to accept brain death as the ultimate moment and take into consideration total death only. They want to be absolutely sure that death has occurred and, therefore, reject the idea of explanting organs that are being kept artificially alive [5–7]. So Prof. Josef Seifert from the Akademie of Philosophy in Liechtenstein says that brain death as such is not man's death, which, according to him, can be proven by means of many cogent and some plausible arguments. So he concludes that even if the theoretical arguments against the identification of man's actual death with brain death did not demonstrate their nonidentity, the opposite position would still be uncertain, at least. Therefore, in view of this undeniable fact, a minimal ethical tutiorism demands that we must not act, by organ retrievals, on the assumption of the identity of "brain death" – in any of its meaning – with man's actual death. We must avoid those actions which, like killing, presuppose a high degree of moral certainty, concerning death, given that we cannot attain such certainty, as in the case of brain death. Consequently for Prof. Seifert, organ and heart explantations are found to be unethical [8,9].

But such a position is based on mere assumptions and not on proven facts. Today it can no longer be seriously justified. Theologians, therefore, can discard it in defining their position on determining the moment of death. Tutiorism is not to the point. Such position against organ transplantation is not only dangerous, but also unacceptable and not serious, because it reduces people's willingness to act as donors in the case of their own deaths.

Thus, also from the point of view of theology, brain death is the decisive moment from when on vital organs can be explanted, on the condition that the corpse is not dealt with irreverently. In case the deceased person has not declared consent to the organ donation and, in further absence of regulation by law, the consent of those who have been closely related to the donor should be attained.

## The Position of the Christian Churches

In the meantime, the Christian churches in Germany have spoken out. On August 31, 1990, the German Bishop's Conference and the Council of the Evangelical Church in Germany published a common declaration on organ transplantation. In it they welcome the new approaches of medical research and the possibility of helping patients by the transplantation of vital organs. There they state that the awareness of the necessity of organ donation should be reinforced. It is justified "for the earthly life of patients who are critically ill can be saved, if it is permissible to explant viable organs from just deceased persons for the purpose of transplantation. A person who in case of his or her own death consents to the explantation of his or her organs acts with ethical responsibility as he or she helps another person" [10].

We, therefore, should not allow ourselves to be confused by voices claiming that not brain death, but only total death, can be regarded as the true death of man as they block the access to life-saving help for many people. The readiness to donate one's own organs in the case of one's own death is a magnanimous act of Christian charity. It ought to be encouraged by everybody.

## References


1. Migne (1343) Patrologia Làtina 64
2. Sass H-M (1989) Hirntod und Hirnleben. In: Sass H-M (ed) Medizin und Ethik. Stuttgart, p. 160–183
3. Gründel J. Der relative Wert irdisch leiblichen Lebens und der Tod aus theologischer Perspektive, in: Krösl W, Scherzer E (eds.), Die Bestimmung des Todeszeitpunktes. Vienna, pp. 321–327
4. Ebenda 18.
5. Augustine Regan, The basic morality of organ transplants between living humans, in: Stdia moralia III (1965) 320–361; Antonellus Elsässer, Organspende – selbstverständliche Christenpflicht?, in: Theol. Quartalschrift (1979) 231 ff.
6. Dietrich E (ed) (1985) Organspende – Organtransplantation. Percha. Starnberger See
7. Böckle F (1989) Ethische Probleme der Organtransplantation. Arzt und Christ 35
8. Seifert J (1990) Ist "Hirntod" wirklich der Tod? In: Diskussionsforum medizinischer Ethik
9. Seifert J (1988) Hirntod: Ein Beitrag zur Kritik der philosophischen Korrumpierung der medizinischen Technik. Ethik und Technik, Zürich
10. Erklärung der Deutschen Bischofskonferenz und des Rates der Evangelischen Kirche in Deutschland: Organtransplantation, Bonn 1990, 26.

# Philosophical Arguments in Accepting Brain Death Criteria

H.-M. Sass

One thing people traditionally feared more than death, was being buried alive. The *Technisches Museum* in Munich and museums all over the world are full of devices used to differentiate the seemingly dead from the really dead, including coffins with ventilation and communication equipment, bells attached to strings, electric bells and phones, and coffin lids which could be opened from the inside. The traditional determination of pulselessness or the arrest of heartbeat and respiration as signs at face value for determining death, and rightly so, were met with personal and public distrust. Stories of medical malpractice in diagnosing death, of confusing it with sleep, of people suffocating in the coffin or unexpectedly rising from the grave are abundant in the literature over the centuries. Some funeral homes in Munich and other places in Germany were called *vitae dubiae azilia* (havens of doubtful life) and served as repositories for corpses until the process of decomposing was clearly on its way. Resuscitation societies, called Humane Societies, were mushrooming in the eighteenth century, first in Amsterdam, then under royal patronage in London and in many places of the old and the new world (Dagi 1989). The introduction of brain-based criteria for determining death – or better: for determining whether 'to treat people as if they were dead' (Dagi 1989, p. 1) – nearly 25 years ago has changed the scenario of scare. The determination of death now seems to be biomedically sufficient and conclusive, risk free, but its bioethical evaluation in individual cases of prolonging or terminating life in the intensive care parameters still do not prevent fear, anxiety, and scare, this time the fear of being kept alive too long. Humane societies encouraging compassionate resuscitation care and intense life support at the end of life are being replaced by *Right to Die Societies,* discouraging uncompassionate resuscitation care and intensive life support.

Given this complex biomedical and bioethical scenario, we will

1. discuss the biomedical and bioethical need for a precise, uniform, and legal statute to determine when people may be treated as if they were dead,
2. present the philosophical arguments which made the switch to brain-based criteria for determining death culturally and morally acceptable in Western culture,

European Professional Ethics Program, Kennedy Institute of Ethics, Georgetown University, Washington DC 20057 USA; Ruhr Universität Bochum, Director, Zentrum für Medizinische Ethik Bochum, Postfach 10 21 48, 4630 Bochum, FRG

W. Land, J. B. Dossetor (Eds.)
Organ Replacement Therapy:
Ethics, Justice and Commerce

3. discuss ontological and moral problems associated with the existing whole brain death criteria, and
4. propose a reformulation of the Uniform Determination of Death Act which will allow for competent adults to opt out of the 'whole brain, including brain stem' criteria in favor of 'higher brain' criteria.

## Medical and Moral Quests for Somatic Criteria Establishing Personal Death

The beginnings and the ends of human life are not just natural facts anymore; they can be manipulated, extended, prevented, and changed in their nature by biomedical technology. But biomedical technology does not tell us what is right or wrong in bioethical terms. Nor will biomedical facts determine the morally correct course of action in clinical intervention. Biomedical facts need cultural and moral interpretation, and biomedical technologies need stewardship in determining the medical and moral benefits, costs and risks involved in their application. Both biomedical facts and biomedical technology have to be analyzed and evaluated by methods of moral reasoning and consensus formation. The three most important tools to be used in the development of individual moral competence and cultural, legal, and moral consensus are

a) the history of moral argumentation,
b) cultura tradition, and
c) the analytical and evaluative methods of assessing specific moral scenarios at the beginnings and ends of human life.

Modern clinical practice calls for a culturally and morally acceptable and medically and legally significant uniform statute for diagnosing death for four reasons:

a) improvements in resuscitative and supportive measures in intensive care may result in keeping patients alive 'whose heart continues to beat but whose brain is irreversible damaged' so that the benefits to the patient and his or her family are questionable;
b) 'obsolete criteria for the definition of death can lead to controversy in obtaining organs for transplantation';
c) intensive care life support for vegetative human life is extremely costly, it may result in situations of triage, where intensive care unit (ICU) beds are not available for those who have a fair and good prognostic chance to recover quickly if intensive care could be provided;
d) societal consensus might erode if quality of life criteria are not met by intensive interventions in catastrophic cases and may fund preventive rather than acute interventions.

As the definition of death is not only of biomedical or bioethical relevance, but plays an important role in religious and secular cultural concepts of personhood, mortality and immortality, the body-soul relationship, re-incarnation and re-surrection, the biomedical criteria for determining the end of somatic and personal human life can only be of philosophical and moral guidance if they correlate to widely held ontological and anthropological convictions, and only then will they may be instrumental for supporting public policy, regulation, and self-regulation regarding the application or withholding of medical intervention.

## Christian and Secular Concepts of a Body-Soul Dualism in Western Tradition Strongly Support Criteria for Determining Personal Death by Cessation of Brain Functioning

The shift from cardiovascular and respiratory criteria for determining the morally significant end of human life to brain-related criteria can serve as a case study in successfully applying differential moral reasoning and value assessment, based on cultural and moral tradition, to new bioethical challenges developed by biomedical technologies. Traditionally, the death of a person was identical with the arrest of heartbeat and breathing. It was not necessary to differentiate between the cessation of functioning of particular organs and the death of the person as long as cessation of breathing and heartbeat caused a chain of reactions, at the end of which all other organs had to stop working. This was no longer acceptable in the presence of high-tech intensive care medicine and organ transplantation.

In 1968, an ad hoc commission of the Harvard Medical School after bioethical evaluation of biomedical facts of the processes of dying, came forward with a new and more precise biomedical criterion for bioethically defining the death of a person: brain death – more precisely "irreversible cessation of all functions of the entire brain, including brain stem" (Beecher 1968). These criteria have since been accepted, with technical refinements, in most countries (cf. Bundesärztekammer 1982; US President's Commission 1981). The Uniform Determination of Death Act, which supported regulation and self-regulation in dealing with different forms of comatose or vegetative or inanimate life formulates: "An individual who has sustained either (1) irreversible cessation of circulatory and respiratory functions, or (2) irreversible cessation of all functions of the entire brain, including brain stem, is dead. A determination of death must be made in accordance with accepted medical standards" (US President's Commission 1981, p. 2).

The relatively smooth and widely accepted bioethical shift from cardio-pulmonary death to whole brain death was made possible by dormant values and principles in Western tradition, supported by the humanist Greek-Roman as well as the religious Judeo-Christian tradition. It was a dualistic anthropological concept, which either made the difference between form and matter, ratio and body in secular terms or between the mortal body and the immortal soul in religious terms. These values predetermined an anthropological understanding of the ontological "nature" of humans as to be related to the *differentia specifica* of reasoning, communicating, and self-communicating. The concept of man in Greek philosophy was that of *zoon logon echon,* i.e. the animal having as its specific difference reason and communication, cognition and consciousness; the Roman term *animal rationale* confirmed this concept, so do the dominant anthropological and ontological positions of modern philosophy since the Age of Reason. Aristotle (*De generatione animalium II,* 736a32-b29) and, following him, Thomas Aquinas (*Summa theologiae I,* q.118, a.2ad2) are the strongest authorities in Western thought for the dualism on the concept of personhood, which, even in the secular and antimetaphysics Age of Reason, found its expression in the Cartesian concept of psychophysical parallelism, which explained an unconnected parallelism between the *res cogitans* (reason) and the *res extensa* (body).

The Old Testament speaks about the creation of Adam after God's own image. God, in blowing his own breath (*ruach Jahwe*) into his creature after basic gestation, made the human corresponding, communicative to the creator, and different from the rest of creation (Genesis 2, 7). The general pattern of the image of God, the special relationship of the creator with his image was reaffirmed and deepened in Christian belief in Jesus as the son of God, his suffering and resurrection and the eternal kingdom of heaven, as being something spiritual, not biological. Consequently, the Christian doctrine that teaches the departure of the soul from the body at the moment of death strongly supports the brain death concept. In 1957, Pope Pius XII, based on the century-old tradition of the theory of animation, declared that in cases of "prolonged coma", the soul might already have left the body and no "extraordinary means" would be required to support the life of such patients any longer, but that the determination of death should be left to the physicians (Pius XII 1957, pp. 1027–1033). The Christian tradition that differentiated between inanimate or non ensouled and animate or ensouled fetuses could easily differentiate between postanimate somatic life and animate somatic life (Sass 1989). The determination of the biomedical criteria for the difference, which has implications for salvation theory as well as for moral theology, asks, according to Pius XII, for biomedical, not theological expertise and, therefore, was left to the physicians, even though the expression "prolonged coma" might favor stages prior to and beyond whole brain death definitions and include people in persistent vegetative state and the long-term comatose. The President's Commission (1981, p. 42) summarizes: "a statute incorporating a brain-based standard is accepted by theologians of all backgrounds".

Those non-Western traditions which, according to their dualistic concept of man's belief in animation or re-incarnation, such as Parsi and Hindu religions, do not have any essential problems with the understanding that at one time the body is ensouled and that at an other time the soul will leave the body. Hindu teaching of re-incarnation in fact denies individual death in contrast to the death of the biological body. Other non-Western cultural traditions arguing from the point of view of the wholeness and integrity of body and mind have basic problems in making the same moral assessments which allowed for developing brain-based criteria in Western cultures and they will continue to do so. A recent survey, undertaken by the Japanese Prime Minister's office in July 1987, however, showed that of 61% respondents only 24% wanted to wait for heart death, while 24% accepted brain death outright and 37% would make that depending on the patient's or his or her family's will; among those accepting brain death criteria, 90% are in favor of organ transplantation, 74% of these would donate their own organs. It should be mentioned, however, that the idea of the "totality" of the body, which played an important role in Christian teaching against mutilation, had its clearest expression in Pius XI Casti Canubii letter (1930), and was not without discussion superseded by the Roman Catholic acceptance of organ donation or transplant later on.

The new brain-based criteria for determining personal death do not create new moral principles or values, rather they interpret new technologies and new medical findings in the light of well-established ontological and ethical principles and values; they make self-help organizations for resuscitation care, such as the Humane Societies of the past, unnecessary. In addressing the functioning of the lower brain, including the brain stem, they cover the concept of the *integrative functioning* of human life, of body and soul, matter, and form; in addressing the functioning of the higher brain, they cover the concept of the human *ontological distinctiveness of conscience and self-consciousness*. The shift to a brain-oriented definition of death had the following five medical, moral, legal and cultural advantages:

1. Human life that meets the strict and well-defined biomedical criteria of whole brain death does not deserve the same bioethical recognition and legal protection as other humans, while other forms of comatose or vegetative human life, including cessation of neocortical functions are not covered under this formula.
2. Moral, emotional, cultural, social, and economic costs that would have been associated with the artificial extension of brain dead life can be saved.
3. Organs become available for patients, who otherwise would die or face severe suffering, hardship, or inconvenience.
4. One single biomedical criterion serves as a correlate for a bioethical consensus on one specific scenario at the end of human life and the traditional difference between animate and inanimate life: "cessation of all functions of the entire brain".
5. People, whose system of belief does not support whole brain related criteria, at least theoretically, would have the option to be diagnosed by the cessation of circulatory and respiratory functions.

## The Right to Die and the Quest for Higher Brain Death Criteria

The whole brain, including brain stem criteria for determining death, therefore, have found wide support. But they found criticism, also, and increasingly so. The critique came from those positions, who (a) like Hans Jonas did reject any conclusive ontological statement on the dividing line between life and death, or (b) from positions who, as mentioned, emphasize the wholeness and integrity of the entire living person, such as Buddhist or Confucian world views. Both positions consequently have problems in accepting organ procurement and transplantation. A third position critical of the whole brain criteria has found increasing support among physicians, bioethicists and the concerned public and is closely related to the *Right to Die* movement. It was argued that "whole brain theorists appeal only to the brain's integrative role, and not to its role in consciousness" and that, in effect, they employ "a lower brain concept of death, and not a whole-brain concept" (Gervais 1989, p. 12).

The President's Commission, in 1981, had based its moral assessment of a whole brain oriented definition on two arguments, (1) that "it is not known which portions of the brain are responsible for cognition and consciousness" (US President's Commission 1981, p. 40), and (2) that those who still believe in the criteria of spontaneous breathing and heartbeat could live with the new definition. Such an overprotection for moral reasons is quite normal in assessing the use of a new technology for the first time. In fact, in situations without prior moral and technical experience overprotection is morally warranted and may be relaxed later as a result of more moral and technical experience, as we have done in deoxyribonucleic acid (DNA) safety regulations. In requiring the cessation of all brain functions, including brain stem, the Uniform Determination of Death Act determines, in fact, the end of the entire human life, also in its vegetative and animalistic form, not just the end of its animation or ensoulment. The existing statutes, according to Zaner (1989, p. 6) "have opted for a philosophical view which identifies 'human life' with strictly organic, bodily conditions: the 'moment at which the body's physiological system ceases to constitute an integrated whole'".

As has been demonstrated, the philosophical as well as the religious tradition in the Western world rather suggest higher brain based criteria than those relating to the physiological integration of the body's system. Sorenson praises the "conceptual clarity" of higher brain based criteria over whole brain based ones (1989, p. 246). And Veatch, a supporter of higher brain based criteria writes: "What we are really interested in is not the presence of neocortical activity, but the presence of certain functions that, for want of a better term, we often refer to as higher brain functions. Exactly what those functions are is open to much further debate, but they would seem to include capacity to be conscious, to think, feel, and to be aware of other people" (Zaner 1988, p. 172).

Smith, in referring to routinely made decisions to withhold specific intervention such as antibiotics from long-term patients in the vegetative stage, argues that the current legal treatment of brain death is both anomalous and unsound: "It upholds surrogate decisions to terminate life-support systems and nourishment when incompetent patients irreversibly lose all consciousness and cognitive functions, yet it fails to recognize neocortical death". He recommends, to "treat the irreversible loss of higher brain function as legal death, reserving the right of the patient or the patient's family to maintain biological existence", thus making the neocortical criteria the uniform standard, but allowing for opting out by special request from the patient or the family (in Zaner 1988, p. 133).

Indeed, Western traditions favor those criteria which refer to thinking, feeling, and communicating rather than those which refer to mere physiological life. But here is the problem: we have to be aware that in pluralistic societies the evaluation of the significance of 'soul', 'consciousness', 'conscience', 'personhood' and 'being aware of other people' might result in quiet different assessments based on different ontological or cultural positions.

Therefore the biomedical position of whole brain criteria, stressing the integrative functions of all parts of the brain, and not the bioethical position of higher brain criteria, which would have to stress conscious and sentient functions, did uniformly find consensus in public policy and in physician-patient relations. The whole brain formula works with a double safety net. Its reference to lower brain functions allows for disregarding possible technical problems in exactly determining neocortical death criteria; those criteria have been described (Brierly 1971), but not found unanimous expert support. Its reference to higher brain functions protects those patients from 'locked in' syndrome. Both references and their use in argumentation are rather of instrumental character than of ontological nature. Even if 'neocortical death', which for all purposes would be the most adequate correlate to the religious notion of the 'soul' and the philosophical distinction of 'animal rational', could be established without any technical question or risk left, bioethical and world view differences in pluralistic societies favor the ontologically dull and unimpressive biomedical criteria of integrative function of the whole brain. Whole brain death criteria do not need philosophical judgement, or only a minimal one; that is their advantage. However, as the fear of being kept alive in ICUs without any personal benefit or quality of life and the criticism of intensive care medicine will increase, physicians and patients will have to find solutions which are not uniformly covered by the existing statutes.

## Public Policy and Individual Choice in Establishing Criteria for Death

There is a way out of the dilemma which allows for uniform death criteria on one hand but causes great fear of being "tortured" in prolonged processes of dying in the intensive care wards. Also, the inflexibility of the existing statutes might be counter productive to post mortem organ donation. The solution might be the following: having a uniform statute for all clinical and public policy situations and allowing competent adults to opt out of the uniform default position according to their individual belief system. This window of opportunity has been mentioned in the literature (Veatch 1988; Gervais 1989), but has recently been strengthened by a landmark court decision. In the US case of *Cruzan versus Director, Missouri Department of Health* (Colby 1990), the court on the one hand upholds the strict whole brain formula regarding Nancy Cruzan, who has been in a persistent vegetative state since 1983, while on the other accepts the right of a competent person to make explicit advanced directives based on his or her own concept of higher brain death, whole brain death, and persistent vegetative state. If Nancy Cruzan had such an advanced directive expressing her preference for correlating persistent vegetative state to personal death, using Veatch's definition of higher brain oriented concept of death as "an irreversible loss of higher brain functions, i.e. certain functions normally associated with the neocortex that include the capacity to be conscious, to think, feel, and be aware of other people" (Veatch, in Zaner 1988), she would have been allowed to die. Only the accurate determination of cessation of higher brain functions would have been a last technical risk, which she might have wanted to accept after appropriate inormation and subsequent consent, thus stressing the neocortical criteria's "conceptual accuracy and practical helpfulness" (Sorenson 1988, p. 246).

A proposal to redefine the Uniform Determination of DeathAct by Truog and Fletcher stresses the integrative functions of the various parts of the brain over the whole brain concept. They formulate: "People are dead if they have a distinct and precisely definable condition characterized by the absence of integrated brain function, such that somatic death is uniformly immanent" (Truog and Fletcher 1990, p. 208). This position covers anencephalics, but lacks the flexibility which an "opt out" option would provide.

A statute confirming the present criteria of whole brain death, but allowing for competent adults to opt for higher brain criteria, actually reversing the procedure proposed by Smith (Smith, in Zaner 1988, p. 133) can solve most of the remaining dilemmata of existing brain death criteria. It would have at least the following three benefits:

(a) Given the differences in world view, culture, and moral priorities in a pluralistic society, a conscience clause for competent adults would allow for making choices for oneself, based on one's own belief system within the legal parameters; competent adults and their physicians will not sentenced to a slow dying process of vegetative life by legal statutes.

(b) Whole brain death criteria will become even more robust and stable, probably getting even more widely accepted, morally and legally, when they become the uniform default position, which competent adults may opt out of; the fact, that for some intelligent people the choice is less strict for the future determination of their death, signals that the uniform statute might be too strict, but definitely not too loose.

(c) The conscience clause for competent adults, established prior to the event of a catastrophic medical crisis, will improve individual and societal trust in and support of intensive care intervention and care, because citizens, the potential patients, will have an option to make advanced directives regarding the right to die according to one's own belief system and quality of life standards.

(d) The strictness of whole brain death criteria allowing for a conscience clause might facilitate greater public support for post mortem organ donation, as trust in these criteria is increased and patients will be allowed to have an input in their life and death decisions regarding the rather philosophical question: when does human life ends?

In order to allow for a *conscience clause* in the statute, I propose its introduction into the well-established statute of the Uniform Determination of Death Act (cf. US President's Commission 1981, p. 2). A model statute confirming established and widely accepted uniform whole brain death criteria for determining death and resolving remaining moral and medical problems by allowing for self-determination and for making right to die decisions could be formulated this way: "An individual who has sustained either (1) irreversible cessation of circulatory and respiratory functions, or (2) irreversible cessation of al functions of the entire brain, including brain stem, is dead. *Competent adults, using advanced directives may opt for death criteria based on cessation of higher brain functions only; proxy decision for higher brain death criteria is not acceptable.* A determination of death must be made in accordance with accepted medical standards".

## References

Beecher KH (1968) A definition of irreversible coma: report of the Harvard Medical School to examine the definition of brain death. JAMA 205:337–340

Beller FK, Reeve J (1989) Brain life and brain death – the anencephalic as an explanatory example. J Med Philos 14:5–23

Brierly JD et al. (1971) Neocortical death after cardiac arrest. Lancet 11:560–565

Bundesärztekammer, Wissenschaftlicher Beirat (1982) Kriterien des Hirntodes: Entscheidungshilfen zur Feststellung des Hirntodes. Deutsches Ärzteblatt 79:45–55

Colby WH et al. (1990) Cruzan: clear and convincing?. Hastings Center Report 20:5–11

Dagi FT (1989) Death-defining acts. In: Kaufmann HH (ed) Historical and cultural observations on the end of life, pediatric brain death and organ tissue retrieval. Plenum, New York, pp 1–30

Gervais KG (1989) Advancing the definition of death. Med Human Rev 3:7–19

Pius XII (1957) Acta Apostolicae Sedis. 45:1027–1033

Sass HM (1989) Brain life and brain death: a proposal for a normative agreement. J Philos Med 14:45–59

Sorenson JH (1988) The determination of death. In: Monagle JF, Thomasma DC (eds) The need for a higher-brain death definition, medical ethics. Aspen, Rockville, MD, pp 234–248

Truog RD, Fletcher JC (1990) Brain death and the anencephalic newborn. Bioethics 4:199–215

US President's Commission for the Study of Ethical Problems in Medicine and Biomedical and Behavioral Research (1981) Defining death. Government Printing Office, Washington DC

Wolfslast G (1989) Grenzen der Organgewinnung: Zur Frage einer Änderung der Hirntodkriterien. Med R 4:163–168

Zaner RM (ed) (1988) Death: beyond whole-brain criteria. Reidel, Dordrecht, Holland

# What Were the Problems of Getting Brain Death Accepted in Denmark: The Beginning and End of a Controversy

P. Rossel

## Introduction

It is a curious fact that Denmark as the last country in Western Europe accepted the brain death criterion. It just happened this year when the Danish Parliament passed the Minister of Justice's Bill concerning inquest, autopsy, and transplantation, etc. (Law no. 402, June 13, 1990). Before that, there had been a long and heated public debate – a controversy – over death criteria and organ transplantation. Why? Are we Danes so different from other people – more religious or (as we love to think of ourselves) more democratic than the rest of the world – or perhaps just more confused?

Here at the outset, I have to say that I am not going to present a systematic sociological account. Rather, what follows is an attempt to analyze the controversy by an observer and participant in the debate. As being in favor of both the brain death criterion and organ transplantation, I hope that my analysis will not be skewed – though it will be rather critical.

## The Beginning of the Controversy

On October 28, 1987 the Ministry of Justice proposed a Bill concerning inquest, autopsy, and transplantation, etc. With a few changes, this Bill was a reintroduction of a Bill put forward on January 14, 1987. This Bill, however, did not by itself ignite much of a debate. But shortly – and hastily – after the Bill had been proposed, the newly established Danish Council of Ethics issued a booklet *Death Criteria – A Report* [1].

The Danish Council of Ethics had been established in 1988 according to Law no 353, June 3, 1987. It was set up to deal primarily with issues of human reproduction, e.g., protection of human fertilized ova, embryos, and fetuses. But it was also entitled to take up cases on its own initiative and "to inform as well as to encourage debate amongst the population on matters of ethics and

Philosophy of Medicine, The Panum Institute, Bldg. 22.3.22, 2200 Copenhagen N, Denmark

W. Land, J. B. Dossetor (Eds.)
Organ Replacement Therapy:
Ethics, Justice and Commerce

biomedicine". It had to spur debates – suitably for a democratic society. This was just what happened with the questions of death criteria and organ transplantation, but it is not a wild hypothesis that the Council with its report wanted to manifest its existence.

To my mind, the Danish Council of Ethics and its report was one of the central problems. The report is not well argued, it is even confused, and in the following debate members of the council were parading as a kind of "moral experts", e.g., some theologians and a writer, who in a TV interview compared organ transplantation with cannibalism. In others words, it was apt to generate a confused public debate. In *Death Criteria,* a majority of 13 members out of 17 of the Council tried to argue for a cardiac-oriented death criterion. The following statements are among its conclusions:

1. "*A person is dead* when the three functions .. 1. heart and circulatory function, 2. respiratory function, and 3. brain function .. all have ceased totally and irreversibly.
2. The cessation of brain function is identical with the irreversible beginning of the death process. A person in this condition is in the process of death" [1, p. 25].

In short, the majority of the council wanted to stick to the traditional criterion. But at the same time it was – in the opinion of the council – permissible to remove organs, e.g., the heart from a – on its own account – still living person, given a prior consent. I shall return to this last point later.

But to remove the heart from a still living person isn't that to kill the person? How is it possible both to uphold a cardiac-oriented death criterion and to allow removal of the heart? The Council's solution reads: "Such an intervention is cause for the conclusion of the process of death, but is not the cause of death" [1, p. 26].

I have tried to figure out what this means, but I have not succeeded. I can only come to the conclusion that the paragraph is just a linguistic evasion – a playing with words to conceal the inconsistency of the Council's position. But such a playing with words – such a statement by "moral experts" – is surely apt to generate a confused public debate, and so it became.

Under what conditions, then, is it permissible to remove organs from a still living person (a brain death organism)? A necessary and sufficient condition, in the opinion of the Council, must be the prior consent of the brain death organism:

"In other words, a fixed principle that *organs cannot be removed without consent* must be insisted upon. Most consequent would be to require explicit consent from the donor himself or herself. But a natural consideration could be whether the relatives can make the decision in certain cases – for example, when minors are concerned" [1, p. 21].

Therefore it proposes the establishment of a donor register, and only if a person, while alive, has registered should it be permissible to remove his or her organs. Whether or not this should result in a shortage of organs is just the price to be paid. Not even the relatives, except in case of minors, should be allowed to give a proxy consent.

The interesting thing here is that the Council, without putting forward any good reasons, is adopting or applying a certain normative model, a model that is far from obvious from a moral point of view. The whole emphasis is put upon the rights of the potential donor. But what about the moral concern for the still living persons in need of an organ transplantation? This moral concern is totally played down.

It is, in fact, another curious feature that most of the public medical/ethical debates in Denmark tend to focus upon fertilized human ova, aborted fetuses, and what happens to brain death organisms, i.e., before we ever become persons, if at all, and what happens after we have ceased to be persons. As an example of another controversy: the use of brain tissue from death aborted fetuses for research in order to find better treatment for Parkinson's disease. The moral concern in this public debate centered on the dead fetuses and not on the fate of patients suffering from Parkinson's disease, and so it was in the controversy over death criteria and organ transplantation.

Why? My best guess is this: among the persons playing an active role in the public debate over medical/ethical issues in Denmark are some theologians, and as such they seem to be more concerned about the beginning of life (fertilized ova and fetuses) and the end of life (brain death organisms) than in what happens in between, i.e., the span of time when we are persons. An even more unfriendly guess is that as Denmark becomes more and more secularized, these professional Christians are eager to show the relevance of their profession. But, admittedly, this is unfriendly and perhaps unfair. Paradoxically, they often join forces with the left. What seems to unite them is some kind of *antitechnological attitude*.

Perhaps the greatest problem was and still is the linkage of the brain death criterion with the question of organ transplantation. It tends to arouse the fear that doctors would cease treatment too early and declare people dead just in order to harvest their organs. Part of the problem was a certain mistrust in the medical profession and a kind of antiexpert attitude. Conceptually it is, of course, possible to distinguish between those two issues. One can accept brain death as the death of the person without endorsing organ transplantation. This, however, should not serve as an evasion of the real issue. Although one can argue for brain death as the death of the person, the reason why – as a practical issue – one wants it legally accepted as the criterion of death is the possibility of organ transplantations.

To be quite clear, I think that one of the lessons from the Danish debate is the following: one should – of course – argue on independent grounds for brain death as the death of the person. One should not, however, deny that the legal acceptance of the brain death criterion is closely linked to the possibilities of transplantations. Instead of an evasion, one should then argue, I think, for the moral obligation to become an organ donor, if there are sound arguments for this, as I think there are [2].

## The End of the Controversy

How, then, was this controversy over death criteria and organ transplantation brought to a close? What are the effects of the controversy?

The controversy was brought to a, perhaps only temporary, closure by the law enacted on June 13, 1990. Why? The reason is quite simple: we had to stop being free-riders. For some years Danish patients had received organs abroad, e.g., in the Federal Republic of Germany, The Netherlands, and England. As the debate went on and on and on, those countries – according to the newspapers at least – were losing their patience with the Danes. They would not allow more Danes to receive organs abroad. We simply had to stop being free-riders. So the law was enacted. The Danish Parliament thus did not follow the recommendations of the Danish Council of Ethics on the question of death criteria. Nor did it follow the Council's recommendations that a necessary condition for the removal of organs must be a prior consent. In the absence of either a prior consent or refusal by the potential donor, the relatives have to make the decision.

What are the effects of the controversy?

I do not have the exact figures, but there has been a dramatic decline in the donation of kidneys during the debate. How the future will be is, of course, hard to tell.

## Conclusion

What, then, were the problems of getting brain death accepted in Denmark? To sum up:

1. A newly established Danish Council of Ethics that wanted to manifest its existence and therefore hurriedly published a confused report *"Death Criteria"*.
2. Members of the Danish Council of Ethics parading as "moral experts" and being opposed to the brain death criterion.
3. The dogmatic application of a certain normative model with a principle of the right to self-determination as the only or overriding principle.
4. An antitechnological attitude among some of the most active participants in the controversy – e.g., theologians and some people on the left.
5. The linkage of brain death and organ transplantation. Although these issues can be kept conceptually distinct they are – as a practical matter – interwoven. Instead of trying to evade this, one should argue morally for organ transplantation, given that brain death is the death of the person.
6. Finally – and not mentioned before – the politicians fear to decide on these matters. The word "ethics" has nearly become a fetish, something very difficult and above the more mundane affairs of the politicians. So they tried to shift the responsibility to a Council of Ethics.

But perhaps all these features – or at least some of them – belong to an open, democratic society?

## References

1. The Danish Council of Ethics (1989) Death criteria: a report. Copenhagen
2. Rossel P (1990) A moral obligation to be an organ donor and a subject of human research? (In Danish). J Dan Med Assoc 152:3816–3818

# When is a Person Dead?: the Answer of the European Philosophers and Poets

J. Rego-Pedro

Among other European authors, Aristotle postulated that the human being is a ternary compound of spirit, soul, and body. The soul makes the body sensitive and allows it to move. In the *Parva Naturalia,* Aristotle says that death corresponds to the moment when the vital warmth of the soul leaves the body. European culture connects death with the idea of loss of warmth and movement. The principle of life inhabits in the heart, but the heart is neither soul nor life, and, therefore, its beating is no longer an absolute criterion of life. In a culture which claims that the principle of life does not identify itself either with the brain or with the heart or any other organ, the idea of brain death is superfluous. What we nowadays call brain death corresponds to the essence of the traditional image of death: the loss of warmth, the loss of movement as a response. The principle of life is a supernatural one.

In the European languages, death is never assumed as the opposite of life, but as the opposite of birth. The opposite of life is called perfection. Poets like Goethe picture death as a metamorphosis, which contains the idea of perfection. In organ transplantation, when we talk about death, we are usually thinking of the donor. Let us think about the death of the receiver, the death we want to avoid with transplantation, a risky operation. If we do so, we may picture transplantation, for the receiver, as a metamorphosis or a new life, and thus, a chance for his improving of being.

If we think the greatest problem in transplantation is the lack of organs, we will be compelled to apply the laws of the market and to set a price on the organs. But we know that life is priceless. The greatest problem in transplantation is the rejection of the transplant. Transplantation may be seen as the marriage of two souls, for according to Plotinus (IVth Ennead), the donor's soul is present in each part of his own body. There should be an affinity or a sympathy or a compassion between both souls. Using Goethe's words once again, the study of these elective affinities occupies an important place in European literature. It is called alchemy, and it deals with the sacrament or mystery of marriage. The improvement of the qualitative results of organ transplantation depends on the study of the elective affinities between the souls.

---

Apartado 96, 7050 Montemor-O-Novo, Portugal

W. Land, J. B. Dossetor (Eds.)
Organ Replacement Therapy:
Ethics, Justice and Commerce

Finally, let us consider the preaching contained in the Gospel of St. John, referring to the dead body of Christ: "You will not break a single bone of His body:" Christian tradition believes in the resurrection of the flesh, and it connects it very strongly with the survival of individuality. The integrity of the skeleton, that is to say, the absence of mutilation of the body, seems to be an inevitable condition for the preservation of identity.

# Brain Death as Identity Loss

F. La Spina[1], E. Bessone[1], R. Verlato[2], and C. Pizzi[3]

We are researching the psychological effects of the issues on cadaver organ donation among the donors' relatives.

The first stage of the research involves interviewing the relatives of the donors 1 year after the donation, while in the second part we investigate the quality of the relationship between the intensive care unit doctors (who had previously filled in a particular questionnaire) and the families during the hospitalization of the donor. The principal aims of the research are:

- To study the relatives' psychological lives, examining the different aspects of the situation (from the donation request, through the response deliberation, up to the months following the donor's death); and
- To look through the difficulties in the consent and the subsequent psychological and psychopathological problems.

Furthermore, starting from these findings, we are interested in fixing a behavior model (stereotypal and individual) that could be useful to the work of the intensive care unit doctors to develop a better relationship with the families and achieve a larger proportion of donation consents.

Preliminary data allowed us to make some comments about the psychological relationship between families and donors, and observations regarding the difficulty of accepting the operative definition of brain death. Death drives the families to locate imaginarily their dead relative in the recipient; this has always been a placing in accordance with the peculiar space and temporality characteristics of life, characteristics that are absolutely improper for the death concept. We have found that people constantly use the defensive mechanism which involves a projective identification from the donor to the receiver; this psychological condition is induced from the active process of transplantation. The family cannot escape from the thought that their relative lives on in the body of the receiver.

This identification is the initial mechanism of coping with death and cannot last for a prolonged period because of the impossibility of maintaining any kind of relationship with the receiver, and thereby not being able to

[1] Psychiatric Department, University School of Medicine, via Francesco Sforza, 35, 20122 Milan, Italy
[2] Intensive Care Unit, Regional Hospital San Bortolo, Vicenza, Italy
[3] Blood Transfusion and Immunology Center, General Hospital via Francesco Sforza, 35, 20122 Milan, Italy

W. Land, J. B. Dossetor (Eds.)
Organ Replacement Therapy:
Ethics, Justice and Commerce

perpetuate the association of the ego of relative with the transplanted organ.

Not long after this, with the establishment of the consciousness of death and the beginning of the mourning period, this early radical defensive mechanism against death breaks down.

Because of organ donation becomes obvious, transplantation often brings the families to a "lack of attention": they lose track of the deceased relative because they are still persuaded of the survival of his identity, and they feel guilty of having been unfaithful and of having forsaken their relative.

Moreover, our research demonstrates the great number of cases in which there is a pathological disease driven by a delay of the psychological mourning elaboration (complex mourning).

When the doctors suggest the idea of donation supported by proofs of death (understood as brain and not cardiac or respiratory death), the family already has in their thought process the idea of the unacceptability of disappearance. The families do not believe in brain death, not just for the certain value of the regular movement and of the warmth (heart beats, lungs expand, etc.), but also because of the unbearable dismay that the concept of brain death evokes in their mind.

In the common imagination, the establishments of feelings of personal unity, continuity, subjective identity, and existence are placed in the brain where thought is in touch with body.

The concept of brain death (lived as cortical death) evokes the ghost of thought disappearance, of identity annihilation. The families do not have any other defense but denial for this dreadful and painful feature of death.

For that reason, it seems that it would be more suitable to give notice of the death of the potential donor trying to lay stress on the neurological and neuropathological aspects of brain death to veil the most dreadful neuropsychological ones.

# Ethical and Practical Problems of Setting Up a System of Elective Ventilation

H. N. Riad, T. G. Feest, C. H. Collins, M. Golby, A. J. Nicholls, and S. N. Hamad

## Introduction

The Exeter Protocol of elective ventilation for the provision of organs for transplantation has been in operation for 2 years. Here we discuss the ethical and practical considerations met in devising and running the protocol.

Research showed that in our district general hospitals serving 303 000 people, some 8–10 patients each year, dying of cerebrovascular incidents, were potentially suitable organ donors, but as they died in general wards, organ retrieval was not possible. A multidisciplinary working party devised a protocol for transferring these potential donors to the intensive Care Unit for circulatory and ventilatory support until organ retrieval could be arranged. The protocol is described in Appendix A. The effectiveness of this protocol in promoting organ donation has been previously described [1], the organ donor rate in our hospital rising by two and a half times to 37.5 donors per million population per year, a rate which is two and a half times the national average in the United Kingdom. The ethical and practical problems thrown up by such a protocol are discussed here.

## Is It Ethical to Transfer Patients to Intensive Care Units for Forms of Therapy Which Are Not for Their Own Benefit?

We decided this is an ethical practice, provided that:

a) It had been clearly expressed to the family that the patient had no chance of recovery,
b) The family were in full agreement with organ donation and
c) That they were fully aware, before it took place, that transfer to the Intensive Care Unit and subsequent ventilation and circulatory support procedures were entirely for the purpose of maintaining adequate perfusion of the organs until retrieval could be arranged, and offered no benefit to the patient undergoing these procedures.

Royal Devon & Exeter Hospital (Wonford), Barrack Road, Exeter EX2 5DW, Devon, England

W. Land, J. B. Dossetor (Eds.)
Organ Replacement Therapy:
Ethics, Justice and Commerce

All relatives approached who were initially in agreement with organ donation accepted the transfer to the Intensive Care Unit with this explanation. We have subsequently spoken to the relatives of all patients to judge their reactions. Although 40 % of them were initially shocked by the request, none expressed any regrets at the decision they had made, and many felt that the facilitation of organ donation had helped them in coping with the loss of their close relative.

Some Intensive Care staff found this procedure more difficult to accept, but our feeling is that although they may be carrying out procedures which are not for the benefit of the patient receiving attention, a more global view should be taken. The procedure may be for the benefit of up to 5 other patients who will receive organs, although for the Intensive Care Unit staff this is more difficult to grasp as they do not see the recipients who get the benefit.

## Will Patients Be Ventilated Who Do Not Subsequently Fulfil the Criteria for Brain Stem Death?

Many Intensive Care Unit staff fear that patients will be transferred to them and ventilated who do not fulfil the criteria for brain stem death. It would be difficult to cease ventilation in such patients and prolonged stays in Intensive Care Units may ensue, with all the emotional difficulties this raises for relatives and staff. Our physicians believed they could accurately predict those patients who were dying rapidly. Previous confirmation of the diagnosis is an essential element of our protocol. In our experience all the patients electively ventilated through the protocol became organ donors in less than 48 h, and as we have learned from experience the time spent in the Intensive Care Unit has become progressively shorter. One of the early patients transferred did not follow the immediate predicted downhill course, was never ventilated and died slowly over the next 5 days. Close liaison was maintained with the members of his family, and they are still fully supportive of the procedures which were carried out and all carry donor cards.

## How Should Such a Protocol Be Introduced?

Such a protocol can only be introduced if it is widely accepted by physicians, intensivists and nursing staff. It is essential to have it carefully prepared and agreed through a well established hospital mechanism, in our case the Joint Medical Staff Committee. Furthermore, we believe that this protocol can only be introduced in a hospital that has a well established mechanism for the retrieval of organs for transplantation with staff already experienced in the very sensitive task of supporting the relatives through this process.

## Does the Protocol Cause Excessive Demands on the Intensive Care Unit?

Our Intensive Care Unit has five beds serving a population of 303 000, in addition to receiving patients from three other health districts who require a combination of renal replacement and intensive care. However, use of the protocol only adds an average of 6–8 patients per year to intensive care admission. The average length of stay of our patients was 16 h 29 min. It is most important to judge the time of transfer to the Intensive Care Unit to reduce the length of stay there. In a period of 25 months, only ten patients were transferred to the Intensive Care Unit for this purpose, a small increase in workload. In one instance, a transfer was turned down because of a shortage of intensive care facilities.

As an alternative to use of the Intensive Care Unit, it was suggested that a special high dependency area be set aside for elective ventilation. This would be expensive to run for the small number of cases who would go through it. We did not feel it practical to recruit and train experienced personnel who would have to be available permanently, but who would only be called upon infrequently at short notice. Most importantly we felt the relatives would be deprived of the skill and expertise of the Intensive Care Unit staff who have the greatest continuing experience of caring for the families of critically ill patients.

## Can the Protocol Be Maintained?

In the first 18 months of using our protocol, we were highly successful in obtaining organ donors. In the subsequent 7 months the number of retrievals via the protocol dropped. Our research shows that several suitable donors were dying on medical wards without organ donation being considered. We realised that we had neglected to regularly and frequently remind the general medical staff of the existence of the protocol, and to adequately educate the new junior doctors. Over 6 months, five potential donors were missed, compared with only four in the first 19 months of using the protocol. We have now started a regular and recurring programme of information and education of all grades of medical staff.

## Conclusion

We believe elective ventilation for organ donation to be ethical. We have demonstrated that it is very successful in increasing the number of organ donors available. Experience shows that it is possible to select appropriate patients for transfer for elective ventilation and that the increased workload and stress on Intensive Care Unit staff is tolerable and well worth the benefits. Most important of all the relatives of patients who have become organ donors in this way have been very supportive of the system, and have found that the provision of this opportunity for their departed relatives to be an organ donor has been a positive experience for them.

## Appendix A The Exeter Protocol

1. The following recommendations for the provision of organs for transplantation have been agreed by a working group of the Joint Medical Staff Committee and the Divisions of Medicine and Anaesthesia. Please familiarise yourself with the procedures below. If you have any queries, please approach your consultant. Please note that there is no strict age limit for organ donation. Patients aged greater than 70 years may be suitable donors.
2. Criteria for the identification of patients with intracranial vascular accidents as potential organ donors:
   a) Characteristic mode of onset: sudden with rapid development of coma.
   b) Progressive decline in conscious level.
   c) Deep coma: lack of withdrawal response to painful stimuli.
   d) Intracranial vascular accident confirmed by CT scan desirable.
2. Exclusion – Reversible causes of coma.
3. Procedure.
   a) Junior medical staff to discuss the case with the consultant concerned.
   b) Consultant or nominee to discuss suitability of patient as an organ donor with a member of the transplant team.
   c) If patient is a suitable donor, discuss with consultant in charge of ICU.
   d) If all are agreed, the consultant physician or his nominee should make an agreed approach to the relatives.
   PLEASE NOTE THAT THE SEQUENCE OF EVENTS a), b), c) and d) SHOULD BE STRICTLY OBSERVED.
4. Approach to relatives.
   This will need to include a discussion of:
   a) The physician's belief that the patient is unlikely to recover.
   b) Request for organ donation.
   c) Transfer to ICU as the appropriate place for the management of organ donation.
   d) The possibility of the patient leaving ICU for the ward if he/she ceases to be a suitable donor.
5. Management in ICU.
   The degree of intensive treatment carried out in ICU is a matter for discussion between the consultant physician and the consultant in intensive care for each case at the time.

## References

Feest TG, Riad HN, Collins CH, Golby MGS, Nicholls AJ, Hamad SN (1990) Protocol for increasing organ donation after cerebrovascular deaths in a district general hospital. Lancet 335:1133–1135

# Responsible Involvement on a Large Scale: The Gift of Life in Implicit Solidarity

P. Schotsmans

Modern developments in medical technology have the virtually unique character of confronting individual human beings with their personal responsibility. An ethical approach to these developments exhibits two great challenges: the task of rational and critical reflection and the need to respect the conscience of each person.

It seems to us that in the search for the core of our being human, we are best served by recalling part of the history of anthropological reflection. What we find striking about that history is that one can virtually draw a straight line from the source of this systematic reflection on humanity, which more or less coincides with the beginning of the twentieth century, up to the present day, from the recognition of the openness of being human to the importance of social responsibility. This observation may help us to avoid falling into one-sidedness. What we shall try to do here is to suggest a complementary vision on humanity and on being human. For it appears to us to be a dead end simply to stress one or another aspect of what it means to be human. According to this vision, to be human is both to exhibit and to participate in the wonder of a rich many-sidedness: to be human is to be rich in unicity and originality, but at the same time, originality is an empty concept if it does not include openness toward the other and if it does not involve cooperation with others for the exploration of a solidary community.

It seems us to be important to demonstrate how responsible involvement as an important aspect of the interwoveness of personal self-development, relational encounter, and human solidarity can deal with new possibilities of medicine. This approach provides an ethical as well as a pedagogical frame of reference. From this perspective, the responsibility of every human being for the meaningful integration of these dimensions in his or her life project can be taken up. This is the ultimate task of ethical reflection: to offer the opportunity to each person to contemplate his or her own situation in a sufficiently rational way, to become conscious of all the values and disvalues that are present to us as persons, and to open our perspective on the humanly desirable.

The development of techniques for removing and transplanting organs is an illustration of the accelerating (r)evolution of medical possibilities. Once again, ethical reflection is faced with a challenge. Our attention is first drawn

Centrum voor Bio-Medische Ethiek, Kapucijnenvoer 35, 3000 Leuven, Belgium

W. Land, J. B. Dossetor (Eds.)
Organ Replacement Therapy:
Ethics, Justice and Commerce

to what appears to be a generally positive consensus that can be found on this topic in the ethical literature: "Transplanting an organ or tissue from a dead person to a living person presents no ethical problem." This might indicate that ethical reflection has peacefully arrived at a conclusion on this matter. Yet, we should immediately add that this consensus is much harder to substantiate when it concerns living donors. Nevertheless, we would prefer to address another aspect of this problem that has surfaced in the concrete regulation of organ donation as it is fixed by law in Belgium: the presumption of principal agreement or the opting-out system.

Let us first clarify our ethical point of departure: an act is ethically good if it is beneficial to the person, adequately considered in him- or herself, in relation to others and to society at large. The person can never be understood in isolation: to be fully human, one has to situate being human itself between the poles of conscientious freedom and responsible involvement, self-development and solidarity. We stress the basically relational structure of our being human: every human being is a relational being. To become human we need others: to be human we have to be confirmed by others in our existence.

This attitude can also guide us in our position on the presumption of principal agreement for organ donation. If a person has not explicity refused this agreement beforehand, the presumption of agreement holds under the law. If a professional and intensive campaign of information and conscientization has been carried out to reach the general public, than we believe such a legal structure may represent an important step in the promotion of the moral level of a society. On the basis of our ethical understanding that human beings are situated between a striving for self-development and solidarity, building the presumption of solidarity into the law appears, then, to be ethically justified.

We have to admit, however, that another point of view is very frequently taken in the literature. It has been pointed out that we would be better served by a principle of free agreement. It is an ideal that each person have the opportunity to make a conscious choice during their lifetime with respect to the destination of their organs after death. In this, each person would decide for himself or herself whether or not to engage their human solidarity with regard to others. However, applied ethics always has to develop within the givens of reality. It is well known that, notwithstanding major campaigns for donor cards, etc., very little progress has been made. In our own opinion, the legal structure of principal agreement appears to offer an expression of a basic characteristic of the human person. In the present circumstances, therefore, we see no reason to react negatively. Of course, it should be clear at the same time that if the givens with regard to the recruitment of organs change, then the ethical evaluation of this program also will have to be rethought. Meanwhile, one of the fundamental dimensions of our being human – solidary responsibility – is fully expressed by the opting-out system.

This ethical approach offers an alternative to possible abuses and one-sided options. Our anthropological model keeps open the possibility of life for others when we exercise solidary responsibility in the reality that surrounds us. All the elements of this issue and the ethical reflection that has been suggested for dealing with the questions testify to the interwoveness of our being human. Perhaps, medical technology can appear to be threatening. But in the end, it remains the assignment for us all to integrate these creative possibilities in a meaningful project of existence.

# Presumed Consent and Cadaver Organ Donation: Is There a Place for Family Involvement?

J. R. Pena[1], R. Pena[2], and A. Gomes da Costa[3]

## Organ Procurement in Portugal (1980–1990)

In 1976, Portugal adopted presumed consent legislation concerning cadaver organ donation for transplantation. This law took its inspiration from several attempts to introduce a similar contracting-out system in Britain, and from the proceedings of the joint committee of experts of the Council of Europe which led to the Resolution (78) adopted by the Committee of Ministers on the 11 May 1978.

If death occurs in such a way that organs could be suitable for transplantation, every nonobjecting individual becomes a donor under presumed consent legislations. Somebody with a phobia against donation should register as an objector. This philosophy has been widely adopted in Europe, but in some countries the rules demand that family must not oppose, which in practice is the equivalent of giving permission.

In Portugal, with a population of approximately ten million, we could harvest the organs from 133 cadaver donors in 1989 with very little family involvement (Pena 1989).

## Condition of the Cadaver According to the Law

After death, the remaining body is no longer a person: the attributes of personality have absolutely ceased. The body of a deceased person is a thing. It is however a very special thing. Under Roman law, it was sacred (*res religiosa*). This idea had certainly been inherited from older civilizations, and extended through the medieval period within Christianity, and beyond. Respect and restrain in face of a corpse explains much of the difficulties that

[1] Hospitais Civis de Lisboa, Rua Duarte Galvão No. 54, 1500 Lisbon, Portugal
[2] Faculdade de Direito da Universidade Clássica de Lisboa, Lisbon, Portugal
[3] Hospital da Cruz Vermelha Portuguesa, Rua Duarte Galvão No. 54, 1500 Lisbon, Portugal

W. Land, J. B. Dossetor (Eds.)
Organ Replacement Therapy:
Ethics, Justice and Commerce

ancient doctors met in their attempts to develop the knowledge of human anatomy. Even in our days, we are well aware of the negative feelings and reactions against every sort of post mortem manipulation. Sometimes these negative feelings may be exaggerated in what we might call a true phobia.

## Powers of the State and of the Family

When St. Francesco of Sales was a student of law in Padova (in the Seventeenth Century) he made a will to donate his body to the School of Anatomy. This is generally accepted within the limits of law. But this right, recognized for the individual himself, is not transmissible to the family, at least within Portuguese jurisprudence (Caeiro 1960). The body cannot be sold and cannot be inherited. The human body is *res extra commercium*. The body does not belong to the family. The powers of the family on the corpse are transient and precarious: the relatives have the right and the duty of showing their affection. To proceed with the funerals, they must however comply with the rules of sanitary and mortuary state policies.

The body does not belong to the State, either. But it is the concern of the State to impose by means of law a certain number of rules:

- The corpse is human, law protects it from indignity.
- Sanitary rules applying to the funerals.
- Mandatory post mortem examination when death was the result of violence, either by accident or crime.

When these objectives that the State considers a priority are fulfilled, the corpse is rendered to the family and friends, or in some other way the funerals are done.

## Portuguese Law of Graveyards (1840)

States never refrained from passing laws and regulations concerning the cadaver, even when they were difficult to accept by the people. In 1840, Portugal was a constitutional monarchy. One particular government – not very popular – passed legislation forbidding burial to be done inside churches. This was called the law of graveyards. It was the last drop for a upheaval, led possibly by a woman of the people – Maria da Fonte – and the clergy of northern Portugal. The government was overthrown, but quite interestingly the law of graveyards is still in force.

## Medical Use of Cadavers

Beyond the objectives that the State and the law consider traditionally with priority, there are in the cadaver a number of important utilities which for centuries had much to do with the medical sciences. Medicine and surgery could never be what they are today to the benefit of mankind, without the knowledge and development of human anatomy and pathology.

It is also a fact that occasionally doctors and society did not feel at ease with each other when the former needed to get hold of the scientific utilities of a human dead body. It is enough to remember old tales of body-snatchers, who secretely disinterred the bodies of the dead for the purposes of dissection. Dissection was probably taken by society as some sort of further punishment beyond life. It was tolerated when done on the bodies of condemned criminals and poor destitute people.

## Organs for Transplantation

Transplantation has shed an entirely new light on the utilities of the cadaver. Parts of the body can now be transplanted into patients restoring them to health. The results of organ transplantation have improved spectacularly over the last 10 years. Either xenotransplantation will emerge as an useful alternative, or it seems now that society will change its views, rules, and the whole process and practice to salvage live organs from dead people. Harvesting will be an automatic procedure under appropriate circumstances.

## The Problem of Consent (Contracting-In and -Out Systems)

Some countries are still attached to a contracting-in system, through which willing people by means of donor cards make their will of organ donation. When there is no card, the family is approached for granting permission. This turn towards the family might well seem practical and acceptable: however, its legitimacy is not all clear. One understands that relatives and friends might well express their opposition, but it seems controversial, on moral grounds, that they should have the power and possibility of giving permission.

Contracting-out systems have been adopted by a large number of European countries. Every nonobjecting individual becomes a donor if the appropriate technical conditions should ever arise. In these circumstances, involvement of the family is not necessary and should probably be avoided.

## Grief

Grief is a complex procedure, with emotional reactions and somatic symptoms. Grief will resolve eventually with time, but time is not on the side of those who need the organs. In particular circumstances, grief can be pathological. It may be the cause of psychotic reactions (depression, schizophrenia) and can even lead to death when not properly resolved (Lieberman 1983; Marley 1989; Rees and Lutkins 1967). Anger is also part of pathological grief. Cleopatra, the queen of Egypt, had the messengers killed whenever the news were bad.

Among risk factors of pathological grief, some are found in the context of organ procurement: short, terminal disease; sudden death; and fear of mutilation. These matters should be decided in cold blood, long before. Otherwise, the Hippocratic principle *primum non nocere,* which has long been a cornerstone of medical practice, would not apply to the case of the bereaved relatives.

## Conclusion

Permission for organ donation should be granted by law, in the absence of objection by the individual himself. Additional trauma and potential harm should be spared to relatives in mourning.

## References

Caeiro AM (1960) Condição jurídica do cadáver. Boletim do Ministério da Justiça 94:49–78

Lieberman S (1983) Life threatening symptoms due to morbid grief. Br Med J 286:702

Marley J (1989) Grief and how to manage it. Practitioner 233:287

Pena JR (1989) Transplantação renal: o ponto da situação em Portugal. Acta Med Port II Ser. [Suppl. 2]:11–15

Rees DW, Lutkins SG (1987) Mortality of bereavement. Br Med J 4:13–16

# Organ Donation by Presumed Consent: Consequences and Duties to the Society That Legalizes It

A. Mendes and H. Alves

Portuguese law (Decree no. 553/76 of July 13, 1976) has recognized the concept of cerebral death and has accepted the current practice of organ removal by presumed consent, expressing as possible and legally acceptable any mode of opposition to that removal. That opposition is valid only when expressed in life by the possible donor. The family only has the right of expressing that opposition, they do not have the right of denying consent for any surgical act envisaging organ removal.

The Portuguese legislator had expressed the intention of bringing the Portuguese law on this subject up to date making possible the medical movement with transplantation in mind. Public opinion did not actively condemn a possible excess of zeal on this subject, even when some newspaper editors intended to protest against this law. Due to doubts and questions expressed by doctors working in medicolegal area, the concept of cerebral death was legally confirmed and accepted as valid by the high authority named Procuradoria Geral da Republica.

It can probably not be said that all the levels of public opinion have a perfect conscience about the pratical meaning of the application of this law, but we must recognize the first line of thinking, the excellence of intention, and even the correctness of Portuguese law. We accept that the State's right to legalize practical organ removal by presumed consent must be recognized, and we think it is good and natural that the State should believe wholeheartedly in the good moral formation of its people. Such a moral formation would surely lead to the agreement of the deceased, if they could come back to life for a few moments. They would surely agree with keeping their organs alive inside a live sick person, thereby helping him to be a healthy one. The deceased would surely formally reject the alternative for his organs: the whole destruction and complete uselessness.

But, for a State which abolished the death sentence over more than a century ago and now recognizes through ethical and medical motives the right to permit intentional disorganization of a still functional biological structure of a deceased person without any expressed consent, there are some consequent obligations. These obligations arise from this attitude and the State's assumption that the people are good. The State too, being by

Centro de Histocompatibilidade do Norte, Pavilhão "Maria Fernanda", Rua Dr. Roberto Frias, 4100 Porto, Portugal

W. Land, J. B. Dossetor (Eds.)
Organ Replacement Therapy:
Ethics, Justice and Commerce

definition a "good person", must then also be so in practice. The opposite would be an absurd position, not integrated, without objectives, in such a delicate subject as the question of life and death.

The first obligation is that the State, by all its means of legislation, policy statement, advertisement, or counseling must reduce as much as possible, by every means, and on all the organizing social levels the probability of existence of organ donors. For instance, it is an unacceptable attitude that such a State should passively permit traffic conditions which result in a kind of Russian roulette game and which may be played by all the population to find the unlucky potential donors. For example, as far as the emergency services and the intensive care units are concerned the existence of good care is fundamental and all the high risk patients must be cared for with the greatest efficiency and medical attention to ensure the best possible health situation. If one allows the existence of situations which easily generate donors, an illegitimate aspect of organ removal by presumed consent arises. It is completely immoral to assume that those who were ill treated in life and who lacked attention and proper care should have such a good moral formation that they understand the need to donate a good organ instead of wasting it. The practice of human transplantation is motivated mainly by the patient's interests. In those patients, the first to be respected as patients are the probable donors.

The second obligation of the State which approves this law is, at the same time that it makes sure there are no easy donors, to guarantee that conditions are created under which no proper opportunities of organ removal are lost, at least until the quantity of organs meets the needs. Recognizing the later usefulness of the painful situation of death to help somebody, a democratic State has an implicit and fundamental obligation to treat all its patients equally, generating equal opportunities for equal situations, and envisaging the good health of all the people to whom it is responsible. To reach this goal, it will have to supervise and to manage the national resources of organs generated by organ removal which are not specifically declared and so intentionally offered to a specific person.

To manage, to give, to offer: who is the owner? Who owns those organs? To whom is the right of owning the organs of a deceased person transferred? As stated above, it is not held by the family. But the transplant organ is not a gold nugget abandoned in nature without a link with its environment, expecting somebody to perhaps find it, who might ask for it, or who might transform it and own it. So, the organ is not the property of the surgeon, the surgical team, or of the hospital department, either. Nor are patients the property of the hospital: hospitals exist to serve them. The situation of internment does not give property rights. The organs of the deceased persons are not State property, either. The State is not a holy incarnation of people, and they are not cells of it. People as human beings have, relative to the State, a superior dignity, and the State has only the dignity that people confer on it.

Will organs be the property of any organizations for organ sharing? Clearly not. If organ donors when alive did not choose them as the entity to which their organs should be offered, nobody, neither surgeon teams who are not themselves owners of removed organs, nor any other people or institution without those rights can give organ property rights to those organizations.

To whom then should we attribute these rights or who must be recognized as the owner of the organs? If the donation is not expressed and so directed to somebody, but only "presumed" and this presumption is legalized and admitted by the State, then the "gift" is made to all the living population. The organs are the people's property as a whole, and especially the patients' property. One organ only belongs to its receiver when it is correctly chosen for him.

The State has the obligation to guarantee an impartial choice of receptor. This choice must be made according to previously established multifactorial criteria, which must be defined so as to protect the interests of the patients and not professional, medical, or other interests, which might be in conflict with those of the patients. If there are no good scientific motives to impose a criteria of selection which must oblige all concerned in the transplant to choose in a specific way, then the choice must be made based on a common agreement among the various groups of specialists in the area.

Each patient must have the right to know the rules of selection and his position on the waiting list. Since the "donation" is made to the national community, the waiting list must be a national list. Only on that condition can the State guarantee that each citizen on the waiting list has equal opportunity for each organ. Although it may not seem fair that the surgeon who collected the organ should act as its owner, the State should however grant him the right to know the use that the organ was put to, and if the rules for receptor choice were respected in the process. If the rules had not been respected, then this surgeon might legally prosecute the technicians or institutions involved in the incorrect procedure, acting as the State's expert on the subject.

Criteria are not enough to guarantee the receiver's right to equal opportunity, it is also essential that their application be institutionalized and guaranteed. To this effect the State has a practical solution, which derives from the genial conception of Van Rood in 1967 and which makes possible an interdisciplinary cooperation and good choice of the receptor. The Eurotransplant-like organizations are a gift of medical intelligence to help the State in fulfilling well its function. On the other hand, they must be helped by the State as organizations of public and national interest.

Concerning the donor the State has also some obligations. The existence of an "opposers" list is an imperative necessity which must be efficient and operational without causing hindrance to the transplant program. It is imperative for the opposition to be a real and effective right. In the case of an "opposition", the State's attitude must be one of tolerance, but if the same person later finds himself in the position of a receiver, then the priority must not be given to him. In the same way, an assassin must not benefit from the organs of his victim.

In a State where consent is presumed, the use of a donation card or an opposer's card is incoherent and even inadvisable. In the case of a serious medical condition, each citizen should be treated independently of his views on the subject of transplantation. Especially his position on organ donation must only be made known after the confirmation of his cerebral death has been made, so that all patients may be treated with equal attention and rights.

And, finally, it would be desirable for the State to invest its efforts in medical investigation so that medical transplantation should, as soon as possible, become an interesting, but old and useless therapeutical procedure.

*Acknowledgement.* We thank Helena Langford C. S. Vieira for her kind assistance with the translation of this communication.

# Donor Recruitment: Individual Rights on Health Care and the Feasibility of a Presumed Consent and a Required Request System

F. T. de Charro[1], J. E. M. Akveld[1], and D. J. Hessing[2]

## Introduction

The fear of commercialization in donor recruitment has been one motive for politicians in the Netherlands to devote attention to legislation for transplantation. More fundamentally, there is a need to clarify the sometimes conflicting interpretations of Articles 22 and 11 of the Dutch Constitution: Article 22 declares a right to health care, for instance, for patients on the waiting list for a kidney transplantation, and Article 11 states a right to physical integrity for everybody. These rights imply a certain level of protection of living and post mortem donors. The still growing importance of transplantation technologies in medical science demands a solution of the legal issues involved. However solutions of the legal issues can only be assessed from a medical/socio/psycho/legal analysis of the underlying reality. In this paper, donor scarcity in the Netherlands will be analyzed from an economic, a psychological, and a legal point of view.

## Economic Analysis

The end stage renal disease program (ESRD program) in the Netherlands as well as in other countries is an expensive health program. Estimates of costs of ESRD treatments have been made according to the principles of cost-effectiveness analyses (De Charro 1986). The costs of transplantation in the first year are about as high as the costs of hemodialysis in a center, but in the second and later years after transplantation, the costs of treatment diminish substantially to a very low level. By means of Markov chain analysis using EDTA and Eurotransplant data it has been shown that increases in the annual number of transplants do not affect the number of life-years gained by the ESRD program over a decade. The quality of life of transplanted patients, however, does increase substantially. The costs of the ESRD program would diminish substantially if the annual number of transplants in the Netherlands rose from about 27.5 per million to about 40 per million of the population,

[1] Erasmus University Rotterdam, Faculty of Law, Health Policy and Law Program, P. O. Box 1738, NL-3000 DR, Rotterdam, The Netherlands
[2] Leyden University, Faculty of Law, Leyden, The Netherlands

W. Land, J. B. Dossetor (Eds.)
Organ Replacement Therapy:
Ethics, Justice and Commerce

which is medically feasible and desirable. The costs to society of a 5-year ESRD program would diminish by about 60 million guilders (5 %). So kidney transplantation saves society substantial amounts of money and is neutral with regard to the quantity and fruitful with regard to the quality of life. On economic grounds, kidney transplantation should be stimulated as much as possible.

## The Psychology of Organ Donation

The supply of organs for transplantation can be considered a public good. When a considerable number of people become aware that they can profit from a public good without contributing to it, a social dilemma exists, since the number of voluntary contributions will decrease and as a consequence the public good will be undersupplied. Maximizing individual gain in a situation of outcome-interdependence thus results in a collective suboptimum and consequently also in an individual suboptimum.

Hessing combined the two foundations of the neoclassical theory of rational behavior under uncertainty as described by Von Neumann and Morgenstern – the subjective expected utility theory and the game theory – in a so-called social orientation model. In this model organ donation is a private act that concerns self-other allocations. Then the altruistic social orientation is needed next to attitudes to explain the variance in behavior in this social dilemma.

The results of Hessing's research confirmed that the discrepancy between attitude and behavior in the case of organ donation can be explained to a large extent by the influence of personality variables (Hessing 1990). These personality variables are the altruistic social orientation and the fear of death and can hardly be changed because of their central position in the personality structure. A more fundamental solution of the social dilemma of organ transplantation at the level of society seems inevitable.

## Legal Solutions to the Dilemma of Organ Donation

The solution of the social dilemma can be found in two ways. First, one can change the cost-gains structure of this social dilemma by the introduction of an opting-out system. Secondly and additionally one could try to influence the organisation of donor procurement and communication in the hospital with the next of kin.

Ninety-nine per cent of the Dutch interviewees are in favor of transplantation. However, the opting-in system provides too many obstacles at the individual level to transform that attitude into actual social behavior. Cooperative behavior cannot be made productive without a prior decision to solve the social dilemma of organ donation at the level of public policy, as is the case with all collective goods. The most evident and clear solution at the public level, therefore, is the change to an opting-out system, which changes the cost-gains structure of the individual in a fundamental way.

The opting-out system provides an elegant and social justifiable solution for a lack of altruistic behavior in society. In this system, both cooperative and defective behavior are sanctioned on an individual level. Those who want to be a potential donor after death will be so automatically, without having to take action. And those who refuse to take part in the solution of this social dilemma will have to take action to make their objections known.

An opting-out system, however, is neither a necessary nor a sufficient condition for an optimal supply of donor organs, since in European countries with an opting-out system, for instance France, donor recruitment is sometimes lower than in countries where an opting-in system exists. From this it can be surmised that an important bottleneck for organ procurement is to be found in the hospitals. It seems, therefore, necessary to provide incentives for the organization in the hospital. Since so few people carry a donor card, it is not considered worthwhile in many hospitals to search for a possible donor card. One immediately approaches the next of kin to investigate whether they have objections against explantation of organs. An incentive could be provided by a weak version of a required request system. A strong version of this system was introduced in the USA and does have a favorable impact on organ procurement in some states. In many states, the system is ineffective in the strong version in which it is prescribed to approach the next of kin in all hospital death cases, even if organ donation would not be possible. A weak version, limiting the required consultation to cases in which organ donation is considered to be medically feasible could, however, be a useful instrument in the mix of sociolegal policy instrument to increase the number of donor organs and improve donor recruitment procedures.

## Conclusion and Discussion

In general, the conclusion is that economic and psycholegal analyses of donor recruitment seem to indicate a logical place within the socio/psycho/economic/legal policy mix for presumed consent and a weak version of required consultation. In general, an international scientific approach to donor recruitment in which the effectiveness of sociolegal mixes of policy instruments for donor recruitment is compared could be fruitful to provide more insight in factors determining donor organ supply.

## References

Akveld JEM (1985) Transplantation legislation. Is there a choice? Gent

De Charro F, Banta HD (1986) Transplant policy in the Netherlands. Int J Technol Assess Health Care 2

Hessing DJ (1990) The social dilemma of organ donation: opting in or opting out? In: Shanteau J, Harris RJ (eds) Psychological research in organ donation. American Psychological Association, Washington

# Psycholegal Aspects of Organ Procurement Systems

D. J. Hessing[1], F. T. de Charro[2], and P. W. C. Akkermans[2]

## Introduction

Post mortem organ donation can take place in an opting-in system or in an opting-out system. In the strict opting-in system, the organs of the deceased may only be taken out when the deceased has given permission (by means of a donor card or a commitment in a central register). In a strict opting-out system, the explantation of organs is permitted unless the deceased has made objections. To increase the availability of donor organs, the Dutch government has proposed an Organ Donation Bill, which is mainly based on an opting-in system.

Presently in the Netherlands – under an unofficial opting-in system – 20 % of the Dutch population report that they have signed a donor card (group I), 32 % are willing to donate, but do not have a donor card (group II), 41 % are (still) in doubt or have never thought about becoming a donor (group III), and 7 % refuse to donate after death (group IV). This paper presents an estimate of the effective donor percentage (defined as the percentage of donor reportings in which – based on the legal system and the behavior of the next of kin – organ donation can occur) in twelve different legal systems.

## The Attitude Toward Organ Donation and the Effective Percentage of Donation

In order to make an analysis of the effects of variants of systems of organ donation, the following assumptions about groups I to IV are made: if the legal system involves a national registration of donors and nondonors, we make the simple assumption for groups I and II that all of group I will register as donors and none of group II will register as donors. To avoid fictitious precision, group I will be set at 20 % and group II at 30 %. By registering as a donor, there will be a group with an *explicitly positive* attitude, which will be group 1, and a group with an *implicitly positive* attitude, which will be group 2.

[1] Faculty of Law, Leyden University, Hugo de Grootstraat 27, 2311 XK Leiden, The Netherlands

[2] Erasmus University Rotterdam, Faculty of Law, P. O. Box 1738, NL-3000 DRRotterdam, The Netherlands

W. Land, J. B. Dossetor (Eds.)
Organ Replacement Therapy:
Ethics, Justice and Commerce

In general, the direct next of kin will be informed about the positive attitude.

Group III requires further analysis, because the doubt expressed by members of this group can have different sources. This group contains about 40 % of the total number of respondents. One of the sources for doubt can be that the person prefers to leave the decision to his/her next of kin. The decision in this case is, therefore, implicitly delegated. Also the pros and cons of organ donation can be in balance. In this case, the doubt can be defined as a neutral position. In all other cases, the doubt may be related to a resistance to organ donation that one is unwilling to express, and the doubt is in fact a cloak for a negative attitude. The three implicated sources for doubt – delegation, neutrality, and disguised resistance – are for the sake of the argument put at 15 %, 15 %, and 10 %, together again 40 %. These groups can be defined as the groups *implicitly delegating* (group 3), *implicitly neutral* (group 4), and group 5, which is *implicitly negative.*

Some of those who are not willing to donate will probably lack the

**Table 1.** Effective donor percentage of 12 legal systems for organ donation with 50 % or 65 % permission of the next of kin

| System/Definition | Wills observed of groups | Relatives decide for groups | Donation possible | Effective % of donation | |
|---|---|---|---|---|---|
| | | | | Permission | |
| | | | | 50 % | 65 % |
| A Strict opting in | 1 | | 1 | 20.0 | 20.0 |
| B Limited additional opting in | 1 6 | 2 | 1 2 | 35.0 | 39.5 |
| C Broad additional opting in | 1 6 | 2 3 4 | 1 2 3 4 | 50.0 | 59.0 |
| D Limited replacing opting in | 1 6 | 2 3 4 5 | 1 2 3 4 5 | 57.5 | 68.8 |
| E Broad replacing opting in | | 1 6 | 1 | 50.0 | 65.0 |
| F Limited additional opting out | 1 6 | 5 | 1 5 | 87.5 | 89.8 |
| G Broad additional opting out | 1 6 | 3 4 5 | 1 3 4 5 | 72.5 | 79.3 |
| H Limited replacing opting out | 1 6 | 2 3 4 5 | 1 2 3 4 5 | 57.5 | 68.8 |
| I Broad replacing opting out | | 1 2 3 4 5 | 1 2 3 4 5 | 50.0 | 65.0 |
| J Strict opting out | 6 | | 1 2 3 4 5 | 95.0 | 95.0 |
| K Complete decision in opting in | 1 6 | | 1 | 20.0 | 20.0 |
| L Complete decision in opting out | 1 6 | | 1 2 3 4 5 | 95.0 | 95.5 |

motivation to have themselves registered. This underestimation of refusals in a national registration must, for the sake of the analyses, lead to a splitting up of group IV (respondents who are not willing to donate) into a part that will have his/her opinion registered, and a part that will not do so. In general, the relatives will be informed of the opinion of the deceased when no registration took place. This underregistration will be implemented in the analyses by dividing group IV (see Table 1) into two equally large groups (both 5 %) of persons that will (group 6) and persons that will not register (group 5). The part that will not register will be added to the group of doubting persons of which the attitude in fact was an implicit negative one. The result is that group 5 has an implicitly negative attitude that has two sources: 10 % doubters and 5 % refusers who are unwilling to register.

## Legal Systems for Donation of Organs

To describe the effects of several systems for organ donation, a classification of 12 organ donation systems (A to H) is presented (Table 1). When calculating the consequences, two alternatives are supposed for the result of the possible judgment of the next of kin. The first alternative is based on an opting-in or opting-out rate of the next of kin of 50 %, the second alternative on a rate of 65 %. The systems do not only differ in a strict legal division of decisional power, but also with regard to the expectation about the level in which the relatives take into account in their own judgment the judgment of the deceased.

An important question is whether the Dutch Organ Donation Bill – which at present has the characteristics of system D – will result in an increase in the number of organs for transplantation, since the new donor cards will only be effective for those people that now report that they are willing to donate, but do not have a donor card (yet). A negative effect of the obligatory nature of the registration could be the emergence of a 'reactance' under the present donor card carriers because of the loss of the altruistic element in donating.

## Required Request

One of the aims of the Organ Donation Bill is to increase the number of transplantable organs. By choosing some form of consent system, this aim will not be reached. The conclusion, therefore, must be that there is a danger that once this Bill has come into force, a decrease in the supply of organs will result if no supplementary measures are taken. One of these measures could be the introduction of a required request system. This system would imply that, after a potential donor has been declared brain dead, the body-preserving measures may not be stopped before it is checked whether the deceased did have a donor card or not. If such a card is not found, the family must be asked for consent in organ explantation for transplantation.

Since in The Netherlands many people are in favor of a legal power of decision for the next of kin, a required request system deserves serious attention. The required request system as such is not linked exclusively with either an opting-in system or an opting-out system. In the lesser strict variants of these systems consultation of the relatives already takes place.

The Dutch population has a positive attitude toward the introduction of a required request system. Among those who under the present system are willing to donate after death (52 % of the respondents) 67 % consider it to be a good system, 5 % have no opinion, and 29 % consider it not a good system (Hessing 1990). Of those who at present doubt or refuse (48 % of all respondents) 45 % consider it to be a good system, 22 % have no opinion, and 33 % are against such a system. The opponents of a required request system derive mainly from the group that has already more problems with donating organs after death. It can be suggested that their attitude toward such a system is partly the result of their negative attitude toward donation itself.

Introduction of a required request system can take place as an addition to an opting-in or an opting-out system. The obligation to approach the relatives can be preceded by an obligation to consult the donor registration or to search for a donor card.

## Conclusions

It seems highly improbable that the supply of organs will increase significantly by the simple registration of positive and negative wills only. A required request system seems an adequate solution of the Dutch shortage given the predominant positive attitude of the Dutch population toward the introduction of such a system. The system that is going to be introduced in the Netherlands will – in any case – observe the written negative decision of the deceased. For that reason, we believe that the legislator should explicitly state that – for those cases in which there is no written opinion of the deceased – organ donation is given the benefit of the doubt. This can be done by taking the opting-out system as the point of departure for the consultation of the next of kin.

## References

D. J. Hessing, 1990, The legislation of organ donation, Paper presented at the 2nd European Conference on Law and Psychology, Nürnberg, September 13–15.

# Current Practice and the Legal, Ethical, and Religious Status of Post Mortem Organ Donation in the Islamic World

A. S. Daar

## Introduction

In Islamic societies, it is really not possible to separate religion from a discussion of ethics or Islamic law. Therefore, in order to answer the question posed by the title of this presentation, it is necessary first to understand the link between religion and Islamic law and how this affects the ethics of transplantation. From this conceptual perspective, I will then discuss the present ethical and legal situation before finally looking at the current status of transplantation with particular reference to post mortem organ donation.

## Law, Ethics, and Religion Are Linked in Islam

In Islam the law, individual conduct, and professional ethics are all intimately related to the religion itself (Sachedina 1988). In this sense, it differs from many other religions. It encompasses the secular with the spiritual, the mundane with the celestial. It provides a code of life (Al Bar 1991). Islamic law, or *Shariah,* derives its ultimate authority from:

a) the Quran, which is Allah's own word transmitted to mankind through the Prophet Mohammad (*Pbuh*), and
b) examples of behavior and the sayings and teachings of the prophet. These were thoroughly documented by his companions and subsequent compilers and constitute the body of learning known as the *Hadith.*

## Islamic Jurisprudence and Organ Transplantation

From these two sources subsequent generations, through the process of *Ijtihad* (effort) and *Ijmaa* (consensus), have derived and continue to derive

Dept. of Surgery, College of Medicine, Sultan Qaboos University, P. O. Box 32485, Al Khod, Muscat, Sultanate of Oman

W. Land, J. B. Dossetor (Eds.)
Organ Replacement Therapy:
Ethics, Justice and Commerce

laws for the regulation of human conduct amongst Muslims.[1] The end result of the process of study by legal scholars, using the Quran and the Hadith together with certain agreed principles of jurisprudence, is the legal opinion known as the *Fatwa*.

In the matter of renal transplantation, specific practical questions had to wait for the religious scholars to study the issues involved and then announce the Fatwas before doctors could comfortably perform, say, post mortem organ retrieval. This is similar to what happens in Jewish societies using the system of Jewish law, the Halachah (Weiss 1988). The result of these studies by scholars in Islamic jurisprudence have on the whole been very much in favor of transplantation from both the living and the post mortem donor. It is instructive to see the kind of process that was applied in the case of transplantation to arrive at these legal opinions, because this illustrates how it is possible that the Shariah "has never failed to find an answer for any question, an opinion (Fatwa) for any problem and a rule for every situation" (Al Qattan 1984). There is in-built flexibility in Islam to deal with whatever developments may arise in society today, tomorrow, and for all time.

In dealing with a situation such as transplantation, the following principles of jurisprudence were applicable:

1. Need and necessity are equivalent.
2. Necessity allows "prohibited" matters.
3. Injurious "harm" should be removed.
4. Prevention of evil has priority over obtaining benefit.
5. The greater benefit prevails over a lesser benefit.

Another important principle is that in Islam life is sacred, and its preservation, including that of the self, is a necessary and integral aim in jurisprudence. This calls for the adoption of all available scientific methods of treatment to preserve life (Al Qattan 1984). Medical treatment is considered not only a right, but an obligation (Sahin 1990). In support of transplantation the following have been quoted by scholars:

a) The Quran says:
   (i) of the faithful that "they give priority over themselves even though they are needy." and
   (ii) "whosoever saves a human life it is as though he has saved all mankind."
b) From the Hadith we also have these two traditions:
   (i) "The faithful in their mutual love and compassion are like the body... if one member complains of an ailment, all other members will rally in response."
   (ii) "The faithful to one another are like the blocks in a whole building... they fortify one another."

[1] Strictly speaking Shariah law applies only to Muslims; non-Muslim societies (say Christian or Jewish) living within a larger Muslim entity are allowed to be judged by their own law.

## Current Opinions Regarding Post Mortem Organ Donation

### Ethical

The Islamic Code of Medical Ethics, which resulted from the First International Conference on Islamic Medicine in Kuwait in January 1981, strongly sanctioned organ donation thus:

"The donation of body fluids or organs, such as blood transfusion to the bleeding or a kidney transplant to the patient with bilateral irreparable renal damage ... is *Fardh Kifaya,* a duty that donors fulfil on behalf of society," and

"If the living are able to donate, then the dead are even more so; no harm will afflict the cadaver if the heart, kidneys, eyes or arteries are taken to be put to good use in a living person. This is indeed charity."

Most transplanters working in Arab countries, which are predominantly Muslim, would therefore have no problem with the ethics of cadaver organ retrieval and transplantation.

### Legal (Islamic Fatwa)

In Egypt the following Fatwas precede the inclusive Fatwas adopted in 1986 and 1988 by the International Conference of Islamic Jusists (Al Bar 1990):

(i) Fatwa No. 1065 of 6th June 1959 by the Grand Mufti of Egypt sanctioned blood transfusion (normally in Islam blood is considered dirty, *Najs*).

(ii) Fatwa No. 1087 of 14th April 1959 by Sheik Hassan Maamoon, the Egyptian Grand Mufti, sanctioned corneal transplantation from cadavers of unidentified persons and for those who agree to donate after their death.

(iii) Sheikh Hureidi, the succeeding Grand Mufti, extended in 1966 Fatwa 1087 of 1959 to include other organs.

(iv) Fatwa 1323 of 5th December 1979 by another Grand Mufti, Gad al Haq, sanctioned donation of organs from the living provided no harm was done, the donation is done freely, in good faith and for the love of God and human fraternity. He also sanctioned cadaver donation provided there was a will of testament or the consent of the relatives of the deceased. In case of unidentified corpses, an order from the Magistrate should be obtained prior to harvesting of the organs.

The Senior Ulamaa (Scholars) Commission of the Kingdom of Saudi Arabia, in Fatwa number 99 dated 9.11.1402 in the Hijra Muslim calender (equivalent to 25 August 1982) resolved by majority the following:

"The permissibility to remove an organ or part thereof from a dead person for the benefit of a Muslim, should the need arise, should the removal cause no dissatisfaction, and should the transplantation seem likely to be successful."

With regard to the question of brain death criteria and the definition of death, the Third International Conference of Islamic Jurists meeting in Amman, Jordan, on 16 October 1986 in its resolution No. 5, declared the following:

"A person (is) considered legally dead, and all the Sharia's principles can be applied, when one of the following signs is established:

1. Complete stoppage of the heart and breathing, and the doctors decide that it is irreversible.
2. Complete stoppage of all vital functions of the brain, and the doctors decide that it is irreversible, and the brain has started to degenerate."[2]

It can therefore be seen that from the religious point of view both the concept of cadaver organ donation and that of brain death would be acceptable to the majority of Muslims (Daar 1990). What is also interesting is that the definition of death is left not to legal scholars but to doctors, in recognition of the division of scholarship and expertise in Islamic societies.

## Legal (Secular Law)

In many Arab countries today there is a duality of legal process: on the one hand there is *Shariah* law, which is applied in certain specified circumstances, and on the other there is secular law, whose promulgation is often, but not always, influenced by the former. For example, in Kuwait in 1979, a Fatwa sanctioning transplantation of organs from both the living and the dead was announced by the Minister of Islamic Affairs, and this was then followed by Law No. 7 of 1983 by the Kuwaiti Parliament. This was summarized recently by Dr. M. Al-Arjawi of Kuwait University as follows:

1. Removing organs from a dead body is permissible, if it will save the life of another.
2. Donation should be free of charge.
3. The procedures should be carried out under qualified medical supervision, and
4. Prior consent of the deceased, or the consent of relatives, is a prerequisite.

[2] Apparently the Islamic League Conference of 1987 was not in favor of removing organs prior to complete cessation of circulation and respiration. However, all previous Fatwas were sanctioned. The most detailed Fatwa on this subject was again by the 4th International Conference of Islamic Jurists meeting in Jeddah in 1988. This Fatwa again endorsed previous ones, (including the landmark Fatwa of 1986, which sanctioned cadaver donation and brain death criteria), clearly rejected any trading or trafficking or organs, and stressed the principle of altruism (Al Bar 1990). It is to be noted also that, since there is no central authority (such as the Pope in the Vatican) in Islam, and since in some instances different scholars or groups of scholars (not individuals without special learning) may arrive at different Fatwas (opinions) regarding the same matter, Muslims are permitted to choose between these options.

The United Arab Emirates announced a proposed law on cadaver organ donation on 4th February 1990. The provisions of this law are quite similar to the Kuwaiti Law.

Since transplantation was spreading rapidly in the Middle East in the 1980s, various countries started to discuss similar laws. In order to try and have some uniformity, the 12th session of the Council of Arab Ministers of Health meeting in Khartoum 14–16 March 1987, having discussed the development of a legal instrument to regulate human organ transplants as a response to the World Health Assembly resolution WHA 40.13, came up with the Unified Arab Draft Law on Human Organ Transplants (A.40/INF.DOC/6 – 30 April 1987). Article 1 (after the preamble) states:

"specialist physicians may perform surgical operations to transplant organs from a living or dead person to another person for the purpose of maintaining life, according to the conditions and procedures laid down in this law."

Article 5 reads:

"organ transplants may be performed from a dead body, provided that consent is obtained from the next of kin, under the following conditions:

1. Death has been definitely established by a committee of three specialist physicians, including a neurologist. The physician who is to perform the operation must not be a member of the committee.
2. The deceased, while alive, did not object to the removal of any organ from his body."

Article 6: "In cases other than those provided for in this law, organ transplantation from a dead body to a living body in urgent need of the organ for the purpose of preserving life may be performed on the decision of a committee of at least three specialist physicians, who should determine the urgency of the patients' need of the organ before the transplant is performed."

In subsequent articles the Ministry of Health in each member country is then expected to designate medical centers where transplants shall be performed (Article 8) and the conditions and specifications that must be fulfilled in those places where organs are preserved, including criteria for the utilisation of such organs (Article 9).

It can thus be seen that both secular laws (where they have already been adopted or ratified) and religious opinions have taken into account developments in transplantation and have sanctioned both living and cadaver donor transplantation, including the adoption of brain death criteria. These laws are more liberal and facilitating of organ donation than the laws of many other countries.

# Organ Transplantation in the Islamic World

## Middle East/West Asia

### *In History*

It has been pointed out that transplantation is not new to Arabs or Muslims (Al Bar 1990). Arab surgeons a thousand years ago were experts at the technique of teeth transplantation. Both teeth and bone transplantation, also practised by Muslim surgeons a millenium ago, were sanctioned by Muslim jurists. Imam Nawawi (631–671 AH, equivalent to 1233–1272 A. D.) discussed fully the subject of bone and teeth transplantation in both his voluminous reference textbook of jurisprudence (*Al Majmoo*) and his concise book, *Minhaj Attalibin*. Zakaria Al Qazwini (600–682 AH/1203–1283 A. D.) advocated the use of porcine bone grafts (as these took much better than other xenografts) despite the injunction in Islam against the use of porcine products (see principles of jurisprudence, above).

### *In Recent Times*

In the modern era, however, transplantation in the Middle East is quite a recent phenomenon. Apart from Jordan, which slowly began kidney transplantation in 1972, most countries started from around 1979, although they had dialysis programs for several years prior to that. The following countries started transplantation in the years shown: Egypt 1976; Kuwait and Saudi Arabia 1979; Syria and United Arab Emirates 1985; Iraq (1973) 1978 (Al Ali 1990); Oman 1988. Limited transplantation activity started about 1986 in the North African Muslim countries of Tunisia (Ben Ayed et al. 1990), Morocco, and Algeria.

In many cases, as exemplified by Kuwait, Saudi Arabia, United Arab Emirates, and Oman etc., the history of transplantation has followed fairly distinct patterns (Daar 1988) going through the following stages:

1. Transplantation of patients abroad, mainly Europe and USA, where they somehow obtained cadaver organs.
2. Help from abroad in establishing local living-related transplant programs.
3. Supplementing local living-related transplants with imported cadaver kidneys (generally from established North European and American centers, which donated organs not used in their countries of origin because of vessel abnormalities, damage or relative contraindications in the donors, including chest infections, diabetes and hypertension).
4. Continuing transplantation of patients in some countries where commercialized living non-related organs continue to be available, and
5. Very recently, the establishment of cadaver programs locally.

W. Land, J. B. Dossetor (Eds.)
Organ Replacement Therapy:
Ethics, Justice and Commerce

**Table 1.** Kidney Transplantation in Saudi Arabia (1 July 1987–15 April 1990)

| Hospital | Live donors | Cadaveric | Total |
|---|---|---|---|
| Riyadh Armed Forces Hospital/Riyadh | 230 | 130 | 360 |
| King Faisal Specialist Hospital/Riyadh | 143 | 54 | 197 |
| Al Shaty Teaching Hospital/Jeddah | 48 | 40 | 88 |
| King Fahd National Guard Hospital/Riyadh | 28 | 14 | 42 |
| Khamees Mushyt Military Hospital/ Khamees Mushyt | 4 | 5 | 9 |
| Dammam Central Hospital/Dammam | – | 4 | 4 |
| Riyadh Central Hospital/Riyadh | 3 | – | 3 |
| King Fahd Hospital/Madina | – | 3 | 3 |
| Total | | | 706 |

Currently, living related donor transplantation predominates and thus cadaver organ donation is historically an even more recent phenomenon. However, Saudi Arabia has entered this field in a very big way, mainly because of the work of a well-organized and well-funded National Kidney Foundation. This foundation does have political support from the government and has a lot of resources backing it, with the result that a very significant contribution is made by cadaver donation (see Table 1). Furthermore, it is important to note that these cadaver donations are done on the basis of brain death criteria (Al Otaibi et al. 1985).

Cadaver organ donation has also been carried out regularly, but on a lesser scale, in Jordan, (both Saudi Arabia and Jordan have heart transplant programs). Some cadaver renal transplants have also been done in Turkey (Sert et al. 1990). Kuwait, after having gone through all the five stages of development mentioned above, had just embarked on a serious cadaver organ donation program when politically disruptive events intervened in the summer of 1990. The United Arab Emirates, having utilized a few cadaver kidneys from Europe, has not yet started local harvesting. In Oman, we have already done some locally harvested cadaver kidney transplants, and at the beginning of 1991 we hope to start a systematic program. Recently Tunisia has reported some cadaver kidney transplants (Ben Ayed et al. 1990). Egypt, surprisingly, has virtually no cadaver organ transplantation despite having been one of the first of the Muslim countries to have had Fatwas enabling this.

## Other Muslim Countries

Malaysia has had a purely living related donor program since 1975 and has not established a cadaver program. In Indonesia, a few cadaver donors have been utilized, but again no systemic program has been carried out. Pakistan is seriously looking into this, and recently both Walter Land and I were invited to participate in a symposium in Karachi to begin the process of publicizing the need for cadaver organ donation. The 15 % of the population of Singapore who are Muslims chose to remain outside the provisions of the Singaporean opting out law, and recently I have been working closely with the National Kidney Foundation of Singapore to encourage Muslims there to opt into the program so that more Muslim cadaver donors can be utilized, and therefore more Muslims will receive kidney grafts. Singapore has now also appointed Muslim transplant coordinators to help with this effort.

## Conclusion

It would appear therefore that, on the whole, there are no legal, ethical, or religious obstacles to post mortem organ donation in the Islamic world. However, cadaver kidney transplants are not yet widespread, and part of the reason for this is that modern transplantation per se is still young in Islamic countries. Factors that may contribute to the slowing of cadaver donation, though, include the following:

1. The citizens of these countries are not yet familar with the whole question of transplantation and are not really aware of the legal and religious laws pertaining to cadaver donation. A public education program is a prerequisite to any successful cadaver program.
2. The number of doctors and nurses properly trained in the discipline of transplantation is still very small. The recognition by health authorities of the contribution of transplantation to the management of end stage renal failure should result in better support for training programs. Local and regional societies, such as the Arab Society for Nephrology and Renal Transplantation and the Middle East Society for Organ Transplantation should also help in encouraging more people to take post mortem organ donation seriously. The (International) Transplantation Society also is keen to help with training.

The future, I think, is quite bright where post mortem organ donation in Islamic countries is concerned. However, much more ground work needs to be done, particularly in the education of the public and of health authorities.

## References

1. Al-Ali MAM, Al Shamma SM, Al Shamma IAA et al. (1990) Renal transplantation at Al Rashad Military Hospital (100 cases). 2nd International Congress of the Middle East Society for Organ Transplantation. Kuwait, March 11–15, 1990 (Abstract No. 110) (in press)

2. Al Bar MA (1990) Islamic view of organ transplantation. 2nd International Congress of the Middle East Society for Organ Transplantation. Kuwait, March 11–15, 1990 (in press)
3. Al Otaibi K, Al Khader A, Abomelha MS (1985) First Saudi cadaver donation. Saudi Med J 6:217
4. Al Qattan M (1984) The juristic Ijtihad regarding transplantation of organs. In: Abomelha MS (ed) Organ transplantation. Proceedings of a symposium held in Riyadh, 1984. Medical Educational Services, Oxford
5. Ben Ayed H, El-Matri A, Ben Abdallah T et al. (1990) Renal transplantation in Tunisia: a three year experience. 2nd International Congress of the Middle East Society for Organ Transplantation. Kuwait, March 11–15, 1990 (Abstract No. 069) (in press)
6. Daar AS (1988) Management of end stage renal failure in the Middle East. 2nd Conference (Kountz symposium) on Renal Failure and Transplants in Blacks. Crystal, Virginia. March 1988
7. Daar AS (1990) Renal transplantation in Islam: the basis for recent legal opinions. Emirates Med J 8:1–3
8. Sachedina AA (1988) Islamic views on organ transplantation. Transplant Proc 20(1):1084–1088
9. Sahin AF (1990) Transplantation: islamic ethics. Transplant Proc
10. Sert A, Gulay H, Karamehmetoglu M et al. (1990) Living unrelated kidney transplantation. 2nd International Congress of the Middle East Society for Organ Transplantation. Kuwait, March 11–15, 1990 (Abstract 042)
11. Weiss DW (1988) Organ transplantation, medical ethics, and Jewish Law. Transplant Proc 20(1):1071–1075

# Resistance to Cadaveric Organ Donation: Experience in a Developing Country

S. Adib Rizvi and S. A. Anwar Naqvi

Pakistan has a population of 100 million and a predominantly Muslim population which is growing at a rate of 3 % annually. The adult literacy rate is 22 %. Per capita income is US $350 annually. Potable water is available to 77 % of the population in the cities and towns, but only to 22 % of persons living in rural areas. The Government spends 1 % of the gross national product (GNP) on health of the nation. Resistance to cadaveric organ donation should be viewed against this backdrop of illiteracy and poverty.

## Problem of End Stage Renal Disease

The enormity of the problem can be assessed by the fact that an estimated 10 000 new patients of end stage renal failure (ESRF) require renal support in the form of dialysis or transplantation. By the same token, an estimated 6000 ESRF patients will require transplantation in order to maintain a stable dialysis population.

The reality, however, is very different. Due to urban bias in the health delivery system, only 25 % of the ESRD patients are able to reach a dialysis facility. Health facilities in rural areas, where 75 % of the population lives, are meagre and few facilities for the diagnosis and treatment for renal failure exist.

## Factors Responsible for Resistance to Cadaveric Donation: Ignorance and Illiteracy

In a country where only 22 % of the adults are literate, ignorance about transplantation is understandable. Only 2 % of the population finishes high school, and only 0.2 % go to college. Knowledge about transplantation through books, periodicals, and newspapers does not have the desired impact. This leaves television, which remains the most powerful medium for the uneducated. Unfortunately, this medium is state-run and subject to the

Institute of Urology and Transplantation, Dow Medical College and Civil Hospital, Karachi, Pakistan

W. Land, J. B. Dossetor (Eds.)
Organ Replacement Therapy:
Ethics, Justice and Commerce

whims of a bureaucracy which is not keen to propagate the cause of transplantation.

## Reverence for the Dead

One of the obstacles to kidney donation has been the local tradition of not parting with organs after death. There is no religious sanction in Islam against organ donation and, in fact, the senior clergy in Saudi Arabia, Jordan, and Pakistan have permitted organ donation. Removal of an organ is considered mutilation of the human body, which is perceived to be sacred after death. This appears to be an Asian attitude and is sufficiently deep-rooted to become an obstacle to organ donation.

## Lack of Intensive Care Units

With the Government spending on health limited to 1% of GNP, health infrastructure in state-run services is very meagre. Intensive care units are limited to teaching hospitals and are ill-equipped to handle patients with brain death. Since patients who could be potential donors can only be found in such specialized units, the paucity of such units means less numbers of potential patients.

## Indifferent Professional Attitude

Of the questions asked to professionals about kidney donation, correct responses about number and success were in the region of 33%. The professionals responded better regarding the number of patients on dialysis. Their knowledge about the success of liver, heart, and lung transplantation was very poor (less than 25% responded correctly).

## Negative Impact of Media Publicity

The population in Pakistan depends heavily on television for information regarding science and technology. Films such as *'Coma'* had a very negative impact on educated persons, and they felt that doctors might have a vested interest in cadaver donation. Similarly the controversy about a 'dead man' becoming alive and the Turkish donor scandal all contributed to a negative impact on the whole transplantation scene.

# The Ethical Virtues of a Futures Market in Cadaveric Organs*

L. R. Cohen

Over the last 35 years, we have witnessed extraordinary developments in transplant surgery. But in the wake of this medical miracle has come a tragic and growing shortage in the supply of transplant organs, and an ever wider recognition of that shortage. Numerous solutions have been offered, and some adopted, including advertising campaigns presumed consent, and required request. Although some increase in organ procurement has resulted, the essential problem remains, that is, the vast majority of organs that would be suitable for transplantation are not harvested. Indeed, the problem has become more severe, for with the progress in transplant techniques, principally the development of immunosuppressant drugs, the number of people who now die and suffer for want of viable organs that are instead buried and burned is growing apace.

The varied reform proposals, both academic and legislative, are based on a widespread recognition that the insufficient supply of transplant organs to meet the demand, is not the result of a natural barrier. It is not an unfortunate but unalterable circumstance of life, like gravity, for which there is neither a medical nor a legal solution. Instead it is believed, and I think correctly, that it is a problem that results from social mores and legal institutions, and is amenable to legislative solution.

The central focus of this article is a call to create a market in transplantable cadaveric tissue, and a moral defense of such a market (for more details see [1]). My specific proposal is to establish a futures market in which healthy individuals would be given the opportunity to contract for the sale of their body tissue for delivery after their death. If the vendor's organs are harvested and transplanted, a payment in the range of US $ 5000 for each major organ and lesser amounts for minor tissue would be made to his estate or designee. I would also require others in whose custody this valuable property is placed to take appropriate care with it. The hospital in which the vendor dies, as any bailee entrusted with valuable property, would have the legal duty, enforced by tort liability, to preserve his cadaver in a manner suitable for organ harvesting and to notify the purchasing agency of the decedent's condition so

* Funding for this article was provided by the Marshall Ewell Research Fund at IIT Chicago-Kent College of Law.

Chicago Kent College of Law, Illinois Institute of Technology, 77 South Wacker Drive, Chicago, IL 60606, USA

W. Land, J. B. Dossetor (Eds.)
Organ Replacement Therapy:
Ethics, Justice and Commerce

that it may harvest his organs. The proposal speaks to the harvesting of organs, not to allocating them. Consistent with my proposal, the harvested organs may be purchased by a state agency, an unregulated private entrepreneur, or something in between, and may be allocated by the market, doctors, a lottery, or any other conceivable means.

At last count about 3000 cadavers per year were being harvested in the United States. At present levels of medical technology, this represents only about one-eight of the number potentially available on grounds of medical suitability [1]. But medical suitability cannot be the only criterion of available supply. A significant barrier to organ retrieval may be social mores. And as a general matter, social mores are not to be taken lightly. Most of us ascribe to the notion that people have the right to dispose of their bodies as they see fit. Thus, a widespread and deeply held opposition to post mortem harvesting of organs, if it existed, would be a powerful constraint on organ availability.

Are there strong religious, aesthetic, psychological, or pragmatic objections to post mortem organ donation? The answer, at least in the United States and I suspect in Europe as well, is an unequivocal no. I do not say that these considerations carry no weight in people's minds. Rather, I believe, that they are simply not very strong barriers to organ donation. Given even a rather weak incentive to donate people will accede to the request. What evidence do I have to support this?

The Gallup poll consistently shows that over 75 % of Americans have no objection to organ donation [2]. In the state of Colorado, where those who apply for a drivers' license must state whether or not they are willing to have their organs harvested, over 60 % answer in the affirmative [3]. A similar percentage of the families who are asked for the right to retrieve organs from deceased loved ones accede to the request [1].

If the failure to harvest organs is not the result of an unwillingness to donate, then why are we getting only 12 % of the available organs? The fundamental root of the problem rests on property rights and incentives. Neither the original possessor nor anyone else is granted a property right in potential transplant organs. The law in the United States prohibits any and all from selling organs for value. As a result, while we would like people to donate their own organs, and we would like doctors to harvest organs when people sign donor cards, and we would like the doctors to ask the next of kin for permission when the deceased has not signed a card, and we would like the next of kin to accede to the request, none of these people is, or may be, offered any material reward for their active participation or cooperation. Nor are they compelled to suffer a material penalty for their failure to participate and cooperate. All personal incentive is absent from the current system.

In Europe, a number of nations have adopted a policy of presumed consent, a system which, in theory, eliminates the need for doctors to ask next of kin for permission to harvest. Despite this more favorable legal climate, medical personnel still lack sufficient incentive to overcome their quite natural reluctance to dismember their patients' bodies without their express consent, or that of their family.

My proposal is to overcome this problem by granting people more extensive property rights in their own bodies, specifically to allow them to profit from its disposition after their death. In this way they will have an incentive to provide for the most valuable and efficient disposition.

Mine is a market solution. Markets have substantial economic virtues. By that I mean that they succed in delivering more and better goods and services at less cost than alternative institutions. But this discussion will not focus on the economic virtues of markets in general, or of a market in transplant organs in particular, for I take it that the economic virtues of markets are much more widely accepted and less controversial than their ethical virtues or even propriety. Therefore, it is those ethical arguments and concerns that must be addressed first.

First, I wish to emphasize that the market I propose, in addition to meeting the ethical objections leveled against some markets in transplant organs, has substantial ethical virtues of its own. First, markets in general and this one in particular give great respect to the autonomy of participants. Unlike a system of presumed consent or required request, a market requires no affirmative act on the part of a potential donor in order that he avoid donating his organs. Second, unlike required request, it compels neither doctors nor next of kin to suffer unpleasant discussions of organ donation at the time of a patient's death.

But what of the moral objections to an organ market? What are they, and how does my market accommodate or answer those objections? There are, I believe, four species of objections to markets in general. At least three of them have been asserted to apply to an organ market. I will refer to them as:

1. The poor man's sale;
2. the rich man's purchase;
3. the sale of what is not yours; and
4. the sale of what cannot be sold.

First, the poor man's sale. Many of us view it as an outrage that some desperately poor person would choose to sell one of his kidneys. A kidney seems too valuable a thing to sacrifice for any amount of money. So, out of a kind of paternalism we would ban such sales. It is in the same spirit that we do not honor contracts in which someone purports to sell himself into slavery.

Such an objection could be countered by a variety of moral arguments. For example, one might note that we currently permit people to sell blood. So why must we ban the sale of bone marrow. It is after all a replaceable bodily fluid much like blood. One could also point to any number of dangerous occupations such as coal mining and lumberjacking that we permit people to engage in for money despite the fact that these activities are far more likely to shorten one's life than would the removal of a kidney.

But rather than trying to convince you that the moral objection to the poor man's sale is unwarranted, I will accommodate the objection. The market I favor is one in which organs are in effect only purchased from the dead. No one need be permitted or induced to sacrifice his health for money. Cadavers are neither rich nor poor, merely dead. Those who currently donate organs at death are, disproportionately, the rich and well educated. If such donation is not now considered an indignity when engaged in by the rich, then I cannot see why it would be so when engaged in by the poor, merely because their estates receive compensation.

Precluding the sale of organs by the living will cost little or nothing in terms of efficiency. The plan I favor is likely to yield more than enough of all transplant tissue with the possible exceptions of bone marrow and hearts to satisfy the demand without resort to gathering organs from live donors. A market in hearts from live donors can be dismissed for obvious reasons. The sale of bone marrow by live donors is not so easily sacrificed. Some potential recipients will die as a result of the absence of a market from live donors. But if banning all purchases from live donors including those who would sell bone marrow, is necessary in order to gain political acceptability then I am reluctantly willing to accept that in order to realize legislative enactment for the remainder of the plan.

In some sense the converse objection to "the poor man's sale" is "the rich man's purchase." The former in effect says the price of the organ is too low, while the latter objects that the price is too high. That is, if the organs are allocated on the basis of willingness to pay, the rich will be able to buy organs that the poor are precluded from obtaining. Some things, it is believed, are literally too vital to permit their allocation by ability to pay. For much the same reason, we no longer permit people to buy substitutes to avoid the military draft. The moral objection to the rich man's purchase, like the objection to the poor man's sale, can be countered by moral argument. For example, one could point out that we currently allow many life-supporting activities and goods to be allocated on the basis of willingness to pay, including food, clothing, shelter, exercise equipment, and until recently all transplant operations. So why single out transplant organs for an absolute prohibition?

Here too, however, I would rather accommodate the objection than persuade you of its error. My plan does not address the question of how the organs will be allocated, only that they will be purchased for value from the original owner and possessor. My proposal is consistent with and can accommodate allocation by any conceivable means. The organs can be acquired by private profit-making institutions or by government agencies, and can be allocated on the basis of medical, social, or economic criteria, and provided to recipients either at market prices or at no charge.

I am largely indifferent to how the allocation decision is made, because in the case of transplant organs most of the benefits of using markets and most of the costs of failing to do so are to be found on the supply side rather than on the demand side. Many of the inefficiencies that would usually plague a market that did not employ price to allocate goods are trivial in the case of an organ market. Because the demand for transplant organs is, in the language of economics, highly inelastic at low prices, the quantity of organs that sick people will purchase will be largely unaffected by price. Unlike a market in edible chicken livers purchased as food in which lowering the sales price to zero will induce people who do not really crave chicken livers to purchase them, a zero price for human livers is not likely to result in anyone buying an extra liver or replacing a healthy one. Therefore, in order to garner most of the gains of a market economy, we need only have the market operating on one side, the supply side. All we require is that the original possessor of the organ be able to sell it for a reasonably substantial fee. In addition, I believe, that the market I propose will succeed in making enough organs available so that, regardless of how organs are allocated, it is unlikely at current levels of medical expertise that anyone who would benefit from a transplant operation will have to forgo one for lack of an organ.

These first two moral objections, the poor man's sale and the rich man's purchase, must be accommodated primarily for political, rather than economic, reasons. I mean by that these objections only make their presence felt as the wishes of those who would like to legally prohibit certain transactions by others, not as a reluctance of the parties themselves to engage in the transaction. Were a broker to approach poor George and rich Martha with the proposal that he sell one of his kidneys to her, neither of them would raise either of these moral objections. Martha would certainly not argue that George should not part with so valuable a thing as a kidney, and though George might decline to sell for precisely that reason, coming from him it would not represent a moral argument, but an economic one, that is, he values his kidney more than the price he is being offered. If George agreed to sell his kidney, he is extremely unlikely to argue that it should be sold at a lower price to someone poorer than Martha.

Were a totally unlimited market in transplant organs legally permitted, the objections to the poor man's sale and the rich man's purchase would only surface as the complaints of third parties. As such they would not be decisive factors in preventing the market from operating. Morality would play the same role that it does in the market for abortions. Right-to-life sorts object to the transactions between women and their abortionists, but the transactions take place largely unimpeded. Even now when the sale of transplant organs is illegal, were not so many strangers and institutions necessary to effect the transfer of organs, such sales would take place in far greater numbers and in more open forms than they do, much as is the case in the markets for illegal drugs and prostitution.

The third moral objection, and one that I have not heard voiced by others, is that you may not sell what is not yours. This is of a different order than the first two. It must be accommodated not merely, or most importantly, for political reasons, but in order that people will voluntarily participate in the market. How would such an objection surface? Imagine an agent of an organ procurement firm approaching the mother of a boy who is lying brain dead in a hospital following a motorcycle accident and offering her US $ 5000 for her son's liver? She has custody, but not ownership of his body, not merely as a legal matter but more importantly as a moral one. Therefore, we, and more poignantly she, will feel that she has no right to profit from her decision as to its disposition. Thus, not so much to meet the political objections to permitting mothers to sell their sons' livers, but primarily because we will have great difficulty overcoming the mother's own moral objections, a market in which organs are purchased from next of kin should be rejected as a first choice.

The market solution I propose does not require that people sell what is not theirs. Instead, it is one in which people contract to sell their organs when they are healthy for delivery after their death. Unlike your mother you normally do believe that you have a property right in your own body.

The fourth and final moral objection is to the sale of what cannot be sold. The very act of selling or purchasing certain goods transforms and degrades them. Such goods or services, are usually, if not exclusively, in the nature of relationships. As a result they can only be transferred in a donative fashion. For example if tonight I wanted to make love to my wife and she were disinclined, were I to offer her money as an inducement it would be hardly likely to improve our marriage. Or consider an illustration I recall from my youth: I remember a playmate saying, "if you share your potato chips with me I'll be your best friend." The instinctive and correct reaction to such an offer is that friendship is not the sort of thing that can be sold and offering to sell it makes transparent that it is not there to be purchased.

Although some writers disagree, I believe, that this last category of morally suspect exchanges does not have natural and necessary public policy implications. Attempting to exchange goods like friendship and love across a market merely evinces the absence of the proper spiritual stance rather that creating that absence. Thus it would hardly make sense to outlaw the exchange of potato chips for friendship in the hope that we would then get more friendship. We would not, instead we would only get less evidence of false offers of friendship.

Even if you find some public policy aspect to this category of objection appealing, it is hard to see how it has any application to an organ market. A transplant organ is not a relationship. It is not degraded by a market transfer. Recipients of transplant organs are generally not much interested in entering an emotional relationship with the donor. They are largely indifferent to the inner spiritual stance of the donor. They want the organ little else. In fact analogizing from certain other similar medical procedures such as sperm donation, or surrogate motherhood, typically the last thing that the recipient wants is an emotional attachment on the part of the donor.

To the extent that anything is lost by sale rather than donation, it is the awareness of a charitable impulse in the giving. And though such a lack of a charitable impulse may actually be a benefit to the recipient it counts as a significant defect of markets in the minds of some commentators. To them I say that even if the encouragement of charity and a sense of community is to be highly valued in general, the effect of a market in transplant organs on such a sense of community is trivial on two counts. First, and most important, by permitting people to sell food, clothing, and shelter rather than insisting that they may only be donated, we suffer the exact same loss of community. We recognize in those cases, as we should in this, that the efficiency gains in terms of lives saved and suffering ameliorated is worth the marginal sacrifice of a sense of community.

Second, even if we accept the notion that the donation of organs should be encouraged because charity in all its forms is a good thing, it hardly follows that sale should be prohibited. Permitting sale does not mandate it. Charitable donation of organs not only remains possible, it becomes a more noble act when sale is permitted. Prohibiting sale only encourages donation to the extent that it diminishes its character. It is hardly an act of great generosity to donate that which you cannot use and may not sell. So, with regard to this fourth moral objection I cannot accommodate it in my market, but I find no substance to it. It seems to me to be the fabrication of the overactive intellects of academics who have never seriously addressed the possibility that they or their loved one might one day need a kidney and find none available for lack of a market.

In proposing that payment should occur at the time of death only for harvested organs, I have rejected two alternative payment schemes:

1. payment at time of contract for the right to harvest at death; and
2. payment at death to the estate or designee of the vendor for the right to harvest whether or not any tissue is taken.

The principal advantage of payment for the harvested organs is that it would entail only about 1 % of the number of cash transactions of the other schemes and thus will have a much reduced transaction cost. In addition, because the estate will only be paid for successfully harvested and transplanted organs, that payment would be perhaps one hundred times larger than a payment for the mere right to harvest the organs payed to every decedent's estate. Therefore it is much less likely to result in efforts by next of kin to void the contract.

I have suggested that US $ 5000 be paid to the estate or designee for each major organ. This figure is not cast in stone. The actual price could either be determined by the market or set legislatively. In either case, I believe, it will not pose a major problem. My guess, and that is all it is, is that about US $ 5000 per major organ will elicit organ sales from at least 90 % of potential donors. Within several years, most people would sign on for what would in effect be a 1 %–2 % chance of leaving as much as an additional US $ 30 000 to their estate. Nor is US $ 5000 per major organ a politically intolerable figure. It would not add inordinately to the budgetary cost of transplant operations.

Now a savvy student of the problem might correctly point out that my plan makes the same error as most of its predecessors, in that it fails to attack the right problem. The primary roadblock to acquiring organs at present is not the unwillingness of people to donate, but the reluctance of doctors to make the necessary inquiries, and to take the initiative in harvesting organs. Thus the mere creation of a market in organs may seem largely irrelevant to the problem. My response is that we must rely on a natural concomitant to property rights, tort liability, to solve that problem. Once we recognize that a person's body is a valuable piece of property in which he has certain standard property rights, it is only sensible and fully in keeping with traditional common and civil law notions that appropriate tort liability be imposed on those responsible for that property. I propose that doctors and hospitals that negligently fail to preserve the cadaver or inform the organ procurement agency of its status should be liable to the estate of the deceased for the value of his organs. Particularly, when writing for an audience of physicians, I must emphasize that this is not meant to be a new and arcane category of medical malpractice, calling for some difficult medical decisions by doctors and hospitals. I only propose that hospitals be required to exercise the same care with the patients' body as they would with his wallet, rings, or watch, that is to preserve it and transfer it to the appropriate custodian.

This tort remedy highlights and captures one of the many virtues of a market solution, its robustness, that is, its purpose and effect are not to identify and respond to a particular cause of the shortage, but rather to create a system that naturally and automatically responds to any potential cause. Thus unlike, advertising campaigns and presumed consent, which were intended to respond to people's presumed reluctance to donate, which as it turned out was a largely nonexistent problem, or required request, which was intended to respond to doctor's reluctance to raise the issue of donation with next of kin, a well-functioning market will automatically respond to a wide variety of potential problems. By defining and extending private property rights in the body, we will allow economic incentives to work as a blast of water through a clogged pipe, flushing out any reluctance to participate in the transplantation process. If everyone in the chain from donor to recipient is provided with the economic incentives that normally and naturally grow out of a property rights system, the organs will be put to their most valued use.

How much will this proposal cost? Virtually nothing. How can that be if we are to pay US $ 5000 per organ? The answer rests on the distinction between budgetary and economic cost. If 20 000 cadavers are harvested, and US $ 20 000 is paid to the estate of each donor, checks will have to be written for US $ 400 million each year. This is the budgetary cost, but it does not represent a real economic cost. To an economist the real cost of any activity is what is given up in its stead. In other words the real cost of a CAT scanner is the alternative use that the resources that went into the CAT scanner could have been put to. In general, the market price of any item is a good reflection of the value of the best alternative use of these resources or, to use the jargon of economics, its opportunity cost. In the case of an organ market, however, the checks that will be written do not represent a true forgone opportunity, the only opportunity lost by donating an organ is having it eaten by worms. These US $ 20 000 payments, therefore, represent a pure and small wealth transfer rather than a true cost.

This proposal is intended as a realistic and morally acceptable way to solve the organ shortage. The author is eager to join with others to make it a reality. Space constraints do not permit me to discuss many of the issues that arise from my plan. The interested reader will find many of them addressed in [1]. Examples of those neglected questions are:

1. Does the shortage of organs serves as a useful natural gatekeeper, in that if more organs were available it would become politically impossible to deny people access to un-cost-justified transplant operations?
2. Will a market in transplant organs induce suicides and murders?
3. How can my market respond to the problem of acquiring needed tissue from stillborns, infants, and children?
4. Can my market succeed in acquiring organs from some of the most attractive potential donors: the disaffected and violent young, who are unconcerned with their estates, e.g., motorcycle gang members?

## References

1. Cohen LR (1989) Increasing the supply of transplant organs: the virtues of a futures market. George Washington Law Rev 1
2. Mathieu D (1988) Introduction. In: Mathieu D (ed) Organ Substitution Technology
3. Overcast, Evans, Bowen, Hoe, Livak (1984) Problems in the identification of potential organ donors. JAMA 251:1559–1560

# General Discussion: The Dilemma of Post Mortem Organ Donation: Are There Any Donation-Facilitating Factors Which Are Potentially Suppressed on the Basis of Ethical or Legal Considerations?

*McMaster:* There are four areas that we might structure so that we can concentrate our efforts. We began the morning with the concepts and philosophy of brain death and the theological approaches to that. We then moved on to cultural and religious aspects of the organ availability, then social and economic factors were addressed, and finally in our invited presentations, we had a marked solution to our problems. Now, we have a number of questions that have come forward. Let's begin with Dr. Jacobsen, who is confused about what life and death is. Is that right? Would you like to put your comment or question forward?

*Jacobsen:* The question is really to the panel and also to the congress. I am a bit confused about the use of the word "brain death," because it seems to indicate that that kind of death is different from any other kind of death. Or at least the public might be confused and think that we have introduced another level of death just because we would like to whip out organs. I thought that really one was either alive or dead. I would like to see the right expression being used, and I think the correct and right expression is that we are talking about death, diagnosed as due to total destruction of the brain by infarction. I would like to hear the panel's comments.

*McMaster:* Yes, death is the total destruction of the brain. What is your opinion, Dr. Dickens?

*Dickens:* There is a link between the physiological and the neurological aspects. Certainly as a lawyer, I am familiar with the concept of the moment of death, but I think one has to recognize medically that death is a process. The question is at what time in that process should certain initiatives be taken. It may be objectionable that one defines death differently for different

---

The general discussion sessions were transcribed from tape recordings made during the conference. In the interest of a rapid publication, the individual speakers/discussants did not see their own comments and questions before the book went to press. One of the editors (W. Land) tried to make obviously necessary corrections in the manuscripts derived from the tape recordings and then authorized the publication of the sessions in their present form. Therefore, incorrect publication of the comments or questions with regard to style, content, etc. might be possible in the view of the speakers concerned. We apologize for any possible inaccuracies.

W. Land, J. B. Dossetor (Eds.)
Organ Replacement Therapy:
Ethics, Justice and Commerce

purposes, and the objection may be taken to identifying brain death when organs are alive for the sake of harvesting those organs. But the concept seems to have value in that if focuses on one of the indicators of death. It could well be that one could link cause and effect in different ways, but targeting which particular failure is the indication for further events could be useful. The idea that you are either alive or dead was true historically, but these days I think we think of the different stages in the process of dying. When different initiatives become appropriate.

*McMaster:* Prof. Eigler is not convinced by that?

*Eigler:* Oh yes, I am convinced, and I would like to point out that we also speak of heart death. We are used to this term, and it refers to the main thing which led to death. But I would like to stress here that the definition of death should be done independent of any purposes. I am always a little bit surprised that the theologians and the philosophers don't see the task of having a definition of death in any way, but it has to be in accordance with medical knowledge, I think. But I would also like to stress that a whole brain death, as it was defined, means not only the death of human beings, but also death of a mammalian organism. I think this is important to stress this so that society accepts this, because that means that we do not have a very sophisticated definition, but rather that the mammalian organism is dead when brain death has occurred. The third statement is that society has a right to be sure that we do not take away organs from dying, but only from dead bodies. I would like now to put a question to Prof. Sass. Would he suggest that the right for people to accept special damage to the cortex as death includes the admittance that organs may already be harvested in these stages? I do not think this was quite clear to the audience, and I would like to know whether he could stress on this point. I think it is one thing to say that somebody doesn't want to be treated anymore but another if you go ahead and say, well in these situations you could harvest. I have many reservations on the second part.

*Sass:* Well I think life is not without risk. Once in a while we make choices which we regret later, other choices we are proud of later. What I recommend when I recommend a conscience clause is not a recommendation for either active or passive euthanasia. That has to be taken care of in other parameters if one wants to do that. What I would rather recommend is to have the existing formula as a default position out of which you can opt. And the two perspectives, first under the perspective of sustained suffering without any sense, and definitely without any associated quality of life, for myself. If I opt then personally, not for others, just for myself for higher brain death criteria, I feel I have the right to do that. Now if, then, I also decide in a non-acute situation, a long time before the catastrophe occurs that I, for whatever moral or altruistic reasons, would not be against being intubated and also having my organs taken out prior to whole brain death, including brain stem criteria having occurred, I can envision such a personal choice by people. But not necessarily has a choice to be diagnosed by higher brain criteria, it has to be the end of my personal life, that does not necessarily have to be associated with organ donation, but it could be.

*Cortesini:* I mentioned at the beginning of this session the importance of the definition of brain death. Really, what we decided in a meeting of the Vatican last year was really a consent that total brain destruction as a definition must not be employed only for the situation of transplantation; this is very important. It is also valid for all other problems, such as in legislative problems. We have tried to put in the different legislations all over the world in the different nations the concept that cerebral death is the death of a human being, of a person. But we will have a lot of disadvantages in dividing and separating the concept from transplantation absolutely! Otherwise there are some damaging effects.

This morning, different speakers, especially the speaker from Denmark, Dr. Rossel, have raised some of these questions. This is the first point. I repeat that after 5 years of working, we have finally agreed that a person is dead when he has suffered total and irreversible loss of all capacity for integrating and coordinating the function of the body. It is the human person, the personality that is directly correlated with these functional units, both physical and mental, which characterizes the human being, the human person. It is a complete definition. If we go further, in the neuroanatomical substract, because there is a substract as we have discussed with Sir John Eccles for a long time, is the unity between the cortex and the radicular system in the brain stem. It is the functional unity between the cortex and the brain stem that is, together with this neuroanatomical network, the background of this functional unity. Sometimes some areas may be destroyed, and others not, but when you completely and irreversibly destroy them, you destroy the neuronal connection that is the fundamental and neuroanatomical background in which the human being has all these capacities of integrating and coordinating all the functions of the body, mental and physical. Just to explain that the destruction has to be in these vital areas.

*McMaster:* Thank you. I don't think any of us are going to disagree that total destruction of the whole brain stem is death, the question is whether less than that equates. Dr. Sass, you felt that people should have the right to opt out into a system. Is that really a practical thing that we are going to introduce in our legislative framework?

*Sass:* I think that this is a very realistic choice, and I think it is the only realistic choice we have, because our experience with our brain-based death criteria is only 25 years old and, given our cultural and moral history, 25 years is a very short time. But there are dormant values, in our Western culture at least, and these are indicated by those who believe in reincarnation and in the immortal soul in other cultures which can also have similar positions. The problem is that we want to avoid what I called in my introductory statements the fear and the scare to be buried alive or to be cut open for the use of our organs while still alive. And, therefore, the intellectually and theologically rather uninteresting and dull and boring definition of entire brain death, including brain stem is the safest default position we can have. Making higher brain criteria required by law for each and every one of us would again open the floor for all kinds of fights of the kind which, by the way, we see at the beginning of human life; there we unfortunately do not have such a uniform, widely accepted standard for the protection of early human life as we have found in the dormant values at the end of human life. I think we should also recognize the technical problems the people at the Harvard Ad Hoc Committee had over 20 years ago and maybe Prof. Angstwurm can comment more on that. It was very difficult and inconclusive to diagnose cessation of higher brain functions only. As far as I understand this technology has improved, not only technology of electroencephalograms but also other forms to look into the brain and into the cortex and neocortex and the higher brain, so that diagnosis is much more conclusive. We can probably offer competent adults various parameters and schemes under which they would be very safe to opt out of the default position.

*McMaster:* Yes, we can always be safe, can't we? The speed of the convoy is going to be dictated by the slowest ship of all, and the "destroyers", if I can use that term, will get frustrated.

*N. N.:* I wanted to comment on the use of self-determination a little further to solve this issue of degrees of brain death. I see it really as avoiding reaching a conclusion on this problem, and I think this poses three obvious problems that Prof. Sass commented on. Firstly, does he feel that many individuals in any society would actually possess the intellectual competence to make a self-determinist choice in an issue as complex as this, given the difficulties we are having today to reach any sort of consensus decision.

*McMaster:* Shall we take that? Are human beings going to be competent to take this sophisticated judgment?

*Sass:* I think that this is the condition under which we are here at this conference, and that is the condition under which the societies in which most of us live rest upon. Otherwise we would have to live in a Confucian society; in paternalistic societies where this is not generally common sense and widely held. But the societies we live in hold widely that we are educated citizens who make educated choices and who once in a while make the wrong choices, but this is the risk we have to take when we want to exercise our capacities to freedom and liberty.

*N. N.:* Given that, how can an individual's decision be communicated? This is a more practical problem and we are all aware of the existing difficulty that we have with opting-in systems of donor cards in organ donation. Self-determination would then be communicated to his descendant's or daughters who are looking after him in that situation. Maybe I will follow that with a third point which arises when the individual's self-determined wish was not known, is a third party then allowed to decide for him? This is quite against the principle of self-determination. And if a third party is to be allowed to decide, who is to be allowed and when are they to be allowed to do this.

*Sass:* If a person does not exercise his or her right to self-determination, I feel there should be the safest possible default position, and I feel, boring as it is and intellectually uninspiring as it is, the existing formula, which is more or less a biological formula of immediate disintegration of the entire body correlating to the disintegration and then final total cessation of all brain tissue, is the default position. This is one of the options we always have in free societies, not to make choices. But then society will provide a default position.

*Dickens:* I don't think that one has to be very neurologically sophisticated to be able to express preferences. Certainly in North America in the context of the Cruzan case, never a comparable rhetoric in the UK, people can say, "I wouldn't want to be a vegetable." The question raised of the third parties making decisions is correctly phrased negatively: third parties cannot make these decisions. The role of third parties is simply to evidence what the patient him- or herself said, and to that extent they are merely witnesses to the patient's wishes. The patient is not at the disposal of third parties' wishes.

*N. N.:* Are governments third parties?

*Dickens:* No, they wouldn't be. Governments can intervene to protect their interests, not the patient's interests. They may have interests that are a public policy agenda, but they are making decisions that will be binding on individuals, they are not the individual's decisions.

*Pflanz:* I think there are two parts to what Dr. Sass said. One is that a person may opt out of the whole brain death criteria. Thinking that practical problems are to be solved, which I don't believe are solved now, I think it is still very difficult. Assuming, however, that this is the case, the second part, giving a person the liberty to say "and then my organs can be taken" opens up a whole new box of questions, because then medical profession would have to change their rules. They would then be taking organs from a living person, since the person is not dead yet. If you accept that a person is dead when all brain functions have ceased, and the patient had said, "I don't want to have any treatment continued, let me die," treatment could be stopped. But if the physician is to take out organs while according to the agreement the person is not dead, that means the doctor would have to get a license to kill the patient, because by taking out the organs you will kill the patient.

*McMaster:* Dr. Sass, license to kill?

*Sass:* No, definitely not. Your argument comes from a statistic and legalistic concept of definition of death. Rather, it will be the individual's definition of death. And indeed then personal death and full death. There can be no 50 % pregnancy, and there can be no 50 % death. It is judged according to this particular individual's 100 % death, and he or she might have decided also to have organs taken out and to be intubated. This would be done to what I call my "cadaver"; this is my definition and is much more loose, but I think it is good enough for me. In addition, there is the prescribed definition of death by the state. So, that is the reason I argue for a very strict official definition of death, and a more loose individual one. And that is also the reason that I cannot agree to proxy decision making for this, because it is a high-risk area. Your immortality, your life after death, and your being in the grey zone between life and death might very much depend on this, and I don't want to continue in theological or religious terms. This is a great risk, probably the greatest risk you have in life.

*McMaster:* Bear with me, please. I certainly don't want to get into life after death, otherwise we'll be here until tea time. I think there is a feeling that we have ducked the classical example of this rather, namely the anencephalic who has an absence of higher centers, but the vital brain stem that you feel so critical maintains function. Would you comment on that, Dr. Angstwurm?

*Angstwurm:* In anencephalic children, brain death does not occur before these children stop breathing. The definition of brain death is, namely, essentially that all functions of the brain stop, the functions of the brain stem as well as the functions of the cortex.

*McMaster:* So the child is alive and should receive full medical support and feeding? Dr. Dickens, is that wrong?

*Dickens:* If the treatment is likely to be futile, then one could undertake minimal rather than maximum care.

*Daar:* I am disturbed by the ongoing discussion. We have gone so far as to say that we will accept people who are *brain dead* as donors, but the *persistent vegetative state* was discussed very carefully in Ottawa, and it was clearly stated by all the people there that this is not an acceptable donor. So the two states are totally different, and by current standards I think everyone would agree that the person in a persistent vegetative state is not a potential donor.

*McMaster:* Yes, indeed, the persistent brain stem function, the vital signs, and the respiratory function you referred to are specifically, I think, excluded.

*Veatch:* I think it should be clear to everyone that in virtually all countries, whole brain death is the current law, and organs cannot be procured before whole brain death. It doesn't follow that this is philosophically or ethically the correct position. There is a substantial body of individuals who hold that a person should be treated as dead when there is a separation of mental function from bodily function, and there is no scientific refutation of that view. There are many others – or at least a few of us in this meeting – who feel that law should be changed to permit the pronouncing of death, at least based on the discretion of an individual expressing his wishes while conscious. That would authorize or in fact require the pronouncement of death when the capacity for mental function is lost. We are talking essentially about the persistent vegetative state patient. That is clearly scientifically measurable, at least according to the consensus of neurological opinion. It is probably more accurately measurable than irreversible cardiac function loss. If such a person were pronounced dead, i.e., if laws were changed to permit such a death pronouncement, then that individual should be treated as a cadaver and anything that one could do to a cadaver would be legally and ethically permissible. As Dr. Sass says that could include, at the individual's discretion, the procurement of organs by a physician who is willing to procure organs under those circumstances. I don't want this meeting to go on record with the assumption that everyone favors a law that would require whole brain rather than higher brain death.

*Dickens:* Could I ask Dr. Veatch a question? If a child that has a functioning brain stem but is anencephalic or if it is a person in a persistent vegetative state has a spontaneous brain stem function and is breathing, would you consider burial appropriate?

*Veatch:* There are many conditions under which it would be unethical and unaesthetic to bury cadavers, for instance if a patient's heart stops while he is on a ventilator, I would not bury him until I had disconnected the ventilator. Likewise for a patient with brain stem function, I would not bury that deceased person, for aesthetic reasons, until spontaneous ventilation stopped.

*McMaster:* There is a lot more to discuss, but Dr. Otte, perhaps the last comment or question on this aspect?

*Otte:* I am dissatisfied regarding the answer about the anencephalics. It is quite evident that for all of us the concept of the whole brain death is not applicable to an anencephalic. However, we have sometimes proposed that organs be removed from anencephalics, and we know that in some centers in Europe, organs from anencephalics are used. I would, therefore, propose that we as a group decide to stop using organs from anencephalics. The question has been addressed completely and with a recommendation from the European Organ Transplantation Society or the Transplantation Society. But the question may not be left aside.

*McMaster:* Thank you. Indeed that is the position in Great Britain at this time. I am going to pause at that point, because there are so many other issues. I will just turn to the social and cultural and religious concerns that there are about transplantation. Mr. Fluss, would you like to put your question to Dr. Daar?

*Fluss:* Prof. Daar, a very eminent Islamic scholar, Prof. Dr. Mohammed Naims Jassin, who is the chairman of the department of jurisprudence in Shari in Kuwait, has published a major article, in which among other things he pleads for a regulated system of donor compensation based on predetermined values. This is for living donors. I wonder if this is a widely held view in the Islamic world or if it is very much an individualistic view?

*Daar:* I am not familiar with the work that you quote. I have not met many people who have that view, but then I don't think anyone has ever done a systematic study or a survey. The answer to your question as far as I am concerned is, I don't think anyone knows. I do not perceive such a commonly held view amongst Muslims. I don't know if Dr. Abouna wants to add anything to that.

*Abouna:* I do not know the person that you mentioned, but I do know what Dr. Daar explained extremely well today, namely the Islamic view, because in some of those I was involved in an indirect way. The view in all the meetings, in the councils which Prof. Daar mentioned, was that the sale of human organs is prohibited, and there are many reasons for this. One, of course, is a social reason and the effect on society, but the other one is because in Islam, like some other religions, it is believed that the organs we have are not ours for sale. They belong to Almighty God, and, therefore, we do not have the power to sell what is not ours.

*McMaster:* One of the problems that we face in a big metropolis in England with many cultural groups is that, because of the Islamic approach, individuals and individual religious advisors may take a different view, and in a big extended family it is not unusual for one member of the family to take a slightly negative view. We have harvested organs from one Asian individual in 10 years, and yet Asians represent nearly one-quarter of our dialysis population. Dr. Daar, how do we overcome the individual interpretation of the Koran? I understand what you have shown us this morning, but can the individual family or advisor still inject a hesitation?

*Daar:* It is not an individual interpretation, it is a lack of any interpretation, because they are not aware of what happens. I think in the context of the UK what I would advise is to ask perhaps the Islamic center in London, which has a very enlightened person called Zaki Bodowi and ask him to give you the guidelines which you can then use to educate a potential donor's family. My understanding would be that the majority of your potential donors don't know anythink about the subject.

*Abouna:* I would like to reinforce what Dr. Daar said, it is really lack of education by the public of their own religious rulings. We met this in Kuwait, too. We had a great deal of difficulty obtaining consent, because some people told us, "this is not allowed in Islam." There is, of course, the *Dophedan,* but they were not aware of it. So it is a problem of education. In addition, a conference was held in March this year in Kuwait where two issues were discussed which you are now just dealing with. One was the payment for transplantation as a contract between the donor and the recipient and the donor and the doctor. And the other one was about anencephalics. I was at that meeting. The decision was that anencephalics are not dead individuals, and, therefore, they should not be used as a donors as long as they have spontaneous respiration. With regard to payment, it was ruled that any predetermined contract between donor and recipient and the donor and a hospital is not allowed, because this violates the principle of a gift of altruism which Islam encourages a great deal. This was in March 1990. I thought you should have that information.

*McMaster:* That was very helpful. Let's turn away from the Islamic world, has Israel got its act together now?

*Aiallam:* As far as Judaism is concerned, I think that we have seen in recent years quite a change in the attitude of religion towards organ transplantation. One has to understand that in Judaism there are 613 commandments: things that you are not allowed to, but you have to do. Now, one of these commandments is the saving of life. And this commandment basically overrules any other commandment, except for three. One is the worship of God, the second one is adultery, and the third one is killing another person. In other words, you may not save one's life at the expense of another one's life. Here lies the basic conflict as far as organ transplantation is concerned, because it depends very much on the definition of death, whether you accept the definition of the death of the brain as a criterion for the establishment of death. In this respect I think quite a major move forward has occurred now, and that is, first of all, that the chief rabbinate in Israel has accepted the declaration of brain death as a criterion for the establishment of death under certain conditions. They require that there won't be two but three physicians in the committee, and they require also at least one objective test, and usually the auditory potentials are used for that. But basically they have accepted the principle of brain death and this now does not *allow* the Jews to donate, but *obligates* them to do that: it is now a *mizveh,* a commandment to do that. So in this we have seen quite a major step forward, and this applies also to the very ultra-orthodox Jews who were very much opposed to organ donation and to transplantation, especially as far as the heart is concerned. They came out with big declarations that that is a double murder, i.e., of both the donor and the recipient. But nowadays they tolerate organ transplantation; they don't go for it, but at least they don't object any more. So those are major steps forward. At the moment in Israel, I don't think that we get more permission from secular families to donate organs than from religious families. I would also like to state that the Israeli law does not require consent from the family. It just requires that the doctors will inform the family about the intention to remove organs. The family, however, has the right to object. This may seem the same, but it is not exactly the same. It sometimes makes a psychological difference that the family is presented with the fact, which they can either accept or object to. They don't have to actively agree to the act of organ donation.

*Karlsberg:* Briefly, I wanted to ask our last speaker a question regarding the position in Israel. Is it accepted that a kidney transplant is a life-saving procedure, because it seems to me that in an area where dialysis facilities are available, it could at least be argued that it is an economy, an improved quality of life, but it does not necessarily save life as distinct from say cardiac or liver transplantation.

*McMaster:* Is a kidney transplant a life-saving procedure in Israel?

*Aiallam:* The answer is yes, it is considered as a life-saving act. But this does not only refer to a kidney transplant. Cornea transplant also comes under the same law that governs this problem of transplantation for life-saving procedures, because for religious Jews, somewhere in Judaism it is stated that the blind are considered as dead. So even for cornea transplant this is considered according to Judaism and the law a life-saving procedure.

*McMaster:* Dr. Karlsberg now, legal aspects in countries.

*Karlsberg:* Sweden was the second latest country to accept the legal concept of brain death in North West Europe; the law was in effect from 1988. However, already 10 years earlier we were about to have legislation, but it was not accepted. The reason was that we were trapped in the same trap as Denmark, the trap of two deaths, one real death and one equal to that, or as the ethical committee in Denmark stated, irreversibly dying. It was not until 1987 when the link between organ transplantation and death concept was broken that a law on human death could be generally accepted. It was then shown that 1500 persons in our country died yearly with beating heart, ventilated in intensive care units. Only 10 % were potentially organ donors. So it was possible to draw a crystal clear line between the death concept and the diagnosis of death on the one side, and organ retrieval on the other, in two different laws. In Denmark, I would like to point out to you, the law and its practical instructions are linked to transplantation. If a dead person is going to be a heart-beating organ donor, a specific set of diagnostic procedures are demanded. On the other hand, if ventilation has just stopped, another quality of diagnosis is used. I would like to know if this is common in other countries also, the connection between the death concept and transplantation. I think you will never get back to the organ donation figures you had 5 years ago until you break the link between the death concept on the one hand and organ transplantation on the other. And I ask you when are you going to correct this law?

*Rossel:* When? I don't know. I don't know whether I understood you correctly, but I said that the reason why we got this law was the connection between these two issues, brain death and transplantation. I think that it is not for the lawmakers, but for philosophers and others to argue that there are two distinct issues, and that we can accept brain death criteria without organ transplantation. So that it can go into the public.

*McMaster:* I think you have answered sufficiently. Prof. Eigler, you are concerned now about the situation in Belgium and information for the public.

*Eigler:* I would like to put the question to Dr. Schotsmans. How is the public continuously informed about the possibilities of presumed consent? That is the one question. The other issue arises from his making it clear that this presumed consent is adopted elsewhere, too. Perhaps I am not correct, but I was informed that in Sweden the law was changed. There was first presumed consent and now it has been changed to something like required request, a movement by personal intensive care units. I don't know whether this is correct, but I think it is.

*McMaster:* Is that correct?

*Karlsberg:* We used to have quite a liberal law with presumed consent and it was switched a little when the brain death criteria were accepted. We are now in the process of getting a new transplant law, and the main thing is that the will of the deceased person will be strengthened, so the possibility for the next of kin to act will diminish.

*McMaster:* How do we continuously educate people in Belgium?

*Schotsmans:* I must admit that this is one of the essential elements of an ethical application of the presumed consent. It is essential for how you integrate presumed consent in a society. In the beginning, of course, when the law was voted, this was very strong. And the risk is then solely on this information, and this education is not coming through. That is one of the risks. Now, this you can prevent, first of all by what we could call self-help groups of kidney insufficiency patients who organize campaigns. It can also be prevented by general education in the context of what you could call a media program, where you regularly inform people about this possibility and this reality, and the way how the law is organized. Thirdly I would join a little bit what Dr. Sass has said: we are adult and competent citizens, I think, in Western societies. I think that every citizen has also the duty to know what are the laws of his country. That is the third reaction, but I think this is the most negative, perhaps, for you. For you doubt strongly that this would be the case. If you continue, however, with media programs, and with what you could call patient groups, then I think that the people are generally informed about the fact that the law isn't that way.

*McMaster:* Thank you. Can I ask Prof. Dickens the questions from the floor, namely what about the people who are not fully grown up, in other words, children under 18 years old. Who is responsible for their decision? One parent, both parents, divorced parents? Who is responsible for children's decisions?

*Dickens:* In the ordinary setting, there would be joint custody, and either parent could give legal authority insofar as legal authority is appropriate. Most laws in fact prohibit minors being donors of organs, meaning solid organs, but many laws cover only organs and don't deal with tissues, which are generally defined as naturally replaceable materials, including blood, but more particularly bone marrow. One of the problem is, of course, that parents may be in a conflict of interest in that they have two children, one of whom is very sick and needs the bone marrow transplant, but only the other child is compatible to offer. And there are mechanisms for supervising parental decisions to volunteer their child to be a donor to another child.

*McMaster:* Sorry, who is legally responsible?

*Dickens:* Either parent will be empowered.

*McMaster:* So if one says yes and the other says no?

*Dickens:* Then one could proceed on the basis of the one who says yes, but if either of them say yes that decision could be reviewable in that there still has to be an established benefit for the child: psychological benefit of contributing to the survival of the sibling could be sufficient. But there was a well-known case in the US in the early 1970s in which the donor child had Down syndrome and had never lived at home, and the recipient child had always lived with the parent. In that case the parents approved the donation from the child – this was not bone marrow, this was a solid organ, a kidney. Although there was the legal power to do it, the general conclusion is that that case was an abuse, and today if parents volunteer their child to be a donor, even bone marrow, with pain and some risk, that could arouse the attention of child protection societies, which may then want a judge to look through the circumstances.

*McMaster:* Thank you. Let us turn to Dr. Lloyd Cohen's presentation. I very rudely curtailed him in midstream, as the urologists would say. Dr. Michielsen, you have comments and questions. Perhaps we could begin with your question or comment to Dr. Cohen about the market.

*Michielsen:* It is more a comment than a question. We have just condemned the opening of a market for living donor's kidneys, and now what is proposed is to open a market for the cadaver organs. I think for the same reasons as we rejected the first one we have to reject the second, but I must say that I feel somewhat uneasy about something which I feel personally as a hypocrisy. While we strongly condemn the selling of organs in India, for instance, someone with a little bit of money in the Middle East can buy himself a kidney in India. We disapproved this, we condemned this, and we expelled the doctors who do this from the Transplantation Society. When someone in the Middle East has much more money, he goes to the US, and although there is a shortage of cadaver organs there, the recent task force which examined these problems came to the conclusion that 10 % of these organs could be used for non-residents. Well, we know what happens: you go there, and you do not pay for the cadaver kidney, of course. And the relatives will not get a single franc. The surgeon will not sell the kidney, but he will receive a fee for service, and the service fee is very high.

*McMaster:* Dr. Cohen would you like to comment on that?

*Cohen:* I really have no response. I think I answered the initial remarks in my address, as for the second part it really doesn't bear on my proposal, so I would really rather go on to another question.

*Abouna:* I have a comment on this organ sale and also indicate some reasons why I think, as Dr. Michielsen said, it is dangerous and not helpful. I think it raises more issues and problems than it actually solves, and some of these were already anticipated by Dr. Cohen in his presentation, especially the sale of what is not yours and who owns the organ, the individual, the family or, of course, as in some religious and as I already mentioned, Almighty God and his reverence of the human body. But what I think the idea brings is a concept which at present I think will be objectionable to the majority of the public and of the profession. It brings an idea that human organs like a commodity can and ought to be sold in the market place for a price which was US $ 5000 in 1990. That will go up with inflation and so on and so forth. Now I think, as I mentioned earlier today, the introduction of any such direct open sale of human organs will have a very strong negative feedback on voluntary and altruistic organ donation. We have seen that on a small scale, at least in our experience as I mentioned earlier, I think it will be on a much larger scale in the United States. Now what is the problem in the United States, Canada, and some other countries? There are plenty of cadavers, as you mentioned, in fact in 1989 there were 14 000 cadavers in the United States, but only 4300 of these were used. So there is a shortage in the midst of plenty. What is the reason? There is, as we heard from the European experience, a lack of utilization, coordination, and indication at two levels. One of them is the medical sector, the organ procurement organizations, the emergency rooms, the trauma centers, and so on. And there is an enormous difference in the

United States now between one state and the other. You mentioned the state of Colorado. The state of Colorado last year for example was able to obtain 46 cadavers per million population, whereas across the United States it is only 18 per million. And if every state in the United States could work as hard and educate as well as the organ procurement in the state of Colorado, there would be no shortage of kidneys in the United States. The only way to do it is to double the amount of cadavers available today.

The other example is the refusal of families for cultural and education reasons. The solution here again has to be taken from the Europeans. We have to introduce presumed consent or the opting-out law. If you are going to introduce any incentive, as I mentioned earlier and as other people have, it has to be non-cash payment, a nonpredetermined contract between donor and recipient to be acceptable at all in our society. This is based on two principles. One is that it is a compensation of loss of work, or of some expenses which you have to incur as a funeral expense. The second one is exemption from compulsory obligations that all of us have to the state, such as taxes. I think those two might be accepted as incentives after the event and not before.

*Riggles (UK Transplant Service):* The question for Dr. Cohen is, would this market suggestion mean that organs such as the kidney would be treated as property in the same way as a gold watch and, therefore, there would be the same obligation on a doctor to ensure that it is actually correctly disposed of after the death of the individual. And the second question was, does Dr. Cohen feel that the payment in this way removes the comfort that bereaved relatives would get on helping others after death or would the universality of the payment leave the emotional support intact?

*Cohen:* There were simply too many points for me to remember them all.

*McMaster:* The first one is the gold watch.

*Cohen:* The gold watch is very critical here. What we are dealing with here is a situation in which we have many people carrying the ball and the ball has to be handed off. We have the decedant before he dies, and we have his family. We have transplant surgeons, we have recipients, we have organ procurement agencies, and we have attending doctors and nurses when the decedant donor dies. One can try to do very partial solutions to attack what they take to be the problem in one particular place, and I think that is a technique we have followed in the past unsuccessfully. What I wish to do is make a kidney a piece of property which a person can dispose of after his death as he would his Rolex watch. Now, what is incumbent in this is that right. I think, the single greatest road block to organ donation at least in the West (I cannot say what it is in Moslem countries) is not an unwillingness of people to donate. And it is not an unwillingness of families to acquiesce in donation. The single biggest road block are physicians. The physicians don't want to ask, and I don't blame them. It is a very unpleasant task. Well, I want to make them ask. And the way in which I make them ask is I make them take the same degree of care with a valuable asset, a body, after its death, as they do with their Rolex watch. If when a person goes into an emergency room his Rolex watch is taken off and just laid on the ground, and someone walks away with it, the physician and the hospital are negligent and will be found liable. So I wish to create the same property obligations with regard to a body. That is if you agree to sell your organs after your death and the physicians and doctors simply ignore your request, don't inform organ procurement agencies of your intention and your body simply decays and is buried and burned, the estate should have a cause of action for that which would amount to about US $ 30 000. That would cure the reluctance of doctors to participate in the process. As for the second notion with regard to taking away the satisfaction of the family with regard to donating the organs, I think that there are some people who get a joy out of that satisfaction, I don't think that would be much diminished if it turns out that all of this is done automatically because of the stated desires of the donor. An earlier point, as to whether this would effect the donative market, it might, but I don't feel that is a problem. Some people now will take money who wouldn't have taken money before, but in the grand scheme of things it is a trivial amount of money. I cannot go into this too much right now, but as an economist, and as the only economist in the room I will tell you that in fact it is a mythical amount of money in the sense that the real cost of anything to an economist is the opportunity cost, that is to say what is given up. That is if I tell you that building another Mount Everest north of Munich, just as building Mount Everest will cost US $ 30 billion, the cost is not the dollars that are printed, the cost is ultimately the resources used to do that. Those resources could be used for something else. To an economist that is known as the opportunity cost. By paying people to donate their organs, we are incurring no opportunity cost. That is to say, the resources are being used. The next best opportunity for the organs, is being fed to worms. And that is an opportunity of zero value, hence the true cost of this is zero.

*McMaster:* Thank you. The kidney should be treated as property like a gold watch. Panel, is one of the concerns that this system might actually work? Dr. Dickens, would this work, the motives of man, money, sex?

*Dickens:* That requires the discipline of the interaction of law and economics, which is Dr. Cohen's background. Lawyers cannot tell you what works, they can tell you what seems to be fair. Many legal schemes have been confounded by the fact that they were fine in theory, but didn't operate in practice. The problem, of course, is that if you try to test this market, then you have established the market in the course of testing it. If you conclude it is a bad idea, it could be hard to make it go away.

*Cohen:* I am persuaded it is going to work, markets work all the time. We are surrounded by markets; it is hardly a stringe assertion that this market will work. That is how we provide ourselves with food, and clothing and shelter. The only reason that we don't have this market now is a mere historical accident. The valuable use of body tissue is a new thing, and that is why it has been treated in a different way.

*Gomes da Costa:* Dr. Cohen, are there any places in the United States where doctors are paid for referring cadaver donors, and, if so, do those places produce larger amounts of donors or not?

*McMaster:* Dr. Cohen, are all the surgeons not paid for harvesting organs in the United States?

*Cohen:* I believe they are. There is however, no "finders' fee" that is paid at present, although some people have suggested that. This really strikes me as unseemly in that it would be a case of granting the doctors a property right in the cadaver which they can make money from but in which the decedant cannot.

*McMaster:* I will leave the last question to you.

*N. N.:* A few clarifications. If you market this whole thing, assuming that the heirs are the owners, how would you find the heir to decide or how would you reconcile between the heirs? They will stop discussing, one will want US $3000, the other one wants US $1000. It will take time, you will lose the donor. And then to whom do you sell the organ? You may have to shop around, perhaps you will find an agen'cy pays more. It will take time, so you lose the donor again. How about the surgeon, if you injure the kidney while removing it, you are liable to be sued because you damaged his gold watch. Or you may judge that the organ is not good for transplantation, it is not a gold watch, it is a tin watch. So you may be judged or sued for lack of judgment. How do you reconcile these things?

*Cohen:* There always will be practical questions and an implementation, but I view them as relatively minor. First of all, if I understood your first point, who is going to authorize this? The important aspect of my plan is the relatives play no role whatsoever, and doctors may initially wish to go to the relatives and ask their permission. I will cure this very quickly, i.e., the person cannot agree to sell and specify any designee to receive the money from this. The donor can designate any organization, any person to receive the money. The doctor will go to the wife and say is it all right with you if we take the organs and the wife will say no. The doctor will not take the organs, will not inform the organ procurement agency, and what will happen? It will turn out the designee is not the wife, it is some foundation, or a child. They will sue and the doctor will be liable. That will cure doctors very quickly of attempting to get reinforcement here. As to the question of if it turns out that the organ isn't good, all of that has to be specified by the contract, what it is you are paying for. My own presumption is that the payment be for successfully harvested and transplanted organs. With lesser fees for simply harvested tissue, which is not used for transplantation but may be used for some other therapeutic or investigative work, for children, that creates a problem. But there is a solution to it, and it is a solution that has a legal precedent. It is the solution that children cannot contract away in the form that I suggest. Now, it would be unseemly, unacceptable, and immoral if parents could contract away for their children independently. But what is not unseemly and what there is legal precedent for in other similar sorts of situations is families contracting away for all of their members simultaneously. That is, the parents in effect agree to sell their own organs if they die under these circumstances, and simultaneously agree that their children's organs shall be harvested in precisely the same fashion. If some people find that unacceptable, then OK, we won't get children's organs. I am willing to compromise, but I find it acceptable.

*McMaster:* Ladies and gentlemen, we have had a long morning and I think a very stimulating one. To the clinicians who come here, who fight in the trenches, as it were, in the war, I am sure we were looking for advice and suggestions as to how we go forward with our battles. I think we have heard quite a lot of comments this morning, many of which, I suspect, we feel quite uncomfortable about, but which require very careful thought indeed. Of course, because of the economic and market forces that I as an Englishman have come to grips with in these last years, I have become very conscious that the benefits you see on the one hand can sometimes be more than mitigated by the negative aspects on the other. But on your behalf I thank the whole panel and all the presenters this morning for what has been a very stimulating session. Thank you.

# *V. Allocation Issues in Organ Transplantation and Dialysis*

# Who Empowers Medical Doctors to Make Allocative Decisions For Dialysis and Organ Transplantation?

R. M. Veatch

There is a short answer to the question of who empowers medical doctors to make allocative decisions for dialysis and renal transplantation?, and that answer is no one. Rather than simply ending my presentation at this point, I would like to develop the argument why, in my opinion, it is a serious mistake for the public to expect clinicians to take on the responsibility for allocating any health resource including dialysis and transplantation.

## The Reality of Allocation

The reality, at least in the United States, the health care system of which I am most capable of speaking, is that no physician in his or her role as clinician is ever expected to allocate either a dialysis machine or an organ for transplantation. The normal limiting factor for dialysis is the availability of machines and the funding to operate them. The United States Congress has, through an amendment to the Medicare laws, categorically covered all appropriate dialysis patients. Of course, clinicians will continue to be expected to determine which patients will benefit medically from dialysis, but in the normal sense of rationing – as we were forced to allocate scarce hemodialysis machines in the 1960s – allocation need not take place. In other countries, there may be fewer machines available, but even then, I shall argue, physicians ought not be the ones who allocate.

For transplantation the story is quite different. Organs are inherently scarce. It is not a matter of money, but of the availability of the organs themselves. The problem has recently become more acute since organ procurement has decreased significantly in the past year. Even if organ availability were maximized through freedom-infringing routine salvaging of cadaver organs, we probably would not have enough – or would not have enough if technical problems were solved. Someone must allocate.

Kennedy Institute of Ethics, Georgetown University, Washington, D.C. 20057, USA

W. Land, J. B. Dossetor (Eds.)
Organ Replacement Therapy:
Ethics, Justice and Commerce

Still it does not follow that clinicians are expected to do the allocating. By law, in the United States all organs are made available through organ procurement organizations in cooperation with the national United Network for Organ Sharing (UNOS). Its board sets the principles for allocation of scarce organs and creates a formula for allocating them. Local practices must conform to the UNOS policies or to authorized variances. No clinician can gain access to an organ for transplant unless he or she conforms to the decisions of the local procurement organization and UNOS.

To take kidney allocation as an example, whenever a kidney becomes available in a local procurement organization, a nationally approved formula determines a priority list of possible recipients. The formula takes into account histocompatibility, panel reactive antibody levels, logistics, waiting time, and, under special circumstances, medical urgency. Whenever a kidney becomes available, a computer generates a priority list among all eligible patients awaiting kidney transplant. The organ procurement organization is required to offer the organ to the person scoring highest according to the allocation formula. This has the advantage of eliminating any charge of special ad hoc considerations or prejudices influencing the allocation. It also has the effect of completely removing the clinician from the allocation decision at the local level. To be sure, physicians are well represented in both the local and national boards that establish and operate the allocation formulas, but they do no direct allocating involving their own patients. I am convinced that this is the only morally defensible arrangement. My only quarrel is with the way points have been assigned in the formula. I would like to summarize the argument that leads to this conclusion.

## Allocation as a Moral Rather than Technical Matter

In order to understand why clinicians should have no role in allocating dialysis machines or transplantable organs, we need to understand why someone might be inclined to assign this life-and-death task to them. I think the working assumption of those who would expect clinicians to be allocators is either that allocations can be made on the basis of factual medical information about patients or that allocations should be made on the basis of the values of physicians. The thesis of my presentation is that key features of allocations are not factual in the medical sense; they are necessarily evaluative, but should not be made on the basis of the personal values of physicians.

### The Role of Medical Facts in Allocation

Surely medical data are relevant in deciding how to allocate scarce medical services. We should continue to expect clinicians to determine the probable effects of dialysis or transplant in patients who are potential candidates for these services. It should certainly hold that no patient should be a candidate for these procedures whose medical condition will not be affected by them. But the patient who would not be affected is not likely to want the procedures anyway. The real debate is over how to allocate in cases in which more patients wanting care have medical conditions that will be affected than there are machines or organs to respond to those needs. The issue is particularly controversial when we can expect different patients to benefit in different degrees, yet all of the potential recipients will benefit to some degree.

If we could assume that the scarce resource should automatically go to the person who would benefit most, it might appear that clinicians would be in a good position to play a role in deciding who should get the organs. Even this assumption proves false, however. Determining what counts as a benefit is inherently controversial and independent of medical facts. One patient may have the greatest chance of survival of acute illness; another may have the greatest predicted years of survival; still another may receive the greatest relief from suffering or morbidity and another may get the most satisfaction. Medical facts alone cannot tell us which of these patients will benefit the most from dialysis or transplant.

More critically, even if we knew which patient would benefit the most medically from the procedure, we cannot automatically conclude that that patient should receive the medical procedure. Social utilitarians would insist that we take into account social and other non-medical consequences of assigning the scarce resource – a determination about which physicians surely are not expert.

Critics of social utilitarianism may insist that the allocation be made solely on the basis of patient-centered reasons. Still that does not imply that the organ should go to the one who would benefit the most medically. Major theories of ethics insist that other considerations are morally relevant. Most importantly, they insist that fairness or justice be taken into account as well as medical or social utility in deciding what is an ethical allocation of organs.

For example, some might argue that justice requires that each candidate receive an equal chance of getting a scarce, social, life-saving resource such as a kidney even if not all have an equal chance of benefiting. They may insist that those who have waited longest or those who are sickest get priority, recognizing that these patients may not be the ones who would predictably benefit the most.

We need to solve the complex ethical problem of what is the correct basis for allocating scarce resources. The point here is merely that, in principle, even perfect knowledge of the medical facts about the patients who are candidates cannot determine which patient should receive an organ or a dialysis machine. If the presumption of a clinician role in allocation is based on their expert medical knowledge of the patient, that cannot provide an adequate basis for defending a role for clinicians in the allocation decision. This perhaps suggests an important role for the clinician in providing medical data about the medical condition of the patient, histocompatibility, prognosis without treatment, and likely outcomes with treatment, but these alone cannot determine the appropriate allocation. On this basis the clinician should provide data for those who create and run the allocation system; they should not make the allocation itself.

## The Role of Clinician Values in Allocation

Sophisticated clinicians, especially those with knowledge of contemporary medical ethical literature, will readily concede that all medical judgments require ethical and other value judgments and that this includes decisions about dialysis and transplant. They argue at this point that there are values inherent in the medical profession that provide the clinician with a basis for deciding (Kass 1985; Pellegrino and Thomasma 1988; Dyer 1985). They point to the traditional values of preserving life, relieving suffering, and maintaining health.

There are serious problems, however, with permitting allocations to be made on the basis of the clinician's interpretation of these traditional medical professional values. First, the medical values, in the interesting cases, lead to contradictions among themselves. The allocation that most preserves life may not be the one that best relieves suffering or promotes health. Clinicians will differ among themselves over how these conflicts should be resolved. Even if they could agree completely, it would not follow that lay people – the ones whose lives are at stake and the ones who created the pool of resources to be allocated – would concur in the ranking.

The problem is even more severe when one realizes that it is not at all obvious that the goal is to maximize medical values. If clinicians can disagree among themselves and can disagree collectively with the general public over the ranking of medical values, they can disagree much more dramatically over the question of how medical values would relate to social, nonmedical goods and over how pursuing the maximum good should be related ethically to other moral norms such as promoting a just allocation. Since these choices have nothing to do with medical knowledge, there is no reason why clinicians should be the ones making them. It is the general lay public that creates the money pool to support dialysis and creates the pool of cadaver organs to be allocated. They should be the ones making the moral choices relating medical to non-medical goods and relating the pursuit of maximum benefit to maximum justice or fairness in allocation. Clinicians should remain free to give undivided loyalty to their patients. That is incompatible with asking them to be resource allocators.

## The United States Kidney Allocation Formula: An Example

To make the nature of the problem concrete, imagine two patients under the care of different nephrologists in the same community, both of whom are awaiting kidney transplants when a single kidney becomes available. Patient A, 30 years old, has a 2 AB, 2 DR match with a potential donor and has been waiting 3 months for a kidney. Patient B is 58 years old, has a 1 AB, 1 DR match with the donor. He has 80 % panel reactive antibodies (PRA) but is a negative cross match with the donor. In part because of the high PRA, he has been waiting for 18 months for a transplant. His medical condition has deteriorated during the wait so that his condition is now described as urgent. Nevertheless, considering the deteriorating medical condition and cross-match history, and his age, his probability of successful graft survival is considered less than Patient A. What contribution could the physicians for each of these patients make to the allocation decision?

Each historically has an ethical duty to serve the interests of his own patient. Presumably, each would make the argument that served those interests. Patient A's physician would emphasize the greater likelihood of success; Patient B's would emphasize the equity issues related to long waiting time, high PRA, and more serious medical condition. Even if either really believed in the moral case the other made, it is doubtful he should be swayed by that belief to abandon his own patient. Even if both physicians came to the conclusion, for instance, that medical benefit took precedence over equity, that might simply reflect the unique value perspective of medical professionals as a group. It cannot be taken to imply that the general public would support the priority of medical benefit over equity. The present United States formula assigns two-thirds of its points to medical benefit.

An earlier formula used in the United States gave much more emphasis to matters of fairness with patients who had special needs (Starzl, et al. 1987). In rough terms three-fourths of the weight was given to equity, only one-fourth to predictors of good medical outcome. Today we need not determine what the correct balance of points is. For our purposes the question is whether individual clinicians or clinicians as a group should be empowered by the general community to choose the principles upon which allocations will be made. In the case of a formula for organ allocation, the critical question is what should be the relative number of points given to medical benefit and to need or equity. I would propose that as a compromise equal weight be given to each of the two considerations. Regardless of the answer, there seems to be no reason why clinicians should be empowered to make the choices. They are not related to the relevant medical expertise of the clinician; on the contrary the clinician ought to be committed to the welfare of his or her patient and, therefore, ought to come up with the wrong allocation decision. When we realize that any specialized professional group is likely to have ingrained commitments that lead it to unique answers to the key ethical question, I cannot see any reason why we should empower the medical professional to make allocative decisions.

## References

Dyer AR (1985) Virtue and medicine: a physician's analysis. In: Shelp EE (ed) Virtue and medicine: exploration in the character of medicine. Reidel, Dordrecht, Holland, pp. 223–235

Kass LR (1985) Toward a more natural science. Free Press, New York

Pellegrino ED, Thomasma DC (1988) For the patient's good: the restoration of beneficence in health care. Oxford University Press, New York

Starzl TE, Hakala TR, Tzakis A, Gordon R, Steiber A, Makowka L, Klimoski J, Bahnson HT (1987) A multifactorial system for equitable selection of cadaver kidney recipients. J Am Med Assoc 257:3073–3075

# A Central Paradox in Medicine: The Ethical Tension Between Self-Interest and Altruism

J. B. Dossetor

## The Underlying Dilemma

I take as my premise that most chronic renal failure patients are suitable for renal transplantation if they desire it. This is said in the face of the 1988 statistic of the EDTA-ERA combined report (EDTAERA 1988) that only 26000 out of approximately 100000 dialysis patients were on the cadaveric transplant list. Even if the overall patient longevity is not greater with renal transplantation (Hutchinson et al. 1984; Burton and Walls 1987; Kjellstrand, personal communication), it is certainly no worse. Others claim increased longevity after transplant even for diabetic patients (Khauli et al. 1986), albeit not without challenge (Parfrey et al. 1985). Further, the quality of life for renal transplant recipients is better than for those on dialysis (Churchill et al. 1987; Evans et al. 1985; Molzahn 1989), and the overall annual cost is reduced (Schippers and Kalff 1976; Optenberg and Jaffers 1986). This also holds for the end-stage renal failure population in the older age groups, when suitably age-adjusted (Delmonico et al. 1975).

Thus, one would expect that, *in the absence of special reason,* transplantation rates from a dialysis population should be comparable from country to country, with the limiting factor being the supply of cadaveric kidneys. In fact, in the figures for 1988 from the 19th EDTA report the number of grafts done (in 13 selected European countries) varied from 8 per million population (pmp) to 43 pmp, with a mean at 30.6 pmp. Also, the proportion of total renal failure patients who were living with a renal allograft in that year varied from 18% to 57%, in these selected countries, with a mean of 40.5% (see Table 1).

I submit, and will support with arguments, that there are two components to notion that patients can be "trapped in dialysis":

1. The personal and group financial self-interest of nephrologists, even though this has become 'covert' to the patient, and therefore no longer creates tension in the physician-patient relationship.

Bioethics Project, University of Alberta, 222 ANR, 8220 114th Street, Edmonton, AB, T6G 2J3, Canada

W. Land, J. B. Dossetor (Eds.)
Organ Replacement Therapy:
Ethics, Justice and Commerce

**Table 1.** Data from the 1988 Combined Report of Regular Dialysis and Transplantation in Europe for 13 selected Countries

| Country | Chronic renal failure × pmp | Percentage of chronic renal failure on home dialysis | Percentage of chronic renal failure on transplant | Transplants pmp | Transplants pmp done in 1988 |
|---|---|---|---|---|---|
| Austria | 412 | 3.0 | 38 | 160 | 43 |
| Belgium | 447 | 8.6 | 35 | 158 | 41 |
| Denmark | 325 | 28.9 | 50 | 166 | 28 |
| France | 360 | 19.1 | 23 | 82 | 33 |
| FRG | 440 | 8.0 | 21 | 95 | 29 |
| GDR | 182 | 0.1 | 31 | 57 | 17 |
| Italy | 330 | 14.1 | 18 | 61 | 8 |
| Netherlands | 374 | 22.4 | 45 | 172 | 28 |
| Norway | 301 | 13.7 | 83 | 252 | 40 |
| Spain | 351 | 9.6 | 31 | 109 | 26 |
| Sweden | 395 | 19.7 | 57 | 226 | 42 |
| Switzerland | 432 | 23.1 | 43 | 189 | 32 |
| UK | 284 | 66.9 | 52 | 147 | 31 |
| Mean | 356 | | 40.5 | 144 | 30.6 |

pmp, per million population

2. A genuine conviction in the minds of nephrologists that the dialysis option is better for many classes of renal failure patient.

I will follow these notions through six stages.

## Changes in the Ethics of the Physician-Patient Relationship in Respect to Payment of Doctors

Physicians are required by their Codes of Ethics, and by their professional relationships with patients, to act with integrity when patient autonomy has been weakened by illness. Despite their vulnerability, competent patients should make their own choices concerning treatments on the basis of full information. Understandably, such information usually comes from their physicians, and patients often seek the physician's advice in coming to their decisions. Physicians, for their part, unwittingly and without malintent, may subconsciously promote their own self-interest by the way in which they give advice and its effect on patient decision-making.

The 'power' imbalance of such situations precludes such encounters from being 'contracts in the market-place'. They are not contracts between negotiating equals, nor does the patient meet the description of 'client'. For this reason, May (1983) deems the concept of *covenant* rather than contract to be a better description, especially in regard to persons suffering with severe or acute illness. Within such a covenantal arrangement, beneficence requires that physicians place the interests of their patients ahead of their own when these two sets of interests come into conflict.

Historically, patients needed to recompense their physicians for their services, usually by direct payment of money. This brought ethical tension into the covenant – a de facto conflict of interest (Pellegrino 1988). The doctor's financial interests were always advanced at the expense of the patient's own resources, despite the existence of the covenant. When patients directly paid their doctors, fee negotiation was usually out in the open, and the ethical tension between the doctor's altruism and self-interest was 'overt'. If patients' lacked money, their doctors often would modify or even forego their fees. In this way, the ethical tension in the covenant was recognized and managed within the boundaries of beneficence. In other situations, the physician would refuse to establish a relationship, denying altruism, except in emergencies.

## Covert Ethical Tension When Payment is Transferred to Third Party Agencies

With the advent of Western third party payment systems, direct payment of the doctor has become a rare event. Removing monetary transactions from the personal doctor-patient covenant has dissipated the formerly 'overt' ethical tension. In these transactions, now contracted between physicians and third party payment agencies, payment of one's physician has become a 'covert' aspect of the physician-patient relationship. The central paradox disappears.

Further, thinking of the third party payers as having "deep pockets" with a more or less inexhaustible supply of cash for impersonal distribution to physicians on behalf of patients, the physician sometimes may develop ethically flawed attitudes towards payment agencies. Whereas the third party payment system has enormous advantages for those insured, nevertheless the former 'overt' tension did have value. It required face-to-face justification of 'what it all costs'. It prevented dissociation of patient service and benefit, on one hand, from what is now called 'the cost to the system', on the other.

Nowadays, patients are no longer aware of what things cost; nor do dialysis patients know how much their physician earns each year from looking after them.

## The Effect of Group Practice

Another significant change in the physician-patient relationship is that associated with group practice, with shared responsibility for patients. Dialysis, a repetitive procedure for each patient and conducted over periods of many months to many years, does not demand continuous involvement of the same physician. Physician group arrangements are common where a given nephrologist provides coverage for other nephrologist's patients on a rotational basis.

One possible consequence of this is that physicians' personal responsibility for individual patients may become blurred. Dialysis patients may come to be regarded as a group. A philosophy may develop which, in effect, says, "We, as a group, will look after you, as a group." In ethical terms, one might term this the development of a communal solidarity of mutual interest and concern. And this must be considered to be a good, to all. Group altruism is grafted onto individual altruism. Equally, a physician who does not subscribe to the feeling of group altruism might find him or herself in an ethical vacuum. Thus, by subtle means, nephrologists could come to see dialysis patients as a resource by which all live – the patients live because of dialysis, the dialysis physicians live because of the patients, and the nurses cement the whole human collectivity together by their hard work and sense of commitment. For the physicians, group altruism also becomes synonymous with group financial interest. No longer is there ethical tension. They are operating within a stable system, provided the group of patients does not alter substantially.

For the patients, what may be at stake in such a system are the principles of individualization of care and flexibility of treatment options. Is it possible, in such a system, for there to be an inadequate appreciation of other treatment options?

## Restriction and Inflexibility in Physician Proffered Treatment Options

How could it come about that physicians might, unwittingly, hold views of renal transplantation outcomes so as to limit renal transplant opportunities? I believe this can come about because of the operation of one or more of the following factors:

1. Ignorance of transplant results for different causes of renal failure at different decades of life; this might happen if one's focus was entirely centered on the problems of dialysis, and how to resolve them;

2. Too ready acceptance of the start-up difficulties in initiating or interacting with a transplant program, especially when local programs have 'problems';
3. Insufficient interest in playing an active role in cadaveric organ procurement – in some cultures, e.g. Japan, there may philosophical or religious prejudice against the practice, as well as lack of agreement on the determination of death from cerebral causes (brain death);
4. Self-exclusion from the immunological aspects of pretransplant work-up, if one's interests have been mainly in mineral, electrolyte, and metabolic areas of dialysis medicine;
5. Conviction that one is best employed in total dedication to the patients whose dialysis care is one's main responsibility.

## How Would the Method of Physician Payment Influence the Situation?

There are three ways by which physicians are rewarded: (1) Fee-for-service – payment for each medical act; (2) Capitation – payment according to each person registered with a health agency, whether ill or not, during periods of time (e.g., for a year); or, (3) Salary – payment based on contract with individual physicians for services during specified periods of time (e.g., for a year), regardless of numbers of persons to be served. In a fee-for-service system, the payment may be made by the individual, or by an insurance agent, or by government. In a capitation system, the physician is paid by a central agency (which could be private or public) on the basis of the numbers of those insured with the agency; profitability depends on the agency not spending more than the bare necessity on specific illnesses or medical acts. Income fluctuates in proportion to the number registered and the net cost of their illnesses. In salaried systems, the physician's income is fixed for specific periods, and there is no financial interaction with patients, directly or indirectly.

The motive of physician self-interest operates strongly in fee-for-service in such a way as to carry out more services and to retain patients under one's care for as long as can be justified. In the past, when all fees were paid privately, the victim was the patient who could not afford to pay. Even now, in the United States for example, the victim is the patient who cannot afford to buy adequate health insurance. Absence of victimization of sick persons only occurs in a fee-for-service system when insurance is universal, and with an agency which has a 'very deep pocket', such as government.

In capitation systems, by contrast, there is both physician and agency self-interest in making treatment as inexpensive and as short as possible and to avoid long-standing cost commitments.

With salaried physicians, there is no financial self-interest operating on the services to patients; the extent and quality of physician dedication now depends on factors unrelated to monetary reward – factors such as beneficence, dedication, and genuine altruism. Thus, on the face of it, the two best systems (for patients) might be "deep pocket" universal insurance coupled with the fee for service principle, or a salaried system.

## How Would One Look for Evidence for "Trapping in Dialysis"?

If the arguments developed so far are valid, one can conjecture certain avenues of exploration to see if they are valid for dialysis practices as they exist today. These avenues are as follows:

1. In countries where dialysis physicians are salaried, is there a higher transplantation rate of the dialysis population than in countries where dialysis physicians earn their income by other methods of remuneration?
2. If there are two types of dialysis funding of units within a single fiscal area (country): (a) dialysis physicians funded by fee-for-service from third parties, and (b) dialysis physicians funded by government salaries, is there a higher transplantation rate in (b) type units than in (a) type?
3. In countries where most dialysis is done in dialysis centers (as contrasted with those promoting home dialysis, actively) is the transplantation rate lower?

## Conclusion

Throughout medical history there has been conflict for physicians between the desire to treat patients altruistically and the need to make money from them in order to live. I have described this as an ethical tension in the traditional doctor-patient relationship. In recent decades there has been progressive dissociation of the patient's responsibility for paying the doctor and the doctor's direct dependency on the patient for his living. Third party paying agencies have been brought in to recompense the physician, whether the basic remunerating system is fee-for-service, capitation, or straight salary. Each payment system would set different limits for what it would consider to be legitimate as the range for dialysis physicians' earnings, but it would be highest when the basis is fee-for-service, and lowest when by salary.

In addition to these changes, in recent decades the practice of medicine has taken on certain shared-practice features. This leads to fragmentation of care (when physicians share responsibility for patients with a wide variety of diseases and individualized needs, using a rotational system), but can lead to an improved continuity of care when patients share many features in common, such as in a dialysis unit. Indeed, the latter may reflect an ethic of human solidarity which is both valuable and ethically understandable. However, it is also possible that such an expression of solidarity could lead to inflexibility of treatment options being offered to patients – especially offering the transplantation option.

This inflexibility would not be a matter of concern if it could be shown that dialysis was associated with improved longevity, using comparable patient populations. However, if longevity is found to be equal or less – not greater –, then the phrase 'trapped in dialysis' would apply. This is because the transplantation option has been shown to be associated with a higher quality of life and to be less expensive.

## References

Burton PR, Walls J (1987) Selection-adjusted comparison of life-expectancy of patients on CAPD, haemodialysis and renal transplantation. Lancet i:1115–9

Churchill DN, Torrance GW, Taylor DW, Barnes CC, Ludwin D, Shimizu A, Smith EK (1987) Measurement of quality of life in end-stage renal disease: the time trade-off approach. Clin Invest Med 10:14–20

Combined Report on Regular Dialysis and Transplantation in Europe, XIX, 1988. Nephrology, Dialysis, Transplantation 1989:4, Supplement 4(5–40)

Delmonico FL, Cosimi AB, Russell PS (1975) Renal transplantation in the older age group. Arch Surg 110:1107–9

Evans RW, Manninen DL, Garrison LP, Hart LG, Blagg R, et al. (1985) The quality of life of patients with end-stage renal disease. N Engl J Med 312:553–9

Hutchinson TA, Thomas DC, Lemieux JC, Harvey CE (1984) Prognostically controlled comparison of dialysis and renal transplantation. Kidney Int 26:44–51

Khauli RB, Steinmuller DR, Novick AC, Buszta C, et al. (1986) A critical look at survival of diabetics with endstage renal disease. Transplantation versus dialysis therapy. Transplantation 41:598–602

May WF (1983) The physician's covenant: images of the healer in medical ethics. Westminster, Philadelphia

Molzahn A (1989) Perceptions of patients, physicians, nurses. Thesis, University of Alberta

Optenberg SA, Jaffers GJ (1986) A prospective cost comparison between renal transplantation and chronic hemodialysis as Wilford Hall USAF Center. Milit Med 151:630–3

Parfrey PS, Hutchinson TA, Harvey C, Guttmann RD (1985) Transplantation versus dialysis in diabetic patients with renal failure. Am J Kidney Dis 5:112–6

Pellegrino ED (1988) The physician as gatekeeper. In: Pellegrino ED, Thomasma DC (eds) For the patient's good: the restoration of beneficence in health care. Oxford University Press, Oxford

Schippers HM, Kalff MW (1976) Cost comparison haemodialysis and renal transplantation. Tissue Antigens 7:86–90

# The Role of Entrepreneurial Factors in Health Care Systems

H. Kütemeyer

The creation of health care systems by government throughout the world in the course of this century has not only assured medical treatment for the ill, regardless of their financial possibilities, it has also decisively changed medical practice for the physician.

In most countries, doctors' fees and reimbursement rates are fixed and controlled by social insurance systems or by health authorities themselves. The majority of physicians in modern industrial nations today are either hospital employed or civil servants or have a fixed contract with social insurance systems. Physicians looking to use new treatment methods or a new diagnostic procedure are very often faced with the fact that health authorities have not yet incorporated these methods into their system.

While it is not the nature of a physician to go and look for business opportunities, it lies in the nature of health care systems to only reluctantly adopt new treatment methods into their system. That is why physicians sometimes have no alternative but to undertake their own business to finance a new treatment method. Once this treatment has proven itself, health care authorities are willing to reimburse the cost. Many new treatment methods or diagnostic procedures were initiated into medical practice in this way. Many physicians have had to learn this strategy also bears the risk of financial failure. During the last two decades many therapies previously performed only in hospitals could be moved to outpatient centers or completely into the home care setting.

Recently, health care societies have started to offer incentives to physicians or private organizations managing treatment outside hospitals. On the other hand, many countries offering a complete scope of medical treatment for their population through national health care services have experienced a veritable boom of privately run and organized hospitals offering their services to an increasing number of patients not qualified for or not satisfied with the universally available treatment quality or the treatment methods of the existing healt care system.

One could continue endlessly naming examples of private enterprise in medicine, even such bizarre situations of socialist countries offering well-to-do patients paying with foreign currency treatment otherwise not available to their own population. At the same time one cannot ignore the most

Dialyse-Institut, Pillauer Straße 6, 7530 Pforzheim

W. Land, J. B. Dossetor (Eds.)
Organ Replacement Therapy:
Ethics, Justice and Commerce

important part of entrepreneurial factors in health care systems today, namely, the continously growing health care industry.

Since this conference addresses entrepreneurial aspects of renal replacement therapy, I would like to discuss private enterprise in regard to dialysis treatment more in detail. When, at the end of the 1960s dialysis treatment had proven itself as a save and beneficial treatment for terminal kidney disease, society in those countries able and willing to offer their population this therapy was faced with two major problems. One was the lack of sufficient treatment capacity, the other was the absence of reimbursement regulations by health care authorities and the need to keep treatment costs as low as possible. Different countries adopted different measures to cope with and solve these problems. Moving treatment out of the hospital into less intensively staffed treatment centers or into the home of the patient himself was one way of solving both problems at the same time.

Not all countries had the same determination or structure in their health care systems to be able to solve both capacity problems and cost containement in this simple fashion. Looking at the situation of where treatment is performed and which organizations offer treatment in three different industrial nations today, we can see that the originally adopted methods in these countries still reflect on the situation today. In the United Kingdom, where health care authorities very early and rigorously propagated self-care treatment, almost 80 % of patients receiving dialysis treatment are on some kind of self-care method. Organization and medical care of these patients is run and regulated by hospital centers of the National Health service. The small number of privately organized centers offer their services to those patients not willing to accept self-care treatment as the only available therapy. In the United States almost half of all treatment centers are run on a private profit-oriented basis, with hospitals and Veteran Organisations making up the other half. In Germany, capacity problems were again solved differently with private non-profit-making organizations treating most patients and hospitals, and private centers treating the rest.

Although treatment capacity problems were solved differently in these three countries, reimbursement is regulated by state-controlled authorities in all three countries alike. There are no significant differences in the amount reimbursed for identical treatment to the different organizations, be they profit-oriented or nonprofit-organized. It would seem, then, that the different methods adopted originally had no significant result on cost development. Looking at the newest patient survival rates for those receiving kidney replacement therapy in these three countries, I would, however, be very reluctant to state that there are no differences in treatment quality and safety.

Another widely discussed problem of profit-oriented medical practice in this field is the question of whether patients of private institutions are not admitted for transplantation by their physicians because of economic considerations. Data available from private centers in the United States suggest, however, that rather than keep patients on dialysis and not admit them to transplantation, the most frequent strategy in the case of economic problems is to shorten treatment time.

The data available to me for the situation in Germany clearly contradict such assumptions. In Germany, with patients having enough treatment capacity to choose a center of their liking, any physician keeping his patients away from transplantation would be shortly without patients to treat. Hopefully, the other presentations at this conference and the resulting discussion will be able to further clarify this issue.

# What Could Be Done to Regulate Profit in Dialysis Centers? Propositions From Some French Realities

G. Dixsaut[1] and D. Cordonnier[2]

Chronic dialysis of uremic patients in France is a very expensive activity, certainly one of the most expensive in the world. It can be a profit-making activity. It is one reason for which those interested in that type of treatment could be tempted to keep patients away from self-care dialysis or transplantation. About 19500 uremic patients were treated in France in 1989 by hemodialysis; of these 15650 are treated in center facilities (i.e., private or public hospitals or nonprofit but nonpublic centers) and 3850 are treated at home or in self-care facilities [1, 2]. The financial burden of dialysis in France was estimated for the year 1989 at 8225 million FF. Transportations, drugs, and laboratory tests are included in this total, but hospitalizations in public hospitals are not [6]. Out of this sum, only 975 million FF were paid by the *Assurance Maladie* (public insurance) for home and self-care facilities [6]. One could understand that the public health authorities care about making an in-depth examination of the reasons for an insufficient and inadequate drain of patients from the expensive methods of treatment (i.e., in center dialysis) to cheaper ones (out-center dialysis or transplantation).

A total of 1957 renal transplantations were performed in France in 1989, 57 of these with kidneys of related living donors. This is by far not enough to satisfy the needs of more than 4000 patients waiting on the French list [4]. In this paper we discuss successively:

1. How the price of dialysis has been fixed differently in different parts of France.
2. How excessive profit (but not only profit) can induce doctors to be reluctant to guide patients to home dialysis or to transplantation.
3. What could be done to regulate these practices which prevent some patients from getting the best treatment they need, thereby increasing public expenditure excessively.

[1] Ministère des Affaires Sociales et de la Solidarité Nationale, 1 place de Fontenoy, 75350 Paris 07 SP, France
[2] Service de Néphrologie, Dialyse et Transplantation, Centre Hospitalier Régional et Universitaire, BP 217 X, 38043 Grenoble Cedex, France

W. Land, J. B. Dossetor (Eds.)
Organ Replacement Therapy:
Ethics, Justice and Commerce

## The Price of Dialysis

The price of dialysis is fixed as a set price by agreement between the Social Security Office (*Caisse d'Assurance Maladie*) on the one hand, and on the other the institution depending upon its status [5]. For profit organizations, there is a ceiling price of 1690 FF for one session, to which are added 250 FF as medical fees and 135 FF for laboratory tests, which makes a session of 2075 FF (transportation not included). This set price was established years ago when dialysis was a rather complicated method and reevaluated automatically each year. Detailed examinations of the costs established by some of these institutions (not necessarily at the ceiling price) show that they have been artificially set. These include excessive investment forecast, and high budget or high rental rates for property companies. The persons in charge of these dialysis centers are often members of these property companies.

In public institutions, the price of dialysis is not precisely established but included in what is called *"budget global"*. This annual budget is fixed each year based upon the analytical cost of every medical or housing act, which includes wages and salaries. This analytical cost shows that the price rate of dialysis can vary widely from one to another hospital depending upon what is calculated in it [6].

## Reluctance to Guide Patients to Home Dialysis and Transplantation

Reluctance to encourage people treated by in-center hemodialysis to switch to cheaper forms of treatment comes from two kinds of attitudes; one is profit, the second is power. Very different kinds of policies are adopted by different nephrologists in different parts of France. The following examples illustrate these differences. Let us first compare Provence Alpes Côte d'Azur (PACA), where the vast majority of dialysis centers are private, and Limousin, where the vast majority of dialysis centers are public.

In PACA, only 18 % of uremic patients are treated outside the centers [7]. The argument developed to explain this low rate is that patients are mostly elderly. Doctors claim that it is difficult for elderly people to be dialyzed outside centers. But in Limousin where they are still older (half of them are more than 60 years old), more than 50 % are treated outside the centers. The doctors there argue that self dialysis, limited care dialysis, and peritoneal dialysis are the best methods to diminish hospitalism [8]. Therefore, the same argument is used for the justification of two opposite attitudes.

Let us now compare two cities in the same north-eastern part of the country. In one large city almost 100 % of the patients are treated in only one center. There are virtually no transplanted patients coming from this public center. The percentage of home dialysis in this city and neighborhood is also extremely low. It is obviously a matter of policy of the nephrologists since there is a very efficient transplant center in the same city (treating patients from other centers of the region) and since in another city situated at only 100 km from the first one, less than 10 % of new patients are treated in the private clinic, more than 90 % being immediately oriented towards transplantation or out-center dialysis methods.

One argument of the doctors who keep patients outside transplantation is that there is a shortage of available organs, which is in part true, but could be modified by some regulations. In theory, the only limiting factor in France is the number of kidneys available, which is around 2500 since there are about 1250 brain deaths per year available, given the present possibilities of mobile emergency facilities and rescuscitation centers [4]. These possibilities are quite good in the main and middle-sized towns. A small increase is still possible, but will be hard to reach.

In 1988, 320 transplantations were performed for nonresident foreigners, in 1989, 330 out of 1957. In some hospitals, the percentage of grafted foreigners is closed to 0. In others it could be very close to 100 % [9]. Explanation of the later situation is complex since responsible doctors claim that the transplantation activity needs to be regular to be correctly performed and that French residents are not registered on waiting lists because of the policies in dialysis centers we have already analyzed. In fact, French residents registered on waiting lists complain angrily that they wait much longer than foreigners. This is true in some centers. In Paris, only 17 % of foreigners are still on the waiting lists at the end of the year, which means that they have been transplanted faster than French persons, far more than 33 % of whom are still on the list. Some of these patients could have been treated preferentially. This assertion needs investigation.

This nonhomogeneous attitude vis-à-vis nonresident foreigners has harmful effects that could and must be modified. It reinforces the wish by some nephrologists to keep their French patients off the waiting list. It enables some foreign countries to find too easy solutions to their own problems, to delay their own organ harvesting programs, and, finally, in some cases it is a waste of time, energy, and money since some of the patients are not properly followed up after transplantation when they come back to their own countries. Furthermore some countries don't pay their debt.

## Possible Solutions

What can we do to modify these unsatisfactory attitudes and move towards low cost treatment, which is also often best suited for the patients? Since these attitudes are not illegal, and are only a drift from a status established over years, only two ways can be implemented: social pressure and more rigorous official regulation. Obviously the very good results of transplantation and home dialysis or self-dialysis, even among persons getting old, cannot be ignored by the patients provided they belong to patients' associations. Diffusing and broadcasting information on the techniques, the practices, the different attitudes, and the cost of each particular aspect would help patients to become more aware, and they would ask for optimal treatment. This kind of pressure has been efficient in the past for a small but significant number of patients, even in the more reluctant centers. To modify these attitudes, regulations and laws are being carried out in France for both dialysis and transplantation.

*Concerning dialysis.* The legal number of dialysis machines in centers in France has nearly reached its full quota, which is 45 in-center machines per million/population [3]. Meanwhile, the number of patients continues to increase slowly. It has been decided not to increase the number of dialysis centers (public or private), but to allow only redeployment of the therapeutic technics [10]. Home dialysis is less popular among autonomous patients because of the burden imposed on spouses. Self-dialysis facilities can only spread slowly now, probably because the number of autonomous patients cannot be increased very much. Therefore, we in France are introducing a new concept, called *les centres allégés de dialyse* (CAD) whose main characteristics are the following. CAD are designed for "well-being dialyzed patients", who are not sufficiently autonomous to be able to use self-dialysis, but who are willing and able to take part more or less in their treatment. These CAD will be located outside public or private hospitals. They will need less equipment and less medical or nursing staff. In short, these will be limited care facilities. The price rate for one session will be set at a ceiling price of around 1200 FF and the responsibility for the running of the CAD will be handed to the nonprofit associations which already have good experience of home dialysis. The official regulation has not been issued yet.

*Concerning Transplantation.* Decrees have been issued recently [10–12]. The opening of new transplantation centers needs public authorization, thereby, limiting the number to 39. This was not the case before [13]; the technical conditions needed for a center to be authorized are very strict [14]. Patients will be obligatorily registered on an official list (under the responsibility of the hospital director) before being transplanted. This list will be managed by the regional subdivisions of France Transplant. Financing France Transplant and these regional subdivisions will be the responsibility of these authorized hospitals [15, 16]. In this way, the Ministry of Health hopes to avoid the following points: nonofficial lists of patients transplanted quickly for nonmedical reasons, particularly nonresident foreigners and, particularly, rich foreigners; uncontrolled enrolment of too many nonresident foreigners on the list at the expense of French citizens; nondevelopment of transplant programs in countries which send us their patients; nonpayment or insufficient payment by these countries.

## In Conclusion

It is easy to claim that our aim is to treat the citizens, when they need to be at a reasonable cost. But we, as persons or as groups, are often balancing between two attitudes to achieve the result. The first one is to facilitate the authorizations of private or even public centers; for that, we need, ask for, and sometimes get the help of elected politicians and even administratives; this is the easy but wrong way. The better one is hard because there are few or no beneficiaries, and, therefore, little help to develop self-dialysis and transplantation.

One could expect that more and more financial control and transparency will help. It is apparently contradictory with an essential principle in medicine which is anonymity. However, the use of data processing helps the administration to have a better knowledge of what is exactly going on in these centers, without knowing the names of the patients. This is the means for more efficient control, but also for a better democracy, with the patients' associations participating.

Finally the key issues seem to be the following:

1. How do we distribute better the harvested kidneys which do not belong to us?
2. How can we transplant our own citizens and residents at the right time or dialyse them in their own actual interest?
3. How do we help other countries, and especially Eastern or Southern countries, to develop their own transplant programs and become more autonomous in this field. This latter point is an essential challenge for the last decade of this century.

## References


1. Jacobs C, Selwood NH (1990) Evalutation démographique et méthodes de traitement de l'urémie chronique au stade terminal chez les sujets âgés de plus de 65 ans en France au cours des années 1980. Néphrologie prospective, Paris, 15–16 March 1990
2. Leroy H (1989) Dialyse à domicile; enquête statistique. Fédération des etablissements hospitaliers et d'assistance privée, Paris
3. Anonymous (1984) Arrêté du 9 avril 1984, fixant l'indice des besoins pour le traitement pour l'hémodialyse en centre de l'insuffisance rénale chronique des adultes. Journal Officiel du 21 avril 1984
4. France-Transplant 1989 Annual report
5. Anonymous (1978) Arrêté du 29.06.1978. Critères et procédures de classement applicables aux établissements hospitaliers privés mentionnés à l'article L 275 du code de la Sécurité Sociale, arrêté des ministères de la Santé de l'Economie, du Budget et de l'Agriculture. Journal officiel de la République Française, 18.07.1978
6. Dautel MM (1988) Le traitement de l'insuffisance rénale chronique. Diplôme d'Etudes Supérieures Spécialisées en Gestion et Economie du Système de Santé. Diploma, University of Paris, Panthéon Sorbonne
7. Anonymous (1987) Mise à jour de l'enquête sur la situation du traitement de l'insuffisance rénale chronique dans la région Provence-Alpes-Côte d'Azur. Direction régionale des affaires sanitaires et sociales 26.10.1987

8. Anonymous (1990) Prise en charge de l'insuffisance rénale en Limousin, 1989 survey. Direction Régionale des Affaires Sanitaires et Sociales, June 1990
9. Anonymous (1990) Nombre d'étrangers non résidents transplantés en France en 1988 et 1989. Annual reports of public hospitals. (Unpublished data)
10. Anonymous (1984) Elaboration de programmes régionaux pour le traitement de l'insuffisance rénale chronique. Circulaire du Ministre des Affaires Sociales et de la Solidarité Nationale. Secrétariat d'Etat chargé de la Santé, 21 June 1984
11. Anonymous (1990) Décrêt n°90 845 du 24.09.1990 relatif aux activités de transplantation d'organes nécessitant un traitement immunodépresseur. Journal officiel de la République Française, 25.09.1990
12. Anonymous (1990) Arrêté n°1955 du 24.09.1990 relatif à la composition du dossier de demande d'autorisation d'effectuer des transplantations d'organes. Journal Officiel de la République Française, 25.09.1990
13. Anonymous (1990) Arrêté n°1954 du 24.09.1999 fixant le numbre des unités de transplantation rénale, cardiaque et hépatique. Journal officiel de la République Française, 25.09.1990
14. Anonymous (1990) Arrêté n°1951 relatif aux modalités d'évaluation des activités de transplantation d'organes. Journal officiel de la République Française, 25.09.1990
15. Anonymous (1990) Arrêté n°1952 relatif à l'organisation de l'activité de transplantation d'organes par établissement et par unité à l'exception de l'activité allogreffe de moelle osseuse. Journal officiel de la République Française, 25.09.1990
16. Anonymous (1990) Arrêté n°1949 du 24.09.1990 relatif à la gestion et au financement de la liste des patients en attente de transplantation. Journal officiel de la République Française, 25.09.1990

# Excuses of Nephrologists Not to Transplant

G. Thiel

The initiator of this congress is a committed transplantation surgeon who has complained to me about nephrologists from time to time for many years. He and several other transplant surgeon colleagues mentioned some practising nephrologists – perhaps it would be better to call them dialysis physicians – of not registering some of their chronic dialysis patients for kidney transplantation for unconvincing reasons. It is, therefore, right to talk about this topic today. It is a good thing that a nephrologist rather than a transplantation surgeon is giving this paper. However, the topic is very sensitive, and a nephrologist is ill-advised to be prepared to talk about it. He must reckon with vehement criticism from his own profession. I am nevertheless presenting this paper because I hope to give moral support and encouragement to some colleagues and conversely to obstruct the activity of those who are criticized in this lecture.

So then, what are the excuses why dialysis patients are either not registered for kidney transplantation, or are not released for operation after registration when a cadaver kidney is available?

## High Age

The most frequent excuse for rejecting transplantation is that the patient is too old [1] and transplantation, therefore, too risky. Fortunately, the 50-year limit for transplantation has been abandoned; however, some nephrologists still work with 60, 65, or 70 year limits. Are there objective reasons for this? Various investigations show an increased mortality of transplantation with increasing age, but the recent reports are in favor of transplantation in older patients [2, 3].

An analysis of the Basle patients [4] are shown in Figs. 1 and 2. They reveal that the survival with a functioning graft at 5 years even in the last years before the cyclosporine era was just as high in patients over 60 years as in an middle-aged class of patients 46–50 years old. The difference merely consisted in a higher mortality. The risk of dying in the over 60 year olds was 12 % during the first year after transplantation in Basel, or 7 % greater than in the

Director, Division Nephrology, Department of Medicine, Kantonsspital Basel, University of Basel, CH-4031 Basel, Switzerland

W. Land, J. B. Dossetor (Eds.)
Organ Replacement Therapy:
Ethics, Justice and Commerce

middle-aged class, which is around 4 %. Certainly, 12 % mortality is a serious risk. However, the mortality in dialysis is not equal to zero, and we will come to that later.

One should be quite honest with old patients who are fed up with dialysis and who inquire about a kidney transplant: if the transplantation is successful

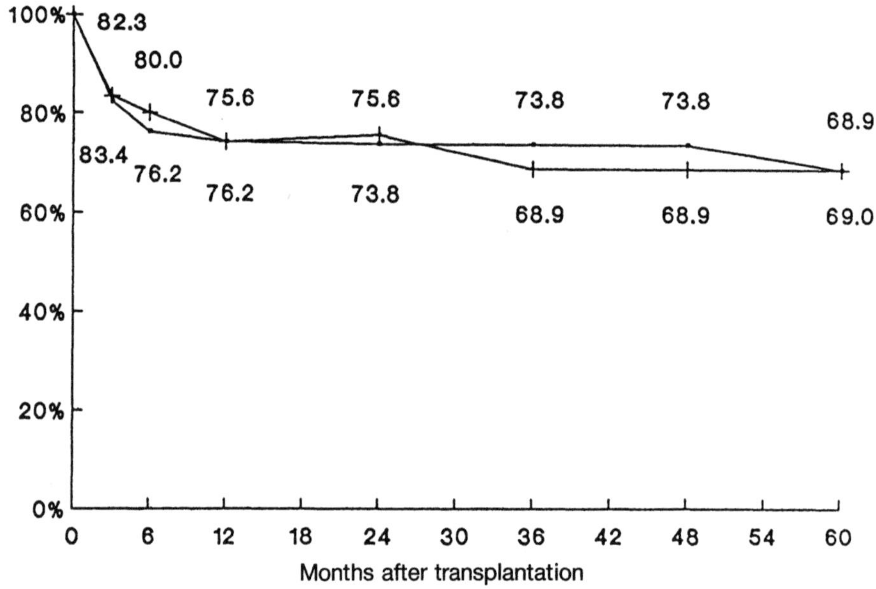


**Fig. 1.** Actuarial renal transplant survival of two age classes in Basle: 46–50 years old (-●-, $n = 45$) and 60–67 years old (+, $n = 42$). Transplantation was performed from 1978 till 1986

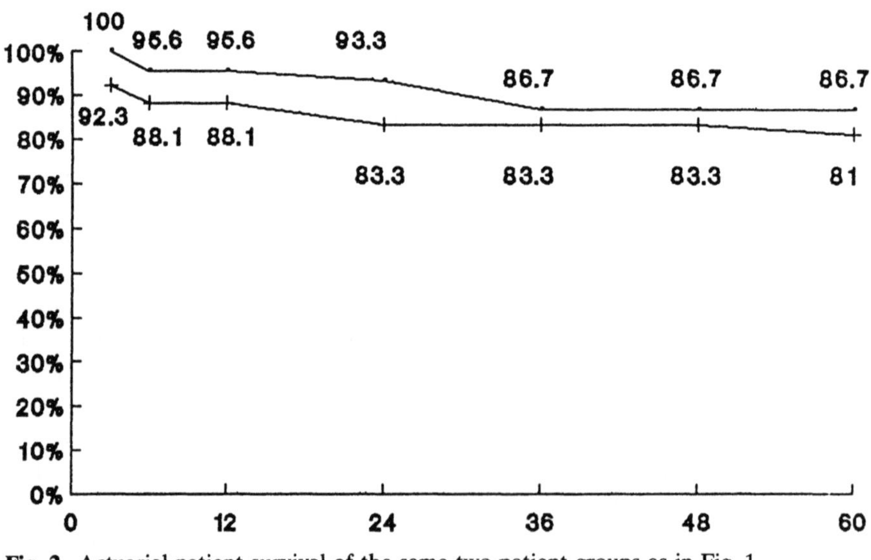


**Fig. 2.** Actuarial patient survival of the same two patient groups as in Fig. 1

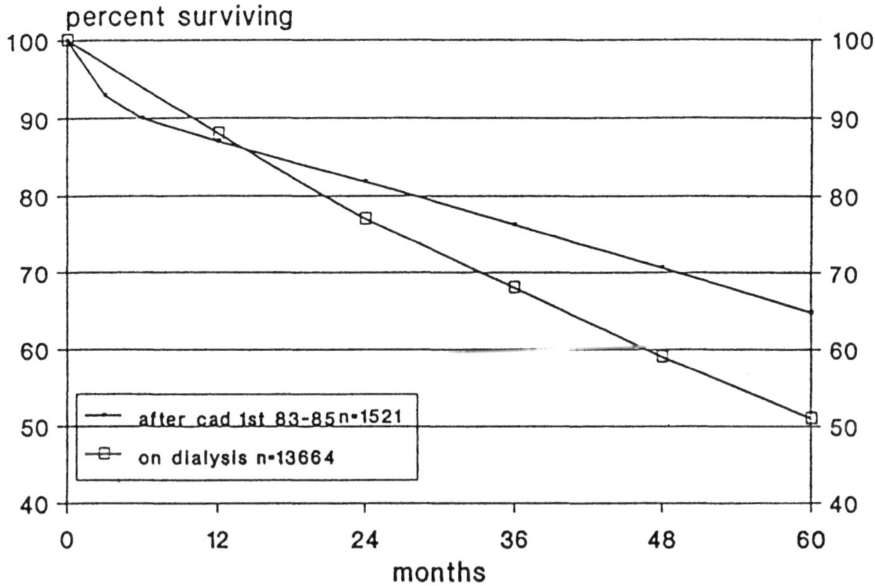


**Fig. 3.** Survival of patients on dialysis, aged 55–64 years at start of dialysis, compared with survival after first cadaveric transplantation at age 55–64. Patients with diabetic end-stage renal failure were excluded in both groups. (Data kindly provided by Prof. Felix Brunner from the EDTA Registry, London)

and the chances of this is around 80%, the quality of life is appreciably increased. If it fails, the patient must reckon to die. But why should elderly patients not be offered the advantages of kidney transplantation if they are prepared to accept some increased mortality as the price for a higher quality of life? The old patient must be given the chance to participate in the decision.

The best argument with regard to the age limit is the lack of kidneys. Should they therefore be distributed amongst younger people? I cannot accept this argument nor all the complaints about the insufficient number of cadaveric donors when expressed by a dialysis physician, as long as he himself does not do anything in his local region to promote organ procurement and transplantation. As long as he is only concerned to extend his own dialysis capacity, his argument sounds hypocritical.

Another inacceptable and hidden argument against transplantation in old people is the concern to worsen the own success statistic in comparison with other centers who refuse to accept risk patients. Indeed, when results of centers are compared in any congress or given paper, little attention is paid to differences in mean age and other risk factors. It is important to realize this difference, since the meaning of an 85 % yearly success rate is very different, if you achieve that with or without including aged and poor-risk patients. It is OK to look for good results and to try to improve them, but it is a poor solution, to achieve good results by excluding old patients from transplantation.

How much higher is the mortality for elderly people than in those who remained on chronic dialysis? This question can best be answered with the analysis from the EDTA registry shown in Fig. 3. The 5-year survival rate for uremic people in the age class of 55–64 is given for people staying on dialysis or for those who received a first cadaveric kidney. The survival rate with a first cadaveric transplant is only lower in the first 12 months. Then the line of transplant survival crosses the dialysis line and achieves a 15 % better survival at 5 years after transplantation.

A dialysis physician, who is used to warning his patients about the increased risk of dying after transplantation should rather show this figure based on 1521 transplanted patients and 13 664 dialysed patients. If he is further used to warning his patients about the increased malignancy rate after transplantation, he should also be telling them about the risk of more than 90 % of developing amyloidosis of bones and ankles after 10 years of dialysis [5].

## HLA Matching

Human leukocyte antigen (HLA) matching takes one of the foremost places in the hit list of excuses not to transplant. The more easy and uncomplicated it is for the staff to dialyse a truly congenial patient, the greater the probability that in the crucial telephone conversation in which his dialysis physician is offered a kidney, he will answer: "No thank you, we should prefer to wait for a better match for him."

It is certainly not the purpose of my presentation to challenge some benefit of HLA matching in Necrokidney transplantation. What I would like to do,

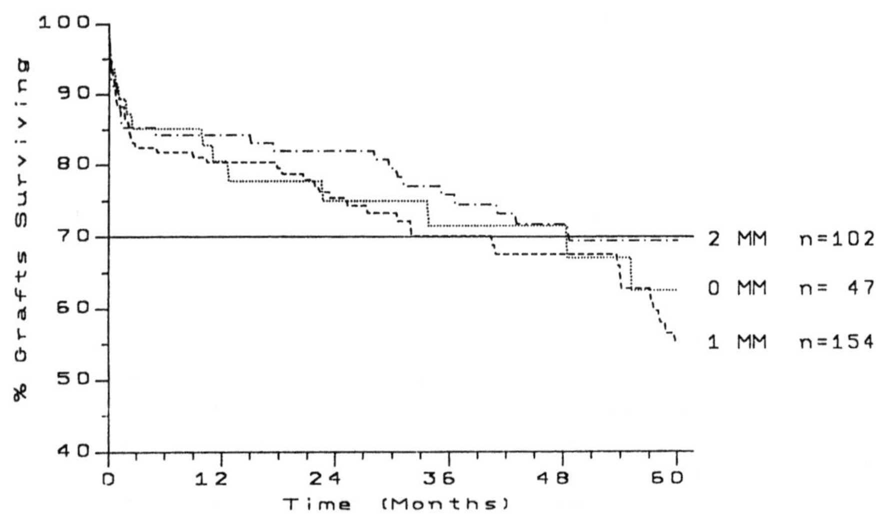


**Fig. 4.** Percentage of 5-year graft survival of first cadaveric renal transplants in Basle, separated according to the number of HLA-DR mismatches. (Data from the CTS-Registry, kindly provided by Prof. Gerhard Opelz, Heidelberg)

however, is to attack the habit of some nephrologists, whenever they use the "not good enough HLA match" argument, when the true reason to refuse the kidney offer is simply based on the necessity of fully utilizing the dialysis equipment in order to pay all salaries and debts, to fulfil some contracts, or to continue a research program paid in part by dialysis-related earnings.

I should like to illustrate my argument on the basis of the Basle figures. Gerhard Opelz was kind enough to analyze the data of all Basle first cadaver kidneys since we have participated in the CTS registry. In Fig. 4 the role of HLA-DR mismatches is shown. The grafts with two HLA-DR mismatches do best and at least as well as the patients with the zero-DR mismatches. The argument that bad mismatching is having its bad influence only late, after 2–5 years, does not show up at all.

The same applies to the transplant survival in Fig. 5. Four HLA-B-DR mismatches, that is complete B-DR mismatching, which is avoided by several institutions, have at 5 years no different outcome than the zero mismatches. Graft survival at 5 years for complete B-DR mismatches is 70 % which is not too bad for cadaveric kidneys.

Some may think that the poor matches need more rejection treatment, give rise to more complications, and have poorer kidney function because of chronic rejection, etc. All this is quite incorrect, as can be seen in Table 1. This table contains two subgroups of our first cadaver kidney recipients: One subgroup consists of our best-matched class, which fulfils Opelz's HIT criteria for hyperimmunized patients, that is maximally one mismatch at the HLA-A, HLA-B, and HLA-DR locus. There have been 60 such well-matched cadaveric kidney transplants since 1984. The other extreme subgroup is

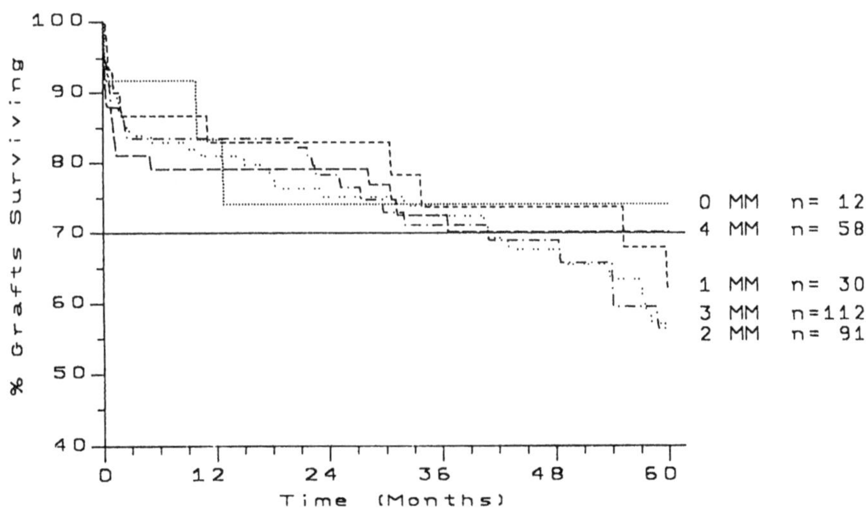


**Fig. 5.** Percentage of 5-year graft survival from the same patients as in Fig. 4, separated according the number of HLA-B-DR mismatches. (CTS registry, kindly provided by Prof. G. Opelz)

**Table 1.** Cadaveric renal transplants in Basle

| Parametrs | Well matched[a] | Full house mismatches[b] |
|---|---|---|
| $n$ | 60 | 29 |
| Mean age (years) | 48 | 51 |
| 12-Month survival (%) | | |
| Patient | 91 | 96 |
| Kidney | 84 | 86 |
| p-Creatinine at 12 months (μmol/l) | 162 | 141 |
| methylprednisolone 0.5 g pulses/12 months | 9.6 | 6.7 |

[a] Maximum one mismatch at HLA-A, -B, or -DR loci
[b] Six-mismatches at HLA-A, -B, or -DR loci

formed by our 29 full house mismatches from the same period, that is a total of six mismatches for the HLA-A, -B and -DR loci. The match of the latter group could not be worse. However, transplant survival and mortality is the same for both. Also the number of Methylprednisolone pulses given to treat rejection is the same. This also applies to kidney function, as reflected by serum creatinine. There is no trend in favor of the good match group, of which one might say, that perhaps larger numbers are required in order to attain significance. Whenever their is a trend, it is in favor of the full house mismatches.

All successful Basle full house mismatches would not have been transplanted in the first place in most of West Germany's transplant clinics, since even five mismatches are regarded as medically irresponsible. Although statistics using very large numbers may show some benefit of HLA matching in first necrokidneys, the effect is too small (or even invisibel) on a single center base to justify any prolongation of dialysis for a patient who wants to be transplanted.

This message is important, especially for third world countries with little funds for starting transplant programs. They need to be encouraged to go ahead without spending monney to send necrokidneys around for a better HLA match, except for their hyperimmunized patients and rapid rejectors of former kidneys. In well-developed countries, HLA matching should no longer remain a good excuse for dialysis physicians who in reality want to fully utilize their dialysis center and will only free the patient, if another uremic patient is ready to replace him.

It may be argued that good matching is not an obstacle to transplantation, but is merely an effort to achieve optimal allocation. That sounds good, but I am not sure whether it is good. Matching on the basis of still inadequate typing technique [6] looks to me like a dispensable and costly obstacle for first cadaver kidneys transplantation in recipients without cytotoxic antibodies.

## The Growing Waiting List for Necrokidneys

Another excuse is the reference to the long and still growing waiting list (10 000 patients in 1989 in Eurotransplant [7]), in which the patient cannot be expected to accept a position at the back of the queue, and would merely arouse false hopes. Of course, this is wrong. Patients who are not put on the waiting list have no chance at all ever to receive a kidney.

## Refuse to Accept Living Related Kidney Donation

From Gerhard Opelz I have the analysis of the Basle living related donors as compared to cadaveric donors (Fig. 6). The difference is impressive and needs no statistic.

The strict rejection of the use of live kidney donors from close relatives is connected with the topic of shortage of kidneys and the lack of readiness to do anything about this. When someone is prepared of his own accord to make a donation out of love, this chance to help should be supported. I am thinking particularly of parents, but also of adult brothers and sisters who are prepared to donate a kidney. As a nephrologist, one should indeed point out this possibility as soon as the progression of renal failure cannot be stopped, and

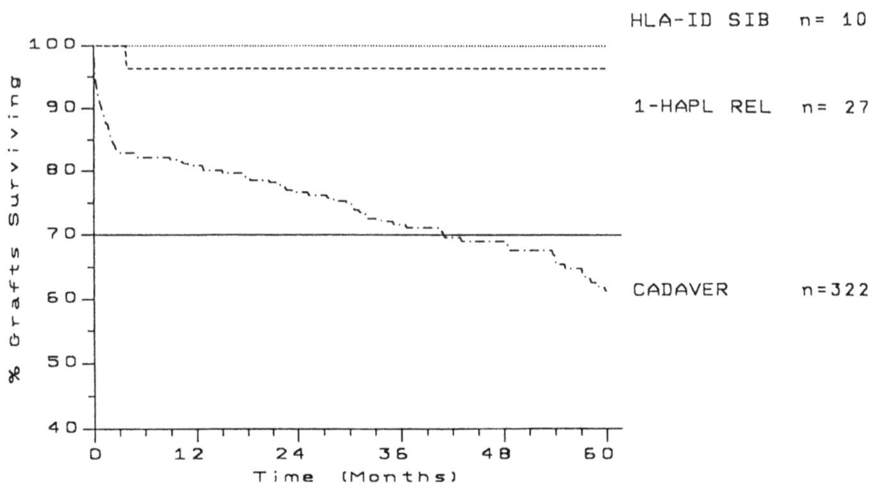


**Fig. 6.** Percentage of 5-year survival of first renal transplants in Basel, separated into cadaveric kidneys and living related donnor kidneys (HLA-identical siblings and haplo-identical relatives). (CTS registry, kindly provided by Prof. G. Opelz)

the time of necesary beginning of dialysis can be foreseen in the near future.

A well-time organized donation from a closely related live donor frequently even enables us to avoid dialysis completely, another frightening concept for some dialysis physicians. In such a way, the continuous full ability of the patient to work can be preserved best. Whoever has ethical objections to donations from closely related live donors should first of all prove that he himself is doing everything in order to promote the procurement of cadaver organs and cadaver organ transplantation in the area within which he has influence. Otherwise the ethical position loses some of its lustrous attraction.

A completely different method for preventing transplantation is the overrating of diseases concomitant to uremia.

## Nonrenal Diseases Used as Excuses

In Table 2, several concomitant diseases are listed which in accordance with my experience are used in good faith or overrated for less noble motives in order to withold a place on the transplantation waiting list from a dialysis patient desiring to have a transplant. These patients are called "clinically unsuited" [1].

Let us mention cardiac failure first. There are well-founded cardiac reasons, e.g., an ejection fraction under 20%, a progressive myocardial amyloidosis, or other similarly hopeless cases. However, the election criteria may not be very stringent, since most simple cardiopathies profit from the elimination of the uremia with hardly any increase in risk of operation. The same applies to peripheral arterial occlusive disease. It is astonishing how well and how long transplants can function when sutured on to the sclerotic iliac vessel only after extensive endarteriectomy.

Vesical atrophy or other bladder anomalies are also used sometimes as a contraindication for transplantation, although the results of transplantation in diversion of the ureter into an ileum conduit are very satisfactory. Psychological and mental diseases also belong on this list. Whoever advocates inclusion of a schizophrenic invalid in the chronic dialysis program, should not specify the same disease as a pretext for not carrying out kidney transplantation. Uremics with severe psychological impairment are also glad to be

**Table 2.** Nonrenal diseases used as excuses

1. Heart diseases
2. Occluding arteriosclerosis
3. Bladder alterations
4. Mental disorders
5. Others

freed of dialysis. An exception are only those whose regular long-term intake of immunosuppressants is not ensured or in whom it cannot be organized. However, it is in any case easier to add immunosuppressants once a day to the tablets which are prescribed anyway, than to dialyse three times a week.

Finally, the arbitrarily made up medical contraindications against transplantation are beyond serious discussion. I am thinking for example of the dialysis patient from a German city who undertook the long journey to Basle to my consultation only to hear from a neutral specialist whether bilateral cystic kidneys are really a contraindication to kidney transplantation. For years, his doctor in a large private dialysis unit had been dissuading him from kidney transplantation.

## Discussion

May I devote the discussion to the motives of all these excuses. Establishing a simple common denominator for the motives of any specific phenomenon is always an oversimplification which is open to substantiated criticism. This of course also applies to the phenomenon of dialysing nephrologists who only hesitantly put their patients on waiting lists for transplants. Why is no local political pressure exerted in order to help transplantation to move up in regions of low transplantation activity? The opposite is the case. Pressure is alleviated by enlargement of the dialysis capacity.

I cannot appraise the role of the various dialysis organizations, since we do not have any such organizations in Switzerland. To be honest, we also do not miss them. A few months ago, the head of the nephrology department of a German university hospital serving an area of 150000 inhabitants told me that one of his staff has set up in town his own private dialysis center with about 200 long-term dialysis patients. This business is flourishing. In order to give you an idea of the relative situation: in Basle, a single hemodialysis centre exists with 60 patients and a continuous ambulatory peritoneal dialysis (CAPD) and home dialysis program with a maximum of 30 patients in addition (Table 3). This is sufficient for an area comprising 300000 inhabitants. The equilibrium is only just maintained by continuous transplantation. Instead of extending the dialysis ward, it is always first attempted to carry out transplantations in as many patients as possible. If twice the number of patients can be profitably subjected to long-term dialysis in a population area

**Table 3.** Comparison of the relative situations of two dialysis centers

| University city | Region to cover with chronic dialysis (no. of inhabitants) | Patients on dialysis or CAPD ($n$) |
|---|---|---|
| Basel | 300000 | 90 |
| XY (Germany) | 150000 | ≈200 |

which is only half as large, then one would like to know the reason for this difference. Among other things, there must be a low transplantation frequency and something must be different with the financial remuneration: otherwise the same situation as in this German city would exist in Basle, too. Human beings are not better anywhere. "What's wrong with profit?" may be rightly objected here; "reward for merit" would be another slogan.

However, this is not the salient point: the system or the contracts should be concluded in such a way that the treatment of a given number of terminal kidney patients produces the same profit, regardless of whether they are treated by means of dialysis or CAPD, or checked periodically as outpatients after kidney transplantation. So long as there is a disequilibrium between the earnings of transplantation and the higher income from dialysis, the purported arguments listed in this paper will remain topical.

In the last 10 years, the frequency of transplantation in Western Europe has greatly increased, and the prevalence of the excuses not to transplant cited here is definitely tending to become less. On the other hand, I consider that the actuality of my paper is very great with regard to the territory of Eastern Europe. The relative undersupply of dialysis facilities and transplantation was a common feature of all Eastern Bloc countries. The salaries of the nephrologists of the former GDR are still low. Nothing appears more logical than to improve doctors' income or to obtain a kind of "second salary" by extension of dialysis and teaming up with a dialysis organization in the West. No Eastern nephrologist so far earns anything from transplantation. On the other hand, he would have to carry out time-wasting and unpleasant work to motivate the relatives of patients with brain death as well as overworked intensive care ward nurses and anesthesists, etc., and all this of course, without extra pay. It is of course very much more attractive to establish a private dialysis ward. Campaigning for transplantation with Eastern Europe nephrologists resembles therefore fishing with a hook and no worm.

I hope that everyone understands my reservations. If the funds which are beginning to flow into the former GDR for care of uremic patients would be used half for dialysis and half for kidney transplantation, a real optimum could be attained. However, I am afraid that there will be a quite different development. Instead of establishing kidney transplantation centers in several large citys like Dresden, for example, and developing the local infrastructure for this, more likely many new dialysis units and private profit-making dialysis centers are to be created. The excuses not to transplant specified in this paper will then become very popular to be used shameless. The points I have made were intended to divert this development, but I have, of course, no illusions as to their effectiveness.

## Summary

This paper covers the different excuses, why some chronic dialysis patients are not registered or freed for transplantation by their dialysis physicians. The main excuses are: (1) high age (unfair), (2) waiting for a better HLA match? (often unjustified), (3) the growing waiting list (an obstacle to overcome), (4) refusal to accept living related kidney donation (unjustified), (5) concomitant nonrenal diseases (overrated). The causal mechanism is related to an inadequate system of financial remuneration, which should be totally freed from the number of dialysis performed, but based only on the total number of end-stage renal failure treated independently of the method. The special situation of Eastern Europe nephrologists concerning this topic is discussed.

*Acknowledgment.* The author gratefully acknowledges the great help of Prof. G. Opelz in providing the data from the Basel renal transplants in the CTS Registry. The same is the case for Prof. F. Brunner, who provided the data from the EDTA registry in London. Dr. B. Huser analyzed the data of Table 1. They will be published in full extend later.

## References

1. Brunner FP, Fassbinder W, Broyer M, Brynger H, Dykes SR, Ehrich JHH, Geerlings W, Rizzoni G, Selwood NH, Tufveson G, Wing AJ (1989) Combined report on regular dialysis and transplantation in Europe, XVIII 1987. Nephrol Dial Transplant 4 [Suppl 2]:5–32
2. Roza MA, Gallagher-Lepak S, Johnson CP, Adams MB (1989) Renal transplantation in patients more than 65 years old. Transplantation 48:689–725
3. Shah B, First MR, Munda R, Penn I, Fidler JP, Alexander JW (1988) Current experience with renal transplantation in older patients. Am J Kidney Dis 6:516–523
4. Buder H-W, Landmann J, Mihatsch M, Thiel G (1991) Nierentransplantation bei Patienten im Alter zwischen 60 und 67 Jahren (in press)
5. Floege J, Burchert W, Brandis A, Gielow P, Nonnast-Daniel B, Spindler E, Hundeshagen H, Shaldon S, Koch K-M (1990) Imaging of dialysis-related amyloid (AB-amyloid) deposits with 131I-beta2-Microglobulin. Kidney Int 38:1169–1176
6. Möller E (1991) Advances in and future of tissue typing. Transplant Proc (in press)
7. Cohen B (1990) Eurotransplant Meeting 1990, progress report. Eurotransplant Newsletter Issue Nr. 79.10.90 (October 1990) Eurotransplant Foundation, Bloodbank, University Hospital P.O. Box 9600, 2300 Leiden, The Netherlands

# Unlimited Admission of Patients to the Waiting List for Transplantation

P. Michielsen

Austria, Belgium, Germany, and the Netherlands collaborate within Eurotransplant for the exchange of transplantable organs. The policy of the organization is to obtain the best possible human leukocyte antigen (HLA) match, avoiding, however, a major imbalance between the import and export of organs for each participating country. As in most organ exchange organizations all over the world, there is a growing gap between the number of patients admitted to the waiting list and the number of kidney transplants performed. The introduction in Belgium and in Austria of a transplantation law based on the principle of opting out has resulted in a significant increase in the number of organs retrieved. As this was apparently without effect on the overall waiting list within Eurotransplant, we examined the effect of this increase on the waiting list in Belgium and Austria.

The number of kidneys needed for transplantation is usually estimated at 40 per million inhabitants and per year. Since the introduction of the transplantation law in 1987 the retrieval of kidneys increased in Belgium to 40.9 per million. Notwithstanding this high retrieval rate, the waiting list for Belgian patients continues to increase to the present value of 85.8 per million. In Austria, the 40 per million retrieval rate was reached in 1987. At that time there were 129 patients per million on the waiting list and this value increased to 149 per million, at which level remained stable, with a retrieval rate of 52.1 kidneys per million population (Table 1).

**Table 1.** Number of cadaver kidneys retrieved per year and waiting list. Values are expressed per million population. Data from Eurotransplant. (Annual Reports)

| Year | Kidneys retrieved in Belgium (*n*) | Waiting list in Belgium (*n*) | Kidneys retrieved in Austria (*n*) | Waiting list in Austria (*n*) |
|---|---|---|---|---|
| 1985 | 21.3 | 65.3 | 27.6 | 108 |
| 1986 | 27.4 | 73.1 | 30.9 | 119 |
| 1987 | 37.5 | 75.5 | 42.5 | 129 |
| 1988 | 38 | 79.3 | 39.3 | 149 |
| 1989 | 40.9 | 81.7 | 52.1 | 147 |
| 1990 | | 85.8 | | 143 |

Universitair Ziekenhuis Gasthuisberg, Leuven B-3000, Belgium

W. Land, J. B. Dossetor (Eds.)
Organ Replacement Therapy:
Ethics, Justice and Commerce

**Table 2.** Number of residents and nonresidents on the waiting list in the Eurotransplant countries. Data per million population (July 1990)

| Country | Residents ($n$) | Nonresidents ($n$, %) | Total ($n$) |
|---|---|---|---|
| Belgium | 50 | 36.9 (42.5) | 86.9 |
| Netherlands | 89 | 2.9 (3.2) | 91.9 |
| Germany | 101.5 | 1.5 (1.5) | 103 |
| Austria | 89 | 54 (37.6) | 143 |

The further increase in the waiting list notwithstanding a retrieval rate which is supposed to cover the needs suggests that the needs for transplantation were underestimated. The reason for this underestimation is apparent from the data in Table 2, showing a massive input of nonresident patients. Nonresidents represent 42.5 % of the Belgian waiting list and 37.6 % of the Austrian waiting list. Most of these patients come from Italy, a country with several active transplantation centers, but with a clearly insufficient retrieval of cadaveric organs. Italy does not participate in the exchange of organs within Eurotransplant.

This problem of admission of nonresidents on the waiting list is not limited to Belgium and Austria. It is known to occur also in France and in the United States, although there are no exact data on the extent to which this occurs nor on the conditions on which these patients are admitted on the waiting list. There are also no data on the results of these transplants, for which one could expect long-term follow-up problems. The reasons for which some transplant centers accept nonresident patients on their waiting list are diverse. It is well-known that only very wealthy nonresident patients can have access to transplantation centers in the United States. In a fee-for-service system with private practice, it is not possible to exclude financial incentives for accepting foreign patients. In Europe the situation is less clear. It is evident that compassion is not the only motivation for accepting Italian patients on the Belgian waiting list, otherwise it would be easier, more convenient, and less costly for the patient and his family to ship the available kidney to one of the well-known Italian transplantation centers. The rewards for transplanting these patients do not however necessarily need to be direct personal profit. Other incentives could be the desire to increase the number of transplantations, so as to improve the efficiency of the program, or to obtain more facilities from the hospital administration, or a scientific interest in developing clinical trials for which a high turnover of patients is desirable. Whatever the motivation, the consequences are the same: any addition of nonresidents to the waiting list increases the waiting time for the own patients.

Another aspect to consider is the modality of allocation of the available kidneys between residents and nonresidents. Several modalities of allocation can be considered, from giving foreigners priority to putting them on the bottom of the waiting list. In the United States a Task Force on Organ Transplantation (1986) estimated that there was evidence that giving nonimmigrant aliens priority on a waiting list has sometimes been the actual (though not the stated) policy of some centers. Within Eurotransplant organ allocation is based mainly on the basis of HLA compatibility, but a considerable latitude is given to the individual transplant centers. Here also, the modalities of allocation between residents and nonresidents have not been clearly defined and made public.

The inclusion of nonresidents on the waiting-list and the decision on the allocation of organs raise the ethical problem of to whom the retrieved kidneys belong and who can make these decisions. It is clear that these organs belong to the community from which these organs are retrieved and can thus only be used for the purposes presented to the community when the opting-out transplantation law was voted. Using these organs for other purposes is a breach of trust, and if money or other advantages result from the transplantation of nonresidents this is equal to selling organs which have been received free of charge.

From Table 2 it is also apparent that the number of Belgian patients on the waiting list is only half the number of the other Eurotransplant countries. According to the EDTA Registry (Tufveson et al. 1989). Belgium has one of the highest numbers of new patients with end-stage renal disease admitted every year for treatment (Table 3). The low number of Belgian residents on the waiting list cannot, thus, be the consequence of a lower incidence of terminal renal failure. If we consider per million population the number of new patients put on the waiting list (Table 3), Belgium entered only the same number as Germany and the Netherlands, countries which do not accept a significant number of nonresident patients on their waiting list. If one takes into account the fact that nonresidents make up 42.5 % of the Belgian waiting list, it can be concluded that the Belgian dialysis centers must put a very low number of their patients on the waiting list for transplantation, approximately half the number in Austria, Germany, and the Netherlands. It is not easy to understand the reasons for this unexpected situation. Belgium has a very high number of dialysis centers, and recent data from the Ministry of Health indicate that there are only 2.48 patients per dialysis machine. It is conceivable under these circumstances that hospital administrations and

**Table 3.** Number of new patients with end-stage renal disease admitted for treatment in 1988 and number of new patients put on the Eurotransplant waiting list

| | New ESRD Patients 1988[a] | New Patients on Waiting List 1988[b] | Percent on Waiting List |
|---|---|---|---|
| Austria | 95.7 | 63.4 | 66 % |
| Belgium | 85.2 | 37.1 | 44 % |
| Germany | 77 | 35.9 | 46 % |
| Netherlands | 65.3 | 35.9 | 55 % |

[a] Data from the EDTA Registry
[b] Data from the Eurotransplant Annual Report

doctors are not pushing very hard to have their patients transplanted. There are indications that the lowest input rate of dialysis patients on the waiting list for transplantation is seen in the part of the country where two transplantation centers accept nonresidents on their waiting list. It could be that it is this low input of resident patients which led these centers into accepting foreigners. The opposite could also be true, the overcrowded waiting list of these two centers could have discouraged the dialysis centers from entering their patients. Whatever the explanation, these massively admitted nonresidents come into competition with the other patients for the available organs.

In Austria the situation is different. Per million population, Austria enters more patients on the waiting list than the other Eurotransplant countries (Table 3). This includes however many foreigners. The number of residents on the waiting list is the same as in the Netherlands and Germany (Table 2). This is indirect evidence that the Austrian patients did not benefit from the higher organ retrieval rate achieved in their country.

The example of Belgium and Austria illustrates that solving the problem of shortage of cadaveric kidneys does not automatically solve the problem of access to the best treatment modality. Patients can be trapped in dialysis even in the presence of plenty organs available for transplantation. It is to be feared that if public opinion would become aware of this situation, this could lead to a massive opting-out, ruining many years of effort to increase the number of transplantable organs. In the presence of shortage of transplantable organs, any decision to allow for uncontrolled circulation of patients and organs among countries with different legislation, different retrieval rates, and different reimbursement policies, is likely to result in ethically unacceptable situations.

The ever-increasing gap between the number of organs transplanted and the number of patients on the Eurotransplant waiting list is often used as an argument to stimulate organ retrieval. This information is misleading unless the extent of admission to the waiting list of patients from outside the Eurotransplant region is clearly mentioned.

## References

Task Force on Organ Transplantation (1986) Organ transplantation. Issues and recommendations. US Department of Health and Human Services, US Government Printing Office.

Tufveson G, Geerlings W, Brunner FP, Brynger H, Dykes SR, Ehrich JHH, Fassbinder W, Rizzoni G, Selwood NH, Wing AJ, (1989) Combined report on regular dialysis and transplantation in Europe, XIX, 1988. Nephrol Dial Transplant 4 (Suppl): 4:6

# Foreign Versus One's Own Country Waiting List in the Case of Organ Shortage

S. Bandini, E. Bertoni, L. Comparini,
G. Mancini, A. Rosati, P. Tosi, and M. Salvadori

The organ shortage forces many Italian nephrologists to put their patients on waiting list for kidney transplant in foreign countries. This was the case in our dialysis center until 1982. Since then, considering the increasing number of Italian donors, we have decided to preferentially put our patients on Italian transplant programs (mainly NITp). The aim of this study is to verify the effects that this change in transplant policy had on the cost/benefit ratio.

We reviewed the charts of 120 first cadaver kidney transplant patients followed up by our nephrological center since 1972. In all, 64 patients were transplanted in seven different European centers outside Italy, and 56 patients were transplanted in Italian centers near Florence. The number of transplants as well as the projected time on waiting list year by year were evaluated. The actuarial survival rates for the patients and for the grafts were calculated both for the "foreign" patients and for the "Italian" patients.[1] Data were analyzed by life table techniques to obtain graft and patient survival rates. Probability values were calculated for these values.

Table 1 shows the number of kidney transplants performed in foreign and in Italian centers in the two different periods. The period 1972–1982 was both the period of conventional therapy and the period during which we preferentially addressed our patients to foreign centers because of the severe organ shortage. After 1983, we changed our transplant policy, preferentially addressing our patients to Italian centers. This change in transplant policy resulted in a decrease in the number of transplants. Equally, the projected waiting time (calculated by dividing the number of patients on the waiting list

**Table 1.** Number of transplants

| | "Foreign" | "Italian" | Total |
|---|---|---|---|
| First period (1972–1982) | 42 | 21 | 63 |
| Second period (1983–1990) | 22 | 35 | 57 |
| Total | 64 | 56 | 120 |

[1] From now on to simplify, "foreign" patient means an Italian patient transplanted in foreign countries, "Italian" patient means an Italian patient transplanted in Italy.

Department of Nephrology, Careggi Hospital, viale Pieraccini 18, I-50100, Florence, Italy

W. Land, J. B. Dossetor (Eds.)
Organ Replacement Therapy:
Ethics, Justice and Commerce

by the number of transplants performed by year) increased. The projected waiting time was 1.9, 3.9, and 9 years, respectively, for 1980, 1985, and 1989. The overall actuarial patient survival rate differed only slightly in the two groups studied (Italian vs. foreign) being at 5 years 84% and 78%, respectively. The difference was not significant. On the contrary, we observed a significant difference in the overall graft survival rates ($p < 0.01$) for the Italian and foreign patients (Fig. 1). Considering the patients in cyclosporine therapy alone, we again obtained a significant difference in the survival ratès (Fig. 2).

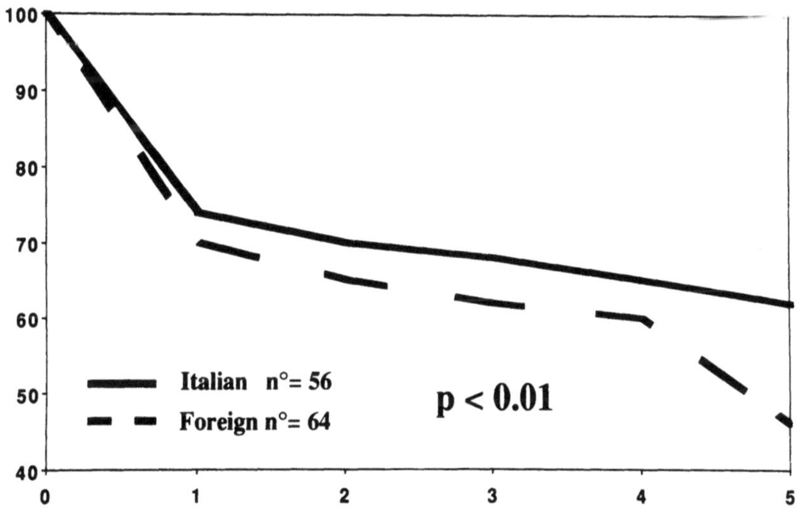


**Fig. 1.** Actuarial graft survival (all grafts) for "Italian" (*solid line*) and "foreign" patients (*dashed line*)

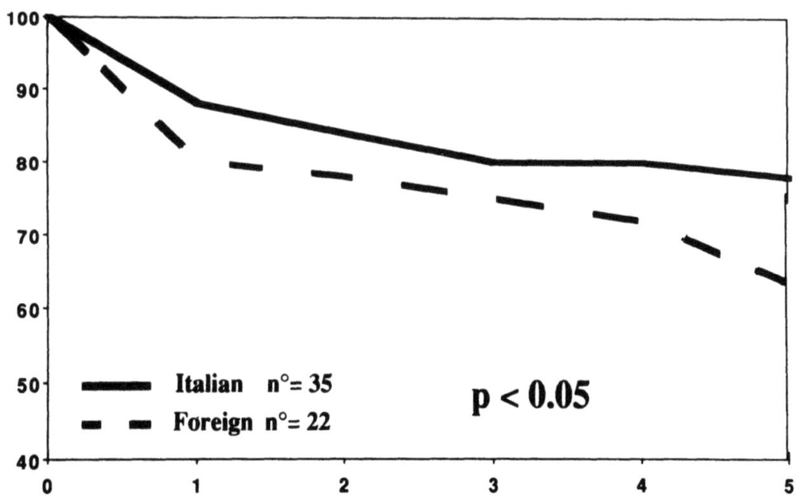


**Fig. 2.** Actuarial graft survival (cya grafts) for "Italian" (*solid line*) and "foreign" patients (*dashed line*)

Each end-stage renal disease therapy should be always reviewed under the aspects of the cost/benefit ratio. This is also the case of a transplant program. Because of the Italian organ shortage, we began our transplant program in 1972, sending most of our patients to foreign countries for transplantation. After 1983, hoping for an increase in Italian donors, we changed our transplant policy, preferentially sending our uremic patients to Italian centers. Therefore, we had the opportunity of comparing the cost/benefit ratio of these two different policies. With regard to the cost of a transplant, it is obvious that each cost is higher in the case of a transplant in a foreign country than for a transplant performed in centers close to the dialysis unit. The benefits of transplantation in foreign countries are much more controversial. The main benefits that a transplant policy should obtain are discussed in the following.

## Number of Transplants

In the second period, we had a decrease in the number of transplants compared with the first period (1972–1982). This fact is even more relevant considering that the number of the renal transplants performed in the world in the 1980s was much higher than in the preceding decade.

## Waiting List

The projected waiting list time increased continuously, reaching its maximum in 1989 with 9 years, which is one of the longest in Europe. The decrease of the number of transplants and the increase of the projected waiting list time were the price we had to pay for our policy to preferentially performing transplants in Italy.

## Patient Survival

The actuarial patient survival rate at 5 years was higher for the "Italian" patients, whether considering all the transplanted patients or the patients treated with cyclosporine (cya) alone. The differences were not significant.

## Graft Survival

The actuarial overall graft survival rate at 5 years was higher for the "Italian" patients than for the "foreign" patients. This difference was significant ($p < 0.01$). According to our experience, the following could be the possible causes of the different survival rates:

**Table 2.** Main difficulties in the follow-up

| |
|---|
| Wide varieties of immunosuppressive regimens |
| Overweighting or underweighting of symptoms by the local nephrologist |
| Overweighting or underweighting of symptoms by the transplant center |
| Disagreement in the diagnosis of complications between the local nephrologist and the transplant center |
| Symptom simulation by the patients |
| Refusal to go back to the transplant center by the patients |

a) more "foreign" patients in conventional therapy. This fact is surely true and depends on our change in transplant policy since 1983. Anyway, this cannot be the only cause of the difference in the graft survival rate between the two groups of patients because there is a significant difference also for the CyA patients alone.
b) More difficulties in the long-term follow-up of the patients transplanted in foreign countries. In our opinion these difficulties, listed in Table 2, could be the main cause of the difference in graft survival rate.

Receiving patients from many different transplant centers with wide varieties of immunosuppressive regimens and a lot of different follow-up criteria can be the cause of confusion and possible mistakes by the local nephrologist. Over- or underweighting new clinical or laboratory data can be made either by the local nephrologist or by the transplant center. The former has less experience, but the advantage of "seeing" the patient and his clinical status. The latter has more experience, but has to form a diagnosis based on referred symptoms and often delayed. Therefore, a disagreement in the diagnosis of complications between the local nephrologist and the transplant center may often arise. In our experience this fact could lead emotionally and psychologically unstable patients to simulate symptoms or, not rarely, to a clear-cut refusal to go or fly back to the transplant center. All the above items show that the approach to a transplant patient is much easier the closer the dialysis and the transplant centers are.

We conclude that beside a "transplant center effect" (Opelz 1975) and a "dialysis center effect" (Burdick 1986; Matas 1988), a "transplant-dialysis-center interrelationship effect" could exist. According to our experience, addressing patients to foreign countries because of organ shortage has the following effects:

Pros
a) Increased number of transplants
b) Shorter time on waiting list

Cons
a) Higher costs for transplantation
b) Worse graft survival, probably due to a worse follow-up

## References

Burdick JF, Williams GM (1986) What causes center effects in kidney transplantation. Ann Surg 203:311–314

Matas AJ, Tellis VA, Quinn T, et al. (1988) The effect of referring dialysis center on cadaver kidney transplant outcome. Transplant Proc 20:375–376

Opelz G, Mickey MR, Terasaki PJ (1975) Comparison of kidney transplant survival among transplant centers. Transplantation 19:226

# The Ethical Problems of Triage for Renal Failure in the United Kingdom

V. Parsons[1], M. Bewick[1], S. Snowden[1], A. Keogh[1], and A. Doherty[1]

Presented by A. M. Davison[2]

Triage is the decision to treat according to outcome; the injured in battle were divided into three: those who would return to the front line, those who would not survive the day and the rest who would need a long period of treatment away from the battle. In the UK various steps were taken to try and rehabilitate those individuals suffering from both acute and chronic renal failure.

In the *acute* field, the Medical Research Council (MRC) supported an acute dialysis unit at Leeds in the face of opposition from other centres, which said it was not worth the time, effort and risk to attempt to dialyse anyone save those with obstetric uraemia. The same arguments are raising their heads again today; we are wasting time, funds and staff on acute renal failure when the patient is elderly or had serious abdominal sepsis coupled with pre-existing vascular or malignant disease. This raises the first ethical problems of justice and equity: does every person, no matter what the preceding scenario and possible outcome, have their renal failure treated and if this leads to less funds/staff for the treatment of other patients in need, is this equable? Should no-one die of renal failure without a trial of replacement therapy? What is the future of prognostic indicators? [1].

Turning to *chronic renal failure,* the history in the UK was that dialysis centres with and without Departments of Nephrology were established between 1964 and 1970, giving approximately one unit to a million people, and even today there is only one unit to half a million people [2]. This led to a restriction in the number of patients that could be taken on by any unit [3]. In studying the effects of this scarcity, the selection procedure was often unconsciously delegated to the physician of first contact – whether he was in general practice or hospital practice. Both groups eased the renal unit's situation by not referring various categories of patients, which included diabetic patients, patients with mental illness or retardation, those with renal failure complicating other diseases with a poor prognosis and, finally, age was a distinct disincentive [4–6].

[1] Renal Unit, King's College School of Medicine & Dentistry, Dulwich Hospital, East Dulwich Grove, London, SE22 8PT, UK
[2] St. James's Hospital, Leeds. UK

W. Land, J. B. Dossetor (Eds.)
Organ Replacement Therapy:
Ethics, Justice and Commerce

There is an interesting interplay here between decisions being made by the physician of first contact and those working in dialysis areas. Various reasons are given to justify the decision to treat, or not to treat:

1. Protecting the elderly patient from the 'new technology', the argument runs: 'Yes, we know you have a condition that could be treated by dialysis and this might prolong your life, but in your case it will only make life difficult for you and for your family or carers'. In this way the physician on the one hand remains in control and is seen to be acting in the patient's best interests. On several occasions patients have been referred in extremis and the relatives' expectation has been minimal: 'I know there is not a lot you can do for him because of his ...' The ethical problem here is truth telling; the facts of survival, rehabilitation and complications are well known and have not been put clearly before the patient or his family [7–9].
2. Protecting the renal unit from being overwhelmed with difficult and complex cases. The listing of the therapy offered for diabetes in the UK is a good illustration of 'you don't want to be troubled with the blind vasculopathy with angina on top of his diabetes'. This has led to a general attitude that diabetic therapy, or lack of it, may be the cause of the complications so why should the diabetic physician look at this group of patients with anything but regret. We have failed – why should you succeed? This impression needs countering; there is strong evidence that some of the major complications have more to do with genetic variation and hypertension than with control, which is slowly overcoming this attitude. Hopefully the poor record of therapy for the diabetic will be reversed [10]. Clearly this is a matter for justly giving treatment to diabetics alongside any other patient despite the complications? Whether elderly patients with diabetes should receive transplants will be discussed later.
3. One of the particular problems in the UK has been the attitude of many units initially, which still persists in some, that they are unable to treat patients with hepatitis B or non-A, non-B. This stemmed from serious outbreaks of hepatitis affecting major units in Manchester, Edinburgh and London, leading to the publication of the Rosenheim Report [11], in turn discouraging the treatment of such patients, save in special areas. This was to avoid the morbidity and mortality among other patients and staff which continued to concern those who managed such patients [12]. This has led not only to such patients being refused treatment, but they have also had to travel hundreds of kilometres to centres where it was made available. How many patients have been denied treatment is unknown, but in view of their normal, or even better, prognosis with therapy, the ethical argument that the risks to the staff are greater than the care of the patient, is unacceptable. The cost of such treatment is known and the risks, with sensible precautions, minimal.
4. Transplants for all. In the UK, the enthusiasm for transplantation as the treatment of choice was based on the fact that it gave the best rehabilitation and, due to the shortage of dialysis facilities, the best use of

> available funds. Given that now we are reaching a ceiling for cadaver organ donation and that live-related donation has never been more than 10 % of donation, we are faced with the best use of the organs donated in good faith by those who become, or surround, the donor [13].

Tissue matching has a part to play in the allocation; group AB recipients have not long to wait and the kidneys can go into no-one else. Group 0 recipients on the other hand may wait several years. Should a kidney from a young donor go into a patient whose prognosis is limited by vascular and other problems? This is the ethical problem again of the best use of a precious resource. It makes sense that if the kidney is likely to 'outlive' the recipient, it would best be matched for a different recipient. The argument is particularly worrying even for the younger diabetic patient who may have unexpected vascular complications [14]. On one occasion the young recipient died and, with permission, the kidney was placed in a second recipient. We have no knowledge of the frequency of such 'second donation', but it would be the answer to the sad waste that is recorded as 'recipient dying with a functioning kidney'.

In this discussion, the pragmatic approach to the delivery of care to patients with renal failure has slowly improved with rates turning around 60 per million per year in many regions. Residual areas of difficulty still to be appreciated are the ethnic minorities who have particularly high rates of renal failure, organ donation from such groups and how we can expand the service without encroaching in other areas of special need, such as special care for neonates and chemotherapy for malignancies. The extent to which such services are using funds is the demonstration that £ 24 million was spent in one teaching hospital on patients who failed to survive more than a year, one-fifth of the hospital and communities budget.

## Summary

Selection of patients for treatment still takes place in the UK for patients with end-stage renal failure because of inadequate facilities for hospital dialysis, a shortage of donor organs compared with demand, and the competing needs of other services with fixed global budgets. The main reasons for de-selection have been age, types B and non-A non-B hepatitis, complicated diabetes, malignant disease, mental illness and, on occasion, non-compliant behaviour and drug-related criminal behaviour. We have had a series of such patients referred to our unit as a final opportunity for treatment, having been refused treatment in other centres. A proportion of such patients have been successfully treated by dialysis and transplantation and the results compare favourably with patients unselected by these criteria. This has led to a change in our attitude to such patients suggesting that selection processes cannot use such criteria for the refusal of treatment. Over a 20-year period, covering over a thousand patients accepted for therapy, 25 % of our patients have had diabetes, 8% hepatitis, 3% malignant disease, and 2% severe mental impairment or disturbed behaviour.

## References


1. Shoemaker WC, Kram HB, Appel PL (1990) Therapy of shock based on pathophysiology, monitoring and outcome prediction. Crit Care Med 18:S19–S25
2. Anderson JL, Parsons FM, Jones IE, (eds) (1978) Living with renal failure. M.T.P. Press, Lancaster
3. Halper T (1989) The misfortunes of others. End-stage renal disease in the UK. Cambridge University Press, Cambridge
4. Challah S, Wing AJ, Bauer R, Morris RW, Schroeder SA (1984) Negative selection of patients for dialysis and transplantation in the UK. Br Med J 288:1119–1122
5. Farmer C, Snowden S, Parsons V (1979) The prevalence of psychiatric illness among patients on home haemodialysis. Psychol Med 9:509–514
6. Davison AM, Read D, Lewins AM (1984) Underutilised hospital haemodialysis resources. Lancet i:723–725
7. Berlyne GM (1982) Over fifty and uremic equals death. Nephron 31:189–190
8. Garcia-Garcia G, Deddens JA, D'Achiari-Rey, et al. (1985) Results of treatment in patients with end stage renal disease. A multivariate Analysis of Risk Factors and Survival in 341 successive patients. Am J Kidney Dis 5:10–18
9. Parsons V, Lock PM (1980) Triage and the patient with renal failure. J Med Ethics 6:173–176
10. Cameron JS, Challah S (1986) Treatment of end stage renal failure due to diabetes in the UK 1975–84. Lancet ii:962–966
11. Rosenheim Report (1970) Hepatitis and the treatment of chronic renal failure. DHSS, London
12. Wing AJ, Broyer M, Brunner FP, et al. (1983) Hepatitis as recorded by the EDTA Registry – an update. Proceedings EDTNA 12:61–69
13. Wing AJ (1990) Can we meet the real need for dialysis and Transplantation? Br Med J 301:885–886
14. Medical Services Study Group of The Royal College of Physicians (1981) Deaths from chronic renal failure under the age 50. Br Med J 283:283–286

# Hypotheses, Basal Conditions, and Facts in the Provision and Allocation of Renal Replacement Therapy in Germany

W. Schoeppe

To analyze a system one must primarily define the purpose or goals which those using the system wish to attain. Renal replacement therapy (RRT) is such a system, and, thus, has to be defined in terms of its clients as well as of the agencies responsible for maximum efficacy for both parties. If one regards the suppositions of RRT presently practised in Germany, the following hypotheses have to be taken in account.

1. *All* uremic patients should receive treatment.
2. *All* uremic patients can be treated.
3. An optimized treatment in adequate form is attainable for *all* uremic patients. That means that an individually necessary treatment – with whatever modifications that are feasible for the special needs of the patient – can be secured without limitation to reach an acceptable degree of well-being and a durable economical basis in provision and management.

There is no doubt that such claims are (and have to be) tested. The motives of challenge are quite different because there are various parties with a variety of interest involved. I will give just some examples. For instance, what means (under point 1) "all uremic patients"? What is the impact of

- Age?
- Nationality?
- Multimorbidity?
- Social-, family-, educational or psychological background?
- Variability of causal chains in regard to prognosis *quoad vitam?*

The second point states that all uremic patients can be treated. Can such a premise be really meant and finally met? Is there a false conclusion based on the illusion what may have been possible in the past will hold true also in the future? Is the argument correct that, within the community of the EDTA registry, those countries with the highest figure of treated patients also represent those in whom the hypothesis in point 2 is fulfilled?

As far as the third point is concerned can a high standard be proclaimed without limitation? Will there be economical conditions to secure such a

J. W. Goethe-Universität, Zentrum der Inneren Medizin, Theodor-Stern-Kai 7, 6000 Frankfurt/Main 70, FRG

W. Land, J. B. Dossetor (Eds.)
Organ Replacement Therapy:
Ethics, Justice and Commerce

system to provide services, restricted only by biological, scientific, or medical conditions?

If one tries to find answers to all these questions, it is reasonable to recall the basic conditions limiting or modifying the system of renal replacement therapy. The basal conditions are:

1. Size of the patient population
2. Growth of the patient population (factors influencing expansion)
   a) New patients demanding treatment
   b) Change of treatment in case of chronic rejection and loss of transplanted kidneys
   c) Medically "new" indications such as systemic diseases, diabetes, severely ill patients or certain age groups
3. Types of treatment
   a) Peritoneal dialysis
   b) Hemodialysis
   c) Kidney transplantation
4. Types of treatment provision
   a) Hospital based
   b) In centers
   c) At home
5. Agencies
   a) Health institutions of public character such as state or community hospitals
   b) Professional but privatly run centers
   c) Nonprofit organizations with or without incorporated medical management
   d) Profit organizations

The different vectors within the system are modified by medical, legal, and socioeconomic components such as the structural elements of the social security act (*Reichsversicherungsordnung*), social background (for instance in home dialysis), medical standard and so forth. As to facts, one can give the following scenario. All the figures given are estimated on the basis of more or less incomplete statistical data of EDTA or state ministries, or information from other institutions. According to these data, there are approximately 25 500 patients (425 per million population, pmp) under treatment and 8000 patients (130 pmp) with functioning graft, making a total of approximately 555 pmp. The patients reaching end-stage renal failure consist of (a) 50 pmp new patients, and (b) 20 pmp of those losing transplants; a total of 70 pmp. There are 34 pmp deceased patients (8 % average all age groups), and the increment per year is 36 pmp.

Projecting into the future, the following conclusions can be drawn:

1. Up to 1994, the dialysis population in the western part of Germany will increase from 25 500 to about 33 000 (Fig. 1).
2. A lower total increase might be reached if kidney transplantation could be increased up to a rate of 3000 kidneys per year. Prolongation of

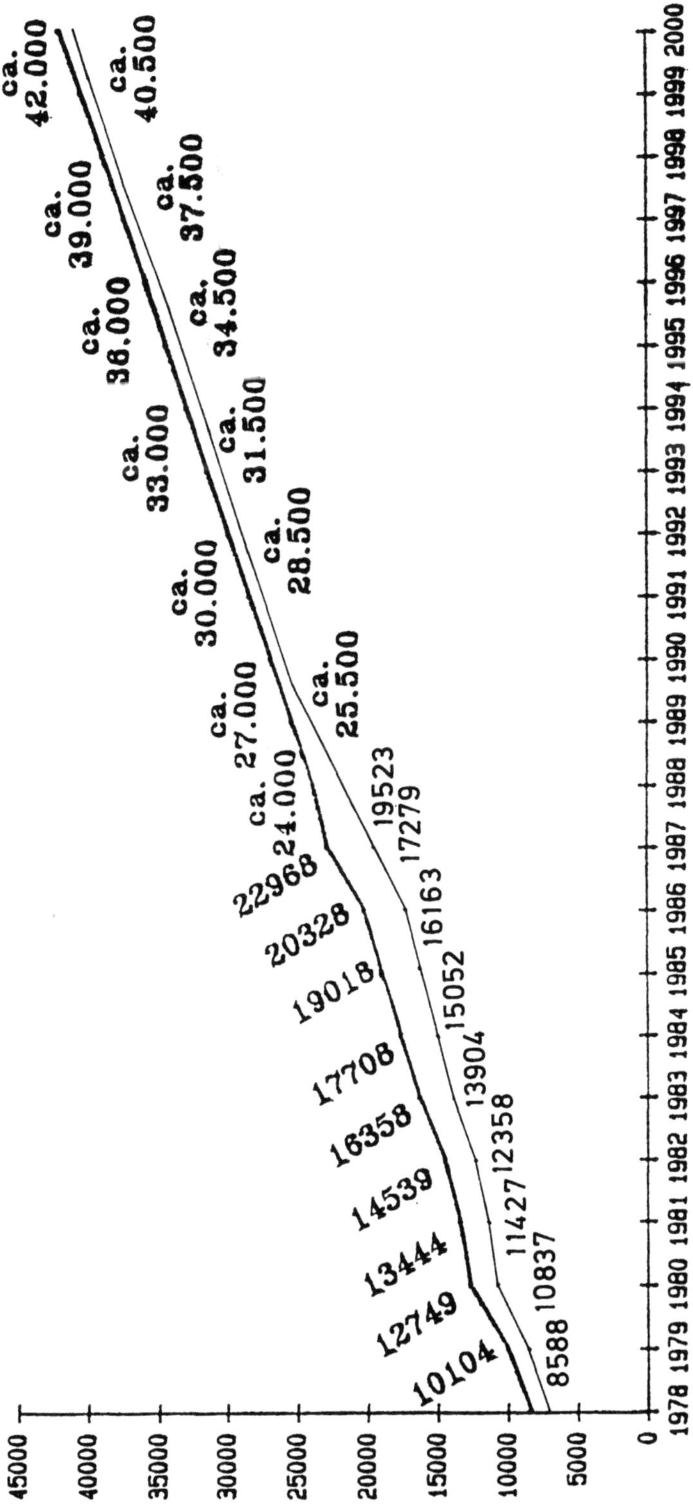


**Fig. 1.** Dialysis patients in the Federal Republic of Germany (old states) according to EDTA registry. The prognosis up to the year 2000 is shown. Yearly EDTA figures are calculated on a 100% basis and linear regression from 1987–2000 estimated. *Thin line* represents actual values according to EDTA and *thick line* represents calculated 100% yearly figures

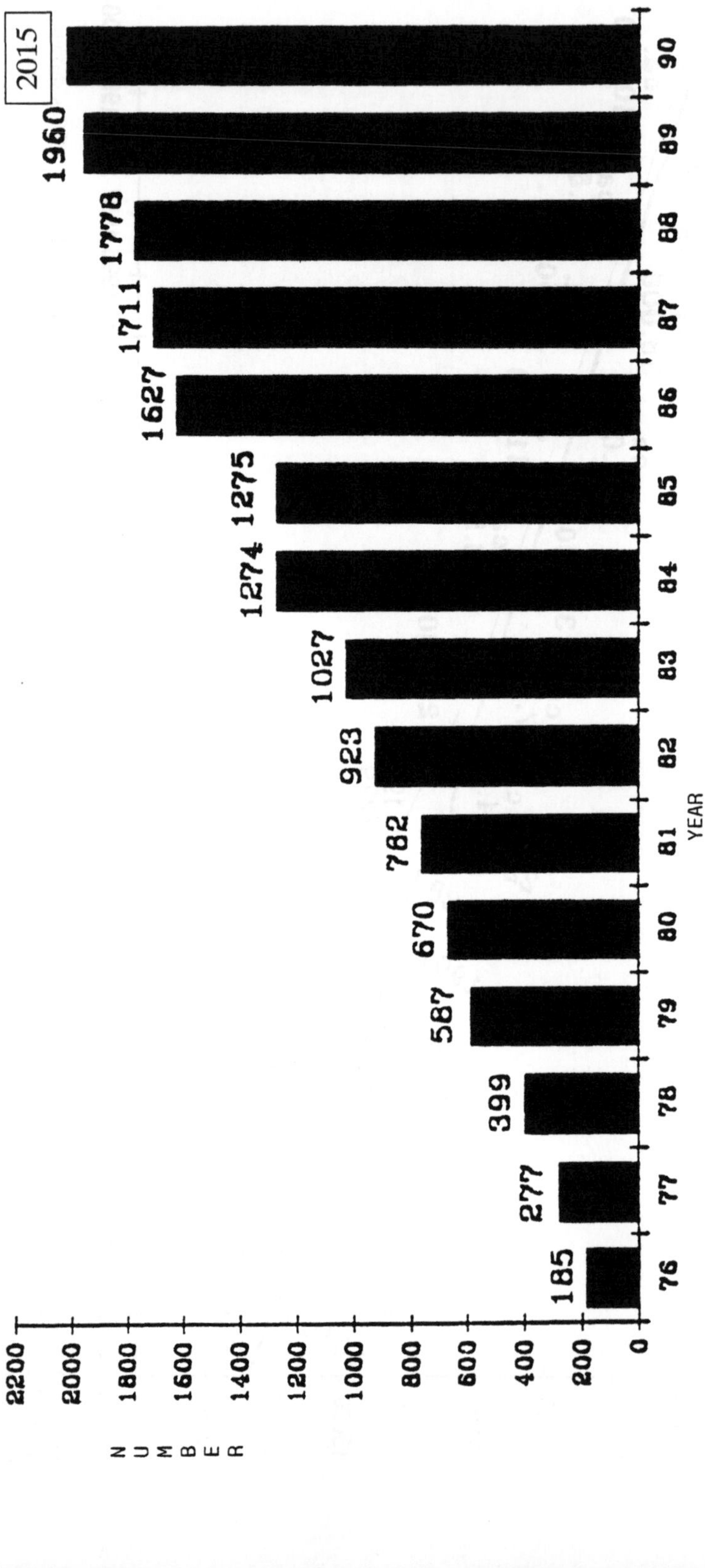


**Fig. 2.** Development of the national kidney transplantation program from 1976 to October 31, 1990

functioning time would further improve the situation, but at the present rate of percentage increase, only 2350 kidney transplantations can be estimated (Fig. 2), so that the total RRT population, now 33 500 will be approximately 45 000 – 47 000.

3. A further modification factor might be a dramatic increase in continuous ambulatory peritoneal dialysis (CAPD). A percentage of 20 % of new patients with this type of treatment would not change the increase in the number of patients to be treated, but would lower investment costs to a considerable extent, whilst only a minor decrease in running costs can be expected. The results in lowering investment costs amounts to about DM 150 – 300 million within 5 years, if costs for one in-center dialysis station are estimated at DM 100 000 – 200 000.

If a comparable standard is expected in the five new states of Germany, this would amount to at least 40 000 patients in dialysis treatment in the whole of Germany from now approximately 32 000 (patients with functioning graft included) i.e., 410 pmp, instead of the 555 pmp in the western states of Germany.

Now one remark on the risks not to be treated: if it is assumed that the incidence of kidney diseases does not change between different countries, and the assumption is also made that at least 400 patients should be treated, the risk of death as a patient exists. Expressed in terms of probability, this means in comparison with those countries where more than 400 patients pmp are treated, the risk in Austria is 8 %, in Sweden 12 %, in France 19 %, in Italy 26 %, in the United Kingdom 36 %, and in the former DDR 59 %. How will the problem we are facing in complying with the hypotheses be solved:

1. Decrease in investment costs was mentioned.
2. Increase in kidney transplants was mentioned.
3. Decrease in costs without loss of quality is a permanent challenge, fulfilled on one side through more CAPD, on the other side through a reduction in the running costs of conventional forms of dialysis treatment. This could, in fact, be shown by the nonprofit organization KfH, where dialysis costs were lowered between 1976 and 1988 by around 25 %.
4. The system of RRT has to be regarded as a continuum where patients must have the opportunity to change safely from one treatment type to another. So the interdependence of hospital unit, and home or center dialysis helps to secure immediate reaction if, for instance, hospital care is necessary. Any economic dependence on a certain size of patients population – just to pay for amortisation, interests, leasing costs, etc. – must be avoided, because selective processes may interfere with early – medically necessary – change of treatment. This holds true for the step from conservative treatment to RRT as well as for the decision to register for transplantation, especially in case of second or third transplantation. As patients on dialysis become older (Fig. 3), the probability of a change within the treatment types decreases (Fig. 4).

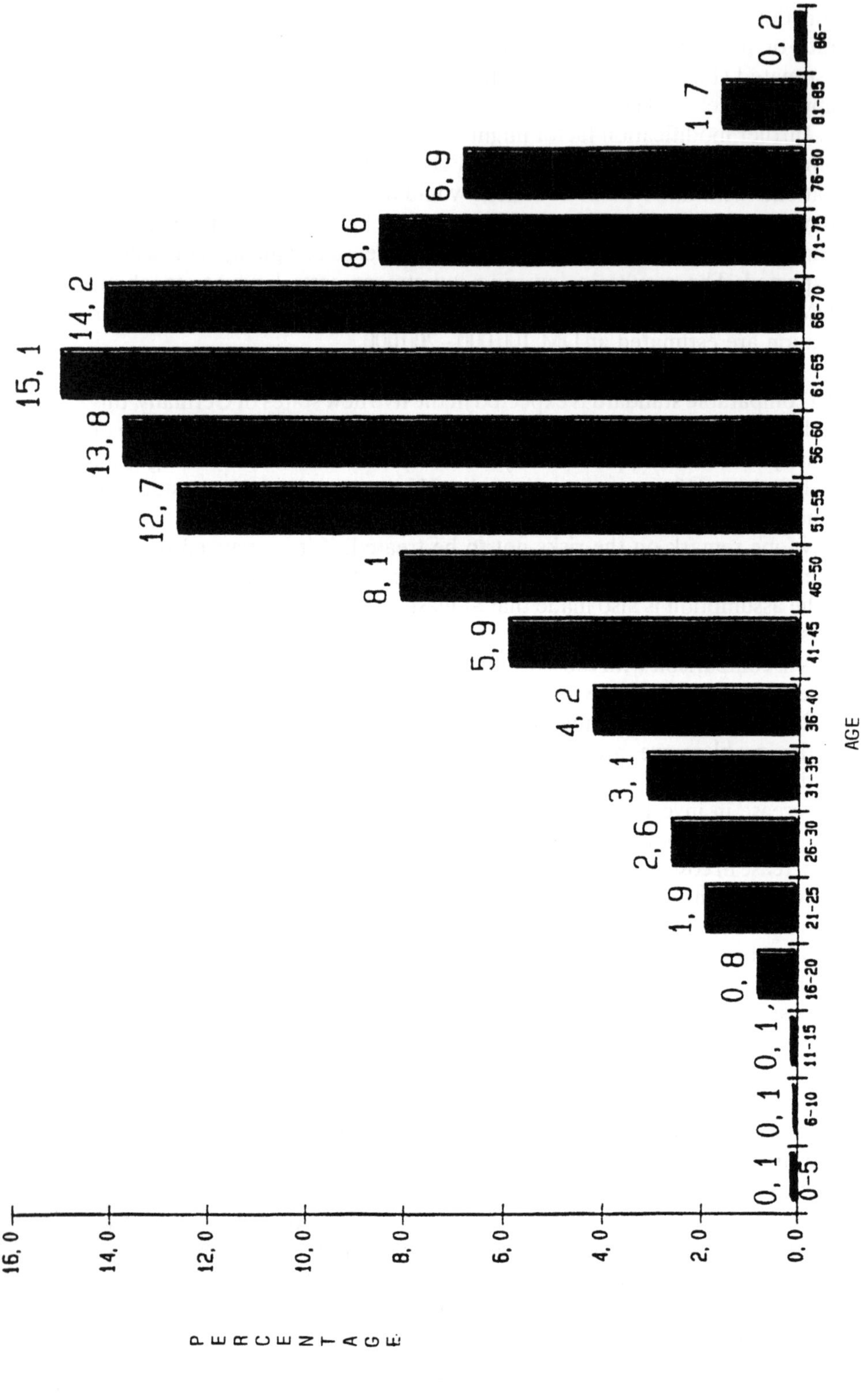


**Fig. 3.** Age groups of dialysis patients in the German state of Hessia in 1988 (figures are shown as a percentage of 2214 patients)

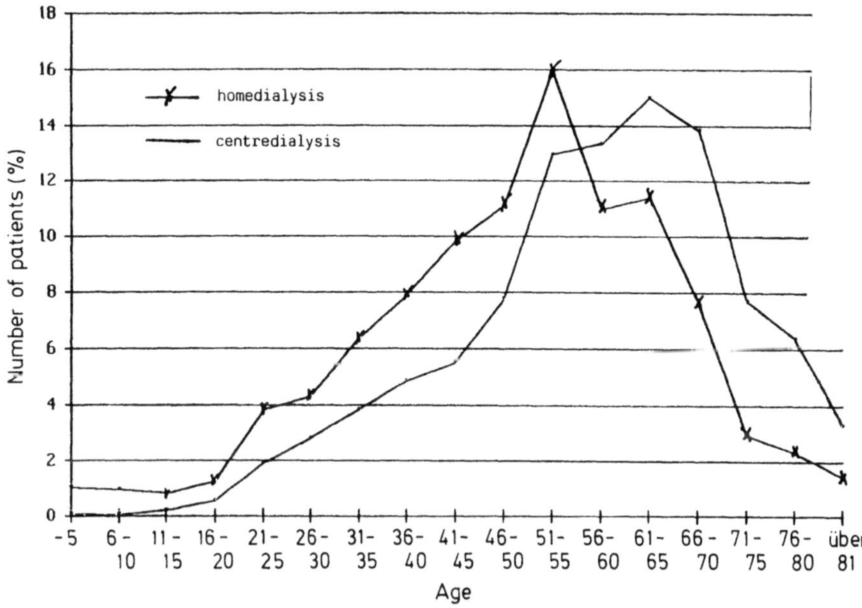


**Fig. 4.** Age of patients of the nonprofit organization KfH. A comparison of the patient groups is presented according to age in homedialysis (*) and center dialysis (–)

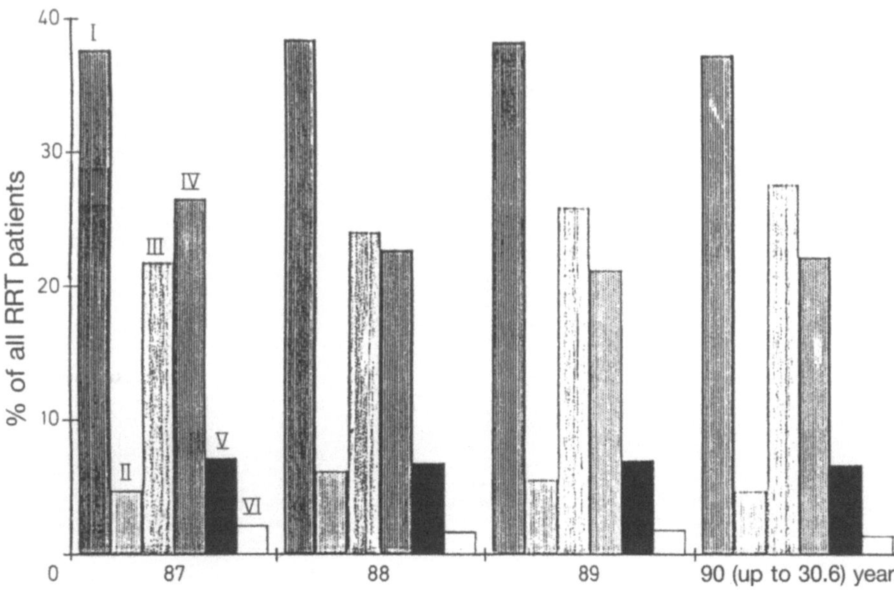


**Fig. 5.** Patients on the waiting list for transplantation between 1987 and 1990 (*I*, KfH centers; *II*, cooperating hospitals; *III*, medical practice affiliated dialysis units; *IV*, hospitals – all dialysis units; *V*, PHV – endowment nonprofit; *VI*, others)

5. As was already discussed today, there is no striking difference between the number of patients put on the transplantation waiting list through the different dialysis organizations. The percentage of patients on the waiting list corresponds roughly to the percentage of patients under treatment within the whole patient population in renal replacement therapy (Fig. 5).

If economic existence must be based on the number of patients alone, any unexpected event will interfere with the stability of continuous treatment. The biological course of events stresses this point. Our patient population changes to higher age groups. This follows from transplantation activities, but also the expansion of limits to accept older patients. This tendency will continue, and standards will be kept under control only if the facilities to treat such patients are provided. This means that medical personel per capita of patients must be increased. This can be done only in terms of joint ventures between ambulatory and intrahospital services. Payment for the latter is at present not provided in necessary amounts by the hospitals. Private or profit-based ventures are not in a position to fill the gap.

# *Allocation and Organ Transplantation*

# Who Legally Owns and Controls Human Organs After Procurement?

B. M. Dickens

## Introduction

This paper will address its topic by reference to the (English) Common Law system of jurisprudence as declared and developed through the courts primarily of England, the United States of America, Canada, Australia, and related countries that claim allegiance to the Common Law tradition. The topic will be approached, furthermore, in point of principle and not by reference to the legislation of any particular jurisdiction, although it will be observed that, for instance, many enacted laws prohibit individuals from selling or buying organs from living donors.

A common distinction is drawn in law between "organs", meaning solid organs such as kidneys, lungs, livers, and hearts that do not regenerate themselves within living bodies, and "tissues", meaning body materials that are naturally regenerative or replaceable in vivo, such as blood, bone-marrow, skin, and reproductive tissues such as sperm and ova. This paper will principally concern solid organs, although many of its propositions will be equally applicable to tissues such as bone marrow, which have considerable value in transplantation therapy. The distinction between organs and tissues appears artificial in light of the fact that a whole liver is nonregenerative, but a segment of a liver may safely be removed from a living donor for successful transplantation into a baby, notably the donor's baby, and will regenerate itself in the donor. Similarly, large skin surfaces and bones are nonregenerative, whereas small areas of skin and segments or slivers of bone that are transplantable from one part of the donor's body to another, and to other persons' bodies, will regenerate themselves.

The paper is limited to consideration of organ replacement therapy, and does not address transfer of sperm, ova, or pre-embryos for purposes of reproduction (see Andrews 1989), although its principles are applicable to transplantations of testicles and ovaries that would lead to procreation of genetically unrelated offspring.

Faculty of Law, University of Toronto, 84 Queen's Park, Toronto, Canada M5S 2C5

W. Land, J. B. Dossetor (Eds.)
Organ Replacement Therapy:
Ethics, Justice and Commerce

## Property Law and Commerce

The legal concept of property has a sophisticated philosophical basis (Munzer 1990), but it may be explained simply in terms of protecting value, which often means economic or commercial value. Historically, for instance, dead bodies were not "property" in law because they had no use. Utility may expose or create scarcity, however, and scarcity creates value, which in law is concretized in terms of property (Dickens 1977). A benefit of enjoying a property right is that the item or entitlement in which the right exists, which is itself commonly described as "property", can be sold; that is, the property right can be traded in commerce. Following the abolition of slavery, people are not property, but people such as professional sports players may sign contracts for the exclusive right to their services, and the right to engage them is a property right that may be traded.

The fear that arises from recognizing human organs as legal property, whether from cadavers or from living donors, is that recognition may create a sinister market in organs and that people themselves will become the subject of commerce. When peoples' dead or living bodies have a commercial value, the way may be opened to the sale of human corpses, to people selling their body parts while alive, and even to people being abducted for removal of especially scarce parts, such as children's small organs. Accordingly, most jurisdictions have legislation that prohibits the sale of human organs and tissues, with a common exception for blood and blood constituents. Such people as sperm donors are paid not for their sperm per se, but for the service of donating them, involving time for testing and out-of-pocket expenses.

In July 1990, in the much-discussed case of *Moore* v. *Regents of the University of California,* the Supreme Court of California ruled that a claim to property rights in a surgically removed spleen and other tissues taken from a patient could not be maintained. The patient's cells had been used, apparently without his consent, in medical research that had produced a cell line that the defendants had patented and that was potentially of a commercial value measured in billions of dollars. The court found that claims for lack of informed consent and for breach of fiduciary duty were available and adequate to compensate any injury to the plaintiff. The claim to a property right in the cells and the research project was rejected on the grounds both of Californian legislation mandating safe destruction of infectious products of surgery, and of public policy supporting medical researchers' access to excised body materials without undue obstructions such as having to ensure the sources' consents.

Neither ground applies to organs or tissues expressly removed and donated for transplantation. These are neither surgical waste products nor dangerous to transplant, as appropriate testing should establish, and public policy may favor donors retaining legal power to ensure that the materials are employed for the beneficial purposes for which they were given. Donation does not obstruct research, but rather serves medical promotion of transplantation therapy in the interests of particular recipients and the general public. The judges observed that, despite rejecting Moore's claim, "we do not purport to hold that excised cells can never be property for any purpose whatsoever" (transcript p. 39). Organ donation may be a case in which recognition of a property interest would be suitable, unless unsavory commerce were involved.

## Abandonment

Patients who suffer but survive surgical or other removals of body materials that may be useful to recipients may expressly dedicate them for this purpose, or insist that they not be so used but, for instance, be destroyed. An express and timely direction to destroy should be respected, and a similar request for use for the benefit of others should be met as far as is practicable. Usually, however, when bodily materials come to exist outside the patient's body through therapeutic surgery or comparable means and can be of no future benefit to the patient, they are deemed to have been abandoned unless the patient shows a contrary intention. They pass into the lawful ownership of the first person or institution consciously to take possession of them, for instance a physician such as a surgeon or a pathologist or a hospital. Whether physicians employed by hospitals acquire rights for themselves or only on behalf of the hospitals depends on the express or, usually, the implied terms of their hospital appointments.

Such materials are rarely useful for transplantation, particularly when derived from sick patients. Placentas available following normal childbirth may be useful for caring for burn patients, however, and transplantable ova may result from hysterectomies. Recently, fetal brain cells from induced abortions have shown promise when transplanted to patients with Parkinson's disease. Physicians may find materials that are not useful to others to be of scientific or research interest, however, and pathologists are usually legally entitled to pass materials to medical or other investigators once they have been examined for the benefit of the patients from whom they came, provided that patients' identities are not traceable. The legal presumption of abandonment may be problematic, however, regarding materials removed from unconscious patients' emergency surgery, since their indifference to customary legal acquisition and disposition cannot necessarily be presumed.

## Live Donation

Legally, ownership and possession are distinguishable. Possessors may enjoy legal rights to possess items of which others are the lawful owners. An agreement by which an owner leaves or gives property to the possession of another (other than a servant of the owner's) is called a bailment. A person who deliberately provides for an organ, bone-marrow, or similarly isolated material to be acquired from his or her living body in order to be transplanted into another's body is the legal owner or bailor from the moment the material becomes tangible outside the donor's body, and a physician or other person who possesses it at recovery from the bailor, during preservation, preparation, or transportation, or at or during implantation into the recipient, is a bailee. A bailee must apply objects of the bailment as directed by the bailor or be in breach of the bailment agreement and, whether or not that agreement is legally enforceable (a free or gratuitous bailment may not be), liable for the tort (or civil wrong) called conversion. If defiance of the bailor's direction is deliberate, a criminal charge of theft may also be considered.

Living donors almost invariably intend that materials they provide will be implanted only into individually identified recipients such as their children, spouses or parents. In contrast, donors who authorize recovery of materials from their bodies following determination of their deaths usually have no specific personal recipients in mind. When a live donor identifies the intended recipient of the donated material, however, no legal interest in the material becomes vested in the designated recipient until substantial implantation has occurred. What constitutes substantial implantation will be determined on the facts of each procedure for implantation. Whether or not the implantation is successful in the long or even short term, the legal criterion of transfer of legal ownership will focus on a stage of implantation when the donated material is physically joined to the recipient's body, such as by substantial connection to his or her blood supply. At this moment, the donor's legal ownership interest will be extinguished, but the recipient's interest will not necessarily arise to replace it because the material will become part of the recipient's living body, which is not the subject of property law.

The designated recipient of donated materials will be owed a legal duty of care to treat them with due skill, not only while they are in transit from the donor's body into the recipient's, but also while they are being removed from the donor, so that any mishandling of the intended donor or of the materials themselves that renders them unfit for transplantation, or any mishandling of the intended recipient that renders him or her unfit to receive the materials when they are ready for implantation, may be legally actionable negligence. Negligence liability requires proof of damage, however, and the intended recipient will have to show evidence, on a balance of probabilities, that, but for the defendant's failure to satisfy the legally determined standards of care in managing the donor, the materials or the intended recipient, the plaintiff, would not have suffered injury such as further sickness. This may require evidence that the transplant would have been successful, at least for a short period. The donor will be unlikely to succeed in a negligence action for personal injury due to failure of transplantation, since he or she had voluntarily accepted the risk of undergoing medical procedures to donate materials to what might prove an unsuccessful transplant. The donor might succeed, however, in a claim for personal injuries if negligent conduct of the surgery for removal caused the materials intended to be donated to become useless for transplantation, or for damage to property rights in the materials themselves due to negligent handling once they were removed from his or her body and were pending implantation into the intended recipient. Where commerce in body materials is legally prohibited, material loss in the latter case might be difficult to show.

An adequately informed donor would be taken to know that, without negligence, donated materials might prove unsuitable for transplantation for medical reasons, and that if they were suitable, the intended recipient might prove or become medically unfit to receive them. In the latter case the donor might be asked to approve their implantation into another, unknown, recipient.

If the donor were unavailable to consent, they might be so used without express consent under legal doctrines of implied consent (in the absence of the donor's express refusal) and of necessity to act in an attempt to save human life. The latter doctrine might prevail to overcome a donor's express refusal of consent when the materials had no equally beneficial and realistic alternative use.

Legislation almost invariably prohibits young persons from donating solid organs, but often permits children to donate regenerative materials such as bone marrow. As legal minors, children may not be able to manage such property interests, nor indeed be able to give their own consent to donation. Their parents or other legal guardians may be legally able to consent to their donation when they will benefit, notably by donation to a sibling or parent whose illness or death would be a source of emotional and/or material loss to them, and such guardians would protect children's legal interests in procured organs or tissues pending implantation into the intended recipient.

## Post Mortem Donation

In the classical Common Law, a dead body was not generally considered to be property (Matthews 1983) and could not be transferred by a will. Sepulchral rights were the area more of Ecclesiastical Law than of Common Law, although a criminal offence was recognized of deliberately causing indignity to a dead body. On a person's death, control of the person's assets and estate passed to an executor, who had charge of the body because of responsibility for the costs of burial, cremation, or other lawful disposal. It is doubtful that an executor could offer the body for medical purposes such as study and research, because in earlier times the Church prohibited dissection of human bodies for medical education, which might constitute causing indignity. Until recent times family members were said to have only a "quasi-property" interest in dead bodies, which coincided with the executor's interest in burial or cremation.

The legal power to donate body parts and intact bodies for medical study and transplantation has been created by legislation. Nineteenth century Anatomy Acts (Meyers 1970) provided for unclaimed corpses, usually of paupers, to be available for medical education, and with the development of transplantation, England's Corneal Grafting Act 1952 and then more comprehensive laws made body parts available post mortem for transplantation. In England, the Human Tissue Act 1961 paved the way, in Canada Human Tissue Gift Acts were enacted to govern both live and post mortem donations, and in the United States, the Uniform Anatomical Gift Act provides a model that states may adopt, with or without amendments, for post mortem donation of organs and tissues. Unlike many countries in Europe that have adopted laws presuming that organs may be taken on death, described as "presumed consent", "opting out" or "contracting out" laws, English-speaking countries tend to have "opting in" or "contracting in" laws that do not presume that a deceased person was willing to have organs taken post mortem for transplantation unless he or she made a positive declaration.

Legislation allows a living competent person to declare that his or her body may be available post mortem for removal of materials for transplantation. The donation may be for transplantation, medical education, and/or scientific research, and be of all body materials or only of specified parts such as identified organs. Ownership and control of organs and like materials will be governed by the terms and implications of the donation. A post mortem gift that states no specific recipient, which is the common form of gift made by a statutory donor card (often attached to a driver's licence), will render the body available to the first physician or medical institution (see above) to exercise lawful control over it for the purpose of recovery of transplantable materials. The physician or institution will be the one taking charge on death in hospital, or the one gaining control when a deceased person is taken to a hospital or mortuary following death at home or, for instance, in an accident. Which physician or institution gains lawful control may be a matter of chance, or be governed by the policy of a health ministry, the police, a hospital, or a coroner when it is known that a deceased person donated his or her body for transplantation purposes.

Any wish the deceased person expressed that his or her body should go to a specified hospital or other institution will be effective when practicable, but if the circumstances do not permit a gift restricted to a specified institution to take effect, the body may not be available to others. This confirms the general principle that any wish a person expresses that his or her body should not be used for post mortem recovery of materials for transplantation should be respected. This applies whether refusal of recovery is general, or is to all but specified institutions. It is considered important that people know that their wishes regarding refusal to approve organ recovery for transplantation will be respected after their deaths.

When a deceased person did not leave a declaration of donation but did not evidence a wish that his or her body not be used post mortem for transplantation, legislation allows appropriate family members to approve recovery of materials from a deceased person's body for transplantation. The family member will usually give lawful authority over materials to the physician or institution that asks for consent to donation. Legislation may permit any defined family member's consent to take effect, or, for instance, priorize spouses, children, brothers and sisters, and parents of deceased persons, perhaps providing that the wishes of a higher priority relative should prevail over those of lower priority relatives, and that a refusal of a relative negates the consent of another of equal rank. That a refusal prevails over a consent of an equal or lower relative reflects respect for religiously based views on preservation of the integrity of dead bodies.

## Ownership and Control

When a deceased person consented to post mortem donation or, in the absence of his or her refusal, a family member consents, a physician or institution will obtain lawful ownership of transplantable organs and like materials. Courts may hold, however, that the lawful ownership is not absolute, but is subject to a trust obligation to use the materials in good faith for the purpose for which they were donated by the deceased or the surviving family member. If donation was to a specified type or class of intended recipient, a member of that class, or a close relative of a member, may be found to have legal standing to enforce the trust in favor of transplantation into an intended recipient, in order to prevent wastage of the material or its application outside the terms of the donation. In any event, the Attorney General of the jurisdiction always has legal standing to enforce trust obligations, and may act independently or at the request of an interested person such as a prospective recipient or relative of such a recipient.

Further, when the terms of a donation cannot be complied with, for instance when a living donor surrenders an organ for a specified recipient who proves unable to accept it, or a donation for post mortem recovery of materials cannot be applied according to its specific terms, courts may be persuaded that, in the absence of contrary evidence, the donor intended a beneficial use as close as possible to the original purpose of donation. The presumption of the donor's general charitable intent may overcome the presumption discussed above that when a deceased person expressed a wish that his or her body should go to a specified institution for recovery of materials for transplantation, but this proves impossible, the body will be unavailable to other institutions for that purpose. A person considered to have a beneficial interest in materials in the lawful ownership of another, or the local Attorney General, may compel the owner to observe the conscientious duty to give effect to the true charitable intention of the original donor.

## References

Andrews LB (1989) Control and compensation: laws governing extracorporeal generative materials. J Med and Phil 14:541–569

Dickens BM (1977) The control of living body materials. U Toronto Law J 27:142–198
Matthews P (1983) Whose body? People as property. Current Leg Problems 1983:193–239
Meyers DW (1970) The human body and the law. Edinburgh University Press, Edinburgh and Aldine Publishing, Chicago
Munzer SR (1990) A theory of property. Cambridge University Press, Cambridge

# Principles Used in Organ Allocation

J. B. Dossetor

Robert Veatch concludes (this volume, p. 331) that physicians should not make allocative decisions. This paper rejects that viewpoint, but admits the social implications of his claim.

It would be an oversimplification to claim that all transplant organs present the same problems and can be dealt with by the same principles. In the case of heart, liver, and lungs, there are questions of matching for size. For these three organs there are also questions of the intricacies of removal from the donor and recipient preparation which are much more complex than for kidney transplants. For renal transplantation, dialysis provides a stable back-up system which is not available for other organs. Thus the "rescue" principle applies more to the latter. Also, for renal transplantation, because of extra time available, it is possible to achieve degrees of human leukocyte antigen (HLA) matching and lymphocytotoxic crossmatching which are not possible (and happen to be less necessary) for the other non-renal solid organs. Thus, the principles of allocation will be described especially in relation to the distribution of cadaveric kidneys.

Allocation can be stratified into three levels or dimensions: microallocation, mesoallocation, and macroallocation. At the microlevel, the issues are personal and individual, the province of doctor-patient relationships, and involve individual patient's values. At the mesoallocation level, issues become "population statistics" and "program related", involving physicians as program directors at institutions, with hospital administrators, health care economists and, hopefully, patient representatives. This is the level of competition with other programs at the institution. At the macroallocation level, issues are political (province, state, or national) and involve wider health care priorities and even the competition between health care and nonhealth related government expenditures. Physicians may be involved as macroallocative consultants. Patients are seen as individuals at the microlevel, program statistics at the mesolevel, and become mere programs at the macrolevel, losing all individuality. In some instances, the term mega-allocation may be used when matters are international and intercultural and related to issues between the developed and developing world.

Transplanted organs are distributed according to ten allocative principles, which have been previously described (Dossetor 1988).

Joint Faculties Bioethics Project, University of Alberta, 222 ANR, 8220 114th Street, Edmonton, AB, Canada T6G 2R3

W. Land, J. B. Dossetor (Eds.)
Organ Replacement Therapy:
Ethics, Justice and Commerce

1. *The "urgency" or "rescue" principle.* This claims priority for those in greatest individual need, whose life is most threatened. This is more a factor in liver and heart transplantation, which have no backup system equivalent to dialysis. The negative cytotoxic crossmatch with >80% PRA is another example. Should the rescue principle always take priority? No – it should be resisted when emotion subsumes rationality.
2. *The medical "efficacy" or "utility" principle.* This principle allocates organs so as to maximize the physical (health) outcome, using such factors as HLA matching, the age of the recipient, complications of disease, other associated disease. Patient compliance, a speculative nonobjective factor, is sometimes introduced under this principle, but it lacks objectivity it is often unreliable, and may be unjust. It is always suspect.
3. *The "fidelity" principle.* Physicians form fiduciary relationships with patients and feel bound to act as specific advocates for their patients because of this. This may be a cause of injustice when the same physician is responsible, at the mesoallocative level, for other patients in a program towards whom he/she does not feel bound to the same extent.
4. *The "lottery" principle.* Random selection, based on chance. Physicians do not like to use this. It seems to negate their expertise, and the prognostic value of laboratory tests, such as HLA. Patients, on the other hand, would probably accept it.
5. *The "time in line" or "queuing" principle.* This principle allocates organs to those who have waited longest on the waiting list – other factors being equal. It is important that entrance to the queue be closely monitored to preserve fairness at this time point. As a principle it denies urgency of need. Patients should not be listed in more than one program's waiting list when this principle is used.
6. *Ability to pay.* Even when transplant programs are government funded (kidney), there are subtle ways in which affluent patients gain priority. As very few government health care programs offer heart or liver transplantation, only the affluent have access to these allografts though sometimes nonaffluent patients are able to raise funds through the media, service clubs, and other charitable sources. In the developing world, ability to pay is the main allocative factor for renal transplants.
7. *Social worth.* When programs are supported by public funds, this form of selection is nonacceptable. In the early dialysis days in Seattle, the principle proved to be capricious, arbitrary, and unjust. Imputation of noncompliance may be evidence of unjust application of social worth. As society tends to disparage older persons, deeming them to be nonproductive, age may unjustly masquerade to discriminate on grounds of reduced social worth.
8. *The "squeaky wheel".* This operates powerfully wherever allocative decisions must be made amidst the competing claims of those in need. Often physicians feel that their fiduciary relationship with patients

entitles them to 'agitate' for special priority. The squeaky wheel process may be defined as 'obtained societal good by active promotion of interests of a specific person, group or agency without primary regard to distributive justice'.

9. *The "needs of the program".* Transplantation programs must succeed to retain their funding. Thus there is a bias towards selecting the low risk case, using the utility principle for the program, rather than the patient. When this is done 'out in the open', as an admitted temporary bias it may be an acceptable public policy, provided recipient patients know about it.
10. *Macroallocative public policy.* These are determinants of organ transplantation programs in the public sector. They are not sensitive to individuals' needs, but constitute the basis of distributive justice in arenas where health care is not the only consideration. Physicians are not usually involved at this level of public policy.

The first two factors, rescue and medical utility, use 'medical values'. The next – fidelity – is based on professional relationship. The next two, the lottery and time on the waiting list are 'value neutral', in sharp contrast to ability to pay, social worth, and the squeaky wheel, all of which are heavily loaded with nonmedical values. The list is completed with two factors relating to public policy at two different levels.

## The Ethics of Gatekeepers to Waiting Lists

The fact that the resource – the transplantable human organ – is limited places great tension on the recipient selection system. One must recognize the ethical traps which may attend the physician as gatekeeper to the waiting list. This brings up the whole question of patients being "trapped in dialysis".

*The medical assessment* is notoriously unreliable, when reviewed over time. For renal transplantation it used to be thought that end-stage diabetic nephropathy would do badly. In fact, there is now abundant evidence that the outcome from both dialysis and renal transplantation in diabetic end-stage renal disease (ESRD) can provide a very acceptable quality of life. This shows how difficult it is to forecast medical outcomes.

For several decades, patients' age was a factor in selection, with renal transplantation being denied to those over 50. Again this has been shown to have been a false assessment factor (Jordan et al. 1985). Although in the 1988 European Registry report only 25 % of dialysis patients are on waiting lists for transplantation, in fact it is likely that over 50 % would benefit from a transplant, and do well, and should certainly be offered that treatment option.

Although physicians may be forced to impose limitations because of the dictates of social utility, care should be taken not to believe that the criteria used are proven medical facts. They usually are not.

## HLA Matching

There is a strong desire or bias towards using medical factors whenever possible, as this avoids having to use social values. The latter are much more controversial. This is one reason why HLA matching, a scientific parameter, receives undue weight in recipient selection. Whilst there is undoubted value to HLA compatibility when it is complete – zero mismatching (Cicciarelli et al. 1987; Gilks et al. 1987) – there is a much less important contribution to outcome when matching is incomplete (van Buren et al. 1984; Harris et al. 1986). This is especially so if the recipient pool is fairly small (i.e., 100–200 patients) as the likelihood of finding a 'zero mismatch' is very small.

## Organ Allocative Problems in India

In countries such as India, where neither dialysis nor transplantation are government priorities (Yadav 1990), the forces of the marketplace are in full operation. Renal transplants are available only to those with the ability to pay, and who must also provide their own live donors. (Unfortunately, cadaveric organs are not used to any appreciable extent because of the expense of maintaining brain donors, not because of religious sanction.) Two systems compete for providing kidneys from live unrelated donors, both driven by donor poverty. These two systems may be described as (a) *rampant commercialism,* with most of the money being retained by unscrupulous entrepreneurial organ brokers, or (b) a less commercialized system, termed *rewarded gifting.* In the latter, selection of donors is carried out by hospitals or institutions on a nonprofit basis and a higher proportion of the recipient's money goes to the donor through a regulated process. The ethics of this second system is much debated (Daar et al. 1990; Johny et al. 1990; Thiagarajan et al. 1990). Clearly, it is largely a matter for that culture to decide for itself. Rewarded gifting has been seen in the West as victimizing of the poor by the rich. It has been condemned on these grounds as well as from more philosophical and religious considerations of self-ownership, self-mutilation, and commodification of one's own body parts. However, that attitude tends to overlook the fact that severe poverty itself is a truly formidable enslaving process and a cause of great victimization. A variation of this practice is its intercultural and international component (Abouna et al. 1990) which has been uniformly deplored. In the ethical dilemma, state or professional paternalism seeks to restrict individual potential donors' autonomous choice to sell a kidney on the grounds that poverty and ignorance render him or her incompetent to give valid informed consent. But, in the Indian scene, there are many complexities which probably will only yield to a state-supported cadaver kidney program.

## Macroallocative Politics

One of the more difficult issues to judge ethically is the activity of physicians in getting new transplant (and other) programs into operation by obtaining funds at the macroallocative level. Clearly they are acting in the interests of their own careers; equally clear is that they are acting for the benefit of patients. Often the pressures of the professional lobby are brought to bear without regard to other priorities, using the media and other support systems to appeal to the prestige of the institution. The first 'outbreak' of heart transplantation in 1969 is an example of this process at its worst. Nevertheless, as shown by the second wave of heart grafting since 1985, programs can be very successful when the time is ripe, even if the acceptance process by society seems to have been largely media dependent.

It is interesting that one state in the United States, namely Oregon, wishes to expand the number of citizens covered by Medicaid by rationing resources to pay only for certain diseases. This would exclude nonrenal transplantation processes, which benefit very few persons (Egan 1990). This plan may prove to be an important precedent in the allocation of health care resources, as it evolves.

## Organ Allocation on the Basis of 'Points'

Kidney sharing by UNOS in the United States uses a number of allocative factors based on "points". This has some similarity to an earlier points system of the Pittsburgh group, which took into account several non-HLA allocative factors (Starzl et al. 1987) in choosing recipients from transplant waiting lists. Such a system is not free of bias, as bias may be inadvertently built into the values used in weighting for points. However, the idea is an attempt at distributive justice and makes for an open policy which is known to recipients.

## Conclusion

This review of allocation principles brings up two further questions: who owns the cadaveric organs which are being allocated, and from what source do those charged with allocation draw their authority? Although the legal aspect of ownership of extirpated organs is unclear (B. Dickens, this volume, p. 385), the ethical premise is that extirpated cadaveric organs belong to the community, not the transplant team. The community then delegates allocative obligations to transplant teams through institutions or agencies. The community also expects that ethical allocative principles will then be applied in a way that is equitable and just.

We must take care not to be unworthy of this public trust and demonstrate willingness to recognize the social dimensions and values of our work. We must allocate by means of open policies and obtain nursing, societal, and patient input and approval of our practices.

## References

Abouna GM, Kumar MSA, Samhan M, et al. (1990) Commercialization in human organs: a middle Eastern perspective. Transplant Proc 22:918–921

van Buren CT, Flechner SM, Kerman R, Vaugh W, Kahan B (1984) Cyclosporine improves outcome in high-risk cadaveric renal recipients. Transplant Proc 16:1162

Cicciarelli J, Terasaki PI, Mickey MR (1987) The effect of zero HLA class I and II mismatching in cyclosporine-treated kidney transplant patients. Transplantation 43:636

Daar AS, Salahudeen AK, Pingle A, Woods HR (1990) Ethics and commerce in live donor renal transplantation: classification of the issues. Transplant Proc 22:922–924

Dossetor JB (1988) Ethics issues in organ allocation. Transplant Proc 20:1053–1058

Egan T (1990) New health test: the Oregon plan. New York Times, May 6 (for commentary: Medical Ethics Advisor (1990) 6:125–127)

Gilks WR, Bradley BA, Gore SM, Klouda PT (1987) Substantial benefits of tissue matching in renal transplantation. Transplantation 43:669

Harris K, Gosling DC, Campbell MJ, et al. (1986) Azathioprine and cyclosporine: different tissue matching criteria needed? Lancet i:267

Johny KV, Nesim J, Namboori, Gupta RK (1990) Values gained and lost in live unrelated renal transplantation. Transplant Proc 22:915–917

Jordan ML, Novick AC, Steinmuller D, et al. (1985) Renal transplantation in the older recipient. J Urology 132:243–246

Starzl TE, Hakala TR, Tzakis A, Gordon R, Stieber A, Makowka L, Klimoski J, Bahnson HT (1987) A multifactorial system for equitable selection of cadaver kidneyrecipients. JAMA 257:3073–3076

Thiagarajan CM, Reddy KC, et al. (1990) The practice of unconventional renal transplantation at a single centre in India. Transplant Proc 22:912–914

Yadav RVS (1990) Transplantation as a health priority in India. Transplant Proc 22:908–909

# Is HLA Matching a Scientific and Relevant Factor for the Allocation of Cadaver Kidneys?

G. Opelz and T. Wujciak

## Introduction

The allocation of cadaver kidneys by the human leukocyte antigen (HLA) match has been questioned, most recently by Matas et al. (1989), who found that HLA matching did not improve the results at their own center. In contrast, large multicenter analyses have shown consistently that better matched grafts have higher success rates than poorly matched grafts (Opelz 1985; Ciciarelli et al. 1987; Opelz 1988a; Sanfilippo et al. 1989). At the recent (August 1990) congress of the Transplantation Society in San Francisco, R. Ferguson argued during the plenary debate on the relevance of HLA matching that, even if it was accepted that HLA matching improved graft survival, the overall graft outcome at 1 year would be a mere 1.5% higher with a policy of matching than with kidney allocation at random. He concurred with the conclusion of Matas et al. that efforts to achieve better matches by means of kidney sharing among transplant centers were not justified.

We reexamined the data of the worldwide Collaborative Transplant Study with respect to the scientific validity and the practical relevance of cadaver kidney allocation by the HLA match.

## Materials and Methods

Cadaver kidney transplants performed from January 1983 to May 1990 at the 274 transplant centers participating in the Collaborative Transplant Study were examined. HLA typing data were provided by the centers' typing laboratories. No exclusions were made.

## Results

Figure 1 shows the impact of matching for the HLA-A, -B, and -DR antigens in first cadaver donor transplants. At 5 years, the survival rate difference between grafts with 0 or 6 mismatches is 20% ($p < 0.0001$).

Institute of Immunology, University of Heidelberg, Im Neuenheimer Feld 305, 6900 Heidelberg, FRG

W. Land, J. B. Dossetor (Eds.)
Organ Replacement Therapy:
Ethics, Justice and Commerce

Figure 2 demonstrates that the quality of HLA typing is important. Transplants that were typed for "broad" (less well-defined) specificities did not show a good correlation of matching with outcome whereas transplants typed for "split" (well-defined) specificities did. Clearly, to achieve the maximal matching effect, typing for HLA antigen splits is required.

Figure 3 shows the impact of HLA matching on retransplants. The difference between well and poorly matched grafts is greater than in first transplants. Figure 4 provides proof that locally obtained kidneys with short cold preservation times (<24 h) perform less well than shared kidneys with prolonged cold ischemia (up to 36 h). Longer preservation incurred because of shipping does not negate the matching effect.

We simulated the distribution of 1000 randomly selected cadaver kidneys according to the number of HLA-A, -B, and -DR mismatches based on a waiting list of 10 000 European patients. HLA antigen splits were considered and the recipient/donor AB0 blood type rules currently in effect within Eurotransplant were adhered to (type 0 kidneys to type 0 or B recipients, type A kidneys to type A or AB recipients). We estimate that it would be possible to transplant as many as 39 % of the patients with 0 mismatch kidneys, 47 % with 1 mismatch, 13 % with 2 mismatches, and 1 % with 3 mismatches. Grafts with 4, 5, or 6 mismatches could be avoided altogether. Based on this estimate, a consistent HLA matching policy would result in a 7 % improvement of the overall 1-year success rate of first cadaver transplants and in a 14 % improvement of the 1-year success rate of second transplants.

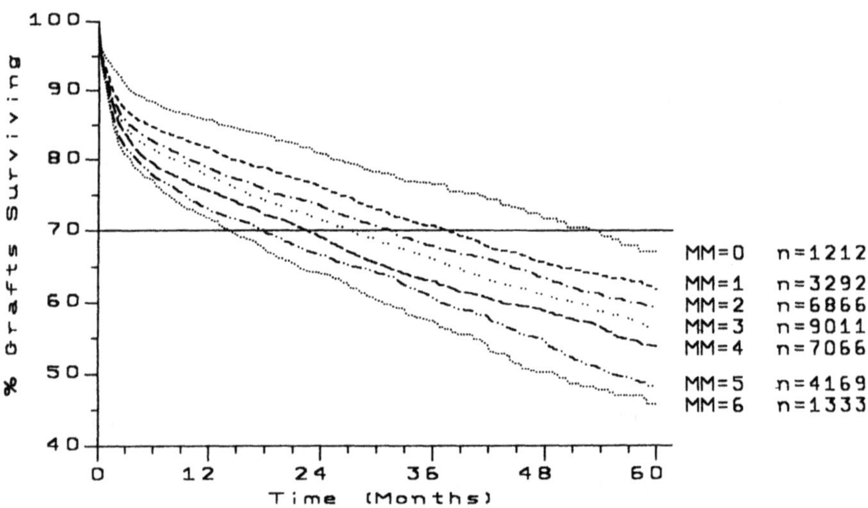


**Fig. 1.** Survival rates of first cadaver kidney transplants according to the number of HLA-A, -B, or -DR antigen mismatches. Recipients and donors were typed for HLA-A and -B antigen "splits", the best defined HLA-A and -B specificities. Numbers of patients studied and numbers of mismatched HLA antigens (*MM*) are indicated ($p < 0.0001$)

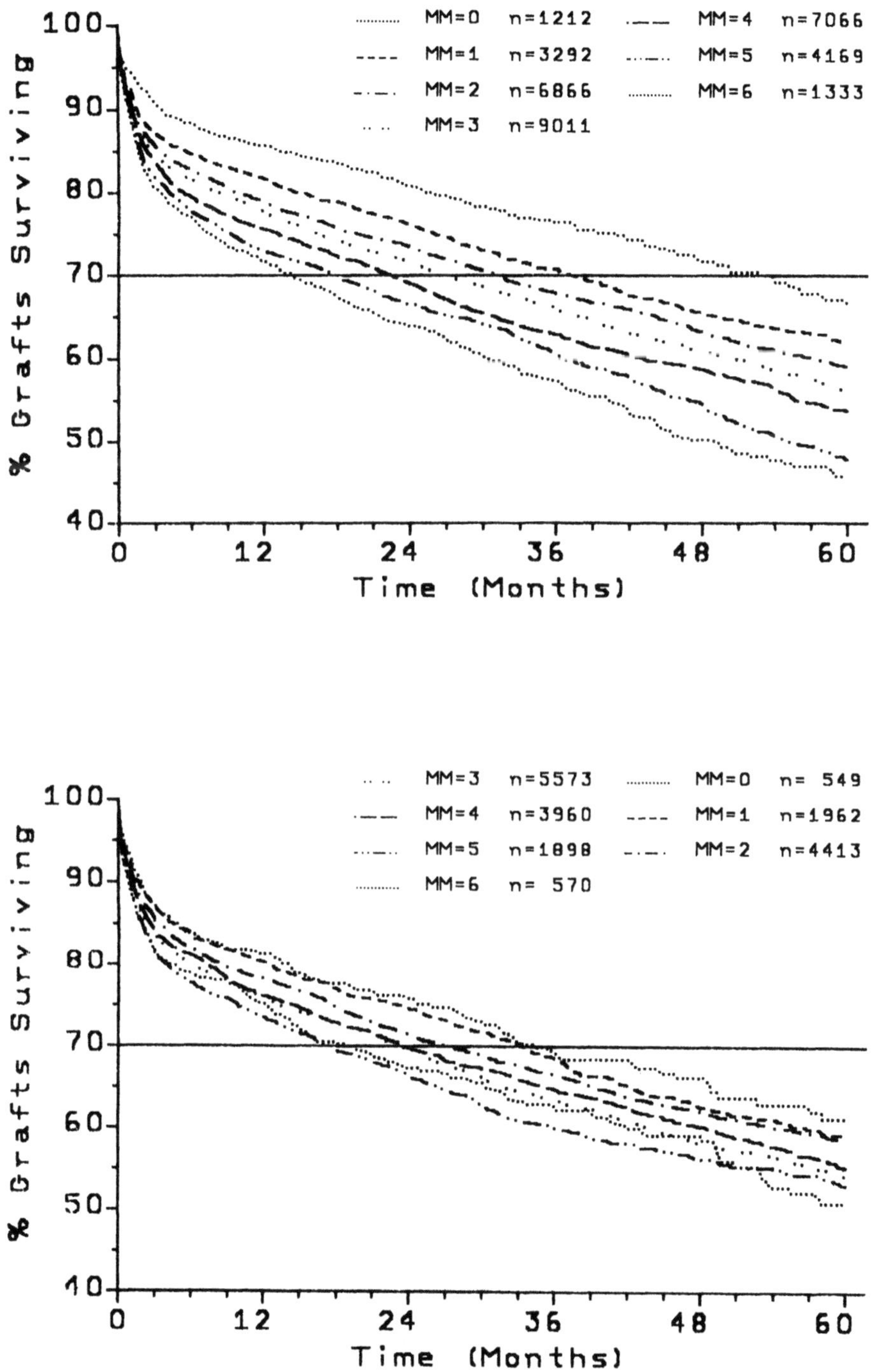


**Fig. 2.** Comparison of HLA analysis in transplants typed for HLA-A and -B antigen "splits" (*left half*) and transplants typed for the less well defined "broad" HLA specificities (*right half*). The matching effect is much stronger in transplants typed for well defined "split" specificities. HLA-A, -B, and -DR mismatches were analyzed

## Discussion

We believe that the scientific basis for the allocation of cadaver kidneys by the HLA match is established beyond doubt (Figs. 1–4). That single-center analyses often fail to show statistically significant associations of matching

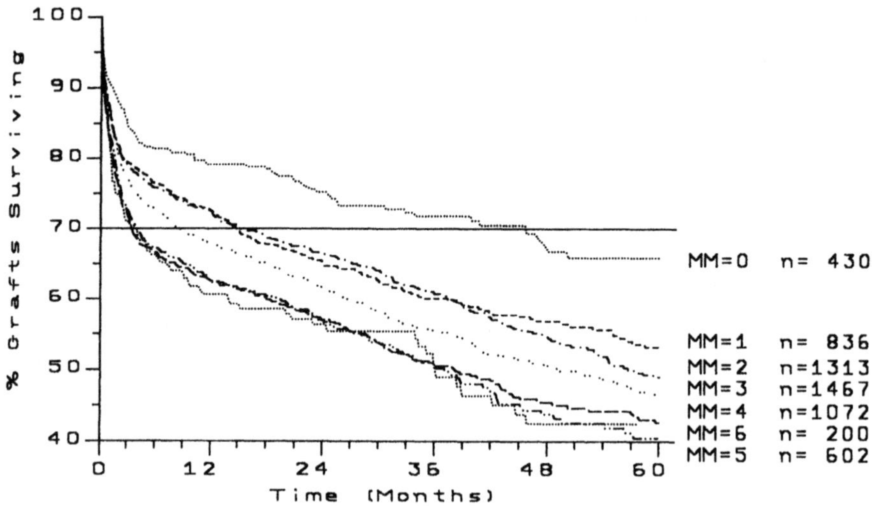


**Fig. 3.** Effect of matching for HLA-A, -B, and -DR antigens (A and B splits) in cadaver kidney retransplants ($p < 0.0001$)

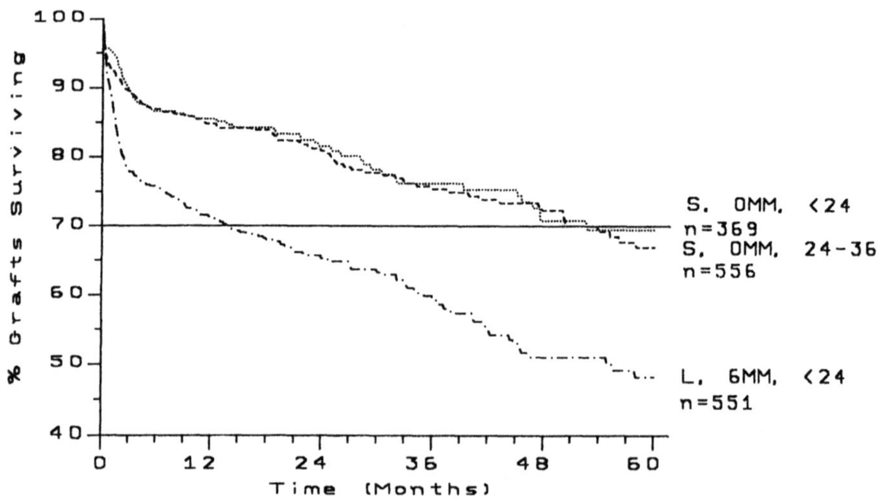


**Fig. 4.** Cadaver transplant outcome in patients receiving kidneys without HLA-A, -B, or -DR mismatches that were shipped (*S*) and in patients receiving kidneys with six mismatched HLA-A, -B, or -DR antigens that were procured locally (*L*). The shared well-matched kidneys did significantly better, even though their preservation times ranged up to 36 h, whereas the local kidneys all were preserved for less than 24 h. Numbers of HLA mismatches and preservation times in hours are indicated

with graft outcome is, in our opinion, related primarily to the insufficient numbers of patients analyzed. Unquestionably, many other factors besides HLA matching exert an influence on graft outcome. These factors are not randomly distributed. Even (or especially) in single-center analyses, the nonrandom distribution of influential factors distorts the analysis of HLA matching. This "disturbance" becomes less noticeable as the number of transplants in the analysis increases. In this context, it is interesting to note that all large multicenter studies have demonstrated a significant improvement effect of HLA matching.

The argument that a center that does not show a matching effect in its own transplants need not participate in a kidney sharing program is flawed. Firstly, it is likely that subsequent transplants at the center would benefit from matching. Secondly, even if a special treatment protocol allowed the successful transplantation of poorly matched grafts, patients at other centers where this is not the case would lose the benefit of matching because of a withdrawal of donor kidneys from the pool. Unless all centers were able to achieve equally superior results with poor matches, the success rates of national and international programs would deteriorate.

Of course, allocation of kidneys by the HLA match must be superceded under certain circumstances by urgency requirements. In addition, special rules may have to be developed for racial minorities because their HLA antigen frequencies differ from those of whites. The available data, however, indicate that HLA matching provides the best basis for an objective and scientifically sound distribution of cadaver kidneys.

*Acknowledgement.* The generous cooperation of 274 transplant centers in 41 countries is gratefully acknowledged. Computer support for the Collaborative Transplant Study was provided by IBM Scientific Center, Heidelberg, Germany.

## References

Ciciarelli J, Terasaki PI, Cecka M, Mickey MR (1987) Is cyclosporine a match for tissue typing centers? Transplant Proc 19:647–649

Matas AJ, Frey DJ, Gillingham KJ, Noreen HJ, Reinsmoen NL, Payne WD, Dunn DL, Sutherland DER, Najarian JS (1989) The impact of HLA matching on graft survival and sensitization after a failed transplant. Transplantation 50:599–607

Opelz G (for the Collaborative Transplant Study) (1985) Correlation of HLA matching with kidney graft survival in patients with or without cyclosporin A treatment. Transplantation 40:240–243

Opelz G (for the Collaborative Transplant Study) (1988a) The benefit of exchanging donor kidneys among transplant centers. N Engl J Med 318:1289–1292

Opelz G (for the Collaborative Transplant Study) (1988b) Importance of HLA antigen splits for kidney transplant matching. Lancet ii:61–64

Sanfilippo F, Vaughn WK, LeFor W, Alexander JW, Pfaff WW (1989) The benefits of HLA matching on renal transplantation relative to cyclosporine use and organ sharing. Transplant Proc 21:661–662

# HLA Matching: A Relevant and Scientific Graft Allocation Factor or Only a Crutch?

D. Albrechtsen

## Introduction

Since grafts are generally not available for all patients needing transplantation (tx) therapy, various selection processes are undertaken. Firstly, for often poorly defined reasons only some patients are placed in the waiting list, while others are not. Secondly, patients on the waiting list are selected to receive an available graft on the basis of various criteria, such as human leukocyte antigen (HLA) match, urgent medical need, or seniority on the waiting list.

Although the present discussion focuses on the role of HLA matching, the overall perspective of patient selection should not be lost. Thus there are

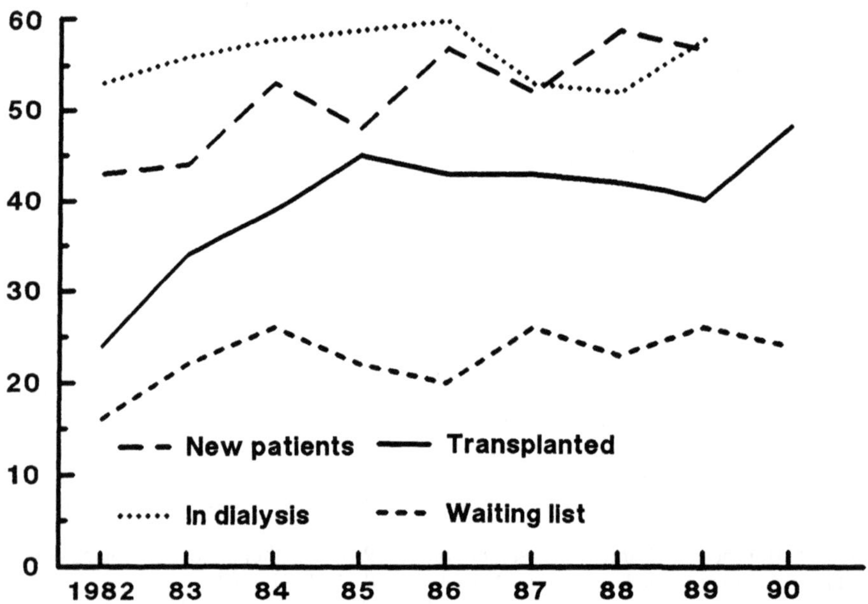


**Fig. 1.** Flow of patients accepted for renal replacement therapy in Norway 1983–1990

Surgical Department, Rikshospitalet, The National Hospital, 0027-Oslo, Norway

W. Land, J. B. Dossetor (Eds.)
Organ Replacement Therapy:
Ethics, Justice and Commerce

really two issues to be analyzed: (1) Does allocation of grafts on the basis of HLA matching improve the probability of success for the individual patient? (2) Does it improve overall results (i.e. patient survival) in the total population of patients needing tx?

Tx scientists have provided much information to resolve the first issue, while the second and even more important one has been less well elucidated.

## Impact of HLA Matching on Kidney Graft Survival

The impact of HLA matching was studied in the renal replacement program providing dialysis and tx service for the population of Norway (Fig. 1). During the 1980s, the annual incidence of patients starting renal replacement therapy increased slowly (presently approximately 60 patients per million

**Table 1.** Graft survival and mismatching for HLA antigens in all living related transplantations ($n = 423$), cadaveric first transplantations ($n = 512$) and cadaveric repeat transplantations ($n = 132$) performed in Norway 1983–89

| | | Patients ($n$) | Graft survival 1 year (%) | 5 years (%) |
|---|---|---|---|---|
| Living related transplantation | | | | |
| HLA identical | | 50 | 100 | 91 |
| 1 haplotype mismatch | | 307 | 91 | 76 |
| 2haplotype mismatch | | 66 | 88 | 75 |
| Cadaveric first transplantation | | | | |
| DR | 0 mismatch | 131 | 78 | 62 |
| | 1 mismatch | 267 | 78 | 57 |
| | 2 mismatch | 114 | 80 | 70 |
| B + DR | 0 mismatch | 30 | 73 | 68 |
| | 1 mismatch | 86 | 72 | 54 |
| | 2 mismatch | 188 | 82 | 62 |
| | 3 mismatch | 145 | 79 | 57 |
| | 4 mismatch | 63 | 79 | 75 |
| A + B + DR | 0 mismatch | 16 | 68 | 68 |
| | 1 mismatch | 40 | 68 | 45 |
| | 2 mismatch | 83 | 76 | 60 |
| | 3–5 mismatch | 357 | 80 | 62 |
| | 6 mismatch | 16 | 75 | 75 |
| Cadaveric repeat transplantation | | | 1 year (%) | 3 years (%) |
| DR | 0 mismatch | 36 | 78 | 63 |
| | $\geq$1 mismatch | 64 | 61 | 55 |

Graft survival was significantly better in HLA identical than in nonidentical living related grafts ($p < 0.02$) and in HLA-DR compatible than in noncompatible cadaveric repeat grafts ($p < 0.05$)

population, pmp). The dialysis population (approx. 55 pmp) and the waiting list for tx (approx. 24 pmp) remained stable, because of a high tx rate (presently 48 pmp). More than three out of four patients needing renal replacement therapy were transplanted, after a mean waiting period of less than 6 months.

In living related tx, superior graft survival (GS) was observed in recipients of HLA identical grafts (Table 1). No difference was observed between grafts mismatched for one or two haplotypes, however. In recipients of cadaveric first grafts, no correlation was found between GS and mismatching for HLA-DR, HLA-B + DR, or HLA-A + B + DR (Table 1). However, although priority was given within Scandiatransplant for HLA-A + B + DR matched combinations, few patients received grafts matched for HLA-(A)-B + DR. Thus, we cannot exclude a potential GS advantage for such grafts, as reported by others (Opelz 1991; Terasaki 1991). On the other hand,

**Table 2.** Graft survival and mismatching for HLA antigens in all cadaveric first tx performed in Norway and Sweden in 1983–1985 (First Scandinavian Multicenter Study, SMCS I, $n = 487$) and 1985–1987 (Second SMCS, SMCS II, $n = 452$). No significant difference was found

| | | Patients *n* | Graft survival 1 year (%) | 5 years (%) |
|---|---|---|---|---|
| SMCS I | | | | |
| DR | 0 mismatch | 197 | 68 | 51 |
| | 1 mismatch | 205 | 73 | 53 |
| | 2 mismatch | 85 | 68 | 53 |
| B + DR | 0 mismatch | 38 | 62 | 53 |
| | 1 mismatch | 121 | 69 | 48 |
| | 2 mismatch | 178 | 70 | 56 |
| | 3 mismatch | 108 | 73 | 52 |
| | 4 mismatch | 42 | 71 | 60 |
| A + B + DR | 0 mismatch | 14 | 63 | 58 |
| | 1 mismatch | 48 | 61 | 42 |
| | 2 mismatch | 107 | 71 | 51 |
| | 3–5 mismatch | 302 | 72 | 53 |
| | 6 mismatch | 16 | 63 | 45 |
| SMCS II | | | | |
| | | | 1 year (%) | 3 years (%) |
| DR | 0 mismatch | 70 | 76 | 70 |
| | 1 mismatch | 225 | 71 | 62 |
| | 2 mismatch | 157 | 80 | 68 |
| B + DR | 0 mismatch | 14 | 79 | 79 |
| | 1 mismatch | 58 | 79 | 65 |
| | 2 mismatch | 139 | 70 | 62 |
| | 3 mismatch | 152 | 75 | 63 |
| | 4 mismatch | 89 | 81 | 70 |

our experience shows that given a limited number of grafts available, a short waiting list and a modest waiting time, rather few patients will actually get the chance of receiving a well matched graft. These findings were confirmed in the First and Second Scandinavian Multicenter Studies (SMCS), which included all cadaveric first grafts performed in Norway and Sweden during 1983–85 (First SMCS) and 1985–87 (Second SMCS) (Table 2). In the Norwegian program, GS in repeat tx correlate to HLA-DR matching (Table 1), consistent with international findings (Opelz 1991).

On the basis of our own experience as well as that of others we conclude:

1. In living related tx HLA identical grafts have a GS advantage of 15%–20% versus mismatched grafts, while there seems to be little difference between grafts mismatched for one or two haplotypes;
2. in cadaveric first tx HLA-(A)-B + DR matched grafts have a GS advantage of 10%–20% versus mismatched grafts, while there seems to be less of a difference between various groups of mismatched grafts;
3. in cadaveric repeat tx HLA-DR matched grafts have a GS advantage of 10%–20% versus mismatched grafts.

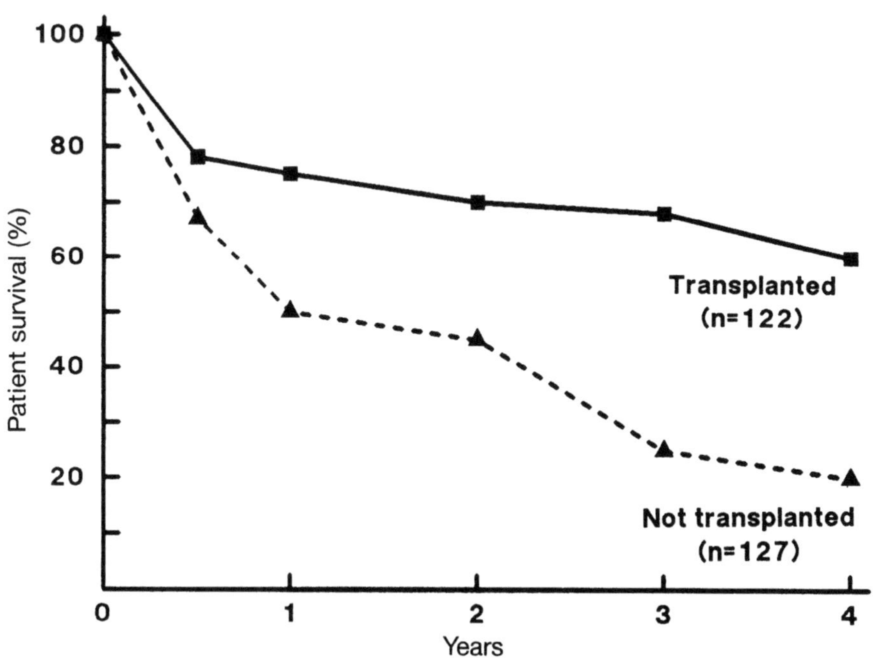


**Fig. 2.** Survival of elderly (>60 years) patients accepted for transplantation in Norway 1981–1985. Survival of those actually transplanted was significantly ($p < 0.01$) better than those accepted on the waiting list, but not transplanted because no graft became available

## Impact of HLA Matching on Overall Survival of Grafts and of Patients Needing Renal Replacement Therapy

In our experience, rather few patients (less than 10 %) will actually reap the benefit of receiving a well-matched graft if the waiting list is short and the waiting time modest. Overall GS would improve by 2 %, if 10 % of the patients received a matched graft. If matching should have much of an impact, matched grafts would have to be provided to a majority of the patients. That would require

1. a much larger donor pool than that provided by Scandiatransplant, and/or
2. an expanded waiting list/prolonged waiting time.

A compelling argument against prolonging the waiting time is depicted in Fig. 2 (Albrechtsen 1988). Elderly patients treated with tx had significantly better survival than those selected for tx, but not transplanted because no graft became available. To delay tx of medically poor risk patients (elderly, extra renal disease) for the purpose of providing a well-matched graft is clearly not to their advantage. For medically good risk patients, waiting time is not so deleterious, and the survival benefit of tx is less evident (Fig. 3). A differential survival benefit of tx for poor versus good risk patients illustrates the moral dilemma in graft allocation: Should a graft be allocated to the patient having the most to gain in survival, or to the patient having the

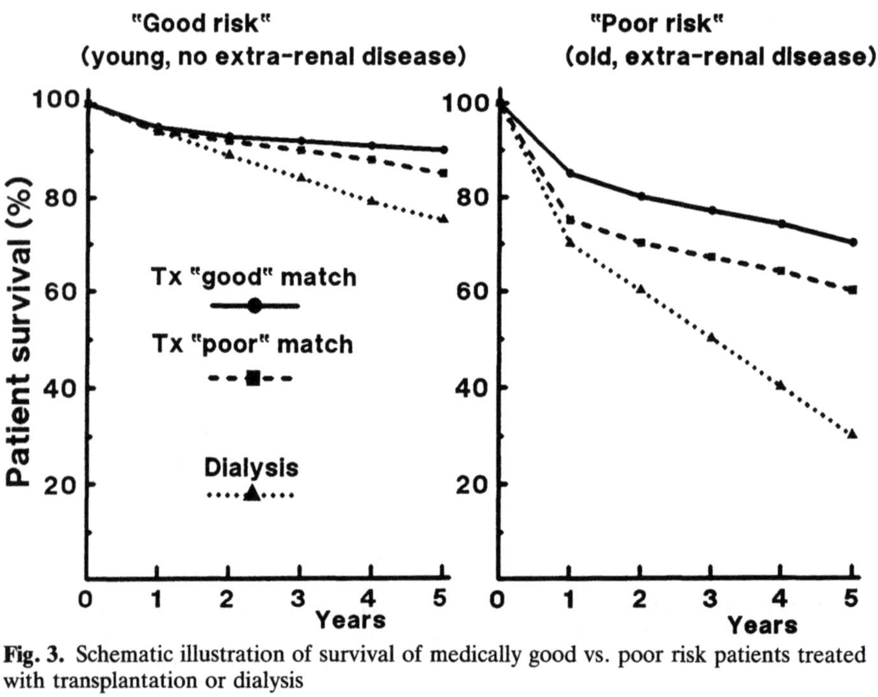


**Fig. 3.** Schematic illustration of survival of medically good vs. poor risk patients treated with transplantation or dialysis

greatest chance of graft survival? Allocation based on HLA matching does not solve this dilemma. In fact it could be argued that more years of life could be saved by allocating a given graft to a poor risk patient irrespective of HLA match, rather than to a well matched good risk patient (Fig. 3).

In my opinion the major objective in graft allocation is to improve overall survival in the total population of patients needing organ replacement, rather than to obtain nice graft survival rates. There is no easy formula to reach that objective. In our clinical practice, we allocate grafts on the basis of the following priorities:

1. No HLA-A + B + DR mismatch;
2. a negative cross match for multisensitized patients;
3. no HLA-DR mismatch for repeat tx, and
4. seniority on the waiting list and medical urgency, irrespective of HLA match.

Most grafts are allocated in the last priority group, reflecting our opinion that HLA matching is but one of several relevant factors in graft allocation.

## References

Albrechtsen D, Fauchald P, Leivestad T, Talseth T, Flatmark A (1988) Renal replacement therapy in elderly patients. Transpl Proc 20:367–369

Opelz G (1991) Is kidney allocation on HLA match justified? Transplant Proc (in press)

Terasaki P (1991) Molecular matching. Transplant Proc (in press)

# Facing Organ Allocation Issues: An Insider's View From the New World

R. D. Guttmann

As therapy for terminal illness, vital organ transplantation has enjoyed spectacular success at least medium term, if not long term, in many cases, having moved from an innovative to a therapeutic medical activity. Concurrent with the recognition of organ replacement as significant therapy, the wide publicity given to its successes and future promise, and the acceptance for financing by most social democratic governments has been a steadily growing demand for vital organ transplants. The number of available organs is far less than those desiring, or defined in need of transplants. Although attempts to maximize the number of multiorgan donors will and must continue, it is likely that demand will far exceed supply. The difficult issue of who shall receive a transplant, which implicitly defines who shall not receive a transplant, will not be easily resolved. Allocation policy determines the potential population to be treated. A fair system must evolve from consideration of those neglected as well as those allowed entry into the system.

The thrust and claim of this paper is that allocation proceeds through a narrow process of decision making, decided upon largely by two groups of insiders, transplant clinicians and transplant immunologists, who use their medical and biological arguments to control the turf. Their public debates are civilized and good natured, based on incomplete information reduced to averages of easily obtained data points, and in reality they speak with one voice. The discourse is preoccupied with parts of rather than the whole of patients; little if any information about those who do not receive transplants, desires of patients, input from certain other professional groups, government or 'the public'. The net effect of this dominance has been the lack of development of a clear research agenda which can help determine a sensible allocation policy. At present, the issue of 'who should receive the next transplant' is not debated in depth from any position of moral philosophy. The current basis for allocation decisions is superficial and rhetorical, and in reality has been formulated from political negotiations which maintain a professionally controlled decision-making mechanism whose moral authority needs to be questioned.

It is my goal to examine the way allocation proceeds using as examples, kidney and heart, in order to reveal the similarities and differences in

McGill Centre for Clinical Immunobiology and Transplantation, Montreal, Quebec, Canada, H3A 1A1

W. Land, J. B. Dossetor (Eds.)
Organ Replacement Therapy:
Ethics, Justice and Commerce

conceptualization and *praxis*. For starters, the statement needs to be made that organ transplants offer at best a finite period of life prolongation, limited by the persistent problems related to slow organ failure associated with chronic rejection as well as immunosuppressive drug-related toxicities and their sequelae.

For years, the issue of 'dialysis versus transplantation' has been debated. This has been the wrong question to ask. Dialysis and renal transplantation are competing therapies by virtue of competing speciality groups. This competition has important implications for the organ allocation issue. The flow of patients to the transplant evaluation process and waiting list for transplantation, i.e., 'through the gate', is controlled and determined by the debate. Unfortunately, the more proper question 'How can dialysis and transplantation as valid therapeutic choices for patients be offered and combined to maximize the quality and quantity of prolonged life?' is usually not posed in medical debates. Technology rather than the patient is debated as the object of interest. The issue of control at the gate may not only involve strong professional biases, but may also be seen as an outcome of turf defense and financial self-interest.

It is clear that if the therapies are seen as complimentary for end-stage renal disease (ESRD) patients, then the next appropriate question, subsumed by the more general question, is 'Who should *not* be considered as a renal transplant candidate?' Transplanters should be heartened by this logic. However, it is at this departure point that important prognostic information is needed, particularly in the area of comorbid processes, on outcome both during the dialysis and the transplant phase of ESRD patients. Recent improvements in the quality of life on dialysis potentially make this issue more complex if seen only from the 'dialysis versus transplant' perspective. Since there are few primary conditions that really contraindicate transplantation, there is the potential for massive demand.

Heart transplantation is a relatively young enterprise and we have little information about conditions at the gate. However, the issue is vastly different than with ESRD. There is no alternative therapy, and it is likely that information about candidacy and appropriate referrals will be rapidly disseminated. The prognostic factors in end-stage cardiac disease (ESCD) may be clear in terms of functional classification and numerical levels of myocardial performance, but as the success of the transplant procedure is recognized, there will undoubtedly be increasing pressure for earlier referral based on considerations of quality of life. Quality of life research is neglected in an end-stage illness where terminal events are often prolonged and associated with considerable suffering. Given the lack of major 'control' issues between the cardiologist and the cardiac surgeon, there is every reason to believe that demand for heart transplants will grow substantially due to evolving criteria of recipient selection as well as earlier evaluation. The net effect will be significant swelling of the waiting lists and equilibration to a steady state will be slow and painful. The drama associated with the wait for a heart is more extreme than a wait for a kidney. Patients not receiving an allograft within months usually die, and during the waiting period terminal complications are poorly managed due to the lack of substantial supportive therapies. A long period of terminal illness before referral and a long wait for an allograft may be associated with a much more difficult and less successful post-transplant rehabilitation.

A further issue in cardiac allograft allocation concerns patient selection. Knowing the approximate number of patients for whom there will be hearts may affect the type of, number of, and rate of patients evaluated by some centers. A new patient may be selected or 'made active' when another is transplanted in order to control the size of the waiting list. The program then has less exposure to the highly charged emotional environment of a long waiting list, and to the suffering and death resulting from an insufficient number of hearts. This control 'at the gate', reflects program concerns. Thus, waiting list numbers do not necessarily reflect potential realities.

There is another important 'at the gate' issue that is relevant to both heart and kidney transplants. In some countries, heart transplant has been considered 'experimental' and is not an insured health service. The implication is that it limits access; only those who are self-insured, i.e., financially capable, will be allowed into programs. In the case of one country's approach to the treatment of ESRD, restriction of the global resources to treat renal failure has led to the necessity of rationing and denying some patients access to dialysis. Physicians, in effect, exercise their judgement about which patient will benefit. Influencing the gate in this way will force allocation until the size of the population deemed in justified need places clinicians in overt conflict.

Having considered allocation issues 'at the gate', next examine the processes of kidney and heart allocation once patients have been accepted. The nature of the allocation process may be substantially different in regions with few programs and a sparse population, compared with regions with dense populations and multiple transplant centers. These centers are often part of several medical faculties, each with its own goals, doing what is perceived to be 'prestige' activity. Where donors are under control of a single center for its own patients, rules of allocation are likely to be more vague. Where there are multiple competing programs, mandated rules are in effect.

The policy used for allocating kidneys has primarily been based on human leukocyte antigen (HLA) match (after ABO compatibility and a negative donor lymphocyte cross-match have been verified). The more antigens matched renders a greater priority score. More recently, the allocation scheme has assigned greater weight to antigens matched at the DR locus, based on the belief that compatibility at that region is more important biologically than at the B or A loci. Of course, the argument goes, DR and B is a better match than DR alone. An allocation system which favors individual HLA antigens is usually justified by the demonstration of correlated life table analyses of allograft survival.

The subloci of HLA are extremely polymorphic. There are 'stronger' regions as well as 'stronger' alleles. Genetic disparity at HLA, given nonidentity, has no serious basis for being viewed as an antigen count to be correlated with outcome. No argument about this. No argument that the biology of graft rejection is modified by prior exposure to antigen, in a graft-rejection as well as graft-prolongation manner. No argument about the necessity for antirejection drugs even when there is HLA identity. No argument about drugs being effective in achieving the desired outcome in many instances of cadaveric transplant where few or no antigens are matched. The point is, there is a substantial biological difference between HLA identity and partial identity.

In many kidney allocation schemes, local discretion allows the use of one kidney and the other is dispatched to a 'pool' or 'organ bank' for distribution. If there is conviction about the validity and value of the HLA matching, then what is the justification for using a kidney locally for a patient when better matches can be achieved? The usual reason given is that the team doing the extensive donor maintenance and surgery should have the right to keep a kidney for one of its patients. It is considered to be an issue of motivation and fairness for the local program. In regions with multiple transplant centers that obtain donors from nontransplant hospitals, the ability to keep a kidney for one's own program leads to competitive behavior and 'control of donors'. Transfer of or access to donors becomes the ticket to keeping at least one kidney, regardless of the allocation scheme. This is effected by professional connections, official and unofficial, rather than any logical principle of relationship.

The system for allocation of cardiac allografts by contrast (after factors of ABO blood group, lymphocyte crossmatch when time permits, size compatibility are considered), generally favors the 'urgent' case, the patient perceived to be at greatest risk for mortality. This assumes that such risk is highly predictable. Various ratings are given, classifying patients on the basis of whether they are on mechanical cardiac support, in an intensive care unit, another hospital unit, or at home waiting.

There are several potential problems with a system favoring the urgent patient. First, it assumes that the clinically sickest patient is in greatest need, and has the greatest risk of dying. Second, this policy could favor selection of a population of patients who have the poorest post-transplant prognosis, although this has not been established given the current criteria for patient selection. Third, locally variable application of mechanical cardiac support devices may influence allocation. It is not inconceivable that the use of an artificial heart assist could be a way for a team, desperate for a heart, to jump the queue. While this would be an abhorrent medical act if done for that reason, as artificial devices become simpler and safer, the tendency will be for application earlier in the time frame of myocardial failure. Fourth, classification honesty, a matter of professional ethics is breached when patients are deliberately misclassified in order to jump the queue. Finally, as with kidneys, the problem of competing for control of donors can be significant: Maintain and/or transfer the donor and keep the organ.

HLA matching is not considered an important factor in allocation of hearts, even though data from registries may indicate that degree of match is correlated with 1- and 2-year graft survival. This is demonstrated when there are hundreds to thousands of cases analyzed, but not as clear in single center series. One obvious reason for the lack of priority for HLA matching is lack of time. Current methods of preservation usually allow less than 6–8 h between donor cardiectomy and transplant and often logistics are such that a complete HLA typing is not available. However, in the very near future, there is reason to think that preservation solutions will allow 12–24 h between donor and recipient procedures, more than enough time for HLA typing and matching. What will the value of HLA be as an allocation factor? Given the dramatic predicament of cardiac patients, I doubt it will be significant.

Having detailed the process, I choose to become a critic of the status quo. There are compelling reasons for being critical. There is a lack of research that could lead to a more transparent and intelligent system. While this lack of information is not due to a lack of potential interest, it is due, in my opinion, to the failure to have 'the system' critically deconstructed and stimulated to a new research agenda. The reasons for this failure to analyze the system will become apparent. We should first begin by asking which voices speak to us about allocation, what are they saying, and what is the nature of the debate?

The current justification for allocation, as detailed above, seems largely to fall into two domains: medical and immunological. And indeed, the discourse about systems of allocation are usually concerned with these issues, debated by the professionals who represent the fields. Each has a professional interest in the outcome of the event, a professional interest which has economic implications for both the individual and the enterprise that is represented.

Examine the system of renal allograft allocation. There is little discussion about matching for ABO group and excluding recipients on the basis of a positive donor lymphocyte cross-match, both biological determinants related to very short-term graft survival. But what about HLA matching and outcome measurements of 1-, 2-, and 5-year graft survival? Registries may even tell us that patient survival as well as graft survival may be related to HLA match. This latter claim is disturbing because, without any other medical facts, if it is due to more severe rejection, resulting in more intense immunosuppressive drug treatment with attendant complications and mortality, then I would suggest that poor medical judgment is being exercised with focus on the treatment of kidneys rather than patients. It seems improbable that mortality rates at experienced renal transplant centers, when adjusted for comorbid pathology, are any greater than for dialysis centers.

What about the survival statistic? It tells us at a point in time whether a graft is functioning or not. It reduces each patient to a point, an *x* and *y* coordinate on a graph, without other information, and then averages these points in time. Quantity of life, not quality of life is considered. It tells us nothing of the level of function of the patient nor the complications that may have been suffered. Furthermore, the validity of the HLA matching claim may be questioned when the definition of 'good match' is seriously examined. It is 'best match', often only 1 or 2 antigens of 6. With so many patients poorly matched doing well, why should we accept the 'biological argument' based on graft survival only?

A pitfall in registry data is illustrated by an example of a patient who undergoes a renal transplant, has an accelerated rejection during the first 3 weeks and transplant nephrectomy is required. The patient is returned to dialysis and to work, and is pleased to await a second transplant. A registry failure. Contrast this with the patient who does well for 2 months post transplant, then has an acute rejection successfully treated, subsequently develops cytomegalovirus (CMV) infection requiring hospitalization, immunosuppression is reduced leading to another rejection which is reversed, then requires frequent clinic visits, has difficulty maintaining a full-time work schedule, and at 1 year has stable but abnormal renal function, hypertension requiring multiple drugs, and is not at all pleased with the outcome. A registry success. While these two cases are not necessarily typical, they are neither unusual nor uncommon. The point is, registries do not tell us about medical or social realities of patients. This is the information badly needed if we are to base an allocation system on more rational criteria.

If the HLA-matching policy aims to produce the highest number of functioning kidneys at a future point in time, one could conceive of 'sharing' widely and at great distances to achieve this goal. If one is truly consequential in position, why not, given the shortage of organs, exclude those with bad prognostic factors, such as the 'immunologically high risk'? Why continue to offer kidneys to patients with significant comorbid pathologies such as those seen in diabetes mellitus?

The reason why this type of extended sharing system based on matching will only be acceptable with severe limits is that a segment of the medical establishment is skeptical about the importance of the one-dimensional graft survival statistic. Extended sharing does not necessarily consider local 'needs', hopefully those of patients as well as programs. Furthermore, HLA antigens are not uniformly distributed in the population. Therefore, as has been claimed, minority racial and ethnic groups may be more difficult to match. This may not be due to their relatively greater numbers awaiting allografts, but may be due to fewer donors available from those communities. Whether there are deliberate or hidden biases in the system can only be revealed as every element in the system is exposed and analyzed.

In allocating renal transplants, the time a patient has been waiting for an allograft may be used to allocate in addition to the HLA match. It can be given an arbitrary weight in a point system, or the system may outrightly favor a long waiting patient. This seems to be a fair criterion superficially, but is it really? One claim for its utilization is that it redistributes kidneys to those who are difficult to match. Does it assume that there are no adverse effects waiting for an allograft? If not, then does the system not bias itself towards a selection criterion which might be associated with an increase in poor prognostic factors in some recipients? Would the nature of these complications be damaging in some way for future rehabilitation? If there are no adverse effects in waiting a long period on dialysis, then why should it have any value in an allocation scheme. Furthermore, waiting time in a given transplant program is a function of the number of allografts done, the number of patients admitted to and leaving the allograft queue. With relatively more being admitted than can be transplanted, the average waiting time will continue to get longer and longer and merely increase the number of transplant recipients who develop complications. The variable of waiting time becomes more significant as indications for transplantation expand. Waiting time is dealt with as if eventually everyone will obtain an allograft, which is clearly not the case. Patients with different prognoses are given similar opportunities to receive allografts. Waiting is not of the same consequence to every patient and has quite a different significance in heart patients.

Allocation schemes adopt criteria which serve the needs of programs to treat a certain population of patients, and allow negotiation for organs from a local donor pool. The reason stated for these allocation schemes is that there is a need to maximize results based on objective criteria rather than allow elements of subjectivity to rule. But these objective criteria are often not related to the medical and psychosocial reality of the patient. There is the aura of consequential action by the proponents of the allocation schemes, yet the criteria chosen relate to a genetic feature of the patient, often the age of the patient (elderly excluded), and how long the patient has been in the queue. Where are the considerations that have to do with the patient as a person? Are there not any other important considerations to support a consequential view? While these distant and numerical criteria are easily manipulated arithmetically, and survival curve correlations are generated by the registries, they give a cold view of what is happening to patients as a group or as individuals having differing prognoses due to factors not considered in the allocation system.

Therefore, to call these systems *consequential* and use this term for their justification is bogus. In fact, the schemes arise, not from consideration of moral positions, but from political negotiations between the two inside factions of the medical establishment. The philosophical arguments for the schemes are weak. A position for consequentialism, nonconsequentialism, or any other stance cannot be developed until there is a systematic approach to data collection in the medical, psychological, and social spheres, to name a few, for all patients eligible for transplant, whether or not transplanted. This should not be a more formidable task than the last 20 years of collecting endless HLA matching and outcome data has been and which has not changed the nature of this debate or significantly changed allocation action. The real meaning of the necessity to allocate is that there are criteria that favor one individual over another individual. No consequential argument can be built which does not account for the outcome of both the individual chosen and not chosen.

The shallowness of the criteria currently used as the basis for allocation and the political nature of the process reveals two things. First, limited medical data is contributed to a limited knowledge base by each of the representatives of the two transplant factions: the clinicians and the immunologists. They use their own data to take action to set allocation policy. Second, there has been no justification about from where this moral authority has been derived. There needs to be a clear dissociation of the highly skilled medical and surgical acts, necessary to achieve excellent outcomes following transplants, and the allocation policy decisions that affect the lives of a patient population. The two groups should contribute their data and present their claims. However, there is little reason why they should continue in their professional hegemony. While the voices of the professionals have been heard, a third voice is emerging, that of the government or insurer. Hard questions are being asked about ethnic and gender discrimination in the system, about foreign patients, about special waiting lists, about justification of costs. Are we really prepared to hear this voice and respond without giving up some measure of control?

What about another unheard voice in the allocation discussion: the voice of the public. Without journeying into the problematic area of 'who is the public?', we should consider their possible contribution. It is the public that supports the health-care system, the system of research support we need, and it is the good-will of the public that allows us to obtain donor organs. Why should not a public voice be part of the chorus?

Finally, the most important voice has not been heard, that of patients. Is it not their concern? Some patient groups have been organized and are beginning to ask questions about the system, but not many challenges have been made. Why have there not been more challenges? Certainly with kidney recipients, there may be no pressing urgency since most patients will tolerate dialysis and 'wait for the good match', a term often used by patients, but not really adequately defined. However, with heart patients who are desperately clinging to their hope of being relieved of a miserable existence within a few months, when a transplant occurs, the response is 'why not me?' This is a statement that must be taken seriously and begs the question of why should prospective as well as post-transplant patients not share their values with us and offer another voice in developing policy. Do they not have as much moral authority as any other group?

The political force of patient should not be underestimated. Witness the situation where a growing number of heart-lung transplant candidates felt that the donor organ allocation system was discriminatory and favored those needing hearts. Their medical advocates working inside a competitive system were unable to change the allocation system to be more equitable, thus the patients directly approached the Ministry of Health. There was a 'sympathetic ear' and an ethical review was ordered. Since such a review would take longer than many of these heart-lung transplant candidates might have to live, it seemed that a future but not immediate politic would be affected. But to the surprise of patients, within 2 years the system suddenly produced a quadrupling in the number of heart-lung transplants. No rational explanation, allocation rules were not changed, but a new voice had been heard by the controlling structure.

What is the message then? First, the allocation system we have speaks with a single voice. The partners are clinical and laboratory professionals contributing certain, but clearly not definitive, data upon which to base allocation policy. Their points and counterpoints maintain control over the debate and the system. Second, the relevant data about prognosis is necessary if, in the future, we want to examine the merits of a consequential view of allocation rather than some other system. Meaningful data must be obtained for all categories of terminal patients whether they are transplanted or not. The tendency to allocate on the basis of easily collectable immunogenetic data rather than factors relevant to the many dimensions of the lives of patients must be reconsidered. Finally, the dominance and control of the professional community over criteria for allocation policy should be challenged.

# Immunological Criteria in Kidney Allocation

A. Gomes da Costa, M. J. Sampaio, A. Sousa, A. M. Correia, and J. R. Pena

## Introduction

In Portugal, shortage of organs is the factor limiting the development of kidney transplantation. As the annual number of new hemodialysis patients acceptable to transplant largely exceeds the annual number of grafted patients [1], waiting lists tend to grow. Kidney allocation is done primarily according to immunological criteria: AB0 blood group compatibility and number of DR, B, and A locus compatibilities in this order. Clinical classification, second grafts, age and duration of hemodialysis come next. Patient priority is defined through clinical classification as Super urgent (SU; only AB0 blood group compatibility and negative crossmatch required); U1, U2, and U3 (1, 2, or 3 human leukocyte antigen, HLA locus compatibilities required); IR (second graft patients), and H (hyperimmunized patients with more than 80% preformed antibodies to a population panel). Using these allocation criteria, 0 group and incomplete HLA locus identified patients should be prejudiced, as 0 kidneys are diverted to other blood group patients, and incomplete HLA-typed patients have less chances to be grafted. In countries with large waiting time to transplant, differences between these groups may became clinically significant, and as a result, we analyzed waiting time to transplant according to the allocation criteria, at the Red Cross Hospital Transplant Unit.

## Material and Methods

Waiting time to transplantation was analyzed for the whole period of functioning, from 29 June 1980 to 29 June 1990, and for the years 1988 and 1989. Patient waiting time was defined either as the difference between transplantation day, death, or withdrawal from the list and the date of acceptance on the active waiting list, or as the difference between the 29 June 1990 and the date of acceptance in active list for patients that were not grafted. For the 1988/1989 period analysis, only patients on the active waiting list at 1 January 1988 or accepted by 31 December 1989 were included, and for those not grafted, waiting time was calculated up to 31 December 1989.

UTR da CVP, Red Cross Hospital, Rua Duarte Galvão, 54, Lisbon, Portugal

W. Land, J. B. Dossetor (Eds.)
Organ Replacement Therapy:
Ethics, Justice and Commerce

A projected waiting time was calculated through the formula:

$$\frac{\text{number of patients in waiting list}}{\text{number of grafted patients/2}}$$

for the period of 1988/1989. Mean waiting time for transplantation and projected waiting time were calculated for each A, B, and 0 blood groups, for the different number of HLA-A, B and -DR identified locus, for the degree of sensitization according to 0+ (0 antibodies against the panel), 1+ (‹25% antibodies), 2+ (›25% but ‹50% antibodies), 3+ (›50% but ‹75% antibodies), and 4+ (›75% antibodies), and for the SU, U2, IR, and H clinical classification. U1 and U3 patients were not included due to their small number. Patients with incomplete or indefined data in one or two allocation criteria were included for analysis of the other criteria. No statistical analysis was performed.

## Results

The results are summarized in Table 1. Although mean waiting time differs for patients in different groups, these changes are not clinically significant.

**Table 1.** Waiting time to transplantation (years)

| | Mean waiting time (80/89) | Mean waiting time (88/89) | Projected waiting time |
|---|---|---|---|
| Group | | | |
| AB0 AB | 0.95 | 1.93 | 5.12 |
| A | 1.52 | 2.45 | 5.2 |
| B | 2.02 | 2.99 | 7.3 |
| 0 | 2.28 | 2.88 | 11.65 |
| DR 2 identified | 1.75 | 2.8 | 5.9 |
| 1 identified | 2.2 | 2.6 | 12.5 |
| AB 4 identified | 1.76 | 2.5 | 7.25 |
| 3 identified | 2.1 | 2.85 | 8.9 |
| 2 identified | 2.0 | 2.93 | 4.77 |
| Sensitization | | | |
| 0+ | 1.2 | 1.64 | 8.5 |
| 1+ | 1.88 | 2.76 | 8.0 |
| 2+ | 2.4 | 3.35 | 6.4 |
| 3+ | 2.3 | 2.92 | 22.5 |
| 4+ | 3.6 | 4.31 | 21.0 |
| Clinical classification | | | |
| SU | 0.48 | 1.22 | 3.1 |
| U2 | 1.8 | 2.6 | 7.6 |
| H | 3.6 | 4.2 | 21.0 |
| IR | 2.1 | 2.47 | 4.3 |

**Table 2.** Number of SU patients grafted

| | Number of patients grafted in 88/89 | Number of patients grafted as SU |
|---|---|---|
| AB0 group | | |
| A | 81 | 9 |
| 0 | 50 | 22 |
| DR locus | | |
| 2 DR identified | 108 | 21 |
| 1 DR identified | 32 | 10 |

On the other hand, projected time presents very large differences between groups. Hyperimmunized, 0 blood group and one DR identified patients have projected waiting time values that exceed the survival time of a large number of patients in hemodialysis or continuous ambulatory peritoneal dialysis (CAPD). This is a discrepancy compared with mean waiting times values of 0 blood groups and one DR identified patients that do not exceed other values. However, the percentage of patients in those two groups grafted with the SU criteria largely exceeds other groups (Table 2).

## Discussion

Mean waiting time in the whole series or in the 2-year period of 1988 and 1989 is not a precise method for the evaluation of differences in waiting time to transplantation between groups. Although the continuous enlargement of the waiting list through the years [2] accentuates differences between patients, making the mean waiting time for the years 1988 and 1989 more sensitive than the whole series, the acceptance of new patients to the active list in this time reduces this effect.

Projected waiting time, although presumptive and subject to error with changes in allocation criteria or in the number of annual transplantations, allows a better estimate of differences between groups. Use of HLA locus compatibility as the first allocation criterion is widely accepted today. Its rationale stands on the correlation of better long-term organ survival with the number of HLA compatibilities between donor and receptor [3]. However, using this criteria makes patients with incompletely identified, homozygotous, or uncommon HLA-DR locus typing more difficult to transplant, and 0 group kidneys will be lost to other blood groups. In the near future, with more sensitive compatibility typing (molecular or epitope) [4], some of these differences will probably be attenuated. Meanwhile, these patients should be given priority to donors sharing uncommon HLA-DR haplotypes or accepted on a priority list after 4–5 years on the active waiting list. As for 0 group patients, 0 group donors should be reserved to them until results of A2 blood group grafting across the blood group barrier is better defined.

The long waiting time for hyperimmunized patients to transplantation can only be solved through the enlargement of the donor pool. With the wide use of recombinant erythropoietin, it is hoped that this population might, in part be lessened.

In conclusion, in Portugal there is a large waiting time to kidney transplantation. Use of the number of HLA compatibilities as the first allocation criterion has an uneven repercussion in patients. 0 group and incomplete DR identified patients have a clinically significant longer waiting time to transplantation.

## References

1. Ponce P, Remedio F, Santos JR (1988) Relatorio do Gabinete de registo do tratamento da insuficiencia renal cronica. Sociedade Portuguesa de Nefrologia. Jornal das Ciencias Medicas 152(3):156–166
2. Pena JR, Correia AM, Costa AG et al. (1984) Actividade e Resultados da Unidade da Transplantados Renal da Cruz Vermelha Portuguesa. 6th Symposium in Nephrology, December, 1984, Oporto, Portugal
3. Gjertson DW (1989) Short- and long-term effects of HLA matching. In: Terasaki P (ed) Clinical transplants. UCLA Tissue Typing Laboratory, Los Angeles, California, pp. 353–360
4. Terasaki PI et al. (1989) Overview and epitope matching. In: Terasaki P (ed) Clinical transplants. UCLA Tissue Typing Laboratory, Los Angeles, California, pp. 499–516

# Age Matching is Fairer Than HLA Matching in Renal Transplantation?

P. K. Donnelly, R. Henderson, A. R. Simpson, P. S. Veitch, and P. R. F. Bell

## Background

To cope with the ever increasing demand for transplantable kidneys, several centres have advocated the increased use of older donors (>50 years) [1, 2]. Unfortunately, older donors are associated with inferior graft survival and renal function compared to younger donors despite human leukocyte antigen (HLA) matching [3, 4]. Optimum matching for HLA antigens is advocated and is the main basis for organ sharing [5]. Inevitably this increases cold ischaemic time, which is a risk factor for graft survival of kidneys taken from older donors [6]. Little attention has been given to the possible benefits of matching for the relative ages of donor and recipient. In this study we investigated the effect of cadaveric donor age on graft survival of Leicester patients whilst allowing for recipient age.

## Patients and Methods

The study comprised 158 consecutive first cadaver recipients transplanted between January 1983 and December 1988 with a minimum 1-year follow-up. Immunosuppressive therapy consisted of cyclosporine in a starting dose of 17 mg/kg and prednisolone 2.0 mg/kg, both tailed over a 6-week period. All patients had been previously dialysed and transfused. Three modes of failure were considered: Immunological failure (biopsy proven), non-immunological failure (e g. graft thrombosis) and death with a functioning (DWF) graft. Donor-recipient ages were compared with other co-variates, i.e. dialysis time, and type, pre- and perioperative transfusions, sex, ischaemic time, sensitivity, donor/recipient ages and HLA-A, -B, -DR matches. So as to investigate donor to recipient age differences, the data were separated into three groups:

a) donor more than 5 years older than recipient,
b) donor within 5 years of recipient, and
c) donor more than 5 years younger than recipient.

Department of Surgery, Leicester General Hospital, Gwendolen Road, Leicester LE5 4PW, United Kingdom

W. Land, J. B. Dossetor (Eds.)
Organ Replacement Therapy:
Ethics, Justice and Commerce

Both univariate statistical methods to investigate the overall effect of a factor and multivariate methods to allow for all factors simultaneously were employed. Univariate methods included product limit survival plotting together with log rank and Breslow tests [7]. Multivariate methods included the Cox proportional hazards model [7] and the Weibull mixed model for heavily censored data [8].

## Results

Donor and recipient details are given in Table 1. Cox regression analysis indicated that the important risk factors determining graft survival (immunological failures only) were;

1. *Donor age* ($p < 0.01$). Kidneys taken from younger donors (<50 years) were associated with a better 1-year graft survival (95 %; $n = 113$) than those from older donors (74 %; $n = 45$).
2. *Donor-recipient age difference* ($p < 0.05$). Even after the effect of donor age was allowed for, the difference between donor and recipient age significantly affected outcome. For example, if the donor was 5 or more years younger than the recipient then graft survival was 95 % ($n = 71$) at 1 year, if the donor was within 5 years of the recipient the survival was 92 % ($n = 41$), but if the donor was more than 5 years older than the recipient the survival was reduced to 78 % ($n = 46$). A consequence is that good results are obtained even with older donors provided recipients are not significantly younger. Thus 1-year survival for donors over 50 was 86 % if the recipient was not more than 5 years younger than the donor, but just 58 % otherwise.
3. *HLA-matching*. Improved 1-year graft survival was obtained with zero HLA-DR mismatches (96 %; $n = 35$) in comparison with one or more mismatches (87 %; $n = 123$) ($p < 0.05$). There was no significant benefit from matching at the A or B loci.

Recipient age did not affect outcome. Similar results were obtained if non-immunological or DWF causes of graft failure were included in the analyses.

**Table 1.** Donor and recipient details ($n = 158$)

| | Mean | SD |
|---|---|---|
| Recipient age (years) | 43.7 | 14.1 |
| Donor age (years) | 34.1 | 17.3 |
| HLA-A (median) | 1 | |
| -B | 1 | |
| -DR | 1 | |
| Pre-transplant transfusion (units) | 13.0 | 16.2 |
| Peri-transplant transfusion (units) | 0.2 | 0.6 |
| Total ischaemic time (hours) | 1177 | 458 |
| Dialysis type (% CAPD) | 41 | |
| Dialysis time (months) | 25.5 | 24.4 |

## Discussion

When cyclosporine was first introduced, many transplant units believed that the immunosuppression was so effective that organ sharing to improve HLA matching was unnecessary. Recently, data supporting the benefits of HLA matching have meant that greater efforts have been directed to obtain complete matches at the HLA-A, -B and -DR loci [8, 9]. This study confirms the benefits of DR matching and supports the view that HLA-A or -B matching is of marginal benefit. Exchange of kidneys between centres to achieve better and better HLA matches increases ischaemic time, which may be detrimental to graft function when older donor organs are concerned [6]. This study has confirmed earlier reports that kidneys taken from donors aged over 50 years are associated with significantly impaired graft survival despite three antigen HLA-matching [3, 4]. More importantly, young patients receiving a kidney from an old donor had inferior graft survival than when a young donor was used. The deleterious effects of using older donors can be partly offset by transplanting older recipients with organs from donors of comparable age. It would seem fairer not to share all kidneys on the basis of maximum HLA match but to accept the limited functional reserve of older donors (>50 years) [10] and aim to transplant them locally for HLA-DR match only. This would ensure optimum function from minimum ischaemic time.

## References


1. Wing AJ (1990) Can we meet the real need for dialysis and transplantation. Br Med J 301:885–886
2. McGeown MG (1990) Prevalence of advanced renal failure in Northern Ireland. Br Med J 301:900–903
3. Foster MC, Wenham PW, Rowe PA (1988) Use of older patients as cadaveric kidney donors. Br J Surg 75:767–769
4. Rao KV, Kasiske BL, Odlund MD et al. (1990) Influence of cadaver donor age on post transplant renal function and graft outcome. Transplantation 49(1):91–95
5. Gilks WR, Bradley BA, Gore SM (1987) Predicting waiting time for a beneficially matched graft. Transplant Proc 19(5):3640–3641
6. Leunisson KML, Bosman FT, Nieman FHM et al. (1989) Amplification of the nephrotoxic effect of cyclosporin by pre-existent chronic histological lesions in the kidney. Transplantation 48(4):590–593
7. Lawless JF (1982) Statistical models and methods for lifetime data. Wiley, New York
8. Farewell VT (1982) The use of mixture models for the analysis of survival data with long term survivors. Biometrics 38:1041–1046
9. Yuge J, Cicciarell J (1987) Kidney transplantation and donor-recipient ages. Clinical Transplant. In: Teraskai P (ed) UCLA Tissue Typing Laboratory, Los Angeles, California
10. McLachlan MSF (1978) The aging kidney. Lancet ii:143

# Donor Factors Determine Cadaveric Kidney Outcome: Should We Use It to Choose Donor-Recipient Combinations?

W. Niebel[1], K.H. Albrecht[1], A. Gille[1], K. Wagner[2], F. W. Eigler[1], H. Grosse-Wilde[3], J. Erhard[1], A. Daul[2], and T. Philipp[2]

## Introduction

Up to the present, the donor-recipient combinations in kidney transplantation have been optimized in most transplant centers according to the histocompatibility system only. It was assumed that the conditions of the organ donation (the circumstances of brain death, the procedure of organ harvesting and shipment) were good or excellent. Other donor criteria were not taken into account. But there are recent studies, which have found a significant influence of donor factors in determining kidney transplant survival rates at a high degree, comparable to that of the HLA system [1, 2]. In this single center study, we retrospectively deal with those donor factors and propose a modified management fo donor-recipient selection.

## Material and Methods

From 1972 to 1988, we performed 1000 cadaveric kidney transplantation in 865 recipients. The basis immunosuppression first consisted of conventional immunosuppression (azathioprine and prednisone) with and without anti-thymocyte globulin (ATG), and since 1983, it has consisted of cyclosporine (CsA) plus prednisone. Rejections were treated with bolus therapy of methylprednisolone, with ATG, or $OKT_3$.

A retrospective analysis of long-term transplant function was done regarding following factors: HLA matching, conventional immunosuppression, CsA therapy; donor factors such as age, sex, blood group, cause of brain

[1] Department of General Surgery, University Clinic Essen, Hufelandstr. 55, 4300 Essen 1, FRG
[2] Department of Nephrology, University Clinic Essen, Hufelandstr. 55, 4300 Essen 1, FRG
[3] Department of Immunogenetics, University Clinic Essen, Hufelandstr. 55, 4300 Essen 1, FRG

W. Land, J. B. Dossetor (Eds.)
Organ Replacement Therapy:
Ethics, Justice and Commerce

death (trauma vs. nontrauma donor), local or nonlocal donor, multiorgan harvesting, blood pressure and creatinine prior to organ harvesting, diuresis during the last 24 h, quality of perfusion, anatomy of the kidneys, and warm and cold ischemia time.

The survival rates of the transplants were estimated according to the life-table method.

The median follow-up is 60 months; no patient was lost to follow-up.

## Results

1. The introduction of CsA significantly improved the 5-year graft survival rates by 25 % (conventional therapy, 38 %; CsA, 63 %). The best 5-year results of 70 % were achieved in a subgroup of patients with a first graft and low-dose CsA and prednisone.
2. HLA matching had only a minor, insignificant effect of 5 % on graft outcome.
3. Donor age below 40 years significantly improved the 5-year graft survival by 25 %, irrespective of the immunosuppressive regimen (conventional therapy, 50 %; CsA, 75 %), while donor sex (male vs. female) had an effect of 8 %. The combination of donor age and sex (age < 40 years and male vs. age > 40 years and female) showed a significant improvement of 30 % (conventional therapy, 45 %; CsA, 75 %).
4. The cause of donor brain death had a significant influence, too. After a traumatic brain death, we found a 5-year graft survival of 73 %, after a cerebrovascular brain death one of 50 %. This difference could only be observed in the CsA period.
5. The combination of the relevant donor factors (age < 40 years, male, traumatic brain death) resulted in a 5-year transplant function rate of 72 %. If the donor factors were age > 40 years, female, and cerebrovascular brain death, we achieved a 5-year transplant survival of 46 %. This difference was highly significant.

## Discussion

The results of the present study can be summarized as follows:
1. Donor factors such as age < 40 years, male, and traumatic brain death play a major role in the posttransplant course, improving the long-term results by about 20 %–30 %.
2. There seems to be a positive correlation between these factors and the immunosuppression, especially if CsA is used.

Since the introduction of CsA in kidney transplantation most transplant centers have achieved 1-year graft survival rates of 80 %–85 %. But it is now becoming more and more evident that half of the grafts are lost in 7–8 years

**Table 1.** Proposal for selection of donor-recipient combinations

| | Recipient stratification[a] | |
|---|---|---|
| Donor criteria | Younger | Older |
| Age < 40 years, male, traumatic brain death | 1st choice | 2nd choice |
| Age > 40 years, female, nontrauma brain death | 2nd choice | 1st choice |

[a] After stratification of the two recipient groups, the definite selection should be based on HLA matching. If there is no acceptable recipient in the preferred group, a recipient of the other group should be selected

after transplantation [3]. This long-term risk seems to be the principal remaining risk of kidney transplantation, and it has to be stressed that this high risk is not affected by CsA. Another major limiting factor in renal transplantation is the shortage of donor kidneys. Therefore, we should think not only of the limits of acceptability of an organ, but also the appropriateness of its use [2].

With respect to good long-term results, the ideal organ donor is male, aged below 40 years and had a traumatic brain death, because there are additive effects of 30 % on 5-year graft survival. Therefore it seems to be justified to choose donor-recipient combinations predominantly according to the donor factors and – in second place – to HLA matching. That means, that the organs of a young organ donor should be offered to young recipients from whom the best HLA match could be selected (see Table 1). This modified management leads to ethical questions which will have to be discussed.

## Conclusion

Donor factors seems to have a major effect on kidney transplant long-term function, especially if CsA therapy is used. Therefore, it has to be discussed if those should be included in the selection criteria of donor-recipient combinations.

## References

1. Cecka JM (1987) Donor factors. In: Terasaki PJ (ed) Clinical transplants 1987. UCLA Tissue Typing Laboratory, Los Angeles, California
2. Lucas BA, Vaughn WK, Spees EK, Sanfilippo F (1987) Identification of donor factors predisponing to high discard rates of cadaver kidneys and increased graft loss within one year posttransplantation – SEOPF 1977–1982. Transplantation 42:253–258
3. Terasaki PI, Mickey MR, Cecka M, Cicciarelli J, Cook D, Iwaki Y, Toyotome A, Wang L (1987) Overview. In: Terasaki PJ (ed) Clinical transplants 1987. UCLA Tissue Typing Laboratory, Los Angeles, California

# Donor Organ Allocation from a Legal Point of View

M. Osinga, J. E. M. Akveld, and F. T. de Charro

## Introduction

Since World War II, the right to health care has become increasingly important as becomes apparent when the embodiment of this right in several treaties and constitutions is taken into account. It is a social right. Such a right gives, in principle, access to health care facilities to all citizens. It has, however, its limits. One of the limits is the limited availability of financial means. Another limit is the absolute scarcity of available donor organs. This leads to conflicts in several forms. One expression of these conflicts are the legal procedures which have been started by some patients [1].

## Selection Criteria

To solve the selection problems, which arise because of this shortage, and to give substance to the right to health care, the government has the duty to further a selection which is as equitable as possible. With regard to the way the government can give substance to its task, different approaches can be found both in literature and in practice.

Leenen, an author who has put to a large extent his mark upon the Dutch legal forming of opinion with regard to health care, distinguishes for example four systems: a lottery system (making the selection by drawing lots), a chronological system (making the selection by first come, first served), a waiting list system (making the choice by taking into account both the urgency of the patient as well as the time he has been waiting on the waiting list), and, finally, a criteria system (making the choice by using criteria) [2]. Annas, an American lawyer, on the other hand, also distinguishes four approaches: the market approach (those get the organ who are able to pay for it), the selection committee approach (making the selection by a lay committee), the lottery approach and the customary approach (making choices implicitly [3]). Leenen gives preference to the criteria system because among others it lends itself the most to legal/ethical judgements.

Centre for Health Policy and Law, P.O. Box 1738, L6B-64, 3000 DR Rotterdam, The Netherlands

W. Land, J. B. Dossetor (Eds.)
Organ Replacement Therapy:
Ethics, Justice and Commerce

With regard to the criteria, both procedural and material criteria can be distinguished. With regard to the material criteria, the following distinction can be made:

1. Medical criteria (e.g., indications and contraindications, physical condition, tissue compatibility, medical seriousness, and medical success). The medical criteria can also be used to mean that they only focus on the effectiveness of a treatment (i.e., the benefit the patient obtains from a treatment in the sense of years of life at a reasonable level of functioning).
2. Personal criteria as far as they are important for the treatment (e.g., psychological ability to comply, motivation, intelligence, and compliance).
3. Daily living conditions as far as they are relevant for the treatment (support at home, the possibility to comply at home, and emotional support, etc.).
4. Significance of the patient for his direct environment.
5. Significance of the patient for the society.
6. Age (e.g., do patients of 55 years and over need a new heart?).
7. Social behavior (e.g., alcohol and drug abuse).

Leenen prefers to use the first five criteria mentioned above in the order of ranking used here, i.e., the medical criteria have to be used first and, if afterwards there are still persons in the pool, the personal criteria are taken into account, and so on and so forth. He is opposed to the use of the age criterion because it is discriminatory. He does not like the social behavior criterion either, because it is too subjective. Annas gives preference to the medical criteria as well, but focuses more on the effectiveness of the treatment in such a sense that the benefit the patient obtains from the treatment in the sense of years of life at a reasonable level of functioning is taken into account. Another suggestion which he makes is to persuade persons not to join the pool. This could be considered as a part of the personal criteria because patients must be extremely motivated to joint the pool in this way. With regard to the age criterion, he is not sure whether to use the age criterion, since it may be impressionistically related to outcome, but as long as this is not proved, this criterion is arbitrary. The same applies in his opinion for alcohol and drug abuse. From this overview we can conclude that Annas focuses most on the effectiveness of the treatment; this follows from the way he uses the medical criteria and the age criterion. A similar approach can be distinguished for Leenen as well. The way he defines the medical criteria makes clear that the effectiveness of the treatment is taken into account by him as well. He also pays attention, however, to other aspects of the medical criteria. Because of the situation, discrepancies in the use of the criteria can arise. Both authors give preference to an explicit formulation of the criteria.

With regard to the procedural criteria, we will only draw attention to the question whether criteria have to be available for the public, and who has to make the choice. The first topic has been answered positively by both Leenen and Annas. With regard to the second issue, Leenen suggests leaving the selection to the medical team treating the patient, possibly in the presence of a lawyer who is impartial. Annas is less explicit in his preference concerning the question of who has to make the selection. He is at least opposed to leaving the selection to a lay committee because of the bad experiences which have taken place in the USA with regard to these committees.

Turning to the Draft Bill on organ donation, which has recently been developed in the Netherlands and which has in the first version as yet only been accepted by the council of ministers in the Netherlands, criteria for selection can also be found. Article 16, part 3, of this Draft Bill states that no other factors will be taken into account apart from blood and tissue compatibility of the donor and recipient of the organ. The medical urgency of the patient and other circumstances which are involved with the condition of the organ or, when these factors do not provide a solution, the time the recipient has been waiting. In the Draft Bill, it can be found that the organ center (i.e., Eurotransplant or Bio Implantant Services) has to decide who gets the available organ. This system is, from the point of view of equal selection, only then equitable if the centers have been supplied with all the available organs. This is, unfortunately, not always the case.

In practice, two levels of selection can be distinguished: first, the answer is given to the question who can get on the waiting list; second, the answer is given to the question who gets the organ first. With regard to the first level, the heart transplantation centers in the Netherlands have developed a protocol in which their criteria for selection can be found. The first nine criteria can be considered to be medical, the other criteria are increasing age, the willingness and the ability of the patient to undergo the treatment, the possibility to communicate with the treating team, and finally the age criterion of 55 years. When the patient is on the waiting list, the medical criteria such as blood compatibility and urgency determine the question of who gets the organ first. The last level looks much like the waiting list system that Leenen introduced and like the system which has been proposed in the Draft Bill. The first level of criteria looks like the first three criteria of the criteria system Leenen proposed, although Leenen proposed to use the next criterion when the former criterion did not provide a solution any more.

## Discussion

One can wonder if the criteria that have been developed in theory and even the guidelines that have been developed by the centers and Eurotransplant improve the equity. In practice sometimes huge discrepancies can be found between the different centers in the number of urgent patients [4]. This may give the impression that criteria are interpreted differently in practice. What should be done about it? A solution might be to introduce a certain form of control, perhaps every 2 or 3 years, at the centers concerned about their use of the criteria to improve the equal use of the criteria. Would this be the best solution?

Effectiveness and equity are also conflicting issues, as becomes clear when one looks at the use of the age criterion. The age criterion here only implies the calendar age (e.g., do patients of 55 years and over have the right to receive a new heart in the case of scarcity?). The biological age criterion is considered to be part of the medical criterion. As can be noticed in the paper, there is no consensus about the question whether the use of the age criterion is justified. Leenen is opposed to its use, while Annas is not sure if it is a correct criterion. Finally, the protocol of the heart centers was the cause of discussion when it introduced the age criterion. One can wonder if the introduction of the age criterion is not equitable. If it were plausible that the elderly have a worse medical prognosis than younger people, would it be unfair to use this criterion? Besides would it not be more discriminatory and less controllable to use the biological age as a criterion, since we have seen how difficult it is even to define medical urgency.

## References

1. Court Den Bosch (1990) Tijdschrift voor Gezondheidsrecht, 19
2. Leenen HJJ (1979) The selection of patients in the event of scarcity of medical facilities – an unavoidable dilemma. Int J Med Law, pp 161–180
3. Annas GJ (1985) The prostitute, the playboy and the poet; AJPH, p 181
4. Eurotransplant Newsletter, no. 79, pp 10–11

# Ability to Pay and Access to Transplantation

J. C. Moskop

Selection to be the recipient of a cadaver organ for transplant is a complex process involving at least three stages: First, referral to a transplant center for evaluation; second, acceptance by the center as a candidate for transplantation and inclusion on that center's waiting list; and third, selection from the list to receive a particular donated organ. A variety of medical, social, and moral considerations influence decisions about a patient's eligibility for transplantation at each of these three stages. Among these are factors designed to increase chances for successful transplantation (such as absence of active infection or neoplastic disease, ability to tolerate major surgery, ability to comply with post-transplant immunosuppressive therapy, blood group compatibility, negative cross-match and human leukocyte antigen (HLA) matching), factors designed to promote individual access to transplantation (such as time on a waiting list, urgency of need, and degree of presensitization), and membership in a particular local or national health care system.

In this paper, I will briefly examine an additional, nonmedical criterion which plays a major role in controlling access to extrarenal transplantation in the United States, namely, ability to pay for one's treatment. Although the Medicare End-Stage Renal Disease Program covers most of the cost of dialysis and kidney transplantation for United States citizens, up to 64 million people, or 26 % of the population of the United States, lack public or private insurance coverage for heart and liver transplantation (Evans 1989). Patients without insurance or personal wealth may not be referred by their physicians for transplant evaluation, or, if they are referred, may not be accepted by a transplant program unless they are able to demonstrate ability to defray a large portion of the cost of their care. Let us consider, then, whether ability to pay is a justifiable criterion for controlling access to transplantation.

If there is a responsibility to insure access to transplantation for all patients who need it, that responsibility presumably belongs to the state or society at large, since the state is charged with promoting the welfare of its members and only the state would be able to carry out such a responsibility. Must the state accept this responsibility? A brief look at the history of the End-Stage Renal Disease Program may explain, if not justify, the reluctance of United

Department of Medical Humanities, East Carolina University School of Medicine, Greenville, North Carolina 27858-4354 USA

W. Land, J. B. Dossetor (Eds.)
Organ Replacement Therapy:
Ethics, Justice and Commerce

States legislators to provide coverage for transplantation of extrarenal organs. The conviction that treatment could save lives, along with very optimistic cost projections, led Congress to establish the End-Stage Renal Disease Program in 1972 (Moskop 1987). In the subsequent years, many lives have been prolonged, but program costs have increased to some $ 3 billion per year. Faced annually with massive federal budget deficits over the last 10 years, Congressional attention has focused on cutting, not expanding, public programs, especially Medicare, because of its large and rapidly increasing costs (Schneider 1985–86). United States legislators are particularly leery of establishing another entitlement program with a price tag as high as that of heart and liver transplantation for all potential candidates.

Some respond to this situation by arguing that United States budget priorities are misguided $\frac{1}{\mathrm{m}}$ that, for example, the federal government should pay for indigent health care, including transplants, by increasing taxes and slashing defense spending. This claim raises, of course, very large issues of assessing competing social goods, issues which I cannot explore here. Even if Congress were willing to raise taxes or shift funds from the military into health care, however, that might only temporarily address the problem of scarcity, since large increases in the number of patients served and in the cost of the care provided might soon exhaust any surplus in this area (Schwartz 1987).

Let us assume, then, that even a nation as wealthy as the United States will not be able to provide all potentially beneficial health care for each of its citizens. It will, then, be unfortunate, even tragic, to refuse some beneficial care to some citizens, but not necessarily unfair, since the state cannot do otherwise (Engelhardt 1984). The obvious next questions are, What kinds of care should the state provide, and what kinds should it choose not to support? Into which of these categories should transplantation fall? Because the interests, values and principles at stake in addressing these questions are complex and often incommensurable, they have no single ideal answer. We must, instead, seek reasonable policies based on informed and sustained moral dialogue and on democratic principles of social choice. In such a moral dialogue, advocates of public support for transplantation can clearly point out the increasing ability of transplants to prolong lives and improve patients' quality of life. They may also point out that end-stage organ failure patients have an urgent need for care, and that transplantation has symbolic value as a highly visible, heroic life-saving treatment. Opponents may point out the relatively high costs of transplantation per patient and the relatively small number of patients able to benefit from this form of treatment. In its report on access to health care, the United States President's Commission for the Study of Ethical Problems in Medicine (1983) noted that support for more inexpensive preventive and primary care programs may improve health and save lives much more cost-effectively than treating an end-stage disease. Acting on such cost-benefit comparisons in 1988, one state, Oregon, restructured coverage under its state-administered Medicaid program of health care for the indigent. Oregon chose to discontinue support for liver, heart, and bone marrow transplantation so that it could provide prenatal care for more low-income pregnant women under this program (Menzel 1990). Given the inescapable reality of resource scarcity and the legitimate social goal of making the greatest overall contribution to the health of its citizens, I submit that societies may, like Oregon, choose to forgo provision of expensive life-saving therapies.

If a state does choose *not* to commit public funds for expensive therapies like organ transplantation, should it allow wealthier individuals to pay for and receive these therapies, either directly or through private insurance? To put this question another way, should the state enforce strict equality in access to health care services, or should it permit some individuals to purchase care that others cannot afford? In most societies, wealthier citizens may purchase a variety of items, including better food, housing, education, means of transportation, and recreation. If, however, we permit great inequalities in access to all of these other areas, why should we insist on strict equality in health care, beyond a basic level of services guaranteed to all citizens? State efforts to enforce equality in health services might need to become invasive, in order to prevent the establishment of black markets in health care, and restrictive, in order to prevent wealthier individuals from traveling to secure health care unavailable at home. It seems incongruous to prohibit citizens from using their resources to purchase life-sustaining health care while we allow them to purchase luxuries like fine wines or fast cars.

Organ transplantation, of course, depends not only on expensive medical technologies like heart-lung machines, but also on the scarce resource of donated organs. Some have argued that individuals and their families will be unwilling to donate organs as part of a public program unless those organs are available to all medically needy patients regardless of their ability to pay (Caplan 1989). This may, indeed, limit the number of those willing to consent to organ donation and hence also limit the number of transplants performed in the United States and other countries in which ability to pay does affect access to transplantation. Even if donors would prefer it, however, it does not follow that the state has a moral obligation to them to make their organs available to all in need. As Daniels (1989) has pointed out, the state may have good reasons to support a practice or program even if it cannot be made available to all who need it. This is, in fact, the case with public support of many areas in medicine besides transplantation.

I conclude that a society may choose to invest its scarce health care resources in those programs that will make the greatest overall contribution to the health of its citizens. If organ transplantation does not qualify for social support as a highly cost-effective therapy, access to transplantation should depend in part on a patient's ability to pay for this therapy.

## References

Caplan A (1989) Problems in the policies and criteria used to allocate organs for transplantation in the United States. Transplant Proc 21:3381–3387
Daniels N (1989) Comment: ability to pay and access to transplantation. Transplant Proc 21:3424–3425
Evans RW (1989) Money matters: should ability to pay ever be a consideration in gaining access to transplantation. Transplant Proc 21:3419–3423
Engelhardt HT Jr (1984) Allocating scarce medical resources and the availability of organ transplantation. N Engl J Med 311:66–71
Menzel PT (1990) Strong medicine. Oxford University Press, New York
Moskop JC (1987) The moral limits to federal funding for kidney disease. Hastings Cent Rep 17(2):11–15
President's Commission for the Study of Ethical Problems in Medicine and Biomedical and Behavioral Research (1983) Securing access to health care. Washington, DC
Schneider AG (1985–86) Commentary: legal and political pressures on health care cost containment. Case Western Reserve Law Rev 36:693–707
Schwartz WB (1987) The inevitable failure of current cost containment strategies. JAMA 275:220–224

# The Ethics of Assessment for Transplantation

V. C. O'Brien, J. P. Scott, N. Caine, S. R. Large, P. M. Schofield, C. Dennis, and J. Wallwork

Over and above the clinical criteria influencing acceptance for transplantation how do we choose recipients? I would like to present the method by which we choose and the process involved.

The objectives of the assessment admission for the transplant team are to educate the patient to the realities of transplantation, to ensure that the result of the process allows the patient to give informed consent, to establish a meaningful relationship based upon mutual trust and to agree a commitment which permits participation of the patient in the decision making process, thus ensuring his active involvement in future care plans.

The objectives for the patient are simple and direct. He seeks information about the procedure, but above all wants to be accepted for transplantation. Although apprehensive about surgery he wants to extend the length and quality of his life. He may well have made an emotional commitment to the procedure before admission believing this to be his only chance to survive.

The current rate of assessment activity is four patients a week. One of the constraints is time, but the over-riding dilemma concerns the number of patients waiting to come in for assessment and subsequently then the numbers currently on our definite waiting lists (Fig. 1; Table 1).

The reasons for non-acceptance are either clinical or because the patient is not ready – he is not ill enough or is not yet committed to transplantation. In the latter case we need to mutually agree a period of re-assessment at a future date.

Patients are admitted for 4 – 5 days accompanied by a close relative. The involvement of family is crucial at this and all subsequent stages of transplantation. Visits to all relevant wards and departments are made to ensure that they fully understand what would be involved at each stage following surgery. Meetings with other transplant patients and their families are essential. Further interviews are undertaken with the medical team, the transplant patient adviser and the consultant surgeon. It is regarded as essential for this procedure to be co-ordinated by an experienced member of the team who can guide the patient through the process, offer information and support, make the necessary organisational arrangements and interpret

Transplant Unit, Papworth Hospital, Papworth Everard, Cambridge CB3 8RE, England

W. Land, J. B. Dossetor (Eds.)
Organ Replacement Therapy:
Ethics, Justice and Commerce

feedback from patients and staff, thus providing continuity for all concerned.

The outcome of the admission for the transplant team is that the patient better understands all that is involved in the transplant procedure, obtains informed consent, which is the ethical foundation of our work with the patient and to establish positive relationships.

The desired outcome of the admission for the patient will be that he will have a more realistic view of transplantation and its problems and will have made the necessary psychological adjustments, relinquishing any preconceived ideas. It will have given him time to consider his present quality of life

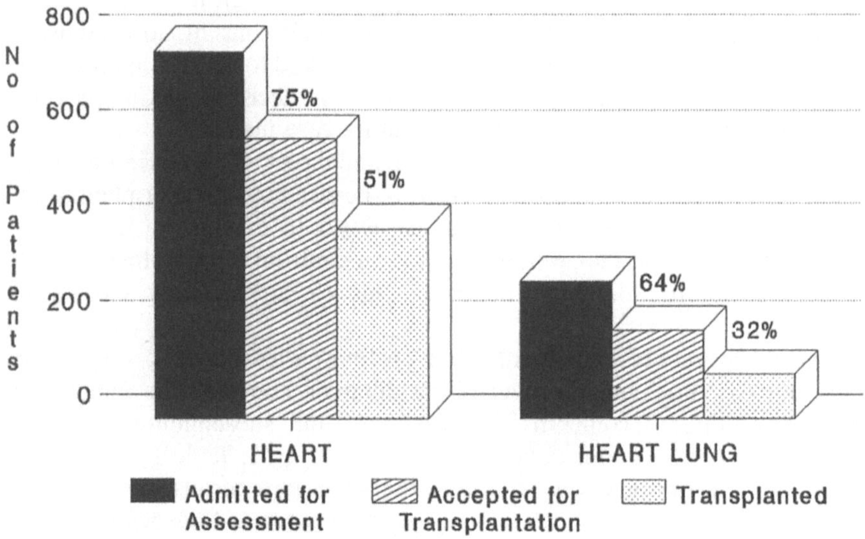


**Fig. 1.** Number and percentage of patients admitted for assessment, accepted for heart or heart-lung transplantation, and who underwent heart or heart-lung transplantation at Papworth between 1979 and September 1990

**Table 1.** Transplantation at Papworth 1979 – September 1990

| | Assessed | Accepted | Transplanted |
|---|---|---|---|
| Heart | 776 | 588 (75%) | 399 (51%) |
| Heart-Lung | 292 | 188 (64%) | 94 (32%) |
| Number of patients awaiting assessment | *n* | Average waiting time (months) | |
| Heart | 38 | 4–5 | |
| Heart-Lung | 91 | 9–12 | |

against the background of high risk surgery and to have taken part in making decisions about his own future.

In summary, the outcome for the team and the patient should result in a mutual commitment which will ensure the active involvement of the patient and his family in future care plans and enable the team to commit themselves to the indefinite post-operative care of the patient's transplant-related needs.

To evaluate the assessment admission, it is necessary to have feedback from the patient which can be used to help monitor its effectiveness. It is essential for this to be co-ordinated by a consistent member of the team.

During the waiting period, evaluation of the system and support to the patient go hand in hand. How the patient copes during this stressful time will demonstrate the strengths of the system and indicate any improvements needed. Anxiously waiting for the operation, he and his family must be helped to face the possibility of dying before a donor organ becomes available.

Following surgery, further evidence of the success of the assessment admission can be seen in the attitude, cooperation and compliance of the patient and his family, and their potential for long-term self care under the guidance of the Out-Patient Department.

The evolution of the system emerged from a careful scrutiny of the many issues which arose from the unique nature of transplantation. Recognising patient and staff views has lead to an enlightened assessment process and an efficient admission procedure. We believe that the procedures followed are soundly based on ethical standards and values, which are not only seen as good practice but accepted as such by all concerned. In addition we have achieved a proficient structured admission during a few short days, which is an investment for both the patient and the team.

The successful outcome of the team's efforts stems from the recognition and acceptance of common values and principles which encompasses the dignity of individual patients, and their right to share in the making of difficult decisions.

# Should Urgent Medical Need Be Used as an Allocation Factor for Liver Allografts?

R. Margreiter

Allocating transplantable and particularly extrarenal life-saving organs has become one of the major issues in transplantation. Every system for distributing organs which were given freely, voluntarily, and altruistically has to be fair, efficient, and practicable. Any policies, practices, or activities that are otherwise imperil the entire enterprise of organ donation and, thus, transplantation. The criteria guiding organ allocation will have to be accepted by the public, that is by those who donate and who receive the organs, and by those who finance transplantation. Everyone agrees that patient selection must be scientifically sound, while these criteria cannot be based on science alone. Many of the most difficult questions are rooted in value conflicts. Therefore, every system must necessarily be a compromise, which ultimately should be acknowledged as being in the best interest of all parties concerned. And public ratification of any such system will very much depend on the manner in which the medical community and all involved in organ transplantation succeed in proving that organ distribution is not based on bias, prejudice, patronage, greed, or publicity consciously or unconsciously masquerading as medical criteria, but rather on the principles of equity and justice. The public will demand the opportunity to review existing policies and to hold those who use them accountable. How difficult fair organ allocation is can be seen from the fact that even seemingly objective medical criteria, such as antigen matching, can produce inequities in those obtaining and not obtaining a transplant. These criteria will always be determined at least partly by social values. Medical objectivity applied in the individual case is in itself no guarantee for the objectivity of the larger scheme, in which medical considerations play an essential role.

At least in the Western world, the concept of allocating transplantable organs by market mechanisms has been explicitly rejected on ethical grounds, which leaves us with three different principles for organ distribution:

1. The so-called queuing principle
2. The principle of optimum utility
3. The principle of urgent medical need

Department of Transplant Surgery, University Hospital, Anichstraße 35, A-6020 Innsbruck, Austria

W. Land, J. B. Dossetor (Eds.)
Organ Replacement Therapy:
Ethics, Justice and Commerce

The queuing principle would be neutral because it requires no background information on applicants for a scarce resource. The only relevant consideration is the date when a patient is put on the waiting list. Since this principle ignores the different medical needs and prognoses of patients and no patient may ever be moved up or down the list, it is inapplicable in practical organ allocation.

Utility as the most relevant and appropiate ethical factor in preferencing potential recipients is defined as maximizing benefits while minimizing losses. In other words, how to ensure the greatest possible graft survival. According to this principle, organs should be given to those patients with the best prognosis in order to maximize the number of lives saved. The complexity of the underlying decision becomes evident when reflecting on whether to give an organ to someone with the greatest possibility of transplant survival, someone likely to enjoy the highest quality of life, someone who is seen as morally most deserving or likely to make the greatest contribution to society, or to someone bearing the greatest responsibility for other lives. Utility as the ethical principle of choice contrasts sharply with prevailing practice and has been criticized in setting recipient allocation priorities [1]. Medical efficacy as the criterion for patient selection is paternalistic and has the potential to reduce to bare statistics the unique value of each human life.

Patients are typically moved up the list as their medical need for a graft becomes more acute. Those whose need for an organ is so urgent that they would die soon without the transplant are given highest priority in an attempt to save them. Since this is literally a "rescue operation", this ethical principle has also been termed the "rescue principle" [2]. For decades, transplant surgeons followed the practice of treating the sickest patient first, and most current allocation systems continue to give priority to the most acute candidates, which is fully compatible with the traditional obligation of physicians toward their patients.

Should urgent medical need be used in future as an allocation factor for liver allografts? Are the principles of utility and medical need mutually exclusive in the context of liver transplantation? Patient selection is primarily required only when resources are limited. According to European but also American experience, this is not yet the case [3]. From January to September 1990, a total of 389 livers were not able to be used by Eurotransplant. In 121 cases, this was solely due to organizational failures. During the same period, a total of 436 liver transplants were performed within Eurotransplant [4]. Thus, a substantial number of livers could not be placed for logistic reasons. As long as we are not able to solve these organisational problems, it is my conviction that we are not allowed to exclude patients from liver transplantation on the basis of medical criteria, provided they meet the minimal medical efficacy criteria. Although liver transplantation must be considered as an established therapeutic measure for a wide variety of diseases, many patients still do not make it on to the waiting list. Patients suffering from end-stage liver disease must first be identified and then referred for evaluation as potential recipients. Suitable candidates for transplantation are selected and finally chosen from the waiting list. Thus, the most important ethical decisions for allocation take place long before an organ actually arrives at a particular transplant center.

As the success of liver transplantation has improved and continues to improve, the number of referrals will certainly increase. In the not too distant future, the number of patients on waiting lists will exceed the number of available grafts. Such circumstances will force transplant surgeons to select recipients of a liver transplant. Are those with the greatest need entitled to the greatest access to scarce resources? Liver patients are categorized according to severity of their illness. Patients suffering from fulminant hepatic failure and those with a nonfunctioning graft or with irreversible early rejection are defined as the group with the highest medical need. Patients with acute fulminant hepatic failure are typically young, previously healthy persons who, through an acute viral infection or exposure to toxins, have developed severe hepatic necroses. Untreated, their mortality exceeds 85 %. Having no portal hypertension and having been in good condition before hepatic failure, these patients are optimal candidates for liver transplantation. In fact, results are excellent [5]. Since complications of cerebral edema may rapidly progress and lead to irreversible damage, these patients should routinely be placed at the top of the waiting list and enjoy priority for an organ. In this case, the patient with the greatest medical need also meets the criteria of optimum medical utility.

How is the situation as far as urgent retransplantation is concerned? Patients undergoing retransplantation for nonfunctioning grafts or irreversible rejection during the immediate postoperative period appear to have a lesser chance of survival than recipients of first transplants. Although efficiency might be of importance, it is long-standing medical tradition that a critically ill patient not be abandoned, all the more so because the transplant team may be partly responsible for graft failure in some instances. It, thus, seems justified to give some recipients a second graft, even though some patients still cannot be saved, while other persons receive no graft at all. This group of patients classified as highly urgent comprises about 20 % of all patients awaiting a liver transplant. Half of these require retransplantation for a nonfunctioning graft and half for fulminant hepatic failure [4]. Irreversible acute rejection of a liver graft is a rare occurrence. Improved preservation techniques and better methods for assessing the quality of the donor liver will help to significantly reduce the number of initially nonfunctioning grafts. Yet, with accurate assessment of liver function and of the potential for organ recovery prior to procurement, the subsequent events such as preservation, surgical trauma at the time of transplant, and reperfusion injury may have an overwhelming influence. However, the criteria used to make the diagnosis of initial nonfunction are poorly defined. The incidence of graft nonfunction may to some extent reflect the surgical attitude towards retransplantation and availability of donor organs rather than the certainty of death without retransplantation. On the other hand, it has been shown that prostaglandin was able to "rescue" some livers considered to be nonfunctioning [6].

Whereas giving priority to this high urgency group of patients can be defended as fair, the problems become more complex with another group of potential recipients who might not survive if they are not given preference, namely those with liver failure from chronic liver disease. Once they require intensive care treatment including respiration, the prognosis is that much less favorable than in patients at home and stable [7]. The value of demonstrating our commitment, however, has its limits since a clear correlation was demonstrated between the grade of illness and 1-year survival rate and the cost for transplantation [8]. It will be one of our major tasks to define threshold criteria of medical efficacy. This should reflect the normative and ethical judgement primarily about the chance of surviving the procedure and secondarily about the length and quality of life that liver transplantation should provide. Since physicians are well situated to assess the risk, benefit, and costs of an organ transplant to an individual patient, it is not inappropriate to have them define these criteria.

Liver malignancy again represents a special form of urgent need. Since tumor growth continues while patients are waiting for a transplant, the waiting period should be kept as short as possible. On the other hand, results of liver transplantation for this indication have shown to be significantly inferior as compared to nonmalignant cases [5]. This has prompted many transplant surgeons to not accept patients with liver tumors.

How can the goal of fair and equitable organ allocation in the field of liver transplantation be achieved when accepting urgent medical need as a selection criterion? Many centers still consider organs procured by themselves as their property. There is, however, increasing recognition that donated organs are a precious community resource. If such a community comprises several different countries, care must be taken to have a similar incidence of organ donors in all participating countries in order to prevent inequities. Whathever criteria and norms are used, it seems clear that a case-to-case evaluation by attending physicians will have to play an important role. Removing the physician from the selection process would be a serious mistake, since only medical experts in the field have sufficient knowledge and experience to guarantee the best possible outcome. Organ allocation requires evaluation of all data in an open process whose fairness is trusted implicitly. For patients with urgent medical need, livers should be allocated by an allocation network. If organ allocation to a non-high-urgency patient, however, is done centrally by a computer, this does not take into consideration the enormous variability of states of illness and thus the degree of need of patients awaiting a liver transplant. This kind of decision remains an integral component of the art of medicine. An alternative would be to offer the organ to various centers on a rota basis and leave the final decision to the transplant team. To avoid abuse of this policy or unconscious bias, a local team possibly including an ethicist should be installed. I would refuse external control as impractical and degrading.

## Conclusion

Urgent medical need should be used as an allocation factor for liver transplants and appears reasonable as the highest priority for potential transplant recipients once minimal medical efficacy criteria are fulfilled. If the likelihood of success falls below a minimal standard, which remains to be defined and eventually redefined, the procedure is not justified. Except for retransplants, organ allocation thus involves the rescue principle as well as medical utility. Standardized medical criteria provide the framework for allocation, with the ultimate factor being the physicians judgement within certain safeguarded limits.

## References

1. Winkler D (1989) Equity, efficacy, and the point system for transplant recipient selection. Transplant Proc 21(3):3437–3439
2. Macklin R (1989) Comment: should selected patients ever be moved up? Transplant Proc 21(3):3395–3396
3. Starzl TE, Shapiro R, Teperman L (1989) The point system for organ distribution. Transplant Proc 21(3):3432–3436
4. Persijn G (1990) Eurotransplant Users Meeting
5. Williams R, O'Grady JG (1990) Liver transplantation: results, advances and problems. J Gastroenterol Hepatology 1:110–126
6. Greig PD, Woolf G, Sinclair S et al. (1989) Treatment of primary liver graft non-function with prostaglandin E1. Transplantation 48:447–453
7. Shaw BW Jr. (1989) Exclusion criteria for liver transplant recipients. Transplant Proc 21(3):3484–3486
8. Williams JW, Vera S, Evans LS (1987) Socioeconomic aspects of hepatic transplantation. Am J Gastroenterol 82(11):1115–1119

# Cardiac Retransplantation: Is It an Ethical Use of Scarce Resource?

P. A. Mullins, P. M. Schofield, J. P. Scott, E. Solis, J. Dunning, D. J. Aravot, S. R. Large, and J. Wallwork

## Introduction

Cardiac transplantation is established as the standard therapy for end stage heart failure. The acute shortage of donors is the limiting factor preventing its wider application at present (Wallwork 1989). Regular audit is necessary to ensure that the best potential is being realised from each organ. We assessed the impact of donor shortage on our cardiac transplant programme. We also noted that retransplanted patients had a particularly poor outcome and attempted to identify preventable risk factors.

## Patients and Methods

The study period is from January 1979 to September 1990. In all, 1318 patients have been referred for assessment for cardiac transplantation at Papworth Hospital in Cambridge, England. Of these, 776 patients were suitable for formal transplantation assessment; 588 patients were accepted onto the cardiac transplant waiting list, 56 patients were placed onto a provisional list, and the remaining 132 patients were rejected. Our reasons for exclusion in the rejected group are shown in Table 1.

**Table 1.** Contraindications for cardiac transplantation

| |
|---|
| Infection (including human immunodeficiency virus) |
| Malignancy (including previously treated disease) |
| Raised pulmonary vascular resistance (>4 Wood Units) |
| Recent pulmonary infarction |
| Extensive cerebrovascular or peripheral disease |
| Active peptic ulceration |
| Psychosocial unsuitability |

Heart Transplant Research Unit, Papworth Hospital, Papworth Everard, Huntingdon, Cambridge CB3 8RE England

W. Land, J. B. Dossetor (Eds.)
Organ Replacement Therapy:
Ethics, Justice and Commerce

Of the group of 588 people on the active waiting list, 399 patients (68 %) received their first heart transplant; 353 of these (60 %) were male. Treatment varied according to the time of operation. Initially steroids, azathioprine, and antithymocyte globulin were used as immunosuppressive therapy. Cyclosporin A was introduced into the programme in March 1982 and used in combination with low-dose steroids (double therapy) until April 1986. After this period, azathioprine was added to the double therapy regime (ie. triple therapy).

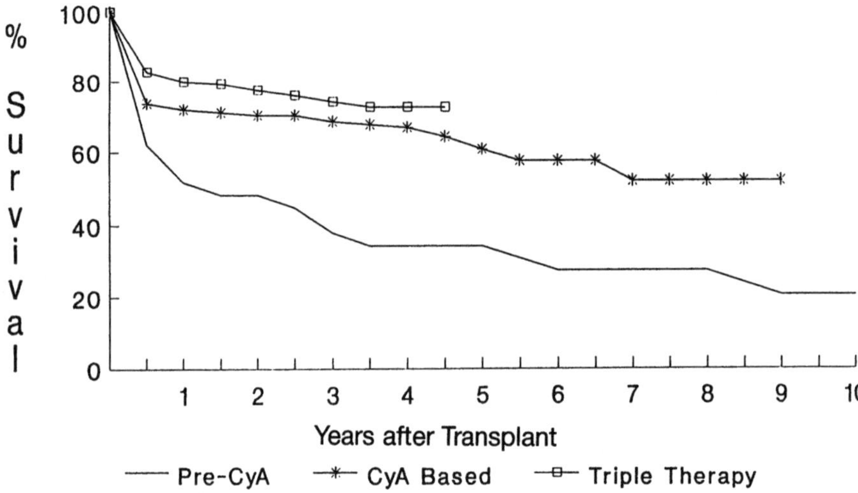


**Fig. 1.** Heart transplant patient survival by immunosuppressive group (*CyA*, cyclosporin A)

The actuarial survival has improved with these treatment changes and is now 82 % at 1 year for patients on triple therapy (Fig. 1). The main causes of early mortality (< 1 year) are rejection and infection. As graft failure from these causes becomes less common after the first year, coronary occlusive disease becomes the most important late complication. All causes of death are shown in Fig. 2.

Although we have no "emergency" group of patients awaiting transplantation, it is our practice to operate on the sickest patient on the list. Despite this policy, 136 (23 %) of patients died while awaiting operation. The mean time from acceptance to death was only 66 days.

## Retransplantation

Twelve patients have undergone cardiac retransplantation at Papworth Hospital: one patient has had a second cardiac retransplant. Therefore, a total of 13 grafts (4 %) of the series are retransplants. Nine patients were male, and the remaining three were female. The mean age was 45 years (range 25–57

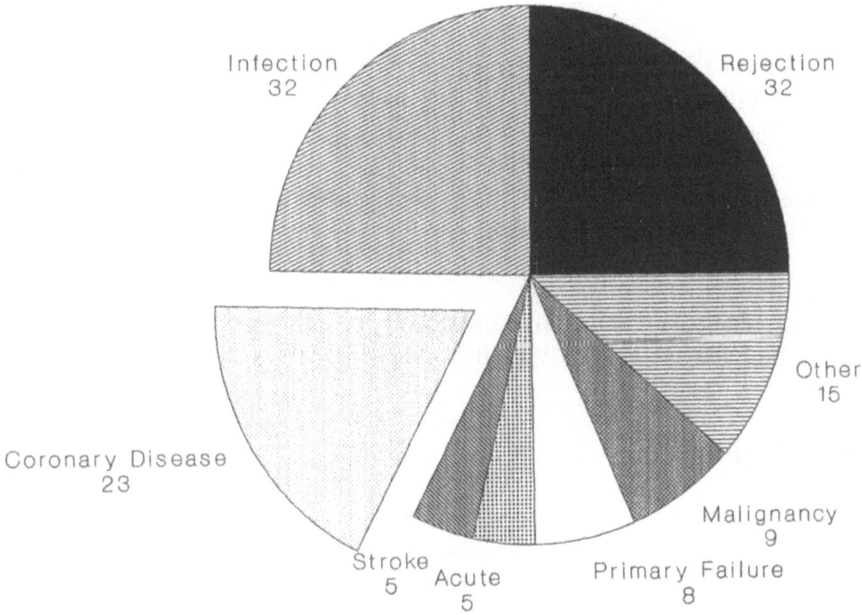


**Fig. 2.** Mortality in cardiac transplants (June 1990; $n = 133$)

years) which is similar to a mean age of 44 years (range 6–63 years) for first-time transplants. All patients were receiving triple immunosuppressive therapy.

## Results

Eight patients died within a year, i.e. 67%. This compares with a 1-year mortality of 17% (38 of 221 grafts) in patients receiving triple immunosuppressive therapy. Seven patients died in hospital soon after reoperation (median 11 days with a range of 0–17 days). Three patients developed "late" graft failure, i.e. after discharge from hospital. One patient died at 93 days from infection, one patient died from acute rejection 2 years after reoperation. One patient developed severe heart failure due to end-stage coronary occlusive disease after 6 years (Table 2). The latter patient underwent a

**Table 2.** Causes and timing of death in retransplanted patients

| | |
|---|---|
| Acute rejection | 3 Patients (median 11 days; range 9–41 days) |
| Coronary occlusive disease | 8 Patients, 9 grafts (median 1833 days; range 191–3232 days) |
| Primary organ failure | 1 patient (1 day) |

**Table 3.** Potential risk factors

| | |
|---|---|
| Age at retransplantation | Creatinine before operation |
| Treatment group | Preoperative infection |
| Number of rejection episodes | Cytomegalovirus status of donor or recipient |
| Original diagnosis | Preoperative hypertension |

second retransplant and is alive and well at present 3 years later. The other two living patients are alive at 9 months and 4.3 years, respectively.

## Risk Factors

Potential risk factors associated with an adverse outcome are difficult to assess in such a small group of patients. Seven patients were operated upon after proper reassessment for transplantation. The patients surviving for more than 100 days are all in this group ($p< 0.001$, Fishers exact test). All the patients in this group were also being retransplanted for end-stage coronary occlusive disease.

It is difficult to manage cardiac transplant recipients with poor renal function postoperatively because of the nephrotoxic side effects of cyclosporin A. However this did not correlate with a poor outcome in this study. Other possible risk factors assessed are given in Table 3. None of these was associated with poor outcome, although the numbers of patients involved are small.

## Discussion

It is apparent that without operation a large proportion of patients who are on cardiac transplant waiting lists will die. The critical lack of donor organs has emphasised that the best potential must be realised from each donated organ. Increasing the donor pool by improving donor management is one approach (Odom 1990). Ensuring that appropriate recipients are selected is also vital. Not only will the inappropriate recipient die, but a potential suitable recipient is denied life-saving treatment. It is, therefore, crurical to direct this precious resource to the recipients who have the greatest opportunity to use it.

International experience with heart retransplantation reflects our own. The Fifth Official Report of The International Society reported a 57 % 1-year survival falling to 53 % at 5 years (Fragomeni et al. 1988). No risk factors were identified in this study.

The high early mortality in retransplanted patients from Papworth Hospital reflects the initial attempts to salvage very sick patients with primary organ failure, rejection and infection. As experience has grown and the donor shortage has become critical, the emphasis has shifted to treating the long-term complication, i.e. coronary occlusive disease. This analysis of the results of retransplantation supports this change in approach.

## Conclusions

Cardiac retransplantation is associated with a high postoperative mortality compared with first-time transplant patients. Patients who have been formally reassessed for reoperation, i.e. patients with coronary occlusive disease, have a better prognosis than patients who undergo emergency operation.

## References

Fragomeni LS, Kaye MP (1989) The registry of the international society of heart transplantation: fifth official report 1988. J Heart Transplant 7:249–253

Odom N (1990) Organ donation I. Br Med J 300:1571–1573

Wallwork J (1989) Organs for transplantation. Br Med J 299: 1291–1292

# General Discussion: Allocation Issues in Organ Transplantation and Dialysis

*Opelz:* There is a question from Robert Sells to Dr. Dickens. In the Moore case, Moore's spleen was removed primarily for his benefit and the benefit for others was secondary. Now a donor kidney is removed primarily for the benefit of the recipient and the benefit to the live donor is secondary. Is this essential difference, such as to make the two models incomparable in common law? Would you like to comment on that, Dr. Dickens?

*Dickens:* There is something of an ambiguity about the Moore case, because the original splenectomy was done on purely therapeutic grounds. The immediate recourse could have had some monetary benefit, and it was the latter treatment that clearly was for the benefit of the commercial interests of the physicians, rather than for Moore himself.

The California Supreme Court seems to have focused primarily on the removal of the spleen and the value of the spleen to conlude the property interest was not appropriate to deal with any injustice that Moore may have suffered.

The Court went on to say, that when Moore was subsequently recalled, it was not for his benefit, but that his rights of action would be for lack of informed consent. The fact that the Court didn't want to be comprehensive in rejecting the property claim, I think, is important, because if one is dealing with a donation, this is primarily for the benefit of the recipient.

Of course, however, there is some benefit for the donor, benefit of a psychological character, once we exclude commercial payments. This is a point that I touched on in fact, regarding minors. Because parental power is not unlimited, parents can use their powers of consenting to medical care for their children to advance the interest of the children, not in a way that is hostile to the interest of the children.

---

The general discussion sessions were transcribed from tape recordings made during the conference. In the interest of a rapid publication, the individual speakers/discussants did not see their own comments and questions before the book went to press. One of the editors (W. Land) tried to make obviously necessary corrections in the manuscripts derived from the tape recordings and then authorized the publication of the sessions in their present form. Therefore, incorrect publication of the comments or questions with regard to style, content, etc. might be possible in the view of the speakers concerned. We apologize for any possible inaccuracies.

W. Land, J. B. Dossetor (Eds.)
Organ Replacement Therapy:
Ethics, Justice and Commerce

The courts may find that there is some kind of psychological benefit in being a donor, e.g., a bone-marrow donor. Equally, if we take live organ transplants, there will be some sympathetic emotional benefit for the donor. That is why it's right to say that the primary purpose is for the welfare of the recipient. The fact that the donor wants the benefit also weighs in the balance. It is not only for benefit of the recipient.

*Sells:* May I comment on what you said, Dr. Dickens, because, forgive me if I'm being a bit dim, I think that you have just repeated my question in a far more adequate way that I could have possibly have said it myself, but I couldn't actually hear the answer to it. Is there anything in the thought that the two cases are really quite different? And if a similar case came up about in the courts which focused on the property interest of the donor in his kidney, is perhaps the dissimilarity between the Moore case and the hypothetical straightforward living related donor, unpaid donor case, such as to render the two cases, hypothetically at least, dissimilar to the point that there would be no obvious precedent in law as result of the Moore case?

*Dickens:* Yes, they are dissimilar, but they are not incompatible. If you take the reasoning that the Court gave for deciding Moore the way they did, in particular public benefit in advance with the medical research not being obstructed by property interests, if one could show that property interests in donors, to achieve their purposes, would advance transplantation therapy, then the Court presumably would be willing to find a property interest. It is a very instrumental judgment in that the Court begins with deciding what it wants, that is, that research will be facilitated and they decide accordingly.

If they decide that transplantation ought to be facilitated, then they would be able to find property interests to serve that goal.

*Opelz:* Another question by Robert Sells to Raimund Margreiter: When a patient who has purposely swallowed a lethal dose of paracetamol is referred to you for transplantation, you inquire about the desire to survive before operation. How does this suicide etiology of such a case affect the priority on your urgent waiting list?

*Margreiter:* It's a very tricky question. Actually we don't have this drug in our country, so we won't be faced with this problem. But in all seriousness, as far as I know, these patients are treated with all methods I can think of such as charcoal absorption and the different methods of dialysis. If we are prepared to do everything to save their lives, why shouldn't we exclude them from transplantation? Personally, I have never been faced with this kind of problem, but I probably would accept him or her for highly urgent transplantation.

*Opelz:* Does that satisfy you? He may want to die.

*Sells:* It doesn't satisfy me, because you don't have the experience, and I wonder if anybody in this room does. I think it is an important issue.

*Margreiter:* It certainly is, but as you are aware, Roger Williams just treats these patients, and does really everything that you could think of to save their lives. What is the difference between this conservative kind of treatment and surgical treatment? I think if we accept them for this kind of treatment, we have to accept them also for surgical treatment.

*Sells:* Presumably, though, you would accept the patient only if he or she wanted to survive in that lucid period after having recovered. Presumably, you would ask the patient whether he or she wanted to be treated. Then, of course, if she said yes, you would go ahead and give the liver.

But I suppose, the second question is more important and that is: You have two patients, one attempted suicide and the other has hepatic necrosis from acute fulminant hepatitis, and you have one liver. If there are no other distinguishing features of either situation which allow you to allocate the organ preferentially to the one, what sort of decision would you make? Will the etiology of this woman's disease affect your decision making?

*Margreiter:* It's probably merely a theoretical question. To be honest, I probably would split the liver.

*Opelz:* Did you have a comment, Dr. Albrechtsen?

*Albrechtsen:* Yes, we have actually treated one such patient in Oslo, but that was in vain, she died. So we didn't get the problem Dr. Sells was alluding to afterwards, unfortunately.

*Opelz:* Perhaps we could then move on to the allocation questions. One actually was to Prof. Klinkmann by Dr. White from Sheffield: Is the failure to refer patients for a transplantation in order to maximize profit from dialysis ethically equivalent to failing to treat a remediable cause of renal failure, for example, obstructive uropathy, before chronic renal failure is established?

*Klinkmann:* I don't think I am in a position to answer this question and I am doubtful if anybody else would feel in the position to answer this question, because the basic failure, if there is a failure of referral from dialysis centers to transplantation, is still very questionable.

After our session yesterday I basically do have the feeling that this is a complicated question which at the present time as a nephrologist I would rather tend to answer by saying that, at least consciously, there is no clear-cut available reason to withhold sending patients to transplantation at the present time.

I have to say, however, that probably starting such a dialogue as we did yesterday, everything did not come onto the table, and the basic discussion is starting, so maybe many questions are being withheld at this time.

*Dossetor:* I would like to comment. I think there is a big difference between the two patients. In the second patient that your question described, there is negligence in my view. In the first patient there is a difference of opinion. There are a number of reasons why people fail to see the advantages of transplantation in this phenomenon of trapping, and some of them can be held with quite ethical conviction, even though I think they are wrong in facts, personally.

*Klinkmann:* I think it would be fair just to mention the discussion which was brought forward yesterday by a colleague from Portugal. He clearly stated that as a dialysis physician at the present time with the quality of transplantation available in Portugal and the difference in quality in dialysis, at the present time he would feel it rather unethical to submit a patient to transplantation, because of the lack of quality and the very distinct difference in life expectancy between transplantation and dialysis in a given region or in a given area. So this may also, of course, influence the decision which has to be taken by the local physician.

*Colleague from Portugal:* If I am allowed to clarify the point, as it was I who yesterday made that point. The problem is that with hemodialysis we can offer a patient a very high quality of duration of life. And when I transplant a young patient in the first year, there is a higher chance of him dying from complications than from hemodialysis. We compared our survival curves in patients I had on the waiting list for transplantation in hemodialysis and transplantation. As we have very long waiting times for transplantation I could make the follow-up: When using azathioprine and prednisolone as the immunosuppressive treatment, clearly we had a higher survival in patients on hemodialysis than in transplantation. With cyclosporine, the results are quite similar, but they are still better for hemodialysis.

*White:* I asked the original question. I must say that having attended the session on Tuesday afternoon, I was slightly shocked at the allegation that seemed to be made, perhaps not explicitly, that people were failing to refer patients for transplantation, because there was profit to be made out of dialysis.

But I want to come back to what Prof. Dossetor has said: If we accept that there are benefits in transplantation, then surely it is just as negligent to fail to refer people to transplantation, who would get those benefits potentially, as it is not to treat their obstructive uropathy.

*Dossetor:* You are throwing out a challenge, and I think it's a fair one.

I tried quite hard to find evidence in the literature that goes back to the beginning of chronic renal failure and tries to make some allowance for dialysis time prior to transplant time, ans shows unequivocal statistical evidence that transplant was better than dialysis in longevity, and there isn't any; at least I couldn't find any data. So it is possible to defend the point of view that dialysis results are better, particularly in an experienced center and particularly if the neighboring center, as in the case of Forensa, may not be that accommodating, right? I mean, it's conceivable, if that's the case then, to hold that point of view is defensible.

Where the case breaks down is if you throw in the factor of overall cost and stop to try and look at quality of life issues, quite apart from personal income by physicians, which is the part that we don't talk about much.

*Opelz:* I think we should go on – yes, Dr. Abouna.

*Abouna:* I find this a little bit contradictory, Dr. Dossetor, because you pleased me today when you were saying in your excellent address today that you felt personally that the percentage of patients on dialysis to be referred for transplantation was so inadequate and it should be over 50 %.

Now, in order to make such an important statement which I agree with 100 %, you must have a reason for it, and the reason must be that transplantation is better than being on hemodialysis. What he is asking you is extremely important, namely if it is *better,* because you said you think that 50 % or more should be referred – rather than the 25 % in Europe and 15 % in the United States $\frac{1}{m}$ then it is negligent.

*Dossetor:* It's not quite as inconsistent as you describe. What I believe is that the majority, over 50 %, should have it fully explained to them so they have the option of transplantation. Some will still elect to stay with dialysis. Others will go with the transplant because of its increased quality, less TDM, and they may not be concerned about costs. But I would challenge anybody to quote the data that unequivocally prove that dialysis is inferior in longevity to transplant.

*Abouna:* Well, it is inferior in two groups of patients, and this has been proven: firstly, in diabetic patients, and secondly, in recipients of a living related donor transplant.

*Dossetor:* Oh, I'm not denying that, but this is still not the major group of patients you are referring to.

*Michielsen:* One short comment on what Dr. Dossetor just said. I think that we must take into account that after 10 years of dialysis, at least 50 % of the patients develop amyloidosis, which is very crippling; the percentage rises to 100 % after 20 years of dialysis. At this moment, if we take all the patients we have had, all the first grafts show a 50 % graft survival at 10 years. So I think there are indications that, at least for these cohorts of patients, the future between 10 and 20 years will be much more comfortable than with dialysis.

But the other point I would like to comment on is that I was astonished to hear that there was no evidence that people could get trapped on dialysis for some reason or another. I think the evidence I presented 2 days ago was quite clear. If you compare both things, with regard to what happens within the Eurotransplant area? For example, in Belgium, the Netherlands, Germany, and Austria, there is nearly the same incidence of end-stage renal disease per million inhabitants every year. Approximately the same number, of patients per million inhabitants are put on the waiting list in Austria, in Germany, and in the Netherlands, but in Belgium this number of residents is only half. So, clearly half the number of patients are trapped on dialysis. The reason why? That's another problem.

*Gäbel:* I would like to comment on the statement that something like 50 % of the dialysis population should actually be on the waiting list for renal transplantation. I think that if you state that, you should have a look at the dialysis population, and that is what we have been doing in Sweden actually.

We have a very active program in Sweden concerning renal transplantation. It couldn't be said about Sweden that we have patients trapped in dialysis because there is no cost benefit in having patients on dialysis in Sweden, since it's all socialized.

Now, 1900 patients in Sweden are living with a functioning allograft. There are 1500 patients on dialysis, 400 of those are on the waiting list for renal transplantation. If we then look at the rest of the patients: 13 % of those patients did not want to have a renal allograft; 35 % of the patients were older than 70 years of age, and, I think, something like 60 % were 60 years or older. I don't think that some of those patients would actually benefit from renal transplantation. I don't think they should be on the waiting list. In order to get better treatment, I think they should be on dialysis.

*Sells:* I have a reference for Dr. Dossetor. I was just searching my data base, and I think that is valid and robust. There is a report by Dr. DuToit from the South African Dialysis and Transplantation Registry which is rather like the EDTA Registry.

The data are really quite unequivocal: The 5-year patient survival rate on dialysis in all racial groups is between 20 % and 25 %. The 5-year patient survival rate in transplantation is of the order of 65 % – 70 %. I guess you probably know these data better than I do, Dr. Opelz.

*Opelz:* Yes, but those data would not look the same here.

*Sells:* Of course not. But it is a particular context in which the answer is given, and the superiority and utility of transplantation in improving mortality rates is very strongly demonstrated, and, therefore, you could argue that, in that particular context, the arguments which have been going back and forth on your point are valid.

*Albrechtsen:* I think there have been some numbers given during this meeting for the mortality on the waiting list. In the United States, it was said that 2000 died every year on the waiting list. If the waiting list is as far as I remember in the order of 15 000 or 20 000, – isn't that correct? – that means the mortality during a year then is at least 10 %. So much for that. And then, some more data: For patients above the age of 60 years, it is known that the mortality in dialysis is much higher if you do not select the patients. In Minnesota, at least in the early 1980s it was in the order of 50 % in the first year. We have in Norway about the same number for unselected patients older than 60 years. I'm sorry, but those are the facts, at least in the early 1980s.

Finally, and that's my most important point, there is an ethical problem here: When you use public funds for health services, you are also making an allocation on health resources. By transplanting that patient you will save at least 150 000 American dollars over a 5-year period. The alternative is dialysis. In other words: You are depriving another patient or another group of patients of that health money from public budgets. That creates a tremendous moral dilemma for the profession, at least in the Scandinavian countries.

*White:* Can I just make one very quick final point to Dr. Dossetor: Would you accept that it is negligent not to give people the option of going on a transplant list and obiously providing them with all the information regarding outcome and so on?

*Dossetor:* I would!

*Michielsen:* Well I would like to comment on the data presented by Dr. Gäbel from Sweden and the possible number of people who could be transplanted.

Of course, if you are under very active transplant activity, very few of the remaining patients from dialysis could be transplanted. But the figure of 50 % belongs to the initial patients. With regard to the new patients admitted every year for treatment of end-stage renal disease; 50 % of those are candidates for transplantation.

*Opelz:* Perhaps we could close this section and move on to something else. I would like to raise a question about something that I have found rather confusing.

I think Dr. Veatch and Dr. Dossetor have argued against the purely utilitarian view that some of us, I guess, have, namely the success rate, the prediction of outcome, is the prime motivating factor for allocation of organs. I think you are saying that should not be the case, that these other things should weigh more than the success prediction. Yet, in the same session here, we have heard from Dr. Margreiter that he would give preference to liver transplant recipients that have the best chance of success. We have heard from the Cambridge group that retransplantation was perhaps not such a good idea, based on the data that were shown by the group.

And yet, if you had a committee of housewives and teachers, they probably would decide that the organs should go into the retransplant patients. How do we reconcile these various viewpoints? Perhaps Dr. Dossetor could comment on that:

*Dossetor:* In other words medical utility as the number one criterion in all cases, right?

*Opelz:* Yes.

*Dossetor:* I think, the answer is no. I mean, medical utilities are a very important criterion. But to make this the absolute and to plug it into the computer and to leave it there for a few years while someone is on the waiting list is too mechanical and denies other values that are important.

*Opelz:* Well, a committee of lay people probably would favor the cancer patients that Dr. Margreiter says are not good candidates for liver transplantatiion. Everyone feels sorry for them and the committee may well decide that these should be the patients who should get those livers.

*Dossetor:* Well, first of all it's a decision made without informed consent or informed choice. You have to take what the patient wants into consideration, I would have thougt. The patient may see transplantation not as a glorious light at the end of the tunnel of despair. And we don't know that. Then there are other factors, surely, personal factors, family factors, transport, distance from center. I would have thought there are many factors that a patient would take into account apart from the medical prognostic assessment, which, after all as we all know, is uncertain. We practise medicine in a sea of uncertainty.

*Opelz:* What is the one thing that we can work on with scientific methods and get a fairly for us at least conclusive answer to? These other things are much more difficult to even weigh against.

*Dossetor:* Isn't that the art of the game?

*Opelz:* That leads on to several questions here that were raised about who should make a decision about allocation. If it is not the medical profession, who should it be? Several people here made the argument that the medical profession is familiar with the situation and is trained to make these decisions and to evaluate the situations. And yet, here we hear, that a decision should be made by people not in the medical field. Again, it's like a jury selection or something. Is that a reasonable approach? Do we all agree with that, because I would not agree with that!

*Klövekorn:* As a transplant surgeon I completely disagree, because as long as the surgeon is responsible for the success or failure of this procedure, he should also be involved in the allocation. Who takes the responsibility, if anyone else makes the decision out of a panel? Dr. Veatch said the medical profession shouldn't do it, but he didn't give an answer on who should do it, and who should be responsible in the end.

*Opelz:* I agree.

*Dossetor:* I will answer for Dr. Veatch by saying that I think he was provoking us by making an extreme statement. What he is trying to say is that when a surgeon has to transplant in a kidney he should also try to evaluate all these other issues. This is an assumption that one shouldn't continue to make without being challenged. I would see his answer being: a social worker, a nurse, a member of the community, a representative of the dialysis group, a representative of a previously transplanted group, or a representative of a previously failed transplant group should be responsible. That doesn't mean that this group would have to suddenly meet in the middle of the night, but Dr. Veatch is, I think, referring to how you establish an allocative policy. I think he would also say that a group like that, lawyers and health care economists and statisticians and so on, were present when a policy was decided upon, and perhaps should be present when a policy of UNOS is decided upon. But obviously physician experts, e.g., surgeons, have to be there.

*N.N.:* I offer a distinction which migth be of some use here. It seems to me that there are two kinds of allocation decisions that we haven't clearly enough distinguished. One kind of decision is the decision about what general criteria will we use, will we weigh? Those include medical success and all the various factors that come under medical success, like HLA match, negative cross-match, decisions about the ability of a patient to comply with treatment, or the absence of active infection or neoplastic disease. All of those things are presumably designed to increase the chances of medical success of survival of the patient.

We also have another set of criteria which I place under that category but under a category of something like increasing the equity of access to an organ. These include, of course, time on the waiting list, and medical urgency, because urgency is a factor which might actually decrease the chances of success. The idea is that we want to give this patient a last chance at access to an organ, and, of course, also a degree of presensitization. We want to give that patient a little bit of an extra chance because the chances of finding a compatible organ are so small.

Those are all more general factors which involve balancing the desire for utility with the desire for equity or equal access. It seems that what Dr. Veatch was saying is that doctors have no greater expertise in balancing those general value issues than do other people in society. It ought, therefore, to be a social choice and not the choice of individual physicians.

Now, I think what Dr. Veatch failed to point out is that supposing those general criteria become established, the UNOS criteria, for example, somebody must apply those criteria in individual situations and decide whether a particular patient can comply with immunosuppressive therapy, for example, or whether there are any other reasons why a particular patient may or may not be a candidate. I believe physicians do have an obvious, natural, unique role in making those kinds of individual decisions. Who is to become a candidate for transplantation in their program, however? We have to allow physicians some discretion in making those individual choices, because society cannot make those choices for individual programs.

That distinction I think is an important one. I think Dr. Veatch overstated his case by not drawing attention to the fact that physicians must make individual decisions, at least in that one area of deciding of who should be a candidate.

*Dickens:* I think the point has been correctly put that there are competing theories. If we consider organs to be a medical resource, then clearly they would have to be allocated by medical criteria. If we consider them to be a social resource, then the social criteria are in the balance.

We are thinking of the positive criteria, but in fact a number of negative criteria are already legislated, and very often defined in national laws, not just ordinary laws, but national constitutions or bill of rights. Of course we also have the whole spectrum of international human rights conventions. These provide for nondiscrimination on grounds of age, physical or mental disability, sex, race, and so forth.

So it may be that doctors can say that one population of potential recipients have a 10 % survival chance after 3 years, another group may have an 80 % survival chance. One may want to calibrate that. We have what are sometimes called quality-adjusted life years, but once medicine has worked out the different arts, everyone is entitled to an equal chance to the best opportunity they have.

By social justice criteria, no one could say that one cannot discriminate upon the number of the grounds that have been discussed. These grounds may be *medically* significant, but that supposes that it is a *medical* decision. If we say that it isn't, but rather that these organs are a social resource to be allocated in accordance with the social value system, then one can see that physicians are not especially privileged to operate that system.

*Michielsen:* I think there are two different aspects of allocation. One is the individual allocation to select individual patients, which is in my opinion a medical decision. But there is another aspect which is a macro-problem. If some surgeons decided to accept a nonresident on their waiting list to the extent that in the end half of the waiting list of the country consisting of nonresidents, I think that this is going beyond the responsibility of the individual doctor. This is a responsibility of the community, which has to decide to accept or not to accept such a situation. In America, they claim that 10% nonresidents on the waiting list is acceptable, this is a decision that cannot be made by the individual surgeons who profit from it, but this decision must be made by the community.

*Opelz:* How has that 10% foreign residents decision been made? Does anyone know here?

*Dossetor:* I think it was made by Dr. Olga Jonasson who was chair woman of a committee that advised on policy for organ sharing.

*Abouna:* Dr. Opelz, I would like to hear your own opinion about the practical aspect which we heard today in an excellent abstract from an English group and another one from a German group, namely that allocation should be done on the basis of age rather than HLA matching. Does this concept constitute discrimination against age or anything like that? If I could have your view about this?

*Opelz:* I enjoyed those abstracts myself and I knew about them. I've talked to both of the speakers before. I have some problems with the subject.

Now, first of all I have a problem inasmuch as it was implied that allocation should be done according to age instead of according to HLA matching. I don't think either of the speakers has the data to separate the two or to compare the two because the numbers are too small for that.

My own reservation to the age-matching effect would be based on the fact that the old patient who receives a kidney from an old donor is really worse off. I think those two studies have more or less shown the same thing. I also cannot quite see why the old patient should get the kidney that is least likely to have a longer term successful outcome, unless you argue that these patients are going to die soon and, therefore, it doesn't matter. Is that correct, Dr. Donnelly?

*Donnelly:* Thanks for the opportunity to reply to that. I think it certainly can be argued that my paper included small numbers. But I find it hard to argue the same case against the 6000 patients from Eurotransplant who were analyzed by the same method and where age difference was shown to be a highly significant risk factor. Then, they did give you the opportunity more than 18 months ago to see if the same stratification of the collaborate transplant data could be shown and again, I am waiting reply on that score.

If we look at the relative values of HLA matching, certainly the DR locus matters, and the Eurotransplant data were important. I think it is hard, however, in other centres to show whether A- or B-matching matters to any great degree, yet we still look for six antigen matches. Certainly DR may matter, but why do we struggle sending kidneys around the world for six antigen units, when we know that 2 DR is perhaps the main factor.

*Opelz:* That's not what we are debating in here. The question here is whether an old patient should get a kidney from an old donor. This is what you are advocating, and the predictable outcome is that this is the worst possible thing you can do to that patient. We all know that if the patient gets a kidney from a young donor, he will do better.

*Donnelly:* Do we really believe that giving a 70-year-old donor kidney to a 20-year-old recipient is just as ethical, given that we know from adequate physiological studies that there isn't any reserve in that kidney. When you allow for the facts of transplant effect itself, acute tubular necrosis, cyclosporine, toxicity, rejection episodes, etc., you can't really expect that kidney to last another 70 years.

*Opelz:* I agree. You would like to transplant a young boy with a young kidney. So, what are you going to do with the old donor?

*Donnelly:* Give them old recipients!

*Opelz:* I think it said in the data that the result was very poor.

*Donnelly:* But not stratified.

*Persijn:* There is another exception to that rule, as Jane Thorogood analyzed, that is category of very young patients.

It is well known that the very young patients benefit most from an adult kidney.

*Donnelly:* I have no argument with that. According to the GFR data presented, the decline starts from adulthood, from 20 – 30 years onwards, once renal function declines. You would have to say that this age-matching effect is only relevant to adults.

*Persijn:* I don't want to take that position. I think ageless matching, matching for HLA-A, -B, or -DR antigens is still more important than age matching.

*Opelz:* Let me just clarify: You are advocating that a 60-year-old or a 70-year-old patient should receive a kidney from a 70-year old donor?

*Donnelly:* No, I am saying that the donor should be no more 5 years older than the recipient.

*Opelz:* I do not agree with that. Let's give Dr. Niebel a chance.

*Niebel:* It's another problem whether a young recipient should get a kidney from an old donor. I would like to mention that our data are retrospectively created, perhaps Eurotransplant should be encouraged to do investigations in a similar way.

*Sells:* May we just go back to Dr. Veatch's point about whether medical decisions, both micro- and macrodecisions really should be responsive to the requirements of the society. I don't think that's an extreme view, I think it is a principle which we should bear in mind all the time, particularly, of course, as we move more and more into cost containment in health services. There is no country which can avoid cost containment; every health budget is not capped. We are forced to at least think of this major consideration, even if we haven't done it in the past.

But if we look at the way in which transplantation ethics, transplant law perhaps, has evolved, as usual the technology has moved forward and the debates have boiled up in its wake.

I think it is tremendously reassuring that intuitive mechanism involved in the decisions, which if you like the transplant fraternity has come to, about these crucial issues, many of which have been dissected out for the first time in the last year or the last 18 months, eventually turned out to be remarkably acceptable. What does Dr. Veatch mean by society expressing a view? Society has to be able to express a view in order for us as a profession to understand it and to decide how far we can go towards it and following that society would like us to do so.

I think the answer is that we have specialists here, and it wasn't really until last year that we actually got qualified specialists who had a broad base in that speciality of law, law philosophy and ethics.

Each individual could come and bring his task to bear, focus very tightly on the issues which *we* as transplant surgeons and physicians have thrown up in the wake of our technology. I think it's very interesting, but also rather worrying, that our science/art has been in existence for 30 years but it was only in 1989 that we had the first congress on transplantation ethics. It's men like Dr. Dossetor and Dr. Stiller who have actually spent a lot of time trying to recruit that intellectual energy from the specialists.

I think it's quite right for Dr. Veatch to say that the profession must be responsive to the requirements of society, but it is actually an irritating and practical problem, isn't it? It's a method of logical inadequacy of society that has not until very recently been able to put the language at our disposal, whereby we can start to communicate and understand the requirements of society. Maybe we are going to move forward now. I don't know.

*Opelz:* Yes, but what people reacted to, and perhaps was not meant, was that it sounded as if the medical profession who had made all the decisions would now be excluded. That was perhaps not the intention. The medical profession would be part of the decision-making process, but others would be involved. That, I think, would be quite acceptable to everyone here.

*Radcliffe-Richards:* I am just joining the long queue of people speaking on behalf of Prof. Veatch in his absence. I think it's often misleading to state the question as who is going to decide. It very often happens in ordinary discourse, and it is very misleading. Whatever answer you give, somebody is going to object. The question is really, what kind of expertise is required to make a particular kind of decision? The trouble with the medical profession is that it has traditionally been supposed to have two kinds of expertise: one is the technical knowledge to produce a certain kind of result and the other is the constraints by such things as the Hippocratic oath, which, as we found for all kinds of reasons, leads to problems now medicine has advanced so far.

To the outsider who thinks about these matters it seems that medicine is a training in a particular area of science. A medical training gives you knowledge about certain causes and defects and about how things work. Like any other such training this gives you the power to bring about certain effects. But the knowledge of how to bring about certain effects doesn't in the least tell you which effect should be brought about. That's an entirely different question, just as being a nuclear physicist doesn't tell you whether it's a good thing to make the bomb, or not. I think Prof. Veatch's point is simply that training in medicine does not constitute training in how to use medicine. This is an entirely separate set of questions, even though, of course, in practice, the medical practicioners are going to have to make most of the decisions on the ground.

It, nevertheless, has to be recognized that this doesn't as such constitute expertise in how to use the knowledge. I think that's the sort of point he was making.

*Schoeppe:* If we think about allocation and as long as we presume that we want to treat all uremic patients properly, be it through dialysis or transplantation, and are then confronted with a shortage of transplantable organs, why does the impetus of the ethicists go in the direction of allocation on medical grounds and questioning the competence of the doctors.

I disagree really with withdrawing medical reasons for allocation, and I know what I am speaking about, because I have to do it on both sides.

Why is this impetus not directed at society and reducing the shortage of transplantable organs? This is in some way parallel to the situation we have in Germany.

I can treat all the patients I can treat, because I don't have any more available organs. I agree with Dr. Michielsen and the Munich surgeon, we have to make these decisions on medical grounds, at present; maybe science will change this and I look to society for a solution. This is a real challenge. What will happen on the basis of HLA when according to Opelz' theory, the 11 % expand to, say, about 20 % or 25 %?

If we don't comply with the HLA compatibility rule, then it would create excess costs for society and transplants would be lost earlier than they should be according to the results of the compatibility tests.

The prognosis involves a tremendous economic impact, and this has to be thought over. The second problem is: What happens to the patients? I have heard no comment on this. What happens to the patients who lose their transplants?

*Opelz:* I think we have to stop the discussion here; we have exhausted most of the issues. Thank you very much.

# *VI. New Frontiers in Organ Replacement Therapy*

# Transplantation of Fetal Dopamine-Synthesizing Cells: Experiment or Therapy of Parkinson's Disease?*

A. Kupsch[1,3], H. Sauer[1,2], and W. H. Oertel[3]

## Introduction

The neuronal transplantation technique represents a potential therapeutic concept against a number of neurodegenerative disorders, e.g., Parkinson's disease (PD; Lindvall 1989; Oertel and Kupsch 1990), Alzheimer's disease (Low et al. 1982; Gage et al. 1984; Björklund and Gage 1987), Huntington's disease (Wictorin et al. 1988; Deckel et al. 1983, 1986; Isacson et al. 1984, 1986), seizures (Barry et al. 1987; Lindvall et al. 1988), and cerebellar or other neurological disorders (for reviews see Lindvall 1989; Olson 1988). Treatments for these disabling neurological disorders are hardly available. As an exception, effective drug therapy is known for PD, especially in its early stages. However, in more advanced stages of PD, antiparkinsonian drugs can be accompanied by serious side effects (see "Drug Therapy" below), and the duration of their beneficial effects becomes shorter. Additionally, no proven treatment has been developed to halt the progression of PD.

PD and relevant animal models are suitable for testing the potential benefits of neuronal cell transplantation, since the lesion in PD predominantly relates to one neurotransmitter system, the dopaminergic nigrostriatal pathway. If it is not possible to ameliorate or even replace the relatively restricted, striatal dopamine deficiency in PD by the transplantation of dopamine synthesizing cells, it will be unlikely that the transplantation technique may be successfully applied to other neurodegenerative disorders, like Alzheimer's disease. In these disorders, the lesions are usually more general and not as restricted as in PD (Lindvall 1989; Quinn et al. 1989).

*Supported by DFG/Oe 95 3-1, 3-2, 4-1, 4-2, German Parkinson Foundation (dPV e.V.) and the German Federal Ministry of Research and Technology (BMFT).

[1]Institute of Physiology, Ludwig-Maximilians-University Munich, Pettenkoferstr. 12, 8000 München 2, FRG.

[2]Institute of Histology, University of Lund, 5 Biskopgatan, 22362 Lund, Sweden.

[3]Department of Neurology, Klinikum Großhadern, Ludwig-Maximilians-University Munich, Marchioninistr. 15, 8000 München 70, FRG.

W. Land, J. B. Dossetor (Eds.)
Organ Replacement Therapy:
Ethics, Justice and Commerce

The following article will summarize the experimental and clinical results of transplantation studies in PD and related animal models. Open neurobiological and methodological questions will be discussed.

## Parkinson's Disease

### Prevalence and Pathology

PD reaches a prevalence of approximately 100/100000 inhabitants and is one of the most commonly encountered neurological disorders, affecting 1 % of the population over 60 years old (for reviews see Tanner 1989). The classical symptoms of PD comprise the triad bradykinesia, rigidity, and resting tremor. The pathoanatomical correlate is an extensive degeneration of melanin-containing, dopaminergic neurons in the pars compacta of the substantia nigra and the medially located ventral tegmental area in the mesencephalon. These neurons innervate the corpus striatum (caudate nucleus, putamen, and the more ventrally located nucleus accumbens). Other brain regions with partly less severe pathoanatomical findings include the noradrenergic locus coeruleus, whose neurons also contain melanin, the pigmented dorsal motor nucleus of the vagal nerve (Forno 1982), the serotonergic raphe nuclei, the substantia innominata, the basal nucleus of Meynert, posterolateral regions of the hypothalamus, and circumscribed parts of the spinal cord and sympathetic ganglia (for reviews see Marsden 1983; Kopin and Markey 1988).

Biochemically, a dopamine deficit is observed in the dorsal striatum (caudate nucleus and putamen), reflecting the degeneration of the nigrostriatal projection. This dopamine depletion must reach more than 70 %, for the cardinal PD symptoms to be observed (Bernheimer et al. 1973). Typically, the putamen is more severely affected by the dopamine deficit than the caudate nucleus (Bernheimer et al. 1973; Kish et al. 1988). While the disease progresses, a decreased catecholamine content is also found in other structures like the nucleus accumbens (dopamine) and locus coeruleus (noradrenaline). Additionally, biochemical alterations of other neurotransmitter and neuropeptide systems have been described (Hornykiewicz and Kish 1987; Agid et al. 1989).

### Drug Therapy

In the early 1960s, the antiparkinsonian activity of L-dopa was discovered (Birkmayer and Hornykiewicz 1961; Barbeau 1961). Initially, the dopamine deficit of PD patients may be satisfactorily treated by L-dopa. However, after approximately 3–7 years of continued L-dopa monotherapy, the majority of the patients suffer from decreased efficacy of L-dopa (e.g., "end-of-dose-akinesia"). At the same time, L-dopa therapy may be accompanied by severe side effects such as dyskinesias and hallucinations. Combination of L-dopa with dopamine agonists (Rinne 1987, 1989a) or inhibitors of the catecholamine catabolizing enzyme monoamino oxidase-B (MAO-B; Rinne, 1989b) may reduce the severity of these side effects. Recently, retrospective (Birkmayer et al. 1985) and prospective studies (Tetrud and Langston 1989; Parkinson Study Group 1989a,b) have suggested that early drug therapy with MAO-B inhibitors may slow down the progression of PD, however, definite proof of this hypothesis is still lacking.

It is evident that the progress of the antiparkinsonian drug therapy has improved the long-term prognosis of PD patients within the last 20 years. The still existing therapeutic problems, however, which have only been touched in this context, underscore the importance of searching for alternative therapies.

## Basic Science: Transplantation

### Transplantation Studies: 6-OHDA Animal Model

Basic insights of the neuronal transplantation research originate from animal models of PD. Unilateral intracerebral injection of the neurotoxin 6-hydroxydopamine (6-OHDA) into the median forebrain bundle induces a striatal catecholamine deficit in animals (Ungerstedt and Arbuthnott 1970; Figs. 1, 2). Lesioned animals display a spontaneous turning behavior to the lesioned hemisphere, which relies on the dominance of the nonlesioned, contralateral brain side. This abnormal rotation behavior (Fig. 1) may be enhanced by systemic application of catecholamine releasing substances, for instance amphetamine, and can be reliably quantified in especially designed automatized rotation boxes. The severity of the rotational behavior corresponds to the striatal dopamine deficit and allows assessment of the efficacy of dopaminergic neuronal transplants (Björklund and Stenevi 1979; Perlow et al. 1979; Freed et al. 1980): the abnormal rotation of 6-OHDA-treated animals may be reversed by intrastriatal grafting of dopamine-synthesizing cells. Experimental experience mainly concerns two different grafting techniques into the striatum: autologous adrenal medulla on the one hand and homologous fetal ventral mesencephalon on the other hand. The latter contains the precursor cells for the substantia nigra and the ventral tegmental area. Experimental findings clearly favor the fetal tissue (for reviews see Lindvall 1989; Quinn et al. 1989). In contrast to adrenal medulla, fetal mesencephalic cells may permanently survive in the striatum as well as reverse an abnormal, 6-OHDA-induced rotational behaviour in rodents. Some prerequisites for a successful neuronal transplantation according to the experimental findings in the rodent model may be summarized as follows (for reviews see Lindvall 1989; Quinn et al. 1989):

1. Unlike peripheral tissue, e.g., adrenal medulla, fetal CNS neurons survive transplantation into the adult host brain only at an early gestational age,

when neurite outgrowth is maximal and extensive synaptic connections have not yet been formed (Das et al. 1980; Quinn et al. 1989). The age of the host seems to be less important (Hallas et al. 1980; Gage and Björklund 1986).

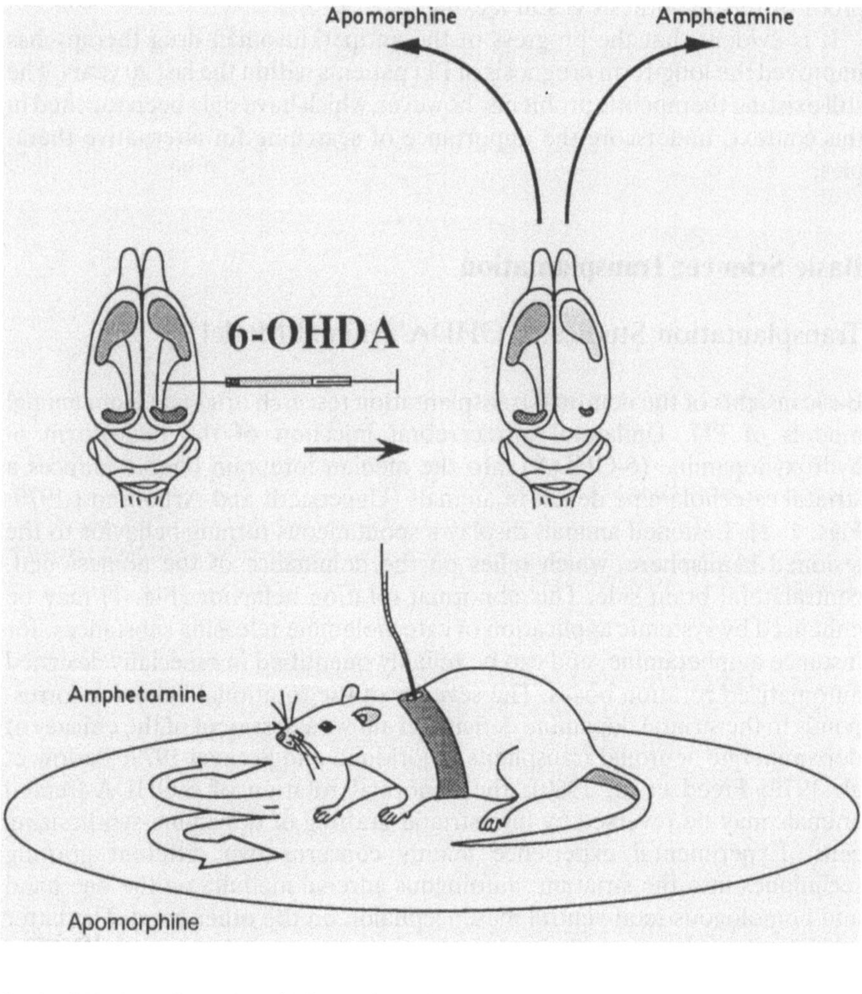


**Fig. 1.** 6-Hydroxydopamine (6-OHDA) model of the rodent. Unilateral, intracerebral injection of the neurotoxin 6-OHDA into the median forebrain bundle induces a spontaneous, slight rotational behavior to the ipsilateral side of the 6-OHDA-lesioned hemisphere that may be enhanced and quantified by systemic application of the indirect catecholaminergic agonist amphetamine. In contrast, the systemic application of the direct dopaminergic ($D_1$/$D_2$)-receptor agonist apomorphine induces a contralateral rotation that is related to compensatory, increased dopamine receptor activity in the lesioned striatum. The rotational behaviour may be assessed and quantified (rotation/time interval) in specially designed rotation boxes both prior to and after transplantation of neural tissues, thus permitting to investigate behavioral effects of grafted tissue

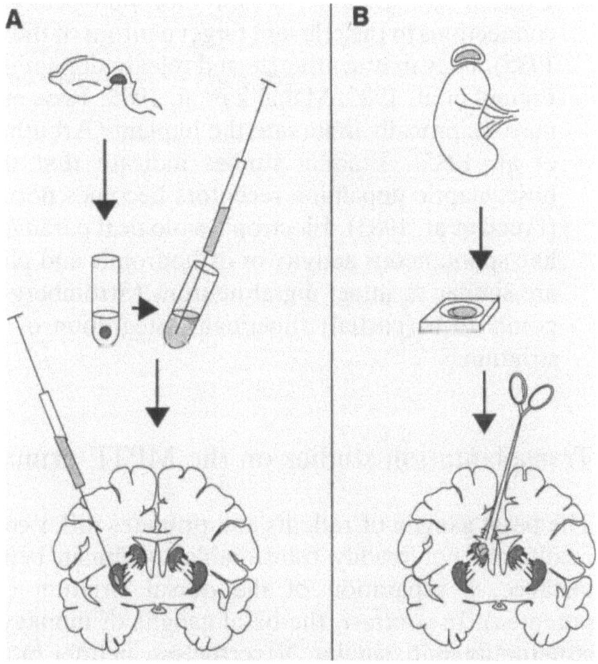


**Fig. 2 A,B** Transplantation techniques. Synoptic diagram on currently applied different grafting techniques in PD. **A** Stereotactic implantation of cell suspensions, which have been prepared from fetal mesencephalon. **B** Transcallosal approach to the caput nuclei caudati and implantation of autologous adrenal tissue fragments into a previously prepared cavity

2. The blood supply of the implant by the surrounding host tissue is sufficient when transplanting cell suspensions or tissue fragments (Björklund et al. 1983; Schmidt et al. 1981). Solid transplants however seem to survive better in ventricular or artificially vascularized environments (Quinn et al. 1989).
3. The immunologically privileged status of the brain (Mason et al. 1986) allows the transplantation of tissues that do not share identical properties of the two major histocompatibility antigen classes with the host. However, immunosuppressive treatment is necessary in cross-species transplants to prevent graft rejection (Brundin et al. 1985/1988; for review see Widner and Brundin 1988).
4. Transplanted cells may reverse an abnormal, 6-OHDA-induced sensory-motor behavioral deficit of rodents that follows systemic application of dopaminergic agonists (Björklund and Stenevi 1979; Björklund et al. 1980; Dunnett et al. 1981a, 1983; Perlow et al. 1979). The transplant-induced behavioral compensation correlates with the number of the surviving neurons and the location of the transplant in the striatum (Dunnett et al. 1981a,b)

5. Grafted cells are able to form morphologically normal looking synaptic connections to the relevant target neurons of the host brain (Mahalik et al. 1985). They may synthetize and release dopamine (Björklund et al. 1983; Freund et al. 1985; Mahalik et al. 1985; Rose et al. 1985). Host neurons may reciprocally innervate the implant (Arbuthnott et al. 1985; Mahalik et al. 1985). Binding studies indicate that the increased density of postsynaptic dopamine receptors becomes normal after transplantation (Freed et al. 1983). Electrophysiological parameters of transplanted cells like spontaneous activity or orthodromic and pharmacological responses are similar to intact nigral neurons (Strömberg et al. 1985). These data points to a (partial) functional integration of the grafts into the host striatum.

## Transplantation studies on the MPTP primate model

The basal ganglia of rodents and primates differ considerably. Thus, rodent results are not readily transferable to human beings, since rats lack, for instance, a separation of the dorsal striatum (caudate nucleus versus putamen). In contrast, the basal ganglia of monkeys and human beings are structurally quite similar. Nevertheless, neither monkeys nor other animals spontaneously develop PD syndromes.

Only recently, after the discovery of the parkinson-inducing properties of the neurotoxin *N*-methyl-4-phenyl-1,2,3,6-tetrahydropyridine (MPTP; Davis et al. 1979; Langston et al. 1983) was a parkinson model established in monkeys (Burns et al. 1983). MPTP causes a bilateral parkinsonian syndrome in human beings and monkeys that is very similar to PD (for review see Langston 1985). The MPTP primate model may answer certain questions posed by the neuronal transplant research which cannot be answered by the 6-OHDA rat model (Bakay et al. 1985, 1987; Bankiewicz et al. 1988a; Redmond et al. 1986, 1987; Sladek et al. 1986, 1987; Fine et al. 1988). Thus, MPTP-treated monkeys may receive focal implants into the putamen or the caput and/or the corpus nuclei caudati. This approach may clarify the clinically important question, which implantation site should be preferred in PD patients. The bilateral MPTP model also allows assessment of the question, if and to what extent a unilateral implant influences the contralateral, nontransplanted side. However, it should be stressed that the MPTP syndrome is not identical with PD (Hornykiewicz et al. 1989). The dopamine depletion in the MPTP syndrome equally affects both caudate nucleus and putamen, while in PD the dopamine depletion is more pronounced in the putamen than in the caudate. Furthermore, PD is typically progressive; in contrast, MPTP-treated monkeys may spontaneously recover to varying degrees which impede the evaluation of therapeutic transplant effects. Therefore, results from MPTP-treated monkeys should be transferred to the clinical situation with caution. Despite these reservations, it is generally accepted that the MPTP primate model represents the best hitherto available animal model of PD. It may help to unravel numerous open, clinically important questions, which can only be outlined here (for reviews see Lindvall 1989; Quinn et al. 1989; Widner and Brundin 1988).

How long may implanted cells survive? How long do therapeutic effects of the transplants last? How many cells have to be transplanted? What – if any – is the role of nondopaminergic cells that are cotransplanted? How does a bilateral implantation compare with a unilateral implantation? Does immunosuppression improve survival of homologous transplants? And if so, which immunosuppressive drugs should be administered? Is it possible to implant a second graft after graft rejection or other failures of the first operation? Does homologous neural tissue in the CNS stimulate the immune response of the host (Bankiewicz et al. 1990a)? Which cells present antigens in brain grafts? Are the major histocompatibility antigens located on neurons or glial cells? How long does the brain-blood barrier stay open after stereotactic or open implantation techniques (Sanberg et al. 1988)? Does precavitation of the implant site induce release of trophic factors or, alternatively, does it enhance vascularization at the implant site, thus improving nutrition and oxygen supply of the transplanted cells and/or of the remaining dopaminergic host neurons? Does a continued L-dopa therapy influence transplant function? How do transplants "work": is the transient therapeutic effect of adrenal implants related to the replacement of catecholamine-releasing cells or to sprouting of surviving host neurons (see Bohn et al. 1987)? And if the last question is to be answered with "yes", may also nonneuronal tissue stimulate dopaminergic host neurons, as has been implicated for amnion tissue and glial cells that are implanted into the basal ganglia (see Bankiewicz et al. 1989, 1990b)? Which type of tissue (fetal mesencephalon, adrenal medulla, superior cervical ganglion, cell cultures, amnion) should be preferred as transplant? And what is the role of trophic factors in this context? Is it possible to successfully cryopreserve the tissue prior to transplantation, which would allow us to avoid the severe logistic problems when transplanting fetal tissue (Redmond et al. 1987; Robbins et al. 1990; Sauer 1990)? Furthermore, histological and microbiological investigation of the prospective transplant prior to host implantation would be feasible.

To answer these topics, systematic studies on rodents and primates are necessary to develop guidelines for prudent clinical procedures. The challenge of basic research is underlined by contrasting 400 operations on human beings with only 100 comparable interventions in nonhuman primates. This contrast is even more striking considering that studies on monkeys frequently lack controlled conditions and are based on small animal numbers per investigating laboratory (Bakay et al. 1988; Bankiewicz et al. 1988a,b, 1990a,b; Dubach et al. 1988; Fine et al. 1988; Redmond et al. 1986; Sladek et al. 1988; detailed descriptions on studies concerning nonhuman primates are summarized by Quinn et al. 1989; Landau 1990; Oertel and Marsden 1988; Oertel and Kupsch 1990).

## The Clinical Situation: Transplantation

### Transplantation Studies on Humans – Summer 1990

A total of 400 transplantations on PD patients have been reported (Sweden: Lindvall et al. 1987, 1989; England: Hitchcock et al. 1988; USA: Allen et al. 1989; Goetz et al. 1989a,b; Mexico: Madrazo et al. 1987/1988; Cuba and China: Quinn et al. 1989): The number of nonreported interventions probably exceeds this number by more than 100% (Goetz et al. 1989a). The results of these operations have been differently evaluated in August 1989 in Cambridge, England, and in June 1990 in Lund, Sweden, by scientists and clinicians. Most scientists press for further insights from animal and other basic research studies. On the other hand, clinicians are daily confronted with patients and their problems and demands, which explains why clinicians seem to be more prone to enter the clinical field. It was, however, generally agreed that

1. Intensive basic research is indispensable to promote the neuronal transplantation technique as a therapeutic alternative that may be promising for both patients and clinicians.
2. Ethical, liable guidelines have to be elaborated if, when, and how fetal human tissue may be used experimentally (and therapeutically).

#### *Adrenal Medulla*

In 1982, the first transplantations of adrenal catecholaminergic cells were performed on two PD patients in Sweden. Even then findings from animal experiments had favored homologous fetal mesencephalon over adrenal tissue as the implant tissue of choice, since fetal mesencephalon warranted better and longer lasting effects than transplants of adrenal medulla (for review see Lindvall, 1989). However, in order to avoid ethical and immunological problems, it was decided to stereotactically and unilaterally graft adrenal tissue into one caudate nucleus. Six months after the operation no difference between the pre- and postoperative condition was recorded, though initially slight improvements had been observed (Backlund et al. 1985). Only shortly after these operations, Nyberg et al. (1983; see also Bernheimer et al. 1973; Kish et al. 1988) showed that the dopamine depletion in PD is more pronounced in the putamen than in the caudate nucleus and that the putamen seems to be more important for motor function than the caudate nucleus (Alexander et al. 1986). Accordingly, the Swedish investigators implanted autologous adrenal tissue stereotactically and unilaterally into the putamen of two PD patients. However, even this procedure did not result in any enduring improvement of the PD symptoms in these patients (Lindvall et al. 1987).

In April 1987, Madrazo et al. (1987) reported dramatic improvements in two unusually young PD patients after transplantation of autologous adrenal medulla. In contrast to the Swedish workers, the Mexican team had prepared a cavity in the right caudate nucleus, following frontal craniotomy. The adrenal tissue was transcallosally implanted in this cavity, which was located at the ventricular border of the caudate nucleus. In 1989, short preliminary statistics concerning neural grafting on PD patients in Spanish speaking countries were published (Madrazo et al. 1989). The report summarizes data from over 135 cases and contends that one-third of these patients experienced good (> 50 % improvement 6 months postoperatively) and on-fourth of these patients moderate (30 %–50 % improvement 6 months postoperatively) improvements of their PD symptoms.

Following the initial Mexican report many patients, especially in the USA and China, have been operated according to the Mexican technique (Goetz et al. 1989a; see also Goetz et al. 1989b, 1990). In contrast to Madrazo et al. (1987), results of these operations from over 13 neurological centers in the USA and in Canada are discouraging. Not one of the over 61 patients (Goetz et al. 1989a) showed spectacular results comparable to the initial publication (Madrazo et al. 1987). Nevertheless, small and moderate success was noticed, for example, a reduction of symptom severity and slight increases in "ON-time" and related decreases in "OFF-time". These improvements have to be weighed against the considerable operative risks. Six patients died during the study, and at least two of these cases were closely related to the operation. The postoperative complications concerned almost all organ systems, pneumonia, depressions, and hallucinations being the most prominent complications. In total, stereotactical implantations of adrenal medulla under local anesthesia entailed fewer side effects and complications than the transcallosal approach after frontal craniotomy with general anesthesia; corresponding advantages were observed for retroperitoneal adrenalectomy in comparison with the abdominal laparotomy. In the few autopsies carried out up to now, dopaminergic surviving neurons within the implantation region could not be demonstrated (Hurtig et al. 1989; Jankovic et al. 1989; Peterson et al. 1989; for review see Quinn et al. 1989). One reason for the relative inefficacy of autologous adrenal transplants may be a lesion of adrenal medullary tissue itself in PD (Stoddard et al. 1989). Determination of post mortem adrenal catecholamine concentrations revealed a significant decrease in PD patients.

In summary, adrenal transplants in PD patients are associated with a mortality of up to 10 % and postoperative complications in most of the cases. In comparison, the therapeutic effects are not convincing.

### *Fetal Ventral Mesencephalon*

Studies concerning transplantation of fetal mesencephalon in humans are still in a preliminary stage (Hitchcock et al. 1988, 1990; Madrazo et al. 1988; Lindvall et al. 1989). One recent detailed Swedish study gives an account of two patients and reports that moderate, but significant clinical improvements may be observed with and without L-dopa therapy. Both patients received mesencephalic cells from a total of four fetuses each via a stereotactical and unilateral approach in two regions of the putamen and one region of the caudate nucleus (Lindvall et al. 1989). Postoperatively, an increased readiness potential was observed, preferentially over the operated hemisphere. In 1990, the same group (Lindvall et al. 1990) reported for the first time clear motor improvements in another transplanted PD patient after stereotactical implantation of mesencephalon from four fetuses (gestational age 8–9 weeks) in three different putaminal regions. The improvements concerned, as expected, preferentially the contralateral body side. This clinical finding correlated with an increased L-[$^{18}$F]-fluorodopa signal at the implantation site, as revealed by positron emission tomography (PET). Basic science findings suggest that this increased signal for L-[$^{18}$F]-fluorodopa may correspond to additional dopamine-producing neuronal structures. Thus, this report could represent the first evidence for surviving dopaminergic transplants by biochemical and imaging techniques. However, it should be stressed that such an increased L-[$^{18}$F]-fluorodapa signal could also be caused by the operation itself, namely by growth of endogenous host dopamine fibers into the implant site. Alternatively, it is conceivable that a postoperative, operation-induced proliferation of small blood vessels or a persistent postoperative defect of the brain-blood barrier could have been responsible for the altered PET signal.

Shortly after the Swedish publication, a research team from Denver (Freed et al. 1990) observed significant improvement of locomotion in one PD patient after transplantation, which was more pronounced on the left body side. A 52-year old patient had received mesencephalic cells of one fetus (gestation age 7 weeks) into ten regions of the right striatum (putamen and caudate nucleus). PET scans, performed on this patient 5 months after the operation, did not permit any conclusive interpretation; a magnetic resonance scan, using gadolinium injection, did not reveal an increased signal, which was considered to be evidence for an intact blood-brain barrier at the implantation site. In contrast to the Swedish patients, the American patient did not receive any immunosuppressive medication. In Sweden, immunosuppressive treatment with cyclosporine, azathioprine, or prednisone (Lindvall 1989; Lindvall et al. 1990) is routinely administered to prevent possible graft rejection. It is not known if this immunosuppressive treatment is actually necessary in humans, since homologous fetal monkey mesencephalon may survive in the brain of adult monkeys without immunosuppression (Bankiewicz et al. 1990a; Fine et al. 1988; Sladek et al. 1988).

Cuban investigators (Molina et al. 1990) have recently reported beneficial effects of intrastriatal fetal mesencephalic grafts in more than 30 PD patients. However, the preliminary studies are not detailed enough to allow a definite evaluation. Further information and long-term follow-up studies are necessary in order to decide whether this approach will be eventually developed into a clinical therapeutic procedure (Oertel and Kupsch 1990; Kupsch et al. 1991).

## Conclusion

Transplantation of fetal mesencephalon aims at a symptomatic permanent compensation of the striatal dopamine deficit in PD. In the future, the technique may allow us to ameliorate PD symptoms by a small surgical intervention and could possibly avoid the systemic side effects associated with the current pharmacological therapies. Before a clinical application may be considered, major issues need to be clarified related to surgical problems, immunological questions, ethical aspects, and many other unresolved points (Landau 1990). Grafting of dopamine-synthesizing cells and the search for possible trophic factors for dopaminergic neurons are certainly fascinating research areas. At present, however, they do not represent an alternative to pharmacotherapy.

## Summary

The transplantation of neural cells into the brain represents a novel therapeutic strategy against a variety of neurodegenerative disorders. Diseases like Parkinson's disease (PD), which is characterized by a relatively restricted lesion of the nigrostriatal system, are particularly suitable to test this potential concept. Recently, animal models of PD allowed substantial insights to be gained on relevant transplantation techniques by implantation of fetal mesencephalon and mature adrenal medulla into the dorsal striatum (caudate nucleus and putamen).

The results with transplantations of autologous adrenal medulla on over 300 patients have not been convincing. Fetal mesencephalon may reverse Parkinsonian syndromes in experimental animal models. Clinical results with homologous fetal mesencephalon on approximately 100 PD patients must be regarded as preliminary.

*Acknowledgment.* The authors thank Prof. Dr. G. ten Bruggencate for his support of this work.

## References

Agid Y, Javoy-Agid F, Ruberg M, Hirsch E (1989) Dopaminergic systems in Parkinson's disease. In: Quinn NP, Jenner PG (eds) Disorders of movement – clinical, pharmacological, and physiological aspects. Academic, London, pp. 85–113

Alexander GE, DeLong MR, Strick PL (1986) Parallel organisation of functionally segregated circuits linking basal ganglia and cortex. Ann Rev Neurosci 9:357–381

Allen GS, Burns RS, Tulipan NB, Parker RA (1989) Adrenal medullary transplantation to the caudate nucleus in Parkinson's disease. Arch Neurol 46:487–491

Arbuthnott G, Dunnett SB, MacLeod N (1985) Electrophysiological properties of single units in dopamine-rich mesencephalic transplants in rat brain. Neurosci Lett 57:205–210

Backlund E-O, Granberg P-O, Hamberger B, Knutsson E, Martensson A, Sedvall G, Seiger A, Olson L (1985) Transplantation of adrenal medullary tissue to striatum in parkinsonism. First clinical trials. J Neurosurg 62:169–173

Bakay RAE, Fiandaca MS, Barrow DL, Schiff A, Collins DC (1985) Preliminary report on the use of fetal tissue transplantation to correct MPTP-induced Parkinson-like syndrome in primates. Appl Neurophysiol 48:358–361

Bakay RAE, Barrow DL, Fiandaca MS, Iuvone PM, Schiff A, Collins DC (1987) Biochemical and behavioral correction of MPTP Parkinson-like syndrome by fetal cell transplantation. Ann NY Acad Sci 495:623–638

Bakay RAE, Fiandaca MS, Sweeney KM, Colbassani HJ Jr, Collins DC (1988) Delayed stereotactic transplantation technique in nonhuman primates. In: Gash DM, Sladed JR Jr (eds) Transplantation into the mammalian brain. Prog Brain Res 787:463–471

Bankiewicz KS, Plunkett RJ, Jacobowitz DM, Kopin IJ, Cummings A, Oldfield EH (1988a) Implant-induced catecholaminergic sprouting in MPTP parkinsonian monkeys: behavioral and histochemical studies. Soc Neurosci Abstr 5:4

Bankiewicz KS, Plunkett RJ, Kopin IJ, Jacobowitz DM, London WT, Oldfield EH (1988b) Transient behavioural recovery in hemiparkinsonian primates after adrenal medullary allografts. In Gash DM, Sladek JR Jr (eds) Transplantation into the mammalian CNS. Prog Brain Res 78:543–549

Bankiewicz KS, Plunkett RJ, Jacobowitz DM, Kopin IJ, Cummings A, Oldfield EG (1989) Behavioural recovery in MPTP-treated hemiparkinsonian monkeys after amnion implantation into the head of caudate nucleus. III[rd] International Symposium on Neural Transplantation, Cambridge Restorative Neurol Neurosci 1 (abstract 33:10)

Bankiewicz KS, Plunkett RJ, Jacobowitz DM, Porrino L, Di Porzio U, London WT, Kopin IJ, Oldfield EH (1990a) The effect of fetal mesencephalic implants on primate MPTP-induced parkinsonism. Histochemical and behavioural studies. J Neurosurg 72:231–244

Bankiewicz KS, Wang J, Plunkett RJ, Jacobowitz DM (1990b) Recovery in hemiparkinsonian rats after intracaudal implantation of neonatal microglia. In: Lindvall O, Björklund A (eds) International conference on intracerebral transplantation in movement disorders, Lund, Shweden (Abstract 31:37)

Barbeau A (1961) Biochemistry of Parkinson's disease. Int Congr Series 38:152–153

Barry DI, Kikvadze, Brundin P, Bolwig TG, Björklund A, Lindvall O (1987) Grafted noradrenergic neurons suppress seizure development in kindling-induced epilepsy. Proc Natl Acad Sci USA 84:8712–8715

Bernheimer H, Birkmayer W, Hornykiewicz O, Jellinger K, Seitelberger F (1973) Brain dopamine and the syndromes of Parkinson and Huntington. Clinical, morphological and neurochemical correlations. J Neurol Sci 20:415–455

Birkmayer W, Hornykiewicz O (1961) Der L-3,4-Dioxyphenylalanin- (L-dopa)Effekt bei der Parkinson Akinese. Klin Wochenschr 73:787–788

Birkmayer W, Knoll J, Youdim Y, Hars V, Marton J (1985) Increased life expectancy resulting from addition of L-deprenyl to Madopar treatment in Parkinson's disease: a long-term study. J Neural Transm 64:113–127

Björklund A, Dunnett SB, Stenevi U, Lewis ME, Iversen DS (1980) Reinnervation of the denervated striatum by substantia nigra transplants: functional consequences as revealed by pharmacological and sensorimotor testing. Brain Res 199:307–333

Björklund A, Gage FH (1987) Grafts of fetal septal cholinergic neurons to the hippocampal formation in aged or fimbria-fornix-lesioned rats. Ann NY Acad Sci 495:120–136

Björklund A, Stenevi U (1979) Reconstruction of the nigrostriatal pathway by intracerebral nigral transplants. Brain Res 177:555–560

Björklund A, Stenevi U, Schmidt RH, Dunnett SB, Gage FH (1983) Intracerebral grafting of neuronal cell suspensions, II: survival and growth of nigral cell suspensions implanted in different brain sites. Acta Physiol Scand (Suppl) 522:9–18

Bohn MC, Cupit L, Marciano F, Gash DM (1987) Adrenal medulla grafts enhance recovery of striatal dopaminergic fibre. Science 237:913–916

Burns RS, Chiueh CC, Markey SP, Ebert MH, Jacobowitz DM, Kopin IJ (1983) A primate model of Parkinsonism: selective destruction of dopaminergic neurons in the pars compacta of the substantia nigra by *N*-methyl-4-phenyl-1,2,3,6-tetrahydropyridine. Proc Natl Acad Sci USA 80:4546–4550
Brundin, P, Nilsson OG, Gage FH, Björklund A (1985) Cyclosporin A increases survival of cross-species intrastriatal grafts of embryonic dopamine-containing tissue. Exp Brain Res 60:204–208
Brundin P, Strecker RE, Widner H, Clarke DJ, Nilsson OG, Astedt B, Lindvall O, Björklund A (1988) Human fetal dopamine neurons grafted in a rat model of Parkinson's disease: immunological aspects, spontaneous and drug-induced behaviour, and dopamine release. Exp Brain Res 70:192–208
Das GD, Hallas BH, Das KG (1980) Transplantation of brain tissue in the brain of the rat. I. Growth characteristics of neocortical transplants from embryos of different ages. Am J Anat 158:135–145
Davis GC, Williams AC, Markey SP, Ebert MH, Caine ED, Reichert CM, Kopin IJ (1979) Chronic Parkinsonism secondary to intravenous injection of meperidine analogues. Psychiat Res 1:249–254
Deckel AW, Moran TH, Coyle JT, Sanberg PR, Robinson RG (1986) Anatomical predictors of behavioural recovery following fetal striatal transplants. Brain Res 365:249–258
Deckel AW, Robinson RG, Coyle JT, Sanberg PR (1983) Reversal of long-term locomotor abnormalities in the kainic acid model of Huntington's disease by day 18 fetal striatal implants. Eur J Pharmacol 93:287–288
Dubach M, Schmidt RH, Martin R, German DC, Bowden DM (1988) Transplant improves hemiparkinsonian syndrome in nonhuman primate:intracerebral injection, rotometry, tyrosine hydroxylase immunohistochemistry. In: Gash DM, Sladed JR Jr (eds) Transplantation in to the mammalian brain. Prog Brain Res 78:491–496
Dunnett SB, Björklund A, Stenevi U, Iversen SD (1981a) Behavioural recovery following transplantation of substantia nigra in rats subjected to 6-OHDA lesions of the nigrostriatal pathway I. Unilateral lesions. Brain Res 215:147–161
Dunnett SB, Björklund A, Stenevi U, Iversen SD (1981b) Grafts of embryonic substantia nigra reinnervating the ventrolateral striatum ameliorate sensorimotor impairments and akinesia in rats with 6-OHDA lesions of the nigrostriatal pathway. Brain Res 229:209–217
Dunnett SB, Björklund A, Schmidt RH, Stenevi U, Iversen SD (1983) Intracerebral grafting of neuronal cell suspensions. IV. Behavioural recovery in rats with unilateral 6-OHDA lesions following implantation of nigral cell suspensions in different forebrain sites. Acta Physiol Scand (Suppl) 522:29–37
Fine A, Hunt SP, Oertel WH, Nomoto M, Chong PN, Bond A Waters C, Temlett JA, Annett L, Dunnett S, Jenner P, Marsden CD (1988) Transplantation of embryonic marmoset dopaminergc neurons to the corpus striatum of marmosets rendered parkinsonian by 1-methyl-4-phenyl-1,2,3,6-tetrahydropyridine. In: Gash TM, Sladek JR Jr (eds) Transplantation into the mammalian brain. Prog Brain Res 78:479–489
Forno LS, (1982) Pathology of Parkinson's disease. In: Marsden CD, Fahn S (eds) Movement disorders. Butterworths, London
Freed CR, Breeze RE, Rosenberg NL, Schneck SA, Wells TH, Barrett JN, Grafton ST, Huang SC, Eidelberg D, Rottenberg DA (1990) Transplantation of human fetal dopamine cells for Parkinson's disease. Arch Neurol 47:505–512
Freed WJ, Ko GN, Niehoff DL, Kuhar DL, Hoffer BJ, Olson L (1983) Normalization of spiroperidol binding in the denervated rat striatum by homologous grafts of substantia nigra. Science 222:937–939
Freed WJ, Perlow MJ, Karoum F, Seiger A, Olson L, Hoffer BJ, Wyatt RJ (1980) Restoration of dopaminergic function by grafting of fetal rat substantia nigra to the caudate nucleus. Long-term behavioural, biochemical and histochemical studies. Ann Neurol 8:510–519

Freund TF, Bolam JP, Björklund A, Stenevi U, Dunnett SB, Powell J, Smith AD (1985) Efferent synaptic connections of grafted dopaminergic neurons reinnervating the host neostriatum: a tyrosine hydroxylase immunocytochemical study. J Neurosci 5:603–616

Gage FH, Björklund A (1986) Enhanced graft survival in the hippocampus following selective denervation. Neuroscience 17:89–98

Gage FH, Björklund A, Stenevi U, Dunnett SB, Kelly PAT (1984) Intrahippocampal septal grafts ameliorate learning impairments in aged rats. Science 225:533–536

Goetz CG, Stebbins GT III, Klawans HL, Koller WC, Grossman RG, Bakay AE, Penn RD and the United Parkinson Foundation Neuronal Transplantation Registry (1989a) United Parkinson Foundation Neurotransplantation Registry. Multicenter US and Canadian data base. Presurgical and 12 months follow up. 1725 West Harrison, Chicago, IL 60612, USA

Goetz CG, Tanner CM, Penn RD, Stebbins III GT, Gilley DW, Shannon KM, Klawans HL, Comella CL, Wilson RS, Witt T (1990) Adrenal medullary transplant to the striatum of patients with advanced Parkinson's disease: 1-year motor and psychomotor data. Neurology 40:273–276

Goetz CG, Olanow CW, Koller CW, Penn RD, Cahill D, Morantz R, Stebbins G, Tanner C, Klawans HL, Shannon KM, Comella CL, Witt T, Cox C, Waxman M, Gauger L (1989b) Multicenter study of autologous adrenal medullary transplantation to the corpus striatum in patients with advanced Parkinson's disease. N Engl J Med 320:327–341

Hallas BH, Das GD, Das KG (1980) Transplantation of brain tissue in the brain of the rat. II. Growth characteristics of neocortical transplants. Am J Anat 158: 147–159

Hitchcock ER, Clough C, Hughes R, Kenny B (1988) Embryos and Parkinson's disease. Lancet i:1274

Hitchcock ER, Clough C, Hughes R, Kenny B, Henderson B, Detta A (1990) Clinical results: the British experience. In: Lindvall O, Björklund A (eds) International conference on intracerebral transplantation in movement disorders, Lund, Shweden (abstract 5:11)

Hornykiewicz O, Kish SJ (1987) Biochemical pathophysiology of Parkinson's disease. In: Yahr MD, Bergman KJ (eds) Adv Neurol 45:607–614

Hornykiewicz O, Pifl C, Kish SJ, Shannak K, Schingnitz G (1989) Biochemical changes in idiopathic Parkinson's disease, aging, and MPTP Parkinsonism: similarities and differences. In: Calne DB, Comi G, Crippa D, Horowski R, Trabucchi M (eds) Parkinsonism and aging. Raven, New York, pp 57–66

Hurtig H, Joyce J, Sladek Jr, Trojanowski JQ (1989) Postmortem analysis of adrenal-medulla-to-caudate autograft in a patient with Parkinson's disease. Ann Neurol 25:607–614

Isacson O, Brundin P, Kelly PAT, Gage FH, Björklund A (1984) Functional neuronal replacement by grafted striatal neurons in the ibotenic acid-lesioned striatum. Nature 311:458–460

Isacson O, Dunnett SB, Björklund A (1986) Graft-induced behavioral recovery in an animal model of Huntington's disease. Proc Natl Acad Sci USA, 83:2728–2732

Jankovic J, Grossman C, Pirozzolo F, Schneider L, Zhu Z, Scardino P, Garber AJ, Jhingran SG, Martin S (1989) Clinical, biochemical, neuropathological findings following transplantation of adrenal medulla to the caudate nucleus for the treatment of Parkinson's disease. Neurology 39:1227–1234

Kish SJ, Shannak K, Hornykiewicz O (1988) Uneven patterns of dopamine loss in the striatum of patients with idiopathic Parkinson's disease. N Engl J Med 318:876–880

Kopin IJ, Markey SP (1988) MPTP toxicity: implications for research Parkinson's disease. Ann Rev Neurosci 11:81–96

Kupsch A, Sauer H, Oertel WH (1991) Transplantation von dopamin-herstellenden Nervenzellen: Eine neue Therapiestrategie gegen das idiopathische Parkinson-Syndrom? Nervenarzt 62: 80–91.

Langston JW (1985) MPTP and Parkinson's disease. Trends Neurosci 8:79–83

Langston JW, Ballard P, Tetrud JW, Irwin I (1983) Chronic Parkinsonism in humans due to a product of mepiridine-analog synthesis. Science 219:979–980

Landau WM (1990) Clinical neuromythology VII: Artificial intelligence: the brain transplant cure for parkinsonism. Neurol 40:733–740
Lindvall O (1989) Transplantation into the human brain: present status and future possibilities. J Neurol Neurosurg Psychiatr (Special Suppl) pp. 39–54
Lindvall O, Backlund E-O, Farde L, Sedvall G, Freedman R, Hoffer B, Nobin A, Seiger A, Olson L (1987) Transplantation in Parkinson's disease: two cases of adrenal medullary grafts to the putamen. Ann Neurol 22:457–468
Lindvall O, Barry DI, Kikvadze I, Brundin P, Bolwig TG, Björklund A (1988) Intracerebral grafting of fetal noradrenergic locus coeruleus neurons: evidence for seizure suppression in the kindling model of epilepsy. Prog Brain Res 78:79–86
Lindvall O, Brundin P, Widner H, Rehncrona S, Gustavii B, Frackowiak R, Leenders KL, Sawle G, Rothwell JC, Marsden CD, Björklund A (1990) Grafts of fetal dopamine neurons survive and improve motor function in Parkinson's disease. Science 247:574–577
Lindvall NG, Rehncrohna S, Brundin P, Gustavii B, Astedt B, Widner H, Lindholm T, Björklund A, Leenders KL, Rothwell JC, Frackowiak R, Marsden CD, Johnels B, Steg G, Freedman R, Hoffer BJ, Seiger A, Bygdeman M, Strömberg I, Olson L (1989) Human fetal dopamine neurons grafted into the striatum in two patients with severe Parkinson's disease. Arch Neurol 46: 615–631
Low WC, Lewis PR, Bunch ST, Dunnett SB, Thomas SR, Iversen SD, Björklund A, Stenevi U (1982) Function recovery following neural transplantation of embryonic septal nuclei adult with septo-hippocampal lesions. Nature 300:260–262
Madrazo I, Drucker-Colin R, Diaz V, Martinez-Mata J, Torres C, Becerril JJ (1987) Open microsurgical autograft of adrenal medulla to the right caudate nucleus in two patients with Parkinson's disease. N Engl J Med 316:831–834
Madrazo I, Franco-Bourland R, Aguilera M, Ostrosky-Solis F (1989) Hispanic registry of graft procedures for Parkinson's disease. Lancet i:751–752
Madrazo I, Leon V, Torres C, Aguilera MC, Vavela G, Alvarez F, Fraga A, Drucker R, Colin R, Ostrosky F, Skurovich M et al. (1988) Transplantation of fetal substantia nigra and adrenal medulla to the caudate nucleus in two patients with Parkinson's disease. N Engl J Med 318:51
Mahalik TJ, Finger TE, Strömberg I, Olson L (1985) Substantia nigra transplants into denervated striatum of the rat: ultra-structure of graft and host interconnections. J Comp Neurol 240:60–70
Marsden CD (1983) Neuromelanin and Parkinson's disease. N Neural Transm 19:121–141
Mason DW, Charlton HM, Jones AJ, Lavy CBD, Puklavec M, Simmons SJ (1986) The fate of allogeneic and xenogeneic neuronal tissue transplanted into the third ventricle of rodents. Neuroscience 19:685–694
Molina H et al. (1990) Clinical results: the Cuban experience – neurotransplantation in Parkinson's disease. In Lindvall O, Björklund A (eds) International conference on intracerebral transplantation in movement disorders, Lund Sweden (Abstract 9:15)
Nyberg P, Nordberg A, Wester P, Winblad B (1983) Dopaminergic deficiency is more pronounced in putamen than in nucleus caudatus in Parkinson's disease. Neurochem Path 1:193–202
Oertel WH, Kupsch A (1990) Transplantation von Dopamin-synthetisierenden Zellen und trophische Faktoren – zukünftige Behandlungsverfahren des idiopathischen Parkinson-Syndroms? In: Fischer PA (ed) Parkinsonkrankheit und Nigraprozesse. 7. Frankfurter Parkinsonsymposium. Roches (in press)
Oertel WH, Marsden CD (1988) Transplantation of dopamine-synthetizing cells – new therapy for Parkinson's disease? In: Przuntek H, Riederer P (eds) Early diagnosis and preventive therapy of Parkinson's disease. Springer, Vienna pp. 283–304
Olson L (1988) Grafting in the mammalian central nervous system: basic science with clinical promise. In: Magistretti PJ (ed) Discussions in neurosciences. Fondation pour l'étude du système nerveux central et périphérique (FESN), vol V, no. 4. Geneva

Parkinson Study Group (1989a) Effect of deprenyl on the progression of disability in early Parkinson's disease. N Engl J Med 321:1364–1371
Parkinson Study Group (1989b) DATATOP: a multicenter clinical trial in early Parkinson's disease. Arch Neurol 46:1052–1060
Perlow MJ, Freed WJ, Hoffer BJ, Seiger A, Olson L, Wyatt RJ (1979) Brain grafts reduce motor abnormalities produced by destruction of nigrostriatal dopamine system. Science 204:643–647
Peterson DI, Price L, Small CS (1989) Autopsy findings in a patient who had an adrenal-to-brain transplant for Parkinson's disease. Neurology 39:235–238
Quinn NP, Dunnett SB, Oertel WH (1989) Studies towards neural transplantation in Parkinson's disease. In: Quinn NP, Jenner PG (eds) Disorders of movement – clinical, pharmacological, and physiological aspects. Academic, London, pp. 225–247
Redmond DE, Naftolin F, Collier TJ, Leranth C, Robbins RJ, Sladek CD, Roth RH, Sladek JR Jr (1987) Cryopreservation, culture, and transplantation of human fetal mesencephalic tissue into monkeys. Science 242:768–771
Redmond DE, Sladek JR, Roth RH, Collier TJ, Elsworth JD, Deutch AY, Haber S (1986) Fetal neuronal grafts in monkeys given methylphenyltetrahydropyridine. Lancet i:1125–1127
Rinne UK (1987) Combined bromocriptine-levodopa therapy early in Parkinson's disease – a five year follow-up. Neurology 39:336–339
Rinne UK (1989a) Lisuride, a dopamine agonist in the treatment of early Parkinson's disease. Acta Neurol Scand 126:165–169
Rinne UK (1989b) Combination of a dopamine agonist, MAO-B-inhibitor and levodopa – a new strategy in the treatment of early Parkinson's disease. Acta Neurol Scand 126:165–169
Robbins JR, Torres-Aleman I, Leranth C, Bradberry CW, Deutch AY, Welsh SW, Roth RH, Spencer D, Redmond Jr DE, Naftolin F (1990) Cryopreservation of human brain tissue. Exp Neurol 107:208–213
Rose G, Gerhardt G, Olson I, Hoffer BJ (1985) Monoamine release from dopamine-depleted caudate nucleus by substantia nigra transplants: an in vivo electrochemical study. Brain Res 341:92–100
Sanberg PR, Nash DR, Calderon SF, Giordano M, Shipley MT, Norman AB (1988) Neural transplants disrupt the blood-brain barrier and allow peripherally acting drugs to exert a centrally mediated behavioural effect. Exp Neurol 102:149–152
Sauer H (1990) Intrazerebrale Transplantation in einem Tiermodell der Parkinsonschen Erkrankung – Optimierung und methodische Studien. Thesis, Ulm, FRG
Schmidt RH, Björklund A, Stenevi (1981) Intracerebral grafting of dissociated CNS tissue suspensions: a new approach for neuronal transplantation to deep brain sites. Brain Res 218:347–356
Sladek JR Jr, Collier TJ, Haber SN, Roth RH, Redmond DE (1986) Survival and growth of fetal catecholamine neurons transplanted in primate brain. Brain Res Bull 17:809–818
Sladek JR Jr, Redmond DE, Collier TJ, Haber SN, Elsworth JD, Deutch AY, Roth RH (1987) Transplantation of dopamine fetal dopamine neurons in primate reverses MPTP-induced parkinsonism. Prog Brain Res 78; Prog Brain Res 71:309–323
Sladek JR Jr, Redmond DE, Collier TJ, Blount JP, Elsworth JD, Taylor JR, Roth RH (1988) Fetal dopamine neural grafts: extended reversal of methylphenyltetrahydropyridine-induced parkinsonism in monkeys. In Gash DM, Sladek JR Jr (eds) Transplantation into the mammalian CNS. Prog Brain Res 78:497–506
Snider WD, Johnson EM Jr (1990) Neurotrophic molecules. Ann Neurol 26:489–506
Stoddard SL, Tyce GM, Ahlskoog JE, Zinsmeister AR, Carmichael SW (1989) Decreased catecholamine content in parkinsonian adrenal medullae. Exp Neurol 104:22–27
Strömberg I, Johnson S, Hoffer B, Olsen L (1985) Reinnervation of dopamine denervated striatum by substantia nigra transplants: immunocytochemical and electrophysiological correlates. Neuroscience 14:981–990

Tanner CM (1989) The role of environmental toxins in the etiology of Parkinson's disease. Trends Neurosci 12:49–54
Tetrud JW, Langston JW (1989) The effect of deprenyl (Selegiline) on the natural history of Parkinson's disease. Science 245:519–522
Ungerstedt U, Arbuthnott GW (1970) Quantitative recording of rotational behaviour in rats after 6-hydroxydopamine lesions of the nigrostriatal dopamine system. Brain Res 24:485–493
Wictorin K, Isacson O, Fischer W, Nothias F, Peschanski M, Björklund A (1988) Connectivity of striatal grafts implanted into the ibotenic acid-lesioned striatum. I. Subcortical afferents. Neuroscience 27:547–562
Widner H, Brundin P (1988) Immunological aspects of grafting in the mammalian central nervous system. A review and speculative synthesis. Brain Res Rev. 13:287–324

# Fetal Islet Cell Transplantation: State of the Art

R. Landgraf

## Why Transplantation of Insulin-Producing Tissue?

The prevalence of diabetes in Western Europe and the United States of America is around 3 % – 4 % of the population, including also type I diabetes mellitus (absolute insulin-requiring disease), which amounts to 0.35 % of the whole population. Despite major advances in the treatment of the various forms of diabetes in recent years, the life of diabetics or their well-being are endangered by vascular, neurological, and connective tissue complications [35]. The severity, rate, and development of these secondary diabetic complications are highly correlated to the chronic metabolic derangements [3, 11]. Normoglycemia is, therefore, an absolute prerequisite for the prevention of diabetic complications. Since even the rather sophisticated methods of insulin replacement regimens, like insulin pumps, are not able to achieve long-term normoglycemia, new therapeutical approaches have been developed or are in progress to reach the ultimate goal of normoglycemia at least in the younger type I diabetics. The main aim of transplantation of insulin-producing tissue is therefore to reverse or halt secondary complications and to improve the quality of life in these patients.

## Why Transplantation of Fetal Pancreatic Tissue?

In recent years, whole or segmental pancreatic grafting has been highly successful, and the pancreas survival rates are very much comparable to those of more established organ transplantations like kidney and heart grafting [30]. However, pancreatic grafting has a number of disadvantages which restricts this method of treatment to careful selected type I diabetics at a rather late stage of their disease [10, 20]. First, there might be a shortage of organs suitable for transplantation. In addition, major surgery is involved in this treatment with a number of possible complications peri- and postoperatively, which are mainly due to the exocrine part of the pancreas. Also chronic immunosuppression is necessary [10, 20]. Therefore, since its feasibility has been proven in animals [9], major efforts have been undertaken

Department of Internal Medicine, Klinikum Innenstadt, University of Munich, Ziemssenstraße 1, D-8000 München 2, FRG

W. Land, J. B. Dossetor (Eds.)
Organ Replacement Therapy:
Ethics, Justice and Commerce

for transplantation of islets [6, 12, 18, 21] or fetal pancreas [6, 22] into diabetic patients. However, adult islet grafting has still a very poor outcome [6], although recently promising advances in islet isolation and purification, islet immunoalteration, and immunoisolation [7, 24, 27] have been reported. But also shortage of human adult islet tissue will be the major restriction for applying human islet grafting to a large population of diabetics even if it would be finally successful.

Human fetal pancreas transplantation remains an attractive alternative with, at least theoretically, no major problems in its availability. It might have additional advantages over adult whole pancreas or islet tissue, since it has been suggested to be less immunogenic, its preparation is technically an easy procedure, and it is enriched in tissue capable of insulin production [15, 22]. Although the fetal pancreas is undifferentiated and contains little insulin-producing tissue, it has been shown that this tissue can grow and differentiate [8, 22, 26]. Fortunately, mainly the endocrine part of pancreas develops after grafting. Human fetal pancreas can be transplanted into athymic nude mice or experimentally induced diabetic rodents where it grows, matures, produces insulin, and reverses diabetes [1, 22, 25, 33].

## Clinical Experience with Fetal Pancreas Transplantation

Human fetal pancreas was first used in 1928 when a young ketoacidotic diabetic was grafted with pancratic tissue from three fetuses [4]. However, this experiment failed. When J. Brown and his colleagues were successful in reversal diabetes in rats after fetal pancreas transplantation [1], new interest emerged in fetal tissue. Since then numerous clinical trials have been initiated, which will be discussed below.

## Details of Transplantation

### Tissue

Human fetal pancreases were obtained from therapeutically or legally terminated pregnancies between 14 and 32 weeks gestation [5, 14, 16, 23, 28, 32]. The methods of termination were water-bag induction, suction curettage, hysterotomy, or prostaglandin induction, followed by aseptic removal of the pancreas as soon as possible after termination of pregnancy, mostly within 2–4 h. After removal of excess connective tissue, pancreas pieces ($\approx 1\ \mu l$) or the whole organ was rinsed with sterile culture medium, and placed into culture dishes for 48 h [16] up to 10 weeks [5] prior to implantation. The quality of the cultured explants was at least in some groups monitored regularly for viability by measuring insulin secretory capacity and performing histological examinations as well as immune staining [16, 32]. Ex vivo testing also incuded microbiological analysis of both the culture medium and the fetal tissue for viruses, bacteria, mycoplasma, and fungi. Maternal serum was tested for antibodies to hepatitis B, human immunodeficiency virus (HIV), cytomegalovirus (CMV), Epstein-Barr virus (EBV), and rubella as well as for toxoplasmosis and treponema pallidum. Lymphocytes from the fetal tissue (spleen, bone marrow, thymus) were tissue-typed for HLA-A, -B, and -DR antigens, and the results compared retrospectively with those of the patients achieving partial or complete mismatches for the A and DR loci [32].

## Tissue Recipients

Clinical details of the patients selected for transplantation are rather limited, especially for those patients treated in the Soviet Union [28] and the People's Republic of China [14]. Only some studies [16, 32] had approval by a local ethical committee and had informed written consent from the patient. The entry criteria varied widely in the clinical trials ranging from young well-trained, well-defined type I diabetics without signs of diabetic complications to older insulin-requiring diabetics with a long duration of diabetes (up to 23 years) and/or severe complications, some of them already renal transplant recipients. Immunosuppression therefore, was necessary in some of the patients [32] including monotherapy with Cyclosporin A (CyA) or duplex treatment with CyA plus prednisone (Pred) or azathioprine (Aza) plus Pred or quadruple treatment with CyA, Pred, Aza, and antilymphocyte globulin for various time intervals. Other fetal explant recipients had no immunosuppression [16] or were treated with "Chinese medicine", an unknown mixture of plant extracts [14]. Also the amount of tissue transplanted varied greatly and ranged from 1 to 20 fetal pancreases. The site of implantation was muscle (forearm, abdominal wall), subcutis (abdomen), liver (via umbilical vein), beneath the kidney capsule, or the free peritoneal cavity. The success of transplantation was documented for short or long time periods posttransplant by reliable parameters such as appearance of significant levels of basal as well as stimulated C-peptide in C-peptide negative diabetics pretransplant. Indicators of success like reduction of exogenous insulin requirement after transplantation are useless.

## Results

A detailed report of the world experience has been given recently [13, 29]. In the meantime, many more cases have been reported to the Islet Transplant Registry [6], which has increased even up to September 1990 to a total of 1582 transplantations in 60 different institutions (Table 1; B.J. Hering et al., personal communication). Only the diabetic patients in the USSR were transplanted with allogenic as well as xenogenic (bovine, pig) fetal tissue, probably only in order to safe exogenous insulin.

**Table 1.** Worldwide experience in clinical fetal islet allo- and xenotransplantation (modified from [6])

| Country | Institution | Cases | Total |
|---|---|---|---|
| USSR | Moscow | 270 | |
| | Kiev | 316 | |
| | Riga | 140 | |
| | Erevan | 65 | |
| | Moscow (Lumumba) | 30 | |
| | Leningrade, Arkhangelsk, Izhevsk, Kharkov | 84 | 1000 |
| China | Shanghai | 75 | |
| | Shengeng | 36 | |
| | Fujan | 15 | |
| | Shanghai/Toronto | 3 | |
| | 27 other centres in China | 307 | 436 |
| Eastern Europe | Szeged | 18 | |
| | Belgrade | 5 | |
| | East Berlin | 2 | |
| | Karlsburg | 1 | 26 |
| Western Europe | Genova | 13 | |
| | Stockholm | 13 | |
| | Frankfurt a.M. | 3 | |
| | Bordeaux | 1 | |
| | Rome | 1 | 31 |
| USA | Denver | 22 | |
| | Dallas | 6 | |
| | Madison | 3 | |
| | Hana Series (Dallas, Denver, Madison, San Francisco) | 28 | |
| | Boston | 8 | |
| | Santa Barbara | 5 | |
| | Kansas City | 2 | |
| | Albany | 1 | |
| | Minneapolis | 1 | 76 |
| Australia | Melbourne | 8 | |
| | Sydney | 5 | 13 |
| | | | 1582 |

The overall results are very disappointing, especially when analyzing critically those cases which have been claimed to be successful. For example, in the largest series ($n = 13$) with a claimed excellent outcome [14], insulin requirement was reduced by 75%–100%, but with basal and stimulated C-peptide levels far below normal values. The data are in addition very difficult to judge, since pretransplant values are in most cases missing, C-peptide analysis is not clearly defined, and the values are comparable with the C-peptide levels observed in those patients with a “good” or “fair” transplant outcome (i.e., reduction of exogenous insulin of 30%–75%). The

**Table 2.** Cases reported to be off exogenous insulin after fetal pancreas transplantation (modified from [6])

| Institution | Year | No.of cases | Period post tx | Comments |
|---|---|---|---|---|
| Bordeaux | 1979 | 1 | 2–14 months | remission phase? |
| China<br>(several centers) | 1981–1987<br>1981–1987 | 5<br>12 | 4–12 months<br>$\geqslant$4–$\geqslant$45 | graft loss due to infection ($n$ = 3)<br>pretransplant characterization of diabetic state unclear<br>(C-peptide negative?) |
| Genoa | 1979 | 1 | off insulin 150 days post tx | no follow-up |
| Moscow | 1989 | 1 | 3 weeks | micropore capsules |
| Santa Barbara | 1988 | 1 | 1st–2nd day | insulin leakage? |

study of Jovanovic-Peterson et al. [16] showed that implanted fetal pancreatic tissue is able to survive and secrete insulin after an adequate challenge (Sustacal) for up to 1 year without immunosuppression, interestingly without appearance of anticytoplasmic islet cell antibodies. A summary of all the cases reported to the International Islet Transplantation Registry assured to be off insulin following fetal pancreas grafting, which amounts to 19 out of 1542 (1.2%) cases up to 45 months posttransplant, is depicted in Table 2 [6].

## Summary and Conclusion

1. The outcome of fetal pancreas grafting is at the moment very poor.
2. The interpretation of the so-called successful transplantations is almost impossible because the documentation of relevant clinical and metabolic data prior to and after grafting is insufficient or missing. Therefore, there is an urgent need for standardization of data collection before adequate evaluation of fetal grafting is possible.
3. For the potential requirement of human fetal pancreases there is and will be an absolute shortage also of fetal organs. But, if the growth of the tissue to be implanted could be markedly stimulated before transplantation, availability could be enhanced and the chance of success would probably increase
4. The methods for isolation of islets from fetal pancreases have to be improved [17], and more experiments ex vivo and in vitro in animals are necessary for a better characterization of the tissue, especially to predict better the outcome of transplantation before clinical trials continue.

5. Human fetal pancreas also shows immunogenicity [15, 32], which might be reduced by several culture procedures or an interim host system [15]. But transplantation of allogeneic fetal material probably needs also immunosuppression of the recipient, comparable with the one in adult tissue grafting or immunoisolation procedures, which have still to be developed, are necessary.
6. The ethical problems involved using human fetal tissue are tremendous and are reflected by the ban on the use of tissue from induced abortions in US federal transplantation research in 1988 [19]. Therefore, xenogenic transplantation of fetal pig pancreas might be a more suitable approach due to its abundant availability, its immunological properties, and its potency to reverse experimental diabetes [2, 31, 36].

## References


1. Brown J, Clark WR, Molnar IG, Mullen YS (1976) Fetal pancreas transplantation for reversal of streptozotocin-induced diabetes in rats. Diabetes 25:56–64
2. Calafiori R, Calcinaro F, Basta G (1990) A method for the massive separation of highly purified adult porcine islets of Langerhans. Metabolism 39:175–181
3. DCCT Research Group (1988) Are continuing studies of metabolic control and microvascular complications in insulin-dependent diabetes mellitus justified? The Diabetes Control and Complication Trial. New Engl J Med 318:246–250
4. Downing R (1984) Historical review of pancreatic islet transplantation. World J Surg 8:137–142
5. Farkas G, Karácsonyi S, Szabó M, Vörös P (1990) Alteration in diabetic retinopathy and nephropathy following islet transplantation. Transplant Proc 22:765–766
6. Federlin K, Bretzel, RG, Hering BJ (1990a) Recent achievement in experimental and clinical islet transplantation. Diabetic Med (in press)
7. Federlin K, Bretzel RG, Hering BJ (1990b) Workshop on methods in islet transplantation research. Horm Metabol Res (in press)
8. Freinkel N, Lewis NJ, Johnson R, Swenne J, Bone A, Hellerström C (1984) Differential effects of age versus glycemic stimulation on the maturation of insulin stimulus-secretion coupling during culture of fetal rats islets. Diabetes 33:1028–1038
9. Gray DWR, Morris PJ (1987) Development in isolated pancreatic islet transplantation. Transplantation 43:322–331
10. Groth CG (ed.) (1988) Pancreatic transplantation. Saunders, Philadelphia, pp 1–413
11. Hanssen KF, Dahl-Jørgensen K, Lauritzen T, Feldt-Rasmussen B, Brinchmann-Hansen O, Deckert T (1986) Diabetic control and microvascular complications: the near-normoglycemic experience. Diabetologia 29:677–684
12. Hellerström C, Andersson A, Korsgren O, Jansson L, Sandler S (1989) Aspects of pancreatic islet transplantation in diabetes mellitus. Baillière's Clin Gastroenterol 3:851–863
13. Hering BJ, Bretzel RG, Federlin K (1988) Current studies of clinical islet transplantation. Horm Metabol Res 20:537–545
14. Hu YF, Cheng RL, Shao AH, Ye RS, Gu ZF, Zhang HD, Zhang ZG, Hen LR, Bi HF, Shi GF (1989) The influences of islet transplantation on metabolic abnormalities and diabetic complications. Horm Metabol Res 22:198–202
15. Hullett DA, Falany JL, Love RB, Burlingham WJ, Pan M, Sollinger H (1987) Human fetal pancreas – a potential source for transplantation. Transplantation 43:18–22
16. Jovanovic-Peterson L, Williams K, Brennan M, Rashbaum W, Peterson CM (1989)

Studies of human fetal pancreatic allografts in diabetic recipients without immunosuppression. J Diabetic Complications 3:107–112
17. Kover K, Moore WV (1989) Development of a method for isolation of islets from human fetal pancreas. Diabetes 38:917–924
18. Lafferty KJ (1989) Islet cell transplantation as a therapy for type I diabetes mellitus. Diab Nutr Metab 2:323–332
19. Lafferty KJ, Mason OJ (1990) Should the fetal tissue research ban be lifted? J NIH Res 2:16–18
20. Land W, Landgraf R (1987) Clinical pancreas transplantation: The world experience. Transplant Proc 19 [Suppl 4]:1–102
21. Najarian JS, Sutherland DER, Groth CG (Guest eds) (1990) Second International Congress on Pancreatic and Islet Cell Transplantation. Transplant Proc 22:569–883
22. Peterson CM, Jovanovic-Peterson L, Formby B (eds) (1988) Fetal islet transplantation – implications for diabetes. Springer, Berlin Heidelberg New York Tokyo
23. Peterson CM, Jovanovic-Peterson L, Formby B, Gondos B, Monda LM, Walker L, Rashbaum W, Williams K (1989) Human fetal pancreas transplants. J Diabetic Complications 3:27–34
24. Ricordi C, Lacy PE, Finke EH, Olack BJ, Scharp DW (1988) Automated method for isolation of human pancreatic islets. Diabetes 37:413–420
25. Sandler S, Andersson A, Schnell A, Mellgren A, Tollemar J, Borg H, Petersson B, Groth CG, Hellerström C (1985) Tissue culture of human fetal pancreas. Development and function of B-cells in vitro and transplantation of explants to nude mice. Diabetes 34:1113–1119
26. Sandler S, Andersson A, Korsgren O, Tollemar J, Petersson B, Groth CG, Hellerström C (1989) Tissue culture of human fetal pancreas. Effects of nicotinamide on insulin production and formation of islet like cell clusters. Diabetes 38 [Suppl 1]:168–171
27. Scharp DW, Lacy PE, Santiago JV, McCullough CS, Weide LG, Falqui L, Marchetti P, Gingerich RL, Jaffe AS, Cryer PE, Anderson CB, Flye MW (1990) Insulin independence after islet transplantation into type I diabetic patient. Diabetes 39:515–518
28. Shumakov VI, Bljumkin VN, Ignatenko SN, Skaletsky NN, Slovesnova TA, Babikova RA (1987) The principal results of pancreatic islet cell culture transplantation in diabetes mellitus patients. Transplant Proc 14:2372–2375
29. Sutherland DER (1981) Pancreas and islet transplantation II. Clinical trials. Diabetologia 20:435–450
30. Sutherland DER, Moudry-Munns KC (1990) International Pancreas Transplantation Registry Analysis. Transplant Proc 22:571–574
31. Thompson SC, Mandel TE (1990) Fetal pig pancreas. Preparation and assessment of tissue for transplantation and its in vivo development and function in athymic (nude) mice. Transplantation 49:571–581
32. Tuch BE (1988) From nude mouse to man. In: Peterson CM, Jovanovic-Peterson L, Fomby B (eds) Fetal islet transplantation. Implications for diabetes. Springer, Berlin Heidelberg New York Tokyo, pp. 127–164
33. Tze WJ, Tai J, Cheung S (1990) Human islet xenograft survival in diabetic rats. Transplantation 49:502–505
34. Weir GC, Bonner-Weir S, Leahy JL (1990) Islet mass and function in diabetes and transplantation. Diabetes 39:401–405
35. WHO Study Group (1985) Diabetes mellitus – report of a WHO study group. WHO Technical Report Series 727
36. Yoneda K, Mullen Y, Stein E, Clare-Salzler M, Ozawa A, Shevlin L, Danitovs J (1989) Fetal pancreas transplantation in miniature swine. II. Survival of fetal pig pancreas allografts cultured at room temperature. Diabetes 38 [Suppl 1]:213–216

# Fetal Tissue Transplantation and the Problem of Elective Abortion

D. E. Vawter, K. G. Gervais, W. Kearney, and A. L. Caplan

Electively aborted fetuses are the most reliable and plentiful source of fetal tissue for transplantation into human recipients [1]. However, many ethical concerns have been raised by the transplantation of tissue from electively aborted fetuses. In this paper, we discuss four widely cited sets of concerns and objections:

1. The transplantation of tissue from an electively aborted fetus is morally inseparable from the morality of the elective abortion.
2. The transplantation of fetal tissue will cause an increased number of elective abortions.
3. The transplantation of fetal tissue will lead to the modification of abortion procedures.
4. The transplantation of fetal tissue will cause women to abort in order to donate.

Each grounded on a belief that the transplantation of fetal tissue either necessarily is, or is likely to become, associated with particular abortions, or with elective abortion in general, in ways that are morally objectionable. The focus of each is a supposed morally relevant connection or interrelationship between fetal tissue transplants and elective abortions. Although several of these sets of concerns include objections to some or all transplantation of tissue from electively aborted fetuses, they do not all call for the prohibition of fetal tissue transplants.

## The Transplantation of Tissue from Electively Aborted Fetuses is Morally Inseparable from the Morality of the Elective Abortion

The first set of concerns states that the transplantation of tissue from electively aborted fetuses is morally inseparable from the morality of the abortions. That is, some kind of necessary connection is said to exist between aborting a fetus and using its tissue, such that it is impossible for the abortion to be immoral and the use of the tissue to be moral. Given this moral

Center for Biomedical Ethics, University of Minnesota, Minneapolis, MN 55455, USA

W. Land, J. B. Dossetor (Eds.)
Organ Replacement Therapy:
Ethics, Justice and Commerce

inseparability, if the abortion is immoral, the use of the tissue is necessarily immoral as well.

This moral objection to the transplantation of fetal tissue is usually raised by those who are morally opposed to all elective abortions. But those who believe that some, but not all, elective abortions are immoral may share the view that it is unethical to use tissue from fetuses aborted for allegedly immoral reasons. They too may hold that the morality of the two activities cannot be separated.

The concept of moral inseparability has not yet been adequately explicated in the literature we have reviewed on ethical and policy concerns raised by the use of fetal tissue. It seems to be used to refer to different things, including logical as well as empirical forms of necessity. Some maintain that abortion is so immoral that a moral taint necessarily transfers to any use of the tissue, or that any use compounds the wrong done to the fetus. Some even suggest that those who use the tissue are accomplices and are morally to blame for the immoral abortions [2]. By using the tissue, they signal that they do not object to the abortions; in fact, they seem to endorse them insofar as they knowingly benefit from them. Thus, on this view, it would be logically inconsistent to use the tissue yet condemn the abortions.

Several responses can be made to such claims of moral inseparability and the objection to all transplants of tissue from elective abortions. First, those who agree with the claims of inseparability, but do not hold that all abortions are immoral might seek methods of procuring and transplanting fetal tissue only from moral abortions. In practice, this would require widespread agreement in the community regarding which abortions are moral and which are not. In some countries there may be sufficient agreement that lawfully performed abortions are moral, that the public can be confident that tissue is used only from moral abortions. In the United States, however, agreement on which abortions are moral would be extremely difficult, if not impossible. Even if such agreement existed, since every woman has a strong moral claim to privacy concerning her own reasons for aborting, it would be impossible in practice to separate fetuses aborted for moral reasons from those aborted for immoral reasons.

Second, if it is impossible to identify or isolate tissue from immoral abortions it can be argued that obtaining tissue from some unidentified immoral abortions might be tolerated if certain utilitarian considerations are relevant. For example, the transplantation of tissue from immoral abortions may be justified if the anticipated benefits are sufficiently significant. The argument is not that the immorality of an abortion is morally separable from the transplantation of fetal tissue, but that additional considerations, such as concern for the suffering of potential recipients may be sufficient to outweigh the immorality of using the tissue [3]. The most conservative, however, maintain that no amount of benefit can outweigh the wrong that is committed when fetal tissue is used from even one immoral abortion [4].

Third, it can be argued that the morality of the use of fetal tissue can be separate from the morality of the abortions from which tissue is obtained.

This view holds that the immorality of the abortion does not necessarily carry over to the use of the tissue. For instance, if those using the tissue do not influence the woman or abortion provider to go ahead with the abortion and if it would be performed anyway for entirely separate reasons, the decision to use the tissue can be judged on its own merits. Under such circumstances, it is argued, the morality of the two activities is not linked.

The morality of using tissue from an immoral abortion is often argued to be analogous to the morality of transplanting the organs and tissues of a murder victim; the morality of the murder is independent of the morality of the transplantation. Moreover, many maintain that it is not merely permissible to use tissue from such sources, but that it is immoral not to do so when someone may benefit, so long as the donor or the donor's family has consented. Others argue that it is morally appropriate to try to reap whatever good is possible from a natural death, accidental death, suicide, murder, immoral abortion, and so forth, in an effort to offset the tragedy.

Disagreement continues over the argument that fetal tissue transplantation and elective abortion are morally inseparable and the corresponding objection to the transplantation of tissue from electively aborted fetuses. Although some maintain that the transplantation of fetal tissue is immoral because the users of the tissue cannot avoid being connected with the immoral abortions from which they obtain tissue, others believe fetal tissue can be used in cases where the abortion was moral or where the benefits outweigh the harms and wrongs. Others have raised strong counterarguments that suggest there is no necessary connection between the immorality of an abortion and the morality of transplanting tissue from the abortion. The arguments concerning the nature of the necessary connection between the immorality of elective abortions and the transplantation of tissue from these abortions deserve further consideration.

## The Transplantation of Fetal Tissue Will Cause an Increased Number of Elective Abortions

A second ethical concern is based on the prediction that the transplantation of fetal tissue will cause a measurable increase in the number of elective abortions and the assumption that an increase in the number of abortions is morally objectionable. As society benefits from the use of fetal tissue, it is argued, many abortions currently considered immoral would gain legitimacy, and restrictive social attitudes and policies regarding abortion would relax. An increase in the number of abortions can be predicted to follow.

The morally objectionable connection that is predicted to develop between the transplantation of fetal tissue and an increase in the number of elective abortions differs from the previous objection in that it is not a necessary connection, but merely a predicted empirical connection. Furthermore, on this view, any particular transplantation of tissue from an electively aborted fetus is not necessarily immoral. Only if transplantation occurs frequently would the number of elective abortions be expected to increase; isolated fetal tissue transplants would not have to be prohibited or restricted.

France and the Council of Europe have each proposed that the transplantation of fetal tissue should be restricted to diseases that are rare and for which there is no equally efficacious treatment [5, 6]. In the United States this concern has been used to justify a complete ban on using federal funds to transplant tissue from electively aborted fetuses [7]. The guidelines of many other countries, however, do not address this concern.

To determine whether the number of abortions would increase, it is necessary to assess any relationship between the transplantation of fetal tissue and public opinion on abortion, and between public opinion and the abortion rate. These relationships may be too complex to accurately measure or even begin to analyze.

We agree with those who argue that until predictions that the transplantation of fetal tissue will lead to more abortions can be empirically supported, they are too speculative to merit major policy restrictions. However, if such a connection were to exist, it still would be necessary to consider whether all such transplants are immoral and whether a partial or complete prohibition on fetal tissue transplantation is justified.

## The Transplantation of Fetal Tissue Will Lead to the Modification of Abortion Procedures

A third type of ethical concern about the relationship between fetal tissue transplantation and elective abortion is that procurers and users of fetal tissue may become immorally involved in abortions (moral and immoral abortions alike). This concern stems from the observation that tissue procurement is most effective when the procurers work closely with abortion clinic personnel. These close working relationships, for example, may lead procurers to encourage abortion providers to modify their procedures to increase the chances of obtaining useful tissue for transplantation. Examples of such modifications include reducing the pressure of the vacuum, slowing the abortion procedure, and increasing the diameter of the cannula. Insofar as a modification is motivated by reasons other than concern for the woman's health, it may constitute a morally unacceptable intrusion in the abortion procedure.

There is nothing inherent in the transplantation of fetal tissue that necessitates that tissue procurers and users of fetal tissue will interfere with abortion procedures or decisions. The alleged connection between these acitivities is merely possible. No general moral objection to the transplantation of tissue from electively aborted fetuses follows from this concern that fetal tissue transplants will lead tissue procurers to interfere in morally unacceptable ways with the abortion procedure.

Several policies have been proposed to restrict the tissue procurer's contact with either the abortion providers or the women considering abortion. In

Britain, one recommendation is to establish a disinterested, government-supported intermediary between the abortion providers and the transplanters to procure fetal tissue. Other proposals would prohibit any modification of the abortion procedure for the purpose of procuring better tissue, or at least prohibit any modification that increases the risk to the woman's health. But it might be objected that if a woman is a competent adult, able to make free and informed decisions, she should be permitted to consent to modifications, including those that increase her risks.

We believe the prospect that tissue procurers and users of fetal tissue may be motivated to interfere in potentially inappropriate ways in abortion procedures is a serious concern. Yet this concern may be particularly amenable to control by public policy, without prohibiting the use of tissue from elective abortion altogether. The chances that the transplantation of fetal tissue will lead some to interfere in the abortion decision and procedures in unacceptable ways largely can be eliminated by restricting the activities of tissue procurers and abortion providers. A question that remains unresolved, however, is whether there are sufficient reasons to prohibit all modifications of abortion procedures, or whether women should be permitted to consent to modifications under some circumstances.

## The Transplantation of Fetal Tissue Will Cause Women to Abort in Order to Donate

The concerns and objections that arise over the prospect that women may abort to donate fetal tissue to relatives or even to anonymous recipients can be divided into two arguments. One argument predicts that the practice of transplanting tissue from elective abortions will necessarily offer women a new immoral reason for abortion, namely, abortion for donation. Providing women with this possible new motive to abort is viewed as a necessary and abhorrent consequence of fetal tissue transplantation.

It may be particularly difficult to morally separate abortions for the purpose of donation from the practice of transplanting fetal tissue generally. It is more difficult for transplanters to argue that they are not causally or morally responsible for abortions to donate, compared with abortions for other reasons. If fetal tissue were not transplanted, fetuses would not be aborted for the purpose of donation. This concern over an alleged necessary connection between the practice of fetal tissue transplants and the occurrence of a new motive to abort to donate may lead some to conclude that all fetal tissue transplants are immoral and should be prohibited. A more moderate policy alternative would allow fetal tissue transplants if mechanisms could be developed that prevent women from aborting to donate and prohibit the transplantation of tissue from such sources.

The second argument consists of the more specific objection that if a fetus is aborted for the purpose of donation, it is immoral to transplant its tissue. As with the argument above, it is assumed that it is always immoral to abort to donate fetal tissue. The objection to transplants of tissue from fetuses aborted for donation might justify policies to prevent women from aborting to donate, or at least policies to prevent the transplantation of tissue from fetuses aborted for donation. This objection to the transplantation of tissue from fetuses aborted for donation, however, does not imply that all fetal tissue transplants are immoral and should be prohibited, but that only a subset of fetal tissue transplants are immoral and should be prohibited.

Both sets of arguments rest on a variety of important moral and empirical assumptions including that abortion to donate is immoral, that women would base abortion decisions on the interests of others, and that transplanting tissue from a biologically related fetus has significant advantages.

To dispute the assumption that abortion to donate is immoral, one can argue the opposite, namely that abortion to donate is moral. For instance, perhaps the needs of actual persons should take priority over the interests of a potential person. If so, when tissue from a fetus is necessary to save or drastically improve someone's life, it may be permissible to abort for this purpose. Under what circumstances, if any, it is morally permissible to abort to donate deserves further consideration.

There is no empirical evidence that women base abortion decisions on the interests of others or that the transplantation of fetal tissue would cause women to abort fetuses they would otherwise carry to term. The factors that influence a woman to have an abortion are complex. Nonetheless, the available data suggest that a woman's decision is highly related to factors such as the effect a pregnancy would have on her life and whether she feels mature enough to be a parent [8]. Donating tissue to help others differs significantly from the usual reasons a woman undergoes an abortion. It is widely held that this motivation is unlikely to be common unless transplanting biologically related tissue proves to be significantly advantageous.

To date no biological advantage has been demonstrated. In fact, there may be disadvantages if the condition being treated is itself a genetically related ailment. However, until fetal tissue transplantation is more successful in general, any advantages to transplanting tissue from biologically related fetuses will remain unknown. Furthermore, it probably will not be possible to answer the question without using tissue from biologically related fetuses aborted for the purpose of donation. Those who hold that abortion to donate is immoral are likely to argue that it is morally impermissible to study whether there are any advantages to using tissue from biologically related fetuses. If the question cannot ethically even be studied, and it remains unknown whether there are any advantages to transplanting tissue from biologically related fetuses, the incentive for a woman to abort to donate to a relative can be expected to be low or nil.

Proposals to discourage abortions to donate (and to protect tissue users from complicity with this type of immoral abortion) aim to:

1. Prevent a woman from designating the recipient of the tissue.
2. Restrict the information a women may have about how the tissue may be used.

3. Prevent a woman from designating how the tissue may be used.
4. Delay discussions of donation until after the woman has consented to the abortion.
5. Eliminate incentives for abortion providers to pressure a woman to abort to donate.
6. Prohibit abortion providers from performing an abortion if the woman's reasons for the abortion include donation.
7. Require a woman who wishes to donate fetal tissue to state that she is not undergoing the abortion for the purpose of donation.

In our view, several of these proposals would impose unjustified restrictions on the information women are permitted to receive and on the decisions they are permitted to make. The restrictions imposed on the donation, procurement, and transplantation of human fetal tissue in response to ethical concerns about the transplantation of tissue from elective abortions should not themselves be morally objectionable intrusions on the rights of the parties concerned. Justifiable policies will be based on good empirical information, be the least restrictive means of achieving the objective, and be consistent with other rights of the relevant parties.

We believe the incentives to women to abort to donate fetal tissue are frequently overestimated, while numerous inherent disincentives are overlooked. Information that should routinely be provided to women before they decide to donate fetal tissue or even before they decide to have an abortion contains significant disincentives to donate fetal tissue and to abort to donate in particular. For example:

1. The chances may be very low that any tissue donated will be used.
2. There is no shortage of fetal tissue.
3. Fetal tissue transplants have had little success and remain experimental.
4. There is no known advantage to transplanting tissue from a biologically related fetus.
5. Donation may pose several risks to the woman's privacy:
   a) The woman's blood is often tested for human immunodeficiency virus and other infectious diseases to establish the quality of the fetal tissue.
   b) Identifiers placed on the fetal tissue make it possible to trace the tissue back to the woman who donated it.
   c) Tissue procurers or others not directly involved in the woman's care may be given access to her clinic record.
6. Donation may increase the risks of pain or injury, if the abortion procedure is modified to increase the chances of obtaining the tissue desired.

More attention should be directed to ensure that women have the information necessary to make fully informed decisions about abortion and the donation of fetal tissue. Incidentally, more complete disclosures will also offer women significant disincentives to donate fetal tissue, and to abort to donate in particular. These disincentives should not be overlooked when considering whether women will abort to donate and what policies, if any, might be necessary to prevent women from aborting to donate.

## Conclusion

Each set of concerns raises important ethical questions about the nature of the relationship between fetal tissue transplants and elective abortion, about whether the transplantation of tissue from some or all electively aborted fetuses is morally permissible, and what policy restrictions on women, abortion providers, tissue procurers, and transplanters may be justified. In particular, we should continue to explore such ethical questions as in what sense, if any, are fetal tissue transplants and immoral elective abortions morally separable from one another, is any increase in the number of elective abortions permissible, is it ever permissible for a woman to abort to donate, and should women be permitted to consent to modifications in the abortion procedure.

## References

1. Vawter DE, Kearney W, Gervais KG, Caplan AL, Garry D, Tauer C (1990) The use of human fetal tissue: scientific, ethical, and policy concerns. Center for Biomedical Ethics, University of Minnesota, Minneapolis
2. Burtchaell J (1988) University policy on experimental use of aborted fetal tissue. IRB 10:7–11
3. Strong C (1991) Fetal tissue transplantation: is it insulated from abortion. J Med Ethics (in press)
4. Bleich JD (1988) Fetal tissue research and public policy. In: Consultants to the Advisory Committee, Director, National Institutes of Health. Report of the human fetal tissue transplantation research panel, vol 1. National Institutes of Health, Bethesda, Maryland
5. Comite Consultatif National d'Ethique pour les sciences de la vie et de la sante (1984) Avis sur les prélèvements a des fins thérapeutiques, diagnostics et scientifiques de tissue d'embryon ou de foetus humains morts. Paris
6. Parliamentary Assembly of the Council of Europe (1985) Opinion on the use of dead human embryos for industrial and commercial purposes. Document 5479
7. Sullivan LW (1988) Letter to Dr. William Raub, Acting Director, NIH
8. Bracken MB, Klerman LV, Bracken M (1978) Abortion, adoption or motherhood: an empirical study of decisionmaking during pregnancy. Am J Obstet Gynecol 130:251–262

# Legal Problems Associated with Abortion: Fetal Cell Transplantation

J. E. M. Akveld

## Introduction

For some time now, induced abortion and organ transplantation have been part of the medical repertory. Lawyers have been of the opinion for a long time that abortion and organ extirpation are forms of medical action requiring legal provisions. A decisive argument for this opinion is that induced abortion and organ removal are not medical actions in the usual sense of the word; medical indication for such actions is generally lacking. This means that, for the permissibility of such actions, further legitimization is needed. Neither the doctor nor the patient concerned can offer this legitimization in a general sense. The legislator can fulfill this legitimizing role. The conditions to which doctors should adhere in performing the actions mentioned above must be laid down in legislation. This creates clarity, both for those who provide aid and for those who ask for aid; moreover, it creates rights and obligations. As, with the actions mentioned above, the interests of third parties are concerned as well, legislation is all the more needed.

On May 1, 1981, the Dutch Parliament passed the Pregnancy Termination Act (WAZ = *W*et *A*fbreking *Z*wangerschap). This act came into force on November 1, 1984. Considering the pluriformity of Dutch society and the widely diverging opinions on the moral permissibility of abortion, it is not surprising that the act represents a great deal of compromise. The Netherlands still have no Organ Transplantation Act, in spite of the fact that there has been talk about it for the last 25 years. At this point in time, the requirement for a donation ex vivo is informed consent on the part of the donor. For a donation ex mortuo the system applied is analogous to the Disposal of the Dead Act (1869) as it holds regarding autopsy and dissection. Summarizing, this means an opting-in system regarding donation.

An Organ Donation Bill has been introduced by the Government. The nature of this bill is one of compromise as well. This is, however, not caused by diverging moral opinions on the permissibility of organ donation, but by varying political opinions on bodily integrity and autonomy of citizens and on the way in which these should take form in the case of organ donation.

Erasmus University, Centre for Health Policy and Law, P.O. Box 1738, 3000 DR Rotterdam, The Netherlands

W. Land, J. B. Dossetor (Eds.)
Organ Replacement Therapy:
Ethics, Justice and Commerce

The notion that fetuses and fetal material, becoming available after an abortion, can be used for scientific purposes or for – often still experimental – transplantation is of a more recent date. Until now, one might think of transplantation through increasing liver, pancreas, brain and bone-marrow cells. In a more distant future, fetal bone parts and organs may possibly be considered for transplantation as well.

Here the juridical problems, connected with the use of fetal tissue and/or tissue suspension as transplant material will be presented. The problem of biomedical research on fetal material will not be considered in this paper. The same holds for questions directly related to the usually experimental character of this form of transplantation medicine. The aim of these observations is to establish whether or not the existing or proposed legal provisions offer a context for the new possibilities of transplantation. To this purpose, the most relevant legal provisions on this issue will be subject to a closer analysis. Successively, the Pregnancy Termination Act, the Organ Donation Bill, and the Law of Property will be considered. The approach will have a juridical and technical character. There is no intention of passing moral judgement.

## The 1981 Pregnancy Termination Act

The Pregnancy Termination Act (hereafter to be called the PTA) makes a distinction between abortion with a so-called vitally indicated character and abortion which is socially indicated. The former category comprises abortions which are the result of an operation which is absolutely necessary for the woman from a medical point of view. It is not exactly indicated in the law when such a necessity arises. Nor was the concept vital indication further clarified during parliamentary discussions about the PTA. For this kind of abortion, the normal regulations hold which apply in the case of regular medical operations.

For abortions which are carried out without a vital indication, the PTA applies. The basic principle of the PTA is that help should be given to women who find themselves in an emergency because of a pregnancy (article 5 of the PTA). In that situation both the woman and the doctor have to act, fully aware of the heavy responsibility they have towards the unborn life and aware of the consequences for the woman, says the Explanatory Memorandum.

The legislator has not laid down a general norm for what constitutes an emergency, nor was that concept worked out in detail during the parliamentary discussions. One of the reasons for this happening is that emergency situations may vary widely and cannot be standardized. The persons entitled to an opinion as to whether or not it is an emergency are the woman and her doctor in the PTA system. The PTA, on the other hand, does comprise a number of procedural guarantees for the protection of the unborn life. These guarantees are mainly directed at making the decision-making process a carefully considered one.

It is seen to be of special importance that a woman arrives at her request for abortion deliberately and voluntarily and that all other alternatives have been exhausted. Pregnancies longer than 13 weeks may only be terminated in clinics specially indicated for this purpose. The law considers it a legal offence to terminate a pregnancy of over 24 weeks with a social indication, when it can reasonably be expected that the fetus is independently viable outside the body of the mother. Finally, it is considered of importance by the legislator that commercial practices are completely excluded.

It may be stated that, in creating the PTA, the Netherlands legislator has hardly paid attention to the possibilities of using fetal material for the purpose of transplantation. That was not anticipated, considering the aims of the PTA. The law is intended to bring about a careful and considered abortion practice and to prevent commercialism. But the result now is that (neither in a forbidding nor in a permissive sense) the act comprises one single regulation regarding the use of fetal tissue for transplantation purposes [1].

## Organ Donation Bill

On February 12, 1990 the Minister of Public Health requested the National Council (Nationale Raad voor de Volksgezondheit) to advise him on the Organ Donation Bill. This bill regulates both donation ex vivo and donation ex mortuo. The bill applies to "a person, dead body or human fetus by whom or regarding whom, by virtue of this act, permission has been granted to remove organs from him or from the body or fetus".

One of the basic assumptions of the bill is the right to inviolability of and self-determination regarding the human body. According to the Explanatory Memorandum, this right, as also laid down in article 11 of the Constitution, does not end at someone's death, but remains valid after death. In practice this means that one may remove organs after someone's death only if an exercise of the relevant person's will is available. If after death no exercise of the will is available, substitute permission for organ extirpation may be given by categories of persons to be indicated in the bill. A comparable regulation also applies for the human fetus. The bill determines that the mother may grant permission where a human fetus is concerned (article 11, paragraph 1). According to the legislator, the fetus may be considered as an organ donor if cerebral death has been established and the woman has granted permission. In any case still-born fetuses will be covered by this bill.

The question remains as to whether or not fetal tissue lies within the scope of this bill. For the bill only applies when organs/material are removed for the purpose of transplantation. Strictly speaking this is not the case with induced abortion. Moreover, the Explanatory Memorandum states that the bill is no "human tissue act", which applies for all kinds of body material, regardless of the way in which, or the purpose for which, the material becomes available. Furthermore, one may argue that fetal material, as it is left after an induced abortion, cannot be put on the same level as the fetus the bill mentions.

Finally, the Explanatory Memorandum states that the problems around material which becomes available in other ways and the desirability of specifically legal provisions in this area will be looked into in the future. In any case, the Organ Donation Bill does not contain an all-embracing regulation for this new problem area. The bill does contain, though, a number of regulations which may offer a first orientation in trying to solve the newly arising possibilities.

## The Human Body and the Law of Property

For some time now there has been a discussion among lawyers about the juridical character of the human body, its removed material, and the dead body itself. The central theme in this discussion has been the question as to which judicial régime should apply regarding these above-mentioned "tissues". There is a high degree of consensus on the legal status of the human body. It has generally been accepted that the right to one's own body cannot be qualified as a right of property. The old maxim *dominus membrorum suorum nemo videtur* still holds. In the current situation the authority over one's body is based on the personal right, and the right to self-determination, as laid down in the Constitution. The status of the dead body does not create many problems either. Without regard to property issues, the legislator has indicated what is lawful in the law on the disposal of the dead. With considerations of public health and hygiene as his starting point, the legislator has carefully laid down which persons are entitled to authority over the dead body.

It is more difficult to indicate what the character of cells, tissues, and organs is once they have been removed from the body. Some authors make a distinction as to whether or not parts of the body are united with the intimate being of a human being [2]. Others distinguish between regenerating and non-regenerating tissues and parts [3]. Another possibility is to discriminate on the basis of removed material. One is more inclined to adopt a regime following the right of property in the case of nails and hair than in the case of sperm, blood, and skin. The problem with these criteria is that the boundaries are often vague and that application of these criteria does not lead to a clear classification into categories [4].

The fact is that after removal, cells, tissues, and organs lose their direct relation with the person from whom they originated. Once separated those matters become liable to actual control. It is usually assumed that these matters become the property of those from whom they originate [4]. It is less simple to indicate what is legal if such a matter comes under the control of a third party. This happens, e.g., in the case of operation remains. In this case, it is assumed that the hospital has implicitly been given permission for control (i.e., destruction or research for the benefit of the patient). It is less clear what is legal if blood has been offered to a bloodbank or organs have been offered to an organ centre. I support Gevers' suggestion that the individual's authority over his own body remains in force. In this line of thought, the will of the person from whom the material originates is decisive in what happens to the material. The control is partly based on the agreement in force between patient and doctor, and partly on the constitutional right to the inviolability of the body. The latter, as it were, becomes an issue in removed cells and organs. Acceptance of this opinion might lead to a legally workable model, also where fetal material is concerned. This solution does not apply if one is of the opinion that the fetus and fetal material have a character of their own, requiring a more precise provision.

## Discussion

As shown above, neither the present laws in force nor the anticipated law indicate which regulations apply regarding the use for transplantation of fetal material after induced abortion. The discussion on this issue has not even started. Some questions, which should be dealt with, will be gone into in this paper.

A first question concerns the position of a pregnant women. It cannot be ignored that, considering a possible transplantation, it might be desirable to continue the pregnancy for a certain period of time, or that it might be preferable to employ a certain abortion technique. From a judicial point of view, few objections can be brought against such a request on the part of a doctor. The doctor must, however, act *lege artis*. This means that a doctor who makes a choice contrary to the medical interests of the woman forsakes his professional duty.

A second question is who is to grant permission for the use of fetal cells for transplantation purposes? Neither the abortion law nor the organ donation bill give clear answers in this respect. The PTA does not provide an answer, since the crucial point in this act is the fact that the woman has the right bestowed upon her to request the termination of her pregnancy [5]. That is the only question the doctor has to consider. It is not clear whether it is also his responsibility to ask permission for transplantation purposes.

The Organ Donation Bill, on the other hand, does not give an explicit answer either on the matter of permission. The only issue which has been regulated is that the woman is entitled to the right to grant permission regarding the use of the fetus as organ source. It is easy to defend the idea of the right a woman has to the final decision regarding the use of fetal material. This would, moreover, be in accordance with the – in itself already central – deciding position, to which the woman has been entitled in both acts. Such a solution would require a legal foundation, and that preferably in the organ donation law.

In this context, I am less than charmed by the solution proposed by the Health Council. The Council reached a remarkable conclusion in its advice on the making available and use of fetal tissue or other mortal remains after abortion for scientific purposes [6]. It says that a distinction should be made between voluntary pregnancy termination and spontaneous abortion in case of a pregnancy which, at least initially, was desired by the woman. In the latter case, states the Health Council, the woman's permission, and possibly that of her partner, must always be asked for the use of fetal material (for scientific purpose). In the opinion of the Health Council, the conclusion would be different if the fetal tissue comes from an abortion of a pregnancy which was unwanted from the beginning. In that case it would be sufficient to inform the woman of the proposed use of fetal cells for transplantation purposes. The woman could, in the opinion of the Health Council, object to such use of the fetal material.

The opinions of the Health Council do raise the question, though, as to whether or not in general, an opting-out system would be preferable. It would spare the pregnant woman a permission interview, which is extremely difficult in most cases.

Recent experience with the use of fetal brain cells raises the question as to whether or not it should be possible for the woman to attach further conditions to her permission, in the sense that the woman designates the recipient of the material. The Organ Donation Bill gives contrary answers in this context. With donation ex vivo it is customary that the donor puts an organ at the disposal of a known recipient. The bill approves this. The provisions for donation ex mortuo are different. Article 16, paragraph 1 of the bill stipulates that the person who diagnoses a donor's death then sees to it that an organ center is immediately informed of the possible availability of an organ. In the future, this center will play an important part in the allocation of the organ to a specific recipient, this allocation being done according to medical criteria. It is important that, by going through an organ center, no direct relation can come into existence between organ donor and organ recipient. This avoids a situation of possible dependence between donor and recipient. Especially this latter consideration argues for opting for allocation via an organ center, also with the use of fetal cells. In this way it would be impossible for material from a certain fetus to be destined for a particular recipient, neither could a pregnancy be arranged with the purpose of creating a source for transplantation material.

A last point is whether or not fetal material should be made available only without charge. The Organ Donation Bill gives an indication on this point. Article 2 of the bill mentioned above stipulates that permission for the extirpation of an organ is void if it is given with the aim of receiving a remuneration which is higher than the costs directly resulting from the removal of the organ. If I take as my starting point that fetal cells are not organs in the sense of this bill, it is still easily defensible to say that the use of fetal cells should not have a commercial aim either. The purpose of such a regulation is to create maximum freedom of decision for the woman. For, if the possibility of obtaining financial gain by making a fetus (or fetal cells) available for transplantation purposes is not ruled out, the woman might find herself in a position of pressure and, because of that, might be constrained in her freedom of decision. Not only, for that matter, is the making available of transplantation material for commercial purposes an invalid agreement in the Organ Donation Bill, such action also has its consequences under the criminal law, since collaboration on such a donation by a doctor is a criminal offence which is subject to a prison sentence of 1 year maximum.

What has not been solved by the bill, is the question: what is legal, if e.g., with the help of fetal cell material, new cell lines are developed which are suitable for transplantation purposes. Although the starting point still holds that also material of this kind must be made available for free, it might be argued that this produces certain – perhaps quite considerable – financial obligations towards the original owner [7].

It seems to me that the judicial answer to the questions raised should be preceded by a point of view in society. "Experimentation with the transplantation of human fetal tissues and organs is not just a matter for the participants. The nexus between a society and its science requires that the broader societal implications of any research programme be recognized (preferably anticipated) and fully considered" [8]. The issue as to whether or not this should then lead to legal provisions should be looked into more deeply. An important consideration in this matter would be to ponder in how far legal provisions could in reality be enforced.

## References


1. Anonymous (1989) Perspectief (editorial, p. 3)
2. Maeyer JMM (1969) Transplantatie van organen en het privaatrecht. (Organ transplantation in private law). Medisch Contact, p. 1325
3. Herten van JHS (1984) De rechtspositie van het lichaam, lijk, stoffelijke resten, organen en niet-menselijke implantaten. (The legal position of the human body, dead body, mortal remains, organs and non-human implants). WPNR 5689:155–164
4. Gevers JKM (1990) Beschikken over cellen en weefsels. (Having disposal of cells and tissues), p. 13
5. Leenen HJJ (1988) Handboek gezondheidsrecht (Handbook of health law), pp. 128–129
6. Health Council (1984) Gezondheidsraad, Den Haag, 19 Sepember
7. Asser-Beekhuis (1977) p. 104
8. McCullagh P (1987) The fetus as transplant donor. Scientific, social and ethical perspectives. p. 211

# Fetal Transplantation: A Model for Medical Ethics Application

J. West, E. Squiers, P. J. Dimmick, S. E. Kelley, R. Latsha, and J. Miller

*"I had sooner play cards against a man who was quite skeptical about ethics, but bred to believe that 'a gentleman does not cheat', than against an irreproachable moral philosopher who had been brought up against sharpers".*

In citing this wonderful quotation from C.S.Lewis' *The Abolition of Man* [1], one can criticize contemporary bioethics as mostly talk and little action; in fact, practitioners in the field of medical ethics have had very little to do until the mid-twentieth century, for only at this time did the biological advances arouse American ethicists from their slumber [2].

In no area are heated debates between medical ethicists and medical practitioners more easily aroused than in that of human tissue transfer (e.g., transplantation). Transplant surgeons in general (and transplant researchers in specific) assume the risk of probing beyond the acceptable and, in so doing, speak from the leading edge of acceptable current medical techniques [3]. Ethical decisions have been an integral part of the history of organ transplantation [4] – Cosmas and Damian, patron saints of medicine who flourished under the Emperor Diocletian (AD 285–305), were beheaded at Cyrus in Syria for their "miracle of the black leg" (transplantation of the leg from a deceased Moor onto a church official who had lost his diseased leg to gangrene); these twin brothers were subsequently canonized by Pope John XV in the tenth century. Subsequent transplant surgeons have not suffered such an extreme fate, but there certainly exists no paucity of nihilists who would receive no small satisfaction in seeing similar sentences carried out! While many of the ethical concerns regarding transplantation have been resolved, the transplantation of fetal tissue seems initially to be more problematic.

## Success of Fetal Tissue Transplantation

That the use of fetal tissue for transplantation purposes has scientific merit is the subject of little or no debate. Transfer of fetal nerve cells into the putamen of a 49-year-old man with Parkinson's disease has reportedly been successful

Geisinger Medical Center, North Academy Avenue, Danville, PA 17822-2111, USA

W. Land, J. B. Dossetor (Eds.)
Organ Replacement Therapy:
Ethics, Justice and Commerce

[5,6]; potentially, such transplants may be extended for application to epilepsy, Huntington's chorea, Alzheimer's disease, etc. These impressive advances in the neurosciences open the floodgates for research into brain cell transplants, stimulation of nerve fiber production, regeneration of nerve pathways, and neuron replacement (with application to other forms of brain or spinal injury). Chinese workers have reported the successful transplantation of fetal adrenal tissue for Addison's disease [7]; extrapolation leads to treatment of other endocrine ailments, the most obvious of which is fetal islet cell transplantation for diabetes [8].

## Why the Use of Fetal Tissue?

With the impressive advances in the neuroendocrine sciences resulting from the use of fetal tissue, other issues are raised. First and foremost, why the use of fetal tissue at all? Because human fetal tissue grows rapidly, is very adaptable, and evokes very little immune response, it is considered an optimal tissue for transplantation. Indeed, the tissue transfer problem that nature itself has provided is the fetus, and "no immunologist handles this problem as efficiently as does nature ...... the maternal decidua plays an immunoprotective role, and the fetal trophoblast is an immunologically-privileged site [not exposed to the host's immune system] par excellence" [9].

## Ethical Aspects of the Use of Human Fetal Tissue for Transplantation

A second issue arising from the use of fetal tissue for transplantation purposes – namely, that of ethics – is seemingly more problematic. As of 1988, federal regulations permitted the use of tissue from *dead* fetuses in experimental transplantation (and all but eight states permitted such research); in March of that year, a National Institutes of Health (NIH) panel was charged with studying questions about fetal tissue research, and in May a virtual moratorium was announced on the use of fetal tissue. Further, federal support for transplantation of fetal tissue was terminated (thereby effectively stymying ongoing fetal transplant research). And, ironically, all of this occurred *despite* the NIH panel's conclusion that fetal tissue transplantation be permissible public policy (with the important caveat that safeguards be enacted to ensure that the prospect of helping a sick person would not persuade a woman to have an abortion). Thus, by administrative fiat research into significant areas of medical advance were aborted [10].

A Stanford University panel issued, by "special report" [11], its opinion regarding the "ethical use of human fetal tissue in medicine", the conclusions being consistent with the prior NIH report. While both the Stanford and NIH panels attempted to separate questions concerning the use of fetal tissue from those involving abortion, the Stanford group muddied the debate somewhat by attempting to sidestep the ethical problems involved in the use of tissue from fetuses of elective (induced) abortions; they recommended that tissue from induced abortions should be avoided if tissue from spontaneous abortions can adequately meet medical demands. But, as Annas and Elias so aptly point out [12]: "the use of tissues from fetuses aborted spontaneously is particularly problematic" as spontaneous abortions generally result from chromosome abnormalities (20 % if in the third trimester), and themselves may have been caused by infection with microorganisms. It goes without saying that neither defective nor infective (infected) tissue should be used for transplantation!

To examine the issue of fetal tissue use, it is necessary to list the sources and clarify these sources [13], be they fetuses from *spontaneous* abortions, fetuses from *induced* abortions, *anencephalic* fetuses (or infants), and *viable* fetuses (or infants):

*Fetuses from Spontaneous Abortions.* Very few ethical concerns are raised over the use of such fetal tissue and those pertain only to appropriateness of the use of potentially defective tissue (mentioned above) with the proviso that the fetus receive the same respectful treatment as would a cadaveric donor.

*Fetuses from Induced Abortions.* Ethical concerns become increasingly complex, as the decision to abort should be made independently of the decision to donate the fetal tissue for research or transplantation. Since fetal tissue is "better" in the second trimester and thereafter [14], there is concern that women would wait until that trimester to abort. Another concern is that a woman may become pregnant specifically to donate fetal tissue or organs to a family member or friend (or for monetary reward); although the National Organ Transplantation Act prohibits any sale, purchase, or brokerage of human organs for transplantation, fetal tissue has not been included (as it indeed needs to be [11]); additionally, federally funded projects are prohibited from offering "inducements" to women for participation in their programs.

*Anencephalic Fetuses.* The condition described as anencephaly is an invariably fatal occurrence characterized by the absence of most of the parietal, occipital, and frontal lobes of the brain (as well as bone and skin covering these areas); usually, the other organs are normal [15]. Two to three thousand anencephalic babies are born annually in the United States, 50 % of whom are born alive (two-thirds of these will die within hours of birth, the remainder within a week, usually). Amniocentesis and ultrasonography can establish the diagnosis in utero, allowing parents to decide whether to continue or terminate the pregnancy. In ending the pregnancy, some of the same concerns apply as in induced abortion. The mother may be asked to terminate pregnancy in the second trimester to prevent spontaneous fetal death or maceration. However, once delivered, the anencephalic infant must fulfil routine brain death criteria and must be provided with adequate medical care. Suggestions for terms such as "brain absent" or "nonviable" are not acceptable alternatives to "brain death" and cannot be used to hasten intervention for tissue or organ removal.

*Viable Fetuses.* This includes the California infant (mentioned by Toufexis [19]) who will be tested at 2 months of age to determine compatibility with her ailing elder sibling.

## Summary

Given the fact of the outstanding progress (and results) in the area of fetal tissue transplantation, it would seem disheartening to abandon these successes by applying Kafkaesquc bureaucratic rules to this and other significant research arenas (in vitro fertilization and the disputes regarding disposition of frozen embryos [16,17]; ongoing research into fetal abnormalities, etc.).

Further ethical issues are raised in cases involving purposeful performance of C-section for organ donation [18], the conception of a child to serve as a bone-marrow donor for an ailing elder sibling [19], and the use of anencephalic fetuses as donors [20]. While there may indeed be no "moral autoclave to sterilize [these embryonic questions] ethically" [21], it would certainly seem that the politics of abortion should not force us to address tangential issues of a tissue's source rather than the central issue of a tissue's use benefiting a sick person.

> As so succinctly worded by Annas and Elias [12]: "Transplantation challenges our ethical precepts, and traditional ethics have taken a back seat to the temptations and incentives to perform transplantations that are the first of their kind. Despite this, the public has generally applauded such transplantation, at least when it is seen as an attempt to save a life that otherwise would certainly have been lost. Transplantation involving fetal tissue is much more problematic, and the public may be less forgiving of ethical shortcuts. Saving a life is usually not at issue, and the source of the tissue, although not illicit, is troublesome to many. The world is watching, and this opportunity to demonstrate good science, good ethics, and compassionate patient care should not be wasted".

Another question might be: Can ethics be taught? "Telling right from wrong in everyday life is not that hard; the hard part is overcoming laziness and cowardice to do what one perfectly well knows one should" [22]. From the Palazzo Apostolico (Vatican City), Pope John Paul II advised the World Medical Association of "the right of man to life .... the first fundamental right, the root and source of all the other rights" [23]. He also reiterated the oath adopted by that body at Geneva in 1948: "I will maintain absolute respect for human life from conception, even under threat. I will not use my knowledge of medicine against humanity".

Finally, the "irreproachable moral philosopher" referred to by C.S. Lewis might feel that all of this transplantation technology is, quite simply, fooling with Mother Nature too much [24]; the idea of one human being fabricating another was pure metaphor when Mary Shelley first wrote *Frankenstein,* but man's mutable nature became more evident with the advent of twentieth century scientific advances:

> "The inconceivable has become conceivable ..... With the miracle that is modern surgery we use patches and parts, manufactured and real, borrowed from ourselves, other living human beings, or cadavers, and we stitch them together with sutures of nylon or pins and staples of stainless steel. The development of such an extraordinary technology that gives ambulation to the lame and life to the dying is the glory of our species" [24].

Presuming that it is our obligation to improve the human condition (Talmudic tradition has it that man alone among God's creatures has the privilege of sharing with the creator in his own design), one must seek new ethics and abandon the purist philosophical approach to treating man as an Absolute. Leonard Bailey (of Baby Fae fame) argues cogently against this purist approach by stating that

> "[Immanuel] Kant was a purist and dealt in absolutes. Biology, by its very nature, is a practical, unpredictable science ..... Organ transplantation is the perfect example. I seriously doubt transplantation ever crossed Kant's mind, and his *Critique of Pure Reason* has yet to make a sick human being whole again" [25].

## References


1. Lewis CS (1978) The abolition of man. Macmillan, New York
2. Kass LR (1990) Practicing ethics: where's the action? Hastings Center Report 20:5–12
3. West JC, Corry RJ (1981) Ethical dilemmas in transplantation. J lowa Med Soc 379–381
4. Diethelm AG (1990) Ethical decisions in the history of organ transplantation. Ann Surg 211:505–520
5. Anonymous (1990) A brain transplant that works (editorial). Lancet 335:445–446
6. Perry TL (1990) A brain transplant that works (letter to the editor). Lancet, 335:1042
7. Yan ZB, Bing ZX, Long WL (1990) A study of cadaveric fetal adrenal used for adrenal transplantation to treat Addison's disease: thirteen cases reported. Transplant Proc 22:280–282
8. Scharp DW et al. (1990) Preliminary results of clinical trials of human islet transplantation. American Society of Transplant Surgeons (Scientific Session), Chicago, June I, 1990, (abstract)
9. Sale GE (1990) The pathology of organ transplantation. Butterworths, Boston, pp. 17–18
10. Beardsley T (1990) Aborted research: ideology seems to have put some medical advances on hold. Scientific American, February, p.19
11. Greely HT, Hamm T, Johnson R, Price CR, Weingarten R, Raffin T, (The Stanford University Medical Center Committee on Ethics) (1989) The ethical use of human fetal tissue in medicine. N Engl J Med 320:1093–1096

12. Annas GJ, Elias S (1989) The politics of transplantation of human fetal tissue. N Engl J Med 320:1079–1082
13. Dimmick PJ (1990) Fetal tissue and organ transplantation. Thesis, Bloomsburg University
14. Drugan A, Evans WJ, Evans MI (1989) Fetal organ and xenograft transplantation. Am J Obtet Gynecol 160:291
15. Cefalo RC, Engelhardt T (1989) The use of fetal and anencephalic tissue for transplantation. J Med Phil 14:28
16. AMA (1990) Board of Trustees report. Frozen pre-embryos. JAMA 263:2484–2487
17. Robertson JA (1989) Resolving disputes over frozen embryos. Hastings Center Report 19:7–12
18. Anonymous (1990) C-section for organ donation (case studies). Hastings Center Report 20:22–24
19. Toufexis A (1990) Creating a child to save another. Time (Ethics Section), p.56, March 5, 1990
20. Harrison MR (1986) Organ procurement for children: the anencephalic fetus as donor. Lancet 1383–1385
21. Beardsley T (1988) Embryonic questions: the experimental use of fetal tissue sparks bitter debates. Scientific American December, pp. 27–30
22. Lewin M (1989) Can ethics be taught? New York Times, November 25, 1989
23. Pope John Paul II (1984) The physician and the rights of mankind (address). JAMA 251:1037
24. Gaylin W (1990) Fooling with Mother Nature. Hastings Center Report 20:17–21
25. Bailey LL (1990) Organ transplantation: a paradigm of medical progress. Hastings Center Report 20:24–28

# Xenografting: Its Future Role in Clinical Organ Transplantation

C. Hammer

The use of animal tissues for transplantation into human beings suffering under end-stage diseases is not futuristic any more. Surgeons are especially interested in xenografts for clinical application because of the shortage of donor organs, both from cadavers and from living donors. Yet, the idea of introducing such foreign organs originates not only from the shortage of grafts (6000 patients in Germany and more than 10000 in Europe have been on the waiting list for a kidney in 1990), but also from the excellent and promising results achieved in allogeneic transplantation.

The idea of substituting destroyed organs with xenografts is, however, not new. For almost a century it has been man's dream to replace diseased organs in end-stage patients by using grafts from animals. Historical trials (Table 1) ventured at the beginning of this century ended mostly in disaster since nothing was known about transplantation immunology or physiology, the surgical possibilities were poor compared with those available today, and not even zoological taxonomy was taken into consideration.

**Table 1.** Cross-species renal transplantation in humans

| Donor | Transplants ($n$) | Survival time | Author |
|---|---|---|---|
| Pig | 1 | 3 days | Jaboulay (1906) |
| Goat | 1 | 3 days | Jaboulay (1906) |
| Macaque | 1 | 32 h | Unger (1910) |
| Sheep | 1 | 9 days | Neuhof (1923) |
| Baboon | 1 | 4 days | Hitchcock (1963) |
| Macaque | 1 | 12 days | Reemtsma (1963) |
| Chimpanzee | 3 | 9 months | Reemtsma (1963) |
| Baboon | 6 | 60 days | Starzl (1963) |
| Chimpanzee | 1 | 1 day | Hume (1964) |
| Chimpanzee | 3 | 49 days | Traeger (1964) |
| Chimpanzee | 2 | 4 months | Goldsmith (1965) |
| Chimpanzee | 1 | 31 days | Cortesini (1966) |

Institute for Surgical Research, Klinikum Großhadern, Marchioninistr. 15, Ludwig-Maximilians University Munich, 8000 München 70, Germany

W. Land, J. B. Dossetor (Eds.)
Organ Replacement Therapy:
Ethics, Justice and Commerce

## Classification of Organ Grafts

Under the evolutionary aspects known today we can distinguish between closely related species and widely divergent ones. In the first case, organs function almost like allografts and are, therefore, called concordant. In this group we include, for example, species combinations like fox and dog, sheep and goat, or chimpanzee and man. The second case would be a discordant combination, a transplantation between widely divergent species, classified as individuals of two zoological orders like pig and dog or pig and man.

Both classes of xenografts, the concordant and discordant, have a different fate. Concordant grafts are rejected like allografts predominantly by cellular components in an acute fashion. Discordant ones in contrast are destroyed by humoral mechanisms, induced by preformed natural antibodies (PNAB) in a hyperacute mode. In widely divergent species this xenogeneic rejection mechanism is extremely complex, if not chaotic. Much has been published especially during the last few years (Auchincloss 1988; Hardy 1988). A therapy realising long-term results does not exist. No real function has been observed in the ultrashort perfusion time.

On the other hand immunosuppressive regimens achieve approximately the same survival time in closely related species, no matter to which zoological family or order they belong. Due to the lack of primates in Europe, we have worked with the combination fox and dog, comparable according to the albumin similarity and other genetic markers with the transplant model baboon and man (Table 2). In this zoological family of canines, if the dog is the recipient fox organs (kidney, heart, and skin) survive for days and weeks. Immunosuppression, in particular with anti-dog lymphocyte sera and antimacrophage sera achieve survival times which could be of clinical interest (Table 3). Chemotherapy is less effective, while total lymphoid irradiation (TLI) can prolong the function of hamster islets in rats up to over 200 days (Bollinger 1989). Optimal modern immunosuppression was able to keep a baboon heart beating for 21 days in the girl baby Fae (Bailey 1988).

**Table 2.** Rates of albumin evolution

| Primate species | Index of Dissimilarity | Canine species | Index of Dissimilarity |
|---|---|---|---|
| Man | 1.00 | Dog | 1.00 |
| Gorilla | 1.09 | Coyote | 1,06 |
| Chimpanzee | 1,14 | Wolf | 1.16 |
| Orangutan | 1.22 | Jackal | 1.18 |
| Baboon | 2,23 | Fox | 1.20 |
| Capuchin Monkey | 5.00 | | |
| Tupaia | 11.00 | | |
| Cattle | 32.00 | | |
| Pig | >35.00 | | |

**Table 3.** Survival time of fox organs in dogs

| Organ | Immunosuppression | Survival time (days) | *n* |
|---|---|---|---|
| Kidney | Control | 6.5 ± 1.2 | 8 |
| Kidney | Xeno BT | 5.6 ± 0.9 | 6 |
| Kidney | Allo BT | 6.3 ± 2.1 | 6 |
| Kidney | ALG | 13.4 ± 1.0 | 9 |
| Kidney | AMS | 15.8 ± 0.7 | 5 |
| Kidney | ALG + AMS | 17.7 ± 0.9 | 7 |
| Kidney | CSA + MP | 10.9 ± 3.0 | 7 |
| Kidney | Deoxyspergualin | 13.0 ± 3.4 | 6 |
| Heart | Control | 8.4 ± 1.9 | 6 |
| Heart | CSA + MP | 20.2 ± 4.1 | 6 |

BT, blood transfusion; ALG, antilymphocyte globulin; AMS, antimacrophage serum; CSA, cyclosporin A; MP, methylprednisolone

It has to be considered that, for a suitable xenograft, it is not only the zoological relationship which is important, it is also the availability of the animals and the organ size. Other genetic aspects deserve to be respected like chromosome numbers and karyotype, deoxyribonucleic acid (DNA) similarity and the major histocompatibility complex (MHC). Animals which hybridize are closely related and ideal transplant models. Proteins and their structure are important as are matching blood groups and enzyme interaction.

## Behavior of Xenografts

Not much is known about long-term behavior in concordant xenografts since few survived for 3 months or more (Reemstma 1964; Starzl 1964). It appears that vascularized organs behave differently (Calne 1970). Livers function even in distantly related species longer than hearts and kidneys. Primary nonvascularized tissues such as skin, bone, cartilage, nerves, heart valves, and bioprotheses are not destroyed in the same way as primary vascularized organs. Their clinical use is already well known and appreciated (Weinhold 1986). Single unprotected cells such as bone marrow, hepatocytes, and endocrine cells, e.g., islets are extremely sensitive to antibodies and can be carried away from the local environment of implantation to different places in the circulation or the lymphatic system. Encapsulation of such cell compartments in alginate would protect them from the large antibody molecules and even more from effector cells. First trials in this direction have been reported (O'Shea 1986)

## Advantages of Xenografts

After extensive studies in this field, the use of xenografts becomes likely and we see the many advantages. The first of these is availability: there would be no shortage of donor organs. Appropriate species could be selected, preferably domestic animals such as pigs or sheep, but monkeys or even kangoroos could also be chosen. First examples in producing transgenic animals have already been reported, mainly pigs in which the human MHC genes were transferred into the pig genome. The organs of such custom-made, MHC-engineered, transgenic animals would be less aggressively rejected as the original xenograft in both concordant and discordant combinations (Hammer 1985).

Xenotransplantation would reduce logistic problems, too. Close to each transplant center, breeding facilities could be established. Donor animals could be manipulated not only in histocompatibility, but also in size, perhaps to miniature horses or pigs or giant rabbits or rhesus monkeys. Under such conditions, the donor animals could also be kept germfree or at least free of specific pathogens in order to prevent resident viral or bacterial infectious diseases in the donor species.

Financial problems would also be small because this type of donor production could be managed in a fast and efficient way. Furthermore, fewer ethical problems would exist. The donor species must, of course, stay under the law of animal protection, but since the animals would be produced purely for transplantation, this type of organ donation would not lead to major problems or opposition.

Which animal or species should be selected in the long run? The optimal and possibly the most sympathetic choice would be the large nonhuman primates. It is, however, a fact that these species are almost extinct in nature and all of them reproduce and grow slowly. Their use would lead to enormous ethical opposition and they will not be available in the near future. Yet what difference would it make if zoologically widely divergent species – let's say pigs – could be modulated by transposed human genes into humanized porcine creatures?

Despite many open questions, pigs represent an attractive species for the future. Pigs reproduce fast and grow quickly, their organs can be used at any size and age, and they are surgically userfriendly. Ethical and even religious problems or opposition would be unlikely or negligible. The future will however show whether other numerous animals such as sheep, goats, or even kangaroos would not be another or additional appropriate choice.

Today we think mainly in terms of the transplantation of vascularized organs like kidney, liver, and heart, but already ideas of using endocrine organs like parathyroids, islets, and adrenals are appearing. Could not cornea, skin, or gut be transplanted from one species to another, and what about whole extremities, which are so similar in the nonhuman primates and man?

**Table 4.** Viruses in primates (Baboon)

| Oncogenic viruses | Effect |
|---|---|
| 1. Rous Sarcoma Virus | Induction of tumors |
| 2. Epstein Barr-Virus | Induction of leukemias |
| 3. Herps Virus Saimiri | Induction of leukemias |
| 4. Herpes Virus Ateles | Induction of leukemias and tumors |
| 5. Herpes Virus Hominis | Induction of leukemias |
| 6. Baboon Herpes Virus | Blastoid cell lines |
| 7. C-Type Viruses | Genome expression |
| 8. Hepatitis A | 0? |
| 9. Hepatitis B | 0? |

## Restrictive Aspects

Today in the era of human immunodeficiency virus (HIV) and bovine spongiforme encephalopathy (BSE), one should not forget to mention the problems of contagious substrates that could be cotransplanted from one species to another, especially under maximal immunosuppression. A list of infectious material for man found also in baboons is shown in Table 4. Less is known about, for example, slow viruses from pigs or kangaroos.

What happens when the organ is accepted? How does the recipient react to the foreign and antigenic products which are synthetized and released into the circulation such as proteins, fat, peptides, and enzymes from the liver, and are they satisfactory in their function? How do they express their antigenicity? Xenogeneic bovine and human growth hormones produced by transgenic mice, for example, are accepted as foreign products due to neonatal tolerance. They function and increase the body size of normal making them into giant animals. However, they also induce marked nephrotic atrophy, obsolescence of numerous glomeruli, massive cystic dilatation of the tubules, and uncontrolled liver hypertrophy because of the production of the hormone which is not down-regulated by physiological inhibitors. Bovine growth hormones, on the other hand, do not function in humans (Wanke 1991).

## What Is the Future Direction of Xenotransplantation?

In *discordant systems* is appears that depletion of PNAB would be of major importance. Absorption columns, lymph drainage, and hemodilution (Messmer 1971) are able to reduce the blood components including PNAB to almost zero values. However, after a few days most of the serum factors return to normal levels or show even rebound effects. Clonal depletion of cells producing antibodies directed against the xenogeneic antigen has been proposed, a procedure as difficult as the induction of antiidiotypic antibodies against PNAB. Chemical destruction of PNAB might be feasible (Hammer 1987). Dithiothreitol has been used to split the sulfur bonds of immunoglobulin (Ig)M-type antibodies in patients who are highly sensitized. In patients in whom these antibodies disappeared, no rejection episodes developed after transplantation. Manipulation of the blood clotting system using antagonists to platelet activating factor (PAF) and drugs inhibiting $Ca^{2+}$ transport has been suggested (Bergmann 1990). Depletion of complement or inhibition of one specific part of the complement cascade has been described (Schilling 1975). The protection of cells or cultured cells against the immune response by membranes like alginate seems to be possible (O'Shea 1986). As yet it appears that discordant transplantation in widely divergent species remains a dream of the future, but when it becomes feasible it will revolutionize medicine.

In *concordant systems,* TLI (Myburg 1984; Bollinger 1989) was used quite successful in a primate and rat-hamster model. Together with potent immunosuppression, this could be a reasonable approach even for the near future. Induction of transplant tolerance or transplantation of bone marrow in order to produce xenogeneic mixed chimeras should not be impossible and has been successfully carried out in rats and mice (Sachs 1989). Transplantation of cultured cells depleted of passenger cells or class II antigens has been shown to be possible in histoincompatible allogeneic systems. Thus, concordant transplantation has an immediate therapeutic future. With our most powerful immunosuppressive strategies, xenotransplantation is ready to be used in desperate situations for a time which is ethically justifiable.

Despite such pioneering experiments it would be naive to believe that xenografting is the solution for tomorrow. The problems are enormous and the mechanisms so complex that they are understood only to a small extent. However, genetic engineering and its rapid progress could allow the use of some organs in a selected manner from special animals of appropriate species to help in desperate cases like bridging the unhepatic phase by using baboon livers or to span the waiting time of a patient with heart disease using a baboon heart.

Encapsulated islets from pigs have been considered and tried experimentally because their product, porcine insulin differs only in one amino acid from that of man. It looks as if genetically manipulated islets could be the first candidates for xenogeneic transplantation. Preserved xenogeneic heart valves and bioprotheses have their firm place in the clinical situation already. This indicates that we are at the beginning of clinical xenografting and it will not be long until xenografting becomes a normal and daily procedure.

## References


Auchincloss H Jr (1988) Xenotransplantation: a review. Transplantation 46:1–20

Bailey MA (1988) Economic issues in organ substitution policy. In: Mathieu D (ed) Organ substitution technology. Westview, Boulder, pp. 198–210

Bergmann R, Saumweber D, Brecht HM, Hammer C (1990) Effects of a PAF-Antagonist (WEB 2086) on hyperacute xenogeneic rejection. Transplant Proc XXII:2009–2010

Bollinger RR, Knechtle SJ, Harland RC, Yamaguchi Y, Halperin EC (1989) New approaches to immunosuppression for xenotransplantation. In: Hardy MA (ed) Elsevier, Amsterdam

Calne RY (1970) Organ transplantation between widely disparate species. Transplant Proc II:550–556

Hammer C (1987) Isohemagglutinins and preformed natural antibodies in xenogeneic organ transplantation. Transplant Proc XIX:4443–4447

Hammer RE, Pursel VG, Rexroad CE, Wall RJ, Bolt DJ, Ebert KM, Palmiter RD, Brinster RL (1985) Production of transgenic rabbits, sheep and pigs by microinjection. Nature (315) 6021:680–683

Hardy MA (1988) Xenograft 25. In: Hardy MA (ed) Elsevier, Amsterdam

Messmer K, Hammer C, Land W, Fiedler L, Klövekorn WP, Holper K, Lob G, Merzel D, Brendel W (1971) Modification of hyperacute xenogeneic kidney rejection. Transplant Proc III:542–544

Myburgh JA, Smith JA, Stark JH, Browde S (1984) Total lymphoid irradiation in kidney and liver transplantation in the baboon: Prolonged graft survival and alterations in T cell subsets with low cumulative dose regimens. J Immunol 132:1019–1025

O'Shea GM, Sun AM (1986) Encapsulation of rat islets of Langerhans prolongs xenograft survival in diabetic mice. Diabetes 35:943–946

Reemstma K, McCracken BH, Schlegel JU. Pearl MA, Pearce CW, DeWitt CW, Smith PE, Hewitt RL, Flinner RL, Chreech O (1964) Renal heterotransplantation in man. Ann Surg 160:384–405

Sachs DH, Thoralf M, Sundt I (1989) Mixed bone marrow reconstituion as an approach to xenograft tolerance. Xenograft 25. Hardy MA (ed) Elsevier, Amsterdam

Schilling A, Land W, Pielsticker K (1975) Experimental xenografting in widely divergent species; interaction of humoral factors in hyperacute xenograft rejection in the rat-dog-system. Res Exp Med 165:79–92

Starzl TE, Marchioro TL, Peters GN, Kirkpatrick CH, Wilson WE, Porter KA, Rifkind D, Ogden DA, Hitchcock CR, Waddell WR (1964) Renal heterotransplantation from baboon to man: Experience with 6 cases. Transplantation 2:752–776

Wanke R, Hermanns W, Folger S, Wolf E, Brem G (1991) Accelerated growth and visceral lesions in transgenic mice expressing foreign genes of the growth hormone family. Ped Nephrol (in press)

Weinhold C, Weingartner J, Hammer C, Gokel JM, Peters D, Reichart B (1986)

In vivo investigation of kangoroo aortic valve xenobioprostheses: An experimental animal model. Yorke Medical Books, pp. 669–676

# The Ethics of Xenografting in Man

W. Cartwright

Is it a morally acceptable way to treat other animals to use them as a source of organs for transplantation into needy human beings? This is the principal, though not the only, moral issue raised by the practice of xenografting. The question can only be answered in the light of some more general understanding of the moral significance of other creatures, and so I begin by trying to supply this.

Moral philosophers characteristically see their task as the development of an adequate theory of morality. Given our propensity to theorise elsewhere, e.g. in science, the search for a theory in the moral sphere is not to be wondered at, though the wisdom of mounting such a search here is open to serious question. This theoretical aspiration is frequently accompanied by an influential conception of the method appropriate to developing a moral theory. We are to begin with our moral views or intuitions and to look for a theory that will account for and systematise those intuitions. Having developed a theory that will accommodate some of them, the method invites us to proceed further, either by adjusting the theory so that it will account for more of our intuitions or, if this is unattractive, by abandoning some of the intuitions in question. The aim is to secure a condition of stable coherence between our intuitions, or as many of them as possible, and the theory. Those of our intuitions which cohere with the theory we may rationally retain, those which do not we must rationally reject. This is the approach famously recommended by the American philosopher John Rawls (1972), who calls it the method of reflective equilibrium.

What, then, are our intuitions about the treatment of animals, and what does moral theory have to say about these intuitions? Not everyone has the same intuitions on this topic, a matter to which I shall return, but there is, it seems to me, a dominant intuitive view which may be succinctly stated as follows: animals matter morally, though less than human beings. This view, which I shall refer to hereafter as the dominant intuition, has two components. First, we cannot do whatever we wish with animals; they have some moral significance which imposes constraints upon how we treat them. But, secondly, their significance is less than that of human beings, and we are, therefore, entitled to prefer our interests to theirs. Now, it is a striking feature

Department of Philosophy, University of Essex, Wivenhoe Park, Colchester, CO4 3SQ, United Kingdom

W. Land, J. B. Dossetor (Eds.)
Organ Replacement Therapy:
Ethics, Justice and Commerce

of contemporary moral theorising that our leading moral theories have difficulty in accommodating this dominant intuition. I take those leading theories, at least in English-speaking philosophy, to be utilitarianism and what has come to be known as contractualism. I shall explain briefly the inhospitability of both theories to the intuition and ponder its significance.

Contractualism, whose most notable exponent is John Rawls (1972), holds that morality is in effect an agreement or contract between rational individuals. The claim is not that each of us has in fact struck any such bargain with the rest – evidently, we have not –, but rather that the best way to conceive of morality is as that set of rules that each of us would rationally have agreed to were we engaged in the process of founding a society. The contract is hypothetical rather than actual. Contractualism, thus, invites us to engage in the thought-experiment of working out what rules it would be rational for each of us to agree to were we beginning social life over again. Such rules have a particular claim upon us as the rules of morality. Contractualists assert that the rules it would be rational for us to select coincide with a significant number of our antecedent moral intuitions. This fact at once confirms the theory and lends rational support to the intuitions in question. Intuitions not so supported should be rejected.

It will be noted that the parties to this hypothetical contract are rational agents, which in practice means people. And the purpose of the contract is to establish a scheme of reciprocal obligations that the rational contractors find it in their mutual self-interest to adopt. This picture of morality excludes animals. They cannot be parties to the contract since, not being rational agents in the sense required, they are incapable of striking bargains. They are then excluded from the scheme of reciprocal obligations that is morality. The human parties to the contract will not find it rational to agree to any obligations towards animals. Why should they when animals are unable to commit themselves to any reciprocal obligations? By its emphasis on rationality and reciprocity, the contractualist vision of morality displaces animals. Contractualism casts doubt on our dominant intuition that animals have a moral importance that imposes constraints on how we treat them.

Utilitarianism, the other leading moral theory, holds, in its simplest and most traditional form, that the morally right act to perform in any situation is the one that produces most happiness or least suffering. The implications of this moral theory for our treatment of animals are more ambiguous. For a utilitarian of the kind described it is the consequences of an action rather than any other feature of it that make it right or wrong. And the only relevant consequences are happiness or pleasure and suffering. Anything capable of experiencing pleasure and suffering is thus an object of moral significance for utilitarians, and the consequences of an action for it must figure in the utilitarian calculation. But animals, or very many of them, are capable of experiencing pleasure and suffering and thus count morally for utilitarians. So far the utilitarian view, unlike contractualism, may seem to endorse the dominant intuition about animals. In fact it does not, for the intuition holds not merely that animals matter, but that they do so less than humans, and the utilitarian seems unable to endorse this second claim. What matters for the utilitarian is pleasure and suffering, and it would not seem to make any difference whose pleasure and suffering is in question. Your suffering is no less important than mine and, furthermore, the suffering of a cat would seem to be no less important than a comparable amount of my suffering. Suffering is suffering. Thus, the utilitarian view seems to deny the dominant intuition by assigning a moral significance to animals that equals that of humans.

But this feature of utilitarianism is counter-balanced by another. In determining how to act, the utilitarian must take account of the consequences of any proposed action for all those affected. The consequences may be mixed – pleasure may be caused to some, while suffering is inflicted on others. An action could still be right, even if substantial suffering was inflicted on some, as long as it was balanced by sufficient pleasure for others. In order for the action to be right, the surplus of pleasure over suffering would have to exceed, or at least equal, any such surplus produced by alternative actions. In principle, then, utilitarians could approve actions that inflicted great suffering on animals if they were counterbalanced by sufficient pleasure for human beings. This approval could extend to actions that the dominant intuition would declare to be unacceptable ill-treatment of animals.

Utilitarianism, then, doubly contradicts the dominant intuition. On the one hand, it assigns an equal moral value to humans and any other animals that can experience pleasure and pain. On the other, it does not construe this value as imposing upon our treatment of animals (or indeed humans) the sort of constraints that the dominant intuition would recognise. Some utilitarians would deny the latter claim. One of the most important contemporary voices speaking on behalf of animals, the Australian philosopher Peter Singer (1975, 1979) rests his case for them on a kind of utilitarianism. Singer evidently supposes that when the utilitarian calculations are done, the quantity of suffering we impose on other creatures in our practices is not outweighed by the quantity of pleasure or avoidance of suffering the practices confer on us. Singer has not, I think, made out his case convincingly; indeed, I doubt that it could be made convincingly. How is one seriously to estimate the quantities of pleasure and suffering involved? The sums are imponderable.

Neither contractualism nor utilitarianism can accomodate the dominant intuition about how we should regard other animals. Some philosophers would take this feature of our two leading moral theories as indicating that rationally we should reject the intuition. This is the best reason we could have, they hold, for thinking that our moral view of animals is mistaken. I shall argue on the contrary that the inability of the theories to accommodate the intuition tells against the theories rather than the intuition.

It is worthy of remark that the leading contractualist, John Rawls (1972, pp. 17, 512), seems to share this view. He recognises that contractualism seems only to cover our relations with other persons and is not apt for dealing with our relations with other animals and nature. He acknowledges the dominant intuition that we have duties towards other creatures, but does not see how the contract doctrine could be extended to embrace and account for these duties. A correct conception of our relations to animals and nature would seem to depend in his view upon a theory of the natural order and our place in it. How far the results of contractualism must be revised once this correct conception is realised he thinks we cannot say in advance. But it is clear from all this that for Rawls the inability of contractualism to account for our moral relations to other creatures is a limitation of the theory.

Those who wish to work the argument the other way from Rawls and myself and to say that the failure of contractualism and utilitarianism to accommodate the dominant intuition gives us reason to reject it, may point out that the intuition is in any case far from undisputed. Rather than supposing that animals have a moral importance which imposes constraints upon how we treat them, many, it may be said, appear to share the view of the great German philosopher Kant (1963, p. 23) that "animals... are there merely as a means to an end. That end is man..." Many, after all, appear to view without perturbation the indiscriminate conversion of animals into our food, our clothing, our pets, our experimental subjects, or our prey. It is one thing, it may be said, for a moral theory to be unable to accommodate a more or less universally shared intuition – this plausibly tells against the theory – but it is quite another for a theory to be unable to embrace an intuition as controversial as the one I have described as the dominant intuition. This surely tells against the intuition.

Such a situation of conflicting intuitions poses a problem for the method of reflective equilibrium which takes the task of moral philosophy to be the achievement of harmony between theory and intuitions. What is theory meant to do in the face of conflicting intuitions? One possibility is that a theory which succeeds in accommodating other intuitions may favour one of the conflicting intuitions. This is a reason for accepting the one intuition and rejecting the other. This is presumably, the thought of those who think that the failure of contractualism and utilitarianism to accommodate the dominant intuition is a reason to reject the latter. But there is another possibility. We may have reason, independently of the preferences of the theory, to suspect one of the intuitions. It may be that those who adhere to the intuition have a special interest which is served by such adherence, and which entitles us to suspect their position. Such may be the case on this issue. Amongst those who reject the dominant intuition are to be found butchers, farmers, hunters, scientific experimenters and others with a vested interest in our current ways of treating animals. By contrast, special interest is rather harder to discern on the part of those who adhere to the dominant intuition. Though the dominant intuition is controversial, these considerations give us some reason to prefer it to the rival intuition and, therefore give support to the view that a theory's failure to accommodate the dominant intuition counts against the theory.

Those still resistant to this conclusion may remark that, while in our culture the dominant intuition is merely controversial, in some other cultures it is not dominant at all. There the prevailing view is that animals lack any moral significance. If the dominant intuition is a culturally parochial one, this may be thought to weaken still further the case for retaining it in the face of the theories that reject it.

I agree with Rawls (1972, p. 512) that a correct conception of our relation to animals depends upon a theory of the natural order and our place in it. I think that in those cultures that assign animals little or no moral importance, there will be found to prevail an implausible theory on these matters. Central to our culture's understanding of these issues now is that there is no fundamental difference of kind between us and other creatures. The differences are rather ones of degree. Indeed, we have an increasing grasp of the complex forms of their lives and of what we share with many of them. This background conception of the natural order makes it grossly implausible to assign considerable moral importance to ourselves and to deny any to them. By contrast, the dominant intuition in our culture is much more congruent with this background. All this gives us reason to discount the intuitions of other cultures that conflict with the dominant intuition of ours, and further reinforces the view that the failure of our theories to accommodate our dominant intuition is a reason for rejecting them rather than the intuition.

I have so far concentrated on defending only one component of the dominant intuition which asserts that animals matter morally. But it will be recalled that there is a second component which asserts that they matter less than human beings. Contractualists can superficially endorse this, but only because they think, contrary to the first part of the intuition, that animals do not matter at all. Utilitarians, however, must reject this component, because they seem committed to holding that animals matter as much as humans, though many utilitarians would be prepared to sacrifice animals to our interests in certain situations. Once again, I think that we have reason to prefer the intuition to the theory.

One familiar way to defend the intuition is to say that the qualities which make humans morally valuable are to be found in other creatures, if they are found at all, only to a lesser degree. If it is our sentience, our intelligence, our rationality, our autonomy, our moral sense, or our capacity for complex social lives, to canvas some of the possibilities, that either singly or in combination make us valuable, then the fact that most of these characteristics are only present in other creatures to a lesser degree, if at all, means that they must have a lesser moral value than humans.

This way of defending the intuition, which to many seems the only one, is precarious because it has to confront a powerful objection. If other creatures are less important than adult humans because they exhibit the qualities mentioned above to a lesser degree, if at all, it follows that some of them are more important than the human fetus or infant precisely because they possess these qualities to a greater degree than the human fetus or infant. It is indisputable, for example, that an adult wolf far exceeds a 1-day-old infant in many of the qualities mentioned earlier. Now this is an embarrassment for the dominant intuition which naturally holds that the 1-day-old human infant is morally more valuable than the adult wolf, and that there are ways of treating adult wolves that are morally permissible in their case, but which never could be in the case of human infants.

Some might be tempted to say at this point, in order to escape the difficulty, that the human infant matters more than the adult wolf because the one is human and the other is not. Others, however, have coined the name 'speciesism' for this move. They think it amounts to a blank and rationally unsupported preference for our own species. They regard it as a prejudice in the same way that racism and sexism are prejudices. If one is going to give moral preference to humans over other animals, it cannot be on the basis of mere species membership, it is said. What, after all, is the moral relevance of that? One has got to find some other quality or qualities that correlate with humanity and that provide a more suitable foundation for moral discrimination in favour of human beings. The list of qualities mentioned above – rationality, intelligence, etc. – then re-presents itself, and so does the difficulty that, by these criteria, human infants turn out to be morally inferior to many adult animals.

The way out of this dilemma is to embrace one horn of it. The reason why humans matter more (to us) than other creatures *is* because they are human and the others are not. Those who regard this as a prejudice do so because they think it represents a failure to transcend the human point of view, which they think must necessarily be partial. Of course, they say, from that point of view humans would seem to matter more. They think that in moral matters we are obliged to take up a more objective stance and, therefore, must support the claim of our greater importance with reasons that are compelling from this objective and dispassionate perspective. They conclude that from that vantage point one cannot plausibly argue that each and every human matters more than each and every animal, for the reasons given above. The flaw in all this is the supposition that in moral matters we should aspire to transcend the human point of view in order to achieve some more objective view of things. But to see the world from a human point of view is a perfectly proper thing for humans to do even, one is inclined to say especially, when it comes to ethical matters. There is no requirement to transcend this point of view, to achieve the point of view of the universe as one might descibe it, a point of view that in fact is no one's. The issue is not about the importance of human beings and animals to the universe, *sub specie aeternitatis* as it were; it is about the importance of human beings and animals to human beings. From that perfectly proper, indeed for us inescapable, perspective, human beings understandably matter more than other creatures. To us as humans, human infants quite properly matter more than adult wolves, even though adult wolves outstrip them in certain respects. The parallel with racism and sexism is a spurious one. The human view of the world is a real one and for us inescapable, but there is no real white or male view of the world which is similarly unavoidable for whites and males.

The upshot of this discussion is that the dominant intuition embodies a defensible view of the moral importance of other animals. They matter, but less than us. What are the implications of this view for the practice of xenografting?

To seek to derive from the dominant intuition precise guidance on this practice, or indeed on any of our other practices involving animals, would be a mistake. Some moral philosophies such as utilitarianism aspire to precision in moral matters, but the aspiration is misplaced. As Aristotle observed, it is the mark of a cultivated man not to expect more precision of a matter than it will admit of. Ethical matters admit of little precision. The obstacles to it in this case include the fact that different animals will have differing moral values on the dominant intuition. Broadly speaking, the more they share with us the more value we shall attach to them. And, furthermore, we can expect no formula to determine what sorts of treatment of animals are permitted or excluded by their varying values. What is required in situations like this is wise and sensitive judgment, as Aristotle also saw. Nevertheless, it would seem to be clear that two key parameters in any such judgment will be the good done to human beings by a practice and the value of the animals involved. The greater the good and the less valuable the animals, the more likely the practice is to be justified. Such balancing may seem to be utilitarian in character, but it is not. Not all moral balancing is utilitarian balancing.

It may help if we compare xenografting with two more familiar practices involving animals: eating them and experimenting on them. In killing animals in order to eat them, we bring to an end lives that have some value on the dominant intuition and our farming practices frequently cause them to suffer. All this is done not in order to keep us alive and healthy – eating meat is not necessary for that – but in order to supply us with gastronomic pleasure. Does this warrant what we do to them? I doubt it. The case for experimenting on them is rather stronger, at least where the aim is to save human life and avoid human suffering in the future through understanding disease processes and developing new drugs. The case for xenografting would seem to be the strongest of the three, since here the purpose of the practice is to save directly the life of an identifiable human being. The dominant intuition would seem at least to allow the judgment that xenografting and some experimentation are permissible, a judgment that increases in strength the less important the animal is. Equally, I can see how the dominant intuition would allow the contrary view. The lesser value of other creatures, it may be said, permits us, for example, to save a human rather than a cat from a fire when we cannot save both, but it does not permit us to seize animals and sacrifice their lives for the purposes of experimentation and transplantation. Such systematic exploitation some will judge to be incompatible with their moral value, less though it is than that of humans. The dominant intuition would seem to permit either of these judgments, and I doubt that the issue between them is capable of decisive resolution. What is clear, however, is that even if one judges these practices to be permissible, the sacrifice of animals that they involve ought to be a matter of moral regret given their value. The moral cost involved should not be forgotten. It follows that if there are alternative and morally less costly ways of realising our goals in these situations, we should embrace them, even perhaps though they achieve our goals less effectively. And if such alternatives do not exist, we should strive to create them. This is an important consideration in the case of xenografting where there are alternative sources of organs. But it may be said that the organs available from those sources are inadequate to meet the demand, whereas the supply from other animals is potentially unlimited. But if what has been said above is correct, xenografting is only morally permissible if we have satisfied ourselves that nothing more can be done to enhance the supply of organs from other, morally less costly, sources. Many think that we cannot yet be satisfied in this respect.

I have suggested that the moral credentials of xenografting may be argued to be superior to those of eating animals and experimenting on them. Anyone, therefore, who thinks, erroneously in my view, that there is nothing wrong with eating animals should find no reason to object to xenografting. Nevertheless, I suspect that many will find xenografting the most shocking of the three practices, and it is worth exploring why this should be so. Perhaps the point is that this practice will strike many people as the most literally exploitative of the three. The varying structures of different forms of exploitation and the moral bearing of that variety is a topic that would repay enquiry. Maybe what will disturb people in this case is the picture of the animals involved that is implicit in the practice. In breeding animals for the purpose of xenografting, we are in effect viewing them merely as vessels bearing organs for our own use, and this may be thought to be a morally shocking picture. But then our practice of farming and eating animals may be thought to incorporate a picture of them as, in effect, meals on four or two legs, and this is not evidently a more edifying vision of them. Perhaps what underlies the sense that xenografting is morally worse than eating animals is that the latter is in some sense natural while the former is not. Eating other creatures is a practice found elsewhere in nature; xenografting is not. Whether or not appeals to what is natural should be allowed any weight in moral argument is a controversial matter, which I shall not pursue here, though I am not disposed to think that there is nothing in such appeals. The sense that xenografting is worse than eating animals may just exemplify the shock of the new. It may just reflect the fact that the latter is familiar, and the former is not. Nothing much follows from this about the relative moral status of the practices.

I shall end my discussion by remarking upon an irony at the centre of our contemporary relations to other animals. Science offers us new ways to make use of other creatures for our benefit and yet it is also science in some of its branches that has enormously enhanced our understanding of the nature and lives of these other creatures. In Britain, at least, this understanding is regularly conveyed in vivid visual form through remarkable television programmes that command very large audiences. There is a tension here that will, I think, increasingly press upon our consciences. What science has so remarkably brought us to respect we may find it increasingly difficult to allow science to exploit.

## References

Kant I (1963) Lectures on Ethics. Harper and Row, New York
Rawls J (1972) A Theory of Justice. Clarendon, Oxford
Singer P (1975) Animal Liberation. New York
Singer P (1979) Practical Ethics. Cambridge University Press, Cambridge

# The Baboon As Cardiac Donor in Man: A Reasonable Approach or an Immoral Desperate Search for Suitable Organs?

H. O. Vetter, H. Reichenspurner, and B. Reichart

## Introduction

There is an increasing need for suitable organs in cardiac transplantation. This scarcity of donor hearts is compounded further in infant and especially in neonatal transplantation; for example, the average prognosis for newborns with congenital lesions such as hypoplastic left heart syndrome is 1 week – 1 month. Current surgical procedures for these babies, who usually have completely normal brain function, are not satisfactory. Immediate heart transplantation (HTx) would be a possible solution to the dilemma. In such cases, xenogeneic heart transplantation (XHTx) using nonhuman primates such as the baboon as donors could become an alternative whenever human hearts are not available.

## Historical Remarks on Clinical Xenogeneic Heart Transplantation

In 1964, pioneering work in the field of XHTx began with the first clinical cardiac transplantation by Hardy [4], who used a chimpanzee heart in man. HTx was performed orthotopically and, therefore, the relatively smaller donor heart could not maintain the adult patient's circulation. In 1977, Barnard [2] performed, therefore, a heterotopic transplantation using the heart of a 30-kg baboon in a patient who could not be weaned off cardiopulmonary bypass after mitral valve replacement. However, the patient survived for only 6 hours. More recently, in 1984, Bailey [1] from Loma Linda Hospital performed an orthotopic HTx in a newborn with hypoplastic left heart syndrome using a baboon heart.

Despite ABO blood group incompatibility (the baby had blood group 0 and the donor baboon group A) Baby Fae survived for 20 days; she eventually died from multiorgan failure due to progressive hemolysis.

---

Department of Cardiac Surgery, Ludwig-Maximilians-University, Klinikum Grosshadern, 8000 Munich 70, FRG

W. Land, J. B. Dossetor (Eds.)
Organ Replacement Therapy:
Ethics, Justice and Commerce

## Specific Problems Associated with Xenogeneic Heart Transplantation

Hyperacute rejection due to the presence of preformed (humoral) antibodies against other species poses one major problem in XHTx. This type of rejection may occur within minutes, as in discordant transplantation. It happens, however, less often if the species are closer related to human (concordant). The terminology of *concordant* and *discordant* xenotransplantation was introduced by Calne in 1970 [3]. Concordant means potentially successful grafts (Fig. 1). This would be in transplantation between closely related species like chimpanzee or baboon. Discordant means potentially unsuccessful grafts like transplantation between sheep or pig and man. The histopathological features of hyperacute rejection show extensive interstitial edema and hemorrhage combined with myocyte necrosis, usually occurring within the first 24 h after transplantation. The second type of rejection is the cellular type – as present in human allograft transplantation – usually observed around the 7th postoperative day. The histology shows perivascular and interstitial mononuclear cell infiltration combined with interstitial edema and/or the presence of myocyte necrosis. A mixed type of rejection can be seen in XHTx, additionally. This type represents a combination of the acute cellular and hyperacute type of rejection.

Therefore, in clinical XHTx, the donors must be closely related to humans within the phylogenetic disparity scale. The chimpanzee, orangutan, or gorilla would be most suitable, even almost matching in size and weight. However, they are endangered and protected animals and, therefore, cannot be considered for XHTx. Baboons or Vervet monkeys are quite common, but

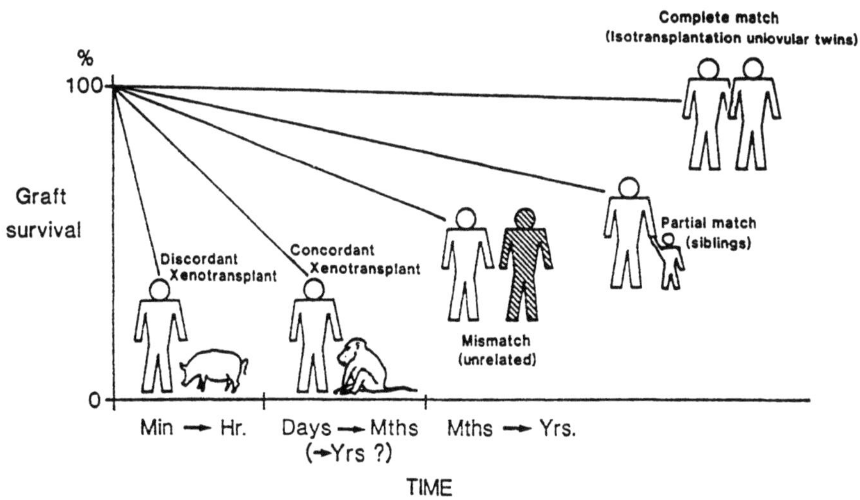


**Fig. 1.** Influence of donor/recipient genetic disparity on graft survival rates in organ transplantation. (From [6])

they are small (body weight 30 kg and 10 kg, respectively). They could be used only in neonatal and infant – or hetertopically – in adult HTx.

ABO blood group compatibility is another precondition for clinical XHTx. Because blood group 0 is very scarce in the baboon and other nonhuman primates, 0 type recipients are almost excluded from xenogeneic transplantation.

Baboons captured in the wild carry numerous viruses, bacteria, and other microorganisms [9]. A virological evaluation of nonhuman primates was described by Human and coworkers [5]. Serum samples were collected from

**Table 1.** Results of serological screening for selected viruses in nonhuman primates. (From [5])[a]

| Antigenetic material | Group A | Group B | Group C |
|---|---|---|---|
| Herpesviridae | | | |
| B virus | 0/10 | 0/10 | 0/14 |
| HSV-1 | 9/10 | 7/10 | n.d. |
| VZV | 7/10 | n.d. | 0/14 |
| CMV | 10/10 | 6/10 | 6/14 |
| EBV | 0/10 | 2/10 | 0/14 |
| SA-6 | 10/10 | 7/10 | 7/14 |
| SA-8 | n.d. | 7/10 | 0/14 |
| Retroviridae | | | |
| $SIV_{mac}$[b] | 0/10 | 5/10 | –[c] |
| SRV-1 | 0/10 | 0/10 | –[c] |
| SRV-2 | 0/10 | 0/10 | 0/14([d]) |
| Reoviridae | | | |
| SA-11 | 8/10 | 2/10 | n.d. |
| Filoviridae | | | |
| Marburg virus | 0/10 | 0/10 | 0/14 |
| Myxoviridae | | | |
| H-Infl. A | 0/10 | 0/10 | 0/14 |
| H-Infl. B | 0/10 | 0/10 | 0/14 |
| H measles | 0/10 | n.d. | 0/14 |
| H mumps | 0/10 | 0/10 | 0/14 |
| Togaviridae | | | |
| Rubella virus | 0/10 | 0/10 | 0/14 |
| Arenaviridae | | | |
| LCM | 0/10 | 0/10 | 0/14 |

HSV-1, herpes simplex virus type I; VSV, varicella-zoster virus; CMV, cytomegalovirus; EBV, Epstein-Barr virus; SA, simian agent agent 8; $SIV_{mac}$, simian immunodeficiency virus; SRV, simian retrovirus; H-Infl, human influenza virus; H, human; LCM, lymphocytic choriomeningitis; n.d., not determined

[a] Results are expressed as a ratio of the number of seropositives against the number of animals tested

[b] Suggests infection by the corresponding AGM strain ($SIV_{agm}$)

[c] Seronegativity preselected

[d] Probable preselection due to close serological relationship to SRV-1

ten Chacma baboons captured in the wild (group A), from a group of ten African green monkeys (AGM), captured in the wild (group B), and from a group of 14 first-generation colony-bred AGMs, selected on the basis of human T-cell lymphotropic virus type 1 (HTLV-1), simian immunodeficiency virus ($SIV^{mac}$), simian retrovirus type 1 (SRV-1), and human immunodeficiency virus type 1 (HIV-1) seronegativity (group C). By a dot immunobinding assay serological testing was performed for herpes simplex type 1 (HSV-1), varicella-zoster virus (VZV), human cytomegalovirus (CMV), Epstein-Barr (EBV), simian agent 6 (SA-6), simian agent 8 (SA-8), and B virus herpesviridae, SRV-1, Simian retrovirus type 2 (SRV-2), and $SIV^{mac}$ retroviridae, simian agent 11 (SA-11) rotavirus, Marburg filovirus, human influenza type A (H-Infl. A), human influenza type B (H-Infl. B), human measles and human mumps myxoviridae, the lymphotic choriomeningitis (LCM) arenavirus, and the human rubella togavirus. The results of this study are given in Table 1. According to our previous investigation, the prevalence of microorganisms in the nonhuman primates are usually not dangerous for humans. There are, however, viruses which are known to cause serious disease or death in man. Colony-bred animals showed a marked reduction of serological evidence to pathogen titers (group C). For successful clinical XHTx, one would, therefore, need a colony of selected potential donors, which is a very costly enterprise.

Ethical aspects are important and thus pose further problems in the field of XHTx. Use of primate xenografts is justified only, if no other method can be offered.

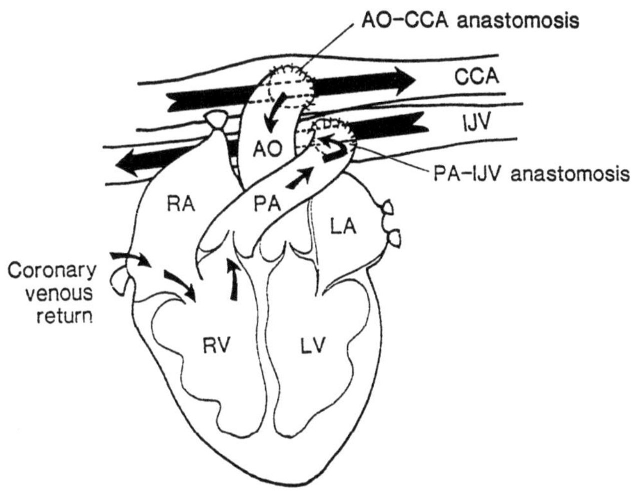


**Fig. 2.** Technique of cervical heterotopic heart transplantation used in experimental xenogeneic heart transplantation. End-to-side anastomoses between the donor aorta (*AO*) and recipient common carotid artery (*CCA*), and between the donor pulmonary artery (*PA*) and recipient internal jugular vein (*IJV*) are performed. Blood flow is via the aorta to the coronary vessels with venous return via the coronary sinus, right atrium (*RA*), right ventricle (*RV*) and *PA*. *LV*, left ventricle; *LA*, left atrium. (From [6])

## Experimental Xenogeneic Heart Transplantation

In an attempt to achieve an optimization of the various combinations of known immunosuppressive drugs, we have tested their efficacy in a model using Vervet monkeys as donors and Chacma baboons as recipients [7]. The donor hearts were transplanted heterotopically into the neck (Fig. 2). Best graft survival was seen when we used an exactly tailored form of immunosuppressive "cocktail", consisting of cyclosporine A, azathioprine, prednisolone, and rabbit antithymocyte globulin (RATG). This shows the necessity of a regimen which is directed towards humoral rejection as well as cellular rejection. A mean survival of 43.3 ± 18.5 days resulted in this group. Therefore, from an immunological standpoint it would be possible to use baboons as a bridge to transplantation for a short time. The longest graft survival (77 days) and less rejection episodes were seen in a group where the animals had been treated additionally with 15-Deoxyspergualin, administered for 10 days following HTx [8]. However, this drug showed major side effects (nausea, diarrhoea), which compromised these animals tremendously.

## Clinical Preconditions for Xenogeneic Heart Transplantation

From our current knowledge in the possible event of clinical XHTx being performed the following preconditions must be considered.

A pretransplant mixed lymphocyte culture is necessary, in which the responsiveness of recipient lymphocytes to cells of several potential donor animals are examined in order to select the most suitable donor. The presence of maternal antibodies must, however, be considered and excluded before clinical evaluation. In addition, the usual direct lymphocytotoxic crossmatch should be performed. ABO blood group compatibility is essential and a conditio sine qua non. A screening for viral and bacterial organisms in the donor animal is obligatory in order to exclude potential infections of the recipient.

Postoperatively, an optimal immunosuppressive therapy should be applied. Rejection monitoring should be very carefully performed. If hyperacute rejection occurs an extra – tested – animal must be available for retransplantation. In the event of blood transfusion, the blood units must be tested for preformed lymphocytotoxic antibodies against the donor animal. Only irradiated packed red blood cells, after four repeated washings, should be used.

## Conclusion

Today the use of xenografts is clearly still under experimental investigation. Therefore, xenogeneic heart transplantation seems not to be as simple, even if one thinks in surgical terms only. It is enormously costly and time consuming. At present, clinical xenogeneic heart transplantation could be used as a bridging procedure until a human organ became available.

## References


1. Bailey LL, Nehlsen-Cannarella SL, Concepcion W, Jolley WB (1985) Baboon-to-human cardiac xenotransplantation in a neonate. JAMA 254:3321
2. Barnard CN, Wolpowitz A, Lossman JG (1977) Heterotopic cardiac transplantation with a xenograft for assistance of the left heart in cardiogenic shock after cardiopulmonary bypass. S Afr Med J 52:1035
3. Calne RY (1970) Organ transplantation between widely disparate species. Transplant Proc 2:550
4. Hardy JD, Chavez CM, Kurrus FE, Neely WA, Webb WR, Eraslan S, Turner MD, Fabian LW, Labecki JD (1964) Heart transplantation in man: developmental studies and report of a case. J Am Med Assoc 188:1132
5. Human PA, van der Riet FJ, Cooper DKC, Kalter SS, Fincham JE, Smuts HEM, Reichenspurner H, Madden DL, Sever JL, Reichart B (1989) The virological evaluation of non-human primates for xenotransplantation. In: Reichart B (ed) Recent advances in cardiovascular surgery. Schulz, Percha, FRG
6. Reichart B, Jamieson SW (1990) Heart and heart-lung transplantation. Schulz, Percha, FRG, 273
7. Reichenspurner H, Human PA, Boehm DH, Rose AG, May R, Cooper DKC, Zilla P, Reichart B (1989) Optimalization of immunosuppression after xenogeneic heart transplantation in primates. J Heart Transpl 8:200
8. Reichenspurner H, Hildebrandt A, Human PA, Boehm D, Rose AG, Odell JA, Reichart B, Schorlemmer HU (1990) 15--deoxyspergualin for induction of graft nonreactivity after cardiac and renal allotransplantation in primates. Transplantation 50:181
9. Van der Riet F, Human PA, Cooper DKC, Fincham JE, Kalter SS, Kanki PJ, Essex M, Madden DL, Lai-Tung MT, Chalton D, Sever JL (1987) Virological implications of the use of primates in xenotransplantation. Transplant Proc 19:4068

# Bridging in Cardiac Surgery: A Reasonable Surgical Procedure or Only a Method for Getting an Emergency Transplant?

J. C. Reidemeister, and H.-R. Zerkowski

Heart transplantation (HTx) has become a well-established clinical procedure for the only actually possible definite treatment of end-stage heart failure. Operative mortality (< 30 days) associated with orthotopic heart transplantation has remained about 10 % during the past 5 years; the mid-term and long-term survival rates of 72 % after 5 years and between 60 % and 70 % after 10 years, respectively, is excellent (Kriett and Kaye 1990). By increasing the number of transplants performed, a donor organ

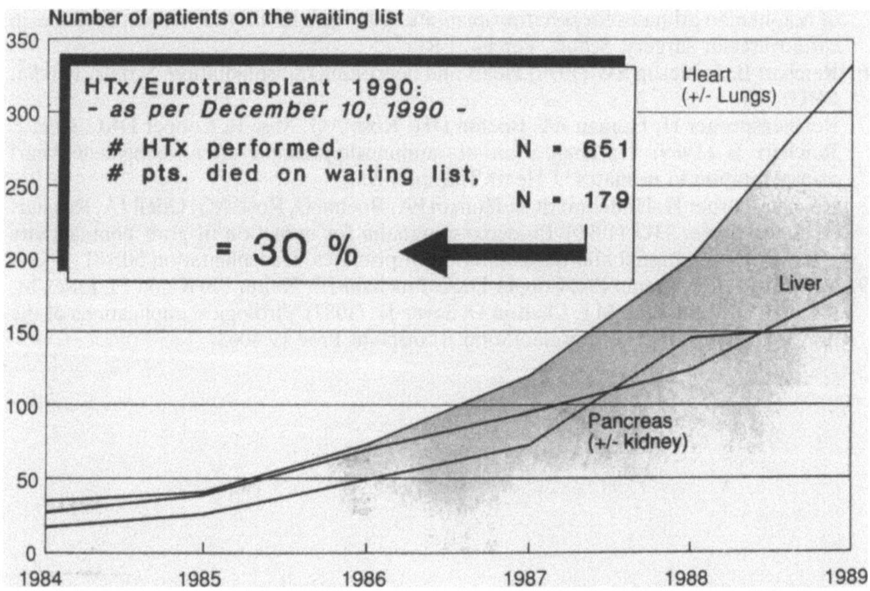


**Fig. 1.** Patients on the waiting list for heart (+/− lungs), liver, and pancreas (+/− kidney) as of December 31, 1989, and the total number of heart transplantations performed as well as the number of deaths on the heart transplant waiting list as of December 10, 1990. (Data from Eurotransplant Foundation Annual report – 1989, and personal communications, respectively)

Department of Thoracic and Cardiovascular Surgery, Essen University Medical School, Hufelandstr. 55, 4300 Essen 1, FRG

W. Land, J. B. Dossetor (Eds.)
Organ Replacement Therapy:
Ethics, Justice and Commerce

demand/supply mismatch becomes even more evident (Fig. 1). The waiting list is still growing, reaching more than 300 Eurotransplant patients overall in 1989 (Persijn and Cohen 1990), but organ donation can not yet supply the need for suitable heart transplants. As of December 10, 1990, 651 heart transplant procedures were performed in the Eurotransplant region, but during the same period of time 179 patients awaiting transplantation died on the list (Eurotransplant Foundation, personal communication, 1990). That means overall 30% dying on the waiting list.

Loisance et al. (1989) were some of the first who made an attempt to realize the vision that some form of bridging to transplant would be able to reduce the number of deaths of patients awaiting transplantation due to heart failure. In his intensive care unit, Loisance was treating 32 patients admitted from all over Paris in severe cardiogenic shock and with maximal catecholaminergic support. First he put them on pharmacological bridging with enoximone, intravenously administered. Indeed, there were some positive responders. These responders had to be re-evaluated and, if they fulfilled transplant criteria, he put them on the waiting list for heart transplantation. If they were not suitable transplant candidates, they continued on oral enoximone therapy. Nonresponders to the pharmacological bridging were those patients where ventricular assist devices (VAD) or artificial hearts were used. And from there, they were put on the transplant list without any re-examination.

The point we want to stress is shown in Fig. 2, i.e., the decision tree of our own institution. Starting with a catecholamine trial first in cases of short-term

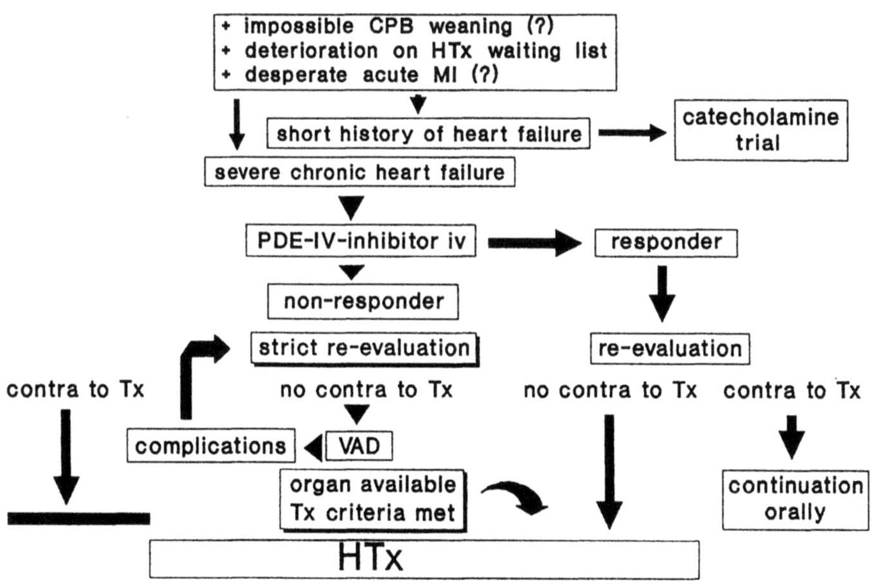


**Fig. 2.** Proposal for decision-making in the treatment of end-stage heart failure as has been in use at Essen University Medical School since 1989 (Zerkowski, Brodde and Reidemeister 1991)

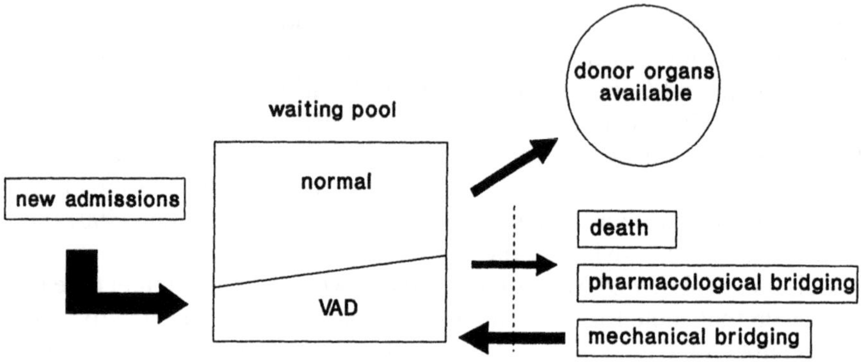


**Fig. 3.** Initiation of mechanical bridging using ventricular assist devices (VAD) reduces the chance of obtaining a suitable organ for patients awaiting elective transplantation by increasing the absolute proportion of poor-risk patients on VAD

acute heart failure, we proceed by administering PDE-IV inhibitors in patients with acutely deteriorated severe chronic heart failure, because in those patients failure of adrenergic support can be predicted (Zerkowski 1991). Coming back to the nonresponders, we insist on a strict re-evaluation, keeping heart transplantation in mind. And if these patients are put on VAD we have to re-evaluate them if complications occur, such as infections or the first signs of multiple organ failure (MOF), etc.. Putting unsuitable patients on the list must be strictly avoided since thereby scarce organs for critically ill patients are wasted.

In 1990, the situation is best described as follows (Fig. 3): The donor organs available are reaching a plateau, and, on the other hand, the admissions to the waiting pool are increasing more and more. Therefore, the pool is made up of normal waiting list candidates and those who are bridged by VAD. A certain number of patients are deteriorating. We have the choice of performing pharmacological bridging or mechanical bridging and, via this therapeutic concept, the number of patients with VAD waiting for HTx is augmented. Because of the shortage of donor organs, one will reach the point that more and more VAD transplantations are to be done.

Mechanical support systems can in fact prolong human life for a limited period of time (Davis et al. 1990). Data have been published on successful VAD support lasting even 6 or 8 months. The underlying vision that bridging reduces the number of deaths due to heart failure in patients awaiting transplantation leads to the fiction that bridging solves the problems of the increasing shortage of donor organs. But on the other hand we rarely demonstrate the inevitable consequence: Bridging reduces the overall chance of survival of all other patients of the waiting pool (for overview, see Wisman and Pierce 1989), that means, the ethically challenging question is: when and whom to bridge, and when and whom to transplant after mechanical support (Pennington et al. 1989).

**Table 1.** Results of bridging to cardiac transplantation. For the original data compiled here see references (For Cabrol 1990, see Muneretto et al; for Hahn 1990, see Meli et al; the Berlin experimental data of Hetzer 1990 were obtained by personal communication, September 1990)

Single center studies

| Author | Center | Year | Type of VAD | N (initial) | Bridge-to-Transplant (*n*) | Transplant (*n*) | Deaths (*n*) | Survivors (discharged) (*n*) | Success rate (% of initial) (*n*) |
|---|---|---|---|---|---|---|---|---|---|
| Griffith | Pittsburgh | 1987 | TAH (J-7) | 6 | 6 | 5 | 1 | 4 | 66.7 |
| Pae | Hershey | 1988 | Pierce-Donachy | 8 | 8 | 5 | 2 | 3 | 37.5 |
| | | | Penn-State heart | | | | | | |
| Pennington | St. Louis | 1988 | Pierce-Donachy | 48 | 11 | 5 | 1 | 4 | 36.4 |
| Kanter | St. Louis | 1988 | Pierce-Donachy | | 11 | 6 | 1 | 5 | 45.5 |
| | | | Novacor | | | | | | |
| Joyce | Minneapolis | 1989 | different | ? | ? | 11 | 2 | 9 | 81.8 |
| Gray | Louisville | 1989 | Pierce-Donachy | 12 | 12 | 7 | 1 | 6 | 50.0 |
| Cabrol | Paris | 1990 | different | 84 | 50 | | | 20 | 40 |
| Hahn | Sion | 1990 | Pierce-Donachy | 34 | 34 | 28 | | ? | |
| Hetzer | Berlin | 1990 | different | 44 | 32 | 23 | 5 | 18 | 40.1 |

Multi center studies

| Author | Center | Year | Type of VAD | N (initial) | Bridge-to-Transplant (*n*) | Transplant (*n*) | Deaths (*n*) | Survivors (discharged) (*n*) | Success rate (% of initial) (*n*) |
|---|---|---|---|---|---|---|---|---|---|
| Farrar | 8 | 1988 | Pierce-Donachy | 29 | 29 | 21 | 1 | 20 | 68.9 |
| Joyce | 22 | 1989 | Jarvik | 100 | 100 | 68 | 37 | 31 | 31 |
| Pae (ISHT) | 62 | 1990 | different | 400 | 400 | 272 | 109 | 163 | 40.7 |

To justify this two-stage cardiac transplant procedure, we have to analyze the data of its short-term as well as mid-term results (Miller et al. 1990). Comparing the post transplant survival rates of the electively transplanted heart transplant recipients with those having been on bridge for transplantation, there seems to be only a difference of 20 % in survival after 2 years. But if all 400 patients forming the data base of these survival curves are analyzed, the following result is obtained: the vast majority of the 400 patients with mechanical circulatory support die before or immediately after HTx, resulting in an overall success rate of only 40 %. As many as 60 % of these 400 patients are lost during the bridging procedure and the higher risk operation of post-VAD transplantation. This overall success rate of only 40 % has to be compared with 80 % survival after elective heart transplantation procedure. Looking at single center studies published from 1987 to 1990, there is an overall success rate of the bridge-to-transplant series in individual units between 36 % and 82 % (Table 1).

The multicenter studies published confirm these data, i.e., the positive aspect is that there are subgroups of patients (young patients suffering from deterioration of chronic heart failure without additional risk factors, MOF, or suspected infections), who may benefit from bridge-to-transplant (Muneretto et al. 1990). The negative aspect remains evident: The amount of wasted organs (i.e., organ loss due to significant incidences of infection and MOF after two-stage HTx) is unjustifiably high. Risk factors can be retrospectively identified (Miller et al. 1990), but no generally accepted list of indications and/or contraindications for staged cardiac transplantation exists.

The dilemma of transplant surgeons since the development of functioning assist devices have been these essential ethical questions: What can we do with mechanical assist devices? What are we allowed to do for the individual patient without limiting the rights and chance of survival of others awaiting transplantation? When are we not allowed ethically to bridge a patient? When is it no longer justified to transplant a patient during bridging?

## Comment

Because the supply of donor organs begins to plateau, and the demand for suitable organs increases, a possible attempt to answer these questions may be given by the following statements:

1. The use of assist devices distorts to a certain degree the distribution of donor organs, with the redistribution favoring poor candidates for HTx.
2. On the other hand, science and medicine are forcefully asked to develop new technology and therapeutic tools despite initially discouraging results.
3. This ethical dilemma can only be justifiably solved by focusing the therapeutic possibilities in patients with calculated risk and predictable outcome (Hill 1988), based on prognostic indices.

4. Bridging to transplant must be understood as a two-stage procedure with indispensable duty for re-evaluation before each step.

Therefore, we think that the community of transplant surgeons is asked to define criteria for the use of assist devices as well as for the initiation of staged transplantation to rule out misuse in organ donation and exchange.

## Summary

Heart transplantation (HTx) has become an established clinical procedure for the definite treatment of end-stage heart failure. Unfortunately, approximately 30 % of patients awaiting transplantation die before a suitable donor heart becomes available. There is no doubt, that, in this situation, mechanical circulatory support (MCS) is able to prolong life for a limited period.

Since 1985, the inception of the combined registry for the clinical use of mechanical ventricular assist devices (VAD) and the total artificial heart (TAH) in conjunction with HTx, 62 centers voluntarily submitted information about their patients to the registry. As of December 31, 1989, data of 400 patients bridged to transplant were available. The overall results are discouraging. They require the analysis of the mortality of the bridging period and the subsequent transplantation period. Only 68 % of all patients on assist devices with the intention to be transplanted could really be transplanted, and out of these (despite significant differences of the survival rates between the different systems used) only 60 % were discharged; i.e., the vast majority (59 %) of patients with MCS died despite any technical support before (30 %) or immediately after HTx (additional 30 %). The overall survival rates of the different surgical groups differ between none and 60 %; the main cause of death was infection during MCS or after HTx (45 %). These results coincide with the extreme shortage of donor organs; i.e., suitable donor hearts are too often transplanted into poor recipients. Therefore, patient selection is the most important factor relating to survival. Criteria for bridging must include criteria for cardiac transplantation. The bridged HTx candidates are reexamined before HTx when a donor heart is offered.

The final outcome is significantly influenced by the pretransplant condition of the patient (occult infection, beginning multiple organ failure). Only well-defined and restricted indications for bridging as well as for post-bridging HTx based on prognostic indices are leading to acceptable results. Otherwise the ethical dilemma will be wasting scarce donor organs to poor transplant recipients. Decision-making in organ sharing must not only include urgency categories, but also accepted prognostic factors.

## References

Cabrol C, Solis E, Muneretto C, Pavie A, Gandjbakhch I, Bors V, Szefner J, Leger P, Cabrol A (1989) Orthotopic transplantation after implantation of a Jarvik 7 total artificial heart. J Thorac Cardiovasc Surg 97: 342–350

Davis PK, Pae WE, Pierce WS (1990) Pulsatile ventricular assist devices. In: Cooper DKC, Novitzky D (eds) The transplantation and replacement of thoracic organs. Kluwer, Dordrecht, pp. 423–430

Farrar DJ, Hill DJ, Gray LA, Pennington DG, McBride LR, Pierce WS, Pae WE, Glenville B, Ross D, Galbraith TA, Zumbro GL (1988) Heterotopic prosthetic ventricles as bridge to cardiac transplantation. N Engl J Med 318:333–340

Gray LA, Ganzel BL, Mavroudis C, Slater AD (1989) The Pierce-Donachy ventricular assist device as a bridge to cardiac transplantation. Ann Thorac Surg 48: 222–227

Griffith BP, Hardesty RL, Kormos RL, Trento A, Borovetz HS, Thompson ME, Bahnson HT (1987) Temporary use of the Jarvik-7 total artificial heart before transplantation. N Engl J Med 316:130–134

Hill JD (1988) Bridge to cardiac transplantation. Ann Thorac Surg 46:131–132

Joyce LD, Emery RW, Eales F, Von Rueden TJ, Kiser JC, Hoffmann FM, Johnson KE, Toninato CJ, Kersten TE, Nicoloff DM, Pritzker MR (1989) Mechanical circulatory support as a bridge to transplantation. J Thorac Cardiovasc Surg 98:935–941

Joyce LD, Johnson KE, Toninato CJ, Cabrol C, Griffith B, Copeland JG, Keon WJ, Tector A, Pifarre R, Semb B, Dembitsky W, Loisance D, Frazier OH, Noon G, Herbert Y, Halbrook H, DeVries WC, Akalin H, Aris A, Phillips SJ, Peterson A, English T, Pennington G, Carmichael MJ (1989) Results of the first 100 patients who received Symbion total artificial hearts as a bridge to cardiac transplantation. Circulation 80 [Suppl III]: III-192–IV-201

Kanter KR, McBride LR, Pennington DG, Swartz MT, Ruzevich SA, Miller LW, Willman VL (1988) Bridging to cardiac transplantation with pulsatile ventricular assist devices. Ann Thorac Surg 46:134–140

Kriett JM, Kaye MP (1990) The registry of the international society for heart transplantation: Seventh official report – 1990. J Heart Transplant 9:323–330

Loisance D, Duboisrande JC, Deleuze PH, Hillion HL, Duval AM, Tavolaro O, Romano P, Castaigne A, Tarrac A, Cachera JP (1989) Pharmacological bridge to cardiac transplantation. Eur J Cardiothorac Surg 3:196–202

Meli M, Odermatt R, Hahn C (1990) Infection and thromboembolic complications in 34 patients under ventricular assistance as a bridge to transplantation. J Cardiovasc Surg 31 [suppl]: 20

Miller CA, Pae WE, Pierce WS (1990) Combined registry for the clinical use of mechanical ventricular assist pumps and the total artificial heart in conjunction with heart transplantation: Fourth official report – 1989. J Heart Transplant 9:453–458

Muneretto C, Rabago G, Pavie A, Gandjbakhch, Miralles A, Tedy G, Bors V, Leger PH, Cabrol C (1990) Indication and patient selection in the use of mechanical circulatory support devices: current status in 1990. J Cardiovasc Surg 31[Suppl]: 22

Pae WE, Pierce WS, Myers JL, Wisman CB, Campbell DB, Waldhausen JA (1988) Staged cardiac transplantation. Circulation 78 [Suppl III]:III-66–III-72

Pennington DG, Kanter KR, McBride LR, Kaiser GC, Barner HB, Miller LW, Naunheim KS, Fiore AC, Willmann V (1988) Seven years' experience with the Pierce-Donachy ventricular assist device. J Thorac Cardiovasc Surg 96:901–911

Pennington DG, Joyce LD, Pae WE, Burkholder JA (1989) Patient selection. In: Pennington DG (ed) Circulatory support 1988. Topical meeting of the society of thoracic surgeons, 6–7 Feb 1988, St. Louis. Ann Thorac Surg 47: 77–81

Persijn G, Cohen B (eds) (1990) Eurotransplant foundation annual report 1989. Available from Eurotransplant Foundation, Leiden, The Netherlands

Wisman CB, Pierce WS (1989) The artificial heart and mechanical circulatory assist devices. In: Yacoub M (ed) Annual of cardiac surgery – 1989. Current Science, London, pp. 62–66

Zerkowski H-R (1991) Zur funktionellen Bedeutung myokardialer Beta$_2$-Adrenozeptoren des Menschen. Thieme, Stuttgart (in press)

Zerkowski H-R, Brodde O-E, Reidemeister JC (1991) Therapie des Herzversagens im Rahmen der kardiovaskulären Chirurgie. Z Thorax-, Herz-, Gefäßchir (in press)

# The Ethics of Domino Heart Transplantation

J. P. Scott, D. J. Aravot, P. A. Mullins, N. Caine, L. Sharples, R. L. Smyth, T. W. Higenbottam, and J. Wallwork

Domino transplantation provides a further source of hearts for transplantation (Dark 1990; Baumgartner 1989; Cavarrochi 1989). It is essential that neither donors nor recipients are disadvantaged as a result of this practice (Sutor 1988; Rhenman 1989). We have studied the first 28 donors and recipients of the domino procedure at our institute and compared them with comparable groups of heart-lung and heart transplant recipients not involved in the domino procedure. Comparison was made of ischaemic time of in-house and distant procurement hearts, of ischaemic time for donors and non-donors of domino hearts, time in hospital and early survival figures at 3 months after transplantation.

We consider that live organ donation places several ethical requirements on the transplantation team. The first and most important is informed consent, including any possible disadvantages to the procedure, one of which may involve the request for coronary angiography if the potential donor is older or has smoked previously. The information given should be the best available to the person obtaining consent, imparted in terms understandable to the patient. The patient may be asked about donation in the assessment week, but his/her acceptance on to this list is not conditional upon agreement to become a live donor. The patient should give final consent, in writing, from home and freed from the pressures of being an inpatient during assessment.

Another difficulty arises in the amount of information a patient should be given following transplantation concerning their donor or recipient. Since, for reasons of uncertainty and confidentiality, this is not an undertaking at the time of consent, the transplant team is under no obligation to make such revelations, although it is unavoidable when both patients are in-house. Accordingly, when patients are both in the same hospital, informing them both in a controlled and deliberate manner when both are stable should reduce potential for conflict.

In analysing the recipient data, we have reviewed the first 28 live heart donors, with 28 non-donating heart-lung transplant (HLT) recipients of similar time post-operatively. We have found that survival is in fact better for donors than for non-donors at 3 months ($p < 0.05$) and in hospital time is

Transplant Unit, Papworth Hospital, Papworth Everard, Cambridge, CB3 8RE, United Kingdom

W. Land, J. B. Dossetor (Eds.)
Organ Replacement Therapy:
Ethics, Justice and Commerce

shorter. This of course may reflect changing management patterns, since the domino procedure is now performed in the majority of HLT procedures.

Underlying diagnosis in the live donors was cystic fibrosis in 17 (61 %), emphysema in 6 (21 %), primary pulmonary hypertension in 4 (14 %) and Eisenmenger atrial septal defect in 1 (4 %). The causes of death for six recipients of domino hearts were infection in three, post-operative bleeding in one, sudden death in one and high pulmonary vascular resistance in one. The causes of death for two live donors of domino hearts were aspiration pneumonia complicated by infection and acute respiratory distress syndrome complicated by tracheal dehiscence.

We consider the domino procedure to be the current procedure of choice for patients with suppurative lung disease and an acceptable method of organ distribution, provided appropriate ethical guidelines are adhered to.

## References

1. Dark JH (1990) History of heart-lung transplantation. Lung 168 [Suppl]: 1165–1168
2. Baumgartner WA, Traill TA, Cameron DE, Fonger JD, Birenbaum IB, Reitz BA (1989) Unique aspects of heart and lung transplantation exhibited in the domino-donor operation. JAMA 261:3121–3125
3. Cavarocchi NC, Badellino M (1989) Heart/heart lung transplantation. The domino procedure. Ann Thorac Surg 48:130–133
4. Sutor S, Wieczorek P, DeMaio K, Gibson J, Michael K, Riddleberger S (1988) Domino transplants. Sequential heart and heart-lung transplantation. AORN-J 48:876–889
5. Rhenman B, Rhenman MJ, Icenogle TB, et al. (1989) Heart-lung transplantation: the initial Arizona experience. J Thorac Cardiovasc Surg 98:922–927

# General Discussion: New Frontiers in Organ Replacement Therapy

*Kootstra:* Mr. Scott, is there any profitable situation for the recipient of a domino heart? Is it a better heart than a third party cadaver heart? I am asking this question because in the donor the heart has always been pumping against the high resistance in the lungs, so there could be some hypertrophy of the right ventricle; this could be an advantage or a disadvantage for the potential recipient.

*Scott:* I think the issue of the so-called rested or stressed right ventricle issue is quite separate from the overall gist of your question. I think it is very debatable whether one is dealing with a pre-stressed or a pre-strained right ventricle, and I think it is extremely difficult to evaluate; I don't know of any effective way of doing that. I think, though, that the broader context of your question, namely that there may be some inherent disadvantage in it, has to be very much weighed against the pros and cons of how we acquire hearts for potential recipients for heart transplantation generally; these hearts almost invariably cannot be properly evaluated. No heart from an older patient will not have had coronary angiography in domino transplantation, and, indeed, the overall issue of quality is probably higher than it is for standard heart transplantation. I think that is the underlying potential benefit for the patient: they are well-evaluated hearts.

*Kootstra:* So, among the potential recipients there are a few who really could profit from getting a domino heart instead of a regular heart. Is that a potential situation, or theoretical?

*Scott:* Profit in the sense of potential for better graft function, yes, it is possible.

*MacPherson:* I would like to ask Dr. Scott about the interesting situation he has when donor and recipient are known to each other. I would like to know what advantages and disadvantages his group has experienced in that situation, because it is unlike other transplant scenarios.

---

The general discussion sessions were transcribed from tape recordings made during the conference. In the interest of a rapid publication, the individual speakers/discussants did not see their own comments and questions before the book went to press. One of the editors (W. Land) tried to make obviously necessary corrections in the manuscripts derived from the tape recordings and then authorized the publication of the sessions in their present form. Therefore, incorrect publication of the comments or questions with regard to style, content, etc. might be possible in the view of the speakers concerned. We apologize for any possible inaccuracies.

W. Land, J. B. Dossetor (Eds.)
Organ Replacement Therapy:
Ethics, Justice and Commerce

*Scott:* I don't know that one can say that there is any inherent advantage in that particular relationship, other than the relationship itself which is going to very much depend on the individuals concerned. I don't think there is any specific benefit, and it is certainly a practice that isn't generally carried out in transplantation as a whole, generally for quite good reasons. It raises a number of difficult emotional issues, particularly if one of the patients is not doing well. If, for example, the heart in a heart-lung transplant patient who perhaps has donated his heart to someone else, does not work well, the situation could be fraught with emotional dilemmas and difficulties, both for the doctors and for the patient. So I don't think there is any particular advantage, it is purely a pragmatic decision. If you are going to maintain good confidence with your patient, then it is much better if you impart that information than if they discover it from a passing plenum. I think that is the difficulty we have there.

*MacPherson:* Just as a comment on that particular point: in the last British Transplant Games, we had the situation of a patient who raced against his own heart. Unfortunately the race had to be abandoned, because the racers lost their way, and we don't know who won. The question that I would like to ask relates to the comments about the ethics of using a donor heart and, particularly, the ethics of the potential donor, that is the person who is going to receive a heart-lung transplant. Could it not be argued that were a person who was to receive a heart-lung transplant to decline to offer his heart as a donor heart, might not his behavior be regarded as so unethical as to disbar him from receiving the heart-lung transplant?

*Scott:* That is a very interesting question because it raises, of course, broader issues. I think that it is difficult for us to place the burden of responsibility for our difficulty in getting transplant organs upon an individual patient. You are asking them to actually undertake a potentially risky procedure, which is not directly going to benefit them. I think the caveat of all of that of course is that it is extremely uncommon for a patient who is going to receive a heart-lung transplant from someone else not to be very happy indeed to donate their own heart; often the patients will offer it. It is, however, very difficult to balance the equation of asking them to undergo the procedure. The usual sticking point is coronary angiography, that is the only point, I think, we have had any difficulty with at all. People perceive this quite rightly, and their second state may be a procedure with some risk. In this case the fallback position is really that we would assess the heart at the time of transplantation. Although that is suboptimal, it is very rare indeed for someone to actually refuse.

*Kootstra:* It does happen that they refuse?

*Scott:* Yes!

*Kootstra:* I think it is part of reciprocal responsibility: if you are willing to accept organs from society you have to be willing to donate to society: that is extremely logical.

*Scott:* Absolutely. But, nonetheless, it is not a burden that should be necessarily be placed upon that patient.

*Kootstra:* That is right too. Let's continue with questions. If abortions were induced for the sake of transplantation, moral capability would be attached to transplanters. Dr. Cartwright demonstrated that there is no difference between eating and using animals. If one produces transgenic pigs, then transplanters are responsible for their use. Now, what happens if the side-products of the meat are disposed of by eating? Are the transplanters then morally responsible for an act of cannibalism? Take your time to think about this question.

*Cartwright:* That is the kind of question I would expect a philosopher to put rather than someone who is not a philosopher, since it has the intricacy characteristic of philosophers. I suppose the answer that strikes me is something like this: this would not be cannibalism in the ordinary sense. Cannibalism is the eating of human beings, and whatever one is eating here, it is not in the fullest sense a human being. Whether or not there is anything wrong with it is another matter, but I don't think it would count as cannibalism.

*Kootstra:* The question was from Dr. Riggulsford, is he satisfied with this answer?

*Riggulsford:* I don't really think that is an answer. You may have to make more transgenic pigs to get over the rejection problems, and the question then becomes *how* transgenic does the pig have to become before it is considered partially human? And what responsibility do all of you as transplanters have for the disposal of the rest of the pig? Is it reasonable to eat those pigs or not?

*Cartwright:* Perhaps the question whether or not it is cannibalism in the end is not the crucial one. This might become a terminological issue of an uninteresting sort, perhaps the substantial issue is the morality of consuming a pig so transformed. Now, I have doubts about the ethics of eating other animals anyway, and I suppose the closer they are to us in the respect mentioned, the greater those doubts become. That is a vague answer, but I am not sure one can make anything sensibly more precise. I doubt that it is cannibalism, and if it is cannibalism, it is only partial cannibalism and I don't think that is the point. The point is the ethics of eating a creature which has been altered in this way, i.e., it may be slightly worse than eating creatures who aren't so altered.

*Riggulsford:* The answer to that would seem to be, therefore, that the philosophers cannot guide us. Can I, therefore, ask the opinion of the utilitarian? John Wallwork, what do you think?

*Wallwork:* Well, I don't think just changing a few genomes in the pig is going to make it any more human than perhaps it is already, or perhaps any more piglike than other people are already. I suspect the crucial issue is that when does a pig become a human, and I would have thought the nearest you can get for that is when you are actually using germ lines to be used for transplantation. Once you start using pig sperm and pig ova for human use, I guess you are getting very near a human-like pig, but until that time I think it is just a chunk of meat surrounded by organs that you need to transplant. That may be rather simplistic, but it seems to be a very pragmatic way of dealing with the problem. I suspect, actually, the meat will not be available because of the way the organs have to be harvested, so as a practical problem it won't occur.

*Hammer:* I just put that as a joke eating a transgenic pig and being a cannibal, but we have to be careful. Growth hormones do not only make animals bigger, they have an impact on various other organs and we do not know what you produce when you change a genome in a special way. The pig may suddenly lose its skin and look very human, or it may get hair, blond curled English hair or something like that. The problem could then suddenly become rather different. That is again very futuristic, but sometimes I dream of that.

*Pflanz:* I think when the question arises whether it is ethically permissible to eat the meat of these pigs, then the question should be is it ethically permissible to change the pig so much that you cannot eat them anymore. I think that is the basic question.

*N.N.:* Could I comment further on this? If the animal in question, the transgenic pig is giving an organ to a human that is causing good, then the transgenic pig has worth to human society. Should we, therefore, not respect it and treat it with the same sort of respect that we would a living donor, for example, and actually reward the pig.

*Kootstra:* I have made a note for myself that there has to be a balance between what science is asking for: the progress in experimental and clinical medicine and the ethical discussion. I think it too ethereal to discuss whether the meat of a transgenic pig ought to be eaten. It is important that the ethical discussion keeps up with the progress in science, but on the other hand there is no reason to be 20 years ahead in the ethical discussion, I am afraid.

*White:* Are there moral problems associated with the creation of transgenic animals and/or the creation of transgenic humans?

*Cartwright:* I am not quite sure how to answer that. My sense is that there are. I had a discussion yesterday evening with various people about the respect one should pay to deep-seated moral anxieties. I think one should pay considerable respect to them, though I also think it is incumbent upon us, including philosophers, to think about these matters, to try and give them a rational voice. Now, I have a deep-seated anxiety, I think, about these sorts of suggestions. I am not sure I can yet give them a rational voice, but I don't disparage the worry. I can think of a number of worries which I don't think get to the bottom of this. I can think of the general worry about interfering in matters whose consequences we do not fully understand; that, I don't think, gets to the bottom of the moral unease, and I am not quite sure what does. But unease I have, and I am sorry to leave it as inarticulate as that, perhaps others can do better.

*Sass:* I don't think it is a very new ethical issue. The Old Testament already talks about breeding programs and ethical issues associated between Lavan and Jacob, for example. One problem we might have with transgenic animals is if it produces severe pain or suffering for these people. We have had some breeding programs with dogs, particularly hunting dogs which had severe spinal malformation when they got older and severe pain. These days, since our survival does not depend on this sort of help in the hunting field, we have to reconsider whether to continue breeding these animals. This is a much more severe problem, as far as I see it, than the issue of transgenic animals. But actually we have in our tradition experience with a responsibility framework, as far as I can see.

*Kootstra:* I would like to ask Dr. Akveld, would it be illegal to farm and breed protected animals?

*Akveld:* I must quite honestly say that I didn't prepare all of those kinds of questions, but I couldn't imagine that it would be forbidden to breed them. I couldn't see a good legal reason for forbidding it, however, there are more legal prescriptions in Holland for animals, it is said, than for people; but that wouldn't mean that there would be strict legal positions that forbid it.

*Hammer:* Did I get your question right? Do you refer to animals that are dying out in nature? We can breed them. It is a must and it is done all over the world, for example, with horses. We have many races of donkeys all over the world that will disappear in the next 10 years. And the fertilized eggs of these animals are deep frozen somewhere in the United States. There is a large program in Munich doing similar things with antelopes. It is a must, and it is one of the reasons why we should keep zoological gardens to do that. But these are not genetically transferred, of course.

*Kootstra:* To keep the species in the world, but my intention is to farm them for the application of being a source for spare parts for human.

*Hammer:* That is not forbidden.

*Kootstra:* Well, that is what I tried to figure out in my question.

*Hammer:* Once again. I have read a lot about evolution. If mankind had developed in an evolutionary sense chromosome by chromosome, we would be in the stage of coli bacteria. There has been something that is called "transduction". When you have a virus coming from an animal to another species, it can take a whole part of the genome of that animal and, therefore, process evolution in a very fast sense. And that is on the other hand also the opposite, because mice, which reproduce very fast, should be far ahead of human beings, which they are not. There is a rather difficult procedure in nature involving artificially transgenic animals, so we have to be careful in that sense. Everybody can change every day by having a new virus. We know that flu viruses from dogs are contagious to man.

*Kootstra:* There is a question from Dr. Comparetti.

*Comparetti:* I represent the Institute of Bioethics in Milazo, in Sicily. The point I wanted to make is that perhaps we should consider fetal tissue transplantation as a sort of bridging in terms of the progress of science, because it is very likely that harvesting fetal tissue mostly from abortion with all the accompanying ethical implications will become unnecessary, since what counts is the transplantation of cells. As we have heard very often, fetal tissue taken altogether is not a purified transplant, but what we need for such cases as Parkinson's disease or Huntington's disease is purified material. If we can have a purified cell line, possibly even genetically engineered, then that is what we must seek and what we can expect in a few years. The problem of donors of aborted tissue will be overcome, since the origin of cells for that purpose is certainly sufficient from spontaneous abortions.

*Kootstra:* Thank you. Who agrees or disagrees? I think cell lines are not going to solve the problem, since we are not talking only about cells. When we talk about islets for insulin production, we are not talking about beta-cells, we are talking about islets.

*Comparetti:* Yes, but you can grow them, and I mean what is needed in general are purified cells rather than whole organs, whole tissue, or graft tissue. We are talking about transgenic animals and we have so many possibilities for genetically engineered cells that I think we could at least advocate that this would be the solution rather than the fetal cell problem.

*Kootstra:* John Noskop from East Carolina University School of Medicine would like to ask a question to Dr. Hammer and others.

*Noskop:* Dr. Hammer, you mentioned – if I understood you correctly – that the most likely current justification for xenotransplantation in human beings would be as a bridge to allotransplantation. You also mentioned the Baby Fae case, which I understood not to have bridging as an option, or not to have been considered in that case. My concern is that we perhaps ought to be more critical of the action in the Baby Fae case, given the absence of that possibility.

*Hammer:* At the moment I would call bridging a time interval of less than 2 years. This is a period which we can achieve sooner or later with xenografting, but that is not the same as a whole life with a new organ. I think in the case of Baby Fae we would have another question. Does the baboon heart grow under the growth hormone of the human being, and how much does it grow? Does it end in the baboon size of 20 kg, while the human grows to 60 kg? That is why I mentioned the growth hormone; I had some ideas behind the stories, and that is why we are interested in growth hormones. Can we transplant a baboon's heart, liver, or kidney into a baby and do these organs grow with the human being? We were interested in transgenic growth hormones for this reason. I have already been attacked that bridging is not enough, but at the moment I see, being very optimistic, no other choice. I would say that bridging could be important in some cases; I know we must disagree.

*Kootstra:* OK, Dr. Wallwork, you don't agree with bridging. During the presentation you explained exactly why you thought that bridging does not solve the problem, neither with xenografting, nor with assist devices. I think using catecholamines or things like that to extend life and to give patients a chance is totally acceptable and sensible. But you do not think that bringing them on to an artificial device is adequate?

*Wallwork:* I think it just highlights the problem of the dilemma of treating your patient to your best ability, and using the scarce resources. I think that is what he is getting at essentially for the heart, because for the heart, and that is what we are talking about here, the total number of donors available is limited. We want to try to get the best outcome and, therefore, it seems to me you are talking about getting the best outcome for the best cost, you are talking about cost benefit and outcome. The outcome from bridging, whichever way you look at it, at the moment is not good. We have more recipients than we need, and as we are providing the health care to a group of patients who have heart disease, it seems to me to be a very expensive way of wasting some organs. Although for an individual it may work, for using scarce health resources for the population of people with heart disease, it does not work. As soon as we provide more donor organs, there is no point in bridging. If you have too many organs and too few recipients, it is a perfectly acceptable way of dealing with things. You have to understand why bridging came about. It is a pity there aren't actually some mechanical people here, because a good argument would come. Bridging came about because everyone was searching for a total mechanical artificial device that was going to be permanent. People use these patients to test their machine – I heard someone say that at a meeting and I think that is terribly wrong. I think people are self-justifying their actions by bridging, and they are also not being able to make those critical decisions about making choices.

We had a lot of discussion yesterday about the fact that doctors don't necessarily make choices. I think it is wrong to assume that just because some doctors over a period of time have made decisions, that all doctors will always make bad decisions. I don't think that it is just for the doctors who have made the choice, and I don't think that it is the choice to bridge or not to bridge in this context. But I do think that you have to think of what you are actually achieving by bridging, and what you are achieving is spending health care money and wasting a resource by getting a less good outcome. I am not so sure you should bridge. It is not because I don't think it can do any individual any good, I think it can: I just think it is not using resources properly and that is the stance I take.

*Kootstra:* I think it would be fair if we asked Dr. Reidemeister to take a position either against or with your statements.

*Reidemeister:* One of the points I would like to make in connection with these statements to Dr. Hammer: I learned that the cytotoxic antibodies on ventricular assisted devices are augmenting, so you have a higher amount of rejection of organs. Perhaps this point will be a normal limitation for doing these post-bridge transplants. Is that right? Have you experience, Dr. Wallwork, with post-bridge-transplants?

*Wallwork:* We had one case, it was an interesting political event.

*Hammer:* I didn't want to mention it. We do experiments in which first we transplant a fox heart to the neck vessels of a dog until it is rejected, and then we do an allogeneic retransplantation, a so-called domino heart on the same day as the other one is rejected. Now guess what happens: it is rejected faster!

*Kootstra:* From a logical point of view there is not much to expect that xenograft bridging makes much sense.

*Wallwork:* I was just wanting to ask a question about transgenics, and wondering whether people thought there would be forbidden genes. In other words, if people don't object to transgenic animals or even doing gene transfers in humans, would there be such a thing as forbidden genes? Perhaps if someone discovered the gene that controls aging in man, and if we could somehow change that gene that would seem to me a forbidden gene to change in man, if it meant we could somehow prevent aging. What do you think about the animals in terms of other attributes than we may give them?

*Sass:* First of all, we have to have the knowledge, but that means we need the entire human genome map. Then it would need a fascistic state to outlaw this, because if you really find something which will prolong your life or your intellectual or sexual capabilities, as long as there are markets and market places, black markets and official markets, these things cannot be suppressed, and I feel they shouldn't be suppressed. Targeted populations should rather find a way to deal with these things in a moral scenario. And there could be anticipatory moral scenario assessments and argumentations and memoranda done, calling for the lawyers and the regulators and legislators and so on. I think this makes things worse, because it decreases our competence to deal with moral issues, while opening a totally new window of cheating on the government and the state which feels that it is strong enough to forbid the trading of certain genes. But the state will not be strong enough to do this if there is real value in these genes and if people feel there is value in them. It is, however, a very interesting question.

*Kootstra:* There is one interesting question to all of us from Dr. Becker from Berlin.

*Becker:* This is just following on from what we just heard. In Germany, investigations on embryonal tissue are prohibited in cases of in vitro fertilization. There are tissue cell conglomerates in which gene manipulation can be done, and this is just what we heard, but they cannot be done in this early state of human developing, since it is forbidden and the medical association has enforced a law that no doctor may do it. I want to know what the situation is in other European or overseas countries on this topic?

*Akveld:* I don't kow about legal regulations, but I would say for Holland, the same is applicable as for Germany. I would say that from a legal point of view, although it is not strictly forbidden because the lawmaker has not thought about it up to now, it shouldn't be allowed in the Dutch situation or in the German situation. I cannot speak for all the other European countries, since I am not informed about them.

*Kootstra:* It is getting late and it is nearly impossible to sum up in a minute what has been the conclusion of this morning. I think we can agree, however, that we had a nice opportunity to exchange opinions. We had very good and interesting papers on various issues, some of which are a little further away, like embryonic tissues, but, nevertheless, there might be a breakthrough and it is good that this society has had time to form its opinion. So, together with the other chairmen I would like to thank you as an audience and the presenters for their contributions to this nice, constructive morning session. Thank you.

# *VII. Congress Resolutions*

At the end of the Congress, an attempt was made to raise Congress Resolutions on the basis of and in accordance with the talks and their discussions during the meeting.

As could be expected, this attempt turned out to become extremely difficult because of all the controversial debates on each topic amongst the participants.

Finally, however, consensus could be obtained in accepting 8 resolutions and 1 recommendation.

Unfortunately, due to the limited time of debate (4 hours!), not all prepared resolutions could be approved by the participants of the Meeting. Thus, the selection of resolutions shown here is incomplete. Nevertheless, it reflects to some extent the intensive discussions we had during those 3 days in Munich. In addition it has to be stressed that we are dealing here solely with Congress resolutions rather than with ESOT/EDTA-ERA resolutions. Both Societies, however, are requested to discuss these resolutions for approval.

*(W. Land)*

# Accepted Resolutions

## Resolution 1

The following congress resolutions are to be understood as subject to:
a) the state of the art of transplantation and
b) national laws

## Resolution 2

The congress supports maintaining a prohibition of commerce to obtain organs or tissues for allotransplantation

## Resolution 3

Genetically related live donor transplantation from adults is ethically acceptable, provided informed and free consent is obtained from both principals or on behalf of recipients unable to give autonomous consent

## Resolution 4

All patients with end-stage renal disease should be informed about ethically accepted treatment options including transplantation so that they may choose for themselves

## Resolution 5

Live donor kidney transplantation between spouses and other emotionally related persons is ethically acceptable

## Resolution 6

The recipient's inability to pay for the procedure should not be a factor in deciding the allocation of organs

## Resolution 7

Countries should be encouraged to develop cadaveric transplant programmes suitable for the needs of their resident population, in accordance with their national health priorities

## Resolution 8

Cadaveric organs procured within a community should be considered assets of the community, and the community rather than just the medical profession should determine their allocation through announced criteria

# Recommendations

## Recommendation

Segmental extrarenal intra-abdominal organ transplantation from live donors is acceptable only in centres with extensive transplantation experience

# Resolution Not Accepted by Participants

"Rewarded gifts" are tolerable/permissible in cultures where they are distinguishable from commerce

# Subject Index

MIX
Papier aus verantwortungsvollen Quellen
Paper from responsible sources
FSC® C105338

If you have any concerns about our products,
you can contact us on
**ProductSafety@springernature.com**

In case Publisher is established outside the EU,
the EU authorized representative is:
**Springer Nature Customer Service Center GmbH**
**Europaplatz 3, 69115 Heidelberg, Germany**

Printed by Libri Plureos GmbH
in Hamburg, Germany